Botswana
Safari Guide

the Bradt Travel Guide

Chris McIntyre

edition
4

www.bradtguides.com

Bradt Travel Guides Ltd, UK
The Globe Pequot Press Inc, USA

BOTSWANA: OKAVANGO DELTA, CHOBE, NORTHERN KALAHARI

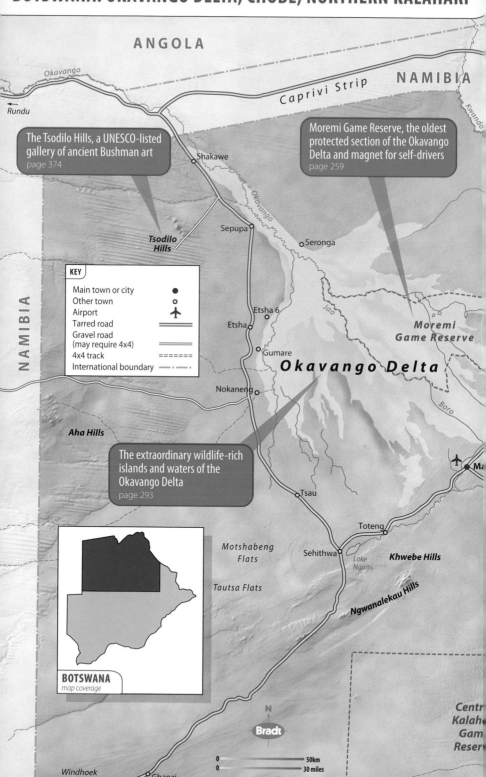

ANGOLA

NAMIBIA

Okavango

← Rundu

Caprivi Strip

Kwando

The Tsodilo Hills, a UNESCO-listed gallery of ancient Bushman art
page 374

Moremi Game Reserve, the oldest protected section of the Okavango Delta and magnet for self-drivers
page 259

Shakawe

Okavango

Tsodilo Hills

Sepupa

Seronga

NAMIBIA

KEY

Main town or city	●
Other town	○
Airport	✈
Tarred road	══
Gravel road (may require 4x4)	──
4x4 track	═══
International boundary	─·─·─

Etsha 6

Etsha

Jao

Moremi Game Reserve

Gumare

Okavango Delta

Nokaneng

Boro

Aha Hills

The extraordinary wildlife-rich islands and waters of the Okavango Delta
page 293

Tsau

✈ Ma

Toteng

Motshabeng Flats

Sehithwa

Lake Ngami

Khwebe Hills

Tautsa Flats

Ngwanalekau Hills

BOTSWANA
map coverage

N

Bradt

Centr Kalahɛ Gam Reser

0		50km
0		30 miles

Windhoek

Ghanzi

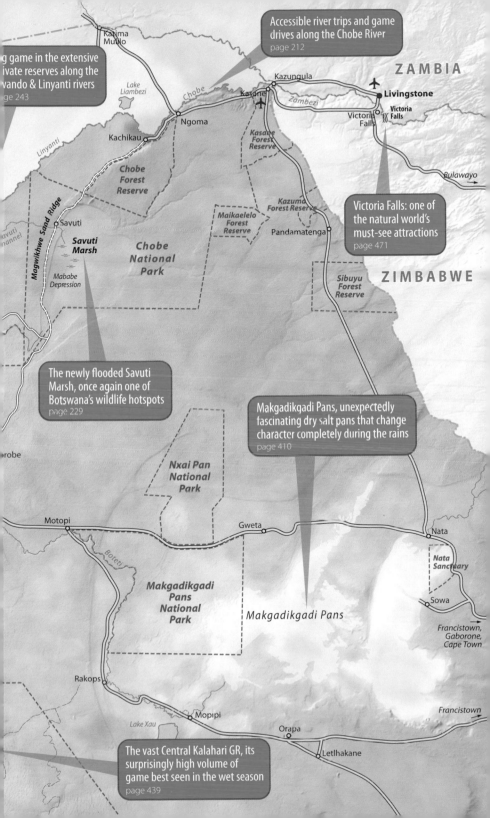

Accessible river trips and game drives along the Chobe River
page 212

ZAMBIA

Livingstone

g game in the extensive ivate reserves along the vando & Linyanti rivers
age 243

Victoria Falls

Victoria Falls: one of the natural world's must-see attractions
page 471

ZIMBABWE

The newly flooded Savuti Marsh, once again one of Botswana's wildlife hotspots
page 229

Makgadikgadi Pans, unexpectedly fascinating dry salt pans that change character completely during the rains
page 410

The vast Central Kalahari GR, its surprisingly high volume of game best seen in the wet season
page 439

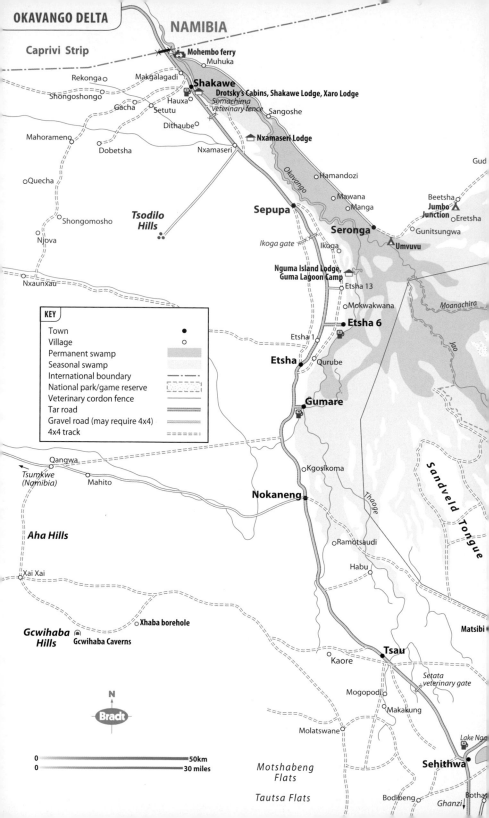

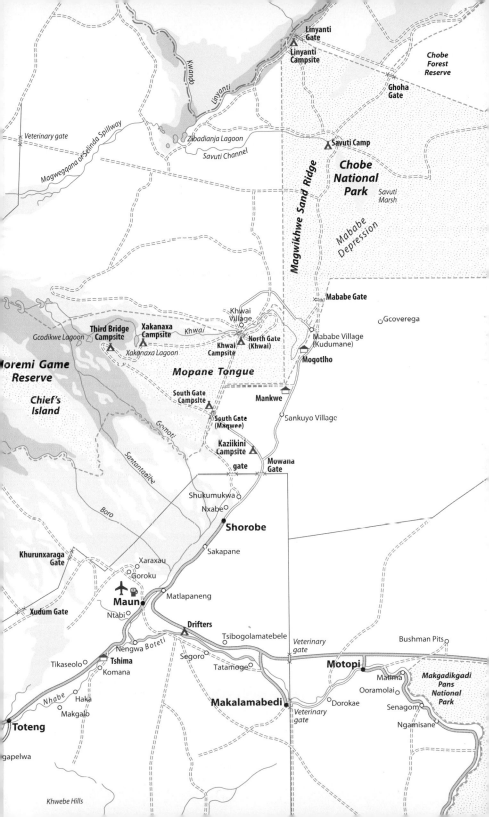

Botswana
Don't
miss...

The Okavango Delta
Extraordinary wildlife-rich
islands and waters, best seen
by *mokoro*
(AVZ) page 259

The Kwando and
Linyanti rivers
In wetter years this is a delta,
providing a refuge for a wide
range of wildlife such as lion
(TH) page 243

Makgadikgadi Pans

Fascinating dry salt pans that can be explored on foot, by 4x4 or on quadbikes

(JG) page 410

Chobe riverfront

A magnet for game, with an increasing number of giraffe

(AVZ) page 212

Moremi Game Reserve

With some of the richest ecosystems in Africa, this reserve is populated by a diverse range of animals, including large numbers of elephant

(TH) page 259

AUTHOR

Chris McIntyre went to Africa in 1987, after reading physics at Queen's College, Oxford. He taught with VSO in Zimbabwe for almost three years and travelled around extensively, mostly with a backpack. In 1990 he co-authored the UK's first guidebook to Namibia and Botswana, published by Bradt, before spending three years as a shipbroker in London.

Since then, Chris has concentrated on what he enjoys most: Africa. He wrote the first guidebook to Zambia for Bradt in 1996, the first edition of their Namibia guide in 1998 and this Botswana guide in 2003; he also co-authors guides to Tanzania and Zanzibar. Whilst keeping these guidebooks up to date, his day job is managing director of Expert Africa – a specialist tour operator which organises high-quality trips throughout Africa for individual travellers from around the world, including a very wide range of trips to Botswana. This also includes the Wild about Africa programme of small guided groups through Botswana.

Chris maintains a keen interest in development and conservation issues, acting as advisor to various NGOs and projects associated with Africa. He is a Fellow of the Royal Geographical Society, and contributes photographs and articles to various publications. Now based in west London, Chris and his wife, Susan, still regularly travel and research in Africa.

Chris can usually be contacted by email on chris.mcintyre@expertafrica.com.

LIST OF MAPS

NOTE ABOUT MAPS

Some maps use grid lines to allow easy location of sites. Map grid references are listed in square brackets after listings in the text, with page number followed by grid number, eg: [94 C3]. Please note, in order to keep the maps legible, not all sites have been pinpointed on the maps. However, grid references have been nonetheless supplied to highlight their general location.

Acknowledgements

Writing this book has been a team effort; I'm indebted to many that have made researching a pleasure and this book possible. Firstly thanks to African expert and fellow author, Philip Briggs, for the original text of the *Wildlife Guide* appendix, and for allowing me to build on it. Similarly, thanks to Wilderness Safaris for kind permission to borrow from their diagrams for the illustrations in *Chapter 3*.

Thanks to all my patient colleagues at Expert Africa. Megan Ingoldby, Nick Hobbs, Tracy Lederer and Chloe Henderson are authorities on Botswana in their own right, and have wrestled to find answers to many apparently trivial queries that make such a difference to the detail of this book.

On a personal note, my wife, Susie, made a great travelling companion during a particularly punishing research trip; I'm looking forward to many more trips with her in the future! In the past, Duncan, Purbs, Occy, Fritz and Simon all helped with different aspects of previous editions; all are remembered here with thanks.

In Botswana, many have helped with the various editions of this guidebook, and its predecessor the *Guide to Namibia & Botswana* – and to them all I owe my thanks. I hope that those who aren't mentioned here will forgive the omissions, but those who have helped most recently include Matt and Lorna Smith from Muchenje; Lloyd Wilmot; Lucille Hattingh from &Beyond; Colin Bell; Hilton Walker and Dereck Joubert from Great Plains; Nicky Keyes and the team at Ker & Downey; Beks Ndlovu and Shelley Cox at African Bush Camps; Sue Smart and Linda Vincent from the Kwando team; Ralph from Uncharted Africa; numerous people at Wilderness Safaris – but especially Grant Woodrow, Caroline Palazzo and Dave van Smeerdijk (seeing the Delta from the ground will never be the same again); Nick Green at Gidichaa; Kristin and Gabi at the Garden Lodge; Alistair Rankin, Malebogo and Comic at Machaba; and all at both Mapula Lodge and Ghoha Hills Safari Lodge. Thanks, too, to James and Geraldine Gifford for helping with so many last-minute queries; to Darkie Kamundunoo at the Tsodilo Hills, for his insightful guiding; and to intrepid cyclist Jon Williamson, who impressed us all with his fortitude in tackling both the Aha Hills and the CKGR, and sent us valuable feedback.

Behind the scenes, a trusty Land Rover kept us on the road – thanks to Charles Norwood at Safari Drive. We're very grateful, too, to Dawn Parr and Dawson Kgosi Ramsden at Botswana Tourism for delving deep to find answers to countless questions.

Thanks also to hundreds of Expert Africa's travellers who have helped with feedback after their trips and allowed us to publish their unedited feedback on expertafrica.com; these online reports now form an invaluable first-hand record of the country's better lodges and camps, from which I learn a lot.

In writing this, I'm aware that there are many above who know much more about Botswana than I. Among them, three experts really stand out: Alec Campbell, Mike

Main and Veronica Roodt. All have written amazing, scholarly works on Botswana which have been a real inspiration, and all kindly offered their help to me. Beside their erudite works (recommended in *Appendix 3, Further information*), this book pales – but I hope that it may introduce Botswana, and their works, to a wider audience.

Finally, Bradt's team who've worked with me on this book – including Sally Brock, David McCutcheon, Maisie Fitzpatrick and Laura Pidgley – have been supremely patient and encouraging. That which is good and correct owes much to their care and attention; errors and omissions are all my own.

AUTHOR'S STORY

Botswana meant little to me at first; it was never in the news. Then, finding myself in Zimbabwe, I remembered an old friend's enthusiasm for the Okavango Delta. So, in April 1988, three of us set off from Victoria Falls and hitched a lift in an open pick-up into Chobe. We were badly prepared, but even our lack of food and close encounters with hyenas added to the magic. No fences here; everything was so wild.

From Maun we splashed out on a few days' camping trip on a mokoro. Whilst the boatman spoke little English, the Delta was magical, almost surreal – like floating on a tropical fish-tank with animals everywhere around. The Okavango's lush greenery contrasted with the harsh dryness of the rest of the subcontinent. Iridescent birds flashed past, whilst terrapins sunbathed and otters played. All added to the feeling of paradise; we left entranced.

Thus started my love affair with the country. Since then I've been lucky enough to return many times. I've been guided by some of the best, learning more about the bush and its animals and plants. I've flown over the dry Kalahari and the verdant Delta, mesmerised by the ancient patterns of watercourses, islands and game trails. And I've walked and driven around, exploring for myself on the ground, exhilarated by the sense of freedom. Yet still I feel as if I've only scratched the surface of Botswana, and I always leave wanting to return.

FOLLOW BRADT

Introduction

It's tempting here, by way of introduction, to list Botswana's main highlights as areas, one by one, describing each to entice the reader. I'd probably start by waxing lyrical about the Okavango Delta being a world-class attraction for exclusive wildlife-viewing; I'd then marvel at the scale of the reserves around the Chobe, Kwando and Linyanti rivers, and perhaps eulogise about the almost spiritual experience of visiting the vast salt pans. But to do this would be misleading. For me, Botswana has just three overriding attractions – which transcend its geography.

First comes the wildlife. Whether this is your first safari or your 50th, Botswana won't disappoint. The sheer variation of the country, from the arid Kalahari to lush, well-watered forest glades, ensures tremendous variety. Botswana is serious about its big game. It has spectacular herds of elephants and buffalo, and prolific populations of predators. Experienced safari enthusiasts can bounce across the bush following a pack of wild dogs: Botswana has probably the continent's best population of these highly endangered predators. Yet often it's the country's smaller residents that will keep you entertained, from tiny painted reed frogs and barking geckos to troops of entertaining meerkats.

Second – and the underlying reason why many come here – is the feeling in Botswana that you're within an endless pristine wilderness, almost devoid of human imprint. For city-dwellers, such space is the ultimate luxury. In Botswana, animals wander freely across vast reserves which are measured in thousands of square kilometres, not merely hectares. Exploring these wilder corners is invariably deeply liberating.

Third, and missed by some, is Botswana's rich history. It's often barely hinted at but, veiled and mysterious, it's all the more enticing. It reveals itself in the paintings at Tsodilo, and the magic that seems to surround those hills. You'll catch a glimpse of it as you search for Stone Age arrowheads on the Makgadikgadi Pans. And standing on an ancient river-bed, or the wave-washed hills around Savuti, it's hard not to look into the geology and wonder what forces shaped this country, long before you, or indeed any people, first set eyes on it.

Back in the present, the world is changing fast. On a very positive note, 2009 and the following two years saw record water levels in the Okavango Delta and Kwando–Linyanti river systems, filling many channels that had been dry for decades. Initially the Boteti flowed for much of its course, the long-dry Magwegqana Spillway filled with water and the Savuti Channel trickled into Chobe National Park once again. Now the channel has reached the Savuti Marsh, transforming this whole area – and its attraction for wildlife.

Despite this good news, most of the earth's great wilderness areas are under threat – and not just from climate change. The 21st century is an age when even the earth's wildest corners must earn their keep, adapt or change irrevocably. Botswana's government has, to date, been a beacon of prosperity and stability within a troubled continent. Financed largely by income from some of the world's largest diamond mines, it has set many examples of how to run a country. However, Botswana's diamonds aren't forever. Current deposits are running out, and whilst new ones are discovered, many expect the industry's output is likely to plateau and decline within a few decades at most. When this happens, it will leave a gaping hole in the economy. Tourism is the obvious way to fill this, but exactly how is not obvious.

As it stands, Botswana's thriving tourist industry is the envy of the continent: minimising impact by admitting only small numbers who pay handsomely to rejuvenate themselves in its pristine environments. Some of the revenue has been channelled back into the poorer communities in the areas concerned. This first-rate approach has been a very responsible one; it hasn't been a quick way for the country to get rich through tourism, but it has been a sustainable one.

In the last decade we've seen the government flirt with the idea of higher-volume tourism in one or two areas. However, the original policy of high-cost, low-density tourism across most of northern Botswana seems to have won the day, and is now being actively applied beyond the Okavango–Chobe region to areas which have previously been regarded as peripheral. Pioneering safari camps have opened in Nxai Pan National Park and the Central Kalahari Game Reserve – and more will be encouraged to follow. Elsewhere, there's a move to encourage new lower-cost properties on the western side of the Panhandle area, thus giving easier and cheaper access to an experience of the Okavango Delta (albeit the edges) from the Shakawe–Sehithwa road.

This bodes well; both steps to increase tourism revenue are moderate, and far from some of the more drastic, damaging proposals that have been mooted. However, as both progress, it remains to be seen if this pace of change will be enough to satisfy the economic imperative for tourism to generate a larger slice of the national income.

So my plea to the reader is twofold. First, go now and support Botswana's small-scale camps and responsible tourism; the country needs you. Second, having committed many of Botswana's secret corners to paper here, I ask you to use this guide with respect. Botswana's wild areas need great care to preserve them. Local people are easily offended, and their cultures eroded, by a visitor's lack of sensitivity. Enjoy – but be a thoughtful visitor, for the country's sake.

NOTE ON DATUM FOR GPS CO-ORDINATES

For all the GPS co-ordinates in this book, note that the datum used is WSG 84 – and you must set your receiver accordingly before copying in any of these co-ordinates.

All GPS co-ordinates in this book have been expressed as degrees, minutes and decimal fractions of a minute. Note that this now differs slightly from the format used by the 2008 edition of the Shell map, which uses degrees, minutes and seconds.

Note that Google Earth satellite images for some of the lodges, camps and key GPS locations in this book can be accessed directly at www.expertafrica.com.

Part One

GENERAL INFORMATION

BOTSWANA AT A GLANCE

Location Southern Africa, between 20° and 30°E, and between 18° and 27°S

Size 581,730km²

Climate Subtropical. Summer (November–March): 19–35°C; winter (June–August): 5–23°C. Rainy season November–March

Status Republic

Population 2,024,904 (2011 census)

Population growth per year 1.9% (2011)

Life expectancy at birth 55 years (CIA World Factbook 2012)

Infant mortality 20/1,000 live births (World Bank, 2011)

Capital Gaborone, population 227,223 (2011 census)

Other main towns Francistown, Lobatse, Selebi-Phikwe, Orapa

Economy Major earners: diamonds, copper, nickel, beef, tourism

GNI US$7,720 per capita (World Bank, 2012)

GDP growth rate 6% (World Bank, 2012)

Currency Pula (BWP, abbreviated to P)

Rate of exchange US$1 = P8.96, £1 = P14.65, €1 = P12.20 (January 2014)

Language English (official), Setswana (national), Shona, other local languages

Religion Christianity, traditional beliefs

International telephone code +267

Time GMT +2

Electricity 220 volts

Weights and measures Metric

Flag Broad, light-blue horizontal stripes, divided by black central stripe bordered by narrow white stripes

National anthem *Fatshe leno la rona*: 'Blessed be this noble land'

Public holidays 1–2 January, Good Friday, Easter Monday, 1 May (Labour Day), Ascension Day, 1 July (Sir Seretse Khama Day), third Monday and Tuesday in July (President's Day), 30 September (Botswana Day), 1 October, 25–26 December

Tourist board www.botswanatourism.co.bw

1

History and Economy

We can learn a lot about Botswana today by looking back into its history. Its far distant past, explaining some of the main features of its landscapes, is covered as part of *The physical environment*, at the start of *Chapter 3*. A potted overview of Botswana's more recent human history is given here, casting some light on its current politics and economics.

HISTORY

EARLY PEOPLES Read about the country's geological history and it's framed in terms of hundreds, or at least tens, of millions of years. Thus it's sobering to realise how relatively recent any human history is, and how much more compressed its timescales are.

Our knowledge about early human life in Botswana is derived from archaeology and from oral histories, which go back about 700 years. Written records date only from the arrival of Europeans in the 18th and 19th centuries. Most of these are personal accounts, which are interesting, but subjective. In many places the story is confused and incomplete, or even deliberately misleading (see *Social groups or 'tribes'*, page 21).

However, archaeological evidence suggests that hunter-gatherer peoples have lived for about 60,000 years at sites like the Tsodilo Hills in the Kalahari. We know, too, that the ancestors of the Khoisan (comprising both the San and the Khoi people; see pages 4–5) were once widely dispersed throughout the continent, and probably had exclusive occupation of southern, central and eastern Africa from about 60,000 years ago up to the last 3,000 years.

Skeletons of a Khoisan-type people, dating back 15,000 years and more, are found throughout southern and eastern Africa. It is believed to be these people who made the rock paintings of people and animals that are found all over eastern and southern Africa and even in the Sahara Desert. The earliest paintings have been found in Namibia (the 'Apollo 11' cave) and are thought to date back 26,000 years.

Rock paintings found at the Tsodilo Hills are evidence that the living was good enough to allow the people to develop a vibrant artistic culture. Most experts believe that many of the paintings have deeper significance, probably connected with spiritual, religious or mythological beliefs. It is impossible to interpret them accurately without an in-depth knowledge of the culture and beliefs of those who created them. Unfortunately no group today claims historical responsibility. The local Zhu Bushmen claim that their god, Gaoxa, made the paintings.

The animals of Africa, such as antelope, eland, rhinos and giraffe, are the subject of many paintings. The images beautifully capture the form and the spirit of each animal. Humans also appear; one painting at the Tsodilo Hills shows a group of

15 men exhibiting the permanent erection, or semi-erection, which is a distinctive feature of San men from birth to death. Later paintings, featuring black men and sometimes war, are thought to depict the arrival of the Bantu farmers.

The San The San were perfectly adapted to their desert environment and had learned to survive its harsh extremes of climate – drought, unrelenting heat and sun in the winter, and heavy rains and floods in the summer.

Predominantly hunter-gatherers, it is thought that at various times, when the climate was more favourable, the San may also have owned and grazed stock. Several times in past millennia the climate of Botswana has been much wetter, and at others much drier than it is at the moment. Periodically the huge pans that are a distinctive feature of the landscape, such as at Makgadikgadi and Nxai, became great lakes, full of water and supplied by several rivers. Probably some San groups took advantage of plentiful supplies of water to acquire stock. Now the rivers have dried up and the Okavango Delta has receded, the pans are full of water only during the rainy season and the San are herders no longer. There are also more recent records of them owning and trading copper from secret mines in the Kalahari, and bartering it for iron.

The Khoi Around 3000BC, Late Stone Age hunter-gatherer groups in Ethiopia, and elsewhere in north and west Africa, started to keep domestic animals, sow seeds, and harvest the produce: they became the world's first farmers.

By around 1000BC these new pastoral practices had spread south into the equatorial forests of what is now the Democratic Republic of Congo, to around Lake Victoria, and into the northern area of the Great Rift Valley, in northern Tanzania. However, agriculture did not spread south into the rest of central/southern Africa immediately. Only when the technology, and the tools, of ironworking became known did these practices start their relentless expansion southwards.

It's thought that during the last centuries BC many Khoi-speaking peoples in northern Botswana converted their lifestyle to pastoralism – herding cattle and sheep on the rich pastures exposed by the retreating wetlands of the Okavango Delta and Lake Makgadikgadi.

It used to be thought that the Khoi acquired their stock during the (black) Iron Age, from Bantu-speaking farmers who are thought to have migrated into their area around 1,500 years ago. However, finds of sheep bone dating back 3,000 years now suggest that the Khoi had obtained stock long before the arrival of the Bantu, probably from east Africa where they had been herded for thousands of years. The Khoi spread, migrating with their livestock through central Namibia, as far south as the Cape of Good Hope, by about 70BC.

When the first Dutch settlers saw the Khoi in about AD1600 they lived in groups with a leader, but were split into smaller clans under their own headman. The clans came together only in times of stress or war. Because water was vital for the stock animals, the Khoi dug wells that were owned exclusively by the clan and group. In times of drought, when water was scarce, fights might erupt over these waterholes. Then each clan sent men to fight to protect the group's interests.

Each clan lived in a village, which was built inside a circular thorn hedge. In the centre were thorn enclosures to pen and protect the stock, surrounded by a circle of houses. Khoi houses are of a 'bender' or dome tent construction type; that is, long flexible poles are bent to form arches and the ends stuck into the ground. They are then covered with mats. When the clan needed to move to find more water or grazing these huts were simply taken down and strapped onto the back of their animals.

Tlou and Campbell (see *Further information*, page 505) describe one such village, which is known to have existed at Toromoja on the Boteti River (about 11 miles east of Rakops) around AD1200. A group of Khoi known as the Bateti lived there and kept long-horned cattle, sheep and goats, but they lived mainly on fish, zebra and other animals which they caught in the pits they dug by the river. They also ate plants, particularly waterlily roots. They had San servants who hunted and collected wild food for them. Sometimes they traded skins and ivory for iron tools, copper and tobacco, with the people living at Maun in the northwest, or the Toutswe people to the southeast.

Archaeologically speaking the Khoisan peoples were examples of Late Stone Age cultures; that is, their tools and weapons were made of wood, bone and stone. The Late Stone Age refers not to a period of time, but to a method and style of tool construction. Human beings had made stone tools for millennia and the name Late Stone Age refers to stylistic refinements and to the manufacture of tools developed for specific uses.

Specifically, experts define the transition from Early to Middle Stone Age technology as indicated by a larger range of stone tools often adapted for particular uses, and signs that these people had a greater mastery of their environment. This was probably in progress around 125,000 years ago in Botswana. They normally characterise the Late Stone Age by the use of composite tools, those made of wood and/or bone and/or stone used together, and by the presence of a revolutionary invention: the bow and arrow. This first appeared in southern Africa, and throughout the world, about 15,000 years ago. Skeletons of some of these Late Stone Age hunters had a close physical resemblance to the modern Khoisan people.

The Bantu-speaking farmers
The next people to arrive in Botswana were the Bantu-speakers. This collective term refers to a number of different tribes, from a related linguistic group, who over the course of thousands of years gradually migrated down into southern Africa from north of the Equator. The date of their arrival in Botswana is hard to pinpoint.

The Bantu were grain farmers (agriculturalists) as opposed to pastoralists or hunter-gatherers and they brought Iron Age technology with them; that is, their tools and weapons were made of iron. Physically these Iron Age farmers were much taller and heavier than the Khoisan, and they became the ancestors of the modern black Africans in southern Africa.

Crucial to the production of iron is a smelting furnace capable of reaching very high temperatures. Associated with the Iron Age is a new kind of pottery, which also had to be fired at high temperatures. Archaeologists use the finds of pottery and iron to date the arrival of the new people on the landscape of Botswana.

It is thought that the Bantu-speakers arrived in two main waves, bringing western and eastern Bantu languages. From west Africa, Late Stone Age farmers on the upper Zambezi were converted to the use of iron tools by about 300BC. From east Africa, Early Iron Age farming spread south along the east coast as far as the Zambezi by around 20BC.

By 200BC, in the Okavango–Makgadikgadi region, people were making a kind of pottery which archaeologists think was Khoi pottery influenced by western Iron Age (Bantu) styles, suggesting an initial contact between the two groups. The major Bantu influx probably occurred around the first few centuries AD, and the ancestors of the Khoisan people, with their simple Stone Age technology and hunter-gatherer existence, just could not compete. Since then the Khoisan have gradually been either assimilated into the migrant groups, or effectively pushed into the areas which could not be farmed. Thus the older Stone Age cultures persisted for much longer in the Kalahari (which is more difficult to cultivate) than in the rest of the country.

In theory, the stronger iron weapons of the Bantu should easily have made them the dominant culture. However, it took a very long time for Bantu language and culture to replace that of the Khoi; as late as the 19th century people were still speaking Khoi on the Boteti River. This supports a theory of communities living peacefully there, side by side, for a thousand years or more. In fact, there is some evidence of inter-marriage or inter-breeding between the two groups. The Batswana today have a mixture of Bantu and Khoisan features and they are noticeably lighter in skin colour than Bantu-speakers further north. They also tend to have the almond-shaped eyes, high cheekbones and thin lips of the Khoisan.

MORE IMMIGRANTS There are numerous problems with compiling a record of Bantu history in Botswana. We are dependent on oral history and archaeological records, and the two sometimes conflict with each other. The situation is very complex because of the number and mobility of the tribes involved.

The earliest dated Iron Age site in Botswana is an iron-smelting furnace in the Tswapong Hills, which is dated to around AD190. There is evidence of an early farming settlement of beehive huts made of grass matting, dating to around AD420 by the Molepolole River and a similar one has been found co-existing with Khoisan sites in the Tsodilo Hills, dating to around AD550.

By the 4th or 5th century AD, Iron Age farmers had certainly settled throughout much of southern Africa. As well as iron-working technology, they brought with them pottery, the remains of which are used by archaeologists to work out the migrations of various different groups of these Bantu settlers. These migrations continued, and the distribution of pottery styles suggests that the groups moved around within the subcontinent: this was much more complex than a simple north–south influx. Many of the tribes roamed over the whole of southern Africa, before various colonial authorities imposed artificial country borders in order to carve out territories for themselves.

This situation was complicated more recently by the prolonged and horrifically bloody tribal wars of the 19th century, known to historians as the Difaquane Wars.

BATSWANA HISTORY The Batswana rose to domination from among a number of powerful dynasties that spread out from the western Transvaal around AD1200– 1400. During the period AD1500–1600 the Phofu dynasty in western Transvaal disintegrated, with junior brothers forming breakaway, independent chiefdoms. Oral history traditions explain this as a response to drought. The archaeological record shows populations expanding into open country in small villages with cattle corrals, but by around AD1700 the settlements were often larger towns built of stone and situated on hills, reflecting the growth of hostile states, and the need for a strong defence.

The Difaquane Wars The whole of southern Africa was subject to increasing disruption, migration and war from about 1750 onwards, as trading and raiding for ivory, cattle and slaves spread inland from the coasts of Mozambique, the Cape Colony and Angola. The tribes often captured opponents during battle and sold them to slave raiders. Some of the battles themselves may have been slave raids against an enemy tribe.

Paramount amongst the aggressors in these wars was an ambitious Zulu leader named Shaka, who controlled a large slice of Natal by around 1810. The Ngoni people, which includes the Zulu nation, refer to the wars which Shaka initiated as the Mfecane, or 'the crushing'. However, the Batswana people, who were amongst the victims of Shaka's wars of expansion, refer to them as the Difaquane, which means 'the scattering'. Because they scattered, so they dispersed others.

A good explanation of this period is covered in John Reader's excellent *Africa: A Biography of the Continent* (see *Appendix 3, Further information*). He summarises the root causes:

> Thus they [the Zulus] were trapped in 'the trans-continental cross-fire of interrelated European plunder systems'. It was the unrelenting advance of settlers from the west, and the predacious demands of slavers in the east – exacerbated by intermittent drought – that set southern Africa in turmoil during the early eighteenth century. Not Shaka, not the Zulus, not the Mfecane.

Eventually, after the wars passed in the 1840s, the Batswana states of Ngwaketse, Kwena and the Ngwato rose to prosperity. They organised their people into wards with their own chiefs, but all paying tribute to the king. The states were in competition over trade benefits for ivory and ostrich feathers, down new roads, south to the Cape Colony. These roads also brought Boer trekkers and Christian missionaries to Botswana.

One of the Batswana kings, Sechele of the Kwena (1829–92), was baptised by David Livingstone, who passed through Botswana on his missionary travels. However it was the Ngwato, who superseded the Kwena in trading supremacy, who produced the most remarkable and famous dynasty and upon whom the following pages will concentrate.

Ngwato dynasty

In *Serowe: Village of the Rain Wind* (see *Appendix 3, Further information*), Bessie Head describes this remarkable dynasty, beginning with the reign of Khama the Great. He was king when the capital of the Bamangwato (Ngwato) moved to Serowe in 1902. Previously the capital had been a hundred miles away at Shoshong, and then at Palapye, but each time the tribe was forced to move on when water sources dried up. In 1902 two rivers, the Sepane and the Manonnye, flowed through Serowe, although both have subsequently dried up.

Khama the Great

Khama was the eldest son of Segkoma I, who was the chief when David Livingstone, the missionary explorer, first moved northwards through Botswana in the 1840s. Whilst the capital had still been at Shoshong, Livingstone had converted Khama and his brothers to Christianity. Although their father had allowed the missionaries to stay with them, and was interested to talk to them, he had refused to give up the traditional ways.

Eventually this led to a war between father and son, which Khama won, becoming king of the Bamangwato. Khama was a poetic visionary who changed the customs of his people in line with his Christian beliefs, and who foresaw the need for strong protection in the colonial carve-up of Africa, and campaigned strongly for the British Protectorate of Bechuanaland. (See also *Chapter 2, People and Culture*.)

Segkoma II

In 1916 Khama was kicked on the knee by a horse. At this time he invited his son Segkoma II, who had been in exile for ten years governing his own branch of the Bamangwato, to come home and rule at Serowe. This he did, and subsequently ruled at Serowe for nine years, although for most of that time he remained in the shadow of King Khama. Most importantly Khama insisted that

Segkoma marry a woman given to him by the Bamangwato, and the heir from this marriage was Seretse, who would later become the first president of Botswana.

Tshekedi Khama Following the death of Khama, and shortly afterwards of Segkoma II, Tshekedi Khama (Khama's son from a late second marriage) stepped in as regent until the four-year-old Seretse should come of age.

Where Khama was a visionary and politician, Tshekedi was full of pragmatic common sense and his rule, from 1926 to 1959, is marked by educational advances and self-help projects. When he first became leader there was only a primary school in Serowe. Then Tshekedi used his own money to send the young people of the village to South Africa for further education. From there they came home to teach in the village school. Later a secondary school and subsequently a college were built, using the voluntary labour of what were known as the age regiments (see page 42). Also known as the *mephato*, these were groups of young men of about the same age, usually formed from those who had graduated from the tribal initiation ceremony (known as *bogwera*) at the same time. They could be called upon to carry out services for the good of the community, ranging from routine community tasks to helping out with emergencies.

Moeng College of Higher Education is exciting for the principles on which it was founded, which gave equal weight to traditional knowledge and craft skills alongside academic instruction. As an experiment in social relations the houses built for the teaching staff were the equivalent of houses for white government officials. It was the only college in southern Africa at the time where houses for white and black teachers were equal and where they lived together in the same hostel.

Seretse Khama During the reign of Tshekedi, a problem arose over the future of Seretse Khama. Seretse was educated abroad, in London, Fort Hare University in South Africa, and Oxford. In 1948 Seretse wrote to inform his uncle that he wanted to marry an Englishwoman, Ruth Williams. Tshekedi opposed the marriage on the grounds that a king or chief could not do as he pleased because he was the servant of the people, and an heir to the chieftaincy was at stake. Traditionally the chief's wife was chosen by the *morafe* or tribal group. Seretse insisted on his right to choose his own wife and married the Englishwoman.

They were still arguing when the British took matters into their own hands. In a case that created an international scandal, the British government barred Seretse from the chieftaincy of the Bamangwato, and exiled him for six years. They invited him to Britain, where they forced him to stay. They also banned Tshekedi Khama from entering the Bamangwato reserve.

Secret documents have since confirmed that this British intervention was in order to satisfy the South African government, which objected to Seretse Khama's marriage to a white woman at a time when the policy of racial segregation, apartheid, was being enforced in South Africa.

Seretse, Tshekedi and their people fought against this banishment. The Bamangwato refused to pay taxes, sent delegations to the British and led protests. They refused to accept a British-nominated chief, and many people, including women, were flogged for this refusal.

Finally Tshekedi visited Seretse in London and the two resolved their differences. Seretse returned to Botswana with Ruth. Although a condition of his return was that he remained barred from the chieftancy, both he and Tshekedi continued to play an active role in the politics of Botswana, and were instrumental in the lead-up to independence.

Traders The earliest Europeans to come to Botswana were adventurers, explorers, hunters and missionaries. Travel in Botswana was very expensive, even then. A year's travel could cost up to £600 – equivalent to what a soldier of the period might earn during 30 years in the army. So early travellers came to trade for ivory, which made them huge profits with which to finance their expeditions. They travelled in wooden wagons, drawn by oxen or horses, and brought guns, beads, clothing and other, less-valuable items, which they bartered for significant amounts of ivory.

One of the biggest problems on the journey was the lack of water. There were often stretches of 50km or more without any. Water would be carried on the wagons, but not enough for both men and beasts. Sometimes the oxen died of thirst. There are stories of the wagons being unhitched and the oxen led to the nearest water – which could be some kilometres distant – and then returning to pull the wagons further. Oxen often died from drinking bad water or from tsetse-fly bite, while horses died of tickbite. A distance of 20km per day was thought to be a good rate of travel.

However, a wagon that did make it could return with about 200 elephant tusks – worth around £1,200 when sold in Cape Town. As they heard tales of huge profits, more traders began to venture into the region and gradually introduced money, which had been unknown until then. Previously barter and exchange systems functioned in the village – one goat equals one woven grass basket, and so on. Subsequently money became important in trade and people were forced to either sell something, or sell their labour, to get money. Little paid work could be found in Botswana, so large numbers of people were forced to emigrate to find work, often in the mines in South Africa.

Meanwhile the traders began to settle in Botswana at Shoshong, though the Bamangwato chiefs, Segkoma and Khama, were keen to prevent them from going further into the interior, so that they could maintain their trading supremacy.

The missions Following the traders came the missionaries, and missionary societies, who were already active in South Africa. Robert Moffat of the London Missionary Society (LMS) established a station at Kudumane, which succeeded in

DAVID LIVINGSTONE

David Livingstone's *Missionary Travels and Researches in South Africa* excited great interest in England. This account of his journeys across southern Africa in the 1840s and '50s had all the appeal that undersea or space exploration has for us now. Further, it captured the imagination of the British public, allowing them to take pride in their country's exploration of Africa, based on the exploits of an explorer who seemed to be the epitome of bravery and righteous religious zeal.

Livingstone had set out with the conviction that if Africans could see their material and physical well-being improved – probably by learning European ways, and earning a living from export crops – then they would be ripe for conversion to Christianity. He was strongly opposed to slavery, but sure that this would disappear when Africans became more self-sufficient through trade.

In fact Livingstone was almost totally unsuccessful in his own aims, failing to set up any successful trading missions, or even to convert many Africans permanently to Christianity. However, his travels opened up areas north of the Limpopo for later British missionaries, and by 1887 British mission stations were established in Zambia and southern Malawi.

prime minister. Within this new administration, a number of senior British public servants were kept on – including the minister of finance and the attorney general, and a senior civil servant in each of the ministries.

This clear victory for the BDP, and stable administration, gave the new government the platform from which to amend the constitution. The new Setswana name of the Republic of Botswana was chosen for the country, and on 30 September 1966, Sir Seretse Khama became the first president.

Politics since independence

1966–80: President Sir Seretse Khama Seretse Khama inherited a poor country. In 1965 the population stood at about 550,000 with a low level of literacy, and the country was gripped by a bad drought. Fortunately Britain was sympathetic to continuing to cover substantial costs of the new nation's administration, although with the discovery of diamonds at Orapa in 1967 by geologists from De Beers, and the subsequent mining operations which began in 1971, this assistance was only needed for six years after independence.

Botswana had long been in the Southern African Customs Union – and in 1969 it succeeded in renegotiating the terms of this, to become more financially independent. (Previously it had received a fixed percentage of total customs union income, rather than the income that was due directly from its own territory.)

During the 1970s Botswana's economy grew steadily, typically by around 12–13%, as Botswana extended its basic infrastructure for both mining development and basic social services for its population. Despite threats from, amongst others, the Marxist-leaning Botswana National Front (BNF), Sir Seretse Khama steered the country on a fairly moderate line – and the BDP was consistently re-elected in generally fair elections.

With civil war in Rhodesia throughout the 1970s, and apartheid regimes in South Africa and South West Africa (Namibia), Botswana's position was tricky. It accepted refugees from neighbouring countries, but refused to be used as a base for resistance organisations. Such neutrality was often severely tried, not least when, in February 1978, the Rhodesian army crossed the border and massacred 15 Botswana soldiers at Lesoma.

Zimbabwe gained independence in 1980, and the same year saw the foundation of the Southern African Development Coordination Conference (SADCC) with the aim of co-ordinating the region's disparate economies in the face of the huge economic muscle wielded by South Africa's apartheid regime.

Sir Seretse Khama died in July 1980 and, as envisaged by the constitution, was succeeded by his deputy, Sir Ketumile Masire. He left behind him an impressive legacy of a stable, prosperous country amidst a changing subcontinent. He had skilfully steered Botswana, with foresight and prudence, during perhaps its most vulnerable period – leaving it with the firm foundations of a democratic tradition, and well-trained executive and administrative branches of government.

The 1980s: President Sir Ketumile Masire Masire's succession was mandated by another victory for the BDP in a general election to the National Assembly in 1984 – although at the same time they lost control of all the town councils except Selebi-Phikwe. This sign of discontent was widely ascribed to the high levels of unemployment.

Just as the 1970s had witnessed upheavals in Rhodesia, so the 1980s saw the intensification of pressure on the white regime in South Africa to give way to majority rule.

Botswana continued to welcome refugees, but refused to harbour bases for the ANC's war on apartheid in South Africa. During this period Botswana had a delicate balancing act to play. Like most countries it was calling for an end to apartheid, and geographically it was one of the 'front line' states in the battle against apartheid. However, Botswana's economy was so dependent on its southern neighbour that it couldn't afford to apply the sanctions which most countries were calling for.

In 1981 tensions arose with South Africa over the supply of military equipment from the USSR for the Botswana Defence Force (BDF), though by 1986 Britain and the USA were offering hardware to the BDF to deter South African incursions into Botswana.

Meanwhile on its eastern border, relations with Robert Mugabe's ZANU government were businesslike rather than terribly friendly. The early 1980s saw Mugabe's notoriously ruthless Fifth Brigade terrorising Matabeleland – the province adjacent to Botswana. Zimbabwean refugees flooded into Botswana including, in March 1983, the leader of ZAPU, Mugabe's opposition in the elections, Joshua Nkomo.

Nkomo left for London rapidly, but later allegations that the refugee camps were harbouring armed dissidents caused problems, culminating in a border skirmish in 1983 between the BDF and 'armed men wearing Zimbabwean military uniforms'. It wasn't until April 1989 that Botswana felt able to revoke the 'refugee' status for Zimbabwean nationals and, soon after, the refugees left – although Botswana continued to have many illegal migrants from Zimbabwe.

Internally, political tensions between the BDP and the BNF peaked in early 1987 with a referendum on constitutional amendments to the electoral system, which was boycotted by the BNF. However, by October 1989, the BDP demonstrated its substantial support by winning 65% of the votes in an election (a result which was again challenged by the BNF in several constituencies). In October the new National Assembly returned Masire to the president's office for a third term.

During this time there were several incursions into Botswana by South African troops – including two raids on alleged ANC offices in Gaborone in 1985 and 1986. But a few years later, tensions began to ease as South Africa's President De Klerk started to set his country on a course for majority rule. One of his first steps was independence for Namibia in 1990.

1990–98: President Sir Ketumile Masire The early 1990s saw several corruption scandals in which a number of ministers resigned – including, in March 1992, the vice president, Peter Mmusi. (Contrast these with the paucity of resignations that occur during corruption scandals in most governments and you'll realise this is a good sign, not a bad one, for the integrity of Botswana's government!)

The general election of October 1994 saw the BNF triumphing in the urban areas, winning 13 seats (37.7% of the vote), while the BDP, with 40 seats (53.1% of the vote), continued to command the support of the rural constituencies. The elections were peaceful, with around a 70% turnout, and at last Botswana had an opposition party capable of a serious challenge to the BDP.

There was some unrest in early 1995, with several days of violence between the BDF and demonstrators (mainly students and the unemployed) during which one person was killed. However, most of this was sporadic and short-lived.

During this time relations with Botswana's neighbours were generally good. However, in 1992 a border squabble arose between Botswana and Namibia over a tiny island (called Sedudu by Botswana, and Kasikili by Namibia) in the Chobe

River. (For details of this argument, see page 196.) A potentially much more serious issue arose in 1996 when Namibia announced plans to construct a pipeline to take water from the Okavango River at Rundu. Given that this would impact directly on the Okavango Delta, the possibility of such a pipeline remains a source of great concern for Botswana.

Then in 1998 an influx of refugees from Namibia's Caprivi Strip arrived, including Mishake Muyongo, who had been suspended as president of Namibia's opposition party, the Democratic Turnhalle Alliance. He and other leading Caprivians had campaigned for independence for the province. By 1999, over 2,000 refugees were living near Gaborone. Namibia's extradition demands were refused, although eventually a settlement was brokered by the UNHCR whereby the most prominent refugees were granted asylum in Denmark, and the rest returned to Namibia under an amnesty.

Internal electoral reform had long been on the agenda in Botswana, with some consensus about the need for it from all the political parties. In 1997 various amendments to the constitution were passed, including a reduction in the voting age from 21 to 18 years old, the establishment of an electoral commission which is independent of the government, and a measure to restrict the president to a maximum of two terms in office.

Masire reshuffled the cabinet slightly in September 1997, and retired six months later, in March 1998. Meanwhile, infighting in the opposition, the BNF, led to a split, with dissident members forming the Botswana Congress Party (BCP). After 11 of the BNF's 13 deputies joined this, the BCP was declared the official opposition in mid-July 1998.

1998–2008: President Festus Mogae
The day after Masire's retirement, his vice president, Festus G Mogae, head of the BDP, was inaugurated. Mogae was born in 1939 and trained at Oxford as an economist. He served as executive director at the IMF for anglophone Africa, and later in various senior government posts, including governor of the Bank of Botswana. His new cabinet was virtually identical to the old one; the only new minister was Lt General Seretse Khama Ian Khama, son of Botswana's first president (the late Sir Seretse Khama), who in 1998 became vice president. Both men remained in office following elections in 1999 and 2004.

In 2003, Ian Khama became chairman of the BDP and five years later, when President Mogae stepped down at the end of his second term in office, he took on the presidency.

2008–present: Lt General Seretse Khama Ian Khama
The new president took office in April 2008. Elections the following year returned the BDP with 53% of the votes, securing 45 seats in parliament. Despite racking up a combined total of 40% of the votes, their BNF and (BCP) rivals came away with just ten seats.

The president was born in the UK in 1953, and went on to train at Britain's military academy, Sandhurst, before joining the newly formed Botswana Defence Force, rising to take charge in the late 1980s. Known as an ardent conservationist, he is actively involved in environmental organisations, and is an opponent of hunting. He has promoted the importance of diversification within Botswana's economy, with a view to lessening the country's dependence on diamond mining. One somewhat controversial initiative, though, has been the introduction of the Directorate of Internal Security, with its own powers separate from the police force. On the international stage, Khama has often taken a hard line against other African countries, occasionally finding himself a lone voice within the African Union. In 2011, he was one of the first to break off relations with Libya's Colonel Gaddafi, and more recently, his government condemned the 2013 elections in Zimbabwe as neither free nor fair.

Botswana's next elections are scheduled for October 2014. While there's every expectation that – like the previous elections – these will be on time, free and fair, the opposition disputes the 'fair', on the basis that access to state-controlled media is unequal. Despite this, the BNF does help to hold the BDP to account, and maintain at least some democratic debate.

GOVERNMENT AND ADMINISTRATION

Botswana's parliament consists of two houses: the National Assembly and the House of Chiefs. Elections to the National Assembly are held every five years, with results based on a first-past-the-post system, similar to that in Britain. As a result, the electoral system affords little chance for minority parties to gain ground, and attempts by opposition parties to pool their resources against the might of the BDP have so far come to nothing.

The president is appointed by parliament rather than directly elected. This is a controversial issue, but in 2008 parliament rejected calls for the system to be changed in favour of a popular vote.

For administrative purposes, the country is divided into a mix of rural and urban districts.

ECONOMY

In economic terms, Botswana is very much one of Africa's success stories, reflecting both the country's natural mineral wealth and a political and social stability which far outweighs that of its neighbours.

In the 30-year period following independence in 1966, the economic growth rate averaged just over 9% a year, marking the economy out as the fastest growing in the world, according to the World Bank. By the turn of the century, the growth rate had stabilised at around 7% a year. Despite plummeting to –7% in 2009, when Botswana's mining sector was reeling from the effects of a worldwide recession, the annual growth rate bounced back to 8% the following year, and in 2012 stood at fractionally over 6%.

Fundamental to this growth has been the exploitation of Botswana's diamond mines, although other growth sectors have been in tourism, cattle farming and financial services.

ECONOMIC DEVELOPMENT Prior to independence, Botswana's economy was primarily based on farming, particularly cattle. Even in 1993, some 46% of the country's land was permanent pasture. Since the 1970s, however, the extraction of mineral resources, particularly diamonds, has become big business, and today the sector accounts for a significant proportion of the country's wealth. Other areas of importance include tourism and cattle raising.

The government is increasingly conscious of the country's narrow revenue base and the need to diversify, in the face of finite diamond resources. In particular, the tourism, technology and financial services sectors have been earmarked for potential development, while the processing of diamonds and semi-precious stones is also targeted.

1

2

People and Culture

POPULATION OVERVIEW

Statistics from the 2011 census put Botswana's population at 2,024,904, with a population growth per year of 1.9% over the last decade.

This growth rate is low by African standards, and results from two conflicting issues. On the plus side, just over half of fertile women use contraceptives, which is exceptional for sub-Saharan Africa and reflects an educated people with a prosperous and generally developed economy. Conversely, average life expectancy is estimated at 55 years which, although a considerable improvement on recent years, is still a long way from the 65 years of the mid-1990s. This downturn reflects the high (albeit declining) incidence of HIV/AIDS, something that the government has sought to tackle both through education and with free anti-retroviral drugs. The good news, according to the United Nations, is that the rate of new cases of HIV/AIDS among Botswana's population fell by 71% between 2001 and 2011. Less positive is that almost a quarter of adults are still living with HIV – the second-highest rate in the world – although this is significantly lower than the peak of around 40%. Currently about a third of the population is under 15.

UNICEF's statistics indicate that 96% of the population has access to safe water, 62% to adequate sanitation, and almost all children under one have been immunised with polio, diphtheria and the BCG triple vaccine shots. These are very good levels by the continent's standards, and are no doubt helped by the government's policy of paying the full cost of all these vaccines.

Health care is provided both by the government and on a private basis, with some facilities built and operated by mining companies. Government expenditure on health amounted to US$734 per person in 2011.

However, these statistics say nothing of what Botswana's people are like. If you venture into the more rural areas, take a local bus, or try to hitchhike with the locals, you will often find that people are curious about you. Chat to them openly, as fellow travellers, and you will find most to be delightful. They will be pleased to assist you where they can, and as keen to help you learn about them and their country as they are interested in your lifestyle and what brings you to Botswana. That said, it's not uncommon, especially in the towns, to find people surly and largely uninterested sometimes … just as they are in London, or New York, or many other modern cities.

SOCIAL GROUPS OR 'TRIBES'

The people of Africa are often viewed, from abroad, as belonging to a multitude of culturally and linguistically distinct tribes – which are often portrayed as being linguists to believe that human language evolved in Africa, and further analysis has suggested that this was probably amongst the ancestors of the Khoisan.

The Khoisan languages are distinguished by their wide repertoire of clicking sounds. Don't mistake these for simple: they are very sophisticated. It was observed by Dunbar in 'Why gossip is good for you' (see *Appendix 3, Further information*) that, 'From the phonetic point of view these [the Khoisan languages] are the world's most complex languages. To speak one of them fluently is to exploit human phonetic ability to the full.'

At some point the Khoisan languages diverged from a common ancestor, and today three distinct groups exist: the northern, central and southern groups. Languages gradually evolve and change as different groups of people split up and move to new areas, isolated from their old contacts. Thus the evolution of each language is specific to each group, and reflected in the classifications described later in this chapter.

According to Mike Main in *The Visitor's Guide to Botswana* (now *The African Adventurer's Guide to Botswana*, see *Appendix 3, Further information*), the northern group are San and today they live west of the Okavango and north of Ghanzi, with representatives found as far afield as Angola. The southern group are also San, who live in the area between Kang and Bokspits in Botswana. The central group is Khoi, living in central Botswana, and extending north to the eastern Okavango and Kasane, and west into Namibia, where they are known as the Nama.

Each of these three Khoisan language groups has many dialects. These have some similarities, but they are not closely related, and some are different to the point where there is no mutual understanding. Certain dialects are so restricted that only a small family group speaks them; it was reported recently that one San language died out completely with the death of the last speaker.

This huge number of dialects, and variation in languages, reflects the relative isolation of the various speakers, most of whom now live in small family groups as the Kalahari's arid environment cannot sustain large groups of people living together in one place as hunter-gatherers.

Genetic discoveries Most genetically normal men have an X- and a Y-chromosome, whilst women have two X-chromosomes. Unlike the other 22 pairs of (non-sex) chromosomes that each human has, there is no opportunity for the Y-chromosome to 'swap' or 'share' its DNA with any other chromosome. Thus all the information in a man's Y-chromosome will usually be passed on, without change, to all of his sons.

However, very rarely a single 'letter' in the Y-chromosome will be altered as it is being passed on, thus causing a permanent change in the chromosome's genetic sequence. This will then be the start of a new lineage of slightly different Y-chromosomes, which will be inherited by all future male descendants.

In November 2000, Professor Ronald Davis and a team of Stanford researchers (see *Appendix 3, Further information*) claimed to have traced back this lineage to a single individual man, contesting that a small group of east Africans (Sudanese and Ethiopians) and Khoisan are the closest present-day relatives of this original man. That is, their genetic make-up is closest to his. (It's a scientific 'proof' of the biblical Adam, if you like.)

This is still a very contentious finding, with subsequent researchers suggesting at least ten original male sources ('Adams') – and so, although interesting, the jury remains out on the precise details of all these findings. If you're interested in the latest on this, then you'll find a lot about it on the web; start searching with the keywords: 'Khoisan Y chromosome'.

Historical and current views of the San Despite much evidence and research, our views of the San seem to have changed relatively little since both the Bantu groups and the first Europeans arrived in southern Africa.

The settlers' view Since the first Bantu farmer migrated south through east Africa, the range of territory occupied by the foragers, whose Stone Age technology had dominated the continent, began to condense. By the time the first white settlers appeared in the Cape, the Khoisan people were already restricted to Africa's southwestern corners and the Kalahari.

All over the world, farmers occupy clearly demarcated areas of land, whereas foragers will move more and often leave less trace of their presence. In Africa, this made it easier for farmers, first black then white, to ignore any traditional land rights that belonged to foraging people.

Faced with the loss of territory for hunting and gathering, the foragers – who, by this time were already being called 'Bushmen' – made enemies of the farmers by killing cattle. They waged a guerrilla war, shooting poison arrows at parties of men who set out to massacre them. They were feared and loathed by the settlers, who, however, captured and valued their children as servants.

Some of the Khoisan retreated north from the Cape – like the ancestors of Namibia's Nama people. Others were forced to labour on the settlers' farms, or were thrown into prison for hunting animals or birds which had been their traditional prey, but which were now designated property of the Crown. This story is told by Robert J Gordon in *The Bushman Myth: The Makings of a Namibian Underclass* (see *Appendix 3, Further information*). He shows that throughout history the hunter-gathering San have been at odds with populations of settlers who divided up and 'owned' the land in the form of farms. The European settlers proved to be their most determined enemy, embarking on a programme of legislation and massacre. Many San died in prison, with many more shot as 'vermin'.

Thus the onslaught of farmers on the hunter-gatherers accelerated between the 1800s and the mid-1900s. This helped to ensure that hunter-gathering as a lifestyle continued to be practical only in marginal areas that couldn't be economically farmed – like the Kalahari.

Western views of the San in the 1800s Though settlers in the Cape interacted with Khoisan people, so did Europe and the US, in a very limited way. Throughout the 1800s and early 1900s a succession of Khoisan people were effectively enslaved and brought to Europe and the US for exhibition. Sometimes this was under the guise of anthropology, but usually it didn't claim to be anything more than entertainment.

One of the first was the 'Hottentot Venus' – a woman who was probably of Khoisan extraction who was exhibited around London and Paris from 1810 to 1815, as an erotic curiosity for aristocrats. A string of others followed – for example, the six Khoisan people exhibited at the Coney Island Pleasure Resort, beside New York, and later in London in the 1880s, and billed as the 'missing link between apes and men'; or the 'wild dancing bushman' known as Franz, brought to England around 1913 by Paddy Hepston (see Q N Parsons' piece in *Botswana Notes and Records*, detailed in *Appendix 3, Further information*).

Impressions of the San from the 1950s In the 1950s a researcher from Harvard, John Marshall, came to the Kalahari to study the Kung! San. He described a peaceful people living in harmony with nature, amidst a land that provided all their needs. The groups had a deep spirituality and no real hierarchy: it seemed

2

like the picture of a modern Eden (especially when viewed through post-war eyes). Marshall was a natural cameraman and made a film that follows the hunt of a giraffe by four men over a five-day period. It swiftly became a classic, both in and outside of anthropological circles.

Further research agreed, with researchers noting a great surfeit of protein in the diet of the Kung! San and low birth rates akin to modern industrial societies.

Again the San were seen as photogenic and sources of good copy and good images. Their lives were portrayed in romantic, spiritual terms in the book and film

TRADITIONAL LIFE FOR THE SAN

Looking at the lifestyle of the San who until recently remained in the more remote areas of the Kalahari, it's difficult not to lapse into a romantic view of ignoring present realities. There are too many cultural aspects to cover here, so instead I've just picked out a few that you may encounter.

NOMADS OF THE KALAHARI Perhaps the first idea to dispel is that the San are nomads. They're not. San family groups have clearly defined territories within which they forage, called a *n!ore* (in the Ju/'hoansi language). This is usually centred on a place where there is water, and contains food resources sufficient for the basic subsistence of the group.

Groups recognise rights to the *n!ore*, which is passed on from father to first-born son. Any visiting people would ask permission to remain in these. Researchers have mapped these areas, even in places like the Central Kalahari.

HUNTER-GATHERERS Any hunter-gatherer lifestyle entails a dependence on, and extensive knowledge of, the environment and the resident fauna and flora found there. In the Kalahari, water is the greatest need and the San know which roots and tubers provide liquid to quench thirst. They create sip wells in the desert, digging a hole, filling it with soft grass, then using a reed to suck water into the hole, and send it bubbling up the reed to fill an ostrich egg. Water-filled ostrich eggs are also buried at specific locations within the group's 'area'. When necessary the San will strain the liquid from the rumen of a herbivore and drink that.

Researchers have observed that any hunting is done by the men. When living a basic hunting and gathering lifestyle, with little external input, hunting provides only about 20% of their food. The remaining 80% is provided largely by the women, helped by the children, who forage and gather wild food from the bush. By the age of 12 a child might know about 200 plant species, and an adult more than 300.

SOCIAL SYSTEM The survival of the San in the harsh environment of the Kalahari is evidence of the supreme adaptability of humans. It reflects their detailed knowledge of their environment, which provides them not only with food, but with materials for shelter and medicine in the form of plants.

Another very important factor in their survival is the social system by which the San live. Social interaction is governed by unwritten rules that bind the people in friendship and harmony. One such mechanism is the obligation to lend such few things as are individually possessed, thereby incurring a debt of obligation from the borrower. The San also practise exogamy, which means they have an obligation to marry outside the group. Such ties bind the society inextricably together, as does the system of gift exchange between separate groups.

The Lost World of the Kalahari by Laurens van der Post (see *Appendix 3, Further information*). This documentary really ignited the worldwide interest in the San and led to subsequent films such as *The Gods Must be Crazy*. All the images conveyed an idyllic view of the San as untainted by contact with the modern world.

The reality was much less rosy than the first researchers thought. Some of their major misconceptions have been outlined particularly clearly in chapter 13 of John Reader's *Africa: A Biography of the Continent* (see *Appendix 3, Further information*). He points out that, far from being an ideal diet, the nutrition of the San was often

Owing to environmental constraints a group will consist of between 80 and 120 people, living and moving together. In times of shortage the groups will be much smaller, sometimes consisting of only immediate family – parents, grandparents and children. They must be able to carry everything they possess. Their huts are light constructions of grass, and they have few possessions.

Because no-one owns property, no-one is richer or has more status than another. A group of San has a nominal leader, who might be a senior member of the group, an expert hunter, or the person who owns the water rights. The whole group takes decisions affecting them, often after vociferous discussions.

HUNTING The San in the Kalahari are practised hunters, using many different techniques to capture the game. Their main weapons are a very light bow, and an arrow made of reed, in three sections. The arrowhead is usually poisoned, using one of a number of poisons obtained from specific plants, snakes and beetles. (Though most San know how to hunt with bows and arrows, the actual practice is increasingly uncommon when it's not done to earn money from observing visitors.)

All the hunters may be involved in the capture of large game, which carries with it certain obligations. The whole group shares in the kill and each member is entitled to a certain portion of the meat.

There are different methods for hunting small game, which only the hunter's family would usually share. One method for catching spring hares involves flexible poles, sometimes 4m long, made of thin sticks, with a duiker's horn (or more usually now a metal hook) fastened to the end. These are rammed into the hare's hole, impaling the animal, which is then pulled or dug out.

TRANCE DANCING Entertainment for the San, when things are good, usually involves dancing. During some dances, which may often have overtones of ritual or religion, the dancers may fall into a trance and collapse.

These trances are induced by a deliberate breathing technique, with a clear physiological explanation. Dances normally take place in the evening, around a fire. Then the women, children and old people will sit around and clap, whilst some of the younger men will dance around the circle in an energetic, rhythmic dance. Often this is all that happens, and after a while the excitement dies down and everyone goes to sleep.

However, on fairly rare occasions, the dancers will go into a trance. After several hours of constant exertion, they will shorten their breathing. This creates an oxygen deficiency, which leads to the heart pumping more strongly to compensate. Blood pressure to the brain increases; the dancer loses consciousness and collapses.

2

Either way, it seemed likely that the government had, at best, been a little 'over-zealous' in its resettlement policy, and at worst may have committed serious injustices to the people in the reserve.

For me, the most pertinent question was 'Why bother?' The official line that the resettlement policy was to protect the game seemed implausible, given the bad press that this generated throughout the world. There were two obvious theories. One recognised that the government is putting an increasing emphasis on tourism, and was concerned that the presence of the San would detract from the tourist's experience. This really doesn't add up, as tourism could integrate well with the communities if given a chance, and provide a real income for them – and the whole process was started many years before tourism to the CKGR on any scale was viewed as a viable prospect. A second suggested that the government wanted to clear the way for the possibility of exploiting mineral claims in the area: diamond prospectors have long been looking for another find like Orapa beneath the Kalahari. This made little sense either; if an economic diamond pipe were found here – which has since proved to be the case – then no regulations would stand in the way of its exploitation! Implausible though it may seem, I believe that the government started by thinking, rather naively, that removal of the San from the CKGR was the 'best thing for all concerned' and were taken aback by the international campaign against it. Then they found themselves unable to backtrack without both losing face and making an exception for one ethnic group, which they didn't want to do.

In 2002, with the backing of the UK human rights organisation, Survival International (*www.survival-international.org*), 243 San people brought a case against the government, asserting their rights under the constitution to return to their ancestral lands. It was a long-running case, but finally, in December 2006, the three judges in the High Court ruled, by a majority of two to one, that the government's action was 'unlawful and unconstitutional', and 'failed to take account of the knowledge and culture' of the San. One judge added, 'In my view the simultaneous stoppage of the supply of food rations and the stoppage of hunting licences is tantamount to condemning the remaining residents of the Central Kalahari Game Reserve to death by starvation.'

Far from being the end of the dispute, however, the judgment served in part to prolong it. Despite the verdict, there was no requirement for the government to provide services such as water for those electing to return to the reserve. On his inauguration in 2008, President Khama sought to find a way forward by calling a meeting between the San and the government (although he is quoted by Survival International as saying that the San's way of life was an 'archaic fantasy'). A draft management plan was circulated among cabinet ministers prior to discussion with local residents' groups and relevant non-governmental organisations (NGOs). Yet despite this initiative, little has changed. The government has provided a new borehole for the small San community. And diamond mining within the reserve has commenced.

Most of those who have 'returned' in fact come and go, spending weeks in the reserve, then leaving in order to collect benefits (known as 'destitute rations' – coupons that can be exchanged for eligible provisions such as oil or flour), or water, or food. They are not allowed to drill further boreholes, to build any permanent structure, to use any form of transport, or to take in any new domestic animals such as goats. Hunting continues to be banned inside the CKGR and, although the San people can apply for special game licences for hunting in the wildlife management areas that abut the reserve, their lawyers argue that they should not have to apply for what is theirs by right.

CULTURAL SENSITIVITY AND LANGUAGE

Cultural sensitivity isn't something that a guidebook can teach you, though reading the section on cultural guidelines at the end of this chapter may help. Being sensitive to the results of your actions and attitudes on others is especially important in this area.

The San are often a humble people, who regard arrogance as a vice. It is normal for them to be self-deprecating amongst themselves, to make sure that everyone is valued and nobody becomes too proud. So the less you are perceived as a loud, arrogant foreigner, the better.

Very few foreigners can pick up much of the local language without living here for a long time. (Readers may already realise that spellings of the same word can vary greatly.) However, if you want to try to pronounce the words then there are four main clicks to master. In the well-documented Ju/'hoansi language, these are:

/ a dental click, a sucking sound, made by putting the tongue just behind the front teeth.

// a clucking sound, like that used in English to urge on a horse.

! a sharp popping sound, like a cork coming out of a bottle, made by pulling the tongue down quickly from the roof of the mouth.

(a soft popping sound, made by putting your tongue just behind the ridge at the back of the front teeth (this is usually the hardest).

In a further blow to the San, in August 2013, their British lawyer was barred from the country, and a month later the High Court ruled that, for procedural reasons, they would not permit the San's latest legal attempt to gain free access to their ancestral land to proceed.

What next? For Survival International, the campaign goes on, underpinned by their claim that 'the government is only allowing the 189 original applicants to the case and their children up to the age of 16, free access to the reserve', whereas 'originally, the government acknowledged that the ruling applied to around 700 Bushmen'.

The situation in the settlements outside the reserve presents different challenges. Around 2,000 people currently live in New Xade, where there is housing, water and government welfare agencies. The children benefit from both primary and secondary schools, and health needs are met by a modern hospital. Nevertheless, many complain that, with no opportunity to practise their traditional skills, the legacy of countless generations is being wiped out. And with no recent farming tradition, self-sufficiency is difficult. Some have found work on cattle farms or game farms and reserves, others in the tourist industry, but unemployment among the San is considerably higher than the national level of 17%. For many, the resulting disenfranchisement has led to situations of extreme poverty, with alcoholism a problem amongst some San populations.

Hope for the future? Perhaps one of the few rays of hope is that as a consequence of the prevailing image of the San, visitors really are willing to pay to see something of their 'traditional culture'. Hence the springing up of various traditional villages and tourism projects in both Botswana and neighbouring Namibia.

These vary from really interesting, genuine insights into the people and their skills, to little more than curiosity shows put on for the benefit of visitors.

I'd probably argue that virtually all are worthwhile for the San – provided that they bring a substantial income into the community involved, and do so without actively harming the people's self-esteem. Meanwhile, from experience of the best, I know they can be absolutely fascinating personal interactions for the visitor, as well as acting to reinforce the community's own self-esteem and value in their own skills, whilst bringing much-needed money into the community.

What's become very, very clear is that making such a tourist–community interaction really successful for both parties needs the permanent commitment of someone on the ground who has been working with the community for a long period – and understands both the community and the tourists. Without this, such projects invariably fail.

The Khoi The San are often described as hunter-gatherers and the Khoi as pastoralists. The distinction between the two Khoisan peoples is not quite so clear-cut, but it is generally useful. The Khoi, who live in central Botswana and Namibia, have herds of cattle, but continue to source some of their food from hunting and gathering, supplemented by milk products. Because of the intrinsic value of the animals, the Khoi milk their herds but do not kill them for food; stock animals are only killed to mark special occasions.

The ownership of property (stock) by the Khoi has created a more rigid and complex social structure than among the San. Property creates wealth, which can be inherited after the death of the owner, and so laws of inheritance have been developed, as well as laws to protect property. Wealth brings with it the power to control others, thus creating leaders. It also leads to a wealth-based economy that depends on the exchange of goods and work that have an economic value. What must be freely given among the San must be bought and paid for among the Khoi.

Little is known about the religious beliefs of the Khoi, though they believe in a Supreme Being and it is thought that some beliefs are similar to the San and can be traced back to a common source.

OTHER SOCIAL GROUPS
Bantu-speaking peoples After a complex history of conflict, a number of tribes of Bantu origin can now be found in Botswana. As discussed on pages 21–3, today the word 'tribe' has colonial connotations, but unfortunately we do not have a suitable alternative. Likewise, definition by ethnic group is not considered politically correct in Botswana; all people are primarily Batswana (the people of Botswana), and only secondarily Bayei, Bakwena, European etc. (Tribal names are frequently preceded by 'Ba', which means 'the people of …'.) Sometimes you'll also see the singular 'Motswana' or 'Matswana', used to mean a person from Botswana.

Batswana Although the same name applies to all the people of Botswana, the Batswana (or Tswana) are also the largest ethnic group in the country. (As an aside, colonial partitioning led to three-quarters of the Batswana actually living in South Africa.) The name embraces a number of different offshoots. The Batswana speak Setswana, which is the second language of Botswana, English being the official language.

The Bakalanga The Bakalanga are the country's second-largest population group after the Batswana, despite having been divided by colonial boundaries.

Today over 80% of them live in Zimbabwe. Those in Botswana live mainly in the area around Francistown, although they are scattered as far afield as Maun, Palapye, Serowe, Mahalapye and Mochudi. Their origins are unclear, though some of them have probably lived in the region of the upper Shashe River for at least a thousand years. For the last 600 years they have been ruled by other peoples, but interestingly their conquerors have always ended by inter-marrying with the Bakalanga and adopting their customs and language.

The Bakalanga are primarily agriculturalists and this is reflected in their religion and culture, but cattle and goats are also kept, usually by the chief on behalf of his tribe. The chief would give cattle to people who had performed services to the tribe, or those who needed them in order to get married or to sacrifice to the ancestors. The primary importance of agriculture is shown by the traditional marital gifts of specially forged iron hoes that were given to the bride's parents to symbolise the continuity of her livelihood.

The Basubiya, the Bayei and the Hambukushu
Around AD1600 these three groups of river-dwelling people all lived close together in the region to the south of the Chobe River. Their closeness is reflected in the similarity of their customs. Significantly, their system of inheritance meant that wealth and status were not passed to the first son, but through to the children of the father's eldest sister. So a man inherited the chieftancy if his mother was the eldest sister of the chief.

The Basublya
According to tradition, after a fight over a lion skin the Bayei were defeated by the Basubiya. They moved away to the Linyanti River, but they still came under the rule of the Basubiya.

Meanwhile, the Hambukushu were driven from their homeland by the expansionist and tribute-seeking chief of the Balozi, whose capital used to be at Katima Mulilo (but is now in western Zambia). To avoid paying the tribute and escape his attentions, the Hambukushu left the Zambezi River and moved nearer to the Chobe and Linyanti rivers, into a region which was already occupied by the Bayei.

In time, the Basubiya grew very powerful and had a large state which stretched westwards from Luchindo on the Chobe River towards the Okavango. Eventually they were defeated by the Balozi and were incorporated into the Lozi empire until its collapse in 1865. According to Campbell, the Basubiya were mainly agriculturalists who also kept some cattle, sheep and goats. They cultivated the floodplains, which they prepared by hoeing in the autumn before the winter floods and planting crops such as millet, sweet reeds and melon when the floods had receded. Today they still live in the Northwest and Chobe districts of the country.

The Bayei (and Banoka)
In response to the Basubiya invasion, the Bayei moved away from the Chobe River, into the Okavango, and between 1750 and 1800 they firmly established themselves in the area of the Okavango Delta around Lake Ngami. This shallower, southern section of the Delta perfectly suited the Bayei, who lived mainly from fishing. They also kept cattle, but used them only as pack animals. In the Delta they encountered a group of Khoi called the Banoka (otherwise known as the River Bushmen), who had adapted their hunter-gatherer skills to the environment of the Delta.

The two peoples seem to have co-existed peacefully and even swapped skills. For example the Bayei taught the Banoka to fish with nets where before they had only used baskets. The Bayei made nets from the twisted fibres of succulent plants, which they then trawled behind their boats, called *mekoro*. A *mokoro* ('mekoro' is the plural form) is a dugout canoe that is poled from the rear. In return the Banoka taught the Bayei how to dig pits, filled with sharp pointed sticks, in the middle of a game trail, to trap unsuspecting animals on their way to the river.

A prize catch for the Bayei was the hippo, which is notoriously bad-tempered and dangerous and is liable to attack if surprised in the water. Sometimes it was hunted from the mekoro, when the Bayei's method, like that of the old whale hunters, was to harpoon the hippo from the boat. Instantly the animal would take flight, towing the mokoro in its wake. The hunters had to kill the hippo with their spears, before it either broke loose or killed them. This they did by attempting to reach the bank in their boats, tying the rope attached to the harpoon to a tree and waiting for the hippo to tire before approaching it with spears. Another favourite method of hippo hunting was to place a spear weighted with rocks suspended from a tree over a hippo trail. This capitalised on the fact that hippos live in the water during the day, but come out at night to graze, when they tend to keep to the same tracks.

While mekoro today are more likely to be transporting tourists for a spot of hippo watching, and may well be made of fibreglass instead of wood, they are still often poled by a Bayei man.

The Hambukushu Meanwhile the Hambukushu found that settling on the Chobe did not take them far enough from the Balozi tribute seekers, so they moved again and settled in the more northerly, upper reaches of the Okavango Delta. Being agriculturalists as well as hunters and fishermen, they preferred the deeper water there. Unlike the lower regions, this area did not flood when the rains came and so was more suitable for agriculture. They cleared the bush and planted crops along the river, such as millet, sugarcane, pumpkins and root crops.

Like the Bayei, the Hambukushu used mekoro, but instead of poling them standing up, they sat down and used paddles to propel them through the deeper water.

Alec Campbell's *The Guide to Botswana* (see *Appendix 3, Further information*) describes how the Hambukushu hunted for elephants:

> They took the blade of a spear which had a barb in it and fixed this into a heavy piece of wood. They dug shallow holes on paths used by elephants and then set these spear blades facing upwards. The elephant stood on this, driving the blade deep into the bottom of its foot, after which it couldn't walk. When it was weak, men came with axes and slashed the tendons in its back legs so that it fell down and could be speared.

Today the Hambukushu are most famous for their beautiful hand-woven baskets, which are internationally recognised for their craftsmanship and design. The wide variety of basket types reflects the numerous purposes for which they were traditionally used, ranging from enormous grain-storage baskets, to tightly woven beer baskets for holding the local brew. Unfortunately, the baskets are now being produced commercially, which enables the makers to earn a reasonable living, but has led to over-exploitation of the natural resources from which the baskets are made. The Hambukushu are also renowned as rain-makers, another skill which they have exploited commercially by selling their services to neighbouring tribes.

The Ovaherero and the Ovambanderu The Ovaherero (or Herero) and their relatives the Ovambanderu are pastoralists, who keep large herds of sheep, goats, and especially cattle, which have a religious significance for them. According to their oral history tradition they seem to have moved southwest from central Africa, probably to escape the tsetse fly which spreads sleeping sickness and kills cattle and people.

The religious life of the tribe was of great importance. The tribe was divided into religious clans under a priest/chief. He owned the most cattle and he maintained a sacred herd on behalf of the tribe. On his death the priesthood and the care of the sacred herd passed to his son. The Ovaherero practised ancestor worship, and one of the priest's main religious duties was appeasing the dead relatives of the tribe.

As pastoralists, the clans led their herds in search of grazing but each clan had a designated area. Within this area the women built round huts from a framework of branches covered with mud. The huts were built in a circle around corrals for the animals. As well as tending the herds, the men hunted with wooden spears (their only iron came from trading with the Batswana). The women also collected wild food and made *omaere*, a kind of sour milk which was their staple food.

The presence of the Ovaherero people in Botswana dates back to the beginning of the 20th century, when they were living in what is now northern Namibia, but were becoming increasingly unhappy about their loss of land to the German colonists. In January 1904 their leader, Samuel Maherero, ordered a Herero uprising against the colonial forces. Initially the Hereros had success in taking many German farms and smaller outposts, and in severing the railway line between Swakopmund and Windhoek. However, later that year the German General von Trotha led a large German force including heavy artillery against the Hereros. By August the Hereros had been pushed back to their stronghold of Waterberg, with its permanent waterholes. On 11 August, the Germans attacked, and the battle raged all day. Though it was not decisive, the Hereros' spirit was beaten by the superior firepower and they fled east, into the Kalahari and towards Maun. Many perished; the rest settled in what is now northern Botswana. They had lost their cattle and were forced to work as servants to another tribe, the Batawana. However they soon rebuilt their herds and also learned agriculture from the Batawana, which they used to supplement their traditional diet of soured milk.

Today, although most of the Ovaherero live in Namibia, some are still to be found in Botswana. The women are recognisable because they continue to dress in the clothes they were taught to wear by Victorian Christian missionaries, including long bulky dresses and elaborate headdresses.

The Kagalagadi This name (not to be confused with the name of the transfrontier park in Botswana and South Africa) is applied to different people of varied descent who currently live in the Kalahari Desert. There are five major groups who have settled in different areas of the Kalahari. They all have their own tribal names and customs and they speak a variety of languages – the combined form of which is a Sotho language, not a dialect of Setswana.

Of these groups, the Bakgwatheng remain in the east of the Kalahari on the fringes of the desert, which receives sufficient rainfall for their crops of sorghum, melons and beans. They also keep small herds of cattle, sheep and goats, and mine and work iron. As iron ore was not available in the heart of the Kalahari, these factors all restricted them to the desert's fringe.

The Bangologa and the Babolaongwe, on the other hand, are pastoralists with large herds of sheep and goats, and a few cattle. They obtain most of their food from hunting and gathering, so they are not reliant upon agriculture and they trade for iron, so they were able to live a nomadic existence within the desert. The other two groups are the Baphaleng and the Bashaga.

For more scientifically minded readers, here's a list of most of Botswana's main language groups, with their linguistic family roots and a few brief notes on where they're spoken. This tells you the history of that language, starting with the main group to which it belongs, and defining it more specifically. Thus English and Afrikaans are both Indo-European languages, and more specifically Germanic and West. That means they both originally derive from one ancient language, West Germanic. The classification of the Khoisan and Bantu languages gives a similar view of their history and relationships. Obviously the information below is best read in conjunction with the whole section on social groups.

BANTU LANGUAGES

Setswana *Classification: Niger-Congo, Atlantic-Congo, Volta-Congo, Benue-Congo, Bantoid, Southern, Narrow Bantu, Central, S, Sotho-Tswana (S30), Tswana.* Around 70% of the population speak Setswana (also known as Tswana). Some official business is conducted in Setswana, the media often use English and Setswana interchangeably, and it's the lingua franca between different citizens who don't speak English.

Tswapong *Classification: Niger-Congo, Atlantic-Congo, Volta-Congo, Benue-Congo, Bantoid, Southern, Narrow Bantu, Central, S, Sotho-Tswana (S30), Tswapong.* Several thousand speakers, in the Central District and Mahalapye Sub-district.

Kagalagadi *Classification: Niger-Congo, Atlantic-Congo, Volta-Congo, Benue-Congo, Bantoid, Southern, Narrow Bantu, Central, S, Sotho-Tswana (S30), Kgalagadi.* Estimated total of about 35,000 speakers in Botswana.

Birwa *Classification: Niger-Congo, Atlantic-Congo, Volta-Congo, Benue-Congo, Bantoid, Southern, Narrow Bantu, Central, S, Sotho-Tswana (S30), Sotho.* Estimated total of about 10,000 speakers in Botswana.

Kalanga *Classification: Niger-Congo, Atlantic-Congo, Volta-Congo, Benue-Congo, Bantoid, Southern, Narrow Bantu, Central, S, Shona (S10).* Estimated total of about 160,000 speakers in Botswana.

Ndbele *Classification: Niger-Congo, Atlantic-Congo, Volta-Congo, Benue-Congo, Bantoid, Southern, Narrow Bantu, Central, S, Ngui.* Estimated total of about 10,000 speakers in the Northeast District, though this is the main language over the border in Zimbabwe's Matabele Province.

Herero *Classification: Niger-Congo, Atlantic-Congo, Volta-Congo, Benue-Congo, Bantoid, Southern, Narrow Bantu, Central, R, Herero.* Estimated total of about 31,000 speakers scattered among other ethnic groups in Botswana, often having their own area in towns and villages. This is one of Namibia's major ethnic groups.

Yeyi *Classification: Niger-Congo, Atlantic-Congo, Volta-Congo, Benue-Congo, Bantoid, Southern, Narrow Bantu, Central, R, Yeye.* Estimated total of about 27,000 speakers in Botswana, with probably another 20,000 ethnic Bayeyi who do not actually speak Yeyi.

Mbukushu *Classification: Niger-Congo, Atlantic-Congo, Volta-Congo, Benue-Congo, Bantoid, Southern, Narrow Bantu, Central, K, Kwangwa.* Estimated total of about 12,000 speakers in Botswana, located in the Northwest District, especially in Gomare and the villages to the north of there, and in the Okavango Delta.

Subiya *Classification: Niger-Congo, Atlantic-Congo, Volta-Congo, Benue-Congo, Bantoid, Southern, Narrow Bantu, Central, K, Subia (L50).* Estimated total of about 12,000 speakers in Botswana, mostly living in the Northwest and Chobe districts.

KHOISAN LANGUAGES

!Xoo *Classification: Khoisan, southern Africa, Southern, Hua.* There are between 3,000 and 4,000 speakers of this Khoisan language, and its related dialects, living in Botswana.

=/Hua *Classification: Khoisan, southern Africa, Southern, Hua.* Around 1,000–1,500 speakers, living mainly in the southern Kalahari Desert and the Kweneng District.

//Gana *Classification: Khoisan, southern Africa, Central Tshu-Khwe, Northwest.* Around 1,000 speakers living around the Ghanzi District, in villages and farms, and in the Central Kalahari Game Reserve. Speakers are also found in the Central District (Boteti Sub-district) and the cattle-posts south and west of Rakops.

/Anda *Classification: Khoisan, southern Africa, Central Tshu-Khwe, Northwest.* About 1,000 speakers live in the Northwest District, mostly around the Khwai River and Mababe Village areas.

Ksoe *Classification: Khoisan, southern Africa, Central Tshu-Khwe, Northwest.* Speakers of this language, often known as the 'River Bushmen', number around 1,700–2,000, and live in and around the Northwest District, mainly in the villages of Gan, Cadikarauwe, Mohembo, Shakawe, Kaputura, /Ao-Kyao, Sikonkomboro, Ngarange, Sekanduko, Xongoa, Cauwe, Moxatce, Dungu, Seronga, Beyetca, Gudigoa, Sikokora, Geixa, /Qom-ca, Tobere, 0/Umbexa, Djaxo and Kangwara.

Deti *Classification: Khoisan, southern Africa, Central Tshu Khwe, Central.* Spoken in the Central District, the Boteti Sub-district, and in the villages which are strung out along the Boteti River.

Nama *Classification: Khoisan, southern Africa, Central Tshu-Khwe, Central.* There are about 200–1,000 Nama speakers in Botswana, mostly in the Kgalagadi Disirct around Tsabong, Makopong, Omaweneno and Tshane villages, and in the Ghanzi District, in the villages along the Ghanzi–Mamuno road. It's also spoken by a much larger population in Namibia.

Ganadi *Classification: Khoisan, southern Africa, Central Tshu-Khwe, North Central.* Spoken in the Northeastern area.

Shua *Classification: Khoisan, southern Africa, Central Tshu-Khwe, North Central.* Counted together with the Tshwa group, there are around 19,000 Shua speakers in Botswana, located in the Central District and Tutumi Sub-district.

//Gwi *Classification: Khoisan, southern Africa, Central, Tshu-Khwe, Southwest.* There are around 800 speakers in villages in the Kweneng and Ghanzi districts.

Naro *Classification: Khoisan, southern Africa, Central Tshu-Khwe, Southwest.* Botswana has an estimated 8,000 speakers of Naro.

Ju/'Hoansi *Classification: Khoisan, southern Africa, Northern.* This is one of the larger Khoisan languages, with 4,000–8,000 speakers in Botswana, and many more in Namibia, around the Tsumkwe area.

=/Kx'au//'ein *Classification: Khoisan, southern Africa, Northern.* There are about 3,000 speakers in Botswana, mostly in the Ghanzi District, both in the villages and working on commercial farms.

EUROPEAN LANGUAGES

English *Classification: Indo-European, Germanic, West, English.* English is the official language in Botswana, the language of government and schools, although official work is increasingly being carried out in Setswana (Tswana).

Afrikaans *Classification: Indo-European, Germanic, West; Low Saxon-Low Franconian, Low Franconian.* There are 20,000 people in Botswana whose native tongue is Afrikaans, mainly on the commercial farms in the Ghanzi District. In addition, many of the white community who have close links with South Africa can communicate in Afrikaans.

MUSIC Botswana's musical traditions are as varied as its culture. In traditional Batswana culture, the teaching of music and dance was incorporated into the initiation rites at puberty, and dancing, accompanied by the beat of drums, was once used to mark special occasions such as hunting or the annual harvest. Today,

CULTURAL GUIDELINES

Comments here are intended to be a general guide, just a few examples of how to travel more sensitively. They should not be viewed as blueprints for perfect Botswana etiquette. Cultural sensitivity is really a state of mind, not a checklist of behaviour – so here we can only hope to give the sensitive traveller a few pointers in the right direction.

When we travel, we are all in danger of leaving negative impressions with local people that we meet. It is easily done – by snapping that picture quickly, whilst the subject is not looking; by dressing scantily, offending local sensitivities; by just brushing aside the feelings of local people, with the high-handed superiority of a rich Westerner. These things are easy to do, in the click of a shutter, or flash of a dollar bill.

However, you will get the most representative view of Botswana if you cause as little disturbance to the local people as possible. You will never blend in perfectly when you travel – your mere presence there, as an observer, will always change the local events slightly. However, if you try to fit in and show respect for local culture and attitudes, then you may manage to leave positive feelings behind you.

One of the easiest, and most important, ways to do this is with **greetings**. African societies are rarely as rushed as Western ones. When you first talk to someone, you should greet them leisurely. So, for example, if you enter a bus station and want some help, do not just ask outright, 'Where is the bus to … ?' That would be rude. Instead you will have a better reception (and a better chance of good advice) by saying:

Traveller:	'Good afternoon.'
Local:	'Good afternoon.'
Traveller:	'How are you?'
Local:	'I am fine, how are you?'
Traveller:	'I am fine, thank you. (pause) Do you know where the bus to …'

This goes for approaching anyone – always greet them first. For a better reception still, learn the greetings in Setswana (see *Appendix 2, Language*), or even the local language. Whilst most people in Botswana understand English, a greeting in an appropriate local language will be received with delight.

Very rarely in one of the towns you may be approached by someone who doesn't greet you. Instead s/he tries immediately to sell you something, or even hassle you in some way. These people have learned that foreigners aren't used to greetings, and so have adapted their approach accordingly. A surprisingly effective way to dodge their attentions is to reply to their questions with a formal greeting, and then politely – but firmly – refuse their offer.

Another part of the normal greeting ritual is **handshaking**. As elsewhere, you would not normally shake a shop-owner's hand, but you would shake hands with someone to whom you are introduced. Get some practice when you arrive, as there is a gentle, three-part handshake used in southern Africa which is easily choral singing is particularly popular, with village choirs often coming together to celebrate national holidays.

With the policy of integration implemented at independence in the mid-1960s came a decline in individual cultural traditions. Since then, however, there has

learned. It consists of taking each other's right hand, as for a normal handshake, but just shaking once, up and down. Then whilst leaving the thumbs linked, the grip is changed by both people raising their hands, until their arms make a right-angle. Each then grasps the other person's thumb and the top of their hand firmly. Then this is swiftly relaxed, with thumbs still interlinked, and the hands are dropped back into one last normal 'shake'.

Your **clothing** is an area that can easily give offence. Most people in Botswana frown upon skimpy or revealing clothing, especially when worn by women. Shorts are fine for walking safaris, but otherwise dress conservatively and avoid short shorts, especially in the more rural areas. Respectable locals will wear long trousers (men) or long skirts (women).

Homosexuality is illegal in Botswana, although no-one – as far as I know – has ever been prosecuted, and same-sex relationships have never been a problem for guests in safari camps. While it's not at all unusual in traditional societies to see two men – or two women – casually holding hands, public **displays of affection** between two people (gay or straight) may create tension and are best avoided.

Photography is a tricky business. Most people in Botswana will be only too happy to be photographed – provided you ask their permission first. Sign language is fine for this question: just point at your camera, shrug your shoulders, and look quizzical. The likelihood is that then everyone will smile for you, producing the type of 'posed' photograph that you may not want. However, stay around and chat for five or ten minutes, and people will get used to your presence and stop posing; then you will get more natural shots (a camera with a quiet shutter is a help).

Note that special care is needed with photography near government buildings, bridges, mines, and similar sites of strategic importance. You must ask permission before photographing anything here, or you risk people thinking that you are a spy. (To be fair to the country, I've never come across such problems in Botswana, though I'd still exercise the same caution as in any other country.)

If you're seeking directions to somewhere, don't be afraid of **asking questions**. Most people will be polite and keen to help – so keen that some will answer 'yes' to questions if they think that this is what you want to hear. So try to avoid asking leading questions. For example, 'Yes' would often be the typical answer to the question, 'Does this road lead to … ?' And in a sense the respondent is probably correct – it will get you there. It's just that it may not be the quickest or shortest way. To avoid misunderstandings, it is often better to ask open-ended questions like, 'Where does this road go to?' or 'How do I drive to … ?'

The examples above are general by their very nature. But wherever you find yourself, if you are polite and considerate to the people of Botswana that you meet, then you will rarely encounter any cultural problems. Watch how they behave and, if you have any doubts about how you should act, then ask someone quietly. They will seldom tell you outright that you are being rude, but they will usually give you good advice on how to make your behaviour more acceptable.

Because he was a deeply committed Christian convert, Khama, the leader of the Bamangwato, began to make changes to the traditional way of life. He reformed the *bogadi* tradition, which had meant that a woman's children belonged to her husband, even those children she had after he had died. He also laid down laws and regulations for his people to live by, including banning the consumption of alcohol.

One of the most significant changes made by Khama was the abolition of the initiation ceremonies for men and women. One elderly man described the men's initiation ceremony or *bogwera*:

> Not only was the foreskin cut and the youths put through endurance tests, but one of us had to remain behind. He was killed in a painful way, in the secrecy of the bush. When we came home, it was made out that the youth had died because he could not stand up to the tests. Everyone knew the truth but it was treated as a deep secret. That was why Khama abolished *bogwera*.

However, the ritual was still important to mark the passing of boyhood into manhood, so Khama preserved the tradition of 'age regiments'. All young men had their coming of age marked by a gathering with prayers and lectures. Those who came of age at the same time formed an age regiment. From Khama's time on, the age regiments began to volunteer to work on community projects such as building schools or churches and many things were accomplished.

It was also largely due to the efforts of Khama that Botswana became a British Protectorate, known as the British Bechuanaland Protectorate. This probably saved the country from becoming another South Africa or Rhodesia (Zimbabwe) and resulted in Botswana's peaceful independence in 1966.

been a resurgence of interest. Dancing is widely taught in schools, and during the 1980s there was a revival of instruments such as the *segaba*, a simple violin used to accompany folk singing. Simpler still are the thumb pianos or *setinkane*, like miniature xylophones made with sheets of scrap metal on a small wooden base, and once widely played.

Recently, there has been an explosion of musical influence from overseas, resulting in a more modern culture of hip-hop artists and performers of *kwasa-kwasa* – a suggestive dance form akin to the rumba.

ARTS AND CRAFTS While the ancient rock art of the Tsodilo Hills has gained international recognition, modern visual arts are much harder to find, at least outside of Gaborone, which is home to the National Museum and Art Gallery.

Visitors, however, should have no problem in finding examples of local crafts, especially basketwork. The tradition stems from items woven for practical purposes such as storing or winnowing grain. Most of these are produced by women from the Bayei and Hambukushu groups in northwest Botswana, where the mokolwane palm – source of the fibres for basket weaving – is widely grown. Now increasingly popular as souvenirs, these baskets can be deceptively complex in construction, something that is reflected in their costs. Many are plain, but others have intricate patterns woven into their design.

Clay pots also have their place in traditional culture, being used both for storing water and for brewing beer, as well as for cooking. In rural villages, such pots were

When the Protectorate was finally granted, Khama expressed his gratitude and laid down the following principles of government, in a document which related primarily to the Bamangwato, but was later applied to the whole country:

> I am not baffled in the government of my town, or in deciding cases among my own people according to custom. I have to say that there are certain laws of my country which the Queen of England finds in operation, and which are advantageous to my people, and I wish these laws should be established and not taken away by the Government of England. I refer to our law concerning intoxicating drinks, that they should not enter the country of the Bamangwato, whether among black people or white people. I refer further to our law which declares that the lands of the Bamangwato are not saleable. I say this law is also good; let it be upheld and continue to be law among black people and white people.

The system of traditional law to which Khama referred in this document was well established. It centred upon the chief, whose position of prestige and power carried with it the obligation that the good of the tribe must be placed above personal desire. The chief held property and land on behalf of the tribe and had always to be available to his people to settle disputes and business affairs.

There was also a tribal court, known as a *kgotla*, to help him make decisions. This consisted of the headmen of the wards into which the village was divided, and of senior tribesmen. Disputes which could not be settled within the ward were brought to the *kgotla*. There was an obligation for people to be open in all their dealings with each other and to act in the best interests of the community.

moulded from natural clays, then baked in the sun to dry, but today potteries such as Okavango Ceramics and the Craft Centre in Maun use kilns to fire their work.

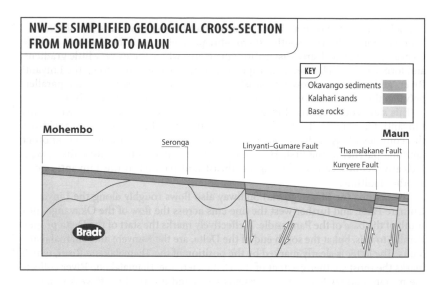

NW–SE SIMPLIFIED GEOLOGICAL CROSS-SECTION FROM MOHEMBO TO MAUN

KEY
Okavango sediments
Kalahari sands
Base rocks

Mohembo

Maun

Seronga

Linyanti–Gumare Fault

Thamalakane Fault

Kunyere Fault

Bradt

as much as 300m. These have acted to 'capture' the Okavango River in a depression where the gradient is very shallow. (As an aside, just north of this, smaller faults, perpendicular to the main ones, act to restrict the Okavango's sweeping meander to the narrow confines of the Panhandle.)

Thus, in time as they gradually formed, these faults diverted the Zambezi and the Kwando rivers, and forced the Okavango to spread into its present-day delta formation.

The great salt pans As its feeding rivers were diverted, the great Lake Makgadikgadi was starved of its sources. This would probably have happened over a very long period of time. We know that the climate in Botswana varied greatly, and during periods of heavier rainfalls the lake might have persisted. Geologists have identified at least five clearly different levels of the lake, each of which has its own identifying features that are still visible. And for each the size of the lake must have been totally different.

But eventually, starved of inflow in a drier climate, the lake shrank. With no known outflows, it would probably have already been very brackish. Now its remaining salts were concentrated more and more, and eventually crystallised out where the last of its waters evaporated – at its lowest point, where the pans are now. Too saline for plants to grow, this residue formed the amazingly flat surface of the great salt pans that are now such a distinctive feature of the northern Kalahari.

The formation of the Okavango Delta The geological history outlined so far in this chapter explains how the Okavango has been constrained by faults, but it doesn't really help to explain how the Delta's strange and wonderful landscapes came about. That's really due to much more recent processes, of which I'll try to give a brief summary here.

From the air Firstly, if you're flying over the Delta, note what you see. There are manmade tracks, like the straight lines of the buffalo fence, which surrounds part of the Delta. Or the close, parallel lines of bush tracks made by vehicles, sometimes curving, sometimes perfectly straight.

You'll also see more erratic, single tracks, often radiating from pans or waterholes; these are clear animal tracks. (Yes, animals have favourite paths that they like to use too.) Deeper in the Delta you'll find more and more winding drainage lines, of water channels which glint in the sun. Catch the light right and you'll realise that areas which you thought were thick, green vegetation are floodplains, which reflect the sky.

Look carefully at the 'browner' areas between these and you'll start to distinguish the dry land and the islands from the floodplains and the water. Look out for the small, round islands that often have a ring of palms around the outside of them. Note that some, at their centre, have barren patches of what looks like white salt.

Many islands will be longer. A few of these may look like a number of the small islands joined together. But many are long and narrow – we'll call them ribbon islands. Note how parallel their sides are, and how the vegetation on the edges looks that much more lush than the vegetation in the middle.

Building islands The Okavango's an amazing sight from the air – and all the more incredible if you understand a little of how its features were formed. Here are the basics of the main two methods.

Biological mechanism: round islands The Okavango's floods are erratic and its water levels variable, sometimes giving the chance for small mounds to develop which, when flooding returns, are above the level of the flood. Often, but not always, these are termite mounds, made by the *Macroternes michaelseni* termite.

Obtruding above the water level of the subsequent flood, the mound allows the termites to survive, and makes a handy perch for birds. Eventually seeds take hold, and grow into shrubs and trees, fertilised by the guano from the birds that rest there. In some areas of the Delta (the Jao flats stand out in my mind) you'll see these small islands at the early stages of their formation everywhere. Often the dominant plants are wild date palms (*Phoenix reclinata*), though *Ficus* species and the usual broad-leafed trees of the Delta will follow.

Once started, the trees will transpire, sucking water up with their roots to fuel photosynthesis. This lowers the water table directly under the island, which then attracts inflows from the surrounding floodplains seeping under the island. However, the tree roots don't take up many salts, and gradually the ground water under the island becomes saturated with salts – especially silica and calcite. Eventually these crystallise out underneath the roots. As this precipitate increases, the level of the ground around the edge of the island is raised.

3

This gradually acts to enlarge the island, raising it above the surrounding floodplains. However, as the island enlarges the groundwater that moves towards the centre of the island becomes increasingly saline – and eventually toxic to plants. The wild date palms die off first in the centre, as they are the least salt-tolerant, then the broadleaved trees, until finally the relatively salt-tolerant real fan palms (*Hyphaene petersiana*) will be the only trees in the centre. When the salt concentrations rise further they, too, die, leaving only salt-tolerant grasses like the spiky sporobolus (*Sporobolus spikatus*).

Capillary action and evaporation force the supersaturated water to the surface of the centre of the island, where salt deposits are now left and no plants can survive. This whole process is estimated to take at least a hundred years. The remaining crystalline salt deposits are known as 'trona' deposits, and are clearly visible as a white crystalline powder from the air or the ground.

Channel mechanism: linear islands The Okavango's water is at its richest in nutrients as it enters the Panhandle and the top of the Delta – as flowing over the nutrient-poor Kalahari sands of the Delta itself won't enrich it. In this Panhandle and upper Delta area, the deep waters are surrounded by the vigorous growth of papyrus (see box on papyrus on page 284 for details).

These live and die fast, forming a mat of thick vegetal matter by the side of the channel. This builds up the sides of the channel, and gradually its deeper stems are compressed and start forming peat. Meanwhile, suspended sediments are deposited on the floor of the channel. Thus the whole channel, floor and papyrus surrounds, start to rise slightly above the surrounding floodplains.

Once this happens it only takes a hippo track, or some other leakage, for the water in the channel to cut through the peat sides of the channel and the papyrus beds find a completely alternative, lower path through the floodplains. This leaves behind a dry,

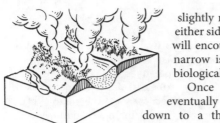

slightly raised line of sandy deposits, lined on either side by high beds of peat. This higher land will encourage plants to grow, forming a long, narrow island, which can be enlarged by the biological mechanisms mentioned above.

Once dry, the peat eventually burns down to a thin layer of nutrient-rich ash, which now lines this island, encouraging what biologists call 'sweet' floodplains. These support nutrient-rich grasses and other high-quality vegetation, and a rich growth of trees and bushes at the edge of these long islands.

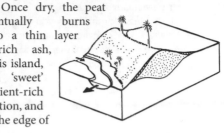

Meandering mechanism: alluvial islands Some islands in the Delta were probably built up first as sandy alluvial deposits during wetter periods in the Delta's history – as the banks beside meandering rivers. Then, when times became drier they were colonised by vegetation, and enlarged by the biological mechanisms mentioned above.

Geological mechanism: Chief's Island Chief's Island, the largest island in the Delta, is thought to have geological origins. Note that its western edge traces out a line which, if continued northwest, would coincide perfectly with the eastern faultline that constrains the Panhandle (see page 49 for a diagram showing this faultline).

Chief's Island was probably pushed up as higher land during the formative rifting/warping of the area, which fits with the observation that it is largely made up of uniform deposits of sand and clay.

CLIMATE Botswana is landlocked far from the coast and mostly in the tropics. It receives a lot of strong sunlight and most of the country is classed as either semi-arid or arid (the line being crossed from semi-arid to arid when evaporation exceeds rainfall). In many respects, most of central and northern Botswana has a subtropical 'desert' climate, characterised by a wide range in temperature (from day to night and from summer to winter), and by low rainfall and humidity.

Botswana's climate follows a similar pattern to that found in most of southern Africa, with rainfall when the sun is near its zenith from November to April, and most areas receiving their heaviest rainfall in January and February. The rainfall is heavier in the north and east, and lighter in the south and, especially, the southwest. The precise timing and duration of the rains is determined by the interplay of three airstreams: the moist 'Congo' air mass, the northeastern monsoon winds, and the southeastern trade winds. The water-bearing air is the Congo air mass, which normally brings rain when it moves south into Botswana from central Africa. Effectively a belt of rain works its way south across the continent, reaching its southernmost point around January or February. If you listen to any local weather forecasts, they'll probably refer to this as the intertropical convergence zone, or the ITCZ. As the sun's intensity reduces, the Congo air mass moves back north, leaving Botswana dry by around April.

Thus **January** and **February** are the wettest months, when many areas will have regular and often torrential downpours in the late afternoon. When there are no clouds, temperatures can peak as high as 40°C. However, it's much more usual for

3

Typical of the pleasant climate in northern Botswana, here are the average maximum and minimum temperatures for Maun – although as elsewhere in the world, things are changing, with temperatures of 40°C or more no longer particularly unusual in October. Nevertheless, Maun's temperatures are slightly less extreme than you might expect for somewhere in one of the Kalahari's drier environments. Similarly, expect the highs and lows of somewhere in the heart of the Delta to be more moderate than this (lower highs, and higher lows!):

	Temp °C		Temp °F		Rainfall
	max	min	max	min	mm
January	33	19	91	68	101
February	32	19	90	70	101
March	32	18	90	65	51
April	30	15	87	60	26
May	28	10	82	50	0
June	25	6	78	42	0
July	26	6	80	42	0
August	27	9	81	48	0
September	34	14	93	58	0
October	38	19	100	68	0
November	37	20	98	69	25
December	35	20	95	69	76

them to be moderated by afternoon cloud cover and to stay between about 20°C and 30°C. Humidity fluctuates during the day, typically from about 50% to 80%.

By **March** the rainfall is decreasing, though still the afternoon clouds are around. Mornings and early afternoons will often be cloudless, and a few of the nights will go below 10°C even though the average of the nightly minimums is nearer 18°C.

April and **May** are lovely months. You may catch the odd afternoon shower in April, but these are gone by May – as are most of the clouds. The maximum day temperatures are around 33°C, and while the nightly minimum average is between 10°C and 15°C, this hides the occasional chilly nights when areas of the Kalahari will record temperatures just below freezing.

June and **July** are the coolest months, with daytime average highs around 25°C concealing the occasional day when the mercury just reaches 30°C. You'll still need your shorts, T-shirt, sunhat and suncream for the middle of the day, but as dusk approaches you'll quickly need warmer clothes. The average night goes down to about 6°C, but cold snaps of well below freezing (typically –5°C) are common – especially in the drier areas of the Kalahari. **August** is very similar, though not quite as cold. You'd be very unlucky for it to go below freezing, even at night, and the days will often creep over 30°C.

September and **October** are really the heart of the dry season, and the daytime heat gradually builds as these months wear on. Typical early afternoon temperatures are in the low 30s (°C), and nights will seldom fall below 10°C, though most will be nearer to 20°C. The humidity is usually very low, typically 20–40%.

November is always interesting and can be unpredictable. Often much of it will simply be a continuation of October's heat and dryness. But eventually the humidity will build and clouds start to appear in the afternoons. These will block the sun, cool the temperatures, and eventually produce some showers in the late afternoon. November mornings will generally remain fine and hot, with blue skies.

During **December** the temperatures will usually stay around 20–30°C, day and night, and rain will be an increasingly regular occurrence in the afternoon. Humidity is normally 50–60%. The hottest days may just reach 40°C, but even so the coolest nights won't go below about 10°C.

FLORA AND FAUNA

FLORA In many ways a brief description of some of the main habitats for plants is really a step through the various types of environment that you'll encounter in Botswana.

As with animals, each species of plant has its favourite conditions. External factors determine where each species thrives, and where it will perish. These include temperature, light, water, soil type, nutrients, and what other species of plants and animals live in the same area. Species with similar needs are often found together, in communities which are characteristic of that particular environment. Botswana has a number of different such communities, or typical 'vegetation types', within its borders – each of which is distinct from the others. The more common include:

Mopane woodland The dominant tree here is the remarkably adaptable mopane (*Colophospermum mopane*), which is sometimes known as the butterfly tree because of the shape of its leaves. Although it doesn't thrive on the Kalahari's sands, it is very tolerant of poorly drained or alkaline soils, and those with a high clay content. This tolerance results in the mopane having a wide range of distribution throughout southern Africa; in Botswana it occurs mainly in the Okavango–Linyanti region, and throughout the eastern side of the country.

Mopane trees can attain a maximum height of 25m when growing on rich, alluvial soils. These are then called cathedral mopane, for their height and the graceful arch of their branches. However, shorter trees are more common in areas that are poor in nutrients, or have suffered extensive fire damage. Stunted mopane will form a low scrub, perhaps only 5m tall. All mopane trees are deciduous, and the leaves turn beautiful shades of yellow and red before falling during the late dry season. Then, with the first rains, the trees become tinged with light-green young leaves. They flower around December and January, with clusters of small, yellow-green flowers.

Ground cover in mopane woodland is usually sparse; just thin grasses, herbs and the occasional bush. The trees themselves are an important source of food for game, as the leaves have a high nutritional value – rich in protein and phosphorus – which is favoured by browsers and is retained even after they have fallen from the trees. Mopane forests support large populations of rodents, including tree squirrels (*Peraxerus cepapi*), which are so typical of these areas that they are known as mopane squirrels.

Pan Though not an environment for rich vegetation, a pan is a shallow, usually seasonal, pool of water without any permanent streams leading to or from it. Mopane woodlands are full of these small pans during and shortly after the rainy season, the water being held on the surface by the clay soils. They are very important to the game that will feed here during the summer, but will dry up soon after the rains cease.

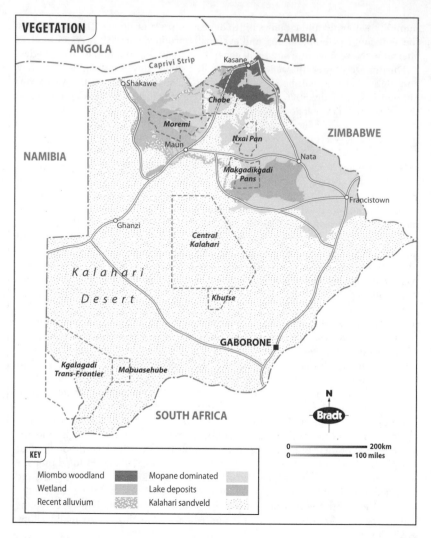

KEY

Miombo woodland	■ Mopane dominated	
Wetland	Lake deposits	
Recent alluvium	Kalahari sandveld	

Salt pan A salt pan is, as its name implies, a pan that's salty. The huge Makgadikgadi Pans are the residues from ancient lakes. Because of the high concentrations of mineral salts found there – there are no plants there when they are dry. When they fill with water it's a slightly different story as algal blooms appear, sometimes attracting the attention of specialist filter-feeders like flamingos.

Miombo woodland Although this would be the natural vegetation across most of neighbouring Zambia, in Botswana miombo woodland, and its associated *dambos* (see below), is uncommon. There are patches in central Chobe and the northeast of the country. It is found in areas where the soils are acid and not particularly fertile. Often they have been leached of minerals by the water run-off.

Miombo woodland consists of a mosaic of large wooded areas and smaller, more open spaces dotted with clumps of trees and shrubs. The woodland is broadleaved and deciduous (though just how deciduous depends on the available water), and the tree canopies generally don't interlock. The dominant trees are *Brachystegia*, *Julbernardia* and *Isoberlinia* species – most of which are at least partially fire-resistant. There is more variation of species in miombo than in mopane woodland, but despite this it is often known simply as 'brachystegia woodland'. The ground cover is also generally less sparse here than in mopane areas.

Dambo A *dambo* is a shallow grass depression, or small valley, that is either permanently or seasonally waterlogged. It corresponds closely to what is known as a *vlei* in other parts of the subcontinent. These open, verdant dips in the landscape often appear in the midst of miombo woodlands and support no bushes or trees. In higher valleys amongst hills, they will sometimes form the sources of streams and rivers. Because of their permanent dampness, they are rich in species of grasses, herbs and flowering plants, like orchids – and are excellent grazing (if a little exposed) for antelope. Their margins are usually thickly vegetated by grasses, herbs and smaller shrubs.

Teak forest In a few areas of the far north of Botswana, including the northern side of Chobe National Park, the Zambezi teak (*Baikaea plurijuga*), also known as Rhodesian teak, forms dry semi-evergreen forests on Kalahari sand. Often these woodlands occur on fossil dune-crests. As this species is not fire-resistant, these stands are only found where fire is rare, and slash-and-burn-type cultivation methods have never been used. Below the tall teak is normally a dense, deciduous thicket of vegetation, interspersed with sparse grasses and herbs in the shadier spots of the forest floor.

The teak is a lovely strong wood, with an even texture and deep red-brown colour. It is expensive, often exported, and widely used – from furniture to classy wooden floors.

Kalahari sandveld A number of trees and bushes thrive on Chobe's extensive areas of Kalahari sand, including various *Acacia*, *Terminalia* and *Combretum* species. 'Kalahari sandveld' is a general term that I'll use to describe any of these plant communities based on sand.

In appearance they range from a very open savannah with a few tall trees separated only by low undergrowth, to quite dense tickets of (often thorny) shrubs which are difficult to even walk through. If you want to be a little more technical about this, then biologists will often divide this into distinctive subgroups, including:

Terminalia sericea **sandveld** occurs where you find deep, loose sand – these are unfertile areas which cover large areas of the Kalahari. The main species found here are the silver terminalia (*Terminalia sericea*), or silver cluster-leaf as it's sometimes called, and the Kalahari appleleaf (*Lonchocarpus nelsii*). These generally occur with wild seringa bushes (*Burkea africana*) and the bushwillow (*Combretum collinum*). Underneath these you'll often find the rather beautiful silky bushman grass (*Stipagrostis uniplumis*).

Acacia erioloba **woodlands** also occur on sand, but often where there are fossil river valleys that have an underground supply of water throughout the year. Camelthorn trees (*Acacia erioloba*) have exceedingly long taproots that reach this, sustaining large stands of these mature trees reaching an impressive 16–17m in height. They grow slowly but give good shade, so the bush cover beneath them is fairly sparse.

Acacia tortilis **woodlands** are not found on such deep sand; instead they prefer the fine alluvium soils, which water has deposited over time. Although

3

it forms homogenous stands less often than the camelthorns, a number of the very distinctive, flat-topped umbrella thorns (*Acacia tortilis*) can often be seen together. Between these you'll find low grasses rather than much undergrowth. This results in a beautiful, quintessentially African scene which fits many first-time visitors' picture of the continent as gleaned from the blockbuster film *Out of Africa*.

Moist evergreen forest In the areas of higher rainfall and (as is more likely in Botswana) near rivers, streams, lakes and swamps, where a tree's roots will have permanent access to water, dense evergreen forests are found. Many species occur, and this lush vegetation is characterised by having three levels: a canopy of tall trees, a sub-level of smaller trees and bushes, and a variety of ground-level vegetation. In effect, the environment is so good for plants that they have adapted to exploit the light from every sunbeam.

This type of forest is prevalent in the Okavango and Linyanti areas, and beside the country's larger rivers. It's perhaps worth distinguishing here between two very different types of this forest:

Riverine forests (occasionally called riparian forests) are very common. They line many of Botswana's major rivers and are found throughout the Okavango–Linyanti area. Typical trees and shrubs here include the jackalberry (*Diospyros mespiliformis*), African mangosteen (*Garcinia livingstonei*), sausage tree (*Kigelia africana*), large feverberry (*Croton megalobotrys*), knobthorn (*Acacia nigrescens*), marula (*Sclerocarya birrea caffra*), raintree (*Lonchocarpus capassa*) and various species of fig. Move away from the river and you'll find riparian species thinning out rapidly.

Swamp forest – or something very akin to it – occurs in tiny patches on small islands in permanently flooded areas of the Okavango. These islands, which will themselves occasionally be flooded, might include a mixture of fig and waterberry species, plus lots of wild date palms (*Phoenix reclinata*) and a few tall real fan palms (*Hyphaenea petersiana*).

In the centre of slightly larger small islands, where the ground is salty from trona deposits (see page 52) you will find only spiky *Sporobolus* grassland (*Sporobolus spicatus*) – no trees at all!

Floodplain Floodplains are the low-lying grasslands on the edges of rivers, streams, lakes and swamps that are seasonally inundated by floods. The Okavango and, to a lesser extent, the Linyanti–Chobe region has some huge areas of floodplain. These often contain no trees or bushes, just a low carpet of grass species that can tolerate being submerged for part of the year. In the midst of most of the floodplains in the Okavango you'll find isolated small 'islands' slightly raised above the surrounding grasslands. These will often be fringed by swamp forest (see above).

Sometimes the communities of vegetation will be 'zoned' to reflect the extent and frequency of the flooding. In areas that become submerged for long periods you'll find species like wild rice (*Oryza longistaminata*) and the sedge *Cyperus articulatus*. Grasses such as *Imperata cylindrica* often dominate places that generally spend less time under water.

Channels Vegetation found in permanent channels includes the giant sedge or papyrus (*Cyperus papyrus*), which dominates large areas of the Okavango, plus species like the distinctive cylindrical hippo grass (*Vossia cuspidata*), the tall maize-like phragmites reed (*Phragmites australis*), used for thatching, and the unmistakable bulrush (*Typha capensis*).

Lagoons Where the water is more still, in deep lagoons and side-channels where the surface is open but the water doesn't flow much, the bottom will often be covered with fairly stable peat deposits. This gives a stable base for many species of aquatic plants. Some are strictly submerged whilst others have floating leaves. An obvious indicator of this type of environment is the presence of waterlilies.

FAUNA

Mammals Botswana's large mammals are typical of the savannah areas of southern Africa. The large predators are here: lion, leopard, cheetah, wild dog and spotted hyena. Cheetah are found in higher densities here than in most other areas of the subcontinent, and northern Botswana has one of Africa's three strong populations of wild dogs.

Elephant and buffalo occur in large herds that roam throughout the areas where they can find water. Rhino had largely been wiped out throughout the wilds of northern Botswana, though are now being slowly reintroduced into one of the private areas of Moremi, and on the western edge of the Makgadikgadi Pans National Park. Initially, only white rhino were brought in, but black rhino are now being reintroduced too.

Antelope are well represented, with impala, springbok, tsessebe and red lechwe all numerically dominant in different areas – depending on the environment. The sheer range of Botswana's ecosystems means that if you move about there is a really wide range of totally different species to be seen. For more details on these and many smaller mammals, see *Appendix 1, Wildlife guide*, pages 477–500.

Because the Okavango area is so well watered, its natural vegetation is very lush and capable of supporting a high density of game in the dry season. This spreads out to the surrounding areas during the earlier months of the year accounting for the sheer volume of big game to be found in northern Botswana's parks and private reserves.

Game migrations: historical factors Like most of Africa's big game, some of Botswana's larger animals have major seasonal migrations – or at least used to have, until relatively recently. The 'big picture' was that large numbers of big herbivores put a great strain on the vegetation in any given locale, and so moving around gave the plants time to recover. Thus the basic patterns were for the game to move out into the Kalahari's drier areas during the rains, when they would have no difficulty finding small pools to drink from, and then to gradually migrate back to sources of permanent water as the dry season progressed.

The main species involved were elephant, buffalo, zebra, wildebeest and hartebeest. These migrations still occur, and do affect the game densities in many areas, although they're much reduced due to two main factors.

First, competition for land from humans and their domestic stock, which has reduced the possible range of the wildlife, and caused particular problems by monopolising some of the few areas of permanent water in the Kalahari.

Second, the erection of long, game-proof, disease-control fences which have appeared across historical migration routes in the Kalahari. The first of these was in 1954, in response to insistence by European trading partners that, to import Botswana's beef, the country must have an effective strategy for containing and dealing with outbreaks of foot-and-mouth disease.

The relative damage done by these two factors is still a hotly debated issue in Botswana, but the results were serious. In some years tens and possibly hundreds of thousands of animals, mostly wildebeest, died of thirst or starvation, many in very

3

close proximity to the fences. (See page 442 for further comments.) Some blame the fences directly; others regarded them as a scapegoat for the real cause – the scale of human encroachment on the Kalahari. Whatever the cause, Botswana no longer has migrations of this scale.

See Mike Main's *Kalahari: Life's Variety in Dune and Delta* for a rational overview of this debate; various issues of *Botswana Notes and Records* (especially 1984) for more detailed partisan arguments; and Mark and Delia Owens' book *Cry of the Kalahari* for an impassioned but one-sided view of the people who observed it at first hand.

Game migrations: the current story Mention the word 'migration' and there's a tendency to picture millions of wildebeest in the Serengeti, fording rivers of waiting crocodiles and filling endless flat plains. That's not what you get in Botswana, so forget those images.

What you do find is a modest but noticeable drift of game away from the main water points of the Chobe, Linyanti and Okavango around the start of the rains – usually somewhere around November – and a gradual return as the dry season progresses. However, the precise details vary with the species of game.

Elephant and **buffalo** have broadly similar movements. As the rains come their large herds split into much smaller family groups, of which some move away from the Linyanti and Okavango systems. They spread out into the drier areas, especially the vast swathes of land dominated by mopane which lie between these areas (Wildlife Management Areas NG14/15/16/18/20; see page 63 for an explanation of WMAs). Those from the Chobe riverfront areas similarly split, heading into the Chobe Forest Reserve and the rest of Chobe National Park, while some move east of Chobe National Park into Zimbabwe's Hwange National Park, and the Matetsi area between that and the Zambezi.

From around May the animals start to head back, and gradually join up into larger herds, until by September and October the riverfronts of the Chobe and Kwando–Linyanti have some of the most amazing densities of buffalo and (especially) elephants that you'll find anywhere in Africa.

The migrations of **zebra** are somewhat more complex, and still the topic of research, but it seems that during the rains large herds of zebra congregate on both Makgadikgadi and Nxai pans, forming an amazing spectacle (if you can find them). During the dry season these animals congregate in numbers beside the Boteti River, the western boundary of Makgadikgadi National Park. Separate populations from the Okavango, Chobe and Linyanti areas move to more open areas of the Kalahari. Some of these groups always seem to pass through the sweet grass plains of the Savuti area around April–May, and often this coincides with their foaling season.

Wildebeest in the north of the country follow a similar pattern to the zebra, but those in the centre and south of the Kalahari are effectively now a separate population. It seems that numbers in the central area of the Kalahari have fluctuated wildly since records began; before the fences there was probably a big annual migration northeast in the dry season to Lake Xau – the nearest water point to the CKGR. Like **hartebeest** in the Central Kalahari, they certainly move around with the season, but the complexities of their current migration patterns are unclear.

Animal tracks A good guide can make animal tracks come alive, helping you to make sense of what you see in the bush. Showing you, for example, that cats' tracks have three lobes at the bottom, whereas dog and hyena tracks feature only two; pointing out the cheetah's claws, usually absent from other cat tracks; or the direction in which an elephant's walking from small scuff marks around its track. The more you learn, the more you'll enjoy about the bush.

The tracks illustrated on pages 478–9 are shown in relation to each other, sizewise, and are intended as a simple introduction to the many signs of wildlife that may be seen around a waterhole, or in the sand.

Birdlife Large areas of Botswana are still covered by relatively undisturbed natural vegetation, and hunting is not a significant factor for most of Botswana's 560 recorded species of birds. Thus, with a range of natural habitats, Botswana is a superb birding destination.

There are fairly clear distinctions between the birds that you're likely to find in areas of swamp or open water, those that frequent riverine forest, and those found in the drier areas. None are endemic, though several have very restricted distributions. These include the slaty egret and the wattled crane, which are restricted to the Okavango, Linyanti and Chobe river systems, the brown firefinch, and the Natal nightjar. The Okavango Delta is a particularly good place for birdwatching as the habitats change from dry, to flooded, to deep-water over very short distances.

In addition to its resident bird species, Botswana receives many migrants. In September and October the Palaearctic migrants (ie: those that come from the northern hemisphere – normally Europe) appear, and they remain until around April or May. This is also the peak time to see the intra-African migrants, which come from further north in Africa. The rains from December to around April see an explosion in the availability of most birds' food: seeds, fruits and insects. Hence this is the prime time for birds to nest, even if it is also the most difficult time to visit the more remote areas of the country.

Field guides Finding good, detailed field guides to plants, animals and birds in Botswana is relatively easy within the country. There are now very comprehensive guides on the flora and fauna of southern Africa, which usually cover Botswana, and several guides dedicated just to Botswana.

See *Appendix 3, Further information* for recommendations and details, but top of your list should be Veronica Roodt's *Trees and Shrubs of the Okavango Delta*, even if you're not that interested in trees or shrubs. For birds, I've always used *Newman's Birds of Southern Africa*, by Kenneth Newman. Finally, if you have room and lots of time, then Richard Estes' *The Safari Companion* is a great general book on mammalian behaviour.

CONSERVATION

A great deal has been written about the conservation of animals in Africa; much of it is over-simplistic and intentionally emotive. As an informed visitor you are in the unique position of being able to see some of the issues at first hand, and to appreciate the perspectives of some of the local people. So abandon your preconceptions, and start by realising how complex the issues are.

Here I shall try to outline a few ideas common to current thinking on conservation, and to many areas in the region. Only then will I frame them in the context of Botswana.

BEING PRAGMATIC: CONSERVATION AND DEVELOPMENT Firstly, conservation must be taken within its widest sense if it is to have meaning. Saving animals is of

minimal use if the whole environment is degraded, so we must consider conserving whole areas and ecosystems, not just the odd isolated species.

Observe that land is regarded as an asset by most societies, in Africa as it is elsewhere. (The San are a notable exception in this regard.) To 'save' the land for the animals, and use it merely for the recreation of a few privileged foreign tourists, is a recipe for huge social problems – especially if the local people remain excluded from benefit and in poverty. Local people have hunted animals for food for centuries. They have always killed game that threatened them or ruined their crops. If we now try to protect animals in populated areas without addressing the concerns of the people, then our efforts will fail.

The only pragmatic way to conserve Africa's wild areas is to see the *development* of the local people, and the *conservation* of the ecosystems, as inter-linked goals. In the long term, one will not work without the other. Conservation without development leads to resentful local people who will happily, and frequently, shoot, trap and kill animals. Development without conservation will simply repeat the mistakes that most developed countries have already made: it will lay waste a beautiful land and kill off its natural heritage. Look at the tiny areas of undisturbed natural vegetation that survive in the UK, the USA or Japan. See how unsuccessful we in the northern hemisphere have been at long-term conservation over the past 500 years.

As an aside, the local people in Africa are sometimes wrongly accused of being the only agents of degradation. Many would like to see 'poachers' shot on sight, and slash-and-burn agriculture banned. But observe the importation of tropical hardwoods by the West to see the problems that our demands place on the natural environment in the developing world.

In conserving some of Africa's natural areas and assisting the development of its people, the international community has a vital role to play. It could effectively encourage African governments to practise sustainable long-term strategies, rather than grasping for the short-term fixes which politicians seem universally to prefer. But such solutions must have the backing of the people themselves, or they will fall apart when the foreign aid budgets eventually wane.

In practice, to get this backing from the local communities it is not enough for a conservation strategy to be compatible with development. Most rural Africans are more concerned about where they live, what they can eat, and how they will survive, than they are about the lives of small, obscure species of antelope that taste good when roasted.

To succeed in Africa, conservation must not only be *compatible* with development, it must actually *promote* it. Conservation efforts must also actively help the local people to improve their own standard of living. If that situation can be reached, then local communities can be mobilised behind long-term conservation initiatives.

Governments are the same. As the famous Zambian conservationist, Norman Carr, once commented, 'Governments won't conserve an impala just because it is pretty.' But they will work to save it *if* they can see that it is worth more to them alive than dead.

The continent's best current strategies involve trying to find lucrative and sustainable ways to use the land. They then plough much of the revenue back into the surrounding local communities. Once the local communities see revenue from conservation being used to help them improve their lives – to build houses, clinics and schools, and to offer paid employment – then such schemes rapidly get their backing and support.

Carefully planned, sustainable tourism is one solution that is working effectively. For success, the local communities must see that the visitors pay because they want the wildlife. Thus, they reason, the existence of wildlife directly improves their income, and they will strive to conserve it. It isn't enough for people to see that the wildlife helps the government to get richer; that won't dissuade a local hunter from shooting a duiker for dinner. However, if he is directly benefiting from visitors, who come to see the animals, then he has a vested interest in saving that duiker.

It matters little to the average rural African, or ultimately to the wildlife, whether these visitors come to shoot the wildlife with a camera or with a gun. The vital issue in the context of hunting is whether or not it is done on a *sustainable* basis (ie: only a few of the oldest animals are shot each year, so that the size of the animal population remains largely unaffected). Photographers may claim the moral high-ground, but should remember that hunters pay far more for their privileges. Hunting operations, when properly run, generate large revenues from few guests, who demand minimal infrastructure and so cause little impact on the land. Photographic operations need more visitors to generate the same revenue, and so generally cause greater negative effects on the country. Despite this, the Botswana government has announced that all forms of commercial hunting will be banned from January 2014.

HIGH REVENUE, LOW VOLUME In the late 1980s Botswana's parks, and especially the Chobe riverfront area and Moremi, were being badly over-used. Many visitors were self-contained South Africans who would arrive with all their food and kit. They bought little in Botswana except their cheap park-entry tickets, and contributed little to the nation's economy.

In an effort to reduce numbers, and stave off serious environmental (and aesthetic) problems due to too many visitors, it was decided to increase the park fees by a factor of ten. This worked miraculously – reducing the number of visitors and their impact, but retaining the same level of revenue for the parks' authorities.

At the time this was revolutionary, even though now it seems obvious. Thus Botswana's policy of 'high-revenue, low-volume' tourism was born. Access to most of Botswana's wild areas is expensive in order to maximise revenues and keep environments pristine. The country is the envy of Africa for having a good, working system that is delivering increasing revenues as well as many local development initiatives.

This basic policy has been in place for almost 25 years, and there is every indication that it will continue. Indeed, the principle has extended way beyond the national parks and game reserves to embrace virtually the whole of northern Botswana.

NATIONAL PARKS AND RESERVES The national parks, like Chobe, and the game reserves, like Moremi, work on a simple system. Nobody lives in these (the San in the CKGR being the exception). Anyone can visit, provided they pay the fees. These are scaled to be cheapest for citizens of Botswana, reasonable for residents and more costly for visitors. (See *National parks* in *Chapter 4, Planning and Preparation*, for these charges.)

Private concessions or reserves Outside of the national parks and game reserves, northern Botswana has been divided up into a series of wildlife management areas (WMAs). See the map on pages 294–5 for some of these. Those in northwestern Botswana, in Ngamiland, are numbered NG1, NG2, etc, up to NG51. These areas are normally referred to in Botswana as 'concessions' although in this guide I have used this term virtually interchangeably with the phrase 'private reserve' or simply just 'reserve'.

Within each of these the government, via the local 'land board', has defined who owns the wildlife, and what can be done with it. In some hunting is forbidden; in most, limited (controlled and sustainable) hunting is allowed.

Community concessions In most of these concessions, the approach taken centres around Community Based Natural Resource Management (CBNRM), a modern phrase for a strategy which tries to reconcile conflicts over resources between the people and the wildlife in its broadest sense.

CBNRM is based on the premise that the people living next to a resource are the ones best suited to protecting that resource, as they would lose most if that resource were lost, and gain most if it's managed well. There is also an ethical consideration: for example, the people who pay the costs of living near wildlife (destruction of crops and livestock, and loss of human life) should benefit from its conservation. Local people need to be involved in the decision-making process and need to benefit from the areas around them, and CBNRM tries to make this possible.

Thus in most of Botswana's concessions, the local communities now make decisions about how they are run, and they reap the rewards if they are run well and successfully. See the box in *Chapter 12* entitled *The anatomy of a community partnership*, about NG22 and NG23, for an example of one such arrangement.

TOURISM Botswana lies in the heart of sub-Saharan Africa – and its tourism is the envy of the continent in many ways. The country is regarded, quite rightly, as having some of the continent's best wildlife areas, which are still in generally pristine condition.

What's more, the expansion of tourism from the nucleus of the national parks to the areas around them has gradually increased the area effectively protected for wildlife since the 1980s. Areas that were devoted to hunting are now becoming solely photographic. This is enlarging the contiguous area in northern Botswana available for the wildlife, helping to ensure that the game populations increase in size, and become more viable.

A final word here goes to Peter Sandenbergh, who has been running safari camps and tourism operations in this area for longer than most. He observes that 'one of the greatest changes since coming to this area in 1983 has been the remarkable increase in animal numbers and species diversity'.

Changing economics of tourism Tourism isn't yet as important to Botswana as diamonds or beef production. However, it is increasing every year, and is providing substantial employment and also bringing foreign exchange into the country, which gives the politicians a reason to support conservation.

When the diamonds run out – within the next few decades – Botswana needs to have an alternative, and renewable, source of income ... and tourism is one of the most obvious contenders. The difficulty for the government will be trying to increase substantially tourism's revenues whilst still keeping tourism a premium product, and hence at a low density.

With this in mind the government put forward two major proposals in a paper published in 2009. The first, to develop the western side of the Delta, along the Panhandle area, is aimed at attracting more budget travellers, without having a negative impact on the pristine environment of the Delta itself. The second is to create a scenic route down this western side, from Shakawe in the north as far as Lake Ngami, south of Maun. It remains to be seen if either of these will ever materialise.

How you can help more The visitor on an expensive safari is, by his or her mere presence, making a financial contribution to development and conservation in Botswana. When on safari, one very simple thing that you can do to help is to ask your safari operator:

- Besides employment, how do local people benefit from this camp?
- How much of this camp's revenue goes directly back to the local people?
- What are you doing to help the people living near this reserve?
- How much control do the local people have in what goes on in the area in which these safaris are operated?

If more visitors did this, it would make a huge difference. That said, many operators do have programmes to help their local communities, having recognised that the mass of Botswana's people must benefit more (and more directly) from tourism if conservation is going to be successful in Botswana.

For ways in which you can support small local charities which directly help the people of Botswana, see *Travelling positively*, pages 112–14.

Hunting issues Big-game hunting, where visiting hunters pay large amounts to kill trophy animals, has long been practised on a number of private reserves and concessions. Just like photographic tourism, this has been a valuable source of revenue in the long term for people living in the country's concessions.

In practical terms, there is room for both types of visitors in Botswana: the photographer and the hunter. The national parks, and some of the private reserves nearest the parks (eg: NG23, NG27A and NG27B), are designated for photographic visitors; here no hunting is allowed.

In many of the private reserves, controlled sustainable hunting has until recently been allowed, although a few (such as the concessions run by Wilderness Safaris, like NG15 and NG26) have maintained a policy of no hunting. Integral to this approach is that the concessions provide a buffer between the pristine national parks and the land around, where sustainable hunting is allowed. This is designed to protect the national parks' animals from any incursions by poachers, whilst the parks act as a large gene pool and species reservoir for the private concessions.

Despite this long-held policy, the government has imposed a moratorium on commercial hunting, which includes trophy hunting, to take effect in 2014. Effectively, this extends the ban on lion hunting that was implemented in 2002, only to be lifted three years later, but then reimposed in 2007. The decision to outlaw commercial hunting comes as no surprise to many in Botswana, as the anti-hunting lobby has the support of President Ian Khama, who – prior to becoming president in 2008 – declared that he would impose a total ban on hunting.

Poaching Having just mentioned poaching, it's perhaps worth commenting that Botswana has very, very little poaching. There is always a little small-scale poaching of game 'for the pot' by local people ... but large-scale commercial poaching operations are virtually unknown.

Occasionally there's a complaint about poachers coming across the river from Namibia – putting the blame on poachers from neighbouring countries is a very usual tactic in this part of the world. However, the Kwando, Linyanti and Chobe rivers, and the rest of the country's borders, are so well patrolled by the Botswana Defence Force (BDF) that this seems unlikely.

4

Planning and Preparation

WHEN TO GO AND HIGHLIGHTS

There simply isn't one 'best time' to visit Botswana, or any of its wild areas. Most tourists visit during the dry season, from around May to the end of October. Within that season, the period from mid-July to mid-October is definitely the busiest – although Botswana's small camps/lodges and private reserves ensure that it never feels busy, even when everywhere is full. (In fact, the country's capacity for tourism remains tiny compared with that of South Africa, Kenya or Tanzania.)

Most of those visiting outside of this season are cognoscenti, who visit early or late in the season – May to July or late October to November – when the camps are quieter and often costs are lower.

A much smaller number of visitors come during the rains, from December to April, when camps will frequently be quiet for days. This often means that they will give visitors a much more personal experience, with private drives; their rates are often lower too, and they're usually far more flexible about bringing children on safari.

Much of the blame for this 'glut or famine' of visitors lies with overseas tour operators. Many who advertise trips here just don't know Botswana well enough to plan trips which work during the rainy season. It's much easier for them to make blanket generalisations, telling enquirers who don't know any better that it's 'not interesting' or that 'you won't see any game' if you visit in the wet season. None of this is true, as long as you choose your destinations carefully, but of course most people don't know this in advance.

While the rains are not the ideal time for everybody's trip, they are a fascinating time to visit and should not be dismissed without serious thought.

Here is some guidance on various issues to help you decide what the best time for your visit would be. However, one of the biggest reasons for coming to the Okavango – and you may only realise this once you've visited – is not the game or the birds. It's simply the whole general ambience of being able to float over lily-covered lagoons with the sun on your back and a gentle breeze in your hair. This is certainly best when the skies are fairly clear of clouds – from April to November.

WEATHER For a detailed description of the weather that can be expected, see the section on *Climate*, pages 53–5, and note that Botswana's rainy season normally occurs between December and April, with January and February usually being the wettest months.

Dry season (May to November) This is the easiest time to travel, as then you are unlikely to meet rain and can expect clear blue skies. This is ideal if this is your first trip to Africa, or if seeing lots of big game is top of your wish-list.

Within this, you'll find June–August the coolest, when night temperatures in the Kalahari can drop below freezing. Then from September onwards the heat gradually builds up. The interior areas of the Kalahari, including central Chobe and the great salt pans, get very hot towards the end of October. Occasions when it reaches over 40°C in the shade have earned this the tag of 'suicide month'.

That said, note that in the Okavango, where there are large areas of water and green vegetation, the extremes of temperature are much more pleasant and moderated: the nights in August never reaching freezing, and the days in October are never unbearable.

Everywhere November is a variable month. Some days will be hot. Some will be cooler, as gathering clouds shield the country from the sun. Sometimes these bring welcome showers; sometimes they simply build, and with them come tension and humidity.

Wet season From December to March, or even April, the scenario is totally different, although the days can still vary enormously from one to the next. Even within a day, skies can change from sunny to cloudy within minutes and then back again. Downpours are usually heavy and short – and usually late in the afternoon – although there are often a few days when the sky remains grey and overcast. You will need a good waterproof for the rainy season, but I've always felt that the rains are seldom long enough to stop you doing anything.

THE OKAVANGO'S ANNUAL FLOOD

This very complex variable is really a minor point for most visitors – who will find the Okavango Delta enchanting whenever they visit. However, the flooding levels will have some influence on certain activities, and may even influence your choice of where you want to visit in the Delta.

The water levels at any point in the Okavango Delta depend mainly on three variables: first, the local rainfall in your location; second, the height of the seasonal flood of the Okavango; and third, your location within the Delta – the further north you are in the Okavango, the more water you're likely to have.

The local summer rains and the arrival of the seasonal floods are generally out of sync by around two to six months, depending on exactly where you are within the Delta. This represents the time taken for the peak of the rains in the Okavango River's main catchment area – the Angolan highlands – to make it down the Okavango River and into the various areas of the Delta.

These annual floods have for years been monitored very carefully at Mohembo, where the river enters Botswana – see the graph opposite. From this we know that the peak of the flood at Mohembo generally occurs between mid-March and mid-May – just after the local summer rains in the region of the Delta have come to an end. Given the tiny gradient and very slow flow rate, this surge of water from Angola can take up to six months to work its way from the Panhandle to the far extremities of the Delta's waterways.

Hence expect the highest water levels in most areas of the Delta to occur after the rains – from about May to August. After that, levels will generally fall until around February, when the local rains start to slowly raise water levels prior to the main flood.

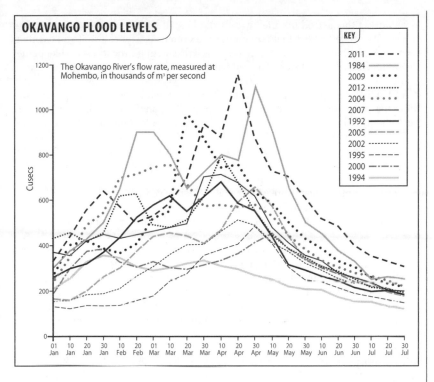

OKAVANGO FLOOD LEVELS

The Okavango River's flow rate, measured at Mohembo, in thousands of m³ per second

KEY
2011
1984
2009
2012
2004
2007
1992
2005
2002
1995
2000
1994

Having said this, on one February visit, the rain didn't ever seem to end, and the skies remained grey for days – so I should perhaps recant this. In fact, I take the view that Africa's weather is just becoming harder to predict, and I was unlucky!

TRAVELLING CONDITIONS Travelling around Botswana in the dry season often has its challenges, but in some places in the wet season it's a totally different game. Then the areas of pure sand are still fine to drive on, and even a bit firmer than they are when it's hot and dry.

Driving yourself In some areas where the soil has a high clay content, the bush tracks become quagmires – the track from Rakops to the Central Kalahari Game Reserve's Matswere Gate near Kuke Corner is a fine example, as are most of the Makgadikgadi Pans. Some tracks, especially those in the Delta–Linyanti region, like the old route between Xakanaxa and North Gate, become submerged completely. Thus travel in Botswana during the wet season requires careful research, and scrupulous attention to your emergency precautions. If you're heading for somewhere remote in the wet season, then travelling with two or more vehicles is wise.

Flying around In contrast, the weather is seldom a problem if you're flying into one of Botswana's safari camps. All are used to the vagaries of the weather and the water levels, although they may affect your activities. Similarly, if you're heading out on a budget mokoro trip or safari, it shouldn't affect your trip significantly – though your vehicle may need the occasional push!

Although there are fewer visitors around during this period, Botswana's flight schedules don't change much, and only a few of its camps will close. (Many will close during this period for a few weeks of planned maintenance or any building work that's needed. Those that remain open are often very quiet – so if you've often been to Africa in the dry season, then this is a fascinating time to visit – like being introduced to a different side of an old friend.)

VEGETATION During the wet season, the foliage runs wild. The Kalahari springs into life as the bush turns many shades of green. Open clay pans become small pools in the bush and it's a time of renewal, when a gentler light dapples Botswana's bush.

When the rains end, the leaves in the Kalahari gradually dry and many eventually drop. More greys and browns appear, and good shade becomes harder to find. Eventually, by late September and October, most plants look dry and parched, coloured from straw yellow to shrivelled brown.

However, note that large areas of the Okavango have their own permanent water supply – regulated more by the annual floods than the rainfall – and so don't follow this pattern so clearly. See box, *The Okavango's annual flood*, page 68.

GAME From the point of view of most herbivores, the wet season is much more pleasant than the dry season. During the wet, most animals live in enormous salad bowls, with convenient pools of water nearby. It's a good time to have their young and eat themselves into good condition.

Visitors who have been to Africa before will often find something special about seeing all the animals when they aren't struggling with thirst and a lack of vegetation. It gives a sense of luxuriance and plenty, which isn't there in the dry season.

Migration patterns Before people started to have a big impact on Botswana's landscape (which, arguably, has only been in the last 150 years or so), many of the animals here used to follow regular seasonal migration patterns, often over very large distances. It was the same throughout Africa originally; many species, and especially the herding species of plains game, would move around to where the best food sources were to be found.

Despite the changes wreaked by man since then, the remnants of these migrations still happen. Understanding them will help you to work out what the best times are to visit the various parks – so first read the section on *Game migrations* in *Chapter 3* for detailed comments.

The finer details of each area are covered under sections entitled *When to go*, which are spread throughout the book, but in very general terms:

Chobe Areas with riverfront are at their best during July–October. Traditionally, the Savuti Marsh area is totally different, with some good game all year, but probably at its best around March–May and (if the rains have arrived) November – when herds of zebra and plains game are passing through.

Kwando/Linyanti Follows the same basic pattern as Chobe's riverfronts – so it is best in the late dry season, when it's the only source of water for miles around.

Okavango/Moremi The central areas of the Delta have permanent water all year, and equally permanent populations of animals. Thus many game species stay here all year, and densities of animals (excluding elephant and buffalo) don't change that much. However, in the dry season the permanent populations of game found on the edges of the Delta are swelled by an influx of animals from the parched

Kalahari. Thus, the game densities on the accessible edges of the Delta often rise significantly as the dry season progresses.

Nxai Pan Can be erratic, but always used to be at its best when wet, from December to March – though often still very good into May and June. However, the artificial pumping of a waterhole a couple of kilometres north of the gate has changed this pattern. During the rest of the year, you'll find plains game staying here in numbers, often accompanied by a few lion.

Makgadikgadi Pans The pans themselves can be superb when wet, December to April; large herds of zebra and other plains grazers appear. On their western border, the Boteti River (or its channel) follows the opposite pattern, attracting game at the end of the dry season, around August to early November.

Central Kalahari Game congregates in the huge grassy valleys here, most famously in Deception Valley, when the vegetation is lush during and shortly after the rains, from about December to May.

Seasonal highlights The bottom line is probably that if game viewing is your overriding priority, or this is one of your first trips to Africa, then you'll be better visiting during the dry season. Then the animals are much easier to spot, as no thick vegetation obscures the view, and they are forced to congregate at well-known water points, like rivers, where they can be observed.

However, more experienced African travellers are missing out if they never travel during the rains – as it's completely different and can be superb. A few specific highlights of Botswana's animal calendar would include:

February–April Most of the herbivores are in their best condition, having fed well on the lush vegetation. It's a perfect time to catch huge concentrations of springbok and oryx on the short grass plains of the Central Kalahari's fossil river valleys.

May–June Probably my favourite time to be in Botswana (and most of southern Africa!). It's a great time to visit Savuti Marsh, and in the Okavango the floodwater moves down the Delta.

July–August Leopard are generally easier to see, as they come out more during the twilight hours. Further into the year, they often wait until it is cool, only appearing later in the evening.

September–October Elephant and buffalo tend to amalgamate into larger, more spectacular herds. (They splinter again just before the rains.) Lion sights become more frequent, as they spend more time near the limited remaining water sources.

November Can be a great month as often the rains haven't arrived, leaving amazing game densities in the riverfront areas (yet visitors are thin on the ground and prices are low). However, too many cloudless days can mean high midday temperatures.

December–January Crocodiles are nesting, and so found on or near exposed sandbanks. Various baby animals start to appear in November, followed by most of the mammals that calve sometime during the rainy season.

BIRDLIFE The birdlife in Botswana is certainly best when the foliage is most dense, and the insects are thriving, ie: in the wet season. Then many resident birds are nesting and in their bright, breeding plumage. This coincides to a large extent with the 'summer' period, from around October to March, when the Palaearctic migrants from the northern hemisphere are seen.

To give you an idea of the richness of the avifauna here, in the Okavango–Linyanti–Chobe areas during the rainy season it isn't difficult for competent ornithologists to record 100 different species between dawn and midday. Really energetic birdwatchers can notch up as many as 200 different species in a 24-hour period in somewhere as rich as the northern Chobe riverfront area. A real enthusiast might count about 320 species (out of the 550 or so which occur) during a two-week trip here.

CHILDREN ON SAFARI

Ten years ago, taking children on safari in Botswana might have been considered unusual, but things are changing, and the country's lodges and camps haven't been slow to pick up on the trend.

The idea of taking a child on safari might at first seem obvious. You'll be out in a wilderness environment, with plenty of animals to watch, and seemingly non-stop entertainment. But that, of course, is part of the problem. The 'entertainment' cannot be guaranteed, so during a typical three-hour game drive, there's often time when things that might fascinate you – colourful birds, the construction of a termite mound, last night's hyena tracks, even a(nother) herd of impala – will be of little interest to a child. And when big game is spotted, instead of being able to leap up and down with excitement, your child is expected to be absolutely quiet and still. Then there's the often unspoken concern of a sensitive child witnessing a kill.

Add to this the rather exclusive make-up of many safari camps, the safety issues within camp (wildlife, high walkways and unguarded pools being just a few), and the lack of opportunity for letting off steam, and the considerations mount up.

So how can it work? Although many lodges still maintain a very adult atmosphere, designating a high minimum age for children, several offer some form of 'family' accommodation. Sometimes that's simply a room with an extra bed or two, rather than anything particularly child-friendly; at others, it's a suite of rooms, either sharing a bathroom or with each of them en suite, and occasionally with their own lounge area. One or two lodges, such as the Shinde Enclave and Linyanti Ebony, have a group of tents or chalets that are slightly separate from the main camp, so work particularly well for families. And more specifically, a handful of places – including Khwai Tented Camp and Kalahari Manor at Deception Valley Lodge – have built entirely separate houses that are exceptionally well suited to families, with space to run around, and your own chef so that you can eat at times that suit your family rather than other guests. Mealtimes in many lodges can be a trial for children, though some will prepare meals early, so that you can dine with the other guests while a member of staff (not a qualified childminder) babysits for you.

Even when lodges do accept families, many insist that those with children under, say, eight years old reserve a private vehicle and guide. If this at first seems draconian, consider too that this is for the benefit of the children, as well as for other guests. With your own guide, you select where you stop and spend time, and if your children want to ask questions, that's fine. At camps run by Kwando

Birding highlights The highlights of Botswana's birding calendar include:

March–July Wattled cranes and other opportunists follow the floods in the Okavango, snapping up drowning insects and reptiles.

August–October 'Fishing parties' of herons, egrets and storks will arrive at pools as they dry up, to feed on the stranded fish.

September–November Nesting carmine bee-eaters colonise soft vertical riverbanks, skimmers nest on exposed sandbanks, and large breeding colonies of storks and herons gather at places like the Kanana heronry and Gcodikwe Lagoon. Migrant waders appear beside the edge of most pans and lagoons.

Safaris, you can organise a specialist guide who will travel with your family and will even keep children occupied during siesta time – which can otherwise be particularly challenging. You'll need to book a private vehicle (from US$200/day for a family of four at Kwando, but rising to a steep US$600 plus at some camps), and a specialist guide will cost a further US$220/day, but your safari experience will be considerably enhanced.

Several camps accept quite young children but insist on a minimum age, for safety reasons, before a child can go on a mokoro trip or bush walk. The smaller camps, such as Motswiri, can often be more flexible here, with guides who will assess the maturity of individual children rather than applying a one-size-fits-all age limit. Other camps, such as those owned by Wilderness Safaris, tend to apply the 'rules' more strictly. Then there's a middle ground: at Moremi Crossing, for instance, a member of staff will look after your children while you do these activities, perhaps taking them fishing or on a boat trip.

Putting children at the heart of safaris, Ker & Downey have come up with their three-day Young Explorers safari for children of seven or older. Based at Shinde Enclave, Footsteps across the Delta or Saile Tented Camp, a specially trained guide will be allocated to your family, focusing on the children both on safari and back in camp. Depending on the ages of the children, activities might include making bows and arrows, fishing, bushcraft and quizzes – but the odd game of football or Frisbee could also be thrown in. The key here is entertainment – bored children are the bane of everyone's life on safari, so be aware that if you opt for a conventional trip, you will need to take plenty to occupy your offspring when in camp.

A couple of other options can broaden the choice. The first is to base yourself in a family-friendly hotel in Kasane, where you'll be rewarded with plenty of wildlife on game drives and boat trips into Chobe National Park without feeling cooped up the rest of the time. The other is to opt for a mobile safari, where children are less likely to feel restrained, and will probably relish the camping element. Three that spring to mind in Maun are Drumbeat Safaris, whose safaris are always exclusive, so even if you book for just two people, you will not be sharing your experience with anyone else; Endeavour Safaris, which has no age restrictions; and Letaka Safaris, who have a special two-bedroom family tent with a lockable entrance, so you and your children will be secure under one roof – which is particularly reassuring with younger age groups. Then, with your children both happy and safe, you can get on with enjoying a family safari.

November–April Most of the weavers are in breeding plumage.

February–April Red bishop birds, yellow-billed storks and the spectacular paradise whydahs have their breeding plumage on display. If the rains have been good then the flamingos may be nesting on Sua Pan; ostriches gather in numbers on the pans of the Central Kalahari.

April–June Juvenile birds of many species abound as this season's young are fledged and leave their nests.

PHOTOGRAPHY I find the light clearest and most spectacular during the rainy season. Then the rains have washed the dust from the air, and the bright sunlight can contrast wonderfully with dark storm clouds. The vegetation's also greener and brighter, and the animals and birds often in better condition. However, it will rain occasionally when you're trying to take shots, and the long periods of flat, grey light through clouds can be very disappointing; you'll get few good shots then. Sometimes it can seem as if you're waiting for the gods to grant you just a few minutes of stunning light, between the clouds.

A much more practical time to visit is just after the rains, around April to June, when many of the advantages remain but you are less likely to be interrupted by a shower. (This is one of my reasons for being a fan of May as a great time to travel!)

The dry season's light is reliably good, if not quite as inspirational as that found during the rains. You are unlikely to encounter any clouds, and will get better sightings of game to photograph. Do try to shoot in the first and last few hours of the day, when the sun is low in the sky. During the rest of the day use a filter (perhaps a polariser) to guard against the sheer strength of the light leaving you with a memory card full of washed-out shots.

During the hotter months around October, you're also likely to encounter more bush fires than normal, which can leave a thin pall of smoke covering a large area. (This can especially be a problem near the border area with Namibia, when smoke from the many manmade fires there can drift across.)

WALKING SAFARIS For safe and interesting walking, you need the foliage to be low so that you can see through the surrounding bush as easily as possible. This means that the dry season is certainly the best time for walking – and even then I'd counsel you to choose where you visit very, very carefully as standards of walking guides can be highly variable. (See my comments on the safety of walking safaris on pages 141–4.)

I wouldn't advise anyone looking for a serious walking trip to visit Botswana in the wet season. Walking through shoulder-high grass is nerve-racking with the best of walking guides, and only two or three operations in Botswana are really likely to have anything like that calibre of guide. The best months for walking are May to October, though away from the moderating influence of the Okavango's waters, October can be very hot for longer walks.

COSTS OF TRIPS Aside from the airfares to get here, which vary in their own way (see *Getting there and away*, page 91), some safari operators also lower their rates when business is quieter. Generally July to October is the peak season when prices are highest; January and February is the green season when prices are lowest, and the rest of the year falls somewhere in between.

PUBLIC HOLIDAYS Botswana's public holidays are as follows:

1 January	New Year's Day
2 January	
March/April	Good Friday and Easter Monday
1 May	Labour Day
May	Ascension Day
1 July	Sir Seretse Khama Day
3rd Monday and Tuesday in July	President's Day
30 September	Botswana Day
1 October	
25 December	Christmas Day
26 December	

ORGANISING AND BOOKING YOUR TRIP

How you organise your holiday depends on what kind of a trip you're taking. Generally the more expensive the trip, the more organisation it needs.

ORGANISING A FLY-IN TRIP Most tourists who come to Botswana for a few weeks' safari fly between a series of remote safari camps; this is by far the easiest and most popular way to visit the country. Combinations of the Okavango Delta, and the Kwando–Linyanti and Chobe areas are most common, with relatively few people venturing further south or west into the Kalahari.

When to book? These trips are not difficult to arrange for a knowledgeable tour operator. If you have a favourite camp or operation, or will be running to a tight schedule, then book as far ahead as you can. Eight to ten months in advance is perfect. Bear in mind that most camps are small, and thus easily filled. They organise their logistics with military precision and so finding space at specific camps at short notice, especially in the busier months, can be tricky.

Unless you're lucky, or book very early, expect one or two of your chosen camps to be full. Usually there will be good alternatives available. That said, it's fairly rare for visitors to have a really bad time in any of the upmarket camps in Botswana, as standards are generally high – so don't be put off just because your first choice isn't immediately available.

The exception to this is usually the rainy season – when camps often close for maintenance for a few weeks; those that do stay open, however, are seldom full.

How much? Safaris in Botswana are not cheap. The standards for an average fly-in safari camp are high, but so are the prices. Expect to pay around US$630–1,400 per person sharing per night in the high season, between June and October. This will include all meals, laundry, activities and local drinks, but note that the very top camps will cost substantially more: up to US$2,500 per person. Light aircraft transfers from Maun to the camps will cost around US$190 one way.

Depending on the particular camps, April, May and November should cost less. At this time of year, expect something nearer US$495–2,000 per person sharing per night – which again includes everything except internal (and international) flights. Prices in the wet season are generally lower (the exception being the camps in the Kalahari); then a rough cost of US$415–1,700 per person sharing per night should be quite realistic.

4

If you stay for a longer spell with some camps (and 'longer' can mean anything from three to seven nights), or groups of camps, then these rates will drop slightly; if you fly between camps every day or two, only spending one or two nights at each camp (not recommended) then they'll rise.

These trips are expensive, so you should expect a good level of service and knowledge from the operator who is arranging it for you. If you don't get it, go elsewhere.

How to book? It's best to arrange everything at the same time, using a reliable, independent tour operator. Many operators sell trips to Botswana, but few know the country and the camps. Insist on dealing directly with someone who does. Botswana's areas, camps and lodges do change, so up-to-date local knowledge is vital in putting together a trip that runs smoothly and suits you.

Booking directly with the Botswana companies is possible, but piecing together a jigsaw of complex transfers and flights can be tricky, and you will have little recourse if anything goes wrong. By contrast, UK and European operators are bonded, so your money is protected if they go broke. (If you're still nervous, pay with a credit card.) Remember, too, that the safari companies are primarily interested in selling space at their own camps and lodges – regardless of whether or not these are the best camps for you, so it's wise to seek out an independent operator. Indeed, most of the bigger groups of camps and lodges work largely with the overseas travel trade, which has special contracts with them. And as if to reinforce the point, many of these groups make it clear on their websites that they don't accept direct bookings, and that these should be made through a specialist travel agent or tour operator. So, paradoxically, the best way of booking a fly-in safari in Botswana is usually by arranging it many months prior to your trip through a specialist tour operator based outside Africa.

European, US and other overseas operators usually work on commission for the trips that they sell, which is deducted from the basic cost that the visitor pays. Perhaps because of the UK's historical links, or the high number of British safari-goers, there seems to be more competition amongst UK tour operators than elsewhere. Hence they've a reputation for being generally cheaper than US operators for the same trips – and the best usually work out much cheaper than similar trips booked directly.

Which tour operator? Botswana looks on the surface like an easy country to sell, and you'll find scores of brochures that feature a trip or two there. The vast majority will include only camps from one local operator – perhaps using only Wilderness Safaris, or only &Beyond camps, or visiting nothing but Desert & Delta places. This is a really bad sign, as no one operator in Botswana has a monopoly of the best camps.

However, start asking detailed questions about the alternatives and you'll rapidly sort the best from the rest. Don't let anyone convince you that there are only half a dozen decent safari camps in Botswana; that's rubbish. If the person you're talking to hasn't been to the camps that you are interested in – or doesn't offer a genuinely wide choice to suit you – then find someone who does.

Here I must, as the author, admit a personal interest in the tour-operating business. I organise and personally run the UK operators Expert Africa and Wild about Africa (see below for details of both). We are currently one of the leading tour operators to Botswana – based on my team's detailed personal knowledge of the country. We organise trips for travellers to Africa from all over the world, especially the UK and America. Take a look at Expert Africa's comprehensive website for probably the most detailed and competitively priced programme of trips to Botswana that are available.

The best Botswana operators are specialists. Their brochures and websites will have unique pictures that you won't find elsewhere, cliché-free text that isn't copied from other websites, and staff who can talk to you from first-hand experience about the camps that interest you. You'll always get the best advice (and the best chance of problem-free trips) from people who know the places that you're thinking of going to personally.

UK tour operators International tour operators featuring Botswana include the following. Whoever you book through, make sure first that the company has in place a 'bond' to protect your money in case they go bust. The most usual form of this in the UK is the ATOL licence; if a company doesn't have one of these, then question them very carefully indeed. All the companies below have good track records, & currently have ATOL bonds for your protection.

Aardvark Safaris RBL Hse, Ordnance Rd, Tidworth, Hants SP9 7QD; ☎ 01980 849160; e mail@aardvarksafaris.com; www.aardvarksafaris.co.uk. Small upmarket operator featuring much of Africa, with good knowledge of Botswana.

Abercrombie & Kent St George's Hse, Ambrose St, Cheltenham, Glos GL50 3LG; ☎ 0845 618 2200; e info@abercrombiekent.co.uk; www.abercrombiekent.co.uk. Large, long-established posh operator worldwide, with a wide choice of Africa trips. (Note that Botswana's Sanctuary Retreats is under the same ownership.)

African Explorations Fraser Hse, Wadham Cl, Southrop, Glos GL7 3NR; ☎ 01367 850566; e info@africanexplorations.com; www.africanexplorations.com. Old-school operator now working worldwide including Africa & the Seychelles.

Audley Travel New Mill, New Mill Lane, Witney, Oxon OX29 9SX; ☎ 01993 838500; e africa@audleytravel.com; www.audleytravel.com. Specialist tailormade operator with worldwide coverage including Botswana.

Cazenove & Loyd 3–11 Imperial Rd, London SW6 2AG; ☎ 020 7384 2332; e info@cazloyd.com; www.cazenoveandloyd.com. Bespoke posh operator with tailormade trips worldwide, including east/southern Africa. Good local knowledge & service with a high price tag.

Cox & Kings 6th Floor, 30 Millbank, London SW1P 4EE; ☎ 020 7873 5000; e sales@coxandkings.co.uk; www.coxandkings.co.uk. Long-established operator famed for its Indian trips. Also features more recent programmes worldwide, including fly-in trips to Botswana.

Drive Botswana (see advert, inside back cover) 34 Birch Valley Rd, Stoke-on-Trent ST7 4GN; ☎ 0161 408 4316; e info@drivebotswana.com; www.drivebotswana.com. A relatively new company, with another office in Botswana, specialising in fully inclusive tailormade self-drive safaris, primarily in fully equipped Toyota Land Cruisers.

Expert Africa (see adverts, page i and 257) 9 & 10 Upper Sq, Old Isleworth, Middx TW7 7BJ; ☎ 020 8232 9777; e info@expertafrica.com; www.expertafrica.com. A team of enthusiastic Africa experts run by Chris McIntyre – this book's author. I believe that we have the best range of fly-in & mobile-safari trips to Botswana!

Hartley's Safaris The Old Chapel, Chapel La, Hackthorn, Lincs LN2 3PN; ☎ 01673 861600; e info@hartleys-safaris.co.uk; www.hartleys-safaris.co.uk. Old-school, established tailormade specialists to east/southern Africa & Indian Ocean islands, with close historical connections to Botswana.

Okavango Tours & Safaris White Lion Hse, 64A Highgate High St, London N6 5HX; ☎ 020 8347 4030; e info@okavango.com; www.okavango.com. Established specialists to east/southern Africa & Indian Ocean. Not part of the Maun company of the same name.

Original Travel 21 Ransom's Dock, 35–37 Parkgate Rd, London SW11 4NP; ☎ 020 7978 7333; e ask@originaltravel.co.uk; www.originaltravel.co.uk. Upmarket worldwide company incorporating the former Tim Best Travel – & including top-end fly-in lodges in Botswana.

Rainbow Tours (see advert, page 394) Laydon Hse, 76–86 Turnmill St, London EC1M 5QU; ☎ 020 7666 1250; e info@rainbowtours.co.uk; www.rainbowtours.co.uk. Established Africa specialists, now part of the Western & Oriental Group, with a varied Botswana programme.

Safari Consultants (see advert, 3rd colour insert, page iii) Africa Hse, 2 Cornard Mills, Mill Tye, Gt Cornard, Suffolk CO10 0GW; ☏01787 888590; e info@safariconsultantuk.com; www. safari-consultants.com. Very old-school tailormade specialists to east/southern Africa & Indian Ocean with a competent Botswana programme.

Safari Drive (see advert, page 132) The Trainer's Office, Windy Hollow, Sheepdrove, Lambourn, Berks RG17 7XA; ☏01488 71140; e info@ safaridrive.com; www.safaridrive.com. Specialist African operator with 1st-class knowledge of Botswana, concentrating on self-drive trips using their own well-equipped Land Rovers.

Steppes Africa 51 Castle St, Cirencester, Glos GL7 1QD; ☏01285 650011; e enquiry@ steppestravel.co.uk; www.steppestravel.co.uk. This posh tailormade specialist covers a wide range of destinations including central, eastern & southern Africa.

Tribes Travel (see advert, page 66) The Old Dairy, Wood Farm, Ipswich Rd, Otley, Suffolk IP6 9JW; ☏01473 890499; e info@tribes.co.uk; www.tribes. co.uk. An interesting company with a selection of trips worldwide, based on strong fair-trade principles, including some Botswana options.

Ultimate Travel Company 25–27 Vanston Pl, London SW6 1AZ; ☏020 7386 4646; e enquiry@theultimatetravelcompany.co.uk; www. theultimatetravelcompany.co.uk. Wide-ranging operator including Africa, from the Nile to the Cape.

Wild about Africa Sunvil House, Upper Sq, Old Isleworth, Middx TW7 7BJ; ☏020 8758 4717; e safari@wildaboutafrica.com; www. wildaboutafrica.com. An offshoot of Expert Africa that specialises in group trips around Namibia & Botswana, from budget small-group departures to top private mobile safaris.

Wildlife Worldwide Capitol Hse, 12–13 Bridge St, Winchester, Hants SO23 0HL; ☏0845 130 6982; e sales@wildlifeworldwide.com; www. wildlifeworldwide.com. Worldwide operator offering tailormade & small-group wildlife holidays to all corners of the globe.

Zambezi Safari & Travel Africa Hse, Poundwell St, Modbury, Devon PL21 0QJ; ☏0800 840 1377; e info@zambezi.com; www.zambezi.com. Specialist safari planners concentrating on east, central & southern Africa.

Other tour operators
USA/Canada

Adventure Center ☏+1 866 338 8735; www. adventurecenter.com. Offices in New York & Canada.

Adventure Travel Desk (ATD) 308 Commonwealth Av, Wayland, MA 01778; ☏+1 800 552 0300; e atd@african-safari.com; www. african-safari.com

Africa Adventure Company (see advert, 3rd colour insert, page i) 2601 E Oakland Park Blvd, Suite 600, Fort Lauderdale, FL 33306; ☏+1 800 882 9453; e safari@africanadventure. com; www.africanadventure.com

David Anderson Safaris 30 W Mission, Suite 8, Santa Barbara, CA 93101; ☏0800 927 4647; www. davidanderson.com, www.focusonafrica.com

Ker & Downey (see advert, page 258) 6703 Highway Bd, Katy, TX 77494; ☏0800 423 4236; e info@kerdowney.com; www.kerdowney.com

Overseas Adventure Travel 1 Mifflin Pl, Suite 400, Cambridge, MA 02138; ☏0800 955 1925; www.oattravel.com. Members-only organisation with group trips for 10–16 participants over 50.

Australia

African Wildlife Safaris 1st Floor, 333 Clarendon St, S Melbourne, VIC 3205; ☏+1 300 363302; e info@awsnfs.com; www.nfs.travel

The Classic Safari Company 124A Queen St, Woollahra, NSW 2025; ☏+1 300 130218; e info@classicsafaricompany.com.au; www. classicsafaricompany.com.au

South Africa

Drifters ☏+27 11 888 1160; e drifters@drifters. co.za; www.drifters.co.za. Specialists in overland trips.

Jenman African Safaris ☏+27 21 683 7826; e info@jenmansafaris.com; www.jenmansafaris.com

Pulse Africa ☏+27 11 325 2290; e info@ pulseafrica.com; www.pulseafrica.com. Tailormade trips to east & southern Africa.

France and Italy

Il Diamante Via 1 Nievo 25, 10153 Turin; ☏011 229 32 40; e info@qualitygroup.it; www. qualitygroup.it

Makila Voyages 4 place de Valois, 75001 Paris; ☏01 42 96 80 00; e info@makila.fr; www. makila.fr

Suggested fly-in itineraries Most fly-in trips to Botswana last between ten days and three weeks, and are often limited more by travellers' available budgets than anything else. The Okavango Delta, Kwando–Linyanti and Chobe areas are the most common destinations, but the Central Kalahari, Nxai Pan and the Makgadikgadi Pans also have their own landing strips and are sometimes added on to the start or end of trips.

Less commonly, it's quite possible to plan a trip that's part mobile or self-drive, followed by a few days of relative luxury at a fly-in camp or two (usually in the Delta).

Concentrating on the fly-in element, the key to an interesting fly-in trip is variation: making sure that the different camps that you visit really are different. For me this means that they're in different environments and have different activities. So mix deep-water camps with shallow-water ones, and forested areas with open ones. That way you'll not only have the greatest variety of scenery, of which there's a lot in the Delta, but also see the widest variety of game.

I also prefer to mix camps run by different companies – one from Wilderness, one from &Beyond and one from Kwando, for example. I find that this makes a more interesting trip than staying at camps which are all run by the same company (sometimes in predictably similar styles).

When flying in, the costs of visiting the camps in the parks are very similar to the costs of those in the private concessions. Because of the ability to do night drives, to drive off-road, and (sometimes) to go walking, I generally prefer to use camps in private areas. Hence I've included relatively few of the camps which are inside the parks here.

For most trips, if you work on spending around three nights at each camp that you visit, that's ideal. Four would be lovely, though often visitors haven't got that much time (or money), whereas two nights is OK for some camps, but a fraction too short for most.

Here I'll give you a few ideas for combinations of areas that I think work well together, giving a real variation to trips. These are **not** lists of my all-time favourite camps; I have deliberately chosen not to pick out just my favourites (simply because the type of camps that I love – the simpler, smaller ones with their emphasis on guiding and wildlife – may not be so ideal for you). Instead, these are trips in which I think the various areas, camps and experiences go well together – and demonstrate what I mean about varying the areas that you stay in and the companies that you use.

Livingstone, Kwando–Linyanti and Okavango Delta: 11 nights/ 12 days

- 2 nights Livingstone, a hotel or lodge
- 3 nights Linyanti Bush Camp, CH1 – riverine areas with a balance of dry and wet areas
- 3 nights Kwara, NG20 – for deep-water motorboat trips plus some game viewing in areas of denser vegetation
- 3 nights Kwetsani, NG25 – for picturesque shallow-water mokoro trips, plus some game viewing in open floodplains

Livingstone, Kwando–Linyanti, Okavango and the Pans: 15 nights/ 16 days

- 2 nights Livingstone, a hotel or lodge
- 3 nights Lagoon, NG15 – dry-land game viewing in mostly riverine forest

- 4 nights Vumbura, NG20 – for some deep-water, some shallow-water mokoro trips, and some game viewing in an open floodplain environment
- 3 nights Sandibe, NG31 – for game viewing in a more forested environment
- 3 nights Jack's Camp – something totally different on the great salt pans

NOTES FOR DISABLED TRAVELLERS   *Gordon Rattray (www.able-travel.com)*

For wheelchair users and people who have difficulties walking, Botswana is a relatively accessible safari destination. It is possible to book through a specialised operator and be sure that your needs are met, or to do enough preparation in advance and travel independently. Either way, with some endeavour, everybody can experience the unique highlights this country has to offer.

TRANSPORT
Air travel Most international travellers arrive via Johannesburg, where the services and facilities for disabled people rival and sometimes better those in Europe. In Maun, the airport has an aisle chair, the staff are extremely efficient and there is a spacious (albeit not officially wheelchair-accessible) toilet.

The shorter flights from Maun to Kasane and into the Okavango Delta are also quite possible; when I went, the pilot helped lift me to my seat and there was room to stow my wheelchair with the luggage. However, these planes are small so a folding wheelchair and soft baggage are essential. Also, do note that airfields in the Delta are usually just a landing strip with few other facilities, and if an aisle chair is needed in Kasane, this should be ordered from Gaborone in advance.

By road Safari vehicles in Botswana are often 4x4, and therefore higher than normal cars. This means that – unless you use a specialised operator with adapted cars and trained staff – wheelchair transfers may be more difficult. My advice is to thoroughly explain your needs and always stay in control of the situation.

It is possible to hire self-drive vehicles, but I know of no company providing cars that are adapted for disabled drivers.

Distances are large and roads are often bumpy, so if you are prone to skin damage you may need to take extra care. Place your own pressure-relieving cushion on top of (or instead of) the original car seat and, if necessary, pad around knees and elbows.

There is no effective legislation in Botswana to help facilitate disabled travellers' journeys by bus.

ACCOMMODATION In **Maun**, Island Safari Lodge (page 162) has two chalets with roll-in showers; Thamalakane River Lodge (page 162) has two chalets with roll-in showers (no hand railing); Maun Lodge (page 160) has two rooms with roll-in shower but both have a 15cm step to enter the rooms; and Riley's Hotel (page 159) has one step-free room with a bath.

In **Kasane,** Mowana Safari Lodge (page 188) and Chobe Marina Lodge (page 188) have adapted rooms; Chobe Safari Lodge (page 189) has two rooms with roll-in showers; and Chobe Game Lodge (page 218) has two rooms with roll-in showers.

There are several lodges and camps in the **Okavango Delta** that have a degree of accessibility, depending on your needs. Motswiri (page 254) has a

Just the Okavango Delta: 8 nights/9 days
- 3 nights Xakanaxa Camp, Moremi – for dry-land game viewing
- 2 nights Xugana, NG21 – transfer from Xakanaxa for deep-water trips
- 3 nights Nxabega, NG31 – for shallow-water trips and game viewing

spacious tent designed for wheelchair users, with handles and a roll-in shower, but is accessible only by air in small Cessna planes. Other camps are accessible by road: Savute Safari Lodge (page 236), which has one tent with a ramp, roll-in shower and plenty of manoeuvring space; Okuti (page 275), which is in general very accessible for wheelchair users, with very spacious rooms and level-entry showers, but the doors accessing the bathroom and shower room are quite tight; and Xakanaxa Camp (page 275), which has ramps to access the main area and roll-in showers in the rooms, but no space next to the toilet for a wheelchair. Outside the Delta, Leroo La Tau Lodge (page 431; accessible by road), has one tent with a ramp, roll-in shower and plenty of manoeuvring space.

In Zambia's **Livingstone**, the Royal Livingstone and Zambezi Sun hotels (pages 464–5) each have two highly adapted rooms.

HEALTH AND SAFETY In general, doctors will know about 'everyday' illnesses, but you must understand and be able to explain your own particular medical requirements. A good first stop for medical advice in Maun is Dr Chris Carey (*Cash Bazaar Centre;* 686 4084/5013). Dr Carey runs his own practice, and being a wheelchair user himself, may have a deeper understanding of some disabilities than most practitioners.

Rural clinics are often basic so, if possible, take all necessary medication and equipment with you. It is advisable to pack this in your hand luggage during flights in case your main luggage is delayed.

Botswana can be extremely hot. If this is a problem for you, be careful to book accommodation with fans or air conditioning. A useful cooling aid is a plant-spray bottle.

Security For anyone following the usual security precautions (see page 129) the chances of robbery are greatly reduced. In fact, as a disabled person I often feel more 'noticed', and therefore a less attractive target for thieves. But the opposite may also apply, so do stay aware of where your bags are and who is around you, especially during car transfers and similar activities.

SPECIALIST TOUR OPERATORS
Endeavour Safaris   (see page 177) The leader in disability travel in Botswana with custom-designed mobile-camping equipment & several adapted vehicles.

FURTHER INFORMATION
www.able-travel.com   Worldwide and country-specific info.
www.globalaccessnews.com   A searchable database of disability travel information.
www.rollingrains.com   A searchable website advocating disability travel.
www.youreable.com   A UK-based general resource for disability information, with an active forum.
www.apparelyzed.com   A site dedicated to spinal injury, but containing info that those with other disabilities will also find useful. It also hosts a hugely popular forum.

4

After reading this book you'll realise there are so many possibilities that you'd be wise to talk through your wishes with someone who knows the camps and can work out what's best for you.

ORGANISING A BUDGET OR BACKPACKING TRIP If you're backpacking then usually you're more restricted by money than by time. Many of the side-trips and safaris that you take will be organised at the time, on the ground – and trying to do too much in advance might be counter-productive.

So, read the book, and head off. Start by heading towards Maun or Kasane, keeping your eyes open and talking to people you meet to see what's going on. And enjoy! Much of the joy is the unpredictability of these trips; if you want everything fixed and arranged then backpacking isn't really for you!

ORGANISING A MOBILE SAFARI Mobile trips in Botswana range from cheap-and-cheerful budget safaris to absolutely top-class operations running privately guided trips for small family groups. Thus generalising amongst them is difficult, although levels of comfort vary. Typically, the cheapest are dubbed 'participation' safaris (where you pitch your own tent and muck in with all the chores). Then there's 'semi-participation', where you'll help but staff will be on hand; and 'non-participation' – where the staff will do everything for you. As a general rule, the more they cost, the further in advance they should be booked. (For an indication of costs, see *Budgeting*, pages 95–7.) The cheaper ones often survive on last-minute bookings from people who turn up; the more costly private ones can be booked up years in advance. Many safari companies are members of HATAB (Hospitality & Tourism Association of Botswana) and/or the Botswana Guides Association (BOGA), both of which operate their own campsites.

Ideally, talk to someone who has been on safari with the mobile operator that you're considering before booking with them. If this isn't possible then don't hesitate to ask a lot of questions before you decide which trip is right for you. You'll be stuck with your guide and group for a week or more, so it's vital to make the right choice.

Most of these companies are based in Maun (see pages 175–9), with only a few elsewhere – like Kasane. The best often have overseas tour operators who know them well, and will sell their trips at around the same price (or even cheaper) than they do directly.

ORGANISING A SELF-DRIVE TRIP Describing the roads in Botswana is like describing Dr Jekyll and Mr Hyde. The tarred main routes, and most of the roads in the towns, are beautifully smooth roads with excellent signposts. They're often delightfully free of traffic: a dream to drive on. They're eminently suitable to potter around in a normal 2WD such as a Toyota Corolla or VW Citi Golf.

However, the tracks through the national parks and more remote areas can become nightmares. Inexperienced or badly prepared drivers will find themselves seriously challenged, with deep sand in the dry season, and glutinous mud when it's wet – often compounded by a complete lack of signposts or directions.

If you want to hire a self-drive vehicle for the trip, then you must treat Botswana's two personas very differently. Your biggest decision is your vehicle, as this will make or break your trip.

Hiring a 2WD If you are sticking to the towns and tar roads then hire a 2WD from one of the normal hire companies – Avis, Budget or Europcar would be the obvious three. Contacting them directly, a medium-sized saloon (Group C) for about two weeks will cost you around US$98/£65 per day, including 'super' CDW (collision damage waiver; see page 84) insurance cover and unlimited mileage, but excluding 12% VAT. See *Car hire* in the chapters on Maun and Kasane for the relevant contact details.

Hiring a 4x4
If you want to explore Botswana in your own 4x4, then you have three options: to hire locally; to rent a vehicle from a South African-based company; or to go with a UK specialist.

The obvious solution would appear to be to hire locally, but think carefully. What you need to drive into the bush in Botswana is a serious, fully equipped vehicle – and what you'd be hiring off-the-peg isn't always, in my view, up to the job. You need a vehicle that you can rely on, with long-range tanks, a high-lift jack, a spade and decent tow-rope, extra fuel cans if necessary and all the other bits and pieces that make all the difference. Perhaps most vitally, you need to have confidence that if anything goes wrong, there's a system in place to help you swiftly.

Local hire Contacting the hire companies directly (see *Chapter 7*, page 158), you'll find a twin-cab 4x4 hired for about two weeks will cost you upwards of about US$140/£95, including unlimited mileage, multiple drivers & standard insurance, but not CDW insurance cover, rising to at least US$170/£115 per day with camping kit – and more for a Toyota Land Cruiser. For full insurance cover, you can expect to pay around US$40 per day. Some companies also charge a premium for the high-season months, usually July to October. Others may charge extra for VAT or for a second driver, or indeed for mileage above a certain level – usually 150km per day.

South African 4x4s Several South African companies specialise in 4x4 hire, including:

🚐**Britz 4x4** ☎ +27 11 230 5200; e maui@iafrica.com; www.britz.co.za
🚐**Bushtrackers Africa** ☎ +27 11 465 5700; e bushtrackers@iafrica.com; www.bushtrackers.co.za

🚐**Drive Africa** ☎ +27 61 066 8578; e mycar@driveafrica.co.za; www.driveafrica.co.za
🚐**Kwenda Safaris** ☎ +27 44 533 5717; e rmath@global.co.za; www.kwendasafari.co.za

Backed-up 4x4s Most of the companies mentioned above simply deal with hiring out vehicles; they may make suggestions, but generally don't get involved with helping you plan your trip or give you any advice. A step up from this, in both price and completeness, are companies that provide not only a vehicle, but also put their expertise at your disposal. They cost more, but if you're not living in southern Africa then it's probably what you need.

Safari Drive are specialist African operators based in the UK who regularly send self-driving clients to Botswana. A second company, Drive Botswana, offers only fully inclusive packages. Both can advise you on self-drive trips from personal experience. For contact details, see pages 77–8.

Safari Drive use probably the region's best fleet of bush-equipped Land Rovers, and their support team has bases in Maun, Livingstone and Windhoek. I've used their vehicles for all my research trips to Botswana, and they come fully equipped with everything that you'll need for comfortable bushcamping, from long-range fuel tanks, roof (or ground) tents and fridges to the washing-up bowls, condiments

4

and crockery that really make a trip comfortable. Included, too, is an extensive starter pack of dried food, such as rice and pasta, tea and coffee, and even biscuits and sweets, as well as 12 litres of bottled water. Each vehicle comes equipped with a satnav device, a satellite phone (you pay just for the calls), and the appropriate tools for getting yourself out of trouble.

Probably more important than the kit is their service. Before you leave, they will help you plan your trip based on detailed local knowledge. They make the tricky campsite bookings with the various private companies as well as the national parks' office. And most importantly, they offer first-rate 24-hour back-up in Botswana – based around a well-connected team on the ground who know all the local operators, and have the contacts and know-how to help you speedily if any problems occur.

Expect these Land Rovers and the service to cost from US$270/£180 per day in low season (November–June) to US$435/£230 in high season, including all the equipment and full vehicle insurance cover.

Checking the fine print
The devil's in the detail, especially if you're looking at any of the cheaper options. You should check any rental agreement very carefully, so that you know your position. Preferably also discuss any questions or queries with someone within the company that is supplying you with the vehicle. A few specific pointers may help.

CDW insurance
The insurance and the collision damage waiver (CDW) clauses are worth studying particularly closely. These spell out the 'excess' that you will pay in the event of an accident. These CDW excesses vary widely, and often explain the difference between cheap rental deals and better, but more costly, options.

Some hire companies have very high excesses (ie: the amounts that you pay if you have a major accident). An 80% CDW is normal – which means that you will always pay 20% of the cost of any damage. However, look around and you should be able to reduce this to zero – although most hiring companies will still want a deposit, in case you damage or lose any of their vehicle's equipment.

Other fine print
Though accidents are fortunately uncommon, they do happen. Then it's very important to get the situation resolved swiftly and carry on with your trip. Some of the companies have quite onerous terms – so be aware of these before you agree to take the vehicle.

Booking accommodation
If you're driving a 2WD on the tar, then you can afford to find a campsite in Maun or Kasane when you get there. If you need a room, then you only need to book one in advance during the busy season. For the rest of the year you shouldn't have a problem finding one.

Generally, finding a campsite outside the national parks is not a problem, though if you're not at a designated private site, you should always seek permission first (see *Chapter 6* for more on this). However, campsites within the national parks **must** be booked in advance (see below) and you should do this as far ahead as possible. Any lodges at which you plan to stay should also be reserved in advance.

National parks
Until recently you could just arrive at any national park and pay your park fees. Then, in January 2009, the authorities decreed that, in line with the campsites (see below), entry fees for the national parks must be pre-booked. Thus it is now essential to organise your trip, and to pay your park fees, before setting off. The policy is strict: no paid permit, no entry. Don't even think of trying to argue with the

park wardens on this; they are not allowed to issue permits at the gate, or to bend the rules, no matter how persuasive you may be. That said, our experience in October 2013 suggests that common sense applies where a genuine problem has arisen.

Park rules and regulations Park opening hours are 06.00–18.30 from April to September, and 05.30–19.00 from October to March. No driving is permitted in the parks outside these hours, so it is imperative to allow plenty of time for your journey, and to be at the gates or your campsite well before closing. Campers may camp only at designated sites, and should leave the park before 11.00, or they will be liable for an additional day's park fees (which are payable to staff at the gates). The speed limit in all the national parks is 40km/h – though you'd be hard pressed to exceed this almost anywhere.

Both walking and swimming are prohibited within all Botswana's parks.

Park fees and permits Most organised trips will include park entry fees in their costs, but if you are travelling on your own then you must pay these directly.

There are usually three sets of park fees: for the people, for your vehicle and for a campsite. These depend on your nationality/immigration status, and where your vehicle is registered. Campsite fees, however, are no longer fixed, so see below for rates at the various privatised sites.

Fees for park permits must be paid in advance at one of a designated number of offices (⏰ *usually 07.30–16.30 Mon–Sat, 07.30–12.00 Sun*). These are located in Gaborone, Tsabong, Ghanzi, Kang, Letlhakane, Maun, Kasane and Francistown. For self-drive visitors, the most accessible of these are likely to be in Maun (see *DWNP*, page 87) and Kasane (where the designated office is at the Sedudu Gate into Chobe National Park). In theory, all these offices accept credit cards (Visa or MasterCard) as well as cash – but it's as well to be prepared for the inevitable occasions when the card machines are not working. Cash payments may be made in pula, US dollars, South African rand or sterling, but do check the rate of exchange offered, as this may not always be favourable.

Park, vehicle and fees for campsites still in DWNP hands have remained unchanged for some time, but are widely expected to increase within the life of this guidebook. In the meantime, fees for the privatised campsites have increased dramatically: see *National parks' campsites* below).

Park entry fees (per person per day)

	Bots citizen	Bots resident	Non-resident
Adult (18+)	P10	P30	P120
Child (age 8–17)	P5	P15	P60
Infant (7 & under)	free	free	free

Vehicle fees (per day)

Foreign-registered vehicle	P50
Botswana-registered vehicle	P10

Camping fees (per person per night, DWNP sites only)

	Bots citizen	Bots resident	Non-resident
Adult (15+)	P5	P20	P30
Child (age 2–15)	P2.50	P10	P15
Infant (under 2)	free	free	free
Wilderness trail	P50	P100	P200

To give you some idea of the total cost of camping within the national parks, the following are based on a foreign-registered vehicle with two adult visitors spending seven days' camping in one or more of the parks – ranging from the lowest possible campsite fees (DWNP sites) to the highest (currently SKL):

Park entry fees	P1,680 (2 x 7 x P120)
Vehicle entry fees	P350 (7 x P50)
Camping fees	from P420 (2 x 7 x P30) up to US$700 (2 x 7 x US$50)
Total costs	**P2,450 (US$281/£188) up to P8,120 (US$933/£622)**

That's an average cost per person per day from P175 (US$20/£13.50) up to (more realistically) P580 (US$66/£44) at the privatised campsites .

National parks' campsites Botswana's national parks have a scattering of campsites where, until the late 1980s, you could just turn up and pay the fees. Then, the introduction of the 'high-revenue, low-volume' policy (see page 63) led to a restriction in the number of campsites at each location. Sites now must be pre-booked; once they're full, you'll be turned away.

Following on from this, in 2009, the DWNP commenced privatisation of the campsites, and by late 2013, most sites in the northern parks were already in the hands of four separate operators, with only a few still handled by the DWNP:

Central Kalahari Game Reserve Lekhubu, Letiahau, Piper, Sunday, Passarge & Motopi campsites (Bigfoot Tours); others (DWNP).
Chobe National Park Ihaha Campsite (Kwalate Safaris); Savuti & Linyanti sites (SKL).
Moremi Game Reserve Xakanaxa & South Gate sites (Kwalate Safaris); Khwai Campsite (SKL); Third Bridge Campsite (Xomae Group).
Makgadikgadi Pans National Park Khumaga Campsite (SKL); Njuca Hills & Tree Island sites (DWNP).
Nxai Pan National Park South Campsite & Baines' Baobab sites (Xomae Group).

For those planning to camp inside the national parks, it remains *essential* to book as early as you can. Sites are very, very limited and often booked out almost a year in advance; you cannot just turn up. Reservations cannot usually be made more than 11 months in advance, but booking this far ahead is usually the ideal.

Each of the operators handles bookings for its own campsites, so if you want to stay at, say, Savuti, Third Bridge and South Gate, you'll need to pull together your itinerary working with three separate operators. Given the difficulty of communications, this isn't always straightforward, so it's crucial to allow plenty of time.

Once you have your campsites lined up, be sure to get written confirmation from each of the operators stating not just the dates of your reservation, but also confirming the number of the pitch reserved. Only then will you be able to book your park permits with the DWNP, who will insist on written proof of your overnight accommodation booking before issuing a permit. You can in theory make these reservations by email (e *dwnp@gov.bw*), attaching your invoices from the various campsite companies, but be prepared to go into one of the DWNP offices in person, or arrange for someone to do so on your behalf.

The new system is not just unwieldy, it's also pretty costly, with camping fees increased tenfold or more at the privatised sites. While the remaining DWNP sites still charge P30 (US$3.50) per person, the lowest fee at the privatised sites for international visitors is around US$35 per person per night – rising to US$50 – and that's exclusive of park fees and P10 per person bed levy. (These rates are for international visitors; locals and residents of the SADAC countries are charged according to a different scale of fees.)

On the plus side, the campsites – and particularly their ablution blocks – do seem to be better maintained than in the past, though inevitably some are cleaner than others. This variation in standards runs through to the efficiency of the individual operators, too. While some seem to be very much on the ball, this is not always the case, so do double check that all your paperwork is in order.

Details of the operators are as follows:

Bigfoot Tours ✆395 3360, 391 0927; m 7224 3567; e reservations@bigfoottours.co.bw; www.bigfoottours.co.bw. Lekhubu, Letiahau, Piper, Sunday, Passarge & Motopi campsites in the Central Kalahari. *US$50 pp.*

DWNP Central booking ✆397 1405; f 391 2354; e dwnp@gov.bw; www.mewt.gov.bw/DWNP. *Gaborone office* ✆318 0774; f 318 0775. *Maun office* ✆686 1265; f 686 1264. *P30 pp.*

Kwalate Safaris ✆686 1448; e kwalatesafari@gmail.com. Ihaha Campsite in Chobe National Park; Xakanaxa & South Gate sites in Moremi Game Reserve. *US$40 pp.*

SKL ✆686 5365/6; e reservations@sklcamps.co.bw, sklcamps@botsnet.bw; www.sklcamps.com. Savuti & Linyanti campsites in Chobe National Park; Khwai (North Gate) Campsite in Moremi Game Reserve; Khumaga Campsite in Makgadikgadi Pans National Park. Arguably the most efficient of the new campsite operators, SKL is also among the most expensive. *US$50 pp.*

Xomae Group ✆686 2221; m 7386 7221; e xomaesites@botsnet.bw; www.xomaesites.com. Third Bridge in Moremi Game Reserve; South Camp & Baines Baobab sites in Nxai Pan National Park. *P300 (US$35) pp.*

All except Bigfoot Tours have offices in Maun (see page 174), so if you do need to visit them in person, you can.

Campsite facilities Each of the parks' campsites has a designated number of pitches or 'campsites'. These are usually very large by European and American standards, and capable of taking several vehicles – perhaps a group of friends travelling together. However, if the campsite is busy, you can expect to share your site with one or even two other vehicles. All the campsites have ablution facilities, most of them relatively modern but some – especially in the CKGR – more rudimentary, and hot water is decidedly hit or miss. Most individual pitches have a firepit, and perhaps a barbecue stand. Regulations prohibit the collection of firewood within all Botswana's national parks and game reserves, so do make sure that you take sufficient with you, along with all the food, fuel and drinking water you will need for your trip. Although the occasional site now has a small shop (Savuti springs to mind), don't rely on it!

Suggested self-drive itineraries If you're driving yourself outside the national parks, and have lots of time, then you can afford to have total flexibility in your route, and plan very little. However, if you're coming for a shorter time, and want to use any of the campsites in the national parks, then you would be wise to arrange your trip carefully in advance. Note that campsite bookings in the national parks can be quite difficult to get, and both payment and dates are fixed at the time of reservation. You cannot just turn up at the national park gates and expect to book a campsite. Further, independent drivers can no longer pay park-entry fees at the park gates (see page 85 for further details). Effectively, this commits you to a specific route and schedule.

Perhaps the most obvious and instantly rewarding trip for your first self-drive trip across Botswana would be between Livingstone and Maun. This is best done in the dry season.

Livingstone, Chobe, Moremi and Maun: 11 nights/12 days This really is the fastest trip that you should consider through this area if you want to have time to enjoy the parks. Allowing more time would be better, and another 3–4 nights camping in the parks (including both Third Bridge and Xakanaxa for a few nights each) would improve it enormously.

- 2 nights Livingstone – hotel/lodge (or campsite)
- 2 nights Ihaha Campsite, Chobe
- 2 nights Savuti Campsite, Chobe
- 2 nights Khwai (North Gate) Campsite, Moremi
- 2 nights Xakanaxa or Third Bridge Campsite, Moremi
- 1 night Maun – hotel/lodge (or campsite)

Of course it can easily be reversed. Some prefer Livingstone at the start, to relax after the flight. Others prefer to leave it until the end, with the highlight of seeing Victoria Falls (and buying curios) at the end. If you do start at Livingstone, then consider picking up your vehicle on the day that you leave for Ihaha, as this could save you a few days of vehicle hire.

I recommend that you use a hotel or lodge, rather than camp, for your first and last few days – I find that this makes my trips much easier and gives me time to get organised more easily at the start and end.

The Panhandle plus Tsodilo, Aha & Gcwihaba Hills: 14 nights/15 days
To visit the hills of the northwest Kalahari, ideally consider a trip based out of Maun:

- 1 night Maun – hotel/lodge (or campsite)
- 2 nights Drotsky's Cabins, Shakawe
- 3 nights Tsodilo Hills – camping
- 3 nights Nxamaseri Lodge or Guma Lagoon Camp, Panhandle
- 2 nights Aha Hills – camping
- 2 nights Gcwihaba Hills – camping
- 1 night Maun – campsite or hotel/lodge

If done in the dry season, August or after, then you might tag on a few days after Maun to visit the Boteti River area, where the game concentrations should then be good. Certainly whenever you go, I'd visit Tsodilo before Aha; it's considerably more accessible. Do remember to fill up with fuel at Etsha 6 or Gumare between your time in Tsodilo and the Aha/Gcwihaba area.

Nxai Pan and the Central Kalahari Game Reserve: 20 nights/21 days
If you're experienced in the African bush, feel a lot more adventurous, and don't mind the idea of spending hours digging yourself out of mud, then consider a trip to Nxai and the northern part of the Central Kalahari Game Reserve. This would probably be at its best between February and May, though going later in that period will make the travelling much easier.

- 1 night Maun – hotel/lodge (or campsite)
- 3 nights South Camp, Nxai Pan – camping
- 2 nights Gweta Lodge or Planet Baobab (campsite or lodge)
- 2 nights Khumaga Campsite, Makgadikgadi Pans NP

- 1 night Meno A Kwena – lodge
- 1 night Deception Valley, CKGR – campsite at north end, CKDEC-01 to CKDEC-06
- 2 nights Sunday Pan, CKGR – campsite
- 1 night Passarge Pan, CKGR – campsite
- 1 night Phokoje Pan, CKGR – campsite
- 2 nights Piper Pans, CKGR – campsite
- 2 nights Deception Valley, CKGR – campsite towards the south side, CKWIL-06 or 7
- 1 night Meno A Kwena – lodge
- 1 night Maun – hotel/lodge (or campsite)

As with any rainy-season trip or excursion into the Central Kalahari Game Reserve, you should be doing this with a minimum of two vehicles, and safety precautions like taking a satellite phone might be a good idea.

RED TAPE

VISAS If you need a visa for Botswana, then you must get one before you arrive.

Currently, passport holders from the following countries **do not need a visa** and will be granted a 30-day entry permit on arrival:

- All EC (European Community) countries
- USA, South Africa, Scandinavian countries
- Most Commonwealth countries (except Ghana, Nigeria, Bangladesh, India Pakistan and Sri Lanka – whose citizens *do* need visas).

For more details, contact your local Botswana embassy or high commission (see below) – which is also the best place to verify that the information here is still current. Alternatively, and to download a visa application form, check on the Botswana government website (*www.gov.bw*).

The prevailing attitude amongst both Botswana's government and its people is that visitors are generally very good for the country as they spend valuable foreign currency – so if you look respectable then you will not find any difficulties in entering Botswana.

Given this logic, and the conservative nature of Botwana's local customs, the converse is also true. If you dress very untidily, looking as if you've no money when entering via an overland border, then you may be questioned as to how you will be funding your trip. Very rarely, you may even be asked for a return ticket as proof that you do intend to leave. Dressing respectably in Botswana is not only courteous, but will also make your life easier.

Visa extensions If you want to stay longer than 30 days, then you must renew your permit at the nearest immigration office. For a visa lasting longer than 90 days, you should apply to the Chief Immigration Officer (*PO Box 942, Gaborone;* 361 1300), preferably before entering Botswana; a fee of P100 is payable. Note that it's a serious offence to stay longer than 90 days in a 12-month period without permission.

Botswana is now quite strict about granting **work permits** only for jobs for which a suitably qualified Botswana citizen is not available; for information, see www.gov.bw. Work permits can be obtained from the Department of Labour and Home Affairs (*Private Bag 002, Gaborone;* 361 1500; *toll free* 0800 600777).

4

BOTSWANA'S DIPLOMATIC MISSIONS ABROAD For an up-to-date list of Botswana's diplomatic missions, see the Ministry of Foreign Affairs' website, www. mofaic.gov.bw, and look under 'diplomatic missions'. Current embassies and high commissions include:

❸ **Australia** (high commission) 130 Denison St, Deakin Act 2600, Canberra; ☏02 6234 7500; f 02 6282 4140; e botaus-info@gov.bw; www. botswanahighcom.org.au

❸ **Belgium** (embassy) 169 Av Tervuren, B-1150 Brussels; ☏02 735 2070/6110; f 02 735 6318, 732 7264; e boer@gov.bw

❸ **China** (embassy) 1 Don San Jie, Sanlitun, Chaoyang District, Beijing 100600; ☏653 26898; f 653 26896

❸ **Ethiopia** (embassy) PO Box 22282, Code 1000, Addis Ababa; ☏011 371 5422/3; f 011 371 4099. Also covers Algeria, Egypt, Libya, Morocco, Tunisia.

❸ **India** (high commission) Plot F8/3, Vasant, Vihar, New Delhi 110057; ☏11 4653 7000, f 11 4603 6191

❸ **Japan** (embassy) 6F Kearny Place, 4-5-10 Shiba, Minato-Ku, Tokyo 108-0014; ☏03 5440 5676; f 03 5765 7581; e botjap@sepia.ocn.ne.jp; www.botswanaembassy.or.jp

❸ **Namibia** (high commission) 101 Nelson Mandela Av, Klein Windhoek, PO Box 20359, Windhoek; ☏061 221941/2/7; f 061 236034

❸ **South Africa** (high commission) 24 Amos St, Colbyn, Pretoria 0083, PO Box 57035, Arcadia 0007, Pretoria; ☏012 430 9640; f 012 342 1845/4783

❸ **Sweden** (embassy) Tyrgatan 11, PO Box 26024, 10041 Stockholm; ☏08 545 25880; f 08 723 0087.

❸ **Switzerland** (permanent mission to United Nations) 80 Rue de Lausanne, 1202 Geneva; ☏022 906 1060; f 022 906 1061; e botgen@ bluewin.ch

❸ **UK** (high commission) 6 Stratford Place, London W1C 1AY; ☏020 7647 1000; f 020 7495 8595; www.gov.bw

❸ **USA** (embassy) 1531–33 New Hampshire Av NW, Washington, DC 20036; ☏202 244 4990/1; f 202 244 4164

❸ **Zambia** (high commission) 5201 Pandit Nehru Rd, PO Box 31910, Lusaka; ☏0211 250019/50555/253903; f 021 1253883/95

❸ **Zimbabwe** (embassy) 22 Phillips Av, Belgravia, PO Box 563, Harare; ☏04 794645/7/8; f 04 793030/416, 705809.

DIPLOMATIC REPRESENTATION IN BOTSWANA There's a list of Gaborone's diplomatic missions on www.mofaig.gov.bw, and in the front of the telephone directory. The following will be of most help to readers:

❸ **Angola** (embassy) 13232 Khama Crescent, Nelson Mandela Rd, P Bag BR 11, Gaborone; ☏390 0204; f 397 5089, 358 1876

❸ **China** (embassy) 3096 North Ring Rd, PO Box 1031, Gaborone; ☏395 2209; f 390 0156; e chinaemb_bw@mfa.gov.cn

❸ **France** (embassy) 761 Robinson Rd, PO Box 1424, Gaborone; ☏397 3863; f 394 1733; e frambots@info.bw

❸ **Germany** (embassy) 3rd Floor, Professional Hse, Segoditshane Way, Broadhurst, PO Box 315, Gaborone; ☏395 3143/3806; f 395 3038; e germanembassy@info.bw

❸ **India** (high commission) 5375 President's Dr, P Bag 00249, Gaborone; ☏397 2676; f 397 4636; e hicomind@info.bw, India2botswana@yahoo. com; www.highcommissionofindia.com

❸ **Kenya** (high commission) 5373 President's Dr, P Bag BO 297, Gaborone; ☏395 1408/1430; f 395 1409; e kenya@info.bw

❸ **Mozambique** (high commission) Robinson Rd, Main Mall, P Bag 00215, Gaborone; ☏319 1251–2/ 1261; f 319 1262; e altocomgamb@info.bw

❸ **Namibia** (high commission) 186 Morara CI, PO Box 987, Gaborone; ☏390 2181; f 390 2248

❸ **Russia** (embassy) 4711 Tawana CI, PO Box 81, Gaborone; ☏395 3389; f 395 2930; e embrus@ info.bw; www.botswana.mid.ru

❸ **South Africa** (high commission) 29 Queen's Rd, P Bag 00402, Gaborone; ☏390 4800–3; f 390 5502

❸ **UK** (high commission) 1079–1084 Main Mall, Queens Rd, P Bag 0023, Gaborone; ☏395 2841; f 395 6105; e bhc@botsnet.bw

☻ USA (embassy) PO Box 90, Gaborone; ✆ 395 3982/7111 (after hrs); f 395 6947

☻ Zambia (high commission) 1120 Queen's Rd, PO Box 362, Gaborone; ✆ 395 1951; f 395 3952; e zamhico@mega.bw

☻ Zimbabwe (high commission) 8850 Orapa Cl, PO Box 1232, Gaborone; ✆ 391 4495; f 390 5863; e zimgaborone@mega.bw

BOTSWANA TOURISM BOARD (*P Bag 275, Gaborone;* ✆ *391 3111; www. botswantourism.co.bw*) In addition to a useful website, and offices in most major towns in Botswana, the tourist board is currently represented by three overseas offices:

☑ Germany Interface International, Karl-Marx-Allee 91A, 10243 Berlin; ✆ 030 42 02 8464; e botswanatourism@interface-net.de; www. botswanatourism.eu

☑ UK Botswana High Commission, 6 Stratford Pl, London W1C 1AY; ✆ 020 7499 0031; e dparr@ govbw.bw; www.botswanatourism.org

☑ USA Partner Concepts LLC, 127 Lubrano Dr, Suite 203, Annapolis, MD 21401; ✆ 410 224 7688; e leslee@partnerconcepts.com; www. botswanatourism.us

GETTING THERE AND AWAY

BY AIR The vast majority of visitors to northern Botswana fly via the gateways of Maun, which has an international airport, and Kasane, which is more effectively serviced by the nearby airports at Victoria Falls (in Zimbabwe) and Livingstone (in Zambia).

The national carrier, Air Botswana, does not fly outside southern Africa, and there are relatively few other airline links to Botswana. A popular routing for visitors to the region is to fly to Livingstone (airline code LVI) via Johannesburg (JNB), then leave from Maun (MUB), again routing via Jo'burg. Botswana's capital, Gaborone (GBE), is relatively rarely visited if you're on your way to or from northern Botswana – although occasionally you might stop in Gaborone as you fly between Maun and Jo'burg.

However you arrange your flights, remember some basic tips. First, make sure your purchase is protected. Always book through a company that is bonded for your protection – which in the UK means holding an ATOL licence (Air Travel Organiser's Licence) – or use a credit card.

Second, note that airlines don't always give the best deals direct. Often you'll do better through a discounted flight centre or a tour operator.

Third, book the main internal flights at the same time – with the same company – that you book your flights to/from Johannesburg. Often the airline taking you to Africa will have cheap deals for add-on regional flights within Africa. You should be able to get Jo'burg–Livingstone flights, or Maun–Jo'burg flights, at discounted rates provided that you book them at the same time as your return flights to Jo'burg. Further, if you book all your flights together with the same company, then you'll be sure to get connecting flights, and so have the best schedule possible. Don't be talked into getting an apparently cheap return to Jo'burg on the basis that you'll be able to then get a separate ticket to Maun; it'll cost you a lot more in the end.

From Europe Johannesburg is invariably the best gateway as it's widely served by many carriers. From Europe, British Airways, South African Airways, Lufthansa and Air France (to name but a few) have regular flights to Jo'burg. Generally these are busy routes which fill up far in advance, so you're likely to get cheaper fares by booking well ahead rather than at the last minute; this is a virtual certainty during the busiest season from July to October, and in December–January around the Christmas period.

For a return from London to Jo'burg with a decent airline, expect to pay around £850/US$1,275 for most of the year, adding perhaps another £80/US$120 or so in October. However, for flights departing after 11 December, you'll be lucky to pay less than £1,400/US$2,100. Unless there's some major international upset, these flights become progressively more expensive as you get closer to the departure. So as with most long-haul destinations, book early for the cheapest flights.

One-way flights between Jo'burg and Maun, with Air Botswana (*www. airbotswana.co.bw*), should cost around £180–220/US$270–330. Between Jo'burg and Livingstone, one-way flights with British Airways (*www.britishairways.com*) or South African Airways (*www.flysaa.com*) should cost in the region of £158–248/US$237–372.

From North America If you are coming from the US then you will certainly need to at least pass through Johannesburg. It's often easiest to also route via London or another European capital. There isn't much of a discounted long-haul flight market in the US, so booking all your flights in the US will not always save you money.

Investigate the flight prices between the US and Botswana bought in the US. Look especially closely at fares with Delta and South African Airways direct from the US to Jo'burg – and talk to 'consolidators' who are the nearest that the US gets to having discounted ticket agents.

Then compare these with buying a US–London return in the US, and London–Botswana tickets from a good source in London. London is Europe's capital for cheap flights, and visitors from the US often discover that flights bought from the UK, as well as trips from UK tour operators, offer better value than those in America.

From Australasia Qantas flies between Jo'burg and Sydney or Perth, whilst Singapore Airlines services routes to Asia, including Singapore.

From Namibia or Zambia It is possible, although rarely either easier or cheaper, to approach Botswana from one of the region's other capitals, Windhoek or Lusaka.

Travel between Windhoek and Maun ought to be easy, as Air Namibia (*www. airnamibia.com.na*) services this route on Monday, Wednesday, Friday and Sunday. However, in practice they use small planes, which are often full months in advance, and they frequently change their schedules with relatively little regard to their passengers' pre-arranged plans. If you intend to use this route as part of a fixed itinerary, you have been warned.

Travel from Lusaka to Kasane is easier and more reliable, though slower. Think of it in two stages: Lusaka to Livingstone, then Livingstone to Kasane. Lusaka to Livingstone is a long six-hour drive (though there are efficient and cheap coaches for the more adventurous) or a short 90-minute flight. There are a handful of good, small Zambian charter companies that will organise a charter flight on this route, or seats on a scheduled charter. Expect a cost of around US$230 per person with Proflight.

See below for options to get between Livingstone and Kasane, but note that it's very easy to arrange to be transferred by vehicle and boat for about US$60 per person one-way. The downside of travelling via Zambia is that most visitors, including those just in transit, will be liable for visa fees, although for those staying less than 24 hours the normal fee of US$50 per person is reduced to US$20.

OVERLAND Most overland border posts open from about 06.00 or 08.00, to 16.00 or 18.00, although some of the busier ones, on main routes connecting with South Africa, stay open considerably longer than this.

To/from Zambia Despite meeting Zambian territory only at a point, Botswana does have one border crossing with Zambia: a reliable ferry across the Zambezi linking Kazungula with its namesake village in Zambia (see *Chapter 8*, page 183).

To/from Zimbabwe Botswana has several border posts with Zimbabwe, of which the two most important are the one on the road between Kasane and Victoria Falls, at Kazungula (⏲ *06.00–20.00*), and the one on the main road from Francistown to Plumtree (and hence Bulawayo), at Ramokgwebane (⏲ *06.00–20.00*). The third is a much smaller post at Pandamatenga (⏲ *08.00–17.00*). This is 100km south of Kasane, and sometimes used by visitors as a neat shortcut into the back of Zimbabwe's Hwange National Park.

To/from Namibia Despite the long length of its border with Namibia, Botswana has very few border posts here. The most important of these by far is the post on the Trans-Kalahari Highway, the route between the towns of Ghanzi and Gobabis. Opening hours (⏲ *07.00–24.00*) are the same at Mamuno, on the Botswana side, as at Buitepos, on the Namibian side.

There are two other main crossings (both ⏲ *06.00–18.00*). One is at Mohembo (north of Shakawe and at the south end of Namibia's Mahango National Park) and the other is across the Chobe River at Ngoma.

Rather less well known are three other possible crossings into Namibia. The first is at the Dobe border post (⏲ *07.30–16.30 Namibian time*), on the road between Tsumkwe, in Namibia, and Nokaneng, on the west of the Delta. This will gradually, and probably radically, alter the options for routes in that whole area. Let's hope it has a positive effect on the Bushman communities in that region, and not the negative one that is widely feared.

The other two, geared to those spending time in lodges right on the Namibian border, are between Kasane and Impalila Island (⏲ *07.30–17.00*), and between Lagoon camp in Botswana's Kwando Concession, and Lianshulu Lodge in Namibia's Caprivi Strip. Visitors are permitted to cross the Kwando River by boat at this point, but only as part of an organised safari with the lodges, with at least one night spent at each lodge.

To/from South Africa South Africa has always been Botswana's most important neighbour politically and economically, and for many years (even before South Africa was welcome in the international fold) it was in a 'customs union' with South Africa and Namibia. Thus it's no surprise to find a range of border posts between Botswana and South Africa. In order from northeast to southwest these are:

- Pontdrift (⏲ *08.00–16.00*)
- Platjan (⏲ *08.00–16.00*)
- Zanzibar (⏲ *08.00–16.00*)
- Martin's Drift (⏲ *08.00–18.00*) to Groblersburg
- Parr's Halt (⏲ *08.00–18.00*) to Stockpoort
- Sikwane (⏲ *06.00–19.00*) to Derdepoort
- Tlokweng, near Gaborone (⏲ *06.00–24.00*) to Kopfontein
- Ramotswa (⏲ *06.00–22.00*) to Swartkopfontein

- Pioneer Gate, near Lobatse (☉ *06.00–00.00*) to Skilpadshek
- Ramatlabama (☉ *06.00–22.00*)
- Phitshane Molopo (☉ *07.30–16.30*) to Makgobistad
- Bray (☉ *07.00–16.00*)
- Makopong (☉ *08.00–16.00*)
- Tshabong (☉ *06.00–18.00*) to McCarthy's Rest
- Middlepits (☉ *07.30–16.00*)
- Bokspits (☉ *08.00–16.30*)
- Twee Rivieren (☉ *07.30–14.00*)

Between Johannesburg and Maun, there's a **long-distance bus** operated via Nata by Mahube Express (**** *+267 392 2660;* **e** *mahube@info.bw; P340 one way*). Buses leave Johannesburg at 10.00, arriving in Maun at 03.30; the return trip departs from Maun at 20.00.

MONEY AND BUDGETING

Botswana has probably Africa's strongest and most stable currency, underpinned by the huge earnings of its diamond industry. The unit of currency is the pula – a word that also means 'rain' in Setswana, and hence tells you something about the importance of water in this country. Theoretically each pula is divided into 100 thebe, although one thebe isn't worth that much, so most prices are rounded to the nearest ten thebe. Notes come in denominations of 200, 100, 50, 20 and 10 pula, with coins of 5, 2 and 1 pula, and 50, 25, 10 and 5 thebe. In August 2009, the Bank of Botswana issued new notes, including an additional denomination of P200. The old notes will remain in circulation for six months, then can be exchanged at banks for the next five years.

The pula's exchange rate is free-floating on the world market, so there is no black market for the currency. Thus don't expect to see any shady characters on the street hissing 'change money' as you pass; I never have. (If you do, then assume they're con men trying to dupe visitors who don't know any better!) As a result, US dollars, euros and UK pounds sterling are easily changed – and most of the more international businesses in the tourism sector set their prices in US dollars. Rates of exchange in January 2014 were as follows: £1 = P14.65, US$1 = P8.96, €1 = P12.20

INFLATION Inflation has generally been relatively modest in Botswana. Between 1993 and 1998 the rate of inflation averaged 10.2%, but in the early 1990s it subsided to below 10% and by June 2002 the rate (based on a consumer price index) was 5.9%. Over the next decade or so it has risen and fallen, largely within these parameters, to stand at 5.7% in July 2013. For the latest statistics, take a look at the Bank of Botswana's website (*www.bankofbotswana.bw*).

Botswana's currency has generally gradually declined in value against the US dollar and the British pound over the last 15 years or so. In 1998, the US dollar was worth P3.64, as against P8.96 in early 2014. Similarly, the rate of exchange against the British pound was P6.22 in 1998, compared with the latest figure of P14.65. By comparison, the pula's rate against the South African rand has been rather more variable, although for several years now this has stabilised at around P0.85 to the rand.

Given the strength of Botswana's economy, this pattern seems likely to continue in the foreseeable future: with the pula gently declining relative to the world's major currencies.

BUDGETING Inevitably, the cost of visiting Botswana varies with the style in which you travel, and the places where you spend your time. However, Botswana's costs are relatively high. VAT (currently 12%) is charged on most transactions.

If you plan to get the most from what Botswana has to offer, you will probably need from US$675/£450 per night for a good mid-range camp in low season, rising dramatically to around US$2,175/£1,450 per night for the top camps in high season. Put into context, this means that an eight-night/nine-day fly-in trip from the UK to a good mid-range camp will start at about US$4,473/£2,982 per person. This is high by African standards, but what you get for it is high quality, and includes everything: your accommodation, activities, food, most drinks (usually excluding spirits and non-house wines), and even the odd charter flight between camps. You'll then be staying at a handful of small safari camps, each of which is situated in a different, but often stunning, corner of a pristine wilderness. This is one of the world's top wildlife experiences – the kind of magical trip at which Botswana excels.

At the other end of the spectrum, if you travel through Botswana on local buses, camping and staying near the towns, then the country isn't too expensive. A budget of US$75–110/£50–72 per day for food, accommodation and transport would suffice. However, most backpackers who undertake trips on this sort of budget won't be able to afford to visit any of the camps or more remote wildlife locations – which means that they'll be missing out on a lot of what makes Botswana unique.

Somewhere in the middle, at around US$150–200/£100–130 per day for a five-day trip, with six participants, you'll find some relatively basic budget-style safaris run out of Maun which will give you a real experience of the national parks and the Okavango Delta. They won't match what you'd find in the private concession areas, or further into the Delta, but they will make you glad you came to Botswana and probably harden your determination to return when you've a lot more money!

One of these mid-range options, though only one for those with substantial African experience, is to hire a fully equipped 4x4. Such a choice enables you to camp, buy food, and drive yourself around. This requires driving ability and planning, and isn't something to undertake lightly. But then four people in a decent vehicle (a slight squash, unless you're very well organised) would cost around US$150/£100 per person per day, including the vehicle, camping kit, equipment, park fees, fuel and food. Such trips are really much better for two people per vehicle, but in that case the daily costs would work out nearer US$250/£165 each.

Budgeting for safaris

Botswana isn't a cheap country to visit. This is due to a combination of the high costs of the logistics needed to operate in remote areas, plus the deliberate policy of the government to maximise revenues from tourism, whilst preserving the pristine nature of the country by using high costs to limit the number of visitors. That said, different kinds of trips need very different budgeting.

For backpackers Camping at organised sites is by far your cheapest way to stay in most areas of Botswana, and always a good bet if you're relatively self-sufficient and have the equipment with you. If you do, then expect to pay around US$7–11/£4.50–7.50 per person camping per night.

Restaurant meals in the towns are cheap compared with Europe or America: expect to pay US$12–16/£8–11 for a good evening meal, including a local beer or two. Imported drinks are always more expensive than those from southern Africa

1

– but as southern Africa has some first-class breweries and wineries, this really is seldom an issue. European wines and spirits, as you might expect, are ridiculously priced (and so make excellent gifts if you are visiting someone here). You will pay well over US$120/£80 for a bottle of decent French champagne!

For self-drivers If you have your own rugged 4x4 with equipment and the experience to use it and survive safely in the bush, then you will be able to camp and cook for yourself. This is then an affordable way to travel and see those remote areas of Botswana which are open to the public.

Your largest expense will be the hire of a decent and well-equipped vehicle. (Taking anything less into remote areas of wild bush is really very foolish.) See pages 82–4 for more comments on this, but expect it to cost from around US$200/£135 per day, including all your camping kit.

Your next largest expense will probably be park and camping fees in the national parks. These can be substantial, especially now that most of the campsites have been privatised. Rates at these vary, but with some of the more popular sites coming out at US$50 per person per night, you'll need to budget P580 (US$66/£44) per day, based on two people. Note, however, that there are still many interesting areas outside of the national parks – including parts of Makgadikgadi, the Tsodilo Hills, Aha Hills, Gcwihaba Caves and various offbeat areas of the Kalahari – where fees are considerably lower – or where no fees are payable.

The cost of food depends heavily on where you buy it, as well as what you buy – but most people will probably do one large shop in Maun or Kasane at the start of their trip, topping up on perishables as they progress. If you are sensible, US$12.50–18/£7–10 per day would provide the supplies for a good, varied diet without having to be at all stingy.

For mobile safaris The question 'how much are mobile safaris?' is as tricky to answer as 'how long is a piece of string?' It depends on where your trip is visiting, what the equipment, staff and guides are like, and how big the group is. In short, these trips vary greatly. To choose you must carefully prioritise what you want, what will suit you, and what you can afford to pay. Note also that prices for higher-end trips are heavily dependent upon the time of year that you travel.

On a bargain-basement trip for backpackers you will put up your tent, do the camp chores and even supply your own sleeping bag and drinks. On this you can expect to visit the parks, but not to have your time there maximised (parks are costly relative to staying outside them!). This would cost you from around US$150–200/£100–130 per day per person sharing, based on a five-day trip with six participants.

By contrast, a luxurious mobile safari, visiting pristine areas in the company of a small group with a top professional guide might cost up to US$600–645/£400–430 per person per day, including superb meals and all your drinks.

Between these two extremes, you ought to be able to get a trip of a decent quality for something around US$300–525/£200–350 per person per night sharing. Then expect to be camping in comfortable tents, with a small camp staff who will organise them, cook your meals and do all the chores.

As a final thought, if you value having a really comfortable bed at night, but still want the continuity of a good professional guide to stay with your group throughout the trip; if you like the idea of putting in a lot of time and energy game viewing in the parks, and don't mind a lot of time in a vehicle, then look at a mobile trip which moves between the lodges. These cost around US$720/£480 per person per day, again including superb meals and all your drinks.

For fly-in safaris to lodges and camps Again, the prices for fly-in trips vary considerably – though they're never cheap, and there's relatively little difference between the few bottom-end camps, and the vast majority of middle-market camps that provide good experiences in good areas.

Expect the most basic camp which offers only mokoro activities (which are cheaper to run than vehicles or boats) to cost up to US$220–325/£140–205 per person per night sharing.

Otherwise a mid-range camp in a good area will usually be around US$515–918/£343–612 per person per night sharing, all-inclusive. By going off-season, or to slightly more offbeat, marginal areas, this can be reduced. However, note that quality of accommodation is only one factor in the price: some of the smallest, simplest bushcamps are amongst the most expensive places to stay.

If money really is no object, then there are a few really top-end places that cost a lot more than this. Abu and Mombo spring to mind. For these, you'll pay double this or more. But then, some would argue, you're getting the pinnacle of what Africa has to offer.

Having said this, there are three obvious caveats. First, none of the prices here include flight transfers. These probably average out at about US$190/£126 per person per transfer, though working them out precisely is a complex business.

Second, you will almost always be quoted a rate for a 'package' of camps and flights; that's normal and often cannot be broken into its components.

And third, note that although the prices for camps given in this guide indicate what you can expect to pay (in 2014) if you book directly, this really should be a maximum figure. You will usually be able to get them a little cheaper – and this is especially applicable to the more costly lodges – if you book through a good tour operator. See the section on *Organising a fly-in trip*, earlier in this chapter, and note that, like airline tickets, the better rates for lodges are usually available indirectly.

Tipping Tipping is a very difficult and contentious topic – worth thinking about carefully. Read the section on *Local payments*, page 148, and realise that thoughtlessly tipping too much is just as bad as tipping too little.

Ask locally what's appropriate; here I can only give rough guidance. Helpers with baggage might expect four or five pula for their help, whilst sorting out a problem with a reservation would be P15–25 (US$2–3/£1–2). Restaurants often add an automatic service charge to the bill, in which case an additional tip is not usually given. If they do not do this, then 10% would certainly be appreciated if the service was good.

At safari camps, tipping is not obligatory – despite the destructive assumption from some visitors that it is. If a guide has given you really good service then a tip of about P35 (US$5–10/£3–6) per day per person would be a generous reflection of this. A similar bonus for a tracker or mokoro poler might be around P20 (US$5/£3) per day per person. And if you'd like to leave something in the communal tip box for distribution to the camp staff, then consider around US$5/£3 per guest per day. Of course, if the service hasn't been that good, then don't tip.

Always tip at the end of your stay – not at the end of each day/activity. Do not tip after every game drive. This leads to the guides only trying hard when they know there's a tip at the end of the morning. Such camps aren't pleasant to visit and this isn't the way to encourage top-quality guiding. It's best to wait until the end of your stay, and then give what you feel is appropriate in one lump sum.

However, before you do this find out if tips go into one box for all of the camp staff, or if the guides are treated differently. Then ensure that your tip reflects this – with perhaps as much again divided between the rest of the staff.

HOW TO TAKE YOUR MONEY Taking your money in the form of both cash (ideally US dollars, but sterling is a reasonable back-up) and credit cards is probably the ideal. Always bring a mixture of US$1, US$5, US$10 and US$20 notes (US$1 notes make useful, if generous, tips for porters). Because of the risk of forgeries, people are suspicious of larger denomination notes, and US$100 and even US$50 bills are often rejected in shops and even banks. South African rand are sometimes accepted, though not as widely as dollars or pounds – and they're not very popular.

While US dollars (and/or credit cards) are most useful for those staying in hotels and lodges, and are usually accepted in restaurants and tourist shops, elsewhere you will really need to have pula, especially for smaller transactions and anything bought by the roadside. In more rural locations, nobody will accept anything else. Many fuel stations will accept only cash in pula; those that accept credit cards are still in the minority.

Travellers' cheques, although arguably preferable from a security point of view, as they are refundable if stolen, are no longer easy to exchange. If you do take them, be prepared for a hefty wait in the banks – we once queued in Kasane for almost two hours.

Credit cards Cashpoint (ATM) machines that work with foreign credit cards can be found in most large towns, including Maun and Kasane. That said, Visa cards are more widely accepted than MasterCard (a notable exception being the Stanbic Bank in Maun), and generally cause fewer problems in shops too, so do bear this in mind when planning your trip. If necessary, you can obtain cash against a credit card inside the banks.

Most tourist lodges, hotels, restaurants and shops accept credit cards.

Banks If you need to change foreign currency, receive bank drafts, or do any other relatively complex financial transactions, then the banks here are perfectly capable and efficient. Their opening times vary, but expect them to start around 08.30 and finish by 15.30 during the week. The bigger banks open on Saturday, too, typically 08.30–12.00.

WHAT TO TAKE

This is an impossible question to answer fully, as it depends on how you intend to travel and exactly where you are going. If you are flying in for a short safari holiday then you need not pack too ruthlessly – provided that you stay within your weight allowance. However, note that smaller, privately chartered planes may specify a maximum weight of 10–12kg for hold luggage, which must be packed in a soft, squashable bag. Once you see the stowage spaces in a small charter plane, you'll understand the importance of not bringing along large or solid suitcases.

If you are backpacking then weight becomes much more important, and minimising it becomes an art form. Each extra item must be questioned: is its benefit worth its weight?

If you have your own vehicle then neither weight nor bulk will be so vital, and you will have a lot more freedom to bring what you like. Here are some general guidelines.

CLOTHING For most days all you will want is light, loose-fitting cotton clothing. Pure cotton, or at least a cotton-rich mix, is cooler and more absorbent than synthetic materials, making it more comfortable in the heat.

For men, shorts (not too short) are fine in the bush, but long trousers are more socially acceptable in the towns and rural villages. (You will rarely see a respectable black man in Botswana wearing shorts outside a safari camp.) For women, a knee-length skirt or culottes is ideal. Botswana's dress code is generally conservative: a woman wearing revealing clothing in town implies that she is a woman of ill repute, whilst untidy clothing suggests a poor person, of low social standing.

These rules are redundant at safari camps, where dress is casual, and designed to keep you cool and protect skin from the sun. Green, khaki and dust-brown cotton is de rigueur amongst visitors at the more serious camps. Wardrobes full of shiny, new safari gear will generally earn less respect than battered old green shirts and khaki shorts.

At the less serious camps you'll see a smattering of brighter coloured clothes amongst many dull bush colours, the former usually worn by first-time visitors who are less familiar with the bush. Note that washing is done daily at virtually all camps, so few changes of clothes are necessary. A squashable hat and a robust pair of sunglasses with a high UV-absorption are essential.

Finally, avoid anything which looks military. Leave all your camouflage patterns at home. Wearing camouflage is asking for trouble anywhere in Africa. You are very likely to be stopped and questioned by the genuine military, or at least the police, who will assume that you are a member of some militia – and question exactly what you are doing in Botswana. Few will believe that this is a fashion statement elsewhere in the world.

FOOTWEAR If you plan to do much walking, either on safari or with a backpack, then lightweight walking boots (with ankle support if possible) are sensible. This is mainly because the bush is not always smooth and even, and anything that minimises the chance of a twisted ankle is worthwhile. Secondly, for the nervous, it will reduce still further the minute chance of being bitten by a snake, scorpion or other creepy-crawly whilst walking.

Because of the heat, bring the lightest pair of boots you can find – preferably of canvas, or a breathable Goretex-type material. Leather boots are too hot for wearing in October, but thin single-skin leather is bearable for walking in July and August. Never bring a new pair, or boots that aren't completely worn in. Always bring several pairs of thin socks – two thin pairs of socks are more comfortable than one thick pair, and will help to prevent blisters.

For mokoro trips, or generally relaxing at camp during the day, rafting sandals or similar – with a strong sole and firmly fitting waterproof straps – are ideal. At night around camp, when you'll need to cover your feet/ankles against mosquitoes, lightweight boots of some sort are best.

CAMPING EQUIPMENT If you are coming on an organised safari, then even the most simple bushcamp will mean tents with linen, mosquito nets and probably an en-suite shower and toilet. However, if you're planning on doing any camping, see *Camping equipment for backpackers* on pages 139–40 of *Chapter 6* for ideas of what you should bring, and note that equipment is easier to buy in Europe or North America.

OTHER USEFUL ITEMS Obviously no list is comprehensive, and only travelling can teach you what you need, and what you can do without. Here are a few of my own favourites and essentials, just to jog your memory. For visitors embarking on an organised safari, camps will have most things but useful items include:

- Sunblock and lipsalve – vital for protection from the sun
- Insect repellent
- Binoculars – essential for game viewing
- A small pocket torch (see page 140)
- 'Leatherman' tool – never go into the bush without one
- A small water bottle, especially on flights (see page 121)
- Electrical insulating tape – remarkably useful for general repairs
- Camera – a long lens is vital for good wildlife shots
- Basic sewing kit – with some really strong thread for repairs
- Cheap waterproof watch (leave expensive ones, and jewellery, at home)
- Couple of paperback novels
- Large plastic 'bin-liner' (garbage) bags, for protecting luggage from dust
- Simple medical kit

And for those driving or backpacking, useful extras are:

- Concentrated, biodegradable washing powder or liquid
- Long-life candles – African candles are often soft, and burn quickly
- Nylon 'paracord' – at least 20m for emergencies and washing lines
- Hand-held GPS navigation system, for expeditions to remote areas
- Good compass and a whistle
- More comprehensive medical kit (see page 118)

MAPS AND NAVIGATION

Finding the right map The best maps of northern Botswana for most visitors are those published in the Shell series, which stand head-and-shoulders above the rest. The first of these was the ground-breaking *Shell Tourist Guide to Botswana*, originally published in 1998, which incorporated a short but very informative 60-page booklet on the country – effectively an impressive mini guidebook – and a serious, well-researched, original map. These were produced by Veronica Roodt, an expert on the flora and fauna of the area (see *Appendix 3, Further information* for her excellent books on the flora). What really made the difference was that, on the reverse, were smaller, inset maps of all the main parks, complete with a number of GPS waypoints. It was this information which revolutionised independent trips around Botswana, and effectively opened the doors for more travellers into some of the country's less-known areas like the Central Kalahari.

Since then Shell have also published more detailed *Chobe* and *Moremi* maps, as well as those covering the *Okavango Delta and Linyanti*, and the *Kgalagadi*. These have much more specific coverage of game-viewing tracks – utilising satellite images, and including bird and animal checklists. All are worth having, in addition to the main Botswana map, if you're visiting these areas.

Because of the general lack of availability of the Shell maps in the UK, Expert Africa (see page 77 for contact details) has imported stocks of them to the UK. These can be sent to any UK postal address – even if you're not travelling with Expert Africa to Botswana. For details, see www.expertafrica.com.

If you want more detailed, Ordnance Survey-type maps, then by far the best plan is to go directly to the offices of the Department for Surveys and Mapping, in either Maun (see page 155) or Gaborone (℡ *395 3251*). Each of these two offices has roughly the same variety of excellent maps on offer, although some are always out of print. A particular favourite is the 1:350,000 map that covers the whole Okavango Delta area in detail. However, many of these maps were made several years ago;

since then, tracks have changed, as has the location and number of safari camps. Therefore, unless you have plenty of time to interpret them, and can afford to carry around lots of maps, they're of limited use.

Many overland travellers with a GPS (see below) would be lost – sometimes quite literally – without Tracks4Africa (*www.tracks4africa.co.za*), a digital mapping software package that covers the whole continent.

More general maps of Botswana, which you're most likely to find in bookshops and map stores outside Africa, are generally fine if you are visiting the towns and simply want to know roughly where the parks are. Amongst these is the Macmillan *Botswana Traveller's Map*. This is certainly easy on the eye, with colour photographs, descriptions, mini street plans, and even a list of lodges and hotels, places of interest, a wildlife identification chart and a calendar of festivals.

In a similar vein is the *Globetrotter Travel Map of Botswana* (New Holland, UK). Again this has clear colouring, showing all the tarred roads and parks beautifully, and includes town plans of Francistown, Gaborone and Maun, and even distance and climate charts.

Similarly, the ITMB map of *Botswana* (aka the *International Traveller Map*) includes sections on the history, geography and people of Botswana, plus a small street plan of Gaborone and paragraphs on each of the main national parks.

However, I view all the above as useless – or worse – if you actually plan to head anywhere remote in the bush. The locations of their tracks and camps are mostly out of date, and the idea of using them to navigate anywhere off the tar is completely fanciful.

GPS systems If you are heading into one of the more remote parks in your own vehicle, then you really should invest in a hand-held GPS (global positioning system). These can fix your latitude, longitude and elevation to within about 10m, using a network of American military satellites that constantly pass in the skies overhead. They will work anywhere on the globe.

What to buy Commercial hand-held GPS units cost from around US$150/£80 in Europe or the USA. As is usual with high-tech equipment, their prices are falling and their features are expanding as time progresses.

I have been using a variety of Garmin GPS receivers for years now. The early ones ate batteries at a great rate and often took ages to 'fix' my position; more recent models not only have endless new functions and far better displays, but also use fewer batteries, fix positions much more quickly, and usually even work when sitting on the car's dashboard. Whatever make you buy, you don't need a top-of-the-range machine.

What a GPS can do A GPS should enable you to store 'waypoints' and build a simple electronic picture of an area, as well as working out basic latitude, longitude and elevation. So, for example, you can store the position of your campsite and the nearest road, making it much easier to be reasonably sure of navigating back without simply retracing your steps.

It will also enable you to programme in points, using the co-ordinates given throughout this book and by the Shell maps, and use these for navigation. See page x for an important comment on datums. Thus you should be able to get an idea of whether you're going in the right direction, and how far away your destination is.

When you return home, if you have a fast internet connection then knowing the GPS co-ordinates for a place will enable you to see satellite images of the place using programmes like Google Maps and Google Earth. See Expert Africa's website (*www.expertafrica.com*) for a demonstration of the satellite images of lodges that are possible.

What a GPS can't do A GPS isn't a compass, and when you're standing still, it can't tell you which direction is which. It can only tell you a direction if you're moving. (That said, some of the most expensive GPS units do now incorporate electronic compasses that can do just this!)

Second, it can give you a distance and a bearing for where you might want to go but it can't tell you how to get there. You'll still need to find a track. You should NEVER just set out across the bush following a bearing; that's a recipe for disaster.

Finally, it can't replace a good navigator. You still need to be able to navigate and think to use a GPS effectively. If you're clueless on navigation then driving around the bush in Botswana will get you into a mess with or without a GPS.

Accessories Most GPS units use quite a lot of battery power, so bring plenty of spare batteries with you. Also get hold of a cigarette lighter adapter for your GPS when you buy it. This will enable you to power it from the car whilst you're driving, and thus save batteries.

Warning Although a GPS may help you to recognise your minor errors before they are amplified into major problems, note that such a gadget is no substitute for good map work and navigation. They're great fun to use, but shouldn't be relied upon as a sole means of navigation. You MUST always have a back-up plan – and an understanding of where you are – or you will be unable to cope if your GPS fails.

PHOTOGRAPHY AND OPTICS
Outside of Gaborone, optical equipment isn't widely available in Botswana – so bring everything that you will need with you. If you're shooting film, and especially if you have a specific film that you want to use, bring a large stock with you.

Pictures taken around dawn and dusk will have the richest, deepest colours, whilst those taken in the middle of the day, when the sun is high, will seem pale and washed-out by comparison. Beware of the very deep shadows and high contrast that are typical of tropical countries – film just cannot capture the range of colours and shades that our eyes can. If you want to take pictures in full daylight, and capture details in the shadows, then you will need a good camera, and to spend some time learning how to use it fully. By restricting your photography to mornings, evenings and simple shots you will get better pictures and encounter fewer problems.

The bush is very dusty, so bring plenty of lens-cleaning cloths, and a blow-brush. Take great care not to get dust into the back of any camera, as a single grain on the back-plate can be enough to make a long scratch which ruins every frame taken.

For further information, see the *Photographic tips* box on pages 104–5.

Binoculars
For a safari holiday, a good pair of binoculars is essential. They will bring you far more enjoyment than a camera, as they make the difference between merely seeing an animal or bird at a distance, and being able to observe its markings, movements and moods closely. Do bring one pair per person; one between two is just not enough.

There are two styles: the small 'compact' binoculars, perhaps 10–12cm long, which account for most popular modern sales – and have only been in production since the 1980s. Then there are the larger, heavier styles, double or triple that size, which have been manufactured for years.

Both styles vary widely in cost and quality. If you are buying a pair, then consider getting the larger style. The compact ones are fine for spotting animals; but are difficult to hold steady, and very tiring to use for extensive periods. You will only realise this when you are out on safari, by which time it is too late.

Around 8 x 32 or 8 x 42 is an ideal size for field observations, as most people need some form of rest, or tripod, to hold the larger 10 x 50 models steady. Get the best-quality ones you can for your money. The cheapest will be about US$60/£40, but to get a decent level of quality spend at least US$300/£200. In a different league entirely are top-of-the range binoculars manufactured by Leica and Swarovski. You will be able to see the difference when you use them.

ELECTRICAL APPLIANCES The local voltage is 220V, delivered at 50Hz. Sockets usually fit plugs with three square pins, like the current design in the UK, though plugs with three large round pins, like those in South Africa, are also widely in use. Ideally bring adapters for both.

When staying in bush lodges and even in the more upmarket camps, you are increasingly likely to have sockets in your room/tent. If you don't, however, it's usually easy to arrange to charge camera batteries etc, as behind the scenes most camps run generators in order to power their kitchen and communications equipment. Don't, though, expect to be able to use a hairdryer out in the bush – few camps can cope with such a high-powered drain on their circuit.

GETTING AROUND

BY AIR There are two ways to fly within Botswana: on scheduled airlines or using small charter flights.

Scheduled flights The national carrier, Air Botswana, operates the scheduled network. This is limited in scope, but generally very efficient and reliable. Air Botswana links Maun directly with Kasane, Gaborone and Johannesburg, while Kasane is linked to both Gaborone and Johannesburg.

Charter flights Small charter flights operate out of the hub of Maun, with Kasane as a secondary focus, and ferry travellers around the camps of northern Botswana like a fleet of taxis. They use predominantly six- to 12-seater planes which criss-cross the region between a plethora of small bush runways. There's no other way to reach most camps, but flights are usually organised by the operator who arranges your camps as an integral part of your trip, and you'll never need to worry about arranging them for yourself.

Several people usually end up sharing these small flights, with timings scheduled by the companies a few days beforehand. Expect them to take under about an hour, during which you may stop at one or two other airstrips before reaching your destination. See my comments under *From the air* in *Chapter 3, The Natural Environment*, page 50, to help you understand a little about the patterns that you'll be able to see in the landscapes below.

BY RAIL There is a railway that links South Africa with Lobatse, Gaborone, Palapye, Francistown and Bulawayo (in Zimbabwe), but that's the only railway in the country – so is rarely used by travellers to northern Botswana.

4

BY BUS Botswana has a variety of local buses which link the main towns together along the tarred roads. They're cheap, frequent and a good way to meet local people, although they can also be crowded, uncomfortable and noisy. In short, they are similar to any other local buses in Africa, and travel on them has both its joys and its frustrations.

There are two different kinds: the smaller minibuses, often VW combis, and the longer, larger, 'normal' buses. Both will serve the same destinations, but the larger ones tend to run to a timetable, go faster and stop less. Their smaller relatives usually wait to fill up before they leave the bus station, then go slower and stop at more places.

PHOTOGRAPHIC TIPS   *Ariadne Van Zandbergen*

EQUIPMENT Although with some thought and an eye for composition you can take reasonable photos with a 'point-and-shoot' camera, you need an SLR camera if you are at all serious about photography. Modern SLRs tend to be very clever, with automatic programmes for almost every possible situation, but remember that these programmes are limited in the sense that the camera cannot think, but only make calculations. Every starting amateur photographer should read a photographic manual for beginners and get to grips with such basics as the relationship between aperture and shutter speed.

Digital SLRs come in different formats, which refer to the size of the sensor. The format of the future is the full-size sensor, but at present all full-size sensor cameras are in the higher price bracket. Different lenses are designed to accommodate the camera sensor sizes.

Always buy the best lens you can afford. The lens, more than the camera body, determines the quality of your photo. Fixed fast lenses are ideal, but very costly. A zoom lens makes it easier to change composition without changing lenses the whole time. If you carry only one lens with a full-size sensor camera, a 28–70mm or similar zoom should be ideal. This corresponds to a 17–55mm or similar for a camera with a smaller sensor. For a second lens, a lightweight telephoto zoom will be excellent for candid shots and varying your composition. Wildlife photography will be very frustrating if you don't have at least a 300mm lens. For a small loss of quality, tele-converters are a cheap and compact way to increase your focal length: a 300mm lens with a 1.4x converter becomes 420mm, and with a 2x it becomes 600mm. Note, however, that 1.4x and 2x tele-converters reduce the speed of your lens.

For wildlife photography from a safari vehicle, a solid beanbag, which you can make yourself very cheaply, will be necessary to avoid blurred images, and is more useful than a tripod. A clamp with a tripod head screwed onto it can be attached to the vehicle as well. Modern dedicated flash units are easy to use; aside from the obvious need to flash when you photograph at night, you can improve a lot of photos in difficult 'high contrast' or very dull light with some fill-in flash. It pays to have a proper flash unit as opposed to a built-in camera flash.

The resolution of digital cameras is improving the whole time and even the most basic digital SLRs are more than adequate for ordinary prints and enlargements. For professional reproduction, cameras with a resolution up to 24 megapixels are available.

Memory space is important. The number of pictures you can fit on a memory card depends on the quality you choose. Calculate in advance how many pictures you can fit on a card and either take enough cards to last for your trip, or take a storage drive onto which you can download the content. A laptop gives the advantage

DRIVING Driving in Botswana is on the left, as in the UK and seatbelts must be worn. The standard of driving is reasonably good. Most roads in the towns, and the major arteries connecting these, are tarred and are usually in superb condition.

Speed limits are generally 80km/h outside towns, and 40km/h in the national parks – though you'd be hard pushed to get near this speed in most places. Variations are clearly signposted. The police have radar equipment, and actively set up radar traps, especially just outside towns. Speeding tickets, which are calculated at P100 plus a further P20 for every kilometre you're over the limit (so P300 for 10km/h over the limit), may sometimes be paid on the spot, against a signed receipt from

that you can see your pictures properly at the end of each day and edit and delete rejects, but a storage device is lighter and less bulky. Bear in mind, however, that digital camera batteries, computers and other storage devices need charging, so make sure you have all the chargers, cables and converters with you. Most hotels and lodges in Botswana have charging points, but do enquire about this in advance.

DUST AND HEAT Dust and heat are often a problem. Keep your equipment in a sealed bag and avoid excessive exposure to the sun. Digital cameras are prone to collecting dust particles on the sensor which results in spots on the image. The dirt mostly enters the camera when changing lenses, so be careful when doing this. To some extent photos can be 'cleaned' up afterwards in Photoshop, but this is time-consuming. You can have your camera sensor professionally cleaned, or you can do this yourself with special brushes and swabs made for the purpose, but note that touching the sensor might cause damage and should only be done with the greatest care.

LIGHT The most striking outdoor photographs are often taken during the hour or two of 'golden light', after dawn and before sunset. Shooting in low light may enforce the use of very low shutter speeds, in which case a tripod might be required to avoid camera shake. That said, some top digital SLRs now give good results with minimal grain when shooting at very high ISO settings, which makes low-light photography a lot easier and reduces the need of a tripod in many situations.

With careful handling, side lighting and back lighting can produce stunning effects, especially in soft light and at sunrise or sunset. Generally, however, it is best to shoot with the sun behind you. When photographing animals or people in the harsh midday sun, images taken in light but even shade are likely to be more effective than those taken in direct sunlight or patchy shade, since the latter conditions create too much contrast.

PROTOCOL In some countries, it is unacceptable to photograph local people without permission, and many people will refuse to pose or will ask for a donation. In such circumstances, don't try to sneak photographs as you might get yourself into trouble. Even the most willing subject will often pose stiffly when a camera is pointed at them; relax them by making a joke, and take a few shots in quick succession to improve the odds of capturing a natural pose.

Ariadne Van Zandbergen is a professional travel and wildlife photographer specialising in Africa. She runs The Africa Image Library. For photo requests, visit www. africaimagelibrary.com or contact her at e info@africaimagelibrary.com.

the officer, but often you'll have to report to the nearest police station within 48 hours. Botswana's police are efficient; it'd be foolhardy not to obey such a summons.

At the time of research, in autumn 2013, the price of fuel in Kasane was P9.88 (US$1.13) per litre for diesel, and P9.70 (US$1.11) for unleaded petrol. The further you travel away from the main centres, the more these prices are likely to increase.

Away from the main arteries, and throughout virtually all of the wild areas covered by this guide, the roads are simply tracks through the bush made by whatever vehicles have passed that way. They are almost never maintained, and usually require at least a high-clearance vehicle – although often a 4x4 is essential. During the wet season some of these tracks can be less forgiving, and become virtually impassable. Travelling on these bush tracks at any time of year is slow and time-consuming – but very much one of the joys of an adventurous trip to Botswana. For more details, see *Chapter 6, In the Wilds*.

For details of vehicle hire and maps, see pages 82–4 and 100–2.

HITCHHIKING Hitchhiking is a practical way to get around the main towns – but very, very difficult as a means of getting around the national parks. Hitching on the tarred roads has the great advantage of allowing you to talk one-to-one with a whole variety of people, from local businesspeople and expats to truck drivers and farmers. Sometimes you will be crammed in the back of a windy pick-up with a dozen people and as many animals. Occasionally you will be comfortably seated in the back of a plush Mercedes, satisfying the driver's curiosity as to why you were standing beside a road in Botswana at all. It can be a great way to get to know the country, through the eyes of its people, though it is not for the lazy or those pressed for time.

Waiting times can be long, even on the main routes, and getting a good lift can take many hours. If you are in a hurry then combining hitchhiking with taking the odd bus can be a quicker and more pragmatic way to travel.

The essentials for successful hitching in Botswana include a relatively neat, conservative set of clothes, without which you will be ignored by some of the more comfortable lifts available. A good ear for listening and a relaxed line in conversation are also assets, which spring naturally from taking an interest in the lives of the people that you meet. Finally, always carry a few litres of water and some food with you, both for standing beside the road and for lifts where you can't stop to eat.

Dangers of drunk driving Unfortunately, drinking and driving is relatively common in Botswana. It is more frequent in the afternoon/evening, and towards the end of the month when people are paid. Accepting a lift with someone who is drunk, or drinking and (simultaneously) driving, is foolish. Occasionally your driver will start drinking on the way, in which case you would be wise to start working out how to disembark politely.

An excuse for an exit, which I used on one occasion, was to claim that a close family member was killed whilst being driven by someone who had been drinking. Thus I had a real problem with the whole idea, and had even promised a surviving relative that I would never do the same … hence my overriding need to leave at the next reasonable town/village/stop. This gave me an opportunity to encourage the driver not to drink any more, and when that failed (which it did), it provided an excuse for me to disembark swiftly. Putting the blame on my own psychological problems avoided blaming the driver too much, which might have caused a difficult scene.

Safety of hitchhiking Notwithstanding the occasional drunk driver, Botswana is generally a safe place to hitchhike for a robust male traveller, or a couple travelling together. However, although safer than in the UK, and considerably safer than in the USA, hitchhiking still cannot be recommended for single women, or even two women travelling together. This is not because of any known horror stories, but because women from outside of Botswana, and especially white women hitching, would evoke great curiosity amongst the local people, who might view their hitching as asking for trouble, whilst some would associate them with the 'promiscuous' behaviour of white women seen on imported films and TV programmes. The risk seems too high. Stick to buses.

ACCOMMODATION

Although northern Botswana's accommodation is dominated by hotels, lodges and campsites aimed at visiting tourists, there is still a considerable variety in terms of both style and prices. Most establishments are graded nowadays, with between one and five stars awarded on the basis of 'furnishings, service and guest care', but inevitably this gives only part of the picture.

Prices quoted in this guide are usually international rates – those payable by visitors from Europe, America and other Western countries. (Some establishments – and especially the national parks' campsites – have a two- or even three-tier pricing system, in favour of nationals of Botswana, and southern Africa.) Where accommodation is not fully inclusive, rates have been coded (see inside front cover), based on the cost of a double room with breakfast. Single supplements average around 20%, but may be significantly higher. A tourism levy, or 'bed levy', of P10 per person per night is usually included in the rates, but in some of the cheaper establishments, or those where you pay per room rather than per person, it may be charged extra. Note that while rates were correct at the time of research, in late 2013/early 2014, many will inevitably rise during the life of this guide.

A final note: following the ban on commercial hunting in January 2014, at least some of Botswana's former hunting camps may well re-open as photographic lodges, potentially creating an upsurge of accommodation over the next few years.

HOTELS AND GUESTHOUSES Hotels in Botswana's towns tend to be aimed at visiting businesspeople, in which case they're functional but boring, regardless of price level. That said, they're also generally clean and rarely unpleasant. Expect costs in Maun and Kasane to be around US$65–160/£43–106 for a double room per night.

In recent years a few guesthouses have sprung up in Botswana's larger towns, including Maun and Kasane, but these are still very limited, and often in such suburban locations that they're only practical if you've got your own vehicle. Some also tend to be on the pricy side, and don't seem to be good value for money.

LODGES AND CAMPS Botswana's lodges and camps vary from palatial residences crafted by top designers to simple spots with a few small tents, and a table in the shade. Given that range, the vast majority have rooms which are at least as comfortable as a good hotel room.

When the words 'tented camp' are mentioned, forget your memories of cramped scout tents and think instead of canvas designer chic. En-suite flushing toilets, running hot and cold water and battery-powered lights are standard, while many have electric fans, and an increasing number have air conditioning. Only the odd old stalwarts, like the delightfully simple mokoro trail camp at Kanana, still use traditional long-drop loos.

Note that expensive does not always mean luxurious. Some of the top camps are very simply constructed. Equally, looking for basic, simple camps won't make your trip any cheaper. You're usually paying for virtually exclusive use of pristine wilderness areas, and will find little cost difference between a tiny bushcamp and the largest lodge. In fact, if anything there's increasingly a premium on space in the smaller camps. These need booking earlier as many find these friendlier than the larger ones.

FOOD AND DRINK

FOOD Talking of any one 'native cuisine' in Botswana is misleading, as what a person eats is dependent on where they live and what ethnic group they belong to. In the Kalahari and Okavango there was relatively little agriculture until recently; there, gathering and fishing, supplemented by hunting, provided subsistence for the various groups.

In the kinder climes east of the Kalahari, where there is enough rain for crops, sorghum is probably the main crop. This is first pounded into meal before being mixed with boiling water or sour milk. It's then made into a paste *bogobe* – which is thin, perhaps with sugar like porridge, for breakfast, then eaten thicker, the consistency of mashed potatoes, for lunch and dinner. For these main meals it will normally be accompanied by some tasty relish, perhaps made of meat (*seswa*) and tomatoes (*moro*), or dried fish. Maize meal, or *papa* (often imported as it doesn't tolerate Botswana's dry climate that well), is now often used in place of this. (In Zimbabwe this same staple is known as *sadza*, in Zambia it's *nshima* and in South Africa *mealie-pap*.) You should taste this at some stage when visiting. Safari camps will often prepare it if requested, and it is always available in small restaurants in the towns.

Camps, hotels and lodges that cater for overseas visitors serve a very international fare, and the quality of food prepared in the most remote camps is usually amazingly high. When coming to Botswana on safari your biggest problem with food is likely to be the very real danger of putting on weight.

Prices for restaurants listed in this guide have been coded (see inside front cover), based on the average cost of a main course.

Self-catering If you are driving yourself around and plan to cook, then get most of your supplies in Maun or Kasane. Both have several large, well-stocked supermarkets and a number of more specialist shops. However, it is important to be aware that northern Botswana is effectively ringed by a veterinary fence – widely known as the buffalo fence – with regular checkpoints along the roads to help prevent infection of the country's valuable cattle herds with foot-and-mouth disease. For this reason, taking red meat across the fence from a buffalo area into an area that is used for cattle farming is prohibited. Campers, take note!

It's usually best to stock up with food at these main centres, as away from them the range will become sparser. Expect villages to have just a bottle stall, selling the most popular cool drinks (often this excludes 'diet' drinks), and a small shop selling staples like rice and (occasionally) bread, and perhaps a few tinned and packet foods. Don't expect anything refrigerated.

DRINK
Alcohol Like most countries in the region, Botswana has two distinct beer types: clear and opaque. Most visitors and more affluent people in Botswana drink the **clear beers**, which are similar to European lagers and always served chilled. St Louis

and Castle are the lagers brewed here by a subsidiary of South African Breweries. They are widely available and usually good. You'll also sometimes find Windhoek lager, from Namibia – which is similar and equally good.

The less affluent residents will usually opt for some form of the **opaque beer** (sometimes called Chibuku, after the market-leading brand). This is a commercial version of traditional beer, usually brewed from maize and/or sorghum. It's a sour, porridge-like brew: an acquired taste, and it changes flavour as it ferments; you can often ask for 'fresh beer' or 'strong beer'. As a visitor you'll have to make a real effort to seek out opaque beer; most bars that tourists visit don't sell it. Locals will sometimes buy a bucket of it, and then pass it around a circle of drinkers. It would be unusual for a visitor to drink this, so try some and amuse your companions. If you aren't sure about the bar's hygiene standards, stick to the pre-packaged brands of opaque beer like Chibuku.

Soft drinks Soft drinks are available everywhere, which is fortunate when the temperatures are high. Choices are often limited, though the ubiquitous Coca-Cola is usually there, along with southern African specialities like Grapetize. Diet drinks are available in the towns, but rarely seen in the small bottle stores which pepper the rural areas – which is no surprise for a country where the rural population are poor and need all the energy their food can give them.

Water Water in the main towns is usually purified, provided there are no shortages of chlorine, breakdowns or other mishaps. It's generally fine to drink.

Out in the bush, most of the camps and lodges use water from boreholes. These underground sources vary in quality, but are normally free from bugs and so perfectly safe to drink. Sometimes it is sweet, at other times the water is a little alkaline or salty. Ask the locals if it is suitable for an unacclimatised visitor to drink, then take their advice.

The water in the Okavango Delta is generally fine to drink. You'll be expected to do so during most budget mokoro trips, which is fine for most backpackers who are in Africa for long trips. There are relatively few people living in the communities in the Delta; contamination levels are very low. However, if you've a sensitive stomach, or are visiting for a short trip, then you'd be best to avoid it and stick to borehole water, or travel with a filter bottle. (I'd recommend that you do not insist on bottled water as the costs/waste involved in transporting it to you are high, and borehole water is generally fine.)

CRAFTS AND CURIOS

Botswana's best bargains are handicrafts, and you'll find a variety. Look especially for hand-woven baskets made from the fronds of the real fan palm (*Hyphaene petersiana*), and the many different handicrafts of the San, like jewellery made from ostrich eggshells.

There's usually a divide between the simpler outlets, perhaps direct from the producers, and the more stylish, well-located shops which often have the best pieces, but invariably charge the highest prices.

If you're starting or ending your trip in Livingstone, then don't miss the curio stalls near the border post to Victoria Falls, or those in Livingstone's Mukuni Park. These are among the region's best places for carvings (though expect to bargain hard). Other places to seek out would be the various curio shops in Maun and Kasese, for excellent baskets, and the small basket shops in towns west of the Delta.

4

There are plenty of shops at the more stylish end of the spectrum, especially in Maun, and many lodges have small shops selling curios. (Ask them if the staff or a local village makes these – and if they do, then buy some to support the initiative!)

Imports and exports There is no problem in exporting normal curios, but you will need an export permit from the Department of Wildlife and National Parks to take out any game trophies. Visitors are urged to support both the letter and the spirit of the CITES bans on endangered species. In any case, without such permits you will probably have big problems when you try to import items back into your home country.

COMMUNICATIONS

POST BotswanaPost (*www.botspost.co.bw*), the government-owned postal service, is reliable, but often slow. They have post offices in all the larger towns, and a network of many agencies in some of the larger villages. In northern Botswana, these include offices or agencies in Ghanzi, Gumare, Gweta, Kasane, Maun, Nata, Nokaneng, Rakops, Sepopa and Seronga.

Letters are classified by size, with a 'standard' one being up to 120mm x 235mm x 20mm, and a 'large' letter up to 229mm x 324mm x 20mm. For postcards and standard letters weighing less than 200g, postal rates are:

Botswana	SADC	Elsewhere
	air	air
P3.50	P7.30	P8.10

SADC – the Southern African Development Community – is a regional grouping of states and includes Angola, the Democratic Republic of Congo (DRC), Lesotho, Madagascar, Malawi, Mauritius, Mozambique, Namibia, Seychelles, South Africa, Swaziland, Tanzania, Zambia and Zimbabwe.

Stamps are sometimes sold in curio shops, and most hotels will post letters on your behalf. There is a post restante service at all the major post offices.

TELEPHONE Botswana's telephone system is generally very good, and you can dial some remarkably offbeat places from overseas.

To dial into the country from abroad, the international access code for Botswana is 267. From inside Botswana, dial 00 to get an international line, then the country's access code (eg: 44 for the UK, 1 for the USA), then omit the first 0 of the number you are calling.

Essential telephone numbers
Ambulance ℡ 997
Police ℡ 999
Fire ℡ 998
Operator ℡ 121 (inc international directory enquiries)
Directory enquiries ℡ 192; m 316 6651; www.bt-phone-book.co.bw

Mobile phones Mobile phone coverage has increased rapidly in recent years, with reception found even in relatively small villages. Outside of these, though, and in the national parks, a mobile phone will be of no use at all.

Local SIM cards can be purchased in Kasane and Maun, significantly cutting the cost of calls from a mobile registered overseas. The major operators are Mascom and Orange, of which Mascom arguably has the better coverage. Expect to pay about P10 for a SIM card, with top-up cards available in various denominations from P10. Calls from one Mascom mobile to another will cost around P1.50 a minute, or P2.50 to Orange.

The presence of public phoneboxes on the streets is all but redundant nowadays. Mobile phones are ubiquitous – and few people have any need for the old-style cardphones.

FAX If you are trying to send a fax to, or within, Botswana then it's often wise to use a manual setting to dial the number. Then listen for a fax tone on the line yourself, and only when you finally hear one should you press the 'start' button on your machine to send the fax.

EMAIL AND THE INTERNET Like most places, Botswana has rapidly adopted email, and a lot of businesses have websites. That said, outside of the main towns, email is often limited to a radio-based service known as 'bushmail', which has a tiny bandwidth and so is only practical for simple text messages. (Never send attachments to any bushmail address!) In general, if you don't get a reply from an email to Botswana within, say, 48 hours, it's a good idea to resend it.

THE MEDIA

With a small population, many in rural locations, the press here is equally small, and partly relies on the larger South African media companies. However, Botswana has several newspapers, radio and television stations.

INDEPENDENCE ISSUES Botswana's small media is generally fairly free and expresses its opinions, even when it disagrees with government policy. Even media which are owned by the government are obliged by law to give basic coverage of opposition views as well as the official versions. That said, disagreements do occur on a fairly regular basis, and clearly the independent press here fights a continuing battle to remain independent.

In May 2001, all government offices were instructed to stop using the two independent weekly papers, the *Botswana Guardian* and the *Midweek Sun*, following their criticism of Vice President Ian Khama. Given that the government is the largest advertiser in these papers, this had significant commercial impact. Shortly afterwards, following proceedings brought against the government by the papers' editors, a High Court judge ruled that the advertising ban was unconstitutional as the authorities were deemed to be applying unfair financial pressure on the papers in order to curtail their right to freedom of expression.

Occasionally the press also comes into the firing line for sensationalism, which is claimed to be fuelling ethnic tensions, and once recently a High Court judge started proceedings against *Mmegi* for defamation.

In late April 2001, the head of news and current affairs at the official Botswana Television (BTV) station quit his job in protest about government interference in the station's editorial policy and programming. He alleged that officials had threatened him, and that the authorities had blocked the broadcast of a documentary on a South African woman who had been convicted of murder by a Botswana court and subsequently executed.

The subsequent, if controversial, establishment of a press council has resulted in a 'code of ethics' for the media, laying out standards of best practice that would seem to be free and fair.

THE PRESS Botswana's most widely read newspapers are the *Botswana Guardian* and *Mmegi* ('*The Reporter*'), both published daily. *Mmegi* also has a sister publication, the *Monitor*, which comes out on a Monday. Other papers include *The Botswana Gazette*, the *Midweek Sun* and the government's free weekday newspaper, the *Daily News*, while the Maun area has the weekly *Ngami Times*. For newspapers on the web, see page 511.

RADIO Botswana has a couple of radio stations that broadcast around the main towns, but there's generally nothing but long-distance shortwave services away from these.

The state-run Radio Botswana has two stations, both mixing Setswana and English in their schedules, and often their programmes. The non-commercial Radio Botswana 1 (RB1) has no advertising and majors on news and current affairs, whilst the commercial station Radio Botswana 2 (RB2) features mainly popular music from ballads, R&B, house, reggae, fusion and jazz to pop and disco. Within this you'll find the usual inane banter, as well as news bulletins at regular intervals.

Alternative independent stations include Yarona FM (106.6FM), Gabz FM (96.2FM) and Duma FM (93.0FM).

TELEVISION Botswana TV is based in Gaborone, and is part of the Department of Information and Broadcasting, which also runs Radio Botswana's two stations.

Apparently in the months preceding the TV station's launch in 2000 there was some doubt about it being on schedule, so a consultancy team from Britain's BBC was brought in. They observed that:

> Ten days before the launch, the general manager and his colleagues laughed at the idea that the launch would take place on time. The government even cancelled plans for a lavish ceremony and speech by the president at the national stadium on launch day. So we booked the stadium and arranged a charity shield football match between the country's two best teams, which attracted a bigger television audience on July 31 than the abandoned show would have done.

This charity shield match has now become a regular fixture.

In Gaborone there is a private channel, Gaborone Television, which is owned by Gaborone Broadcasting Company (GBC) and funded by advertising. Throughout Botswana most people with televisions are connected to one of the large South African networks – like the MultiChoice satellite service. There is no cable television.

TRAVELLING POSITIVELY

Botswana is one of the richer of the developing nations, but despite this you may see scenes of poverty when you are visiting the country, especially in more rural areas. Beggars are fairly rare in the towns, but often the least able are dependent on charity. Whilst giving a few coins to people is one way to put a sticking plaster over your feelings of guilt, this is not a long-term solution.

There *are* ways in which you can make a positive contribution, but they require more effort than giving to someone on the street; perhaps this is the least you can do after an enjoyable trip to Botswana?

There is an established, trustworthy and reliable network of charities, churches and NGOs (non-governmental organisations). If you really want to help, then contact someone and make it happen!

LOCAL CHARITIES WORKING IN BOTSWANA One good source of information is the website of the Botswana Council of Non-Governmental Organisations (*BOCONGO;* ☏*391 1319;* e *bocongo@bocongo.org.bw; www.bocongo.org.bw*), which provides a brief synopsis of many of the country's groups doing valuable work. It doesn't include all charities, but would be a good start to your research.

Helping poorer and disadvantaged communities

Botswana has a whole range of good, small charities working at grassroots level to improve the lot of the poorest members of society here, and help them to develop economically. A good first port of call would be Travel for Impact (*Airport Rd, Maun;* ☏*686 4431;* m *7230 7694;* e *tfibotswana@gmail.com; www.travelforimpact.com*). Established in 2013, they already work with Bana Ba Letsatsi (below), as well as Women against Rape, and Motse wa Tsholofelo, a charity for vulnerable pre-school children, and would be well placed to offer advice on where you can best help.

A few individual charities that concentrate on the north of the country include:

Bana Ba Letsatsi Maun; ☏686 4787; m 7264 3468; e info@banabaletsatsi.org; www. banabaletsatsi.org. A local charity helping with Maun's streetchildren. See pages 152–3.

Chobe Enclave Conservation Trust (CECT) Kavimba; ☏625 0159; e cect@botsnet.bw. A village trust that aims to support the sustainable management of the Chobe Enclave's natural resources for the benefit of the local community.

Ditshwanelo (The Botswana Centre for Human Rights) ☏390 6998; e admin.ditshwanelo@info.bw; www.ditshwanelo.org.bw. Ditshwanelo works with poorer communities all over Botswana on a range of human rights issues, from child advocacy & the death penalty to the case of the San in the CKGR.

Gumare Counselling Centre ☏687 4235. Provides free counselling & HIV-testing services in Gumare & the wider Okavango area, & also works with orphans & other vulnerable children.

Love Botswana Outreach Mission Maun; ☏686 2798; e info@lovebotswana.org; http://lovebotswana.org. Aims to provide leadership development through education, HIV/AIDS care & prevention, economic empowerment & spiritual development.

Thuso Lutheran Rehabilitation Centre Maun; ☏686 0539. Rehabilitation centre for disabled people in the Chobe & Ngamiland community, providing therapy & vocational skills training such as gardening, knitting, sewing & computing.

STUFF YOUR RUCKSACK – AND MAKE A DIFFERENCE

www.stuffyourrucksack.com is a website set up by television's Kate Humble which enables travellers to give direct help to small charities, schools or other organisations in the country they are visiting. Maybe a local school needs books, a map or pencils, or an orphanage needs children's clothes or toys – all things that can easily be 'stuffed in a rucksack' before departure. The charities get exactly what they need and travellers have the chance to meet local people and see how and where their gifts will be used.

The website describes organisations that need your help and lists the items they most need. Check what's needed in Botswana, contact the organisation to say you're coming and bring not only the much-needed goods but an extra dimension to your travels and the knowledge that in a small way you have made a difference.

HELPING THE ENVIRONMENT AND WILDLIFE The first thing to do if you want to help protect Botswana's wilder areas is to travel there, often; the income generated by tourism is the main hope to enable these areas to survive and thrive in the long term.

The second thing to do is to support organisations such as the following that work in promoting knowledge of Botswana's wilder areas, or in campaigning for environmental and social issues:

Birdlife Botswana ☎319 0540/1; e blb@ birdlifebotswana.org.bw; www.birdlifebotswana. org.bw. Their 'tickbird' scheme enables visitors as well as locals to contribute to data collection by entering information about birds identified on a specific day within a clearly defined area on their website.

Kalahari Conservation Society ☎397 4557; e publicrelations@kcs.org.bw; www.kcs.org.bw
The Botswana Society ☎391 9745; e botsoc@ info.bw; www.botsoc.org.bw.

In addition, helping the country's poorer communities (see above) will, ultimately, also help preserve the wildlife areas, as without sustainable economic development there's little long-term hope for the wildlife.

There are also several good small charities that are working for different, small-scale, but nonetheless important projects, including:

Botswana Rhino Reintroduction Project e info@wildernesstrust.com; www. wildernesstrust.com. White & black rhino have

been successfully reintroduced to Moremi Game Reserve (page 289), but inevitably this sort of programme requires significant financial support.

VOLUNTEERING Botswana, like many African countries, hasn't been slow to take advantage of the upsurge in volunteering holidays. Despite this, there are many pitfalls for unwary volunteers, so be sure to do your homework – especially if you are trying to get involved with a local community.

Both Bana Ba Letsatsi and Love Botswana (page 113) have volunteer programmes, and it could well be worth contacting Travel for Impact for other ideas.

More generally, an excellent place to start is www.ethicalvolunteering.org, which also has a downloadable pamphlet entitled *The Ethical Volunteering Guide*. Some of the many issues to consider include:

- For every bona fide organisation there will be others who are willing to take your cash without delivering on their side of the deal.
- Try to be realistic about what your skills are; they will probably define what you can usefully contribute. Communities in Botswana don't need unskilled hobbyists; they need professionals. To teach skills properly takes years of volunteering, not weeks. (How long did *you* take to learn those skills?) So, for example, if you're not a qualified teacher or builder in your home country, then don't expect to be let loose to do any teaching or building in Botswana.
- Most volunteers will learn much more than the members of the communities that they come to 'help'; be aware of this when you describe who is helping whom.
- Make sure that what you are doing isn't effectively taking away a job from a local person.

Time in Botswana will do you lots of good; make sure it's not to the detriment of your hosts.

5

Health and Safety

with Dr Felicity Nicholson and Dr Jane Wilson-Howarth

There is always great danger in writing about health and safety for the uninitiated visitor. It is all too easy to become paranoid about exotic diseases that you may catch, and all too easy to start distrusting everybody you meet as a potential thief – falling into an unfounded us-and-them attitude towards the people of the country you are visiting.

As a comparison, imagine an equivalent section in a guidebook to a Western country – there would be a list of possible diseases and advice on the risk of theft and mugging. Many Western cities are very dangerous, but with time we learn how to assess the risks, accepting almost subconsciously what we can and cannot do.

It is important to strike the right balance: to avoid being excessively cautious or too relaxed about your health and your safety. With experience, you will find the balance that best fits you and the country you are visiting.

HEALTH

BEFORE YOU GO

Travel insurance Visitors to Botswana should always take out a comprehensive **medical insurance policy** to cover them for emergencies, including the cost of evacuation to another country within the region. Such policies come with an emergency number (often on a reverse-charge/call-collect basis). You would be wise to memorise this, or indelibly tattoo it in as many places as possible on your baggage.

Personal-effects insurance is also a sensible precaution, but check the policy's fine print before you leave home. Often, in even the best policies, you will find a limit per item, or per claim – which can be well below the cost of replacement. If you need to list your valuables separately, then do so comprehensively. Check that receipts are not required for claims if you do not have them, and that the excess which you have to pay on a claim is reasonable.

Annual travel policies can be excellent value if you travel a lot, and some of the larger credit-card companies offer excellent policies. However, it can often be better to get your valuables named and insured for travel using your home contents insurance. These year-round policies will try harder to settle your claim fairly as they want your business in the long term.

Immunisations Having a full set of immunisations takes time, normally at least six weeks, although some protection can be had by visiting your doctor as late as a few days before you travel. Ideally, see your doctor or travel clinic (see below) early on to establish an inoculation timetable.

115

Legal requirements There is no risk of yellow fever disease in Botswana, but a certificate for yellow fever vaccine is required for entry into Botswana if you are coming from a yellow fever endemic area (which for immigration purposes currently includes Zambia) or are travelling on a passport issued in a country where yellow fever is endemic. Talk to a registered yellow fever centre to see if the vaccine is suitable for you.

Recommended precautions Preparations to ensure a healthy trip to Botswana require checks on your immunisation status: it is wise to be up to date on **tetanus**, **polio** and **diphtheria** (now given as an all-in-one vaccine, Revaxis, that lasts for ten years), and hepatitis A. Immunisations against hepatitis B and rabies may also be recommended. Immunisation against cholera is not required for trips to Botswana, but there have been several reported cases recently, so may be worth considering if you are spending any length of time in highly populated areas.

    Hepatitis A vaccine (Havrix Monodose or Avaxim) comprises two injections given about a year apart. The course costs about £100, but may be available on the NHS; it protects for 25 years and can be administered even close to the time of departure. **Hepatitis B** vaccination should be considered for longer trips (one month or more), for those working with children, or in situations such as a hospital or contact sport where contact with blood is likely. Three injections are needed for the best protection and, for those aged over 16, can be given over a three-week period if time is short. Longer schedules give more sustained protection and are therefore preferred if time allows. Hepatitis A vaccine can also be given as a combination with hepatitis B as 'Twinrix', though two doses are needed at least seven days apart to be effective for the hepatitis A component, and three doses are needed for the hepatitis B. Again the former schedule applies only to those aged 16 or over.

    Vaccination against **typhoid** is encouraged unless you are leaving within a few days for a trip of a week or less, when the vaccine would not be effective in time. Injectable vaccines (eg: Typhim Vi), last for three years and are about 70–80% effective, while three oral capsules (Vivotif) taken over five days will also last for about three years. However, the capsules may be less effective, although they are a useful alternative for those aged six and over.

    Vaccination against **rabies** is particularly wise for those travelling for extended periods (four weeks or longer), or staying in rural areas (see *Rabies*, page 126). Ideally you should have three pre-exposure injections over a minimum of 21 days, but this is especially important if you intend to have contact with animals and/or are likely to be more than 24 hours away from medical help, since you would need all three to change the treatment following potential exposure. Contrary to popular belief these vaccinations are relatively painless.

    Experts differ over whether a BCG vaccination against **tuberculosis** (TB) is useful in adults: discuss this with your travel clinic.

    In addition to the various vaccinations recommended above, it is important that you should be properly protected against malaria. For detailed advice see below.

    Ideally you should visit your own doctor or a specialist travel clinic (see opposite) to discuss your requirements if possible at least eight weeks before you plan to travel.

Malaria Malaria is the most dangerous disease in Africa, and the greatest risk to the traveller. It occurs throughout northern Botswana, all the year round, so it is essential that you take all possible precautions against it. Key to these are prevention of mosquito bites, and taking a suitable prophylactic agent.

Malaria prevention Prophylaxis regimes aim to infuse your bloodstream with drugs that inhibit and kill the malaria parasites which are injected into you by a biting mosquito. This is why you must start to take the drugs *before* you arrive in a malarial area – so that they are established in your bloodstream from day one. Unfortunately, malaria parasites continually adapt to the drugs used to combat them, so the recommended regimes must adapt and change in order to remain effective. None is 100% effective, and all require time to kill the parasites – so unless there is a medical indication for stopping, it is important to complete the course after leaving the area as directed (usually one to four weeks depending on the regime). Falciparum (cerebral) malaria is the most common in Africa, and usually fatal if untreated, so it is worth your while trying to avoid it.

Seek current advice on the best anti-malarials to take: usually mefloquine, Malarone or doxycycline. If mefloquine (Lariam) is suggested, start this 2½ weeks (three doses) before departure to check that it suits you; stop it immediately if it seems to cause depression or anxiety, visual or hearing disturbances, severe headaches, fits or changes in heart rhythm. Side effects such as nightmares or dizziness are not medical reasons for stopping unless they are sufficiently debilitating or annoying. Anyone who has been treated for depression or psychiatric problems, has diabetes controlled by oral therapy or who is epileptic (or who has suffered fits in the past) or has a close blood relative who is epileptic, should probably avoid mefloquine.

In the past doctors were nervous about prescribing mefloquine to pregnant women, but experience has shown that it is relatively safe and certainly safer than the risk of malaria. That said, there are other issues, so if you are travelling to Botswana while pregnant, seek expert advice before departure.

Malarone (proguanil and atovaquone) is as effective as mefloquine. It has the advantage of few side effects and need only be continued for one week after returning. However, it is expensive and because of this tends to be reserved for shorter trips. Malarone may not be suitable for everybody, so take advice from a doctor. For most people, it can be taken safely for a year or more. It is suitable for children weighing 11–40kg, but may sometimes be prescribed safely for those beneath this weight.

A third alternative is the antibiotic doxycycline (100mg daily). Like Malarone it can be started one to two days before arrival. Unlike mefloquine, it may also be used in travellers with epilepsy, although certain anti-epileptic medication may make it less effective. In perhaps 1–3% of people there is the possibility of allergic skin reactions developing in sunlight; the drug should be stopped if this happens. It is also unsuitable in pregnancy or for children under 12 years.

Chloroquine and proguanil are no longer considered to be effective enough for Botswana but may be considered as a last resort if nothing else is deemed suitable.

All tablets should be taken with or after the evening meal, washed down with plenty of fluid and, with the exception of Malarone (see above), continued for four weeks after leaving.

Despite all these precautions, it is important to be aware that no anti-malarial drug is 100% protective, although those on prophylactics who are unlucky enough to catch malaria are less likely to get rapidly into serious trouble. In addition to taking anti-malarials, it is therefore important to avoid mosquito bites between dusk and dawn (see *Avoiding insect bites*, pages 122–3).

There is unfortunately the occasional traveller who prefers to 'acquire resistance' to malaria rather than take preventative tablets, or who takes homeopathic 'prophylactics' thinking these are effective against a killer disease. However, since homeopathy theory dictates treating like with like, it does not provide for prophylaxis or immunisation in a well person, so bona fide homeopaths do not advocate it. As for resistance, it takes at least 18 months residing in a malarial area for someone to get some immunity to malaria, so travellers to Africa will not acquire any effective resistance.

Travel clinics and health information A full list of current travel clinic websites worldwide is available on www.istm.org. For other journey preparation information, consult www.nathnac.org/ds/map_world.aspx (UK) or http://wwwnc. cdc.gov/travel/ (US). Information about various medications may be found on www.netdoctor.co.uk/travel. All advice found online should be used in conjunction with expert advice received prior to or during travel.

Medical kit Pharmacies in Botswana's main towns, and in Livingstone, generally have good supplies of medicines, but away from these you will find very little. If you're venturing deep into the wilds on an independent trip, then you should take with you anything that you expect to need. If you are on an organised trip, an overlanding truck, or staying at hotels, lodges or safari camps, then you will not need much, as these establishments normally have comprehensive emergency kits. In that case, just a small personal medical kit might include:

- alcohol-based hand rub or bar of soap in plastic box
- antihistamine tablets
- antiseptic, eg: iodine or potassium permanganate (don't take antiseptic cream)
- blister plasters (if you plan any serious walking)
- condoms or femidoms and contraceptive pills
- impregnated bed-net or permethrin spray
- insect repellent
- lipsalve (ideally containing a sunscreen)
- malaria prophylaxis
- Micropore tape (for closing small cuts – and invaluable for blisters)
- moisturising cream
- paracetamol or aspirin (but note that aspirin should not be given in the event of snakebite)
- sticking plaster (a roll is more versatile than pre-shaped plasters)
- sunscreen

However, if you are likely to end up in very remote situations, then you should also consider taking the following – and know how to use them:

- burns dressings (burns are a common problem for campers)
- antibiotics: ciprofloxacin or norfloxacin, for severe diarrhoea
- antibiotic eye drops, for sore, 'gritty', stuck-together eyes (conjunctivitis)
- injection swabs, sterile needles and syringes
- lint, sterile bandage and safety pins
- oral rehydration sachets
- steristrips or butterfly closures
- strong painkiller (eg: codeine phosphate – also use for bad diarrhoea)
- tweezers (perhaps those on a Swiss army knife)
- water purification equipment (see page 121)
- a good medical manual (see *Appendix 3*, page 509).
- tinidazole for giardia or amoebic dysentery (see below for regime)
- malaria diagnostic kits (5) and a digital thermometer

LONG-HAUL FLIGHTS, CLOTS AND DVT

Any prolonged immobility including travel by land or air can result in deep vein thrombosis (DVT) with the risk of embolus to the lungs. Certain factors can increase the risk and these include:

- Previous clot or close relative with a history
- Being over 40 (but risk increased over 80 years)
- Recent major operation or varicose veins surgery
- Cancer
- Stroke
- Heart disease
- Obesity
- Pregnancy
- Hormone therapy
- Heavy smoking
- Severe varicose veins
- Being very tall (over 6ft/1.8m) or short (under 5ft/1.5m)

A deep vein thrombosis (DVT) causes painful swelling and redness of the calf or sometimes the thigh. It is only dangerous if a clot travels to the lungs (pulmonary embolus). Symptoms of a pulmonary embolus (PE) include chest pain, shortness of breath, and sometimes coughing up small amounts of blood, and commonly start three to ten days after a long flight. Anyone who thinks that they might have a DVT needs to see a doctor immediately.

PREVENTION OF DVT
- Keep mobile before and during the flight; move around every couple of hours.
- Drink plenty of fluids during the flight.
- Avoid taking sleeping pills and excessive tea, coffee and alcohol.
- Consider wearing flight socks or support stockings (see www.legshealth. com).

If you think you are at increased risk of a clot, ask your doctor if it is safe to travel.

If you wear glasses, bring a spare pair. Similarly those who wear contact lenses should bring spare ones, also a pair of glasses in case the dust proves too much for the lenses. If you take regular medication (including contraceptive pills) then bring a large supply with you – much easier than hunting for your usual brand in Botswana. Equally, it's worth having a dental check-up before you go, as you could be several painful days from the nearest dentist.

IN BOTSWANA
Hospitals, dentists and pharmacies Botswana's main **hospitals**, in Maun (℡ 686 0444), Francistown (℡ 241 1000) and Gaborone (℡ 362 1400), are capable of serious surgery and a good quality of care; they will also treat you first and ask for money later. However, the public health system is over-stretched and under-funded, so unless your illness is critical, it will take time for you to be attended

to and treated at the public hospitals. Bear in mind, too, that a large number of patients in the public hospitals have serious infectious diseases, so there's a risk of coming away from these with something worse than you had when you arrived.

Assuming that you have comprehensive medical insurance as part of your travel cover – and you should check that you have – it is probably better go to one of the better-funded **private clinics** which are found in each of the main towns. These cater for both affluent citizens of Botswana and expats/diplomatic staff/travellers. They will accept payment from genuine travel-health insurance schemes. The best way to find details of the nearest private clinics is to look up 'medical – private clinics/practitioners' in the yellow pages at the back of the phone book.

In an emergency, contact:

Medical Rescue International ＼992 from a land line, or ＼147 on Mascom; emergency number in Gaborone ＼+267 390 1601; www.mri.co.bw. MRI organises medical evacuations from anywhere. They insure individual travellers, & your own insurance company may pick up the bills if their services are needed, but many lodges are also members, covering you whilst you are staying there (though you will still need your own medical insurance).

Okavango Air Rescue Emergency ＼995, or ＼+267 686 1506 from a satellite phone; office ＼686 1616; e office@okavangorescue.com; www. okavangorescue.com. This new not-for-profit organisation is on call 24/7. Their helicopter has a qualified doctor on board, & can airlift patients out if necessary. Many tour operators include their services, but individual membership costs just P175/year – around US$20/£13.

Alternatively, call an ambulance from a public hospital on ＼997.

Pharmacies in Botswana's main towns (and in Livingstone) generally have a good range of medicines, though specific brands are often unavailable. So bring with you all that you will need, as well as a repeat prescription for anything that you might run out of. Outside of the larger towns you probably won't be able to find anything other than very basic medical supplies. Thus you should carry a very comprehensive medical kit if you are planning to head off into the wilds (see page 118).

Staying healthy
Botswana is one of the healthiest countries in sub-Saharan Africa. It has a generally low population density, who are affluent by the region's standards, and a very dry climate, which means there are comparatively few problems likely to affect visitors. The risks are further minimised if you are staying in good hotels, lodges, camps and guest farms, where standards of hygiene are generally at least as good as you will find at home.

The major dangers in Botswana are car accidents (caused by driving too fast, or at night, on gravel roads) and sunburn. Both can be very serious, yet both are within the power of the visitor to avoid.

It's interesting to note that in recent years the most frequent medical reason for air evacuations from the Okavango Delta, and surrounds, has been the unexpected side effects of the anti-malarial drug Lariam.

The following is general advice, applicable to travelling anywhere, including Botswana.

Food and storage
Throughout the world, most health problems encountered by travellers are contracted by eating contaminated food or drinking unclean water. If you are staying in safari camps or lodges, or eating in restaurants, then you are unlikely to have problems in Botswana.

However, if you are backpacking and cooking for yourself, or relying on local food, then you need to take more care. Tins, packets and fresh green vegetables (when you can find them) are least likely to cause problems – provided that clean water has been used in preparing the meal. In Botswana's hot climate, keeping meat or other animal products unrefrigerated for more than a few hours is asking for trouble.

Water and purification Tap water in Botswana's major towns and borehole water, which is used in most of the more remote locations, is perfectly safe to drink for local residents. However, even the mildest of the local microbes may cause a slightly upset stomach for an overseas visitor so you would be wise to use bottled or treated water at all times – and this includes cleaning your teeth! Two-litre bottles of mineral water are available from most supermarkets; these are perfect if you're in a car. The vast majority of safari camps use borehole water that is extensively filtered, but will usually have bottled water if you insist.

Alternatively, you might want to consider using a bottle with a filter (eg: Aquapure). You can filter anything from river water to tap water without having to wait to drink it and the filter lasts for 350 litres. There is no need to boil the water either. If you don't have such a bottle, then first filter out any suspended solids, perhaps by passing the water through a piece of closely woven cloth or something similar. Then bring it to the boil, or sterilise it chemically with chlorine dioxide. Boiling is much more effective, provided that you have the fuel available. Iodine tablets are no longer advised for water sterilisation.

Heat and sun Heatstroke, heat exhaustion and sunburn are often problems for travellers to Botswana, despite being easy to prevent. To avoid them, you need to remember that your body is under stress and make allowances for it. First, take things gently; you are on holiday, after all. Next, keep your fluid and salt levels high: lots of water and soft drinks, but go easy on the caffeine and alcohol. Third, dress to keep cool with loose-fitting, thin garments – preferably of cotton, linen or silk. Finally, beware of the sun. Hats and long-sleeved shirts are essential. If you must expose your skin to the sun, then use sun blocks and high-factor sunscreens (the sun is so strong that you will still get a tan). Be especially careful of exposure in the middle of the day and of sun reflected off water, and wear a T-shirt and lots of waterproof suncream (at least SPF15) when swimming. The glare and the dust can be hard on the eyes, too, so bring UV-protecting sunglasses and, perhaps, a soothing eyebath.

Prickly heat A fine pimply rash on the trunk is likely to be heat rash; cool showers, dabbing dry and talc will help. Treat the problem by slowing down to a relaxed schedule, wearing only loose, baggy, 100%-cotton clothes and sleeping naked under a fan; if it's bad you may need to check into an air-conditioned hotel room for a while.

Eye problems Bacterial conjunctivitis (pink eye) is a common infection in Africa; people who wear contact lenses are most open to this irritating problem. The eyes feel sore and gritty and they will often be stuck closed in the mornings. They will need treatment with antibiotic drops or ointment. Lesser eye irritation should settle with bathing in salt water and keeping the eyes shaded. If an insect flies into your eye, extract it with great care, ensuring you do not crush or damage it otherwise you may get a nastily inflamed eye from toxins secreted by the creature. Small elongated red-and-black blister beetles carry warning colouration to tell you not to crush them anywhere against your skin.

Skin infections Any mosquito bite or small nick in the skin gives an opportunity for bacteria to foil the body's usually excellent defences; it will surprise many travellers how quickly skin infections start in warm humid climates and it is essential to clean and cover even the slightest wound. Creams are not as effective as a good drying antiseptic such as dilute iodine, potassium permanganate (a few crystals in half a cup of water) or crystal (or gentian) violet. One of these should be available in most towns. If the wound starts to throb, or becomes red and the redness starts to spread, or the wound oozes, and especially if you develop a fever, antibiotics will probably be needed: flucloxacillin (250mg four times a day) or cloxacillin (500mg four times a day). For those allergic to penicillin, erythromycin (500mg twice a day) for five days should help. See a doctor if the symptoms do not start to improve within 48 hours.

Fungal infections also get a hold easily in hot, moist climates so wear 100%-cotton socks and underwear and shower frequently. An itchy rash in the groin or flaking between the toes is likely to be a fungal infection. This needs treatment with an antifungal cream such as Canesten (clotrimazole); if this is not available try Whitfield's ointment (compound benzoic acid ointment) or crystal violet (although this will turn you purple!).

Avoiding insect bites The most dangerous biting insects in parts of Botswana are mosquitoes, because they can transmit malaria, dengue fever and a host of other diseases. Research has shown that using a mosquito net over your bed, and covering up exposed skin (by wearing long-sleeved shirts, and tucking trousers into socks) in the evening, are the most effective steps towards preventing bites. Bed-net treatment kits are available from travel clinics; these prevent mosquitoes biting through a net if you roll against it in your sleep, and also make old and holey nets protective. Mosquito coils and chemical insect repellents will help, and sleeping in a stream of moving air, such as under a fan, or in an air-conditioned room, will help to reduce your chances of being bitten.

DEET (diethyltoluamide) is the active ingredient in many repellents. The optimum concentration, of 50–55%, can safely be used in pregnancy and on babies from two months upwards. Note, however, that it will dissolve some plastics and synthetic materials, and may irritate sensitive skin, so care should be taken. Mosquito repellent must be applied to all exposed skin as mosquitoes will find any untreated skin.

Natural repellents are generally less effective than DEET-based ones and have to be used more frequently. Those who are genuinely allergic to DEET should use a natural repellent with citronella and eucalyptus oils. Other remedies, such as eating garlic or taking vitamin B, are anecdotal and there is no evidence to suggest they work, so never substitute these for DEET.

Mosquitoes and many other insects are attracted to light. If you are camping, never put a lamp near the opening of your tent, or you will have a swarm of biters waiting to join you when you retire. In hotel rooms, be aware that the longer your light is on, the greater the number of insects which will be sharing your accommodation.

Aside from avoiding mosquito bites between dusk and dawn, which will protect you from elephantiasis and a range of nasty insect-borne viruses, as well as malaria (see pages 116–18), it is important to take precautions against other insect bites. During the day it is wise to wear long, loose (preferably 100%-cotton) clothes if you are pushing through scrubby country; this will keep off ticks and also tsetse and day-biting *Aedes* mosquitoes which may spread viral fevers. You can also treat natural-fibre clothing with pyrethoid sprays (eg: permethrin), which will then kill mosquitoes on contact.

Tsetse flies are now rare in the Okavango Delta thanks to a government initiative to eradicate them. The flies hurt when they bite and it is said that they are attracted to the colour blue; locals will advise if they are a problem and whether they transmit sleeping sickness.

Minute pestilential biting blackflies spread river blindness in some parts of Africa between 19°N and 17°S; the disease is caught close to fast-flowing rivers since flies breed there and the larvae live in rapids. The flies bite during the day but long trousers tucked into socks will help keep them off. Citronella-based natural repellents (eg: Mosi-guard) do not work against them.

Tumbu flies or putsi, often called mango flies, are a problem where the climate is hot and humid. The adult fly lays her eggs on the soil or on drying laundry and when the eggs come into contact with human flesh (when you put on clothes or lie on a bed) they hatch and bury themselves under the skin. Here they form a crop of 'boils' each with a maggot inside. Smear a little Vaseline over the hole, and they will push their noses out to breathe. It may be possible to squeeze them out but it depends if they are ready to do so as the larvae have spines that help them to hold on.

In putsi areas either dry your clothes and sheets within a screened house, or dry them in direct sunshine until they are crisp, or iron them.

Jiggers, or sandfleas, are another flesh-feaster, which can be best avoided by wearing shoes. They latch on if you walk barefoot in contaminated places, and set up home under the skin of the foot, usually at the side of a toenail where they cause a painful, boil-like swelling. They need picking out by a local expert.

Snakes, spiders and scorpions Encounters with aggressive snakes, angry spiders or vindictive scorpions are more common in horror films than in Botswana. Most snakes will flee at the mere vibrations of a human footstep whilst spiders are far more interested in flies than people. You will have to seek out scorpions if you wish to see one. If you are careful about where you place your hands and feet, especially after dark, then there should be no problems. You are less likely to get bitten or stung if you wear stout shoes and long trousers. Simple precautions include not putting on boots without shaking them empty first, and always checking the back of your backpack before putting it on.

Snakes do bite occasionally, and you ought to know the standard first-aid treatment. First, and most importantly, *don't panic*. Most snakes are harmless and even venomous species will only dispense venom in about half of their bites. If bitten, you are unlikely to have received venom; keeping this fact in mind may help you to stay calm.

Even in the worst of these cases, the victim has hours or days to get to help, and not a matter of minutes. He/she should be kept calm, with no exertions to pump venom around the blood system, whilst being taken rapidly to the nearest medical help. The area of the bite should be washed to remove any venom from the skin, and the bitten limb should be immobilised. Paracetamol may be used as a painkiller, but never use aspirin because it may cause internal bleeding.

Most first-aid techniques do more harm than good: cutting into the wound is harmful and tourniquets are dangerous; suction and electrical inactivation devices do not work. The only effective treatment is antivenom. In case of a bite that you fear may be both serious and venomous:

- Try to keep calm. It is likely that no venom has been dispensed.
- Stop movement of the bitten limb by applying a splint.

- If you have a crêpe bandage, wrap it around the whole limb (eg: all the way from the toes to the thigh), as tight as you would for a sprained ankle or a muscle pull.
- Keep the bitten limb *below* heart height to slow the spread of any venom.
- Evacuate the victim to a hospital that has antivenom.
- *Never* give aspirin. You may offer paracetamol, which is safe.
- *Do not* apply ice packs.
- *Do not* apply potassium permanganate.

If the offending snake can be captured without any risk of someone else being bitten, take it to show the doctor. But beware, since even a decapitated head is able to dispense venom in a reflex bite.

When deep in the bush, heading for the nearest large farm or camp may be quicker than going to a town: it may have a supply of antivenom, or facilities to radio for help by plane.

DISEASES AND WHEN TO SEE A DOCTOR

Travellers' diarrhoea There are almost as many names for this as there are travellers' tales on the subject. Firstly, do resist the temptation to reach for the medical kit as soon as your stomach turns a little fluid. Most cases of travellers' diarrhoea will resolve themselves within 24–48 hours with no treatment at all. To speed up this process of acclimatisation, eat well but simply: avoid fats in favour of starches, and keep your fluid intake high. Bananas and papaya fruit are often claimed to be helpful. If you urgently need to stop the symptoms, for a long journey for example, then Lomotil, Imodium or another of the commercial anti-diarrhoea preparations will do the trick. They stop the symptoms, by paralysing the bowel, but will not cure the problem. They should be used only as a last resort and never if you have bad abdominal cramps with the diarrhoea.

If the diarrhoea persists for more than two days, or the stools contain blood, pus or slime, and/or you have a fever, you must seek medical advice. There are as many possible treatments as there are causes, and a proper diagnosis involves microscopic analysis of a stool sample, so go straight to your nearest hospital. The most important thing, especially in Botswana's climate, is to keep your fluid intake up. If it is not possible to reach medical help quickly then a dose of norfloxacin or ciprofloxacin repeated twice a day until reaching medical help may be appropriate. (If you are planning to take an antibiotic with you, note that both norfloxacin and ciprofloxacin are available only on prescription in the UK.) If the diarrhoea is greasy and bulky and is accompanied by sulphurous (eggy) burps, the likely cause is giardia. This is best treated with tinidazole (four x 500mg in one dose, repeated seven days later if symptoms persist).

The body's absorption of fluids is assisted by adding small amounts of dissolved sugars, salts and minerals to the water. Sachets of oral rehydration salts give the perfect biochemical mix you need to replace what is pouring out of your bottom but they do not taste so nice. Any dilute mixture of sugar and salt in water will do you good so, if you like Coke or orange squash, drink that with a three-finger pinch of salt added to each glass. The ideal ratio is eight level teaspoons of sugar and one level teaspoon of salt dissolved in one litre of water. Palm syrup or honey make good substitutes for sugar, and including fresh citrus juice will not only improve the taste of these solutions, but also add valuable potassium.

Drink two large glasses after every bowel action, and more if you are thirsty. If you are not eating you need to drink three litres a day *plus* whatever you are sweating *and* the equivalent of what's going into the toilet. If you feel like eating, take a bland diet; heavy greasy foods will give you cramps.

If you are likely to be more than a few days from qualified medical help, then come equipped with a good health manual and the selection of antibiotics which it recommends. *The Essential Guide to Travel Health* by Dr Jane Wilson-Howarth (see *Appendix 3*, page 509) is excellent for this purpose.

Malaria You can still catch malaria even if you are taking anti-malarial drugs so you should do everything possible to avoid mosquito bites. Untreated malaria is likely to be fatal, but even strains resistant to prophylaxis respond well to prompt treatment. Because of this, your immediate priority upon displaying possible malaria symptoms – including a rapid rise in temperature (over 38°C), and any combination of a headache, flu-like aches and pains, a general sense of disorientation, and possibly even nausea and diarrhoea – is to establish whether you have malaria, ideally by visiting a clinic.

A definite diagnosis of malaria is normally possible only by examining a blood sample under the microscope. It is best to get the problem properly diagnosed if possible, so don't treat yourself if you can easily reach a hospital first. Even if you test negative, it would be wise to stay within reach of a laboratory until the symptoms clear up, and to test again after a day or two if they don't. It's worth noting that if you have a fever and the malaria test is negative, you may have typhoid or paratyphoid, which should also receive immediate treatment.

If (and only if) medical help is unavailable, then self-treatment is fairly safe, except for people who are pregnant or under 12 years of age. Should you be travelling to remote parts of Botswana, you would be wise to carry a course of treatment to cure malaria, and a rapid test kit. With malaria, it is normal enough to go from feeling healthy to having a high fever in the space of a few hours (and it is possible to die from falciparum malaria within 24 hours of the first symptoms). In such circumstances, assume that you have malaria and act accordingly – whatever risks are attached to taking an unnecessary cure are outweighed by the dangers of untreated malaria.

There is some division about the best treatment for malaria, but either Malarone or Coarthemeter are the current treatments of choice. In Botswana you should always be able to get experienced local advice to tell you which will be the most effective.

Dengue fever This mosquito-borne disease – and other similar arboviruses – may mimic malaria but there is no prophylactic medication available to deal with it. The mosquitoes that carry this virus bite during the daytime, so it is worth applying repellent if you see any mosquitoes around. Symptoms include strong headaches, rashes, excruciating joint and muscle pains and high fever. Dengue fever only lasts for a week or so and is not usually fatal. Complete rest and paracetamol are the usual treatment. Plenty of fluids also help. Some patients are given an intravenous drip to keep them from dehydrating. It is especially important to protect yourself if you have had dengue fever before. A second infection with a different strain can result in the potentially fatal dengue haemorrhagic fever.

Sexually transmitted diseases AIDS is spread in exactly the same way in Africa as it is at home, through body secretions, blood and blood products. The same goes for the dangerous hepatitis B. Both can be spread through sex.

Remember that the risks of sexually transmitted disease are high, whether you sleep with fellow travellers or locals. About 80% of HIV infections in British heterosexuals are acquired abroad. If you must indulge, use condoms or femidoms, which help reduce the risk of transmission. If you do have unprotected sex, visit a clinic as soon as possible; this should be within 24 hours, or no later than 72 hours, for post-exposure prophylaxis. And if you notice any genital ulcers or discharge, get treatment promptly.

Hepatitis This is a group of viral diseases which generally start with Coca-Cola-coloured urine and light-coloured stools. It progresses to fevers, weakness, jaundice (yellow skin and eyeballs) and abdominal pains caused by a severe inflammation of the liver. There are several forms, of which the two most common are typical of the rest: hepatitis A (or infectious hepatitis) and hepatitis B (or serum hepatitis).

Hepatitis A and hepatitis E are spread by the faecal-oral route, that is by ingesting food or drink contaminated by excrement. They are avoided in the same ways you normally avoid stomach problems: by careful preparation of food and by drinking only clean water. But as there are now excellent vaccines against hepatitis A it is certainly worth getting inoculated before you travel. See *Recommended precautions* on page 116.

In contrast, the more serious but rarer hepatitis B is spread in the same way as AIDS (by blood or body secretions), and is avoided the same way as one avoids AIDS. There is a vaccine which protects against hepatitis B, but three doses are needed over a minimum of 21 days. It is usually considered necessary only for medical workers, people working closely with children or if you intend to travel for six weeks or longer. There are no cures for hepatitis, but with lots of bed rest and a good low-fat, no-alcohol diet most people recover within six months. If you are unlucky enough to contract hepatitis of any form, use your travel insurance to fly straight home.

Rabies Rabies is carried by all warm-blooded mammals (beware the village dogs, and small monkeys that congregate around campsites in the parks) and is passed on to humans through a bite, a scratch or a lick of an open wound. You must always assume any animal is rabid as they can often look well but still be infectious. Seek medical help as soon as possible after any potential exposure. Meanwhile scrub the wound with soap under a running tap or while pouring water from a jug for a good 10–15 minutes. The source of the water is not important, but if you have antiseptic to hand, then put this on afterwards. The soap helps stop the rabies virus entering the body and along with an antiseptic will guard against wound infections, including tetanus.

If you are bitten, scratched or licked over an open wound by a warm-blooded mammal, even if it looks healthy, then post-exposure prophylaxis should be given as soon as possible, though it is never too late to seek help, as the incubation period for rabies can be very long.

Tell the doctor if you have had pre-exposure vaccine, as this will change the treatment you receive. If you have had three doses of pre-exposure vaccine, you will need only a couple of doses of rabies vaccine, ideally given three days apart.

Those who have not been immunised before (see page 116) will need four or five doses of vaccine over 28–30 days and should also receive a product called rabies immunoglobulin (RIG – either human or horse). This is injected round the wound to try and neutralise any rabies virus present and is a pivotal part of the treatment, but it is expensive and may not be readily available in Botswana, so it is important to insist on getting to a place that has it. Another reason for having good insurance. And remember that, if you do contract rabies, mortality is 100% and death from rabies is probably one of the worst ways to go.

Outbreaks of anthrax are relatively common among the animals in Botswana's national parks, but the Botswana authorities monitor the situation very closely, putting affected areas off limits to visitors for a considerable period of time.

To allay any fears, it's worth noting a few facts about anthrax. It is a bacterial disease caused by the spore-forming *Bacillius anthracis*, and is primarily contracted by herbivores such as cattle, goats or sheep; outbreaks among carnivores are rare. Humans can contract the disease only if they come into direct contact with infected animals, their carcasses or material, including soil; it cannot be passed from one human to another. Fortunately the risk for travellers of getting anthrax is very low. Unless you're planning to eat the meat, or to get close enough to touch any animal or part of an animal, you're not at risk – though remember to avoid buying souvenirs made from animal skin, however tempting. For the most part, the disease occurs in the dry season when animals graze closer to the soil, where the spores can survive for a considerable period of time – hence the recurrence of outbreaks year on year. For this reason, proper disposal of carcasses, usually by incineration, is a crucial part of anthrax control measures.

Symptoms of anthrax vary, but usually occur within seven days. Most infections result from a cut or graze coming into contact with the bacteria. In this instance, what appears to be an insect bite grows within a couple of days into a painless ulcer about 1–3cm across, with a black centre, and surrounding lymph glands may swell. This type of infection usually responds well to antibiotics. Rarely, as a result of inhalation of spores, the apparent symptoms of a common cold progress to severe breathing problems, with a bleak outlook. A third form of the disease, which may follow the consumption of contaminated meat, leads to inflammation of the intestine, with potentially fatal consequences. While a vaccine is available, it is not normally recommended that visitors to Botswana should be inoculated.

Tickbite fever African ticks are not the rampant disease transmitters they are in the Americas, but they may spread tickbite fever and a few dangerous rarities in Botswana. Tickbite fever is a flu-like illness that can easily be treated with doxycycline, but as there can be some serious complications it is important to visit a doctor. It is most prevalent in Botswana between November and January.

Ticks should ideally be removed as soon as possible as leaving them on the body increases the chance of infection. They should be removed with special tick tweezers that can be bought in good travel shops. Failing that you can use your fingernails: grasp the tick as close to your body as possible and pull steadily and firmly away at right angles to your skin. The tick will then come away complete, as long as you do not jerk or twist. If possible douse the wound with alcohol (any spirit will do) or iodine. Irritants (eg: Olbas oil) or lit cigarettes are to be discouraged since they can cause the ticks to regurgitate and therefore increase the risk of disease. It is best to get a travelling companion to check you for ticks; if you are travelling with small children, remember to check their heads, and particularly behind the ears.

Spreading redness around the bite and/or fever and/or aching joints after a tickbite imply that you have an infection that requires antibiotic treatment, so seek advice.

Health and Safety   HEALTH

5

Bilharzia or schistosomiasis Though a low risk in Botswana, bilharzia is an insidious disease, contracted by coming into contact with contaminated water. It is caused by parasitic worms which live part of their lives in freshwater snails, and part of their lives in human bladders or intestines. A common indication of an infection is a localised itchy rash – where the parasites have burrowed through the skin – and later symptoms of a more advanced infection may include passing bloody urine. Bilharzia is readily treated by medication, and only serious if it remains untreated.

The only way to avoid infection completely is to stay away from any bodies of fresh water. Obviously this is restrictive, and could make your trip less enjoyable. More pragmatic advice is to avoid slow-moving or sluggish water, and ask local opinion on the bilharzia risk, as not all water is contaminated. It's generally thought that the Okavango Delta is not infected with bilharzia.

Generally bilharzia snails do not inhabit fast-flowing water, and hence rivers are free of it. However, dams and standing water, especially in populated areas, are usually heavily contaminated. If you think you have been infected, don't worry about it – just get a test done on your return at least six weeks after your last possible exposure.

Avoiding bilharzia If you are bathing, swimming, paddling or wading in fresh water which you think may carry a bilharzia risk, try to get out of the water within ten minutes.

- Avoid bathing or paddling on shores within 200m of villages or places where people use the water a great deal, especially reedy shores or where there is lots of waterweed.
- Dry off thoroughly with a towel; rub vigorously.
- If your bathing water comes from a risky source try to ensure that the water is taken from the lake in the early morning and stored snail-free, otherwise it should be filtered or Dettol or Cresol added.
- Bathing early in the morning is safer than bathing in the last half of the day.
- Cover yourself with DEET insect repellent before swimming: it may offer some protection.

Returning home Many tropical diseases have a long incubation period, and it is possible to develop symptoms weeks after returning home (this is why it is important to keep taking anti-malaria prophylaxis for the prescribed duration after you leave a malarial zone). If you do get ill after you return home, be certain to tell your doctor where you have been. Alert him/her to any diseases that you may have been exposed to. Several people die from malaria in the UK every year because victims do not seek medical help promptly or their doctors are not familiar with the symptoms, and so are slow to make a correct diagnosis. Milder forms of malaria may take up to a year to reveal themselves, but serious (falciparum) malaria will usually become apparent within three to six months, and can start as early as one week into a malarial area.

If problems persist, get a check-up at one of the hospitals that specialise in tropical diseases: the Hospital for Tropical Diseases in the UK (*www.thehtd.org*), or in the USA the Centers for Disease Control (*www.cdc.gov*). Note that to visit such a hospital in the UK, you need a letter of referral from your doctor.

SAFETY

Botswana is not a dangerous country. If you are travelling on an all-inclusive trip and staying at lodges and hotels, then problems of personal safety are exceedingly rare. There will always be someone on hand to help you. Even if you are travelling on local transport, perhaps on a low budget, you will generally be perfectly safe if you are careful.

Outside of rougher parts of the main cities, crime against visitors, however minor, is rare. Even if you are travelling on local transport on a low budget, you are likely to experience numerous acts of random kindness, but not crime. It is certainly safer for visitors than the UK, USA or most of Europe.

To get into a difficult situation, you'll usually have to try hard. You need to make yourself an obvious target for thieves, perhaps by walking around at night, with showy valuables, in a less affluent area of a town or city. Provided you are sensible, you are most unlikely to ever see any crime here.

For women travellers, especially those travelling alone, it is doubly important to learn the local attitudes, and how to behave acceptably. This takes some practice, and a certain confidence. You will often be the centre of attention but, by developing conversational techniques to avert over-enthusiastic male attention, you should be perfectly safe. Making friends of the local women is one way to help avoid such problems.

THEFT Theft is not generally a problem in Botswana – which is surprising given the poverty levels amongst much of the population. The only real exception to this is theft from unattended vehicles, which is becoming more common in the larger towns. If you leave a vehicle with anything valuable on view, then you may return to find a window smashed and items stolen.

When staying at safari camps in the bush, you'll often find that there are no locks and keys on the doors and there is a tremendous amount of trust. Regardless of this, leaving cash or valuables lying around or easily accessible is both stupid and

SAFETY FOR WOMEN TRAVELLERS *Janice Booth*

When attention becomes intrusive, it can help if you are wearing a wedding ring and have photos of 'your' husband and children, even if they are someone else's. A good reason to give for not being with them is that you have to travel in connection with your job – biology, zoology, geography, or whatever. (But not journalism – that's risky.)

Pay attention to local etiquette, and to speaking, dressing and moving reasonably decorously. Look at how the local women dress, and try not to expose parts of yourself that they keep covered. Think about body language. In much of southern Africa direct eye-contact with a man will be seen as a 'come-on'; sunglasses are helpful here.

Don't be afraid to explain clearly – but pleasantly rather than as a put-down – that you aren't in the market for whatever distractions are on offer. Remember that you are probably as much of a novelty to the local people as they are to you, and the fact that you are travelling abroad alone gives them the message that you are free and adventurous. But don't imagine that a Lothario lurks under every bush: many approaches stem from genuine friendliness or curiosity, and a brush-off in such cases doesn't do much for the image of travellers in general.

Take sensible precautions against theft and attack – try to cover all the risks before you encounter them – and then relax and enjoy your trip. You'll meet far more kindness than villainy.

very unfair to the camp's staff. Your watch could easily be worth a year's salary to them; make sure you keep such items out of sight and out of the way of temptation.

Should you experience a theft in a camp, report it to the management immediately; but bear in mind that most such reports are solved with the realisation that the property's owner mislaid it themselves!

How to avoid it Like anywhere, thieves in the bigger cities here work in groups and choose their targets carefully. These targets will be people who look vulnerable and who have items worth stealing. To avoid being robbed, try not to look too vulnerable or too rich – and certainly not both. Observing a few basic rules, especially during your first few weeks in Botswana's cities, will drastically reduce your chances of becoming a target. After that you should have learned your own way of assessing the risks, and avoiding thefts. Until then:

- Try not to carry anything of value around with you.
- If you must carry cash, then use a concealed money-belt for your main supply – keeping smaller change separately and to hand.
- Try not to look too foreign. Blend in to the local scene as well as you can. Act like a streetwise expat rather than a tourist, if possible. (Conspicuously carrying a local newspaper may help with this.)
- Rucksacks and large, new bags are bad. If you must carry a bag, choose an old battered one. Around town, a local plastic carrier bag is ideal.
- Move confidently and look as if you know exactly what you are doing, and where you are going. Lost foreigners make the easiest targets.
- Never walk around at night – that is asking for trouble.
- If you have a vehicle then don't leave anything in it, and avoid leaving it parked outside in a city.

Reporting thefts to the police If you are the victim of a theft then report it to the police – they ought to know. Also try to get a copy of the report, or at least a reference number on an official-looking piece of paper, as this will help you to claim on your insurance policy when you return home. Some insurance companies won't act without it. But remember that reporting anything in a police station can take a long time, and do not expect any speedy arrests for a small case of pickpocketing.

ARREST To get arrested in Botswana, a foreigner will normally have to try quite hard. There's no paranoia about foreigners, who are now generally seen as welcome tourists who bring money into the economy.

One simple precaution to avoid trouble is to ask for permission to photograph near bridges or military installations. This simple courtesy costs you nothing, and may avoid a problem later.

One excellent way to get arrested in Botswana is to try to smuggle drugs across its borders, or to try to buy them from 'pushers'. Drug offences carry penalties at least as stiff as those you will find at home – and the jails are a lot less pleasant. Botswana's police are not forbidden to use entrapment techniques or 'sting' operations to catch criminals. Buying, selling or using drugs in Botswana is just not worth the risk.

Failing this, arguing with any policeman or army official – and getting angry into the bargain – is a sure way to get arrested. It is essential to control your temper and stay relaxed when dealing with Botswana's officials. Not only will you gain respect, and hence help your cause, but you will also avoid being forced to cool off for a night in the cells.

If you are careless enough to be arrested, you will often be asked only a few questions. If the police are suspicious of you, then how you handle the situation will determine whether you are kept for a matter of hours or for days. Be patient, helpful, good-humoured, and as truthful as possible. Never lose your temper; it will only aggravate the situation. Avoid any hint of arrogance. If things are going badly after half a day or so, then start firmly, but politely, to insist on seeing someone in higher authority. As a last resort you do, at least in theory, have the right to contact your embassy or consulate, though the finer points of your civil liberties may be overlooked by an irate local police chief.

BRIBERY Bribery is not at all common in Botswana. Indeed, the country is widely rated as the least corrupt in Africa, and the government takes a very strict anti-corruption stance. Certainly no normal visitor should ever be asked for, or offer, a bribe. It would be just as illegal as offering someone a bribe back home. Forget it.

The ultimate way to explore Botswana

Safari Drive has been organising tailor-made, self drive safaris in Botswana since 1993.

With expert knowledge of the roads, driving conditions and routes, Safari Drive gives you the freedom and security to embark on an adventure of a lifetime. Self drive safaris offer versatile, independent travel with the freedom to explore at your own pace.

Personal itineraries are tailored to your time frame, level of 4x4 driving experience and budget.

Choose from a range of accommodation from luxury lodges to camping.

Safari Drive trips include:

- Expedition equipped Land Rovers for up to four people
- In-country briefing & backup
- Satellite phone
- Handbook
- Roof tent
- Water tanks
- Satellite navigation with Tracks 4 Africa
- All camping equipment

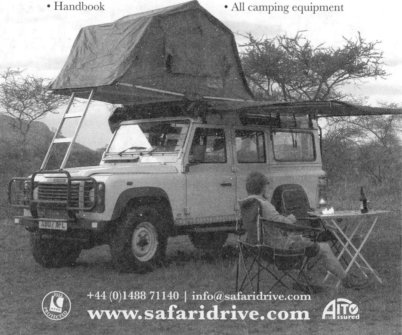

+44 (0)1488 71140 | info@safaridrive.com
www.safaridrive.com

6

Into the Wilds

DRIVING

Driving around Botswana is exceedingly easy if you stick to the network of first-class tarred roads between the towns, but heading into the bush is a completely different proposition, which usually requires a small expedition.

Botswana's bush tracks are maintained only by the passage of vehicles, and aren't for the novice, or the unprepared. However, if you've been to Africa at least once or twice before, perhaps including a driving trip around South Africa or Namibia, then such trips can be a lot of fun provided that you realise that you're embarking on an adventure as much as a holiday.

To explore the more rural areas and remote parks on your own you'll need a fully equipped 4x4 vehicle, stocked with food and water for your trip. Depending on where you are going, some form of back-up is often wise. This might be a reliable satellite phone, a radio (and the know-how to use it), someone tracking your schedule – with frequent call-in points so they can look for you if you don't turn up on time – or the security of travelling in convoy with at least one other vehicle.

Having assessed all the dangers, those who do this kind of trip often get addicted to the space and the freedom; it can be really rewarding and tremendous fun!

For general information on driving in Botswana, see *Getting around* in *Chapter 4*, pages 105–6.

EQUIPMENT AND PREPARATIONS

Fuel Petrol and diesel are available in all of the larger towns, but supplies at fuel stations outside Maun and Kasane can be erratic, so it is wise to fill up frequently. For travel into the bush you will need long-range fuel tanks, and/or a large stock of filled jerrycans. (Only use metal jerrycans for fuel; plastic containers are highly dangerous.)

It is essential to plan your fuel requirements well in advance, and to carry more than you expect to need. Remember that using the vehicle's 4x4 capability, especially in low ratio gears, will significantly increase your fuel consumption. Similarly, the cool comfort of a vehicle's air conditioning will burn your fuel reserves swiftly.

Spares Botswana's garages generally have a comprehensive stock of vehicle spares – though bush mechanics can effect the most amazing short-term repairs, with remarkably basic tools and raw materials. Spares for the more common makes are easiest to find; most basic Land Rover and Toyota 4x4 parts are available. If you are arriving in Botswana with an unusual foreign vehicle, it is best to bring as many spares as you can.

Navigation See the section on *Maps and navigation* in *Chapter 4*, pages 100–2, for detailed comments. There are several good maps designed for visitors that are widely available, while survey-style maps may be obtained from the Department of Surveys and Mapping in Maun and Gaborone. It's wise to take a GPS (see *Chapter 4, GPS systems*), though learn how to use it before you arrive and never switch your brain off and rely on it totally.

COPING WITH BOTSWANA'S ROADS
Wherever you are driving in Botswana, no matter what the road surface, you should always be prepared for animals wandering on to the road and for pot-holes.

Tar roads Botswana's network of tar roads is gradually being extended. Although these roads are generally very good, don't be lulled into complacency; pot-holes do occur, with potentially devastating consequences if hit at speed.

Gravel roads There aren't many good gravel roads in Botswana – most are either good tar, or basic bush tracks. However, the few gravel sections can be very deceptive. Even when they appear smooth, flat and fast (which is not often), they still do not give vehicles much traction. You will frequently put the car into small skids, but with practice at slower speeds you will learn how to deal with them. Gravel is a less forgiving surface on which to drive than tar. The rules and techniques for driving well are the same for both, but on tar you can get away with sloppy braking and cornering which would prove fatal on gravel.

In addition to animals wandering on to the road and pot-holes, be prepared for sand-traps, or an unexpected corner. It is verging on insanity to drive over about 80km/h on any of Botswana's gravel roads. Other basic driving hints include:

- **Slowing down** If in any doubt about what lies ahead, always slow down. Road surfaces can vary enormously, so keep a constant look-out for pot-holes, ruts or patches of soft sand that could put you into an unexpected slide.
- **Passing vehicles** When passing other vehicles travelling in the opposite direction, always slow down to minimise both the damage that stone chippings will do to your windscreen, and the danger in driving through the other vehicle's dust cloud.
- **Using your gears** In normal driving, a lower gear will give you more control over the car – so keep out of high 'cruising' gears. Rather stick with third or fourth, and accept that your revs will be slightly higher than they normally are.
- **Cornering and braking** Under ideal conditions, the brakes should only be applied when the car is travelling in a straight line. Braking whilst negotiating a corner is dangerous, so it is vital to slow down before you reach corners. Equally, it is better to slow down gradually, using a combination of gears and brakes, than to use the brakes alone. You are less likely to skid.

Driving at night Outside of the main towns, **never** drive at night unless it's a matter of life and death. Both wild and domestic animals frequently spend the night by the side of busy roads, and will actually sleep on quieter ones. Tar roads are especially bad as the surface absorbs all the sun's heat by day, and then radiates it at night – making it a warm bed for passing animals. A high-speed collision with any animal, even a small one like a goat, will not only kill the animal, but will cause very severe damage to a vehicle, with potentially fatal consequences. And in the bush, even on main roads, the danger of startling elephants is very real.

DRIVING TECHNIQUES You want a high-clearance 4x4 to get anywhere in Botswana that's away from the main arteries. However, no vehicle can make up for an inexperienced driver – so ensure that you are confident of your vehicle's capabilities before you venture into the wilds with it. You really need extensive practice, with an expert on hand to advise you, before you'll have the first idea how to handle such a vehicle in difficult terrain. Finally, driving in convoy is an essential precaution in the more remote areas, in case one vehicle gets stuck or breaks down. Some of the more relevant ideas and techniques include the following.

When and how to use a 4x4
Firstly, read your vehicle's manual. All makes are different, and have their quirks, and so you must read the manual before you set off. Note especially that you should **never** drive in 4x4 mode with fixed (or 'locked') differentials on tar roads. Doing this will cause permanent damage to the mechanics of your vehicle.

When you do encounter traction difficulties, stop when you can and put the vehicle into 4x4 – usually setting the second 'small' gearstick to '4x4 high' is fine for most situations.

Now get out of the vehicle and check if the front two hubs of your vehicle have, at their centre, knobs to turn. (This is the case with many Toyotas, though some newer vehicles have 'automatic' hubs.) If so, you'll need to turn these to the 'lock' position – a fact forgotten by many novices that causes untold trouble for them, and endless smug amusement for old Africa hands.

When you're past the problem, using 2WD will lower your fuel consumption, though many will use 4x4 the whole time that they're in the bush. Remember to reset your hubs to 'free' before you drive on tar again.

Driving in sand
If you're in 4x4 and are really struggling in deep sand, then stop on the next fairly solid area that you come to. Lower your tyre pressure until there is a small bulge in the tyre walls (having first made sure that you have the means to re-inflate them when you reach solid roads again). A lower pressure will help your traction greatly, but increase the wear on your tyres. Pump them up again before you drive on a hard surface at speed, or the tyres will be badly damaged.

If you have your own vehicle, and thus have a choice, there are tyres designed specifically for driving in sand, so it may be worth considering these – although bear in mind that the sides will bend more easily than those designed for tarmac surfaces, so you'll not want to use these for long distances on the tar.

Where there are clear, deep-rutted tracks in the sand, don't fight the steering wheel – just relax and let your vehicle steer itself. Driving in the cool of the morning is easier than later in the day because when sand is cool it compacts better and is firmer. (When hot, the pockets of air between the sand grains expand and the sand becomes looser.)

If you do get stuck, despite these precautions, don't panic. Don't just rev the engine and spin the wheels – you'll only dig deeper. Instead stop. Relax and assess the situation. Now dig shallow ramps in front of all the wheels, reinforcing them with pieces of wood, vegetation, stones, material or anything else which will give the wheels better traction. Lighten the vehicle load (passengers out) and push. Don't let the engine revs die as you engage your lowest ratio gear. That probably means using '4x4 low' rather than '4x4 high'. Use the clutch to ensure that the wheels don't spin wildly and dig themselves further into the sand.

Sometimes rocking the vehicle backwards and forwards will build up momentum to break you free. This can be done by the driver intermittently applying the clutch and/or by getting helpers who can push and pull the vehicle at the same frequency. Once the vehicle is moving, the golden rule of sand driving is to keep up the momentum: if you pause, you will sink and stop.

Grass seeds in the Kalahari After the rains, the Kalahari's tracks are often knee-high in seeding grass. As your vehicle drives through, stems and especially seeds can build up in front of and inside the radiator, and get trapped in crevices underneath the chassis. This is a major problem in the less-visited areas of the Kalahari. It's at its worst from March to June, after the rains, and in the areas of the great salt pans, the CKGR, and the tracks around Tsodilo and the Aha Hills. The main tracks around Chobe and Moremi are used relatively frequently, and so present less of a problem.

The presence of long grass on the tracks causes a real danger of overheating (see below) and fire. First, the build-up of seeds and stems over the radiator insulates it. Thus, if you aren't watching your gauges, the engine's temperature can rocket. It will swiftly seize up and catch fire. Second, the grass build-up itself, if allowed to become too big, can catch fire due to its contact with the hot exhaust system underneath the vehicle.

There are several strategies to minimise these dangers; best apply them all. First, before you set out, buy a few square metres of the tightly woven window-meshing gauze material used in the windows of safari tents. Fix one large panel of this on the vehicle's bull-bars, well in front of the radiator grill. Fix another much closer to it, but still outside of the engine compartment. Hopefully this will reduce vastly the number of seeds reaching your radiator.

Second, watch your vehicle's engine-temperature gauge like a hawk when you're travelling through areas of grassland.

Third, stop every 10km or so (yes, really, that often) and check the radiator and the undercarriage for pockets of stems and seeds. Pay special attention to the hot areas of the exhaust pipe; you should not allow a build-up of flammable material there. Use a stick or piece of wire to clean out any seeds and stems before you set off again.

Overheating If the engine has overheated then the only option is to stop and turn it off. Stop, have a drink under a tree, and let it cool. Don't open the radiator cap to refill it until the radiator is no longer hot to the touch. Even then, keep the engine running and the water circulating while you refill the radiator – otherwise you run the risk of cracking the hot metal by suddenly cooling it. Flicking droplets of water on to the outside of a running engine will cool it.

When driving away, switch off any air conditioning (as it puts more strain on the engine). Open your windows and turn your heater and fan full on. This may not seem pleasant in the midday heat – but it'll help to cool the engine. Keep watching that engine-temperature gauge.

Driving in mud This is difficult, though the theory is the same as for sand: keep going and don't stop. That said, even the most experienced drivers get stuck. A few areas of Botswana (the road from Rakops to the CKGR's main gate is legendary in this respect) have very fine soil known as 'black-cotton' soil, which becomes impassable when wet.

Push-starting when stuck If you are unlucky enough to need to push-start your vehicle whilst it is stuck in sand or mud, there is a remedy. Raise up the drive wheels, and take off one of the tyres. You should have a hi-lift jack with you, and know how to use it.

Then wrap a length of rope around the hub and treat it like a spinning top: one person (or more) pulls the rope to make the axle spin, whilst the driver lifts the clutch, turns the ignition on, and engages a low gear to turn the engine over. This is a very difficult equivalent of a push-start, but it may be your only option.

Rocky terrain There's not much of this in northern Botswana – but you will find some in the southeast. Have your tyre pressure higher than normal and move very slowly. If necessary, passengers should get out and guide you along the track to avoid scraping the undercarriage on the ground. This can be a very slow business.

Crossing rivers and other stretches of water The first thing to do is to stop and check the river. You must assess its depth, the type of riverbed and its current flow; and determine the best route to drive across it. This is best done by wading across the river (though in an area frequented by hippos and crocodiles this is not advisable). Beware of water that's too deep for your vehicle, or the very real possibility of being swept away by a fast current and a slippery riverbed.

If everything is OK then select your lowest gear ratio and drive through the water at a slow but steady rate. Your vehicle's air intake must be above the level of the water to avoid your engine filling with water. It's not worth taking risks, so remember that a flooded river may subside to safer levels by the next morning.

Driving near big game The only animals which are likely to pose a threat to vehicles are elephants – and generally only elephants which are familiar with vehicles. So, treat them with the greatest respect and don't 'push' them by trying to move ever closer. Letting them approach you is much safer, and they will feel far less threatened and more relaxed. Then, if the animals are calm, you can safely turn the engine off, sit quietly, and watch as they pass you by.

If you are unlucky, or foolish, enough to unexpectedly drive into the middle of a herd, then don't panic. Keep your movements, and those of the vehicle, slow and measured. Back off steadily. Don't be panicked, or overly intimidated, by a mock charge – this is just their way of frightening you away. For detailed comments, see the boxes on *Driving near elephants* in *Chapter 9*.

BUSHCAMPING

Many 'boy scout' type manuals have been written on survival in the bush, usually by military veterans. If you are stranded with a convenient multi-purpose knife, then these useful tomes will describe how you can build a shelter from branches, catch passing animals for food, and signal to the inevitable rescue planes which are combing the globe looking for you – whilst avoiding the attentions of hostile forces.

In Africa, bushcamping is usually less about survival than comfort. You're likely to have much more than the knife: probably at least a bulging backpack, if not a loaded 4x4. Thus the challenge is not to camp and survive, it is to camp and be as comfortable as possible. With practice you'll learn how, but a few hints might be useful for the less experienced.

WHERE YOU CAN CAMP In national parks, there are strictly designated campsites that you should use, as directed by the local game scouts. These must be pre-booked or you are unlikely to be allowed entrance.

Outside of the parks, if no campsites are designated, you should ask the local landowner, or village head, if they are happy for you to camp on their property.

If you explain patiently and politely what you want, then you are unlikely to meet anything but hospitality in most areas of rural Botswana.

CHOOSING A SITE Only experience will teach you how to choose a good site for pitching a tent, but a few general points, applicable to any wild areas of Africa, may help you avoid problems:

- Avoid camping on what looks like a path through the bush, however indistinct. It may be a well-used game trail.
- Beware of camping in dry riverbeds: dangerous flash floods can arrive with little or no warning.
- In marshy areas camp on higher ground to avoid cold, damp mists in the morning and evening.
- Camp a reasonable distance from water: near enough to walk to it, but far enough to avoid animals which arrive to drink.
- Give yourself plenty of time before it gets dark to familiarise yourself with your surroundings.
- If a lightning storm is likely, make sure that your tent is not the highest thing around.
- Finally, choose a site which is as flat as possible – you will find sleeping much easier.

CAMPFIRES Campfires can create a great atmosphere and warm you on a cold evening, but they can also be damaging to the environment and leave unsightly piles of ash and blackened stones. Deforestation is a major concern in much of the developing world, including parts of Botswana, so if you do light a fire then use wood as the locals do: sparingly. If you have a vehicle, consider buying firewood in advance from people who sell it at the roadside – or collect it in areas where there's more wood around.

If you collect it yourself, then take only dead wood, nothing living. Never just pick up a log: always roll it over first, checking carefully for snakes or scorpions.

Experienced campers build small, highly efficient fires by using a few large stones to absorb, contain and reflect the heat, and gradually feeding just a few thick logs into the centre to burn. Cooking pots can be balanced on the stones, or the point where the logs meet and burn. Others will use a small trench, lined with rocks, to similar effect. Either technique takes practice, but is worth perfecting. Whichever you do, bury the ashes, take any rubbish with you when you leave, and make the site look as if you had never been there. (See *Appendix 3, Further information* for details of Christina Dodwell's excellent *An Explorer's Handbook: Travel, Survival and Bush Cookery.*)

Don't expect an unattended fire to frighten away wild animals – that works in Hollywood, but not in Africa. A campfire may help your feelings of insecurity, but lion and hyena will disregard it with stupefying nonchalance.

Finally, do be hospitable to any locals who appear. Despite your efforts to seek permission for your camp, you may effectively be staying in their back gardens.

USING A TENT Whether to use a tent or to sleep in the open is a personal choice, dependent upon where you are. In an area where there are predators around (specifically lion and hyena) then you must use a tent – and sleep completely inside it, as a protruding leg may seem like a tasty take-away to a hungry hyena. This is especially true at organised campsites, where the local animals are so used to humans that they have lost much of their inherent fear of man.

Outside game areas, you will usually be fine sleeping in the open, or preferably under a mosquito net, with just the stars of the African sky above you. On the practical side, sleeping under a tree will reduce the morning dew that settles on your sleeping bag. If your vehicle has a large, flat roof then sleeping on this will provide you with peace of mind, and a star-filled outlook. Hiring a vehicle with a built-in roof-tent is a perfect solution for many, though it can take time to pack when wanting to rush off on an early-morning game drive.

CAMPING EQUIPMENT FOR BACKPACKERS If you are taking an organised safari, you will not need any camping equipment at all. If you're hiring a 4x4, then it's best to hire one here with all the kit. However, for those backpacking, there is very little lightweight kit available in Botswana. Most of the equipment is designed to be sturdy, long-lasting and carried around in vehicles. So buy any lightweight kit before you leave home, as it will save you a lot of time and trouble once you arrive. Here are a few comments on various essentials.

Tent During the rains a good tent is essential in order to stay dry. Even during the dry season one is useful if there are lion or hyena around. If backpacking, invest in a high-quality, lightweight tent. Mosquito-netting ventilation panels, allowing a good flow of air, are essential. (Just a corner of mesh at the top of the tent is *not* enough for comfort.) Don't go for a tent that's small; it may feel cosy at home, but will be hot and claustrophobic in the heat.

I have had the same 'Spacepacker' tent for many years, but sadly they are no longer manufactured. It's a dome tent with fine mesh doors on either side which allow a through draught, making all the difference when temperatures are high. The alternative to a good tent is a mosquito net, which is fine unless it is raining or you are in a big-game area.

Sleeping bag A lightweight, three-season sleeping bag is ideal for Botswana most of the time, though probably not quite warm enough for the very coldest nights in the Kalahari. Down is preferable to synthetic fillings for most of the year, as it packs smaller, is lighter, and feels more luxurious to sleep in. That said, when down gets wet it loses its efficiency, so bring a good synthetic bag if you are likely to encounter much rain.

Ground mat A ground mat of some sort is essential. It keeps you warm and comfortable, and it protects the tent's groundsheet from rough or stony ground (do put it underneath the tent!). Closed-cell foam mats are widely available outside Botswana, so buy one before you arrive. The better mats cost double or treble the cheaper ones, but are stronger, thicker and warmer – well worth the investment.

Therm-a-Rests, the combination air-mattress and foam mat, are strong, durable and also worth the investment – but take a puncture repair kit with you just in case of problems. Do watch carefully where you site your tent, and try to make camp before dark. My trusty Therm-a-Rests deflated badly one night in the Kalahari, sleeping near the Mamuno–Buitepos border. Breaking camp the next morning, I lifted the mat to find a large scorpion in its burrow immediately beneath the mat.

Sheet sleeping bag Thin, pure-cotton or silk sheet sleeping bags are small, light and very useful. They are easily washed and so are normally used like a sheet, inside a sleeping bag, to keep it clean. They can, of course, be used on their own when your main sleeping bag is too hot.

Stove 'Trangia'-type stoves, which burn methylated spirits, are simple to use and light, and cheap to run. They come complete with a set of light aluminium pans and a very useful all-purpose handle. Often you'll be able to cook on a fire with the pans, but it's nice to have the option of making a brew in a few minutes while you set up camp. Methylated spirits are cheap and widely available in Botswana, even in rural areas, but bring a tough (purpose-made) fuel container with you as the bottles in which it is sold will soon crack and spill all over your belongings.

Petrol- and kerosene-burning stoves are undoubtedly efficient on fuel and powerful – but invariably temperamental and messy. Gas stoves use pressurised canisters, which are not allowed on aircraft.

Torch (flashlight) This should be on every visitor's packing list – whether you're staying in upmarket camps or backpacking. Find one that's small and tough, and preferably water- and dust-proof. Headtorches leave your hands free (useful when cooking or mending the car) and the latest designs are relatively light and comfortable to wear. Consider one of the new generation of super-bright LED torches; the LED Lenser range is excellent.

Those with vehicles will find that a strong spotlight, powered by the car's battery (perhaps through the socket for the cigarette lighter), is invaluable for impromptu lighting.

Water containers For everyday use, a small two-litre water bottle is invaluable, however you are travelling. If you're thinking of camping, you should also consider a strong, collapsible water bag – perhaps 5–10 litres in size – which will reduce the number of trips that you need to make from your camp to the water source (ten litres of water weighs 10kg). And to be sure of safe drinking water, consider taking a bottle with a filter (see page 121).

Drivers will want to be self-sufficient for water when venturing into the bush, and so carry several large, sturdy containers of water. If you're driving a vehicle specially kitted out for camping, ensure that the water tank is full at the outset.

See *Chapter 4, Planning and Preparation*, pages 98–100, for a memory-jogging list of other useful items to pack.

ANIMAL DANGERS FOR CAMPERS Camping in Africa is really very safe, though you may not think so from reading this. If you have a major problem whilst camping, it will probably be because you did something stupid, or because you forgot to take a few simple precautions. Here are a few general basics, applicable to anywhere in Africa and not just Botswana.

Large animals Big game will not bother you if you are in a tent – provided that you do not attract its attention, or panic it. Elephants will gently tiptoe through your guy ropes whilst you sleep, without even nudging your tent. However, if you wake up and make a noise, startling them, they are far more likely to panic and step on your tent. Similarly, scavengers will quietly wander round, smelling your evening meal in the air, without any intention of harming you.

- Remember to use the toilet before going to bed, and avoid getting up in the night if possible.
- Scrupulously clean everything used for food that might smell good to scavengers. Put these utensils in a vehicle if possible; if not, suspend them from a tree, or pack them away in a rucksack inside the tent.

- Do not keep any smelly foodstuffs, like meat or citrus fruit, in your tent. Their smells may attract unwanted attention.
- Do not leave anything outside that could be picked up – like bags, pots, pans, etc. Hyenas, amongst others, will take anything. (They have been known to crunch a camera's lens, and eat it.)
- If you are likely to wake in the night, then leave the tent's zips a few centimetres open at the top, enabling you to take a quiet peek outside.

Creepy crawlies As you set up camp, clear stones or logs out of your way with great caution: they make great hiding places for snakes and scorpions. Long moist grass is ideal territory for snakes, and dry, dusty, rocky places are classic sites for scorpions.

If you are sleeping in the open, it is not unknown to wake and find a snake lying next to you in the morning. Don't panic; your warmth has just attracted it to you. You will not be bitten if you gently edge away without making any sudden movements. (This is one good argument for using at least a mosquito net!)

Before you put on your shoes, shake them out. Similarly, check the back of your backpack before you slip it on. Just a curious spider, in either, could inflict a painful bite.

WALKING IN THE BUSH

Walking in the African bush is a totally different sensation from driving through it. You may start off a little unready – perhaps even sleepy for an early-morning walk – but swiftly your mind will wake. There are no noises except the wildlife, and you. So every noise that isn't caused by you must be an animal; or a bird; or an insect. Every smell and every rustle has a story to tell, if you can understand it.

With time, patience and a good guide you can learn to smell the presence of elephants, and hear when a predator alarms impala. You can use ox-peckers to lead you to buffalo, or vultures to help you locate a kill. Tracks will record the passage of animals in the sand, telling what passed by, how long ago, and in which direction.

Eventually your gaze becomes alert to the slightest movement; your ears aware of every sound. This is safari at its best: a live, sharp, spine-tingling experience that's hard to beat and very addictive. Be careful: watching game from a vehicle will never be the same again for you.

WALKING TRAILS AND SAFARIS One of Africa's biggest attractions is its walking safaris – which attract people back year after year. However, because of the danger involved, the calibre and experience of guides when walking is far more important than when driving. Anyone with a little experience can drive you around fairly safely in a large metal vehicle, but when you're faced with a charging elephant you need to be standing behind a real expert to have much chance of survival.

Walking guides I am not confident that Botswana has progressed well towards the implementation of rigorous minimum standards for guides who lead walking safaris. Zimbabwe has for many years led the field, with a really tough training course leading to the exalted status of 'pro guide'; in many ways this is Africa's 'gold standard' of guiding.

Zambia has adopted an alternative, but also very safe, system requiring an armed scout and an experienced walking guide to accompany every walk. The scout controls the problem animal, the guide controls the group of people. It's rarely necessary to even fire a warning shot, and injuries are exceedingly rare.

6

However, Botswana, like South Africa, has minimum standards which I think are too low for walking guides. Thus, in my opinion, the term 'qualified guide' in Botswana doesn't mean that I should necessarily feel safe going walking with them. Thus it's mostly up to the individual safari operation to make sure its guides are experienced.

A handful of operations (Linyanti Bush Camp and its sister camps, the Footsteps operation near Shinde, Motswiri, and the Selinda Reserve, spring to mind) really concentrate on walking safaris. These take their walking very seriously, employ top walking guides, and put safety at the top of their agenda. I'm confident to go walking with such operations.

The rest are a mixed bag; some use good guides, others I've been out with I felt were actually dangerous. One good rule of thumb is the presence of a rifle. If your guide *doesn't* carry one, then I certainly wouldn't walk with them to anywhere where we were likely to see any dangerous game. (The converse doesn't apply though; carrying a rifle does not make an inexperienced guide safe.)

Often you'll see advertising for camps in the Okavango with comments along the lines that your guide is 'a man of the swamps, completely at one with his environment'. This is doubtless true, but doesn't imply that this same guide automatically has the foresight, command and communication skills to look after frightened foreigners whilst avoiding game in a dangerous situation. Knowing how to save himself is different from controlling a small group, and saving *them* from a nasty end.

Thus my advice is that if you want to do much walking in Botswana, go to one of the places that really concentrate on walking safaris. The rest of the time, stick to canoes, boats and driving. Only go walking with guides who are armed, know how to use their guns, and you have discussed the issues with and satisfied yourself that they have sufficient experience for you to be safe.

Etiquette for walking safaris If you plan to walk then avoid wearing any bright, unnatural colours, especially white. Dark, muted shades are best; greens, browns and khaki are ideal. Dark blue tends to attract tsetse flies, so best to avoid that if you can. Hats are essential, as is sunblock. Even a short walk will last for two hours, and there's no vehicle to which you can retreat if you get too hot.

Binoculars should be immediately accessible – one pair per person – ideally in dust-proof cases strapped to your belt. Cameras too, if you decide to bring any, as they are of little use buried at the bottom of a camera bag. Heavy tripods or long lenses are a nightmare to lug around, so leave them behind if you can (and accept, philosophically, that you may miss shots).

Walkers see the most when walking in silent single file. This doesn't mean that you can't stop to whisper a question to the guide; just that idle chatter will reduce your powers of observation, and make you even more visible to the animals (who will usually flee when they sense you).

With regard to safety, your guide will always brief you in detail before you set off. S/he will outline possible dangers, and what to do in the unlikely event of them materialising. Listen carefully: this is vital.

Face-to-face animal encounters Whether you are on an organised walking safari, on your own hike, or just walking from the car to your tent in the bush, it is not unlikely that you will come across some of Africa's larger animals at close quarters. Invariably, the danger is much less than you imagine, and a few basic guidelines will enable you to cope effectively with most situations.

First, don't panic. Console yourself with the fact that animals are not normally interested in people. You are not their normal food, or their predator. If you do not annoy or threaten them, you will be left alone. No matter how frightened you are, you'll probably run slower than whatever is worrying you. So don't try to run; think your way out of the tight spot.

If you are walking to look for animals, then remember that this is their environment, not yours. Animals have evolved within the bush, and their senses are far better attuned to it than yours. To be on less unequal terms, remain alert and try to spot them from a distance. This gives you the option of approaching carefully, or staying well clear.

Animals, like people, are all different. So whilst we can generalise here and say how the 'average' animal will behave, the one that's glaring at you over a small bush may have had a really bad day, and be feeling much grumpier than normal.

Finally, the advice of a good guide is far more valuable than the simplistic comments noted here – though a few general comments on some potentially dangerous situations might be of use.

Buffalo This is probably the continent's most dangerous animal to hikers, but there is a difference between the old males, often encountered on their own or in small groups, and large breeding herds.

The former are easily surprised. If they hear or smell something amiss, they will charge without provocation – motivated by a fear that something is sneaking up on them. Buffalo have an excellent sense of smell, but fortunately they are short-sighted. Avoid a charge by quickly climbing the nearest tree, or by sidestepping at the last minute. If adopting the latter, more risky, technique then stand motionless until the last possible moment, as the buffalo may well miss you anyhow.

The large breeding herds can be treated in a totally different manner. If you approach them in the open, they will often flee. Sometimes though, in areas often used for walking safaris, they will stand and watch, moving aside to allow you to pass through the middle of the herd.

Neither encounter is for the faint-hearted or inexperienced, so steer clear of these dangerous animals wherever possible.

Black rhino Until 2003, there were no black rhino left in Botswana, but at the end of that year four animals were reintroduced into the heart of Moremi. Sightings are exceptionally rare, but if you are both exceptionally lucky enough to find one, and then unlucky enough to be charged by it, use the same tactics as you would for a buffalo: tree climbing or dodging at the last second. (It is amazing how even the least athletic walker will swiftly scale the nearest tree when faced with a charging rhino.)

Elephant Normally elephants are only a problem if you disturb a mother with a calf, or approach a male in *musth* (state of arousal), so keep well away from these. Lone bulls can usually be approached quite closely when feeding. If you get too close to any elephant it will scare you off with a 'mock charge': head up, perhaps shaking – ears flapping – and trumpeting. Lots of sound and fury. This is intended to be frightening, and it is. But it is just a warning and no cause for panic. You should just freeze to assess the elephant's intentions. When it's stopped making a fuss, back off slowly. Don't run. There is no easy way to avoid the charge of an angry elephant, so take a hint from this warning and move away.

When an elephant really means business, it will put its ears back, lower its head, and charge directly at you. This is known as a 'full charge' and they don't stop. It is one of the most dangerous situations in Africa. Then you probably have to run – but elephants are much faster than you, so think while you run. Aim to get behind an anthill, up a tall tree, or out of the way somehow.

See also the boxes on *Driving near elephants*, in *Chapter 9*, for more details of this behaviour with reference to vehicles.

Lion Tracking lion can be one of the most exhilarating parts of a walking safari. Sadly, they will normally flee before you even get close to them. However, it can be a problem if you come across a large pride unexpectedly. Lion are well camouflaged; it is easy to find yourself next to one before you realise it. If you had been listening, you would probably have heard a warning growl about 20m ago. Now it is too late.

The best plan is to stop, and back off slowly, but confidently. If you are in a small group, then stick together. Never run from a big cat. First, they are always faster than you are. Second, running will just convince them that you are frightened prey, and worth chasing. As a last resort, if they seem too inquisitive and follow as you back off, then stop. Call their bluff. Pretend that you are not afraid and make loud, deep, confident noises: shout at them, bang something. But do not run.

John Coppinger, one of Africa's most experienced guides, adds that every single compromising experience that he has had with lion on foot has been either with a female with cubs, or with a mating pair, when the males can get very aggressive. You have been warned.

Leopard Leopard are very seldom seen, and would normally flee from the most timid of lone hikers. However, if injured, or surprised, then they are very powerful, dangerous cats. Conventional wisdom is scarce, but never stare straight into the leopard's eyes, or it will regard this as a threat display. (The same is said, by some, to be true with lion.) Better to look away slightly, at a nearby bush, or even at its tail. Then back off slowly, facing the direction of the cat and showing as little terror as you can. As with lion – loud, deep, confident noises are a last line of defence. Never run from a leopard.

Hippo Hippo are fabled to account for more deaths in Africa than any other animal (ignoring the mosquito). Having been attacked and capsized by a hippo whilst in a mokoro, I find this very easy to believe. Visitors are most likely to encounter hippo in the water, when in a boat or mokoro. (See the other section on hippo, page 146.)

However, as hippos spend half their time grazing on land, they will sometimes be encountered out of the water. Away from the water, out of their comforting lagoons, hippos are even more dangerous. If they see you, they will flee towards the water – so the golden rule is never to get between a hippo and its escape route to deep water. Given that a hippo will outrun you on land, standing motionless is probably your best line of defence.

Snakes Most snakes are really not the great danger that people imagine, and will flee when they feel the vibrations of footsteps; only a few will stay still. The puff adder is probably responsible for more cases of snakebite than any other venomous snake in Boswana because, when approached, it will simply puff itself up and hiss as a warning, rather than slither away. This makes it essential to always watch where you place your feet when walking in the bush.

Similarly, there are a couple of arboreal (tree-dwelling) species which may be taken by surprise if you carelessly grab vegetation as you walk. So don't.

Spitting cobras are also encountered occasionally; they will aim for your eyes and spit with accuracy. If one of these rears up in front of you, then turn away and avert your eyes. If the spittle reaches your eyes, you must wash them out immediately and thoroughly with whatever liquid comes to hand: water, milk or even urine if that's the only liquid that can be quickly produced. See also pages 123–4.

BOATING

Trips on motorboats and mekoro are very much an integral part of a safari trip to northern Botswana – they're both very different, and both a lot of fun. Almost no operators use the paddle-yourself Canadian-style canoes that are popular elsewhere in Africa (Zarafa, Selinda and Motswiri camps are perhaps the exceptions which prove this rule).

BY MOKORO In *Lake Ngami and the River Okavango* (see *Appendix 3, Further information*), the explorer Charles John Andersson describes a mokoro used by him on Lake Ngami in the early 1850s:

> The canoe in which I embarked (and they are all somewhat similarly constructed) was but a miserable craft. It consisted of the trunk of a tree, about 20 feet long, pointed at both ends, and hollowed out by means of fire and a small hatchet. The natives are not at all particular as to the shape of the canoe. The after part of some that have come to my notice, would form an angle of near forty-five degrees with their stem! Nevertheless, they were propelled through the water by the Bayeye (my boatmen were of that nation) with considerable speed and skill.
>
> The 'appointments' of the canoe, consist of a paddle and a pole, ten to twelve feet in length. The paddle-man sits well in the stern, and attends mostly to the steering; whilst his comrade, posted at the head of the canoe, sends her along, by means of the pole, with great force and skill.
>
> The natives, however, rarely venture any distance from the shore in their frail skiffs.

Local inhabitants of the Okavango still use mekoro like this, but for visitors it's more usual to have simply a single poler standing up at the stern and propelling the craft with a long pole. It's very like the punting done at some universities in Britain; a gentle form of locomotion best suited to shallow waters.

Only certain trees are suitable for making mekoro; they must usually be old, straight and strong. Jackalberries (*Diospyros mespiliformis*), sausage trees (*Kigelia africana*) and kiats (*Pterocarpus angolensis*) are favourites, whilst occasionally African mangosteens (*Garcinia livingstoneii*) and rain trees (*Lonchocarpus capassa*) are also used. The wood used to make the poles to propel them is less crucial, though these are often made from silver-leaf terminalia trees (*Terminalia sericea*).

The last few decades have seen a mushrooming demand for mekoro, which began to deplete the older specimens of these species in some areas. Fortunately, fibreglass mekoro, that look very similar, are now being made, and are used by most safari camps today. This is worth encouraging, so if you are given a wooden craft, check with your camp that when it's no longer usable, they intend to replace it with a fibreglass version. The Delta can't afford to lose any of its oldest trees!

BY MOTORBOAT Motorboats are used on the rivers, and in the deeper channels and lagoons of the Okavango. They can be a lot of fun, although – used carelessly – their noise and (especially) their wake can do a lot of damage, so be sensitive to the dangers and don't encourage your guide to speed. (It can be a good idea to state this from the outset.) You'll often see much more by going slowly anyhow.

Interesting variations on this theme include the small, double-decker boat used at Kwara, which affords views out over the top of the papyrus beds, and a similar set-up at Lagoon Camp, which is ideal for sundowner cruises.

THE MAIN DANGERS It's tempting to become concerned about dangerous animals in Africa, but it's foolish to get paranoid. With common sense and a little knowledge, boat and mokoro trips are very safe – certainly no more dangerous than going on a game drive or walking safari. And if these worry you, maybe you shouldn't be heading out into the bush at all!

On motorboat trips, you'd have to try very hard indeed to get into difficulties. Mekoro are also safe, though these craft are smaller and more vulnerable, so you should be aware of the dangers posed to you by hippos and crocodiles.

Hippo are strictly vegetarians, and will usually only attack a mokoro if they feel threatened. Your poler is usually standing up, so he has the best vantage point for spotting potential dangers ahead. It's helpful if you're either silent, or making so much noise that every animal in the bush can hear you approaching!

During the day, hippopotami will usually congregate in deeper water. The odd ones in shallow water, where they feel less secure, will head for the deeper places as soon as they are aware of a nearby mokoro. Avoiding hippos then becomes a fairly simple case of steering around the deeper areas, and sticking to the shallows. This is where the poler's experience, knowing every waterway in the area, becomes valuable.

Really large and deep channels and waterways are seldom a problem, as the hippos can avoid you provided that you make enough noise so that they know you are around. Shallow floodplains are also fairly safe, as you'll see the hippo in advance, and avoid them.

Problems usually occur when mekoro use relatively small and narrow 'hippo trails' where hippos can submerge but can't get away. Then there's a danger of accidentally approaching too close, inadvertently surprising a hippo, and/or cutting it off from its path of retreat to deeper water. Then the hippo feels cornered and threatened, and may even attack. Some camps now send mekoro out in small groups, with an armed guide in the lead mokoro – though others maintain that this isn't necessary.

An angry hippo could overturn a mokoro without a second thought, biting at it and/or its occupants. Once in this situation, there are no easy remedies. So avoid it in the first place.

Crocodiles may have sharp teeth and look prehistoric, but are of little danger to you … unless you are in the water – or very close to the edge. Then the more you struggle and the more waves you create, the more you will attract their unwelcome attentions. They sometimes become an issue when a mokoro is overturned by a hippo; you must get out of the water as soon as possible, either into another canoe or on to the bank.

When a crocodile attacks an animal, it will try to disable it, normally by getting a firm, biting grip, submerging, and performing a long, fast barrel-roll. This will disorient the prey, drown it, and probably twist off the limb that has been bitten. In this dire situation, your best line of defence is probably to stab the reptile in its eyes with anything sharp that you have. Alternatively, if you can lift up its tongue and let the water into its lungs whilst it is underwater, then a crocodile will start to drown and will release its prey.

I have had reliable reports of a man surviving an attack in the Zambezi when a crocodile grabbed his arm and started to spin backwards into deep water. The man wrapped his legs around the crocodile, to spin with it and avoid having his arm twisted off. As this happened, he tried to poke his thumb into its eyes, but with no effect. Finally he put his free arm into the crocodile's mouth, and opened up the beast's throat. This worked. The crocodile left him and he survived with only a damaged arm. Understandably, anecdotes about tried and tested methods of escape are rare.

MINIMUM IMPACT

When you visit, drive through, or camp in an area and have 'minimum impact' upon it, this means that the area is left in the same condition as – or better than – when you entered it. Whilst most visitors view minimum impact as being desirable, do spend time to consider the ways in which we contribute to environmental degradation, and how these can be avoided. Most of these points apply to any areas of rural Africa.

DRIVING Use your vehicle responsibly. If there's a road, or a track, then don't go off it – the environment will suffer. Driving off-road can leave a multitude of tracks that detract from the 'wilderness' feeling for subsequent visitors. Equally, don't speed through towns or villages: remember the danger to local children, and the amount of dust you'll cause.

HYGIENE Use toilets if they are provided, even if they are basic long-drop loos with questionable cleanliness. If there are no toilets, then human excrement should always be buried well away from paths, or groundwater, and any tissue used should be burned and then buried with it.

If you use rivers or lakes to wash, then soap yourself near the bank, using a pan for scooping water from the river – making sure that no soap finds its way back into the water. Use biodegradable soap. Sand makes an excellent pan-scrub, even if you have no water to spare.

RUBBISH Biodegradable rubbish can be burned and buried with the campfire ashes. Don't leave it lying around: it will look very unsightly and spoil the place for those who come after you.

Bring along some plastic bags with which to remove the rest of your rubbish, and dump it at the next large town. Items that will not burn, like tin cans, are best cleaned and squashed for easy carrying. If there are bins, then use them, but also consider when they will next be emptied, and whether local animals will rummage through them first. For this reason, it's probably best not to use the bins at most national parks' campsites; better to carry out all your own rubbish to the nearest town.

HOST COMMUNITIES Whilst the rules for reducing impact on the environment have been understood and followed by responsible travellers for years, the effects of tourism on local people have only recently been considered. Many tourists believe it is their right, for example, to take intrusive photos of local people – and even become angry if the local people object. They refer to higher prices being charged to tourists as a rip-off, without considering the hand-to-mouth existence of those selling these products or services. They deplore child beggars, then hand out sweets or pens to local children with outstretched hands.

Our behaviour towards 'the locals' needs to be considered in terms of their culture, with the knowledge that we are the uninvited visitors. We visit to enjoy ourselves, but this should not be at the expense of local people. Read *Cultural guidelines*, pages 40–1, and aim to leave the local communities better off after your visit.

LOCAL PAYMENTS If you spend time with any of Botswana's more rural communities, perhaps camping in the bush or getting involved with one of the community-run projects, then take great care with any payments that you make.

First, note that most people like to spend their earnings on what they choose. This means that trying to pay for services with beads, food, old clothes or anything else instead of money isn't appreciated. Ask yourself how you'd like to be paid, and you'll understand this point.

Second, find out the normal cost of what you are buying. For example, most community campsites will have a standard price for a pitch. Find out this price before you sleep there. It is then important that you pay about that amount for the pitch – not less, and not too much more.

As most people realise, if you try to pay less you'll get into trouble – as you would at home. However, many do not realise that if they generously pay a lot *more*, this can be equally damaging. Local rates of pay in rural areas can be very low, and a careless visitor can easily pay disproportionately large sums. Where this happens, local jobs can lose their value overnight. (Imagine working hard to become a game scout, only to learn that a tourist has given your friend the equivalent of your whole month's wages for just a few hours' guiding. What incentive is there for you to carry on with your regular job?)

If you want to give more – for good service, a super guide, or just because you want to help – then either buy some locally made produce (at the going rate), or donate money to one of the organisations working to improve the lot of Botswana's most disadvantaged. See pages 112–14 for ideas, but also consider asking around locally and you'll often find projects that need your support.

Many lodges and camps will assist with community projects, and be able to suggest a good use for donations. Increasingly they're becoming more involved in the welfare of the local communities near them, which is something in which you can encourage them.

Part Two

THE GUIDE

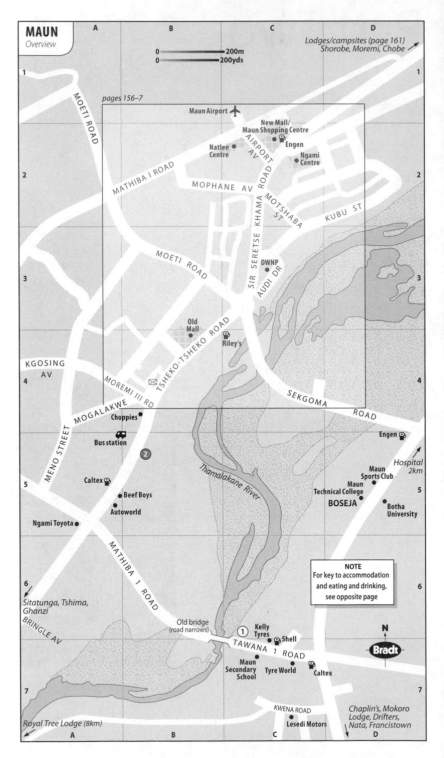

MAUN
Overview

A B C D

Lodges/campsites (page 161)
Shorobe, Moremi, Chobe

0 ——————— 200m
0 ——————— 200yds

pages 156–7

1

MOETI ROAD

Maun Airport ✈

New Mall/
Maun Shopping Centre

MATHIBA I ROAD

Natlee
Centre

Engen

AIRPORT AV

Ngami
Centre

2

MOPHANE AV

SIR SERETSE KHAMA ROAD

MOTSHABA ST

KUBU ST

MOETI ROAD

DWNP

AUDI DR

3

Old
Mall

TSHEKO-TSHEKO ROAD

Riley's

KGOSING
AV

SEKGOMA ROAD

4

MOREMI III RD

MOGALAKWE

Choppies

Bus station

MENO STREET

②

Engen

Hospital
2km

Thamalakane River

Maun
Sports Club

5

Caltex

Beef Boys

Autoworld

Ngami Toyota

Maun
Technical College

BOSEJA

Botha
University

MATHIBA I ROAD

NOTE
For key to accommodation
and eating and drinking,
see opposite page

6

*Sitatunga, Tshima,
Ghanzi*

BRINGLE AV

N

Old bridge
(road narrows)

①

Kelly
Tyres

Shell

Bradt

TAWANA 1 ROAD

Maun
Secondary
School

Tyre World

Caltex

7

Royal Tree Lodge (8km)

KWENA ROAD

Lesedi Motors

*Chaplin's, Mokoro
Lodge, Drifters,
Nata, Francistown*

A B C D

7

Maun

This once-dusty, sprawling town has been the start of expeditions into the wilds since the turn of the century, and it is now the safari capital of the country. Maun's elongated centre is dotted with modern shops and offices, and its suburbs – until recently dominated by traditionally built, thatched rondavels – glint in the sun reflecting off tin-roofed houses.

In the 1980s everywhere and everything here seemed geared towards the tourism bonanza. Maun had a rough-and-ready frontier feel, as contemporary cowboys rode into town from the bush in battered 4x4s. Its focal points were the camps north of town – Island Safari Lodge, Crocodile Camp, Okavango River Lodge – and the old Duck Inn opposite the airport.

Then, as Maun became the administrative centre for the northern and western parts of Botswana, government departments moved here en masse. The town's roads became sealed tar, rather than pot-holed gravel tracks, which opened the door to an influx of saloon cars from the rest of the country. Finally the tourism product itself changed. The pendulum swung away from last-minute budget trips bought in Maun, to upmarket safaris bought in advance from overseas. The new breed of visitors just change planes here; they seldom spend more than a few hours at Maun Airport.

However, for those who are driving themselves, Maun remains a centre to get organised, and perhaps a place to look at what cheaper safari options are available. It also offers an increasing number of activities to interest those who may find themselves with time on their hands between flights, or who are stopping over here before or after a safari.

GETTING THERE AND AWAY

Maun is 950m (3,100ft) above sea level, and fairly easy to reach, however you are travelling.

BY AIR

Scheduled services Maun is well connected by scheduled domestic and international flights, although you can expect frequent changes to the timetables. Air Botswana connects with Johannesburg daily, and with Gaborone daily, and with Cape Town twice a week, on Thursday and Sunday. They also have at least one flight a day to Gaborone, but their service to Kasane is limited to Tuesday and Thursday only.

Flights with SA Airlink between Maun and Johannesburg operate daily in each direction.

Air Namibia schedules four flights a week between Windhoek and Maun, though these are frequently sold out far in advance. Note also that there are inherent risks in relying on these flights to fit in with a complex, 'fixed' trip itinerary in both countries, as the schedules for them can, and do, change relatively regularly.

✈ **Air Botswana** [156 E2] Airport Av; ✆686 0391; www.airbotswana.co.bw. It's generally easier to reconfirm flights & make further arrangements at their main reservations office, near the corner with Sir Seretse Khama Rd, than at the airport.

✈ **Air Namibia** ✆686 0391/0762; www. airnamibia.aero
✈ **SA Airlink** ✆390 5740; www.flysaa.com

Charter airlines Maun also has a number of air charter companies, where you can hire light aircraft for private flights and transfers. These can sometimes be economical if you have four or five people travelling together. I include these and their contact details not because you need to ever book your own flights between the camps; you don't. That's always done for you by the camps concerned, or your tour operator back home; it's better that way. However, you may want to contact them in case of emergency or to take a pleasure flight over the Delta, or even to charter a plane somewhere fairly unusual – like the Tsodilo Hills for the day!

BANA BA LETSATSI   *Tricia Hayne*

To the casual observer, Botswana's society appears to retain much of its traditional, close-knit fabric based on strong family and community ties. Yet currently one in five children are orphans, and because of HIV/AIDS the number of orphaned and vulnerable children in Botswana is rising each year.

When Emily Cusack was working as a nurse in Maun in 2002, she noticed small numbers of children begging on the streets rather than being in school or at home. From her own resources, she set about entertaining them, collecting them up in a borrowed pick-up truck for a couple of hours' activities. Today, the organisation that she founded, Bana Ba Letsatsi (the Sunshine Children: *PO Box HA55 HAK, Maun;* ✆ *686 4787;* m *7264 3468;* e *info@banabaletsatsi.org; www.banabaletsatsi. org*) has over 200 children on its register, aged from two to 21. It comes as a shock to learn that many of the children on the streets are there because begging from tourists is lucrative. They have learned that they can earn enough each day to buy a few tins of glue to sniff and get high, so they see no reason to go to school. Thus the booming safari industry and resulting tourists unwittingly encourage the children to live on the streets.

The children at Bana Ba Letsatsi have often never been to school, or have dropped out, and the charity focuses strongly on education as a means of rehabilitating them. Many are victims of sexual or physical abuse at home or on the streets; they work under age, abuse drugs and alcohol, and beg.

The day begins at 06.30 with the youngest children being picked up, while the others walk to the centre. Here, preparations are made for showers, breakfast, packed lunches and uniforms. Non-formal education begins, children go to school and the carers start sewing and weaving in the workshop or tending to the

Note that booking inter-camp flights through the camps is invariably cheaper than chartering them directly with the airlines. For rough guidance, a five-seater plane (six if you include the pilot!) and an hour's flying time costs around P3,750 (US$430). These basic prices will usually vary very little between the various companies. For details of scenic flights, see page 172.

✈ **Air Shakawe** [156 C2] Mathiba I Rd; ☎686 3620

✈ **Delta Air** [156 E1] Mathiba I Rd; ☎686 0044/1682; e schedules@deltabotswana.com; www.okavango.bw/air. Delta Air has a close association with Lodges of Botswana & usually operates transfers for their camps as well as charter services including pleasure flights over the Delta.

✈ **Helicopter Horizons** [156 C2] Apollo Hse, Mophane Av; ☎686 1186; e info@ helicopterhorizons.com; www.helicopterhorizons. com

✈ **Kavango Air** [156 D1] Maun Airport; ☎686 0323; e aggie@kavangoair.com; www.kavangoair. com. Scenic flights over the Delta.

✈ **Mack Air** [156 D1] Natlee Centre, Mathiba I Rd, ☎686 0675; e reservations@mackair.co.bw;

www.mackair.co.bw. Mack Air maintains a good reputation as a reliable, high-quality air charter company which doesn't have ties to any of the camps. Their planes are 2-, 5-, 7- & 13-seaters, with the smaller planes (allowing a window seat for everyone) also used for scenic flights.

✈ **Major Blue Air** [156 D2] Natlee Centre, Mathiba I Rd; ☎686 5671; e info@majorblueair. com; www.majorblueair.com. Established in 2010, Major Blue operates camp transfers & scenic flights in 3-, 5- & 7-seater planes.

✈ **Moremi Air** [156 D1] Maun Airport; ☎686 3632; e info@moremialr.com; www.moremiair. com. Based upstairs in the main airport building, & linked with Kwando Safaris, this is another charter specialist. Their fleet of 4-, 5- & 9-seater aircraft is geared to both passenger transfers & scenic flights.

vegetable gardens. At lunchtime a meal is served to all the children. Afternoons are spent doing homework with the teachers, in sessions with the counsellors, playing football, receiving medical attention, washing clothes, or doing creative activities. As few of the children have an evening meal at home, a snack is served before they leave.

During the school holidays the centre tries to introduce the children to new experiences, such as going into the Delta to see the wildlife or going on camping trips in to the pans. In a country whose major attraction is its wildlife, most of these youngsters have never seen an elephant, or indeed been near the national parks.

As well as working with the younger children, Bana Ba Letsatsi also runs a successful youth programme for those over 17, offering training in plumbing, carpentry, hospitality or cooking. On completion, the charity works hard to gain them work experience and ultimately employment.

Bana Ba Letsatsi receives no funding from the government, so donations and sponsorship are much appreciated. So, too, are offers of help: the charity welcomes skilled volunteers, preferably for at least six months, but all expenses need to be covered by the volunteer. And if you find yourself with room in your luggage, perhaps you could take something for the Sunshine Children: they would welcome the normal family basics, such as underwear, T-shirts or shorts; plasters and hygiene materials; footballs; pens and pencils. Just phone ahead or – if time isn't on your side – you could drop items at the Ker & Downey office opposite the airport, or call Ruth Stewart at Travel for Impact (m 7230 7694), whose office is further down the same road. How much more rewarding than putting children on the streets in the first place.

✈ Safari Air [156 E1] Mathiba I Rd; `686 0385; e reservations@safariair.co.bw; www.desertdelta. com. Located in the Ker & Downey Botswana complex, opposite the airport, the company operates transfers to their lodges in Botswana in single-engined Airvans, Cessna 206s & Cessna Caravans. They have links with the safari company, Desert & Delta Safaris.

✈ Wilderness Air [156 E1] Mathiba I Rd; `686 0778; e ops@wilderness-air.co.bw; www. wilderness-air.com. Owned by Wilderness Safaris, & based inside the airport gates, Wilderness Air organises virtually all the flights in Botswana for clients to Wilderness camps, making them the biggest 'small' airline here. In an emergency, if they're not available on the number above, try getting hold of them via Wilderness Safaris (page 177).

Maun Airport

[156 D1] On the north side of town, Maun's airport is just a stone's throw from many of the local safari operators, and equally close to a number of bars, restaurants, shops and other facilities.

Following construction of a longer runway to facilitate the arrival of larger planes, there are plans to construct a new terminal building, though no date has yet been set for this. So, for now, the airport remains small and very relaxed, with none of the hassle you sometimes find at larger hubs. Alongside a couple of check-in desks downstairs is a bureau de change, though rates are not the greatest. Avis and Budget both have a presence here, as does Botswana Tourism, where various leaflets are on display. There's also a desk for Okavango Air Rescue (see page 120). Upstairs, there's still a post-office counter, but the café has been closed for some time; try Bon Arrivée just outside the airport gate instead.

The airport itself has no left-luggage facility, but if you're passing through to visit camps in the region by light aircraft, most safari companies will collect any spare baggage from you, and return it to you as you leave.

DRIVING OR HITCHHIKING Ignoring the odd tiny bush track, there are only three significant roads linking Maun with the rest of the country:

Northeast towards Kasane Routing right through Chobe National Park, it's about 360km of bush and thick sand (accessible only by 4x4) northeast to Kasane. For details of this track, through Shorobe to Moremi and Chobe, see *The road north of Maun: to Moremi and Chobe*, at the end of this chapter.

Southwest towards Ghanzi and Namibia It's about 286km of good tar road to Ghanzi, and thence to the Namibian border. About 2.5km beyond the Ngami Toyota garage, you'll pass the Maun Sports Complex on your left (page 172). If you're hitchhiking then consider catching a bus or taxi, or walking this far out as it'll get you beyond most of the local traffic.

East towards Nata and Francistown Nata is about 305km due east, again along a good tar road which crosses between the Nxai Pan and Makgadikgadi Pans national parks. The road crosses the 24-hour police and veterinary control post north of Makalamabedi. Note that you cannot take any red meat through this checkpoint if you're heading east. If you're hitching, then at least cross to the south side of the Thamalakane River as far as the Caltex service station. Then, if you prefer, continue for a few kilometres south until the road starts to bend west and you're beyond the outskirts and the local traffic.

BY BUS Maun's smart new bus station on Tsheko-Tsheko Road [150 A5] has replaced its chaotic predecessor close to the local market. Street vendors have been quick to take advantage of the concrete shelters, selling drinks from colourful coolboxes to thirsty travellers, but otherwise there are few amenities. There are regular departures for the major destinations, stopping at most of the larger towns on the way. The first buses leave at around 05.30, then regularly through the morning, but do check times beforehand, and arrive early. Larger bus companies include JNG Express, Golden Bridge Express and Seabelo Express (✎ *395 7078; www.seabelo.bw*).

Francistown	7hrs, P105 one way; departures between 06.30 & 9.30
Gaborone	10hrs, P195 one way; departures between 05.30 & 11.00
Ghanzi	4hrs, P62 one way; departures at 07.30, 08.30 & 15.30
Shakawe	4½–7hrs, around P89 one way, depending on the company. Departures between 05.30 & 16.30; quickest is Golden Bridge Express leaving at around 08.00.

To reach **Kasane**, hop on a bus towards Francistown and change at Nata.

ORIENTATION

Finding your way around Maun is relatively simple. Though the town straddles the Thamalakane River, most places of interest are on the north bank. Here there are two focal points: the airport area, and the area around Riley's Garage, further south. For the purposes of distances in this guide, we have taken Riley's Garage as the centre of Maun.

MAPS Though Maun has grown a lot in recent years, there have until recently been few good maps of the place apart from the town planners' survey maps, which are too detailed for most purposes, and the maps in this book. However, the new *Maun Guide* (P45) has eight pages of useful maps, so could be worth the investment if you're staying in town for any length of time.

If you want to head anywhere 'off-piste' in Botswana's bush, then there are a couple of options. The Shell maps, by Veronica Roodt, have become the standard references for most travellers, and are sold in most curio shops and garages in Maun. Alternatively, for more traditional survey maps at a range of scales, seek out the **Department of Surveys & Mapping** [156 E2] (*Airport Av;* ✎ *686 0272;* ☉ *07.30–12.45 & 13.45–16.30 Mon–Fri*), the blue-and-white building just to the right of the Air Botswana office; the entrance is round the back. Even if you're not exploring, the large 1:350,000 map of the Okavango Delta makes a great souvenir – though many of the camps on it are long gone. Laminated versions of many of the survey maps are available from Jacana Enterprises (page 16); otherwise, these maps can normally be found only in Gaborone.

TOURIST INFORMATION Botswana Tourism [156 C2] (*Apollo Hse, Mophane Av;* ✎ *686 1056, airport* ✎ *686 3093;* e *maun@botswanatourism.co.bw;* ☉ *07.30–18.00 Mon–Fri, 09.00–14.00 Sat*) has a new office close to the airport, and another within the airport building.

The local newspaper, *The Ngami Times* (*www.ngamitimes.com*), is published weekly at P5, and is useful for details of local sports and entertainment. Like the *Maun Guide* (above), it's available from outlets across town, including the shop at Riley's Garage.

GETTING AROUND

If you're around the centre, between the airport and Riley's, then walking is hot but feasible. Otherwise, you'll need some form of transport, most of which operates

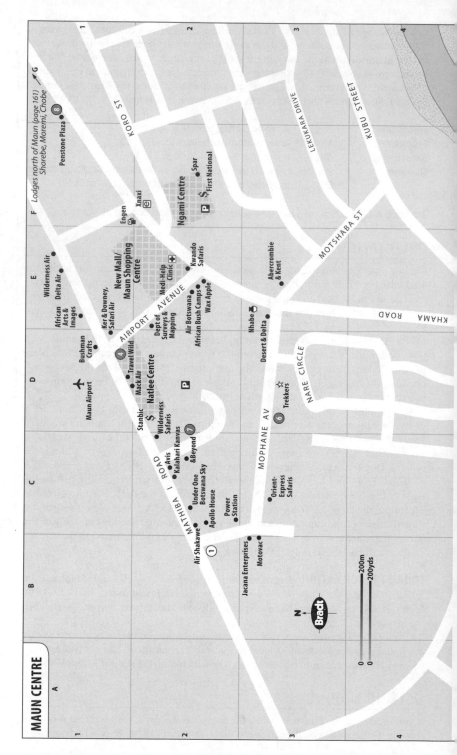

MAUN CENTRE

Lodges north of Maun (page 161)
Shorebe, Moremi, Chobe

Penstone Plaza 8

KORO ST

Wilderness Air
Delta Air

African
Arts &
Images

Ker & Downey,
Safari Air

New Mall/
Maun Shopping
Centre

Engen

Xnaxi

Ngami Centre

Spar

First National

Medi-Help
Clinic

Kwando
Safaris

Bushman
Crafts

Maun Airport

Travel Wild

Mack Air

Natlee Centre

AIRPORT   AVENUE

Dept of
Surveys &
Mapping

Air Botswana

African Bush Camps

Wax Apple

Abercrombie
& Kent

MOTSHABA ST

LEKUKARA DRIVE

KUBU STREET

Stanbic

Wilderness
Safaris

Kalahari Kanvas

Avis

Under One
Botswana Sky

Apollo House

Power
Station

Air Shakawe 1

Jacana Enterprises

Motovac

Orient-
Express
Safaris

MOPHANE AV

Nhabe

Desert & Delta

Trekkers 6

NARE CIRCLE

KHAMA   ROAD

Brack

N

0   200m
0   200yds

7

4

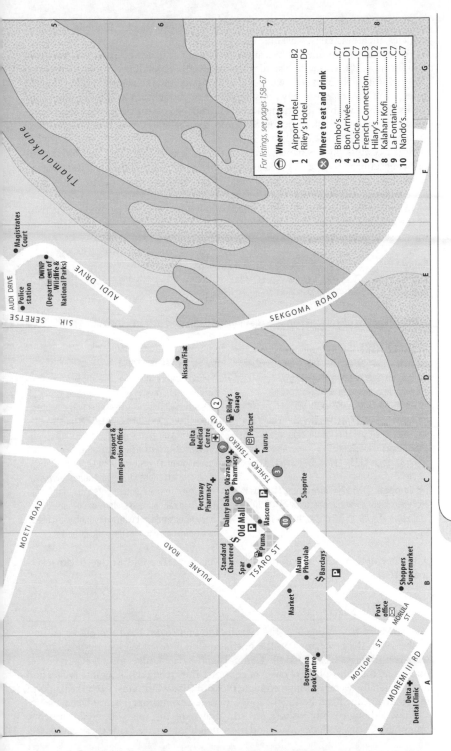

For listings, see pages 158–67

Where to stay

1	Airport Hotel	B2
2	Riley's Hotel	D6

Where to eat and drink

3	Bimbo's	C7
4	Bon Arrivée	D1
5	Choice	C7
6	French Connection	D3
7	Hilary's	D2
8	Kalahari Kofi	G1
9	La Fontaine	C7
10	Nando's	C7

Maun GETTING AROUND

7

out of the new bus station [150 A5] on Tsheko-Tsheko Road. All public-transport vehicles, including taxis, have blue number plates.

For a **taxi** out to one of the camps to the north of town, expect to pay from P40 (or more if there's a long sand track involved), depending on your negotiating powers. If it's a shared taxi – when the driver stops to take another lift at the same time – you can expect to pay considerably less, though not as little as one of the locals. Taxis have their telephone numbers displayed on the doors, and can be pre-booked. If in doubt, ask someone you know for a reliable contact number, as these tend to change all too frequently.

Small **combis** ply frequently between the back of the new bus station and the outlying suburbs. Typically, vehicles leave only when full, but they will drop you on request. Fares are fixed at just a few pula – from the bus station out to Audi Camp, for example, costs about P4.

In theory there are ten clearly defined routes, with numbers painted on the front of the vehicles, but not all were operational at the end of 2013. For the visitor, the most useful routes are as follows:

Route 1	Airport, & north as far as Audi Camp
Route 5	Maun Lodge
Route 7	Letsholathebe II Memorial Hospital

Hitchhiking is also viable on the main arteries in and around town.

VEHICLE HIRE

🚗 **Avis** [156 C2] Mathiba I Rd; ☎686 0039; m 7583 6018; e avismun@botsnet.bw, botswanares@avis.co.za; www.avis.co.za; ⏰ 08.00–13.00 & 14.00–17.00 Mon–Fri. 4x4 hire (group N) from P761 per day, based on 3 days, plus insurance & rate per km (150km inc).

🚗 **Budget** [156 D2] Natlee Centre, Airport Av; ☎686 3728; m 7133 1114; www.budget.co.za; ⏰ 08.00–17.00 Mon–Fri

🚗 **Europcar** [156 D2] Natlee Centre, Mathiba I Rd; ☎686 3366; www.europcar.co.za; ⏰ 07.30–17.00 Mon–Fri, 08.00–12.00 Sat, 16.00–18.00 Sun

🚗 **Maun Self Drive 4x4** ☎686 1875; e info@maunselfdrive4x4.com, info@botswanaselfdrive4x4.com. Also trading as McKenzie Self Drive 4x4, they offer fully equipped camping vehicles with suggested itineraries & the promise of a breakdown service as back-up.

🚗 **Travel Adventures Botswana** (see advert, 3rd colour insert, page ii) ☎686 1211; m 7231 1132; e reservations@traveladventuresbotswana.com; www.traveladventuresbotswana.com. Toyota Hilux twin cabs or Land Cruisers can be rented as they are, or kitted out with everything you'll need for a camping safari into the national parks.

A further option is to hire a 4x4 with driver from The Old Bridge Backpackers (page 164).

 # WHERE TO STAY

Just as Maun has changed in the last decade or two, so have the places to stay. In the 1980s the few camps on the northern side of town felt like outposts in the wilderness. Places like Crocodile Camp, Island Safari Lodge and Okavango River Lodge had the atmosphere of oases of comfort. They seemed like remote lodges and often, when the water was high enough, mokoro trips would start from the banks of the Thamalakane River beside the lodge, to pole adventurers into the Delta.

Now, although many visitors are still drawn to the riverside establishments, times have changed. Better roads and more neighbours have made these camps feel less isolated and more a part of Maun. Less water in the river has for many years put an end to mokoro trips starting in Maun (although since the floods of 2009, transfers have been made by motorboat). Whereas visitors (especially backpackers) used to stop for at least a night in Maun, now many simply transit briefly through the airport to fly in to a safari camp.

Yet while these fine old camps have lost much of their atmosphere, they may still be more interesting than some of the rather bland hotels that have sprung up to serve the business market. More appealing than these is a handful of small-scale ventures that have breathed new life into the accommodation scene: most recently a clutch of small self-catering establishments. Conversely, most of the new B&Bs – with the notable exception of Discovery B&B – are basic and functional, and are too far outside the centre of town to be of interest to tourists.

If you're driving yourself, do be aware that signposts for some establishments only face south, so keep a watchful eye out for any pre-booked accommodation.

HOTELS

The distinction between hotels & lodges is more one of style than of substance. Those listed here include several that have 'lodge' in their name, but which in my view fall within the concept of a hotel in terms of either facilities or simply ambience. Establishments in Maun are normally open throughout the year.

⌂ **Riley's Hotel** [175 D6] (51 rooms) Tsheko-Tsheko Rd; ☎686 0204; e resrileys@cresta.co.bw; www.cresta-hospitality.com. Riley's has always been more of an institution than a hotel. It was founded when Harry Riley arrived in Maun, in 1910. Initially he simply built an extra rondavel next to his own, suitable for one visitor. It had no bed, just reed matting on the floor. A few years later he joined the 2 rondavels together, building a simple dining room between them, & soon he was running Maun's first hotel. In his book *The Lost World of the Kalahari*, Laurens van der Post described Riley's in the 1950s as a 'remarkable little hotel which he [Harry Riley] had founded for the odd, intrepid traveller who had been determined enough to cross the desert, as well as for the score or so of Europeans patient & courageous enough to make Maun the unique outpost of life that it is today'.

Now those first buildings form part of the manager's house, & Riley's is owned by the Cresta group. For the visitor, Riley's has a central location on the main street, & the added benefit of a lovely outdoor swimming pool & pool bar, surrounded by lawns with tables under thatched umbrellas, & a children's play area. Much-needed refurbishment in 2009 saw transformation of 36 rooms, with dark-wood contemporary furniture, leather bed

bases, AC & DSTV, & spruced-up bathrooms. Prices are the same for these as for the older ones, which – together with the rather dingy bar & restaurant – must wait their turn for an upgrade until 2014, when the addition of a gym is also planned. **$$$$**

⌂ **Airport Hotel** [156 B2] (39 rooms, 2 suites) Mathiba I Rd; ☎686 5454; e reservations@airporthotelmaun.com; www. airporthotelmaun.com. Corporate in style, this 2-star hotel catering for the business market couldn't be more handy for the airport: it's almost opposite what is anticipated to be the entrance when the new terminal opens. En-suite rooms are rather stark & functional, with a dbl bed, AC, TV, kettle, fridge & safe – in short, all that you need, but nothing more. There's a bar & restaurant, & free Wi-Fi throughout, but the rather clinical feel isn't helped by a leopard skin draped over a couch in the lobby. **$$$** *exc b/fast (P60–90)*.

⌂ **Sedia Hotel** [map 161] (24 rooms, 8 chalets, camping) Sir Seretse Khama Rd; ☎686 0177; e sedia@info.bw; www.sedia-hotel.com. The attractive, wide-fronted Sedia, with its cream & ochre walls & deep-red blinds, occupies extensive grounds 6km north of Maun, to the east of the main road. Once dubbed the 'Sedi Motel', it has gradually moved upmarket & expanded since the early 1990s. Now, although not quite as costly as Riley's or Maun Lodge, it has a livelier, more colourful atmosphere.

The recently refurbished foyer is all traditional African wall-hangings & squashy sofas, complete with large wooden hippo. Most of the rooms are laid out along 2 wings facing into the hotel's gardens, each with its own outside entrance.

Bright ethnic colours adorn twin or dbl beds, & each room has AC & ceiling fan, tea/coffee station, TV & phone; modern, en-suite bathrooms incorporate a bath with shower. Larger chalets closer to the river boast a fridge & kitchenette (but no cooking facilities), AC, lounge with TV & a shady veranda.

At the back of the hotel, set among gardens with large lawns, is one of the area's best swimming pools, which is now exclusively for hotel & campsite guests. The surrounding decking is a popular venue for dining or just for a drink, while the more formal restaurant comes into its own in the winter. There is also a lively bar with 2 pool tables, & a children's playground.

Beyond the lawns, a large & sprawling campsite leads down to the Thamalakane River, where campers share 5 well-kept showers & toilets. There is plenty of tree shade for your own tent, or their pre-erected tents, which have 2 beds, a table, chair & power point, plus a small, shaded veranda. It's possible to park next to your tent, particularly useful as the campsite isn't well fenced & security didn't seem that tight when I last stayed there, despite the presence of a nightwatchman. (With good locks on the room doors, this wasn't a problem for those staying in the hotel.)

The hotel is the base for Afro Trek (page 179), who operate a variety of budget safaris & mokoro trips. **$$$** *Camping P50 pp; tent P350 dbl.*

🏠 **Maun Lodge** [map 161] (140 rooms, 12 chalets) Tawana I Rd, Boseja; 📞686 3939; e maun.lodge@info.bw; www.maunlodge.com. Massive expansion in 2013 has transformed this established place on the banks of the Thamalakane River into Maun's largest hotel. By & large it does a good job, with friendly staff who try hard.

The high entrance lobby is enhanced by a colourful wall hangings & a trendy metal sculpture of pelicans, but most of the en-suite rooms are rather bland. Twin beds, tea/coffee-making facilities, AC, TV, phone & safe come as standard; newer rooms have a bath or shower, while older ones have a shower over the bath. Similar in style, & particularly good value, are brick-&-thatch chalets, which lack the phone, but have their own parking spaces, with these & the car park patrolled by security guards. (We have, though, received recent reports of theft from the rooms in the main hotel.) More expensive are options overlooking the river, including 2 family chalets & the presidential suite.

A rather formal cocktail bar, restaurant & conference centre are balanced by a small pool & the more appealing open-air Boma bar. Guests may order from a range of light meals here, or from the restaurant's à-la-carte menu, which includes grills, vegetarian options & some local dishes. Live music is played on Wed & Fri. **$$–$$$** *exc b/fast (P115 pp).*

🏠 **Kamanga Safari Hotel** [map 161] (15 rooms) off Sir Seretse Khama Rd; 📞686 4121; e lodge@kamangaonline.com; www.kamangaonline.com. Set back some 200m from the main road, near the Sports Bar, this spotless modern hotel painted in earthy brown opened in 2006. Overlooking a pool set in a small patch of lawn, its en-suite rooms, in 2 blocks, are nicely finished with dbl or twin beds, shower &/or bath, AC, kettle, fridge & TV. There's a restaurant that's open for all meals, a TV lounge with exceptionally elaborate armchairs, & free Wi-Fi throughout – yet somehow it's all rather soulless. The lodge is the base for a tour company under the same name. **$$**

🏠 **Mokoro Lodge** [off 150 D7] (36 rooms) 📞680 0551; m 7175 2728; www.mokorolodge.com. ✪ MOKLOD 20°01.646'S, 23°26.255'E. Out of town on the Nata road, 3.4km from Riley's, this simple but modern motel is set back from the road, with good security. It's primarily a conference venue, but would be a reasonable place to spend the night if you're passing through. Twin & dbl en-suite rooms have all the essentials, plus AC, DSTV, a kitchenette & no-nonsense bathroom. More important for self-drivers is the covered parking space next to the room. **$$** *exc b/fast.*

LODGES AND CAMPS While some of the places featured here fall neatly into the category of lodges, others have been moved to reflect their growing emphasis on chalet accommodation as against their campsites – although several also have excellent camping facilities.

🏠 **Royal Tree Lodge** [off 150 A7] (10 tents, 2 chalets) 📞680 0757; e treelodge@botsnet.bw; www.royaltreelodge.com; ✪ TREELO 20°03.896'S, 23°22.881'E. About half an hour from Maun, the former Motsentsela Tree Lodge is set on a 2km² game farm, a pleasant halfway house between the town & the bush. All profits from the lodge go towards the work of Love Botswana Outreach Mission.

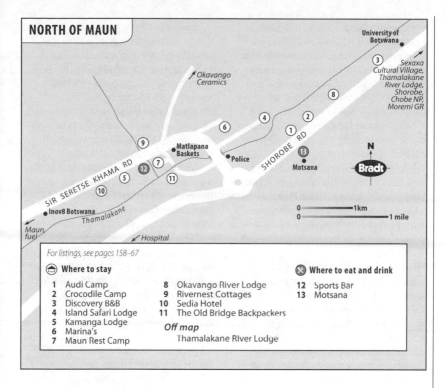

NORTH OF MAUN

University of Botswana

(3) Sexaxa
Cultural Village,
Thamalakane
River Lodge,
Shorobe,
Chobe NP,
Moremi GR

Okavango Ceramics

(8)

(4) (2)
(6)   (1)

(9)   Matlapana
           Baskets   SHOROBE RD
(7)   Police
SIR SERETSE KHAMA RD (12)
(5)   (11)   (13)
(10)   Motsana

Inov8 Botswana
Thamalakane

Maun
fuel   Hospital

N

Bradt

0   1km
0   1 mile

For listings, see pages 158–67

🛏 **Where to stay**

1 Audi Camp
2 Crocodile Camp
3 Discovery B&B
4 Island Safari Lodge
5 Kamanga Lodge
6 Marina's
7 Maun Rest Camp

8 Okavango River Lodge
9 Rivernest Cottages
10 Sedia Hotel
11 The Old Bridge Backpackers

Off map
Thamalakane River Lodge

🍴 **Where to eat and drink**

12 Sports Bar
13 Motsana

Most visitors are collected from the airport & stay just 1 night. Self-drivers, who must have a reservation, will be given directions & the gate code at the time of reservation; you cannot just turn up here. As a guide, leave Maun on the road to Francistown, taking the 1st turning right at the Caltex garage into Kwena Rd (signposted to Land Rover & the lodge). Just before the tar road becomes a dirt track, turn left through a residential area & follow the signs more or less straight for about 8km until you reach a large sign for the lodge. Go right here, leading to a locked gate; beyond, a track to the lodge leads through the farm, stocked with giraffe, zebra, kudu, springbok, impala, oryx, eland & ostrich.

The elongated central building combines a well-designed bar, lounge & dining area, all under thatch. Meals are taken at a communal table, or outside on an extensive deck shaded by trees, & regularly visited by a family of genets. Paths lead to a small pool, & on to large Meru-style tents on stilts, which are dotted around among the trees. Each is accessed from a veranda through a solid door, with mesh windows allowing a through breeze. Inside, set on a varnished wooden floor,

large twin beds with copious cushions recline under a central ceiling fan. Behind, the open-plan bathroom features a dbl vanity unit, a clawfoot bath & semi-private toilet, & outside is a well-screened open-air shower. 2 honeymoon suites follow a different mould – spacious & stylish, these are solid-walled affairs with AC, tiled floors, gecko-printed white drapes & a couple of armchairs. Their bathrooms with deep bath & outside shower are modern yet entirely in keeping, & sliding patio doors lead to a small veranda at the back.

A series of marked walking trails wends through the grounds & down to the river, affording opportunities to watch game or check out the birds; to date, some 400 species have been identified here. Riders of all abilities can take to the saddle on the farm (US40/hr), which is the Maun base for Ride Botswana (page 179), while those interested in the mission's work can ask to visit the orphanage, or even volunteer their time for a few hours or more. Further afield, mokoro trails can also be organised, as can day trips to Moremi Game Reserve with the lodge's own guide. **$$$$–$$$$$** *US$255–300 FB, inc transfers from Maun; sgl supp't US$90.*

🏠 **Crocodile Camp** [map 161] (15 chalets, camping) Shorobe Rd, Maun; m 7560 6864; e sales@crocodilecamp.com; www.crocodilecamp.com. 'Croc Camp' as it's universally known is one of the old institutions of Maun, on a site sloping down to the river some 15km north of town. Its en-suite twin-bedded chalets, set at the top of the site, were once impressive, with imaginative curved walls, mosquito nets, a sofa & ceiling fan, but by 2013, lack of maintenance was taking its toll, There are older chalets, too, also en suite & with mains electricity. Near the car park, a separate campsite with a modern ablution block is set under a few shady camelthorn (*Acacia erioloba*) trees. Some pitches benefit from individual water & power supplies, & overland trucks have their own discrete area.

The camp's thatched bar, overlooking the Thamalakane River, remains a great place for a sundowner, & the swimming pool set in shaded lawns dotted with tables & chairs makes a good spot for families. Less appealing is the restaurant (🕐 06.30–22.00), tucked away from the river. A range of activities can be booked, including motorboat & mokoro trips starting from the camp. **$$$$** *Camping US$15 pp.*

🏠 **Thamalakane River Lodge** [off map 161] (18 rooms, 2 tents, camping) Shorobe Rd; 📞 680 0217; m 7327 3700; e reservations@thamalakane.com; www.thamalakane.com; ⊕ THAMAL 19°53.362'S, 23°33.412'E. Opened in 2007 as Lehututu Lodge, this riverside hotel, some 19km north of the town, has one of the most attractive settings in Maun. That said, in late 2013 the place was looking a little jaded, & though staff remain helpful, it's clear that standards have slipped. The good news is that a change of ownership is said to be imminent, so it's reasonable to anticipate that things will start to look up.

Paths wend through the gently sloping site to twin, dbl & family chalets, set quite close together among well-tended gardens. Stone walls, steeply thatched roofs, tiled floors & ceiling fans help to mitigate the sun's rays, but in the cheaper rooms, glazed sliding doors afford little privacy – even in the shower. On the other side of the plot, a small campsite has a tiled ablution block, & is likely to be extended in 2014. All guests may use the pool set among lawns, & activities in & around Maun can be organised. The lodge can also organise in-room massage.

Popular locally is the restaurant, an open-sided thatched building that spills on to a tree-shaded terrace by the river. With options from steak & seafood to pizzas & vegetarian dishes, there's plenty of choice, but you may need to make a reservation. **$$$$** *Camping US$20 pp.*

🏠 **Island Safari Lodge** [map 161] (12 chalets, 10 rooms, camping) Sir Seretse Khama Rd; 📞 686 0300; m 7332 6719; e isl@africansecrets.net; www.islmaun.com. Island Safari Lodge was a well-established hub when I first visited Maun in 1988, & is now back in the hands of the original owners. It stands in 116ha beside the western bank of the Thamalakane River about 12km north of Maun, under a forest canopy dominated by tall sycamore figs (*Ficus sycomorus*). Coming from Maun you take a well-signposted left turn just before the river, pass through the security gate, then follow a track for almost 2km through old riverine forest (perfectly navigable for 2WD vehicles).

Accommodation is in twin-bedded thatched chalets, set among lawns & indigenous vegetation close to the river. All have AC, sisal flooring, TV, tea/coffee facilities, & en-suite shower – & a bench outside from which to contemplate the sunset. 2 chalets are suitable for disabled visitors. Further back are 6 new 'standard' rooms & the older budget rooms. The shady campsite has 2 ablution blocks, & there are dedicated spaces for overland trucks around the perimeter.

Landscaped gardens lead down to the river, where meals are served in the long bar/restaurant (🕐 06.00–22.00) with sports TV for entertainment, & free Wi-Fi. Cooling off is easy, with a small pool close to the restaurant, & a far larger one by the campsite. Further afield, the lodge can organise boat trips at P119/hr pp (based on 4 people), as well as day trips to Moremi & mokoro excursions. **$$$** *Camping P80 pp.*

🏠 **Marina's** [map 161] (9 rondavels, 2 rooms) Sir Seretse Khama Rd, Maun; 📞 680 1231; e marinas@dynabyte.bw; www.marinascamp.com. Motswana Marina & her Australian husband opened their innovative lodge about 8km north of Maun in 2002, although they no longer run it themselves – so standards & rates can & do vary. Large, well-designed rondavels have dbl, twin or family accommodation with fans & mosquito nets, & en-suite shower & toilet. Two spacious but basic budget rooms sharing a bathroom were added simply to bring the quota up to 11 – the minimum required to be allowed to run a bar & restaurant. Plans to build a campsite were scuppered by the return of water to the Thamalakane – but the new river frontage is now a big plus!

The circular theme continues with the outside bar, & a giant dining rondavel draped with colourful wall hangings, whose ingenious upper balcony would make a great place for alfresco dining – if it's ever completed. For good measure, there's a large pool, & a firepit to guard against the winter chill. **$$$**

B&BS AND SELF-CATERING
As Maun benefits from an increasing range of shops, cafés & restaurants, self-catering has been added to the accommodation mix, alongside a more established & particularly attractive B&B. Often such establishments are too far off the beaten track for visitors, or too far from somewhere to eat, but 2 fulfil both of these needs.

🏠 **Rivernest Cottages** [map 161] (10 rooms) Sir Seretse Khama Rd; ☏ 684 0400; 📱 7149 2623; e rivernestmaun@gmail. com; www.rivernestmaun.com. The name 'cottages' does little to describe this pleasant but unassuming place, set on a compact plot just off the main road, with free Wi-Fi throughout. Built around a small pool, each of its 5 modern chalets incorporates 2 rooms, which have their own lounge area, TV & kitchenette, & an en-suite bedroom with a dbl or twin beds. Guests can relax at the bar with a drink, & meals can be brought in by arrangement, but for a bit of life head for the Sports Bar, just a stone's throw across the road. **$$$** exc b/fast.

🏠 **Discovery Bed & Breakfast** [map 161] (9 chalets) Shorobe Rd; 📱 7244 8298; e discoverybookings@gmail.com; www. discoverybedandbreakfast.com. A taste of Botswana's culture comes to life in this quiet, attractively planted complex, about 17km north of Maun down a 300m track to the west of the main road. Individual wood-framed rondavels, painted inside & out in traditional patterns of browns, ochres, deep reds & greens, are set on a sandy plot around a firepit, in the form of a local village. Inside are twin beds with side lights & a mosquito net, with a toilet & basin behind a reed screen, & open-air showers planned for 2014; until then, there are communal showers in a separate

rondavel. This original 'village' has been extended to a further 4 en-suite chalets in similar style, but with small verandas. Their beds are of rustic wooden poles swathed in mosquito netting, & 1 chalet has a 3rd bed in the roof area. The reception area doubles as a homely b/fast room, & there's a small pool at the back. Sadly, evening meals are no longer available, but there are several options nearby, & activities can happily be arranged. **$$**

CAMPSITES AND BACKPACKERS'
Although many of Maun's hotels, lodges & camps offer camping as well as their normal rooms, one of the dedicated campsites is often a better bet – although the sites at both the Sedia Hotel & Crocodile Camp are also well worth consideration.

Most of the campsites are north of Maun, on the road to Shorobe, with the furthest – Okavango River Lodge – 15km out of town. They're the obvious places to stay if you arrive in your own vehicle, but if you don't have transport, most will provide a pick-up/drop-off service into town at a price. Alternatively, a taxi from town will cost you around P40, or you can take a Route 1 combi for some P4. These pass up & down the main road near the camps every few minutes during the day.

⚊ **Audi Camp** [map 161] (camping, 10-bed house) Shorobe Rd; ☏ 686 0599; e info@ okavangocamp.com; www.okavangocamp. com. While standards at other places tend to to fluctuate, Audi Camp seems to remain one of Maun's constants. It's clean, friendly & well cared for, with the whole multi-level site securely fenced & patrolled at night by security guards. The camp is well signposted about 12km from the centre of Maun on the road north to Moremi & Chobe.

At the top of the complex is a sandy campsite under mopane trees, with a basic camper's kitchen, & ablutions in an intriguingly designed circular block that has open-air showers & hot water. Pitches with power have their own braai & water supply. Bring your own tent, or rent one of their pre-erected tents on solid bases: either bare dome tents with camp beds & no linen (bedding can be rented), or small Meru tents (4 en-suite) with beds & linen, as well as electric lights & fans. Firewood & ice are available, as is a laundry service. If you don't fancy sleeping under canvas, try a room in the 4-bedroom riverside house, which has its own kitchen & bathroom.

The camp has a large thatched bar, & a restaurant area on a lower level which serves meals & snacks all day, from toasted sandwiches to steaks & vegetarian options. Down again, & near the river, is a large & very popular swimming pool. A great little shop sells a range of curios as well as InOv8 (Sibanda) hand-printed fabrics (page 168), while almost opposite is the new Motsana 'village', which incorporates a café & beauty therapist. The camp itself is also the base for Audi Camp Safaris (page 179). *Camping P65 pp, power point P70 per night; dome tent P140/170 sgl/dbl, Meru tent P320/440, en suite P570/690, house P1,900, or P470 dbl, all exc P10 pp/night tourism levy. Transfer from town P140/vehicle.*

⚔ Maun Rest Camp [map 161] (4 Meru tents, camping) off Sir Seretse Khama Rd, Maun; ☎686 2623/3472 (with answerphone); e simonjoyce@info.bw. This nice, quiet campsite on the river is also the base for a small mobile-safari operation (page 178) run by the owners, Simon & Joyce. Find it by heading 7km north of the airport on the road to Chobe & Moremi.

The campsite has 14 individual pitches, each with its own braai & water tap. If you don't have a tent, then Meru ones are available with twin beds, electric lights & carpets, & chairs at the front. 2 clean, brick-built ablution blocks (4 separate showers, loos & basins plus laundry tubs & sinks for dishes – all with copious hot water from a gas geyser) lie under large shady trees. Ask the owners to show you the bird-plum or *motsentsela* tree (*Berchemia discolor*) here, which is indigenous but a little uncommon, with its thick foliage & small, edible fruits.

There's no bar or restaurant here, but the Sports Bar & Restaurant & The Old Bridge are barely 2mins' walk away – so finding somewhere for a drink or dinner isn't a problem. *Camping P75 pp, tent P220/400 sgl/dbl.*

⚔ Okavango River Lodge [map 161] (camping, 8 tents, 6 chalets, dorm beds) Shorobe Rd; ☎686 3707; e info@okavango-river-lodge.com; www.okavango-river-lodge.com. Opened in the late 1970s, this rustic lodge stands on the Thamalakane River, about 15km north of Maun. Leading down to the river under shady acacia trees, its campsite has a thatched gazebo with tables & benches, & an old ablution block.

Set further back are basic en-suite chalets with nets, fans & twin, dbl or family accommodation, while on the other side of the site, twin-bedded tents with electric fans & lights share their own ablution facilities. And if you're on a tight budget, there are always the dorm beds.

Central to the lodge is its lively bar, which can be heaving at w/ends. A bar menu promises a variety of tasty bites, from b/fast or toasted sandwiches to T-bone steaks; the food is good, & service is both prompt & friendly. The small pool is popular with campers & diners, but their quirky Sunday cricket matches, which used to be played on the floodplain opposite camp, have now been relocated thanks to the (otherwise welcome) rise in river levels.

River trips from the lodge's jetty are a lovely way to explore the Thamalakane, costing around P480 for 2hrs (min 4 people). Depending on water levels, there's also the option of a full-day boat trip to Chief's Island, at around P1,000 pp (inc lunch, based on 4 people). Mokoro trips of varying lengths can also be organised, based on the Boro River in NG32. For details, see *Mokoro trips*, pages 172–3 – & note that if you don't have a tent & other camping kit, you can hire this from the lodge. Other activities can be booked at the lodge's new travel desk. *Camping P70 pp, power P30; dorm bed P100 pp; tent P150/280 sgl/dbl; chalet P280/400/500 sgl/dbl/family, all exc b/fast & P10 bed levy.*

⚔ The Old Bridge Backpackers [map 161] (camping, 8 dorm beds, 8 tents) Off Sir Seretse Khama Rd; ☎686 2406; e info@maun-backpackers.com; www.maun-backpackers.com. Maun's best backpacker hang-out by some way is tucked down a tarred lane just north of the river bridge, 10km out of town. It's clearly signposted from the bridge. Owned by David, one of the original partners in Livingstone's Jungle Junction, it was opened in 2005 on a shady site close to the old pole bridge (now a national monument) across the river. At this point, the river flows permanently, & hippos congregate in front of the camp, while fruit bats are attracted by a large sycamore fig tree. The area used to be a vegetable garden; now, around 400 trees have been planted around the site, which offers some lovely walks with good birding.

Alongside space for independent campers, there are 3 pre-erected walk-in tents, each with a dbl or twin beds, some simple dome tents with

2 mattresses & bedding, & a block of individual 'dorm' beds that are useful if it's too wet to camp. All share clean, reed-screened showers & toilets that are open to the stars. For greater privacy, consider 1 of the 5 en-suite tents that stand on the riverbank. A well-used pool table sits alongside the large, thatched central area, where the latest sports are on TV, & tables & chairs are set out under the trees. Food is available all day, from a full b/fast to a range of pasta dishes from around P50; there's also a self-catering kitchen. A small pool & Wi-Fi add to the facilities.

This is a relaxed outfit, young & friendly, & with no shortage of activities. From the campsite itself, you can rent kayaks, or indulge in a sunset river cruise (P500 per 6-seater boat), while further afield, there are several options; for details, see page 179. *Camping P60 pp; dome tent P100 pp; dorm P155 pp; walk-in tent P225/348 sgl/dbl, or P425/505 en suite.*

SOUTH AND WEST OF MAUN
Å **Drifters Maun Camp** [off 150 D7] (camping) Chanoga; m 7230 4472; e drifters@drifters.co.za; www.drifters.co.za. Situated 32km south of Maun, towards Nata, the local base of the overland safari company, Drifters, is also open to independent campers – & is well worth considering if you're heading south. Coming from Maun, take the tar road towards Nata & Francistown, & just beyond the village of Chanoga turn right down a sandy track of about 1km. Here you'll find a wide riverfront location with grassy lawns, where the thatched communal areas are attractively decorated with wall hangings & baskets. There's a small pool, but the greatest attraction is the Boteti River, which when flowing (& it has been for several years), attracts numerous waterbirds – including flamingos, pelicans & knob-billed ducks. Camping is on a small, tree-shaded site, with an extremely clean ablution block & hot water. You'll have use of the bar, but otherwise will need to be self-catering. *Camping €10 pp.*

Å **Sitatunga Camp** [off 150 A6] (12 cabins, 12 chalets, camping) 680 0380; e info@deltarain.com; www.deltarain.com; ⊕ SITAT 20°04.476'S, 23°21.296'E. Within a secure complex, Sitatunga remains a popular choice for overlanders, but for independent campers pre-booking is almost essential. To get there, head southwest from Maun towards Ghanzi, before

turning off the main road about 12km from Riley's Garage. The lodge is about 2km from the main road down a sandy track, & is accessible by 2WD.

The large campsite lies under trees, with pitches well spread out, & basic but clean ablutions. A 2nd small ablution block serves 12 simple twin & dbl chalets, each with nets & power points, which are set on their own away from the bar area. A hefty price hike will bring a brick-walled, canvas-roofed chalet, with twin beds, AC, ceiling fan, mosi nets, en-suite toilet & basin, & outside shower. There's a handy laundry service, & firewood is sold at P15 per load.

A recent fire has provided the opportunity to construct a large, new, airy bar area (⊕ 11.00–late), where the likes of burgers & pizzas are served. There's no self-catering kitchen, but braai facilities are available. As well as a pool by the bar, & a second close to the chalets, darts, volleyball & table tennis are on hand to keep campers busy. *Cabin/chalet P180/P500 (both 2 people max); camping P55 pp.*

🏠 **Tshima Bush Camp** [off 150 A6] (4 tents) m 7484 2079; e info@tshimabushcamp. com; www.tshimabushcamp.com; ⊕ TSHIMA 20°11.449'S, 23°14.430'E. Also on the Ghanzi road, some 30km southwest of Maun, Tshima was opened in June 2012 by Dutch friends Rienie & Michel. It's a friendly, low-key spot in 30ha of land bordering the Nhabe River, where marked walking trails make exploring easy. The occasional elephant crosses through camp, & – very unusually – aardvark are regularly seen, but for many birding is the draw: to date, Michel has identified around 350 species here.

Facing into the bush, Tshima's smart walk-in tents have twin beds under mosi nets, & a modern en-suite bathroom. Each has a table & chairs on the veranda, plus its own picnic bench, so b/fast – brought to your tent in a basket each morning – can be both relaxed & private. In the evening, guests can prepare their own braai, but most opt for a convivial 3-course dinner (P200) under the stars, with fresh salads grown in Tshima's garden.

With easy 2WD access from the tarred road, Tshima is a tranquil place for a spot of R&R – but note that you cannot just drop in: reservations are essential. **$$$**

✖ WHERE TO EAT AND DRINK

Maun's hardly a town for fine dining, but there are several reasonable venues, including some of the hotels and camps. There are also numerous fast-food places, including Nando's, Barcelo's, Bimbo's and more, with KFC expected to open near the bus station in 2014. Expect a decent burger to cost upwards of P30 – and remember that you're in a country which counts beef as one of its main exports.

Of the hotels, pick of the bunch is the riverside restaurant at **Thamalakane River Lodge**, where the pizzas and setting are worth the journey. While both **Maun Lodge** and the **Sedia Hotel** have competent if uninspiring formal restaurants, their open-air offerings are far more appealing. Of these, **The Boma** at Maun Lodge is relaxed and quite rustic, while eating by the pool at the back of the **Sedia** can be fun with a good atmosphere. Of the campsites, **Okavango River Lodge** is generally a good bet, as well as being arguably the town's most frequented watering hole – especially at weekends.

Individual restaurants and cafés add variety to the mix, some specialising in breakfast and lunch, and others open in the evening. Many are within walking distance of the airport, and most are licensed, with vegetarians well catered for almost everywhere.

For **traditional food**, the restaurants at both Riley's and Maun Lodge can oblige, but beat a path to Choice, or the Dine Inn [150 B5], and you're likely to be the only tourist in sight. Or close to the airport, pop out at lunchtime to one of the street stalls just opposite Bon Arrivée; a satisfying serving of pap and stew will be yours for just P20–25.

✖ **Sports Bar** [map 161] Sir Seretse Khama Rd; ☏686 2676; ⊕ restaurant 18.00–22.00 daily, bar 16.00–midnight, & Sat pm. This long-standing favourite about 7km north of town is probably the best restaurant in the area – helped by speedy service & the frequent presence of the owners. The complex is spread over 2 levels, with meals served in the pleasantly air-conditioned restaurant, all dark greens & reds, or in a relaxed beer garden. The extensive menu is known for great pizzas & pasta, fresh bream & some excellent salads, with seasonal specials featuring the likes of kudu carpaccio, or oxtail stew. Entirely separate is the bar with pool tables & big-screen TV, where the big matches are shown live on Sat afternoons. Come on a Fri night when the place rocks; there's usually live music & no cover charge, attracting Maun's younger & more affluent residents & expats (including lots from the safari industry) to dance the night away. **$$–$$$$**

✖ **Bon Arrivée** [156 D1] Mathiba I Rd; ☏680 0330; ⊕ 07.00–22.30 Mon–Thu, 07.00–23.00 Fri–Sun. Opposite the airport, this trendy & unashamedly aviation-themed bar/restaurant has a pretty eclectic menu serving everything from b/fast (P38–57) & burgers, to seafood vol-au-vent & fillet steak. It's also a popular watering hole with expats on a Fri night. If the jokes on the menu are pretty corny, they do at least help to while away the time waiting for a delayed flight. **$$**

✖ **Chaplin's** [off 150 D7] Nata Rd; m 7696 8484; ⊕ 9.30–21.00 Mon–Fri, 14.00–22.00 Sat. Despite its location on an industrial estate, Chaplin's is the restaurant that's on everyone's lips: friendly, welcoming & with good food. Known for its pizzas & 'fantastic burgers', it also does specials that might include ribs, or slow-cooked chicken, & is about to branch out into the likes of surf 'n' turf. Find it about 2km south of the Caltex fuel station. **$$–$$$**

✖ **French Connection** [156 D3] Mophane Av; ☏680 0625; m 7175 4030; ⊕ 08.00–17.00 Mon–Sat. This licensed café/restaurant quite close to the airport is run by Marie & George, a couple of Swiss/Dutch origin, & is highly rated. With seating outside under mopane trees, or inside for inclement weather, it's well screened from the road, with off-road parking. The French-influenced menu ranges from wraps to fresh salads & mouth-watering baguettes. B/fasts, served until 12.00, include an innovative vegetarian version featuring ratatouille & rösti. As an aside the restaurant also sells secondhand books in aid of a charity that spays & vaccinates village dogs around the Delta. $$

✗ **Hilary's Coffee Shop** [156 D2] Off Mathiba I Rd; ☎686 1610; ⏱ 08.30–16.00 Mon–Fri, 08.30–12.00 Sat. Also close to the airport, Hilary's has been serving since about 1995, & is one of the more interesting & reliable places to eat during the day in Maun. Well-shaded tables are outside amongst mopane trees & pot plants. Hilary & her staff make everything on the premises, from mayonnaise & salad dressing to bran muffins; the home-baked wholewheat bread is to die for, & with a little advance notice can be made to order for a camping trip, if you ask nicely ... Expect the best home-cooked breakfasts in Maun, & tasty wholesome lunches, including sandwiches & salads, daily specials & amazing desserts & cakes. $$

✗ **Kalahari Kofi** [156 G1] Penstone Plaza; ⏱ 08.00–17.00 Mon–Fri, 08.00–13.00 Sat. You may need to keep an eye out for this licensed café as it was planning a name change when we visited. But the menu – with coffee & cakes, steaks, burgers, salads & pasta dishes – should remain unchanged. Free Wi-Fi is a bonus. $$

✗ **Motsana** [map 161] Shorobe Rd; ⏱ 08.00–18.00 Mon–Fri, 08.00–15.00 Sat. The licensed café at Motsana 'village' is a quirky spot for b/fast or lunch, or even just an ice cream, with free Wi-Fi & a whole range of shops to add to the attraction – there's even a beauty salon here. Thursday night is cinema night, when they're also open for dinner. $$

✗ **Choice** [157 C7] Old Mall, Tsheko-Tsheko Rd; ⏱ 07.30–22.00 daily. For a hearty helping of traditional food, join the lunchtime queues at Choice. It feels rather like a fast-food joint, with modern wooden tables & benches, but the buffet features a range of Botswana specials, including oxtail, rice & greens. $

✗ **La Fontaine** [157 C7] Tsheko-Tsheko Rd; ☎686 1411; ⏱ 07.00–19.30. Opened to cater for patients at the neighbouring medical centre, the simple La Fontaine is far from the French restaurant that the name suggests. Instead, come for b/fast, sandwiches & local dishes or the likes of spaghetti bolognese, washed down with soft drinks (or bring your own alcohol). $

ENTERTAINMENT AND NIGHTLIFE

Maun doesn't have much in the way of nightlife, except for some lively bars, the most popular being the Sports Bar, with its well-stocked bar and sports TV, and Bon Arrivée. The only nightclub, Trekkers, is on Mophane Avenue. Its reputation for safety is pretty dubious, so if you want to explore, go with a local you trust.

If you're in town on a Thursday evening, it's worth checking to see if there's a film showing at Motsana 'village' [map 161] (*Shorobe Rd*). With its funky Moorish architecture and dark walls, it looks like an imposing fortress from the outside, but step through the gate and you're greeted by a large stage which every Thursday evening at 19.30 hosts a semi-open-air cinema. Seating is in the licensed café, so it's all very relaxed.

For pure relaxation, the same venue also has a beauty therapist, the Lily Pad (m *7172 6046*; e *salonkate@gmail.com*), which could be just the ticket after a week or two in the bush.

SHOPPING

Most shops are open Monday to Friday around 08.00–17.00, and Saturday to midday or thereabouts, with supermarket hours considerably longer. Note that locals have warned of a problem with opportunist theft both near the airport and around the market, so watch your bags in these areas in particular.

FOOD AND DRINK You can buy most things here that you'll find in a supermarket in Europe or North America, although the brand names may be different and the choice (especially of fresh fruit and vegetables) may not be as varied. Several of the

supermarkets are on Tsheko-Tsheko Road to the south of Riley's Garage. These include Maun's oldest, Shoprite [157 C7] (*Tsheko-Tsheko Rd*), and its more recent rivals: Spar [157 B7] (behind Nando's) with a second branch in the Ngami Centre [156 F2]; and Choppies, near the bus station [150 A5] (⊕ *08.00–20.00 daily*), with a smaller branch in New Mall [156 E1]. Most are open daily from 08.00 until about 19.00 or 20.00 midweek, but close earlier on Saturday and (particularly) Sunday.

If you're just after **bread**, try Dainty Bakes on Tsheko-Tsheko Road [157 C7], while for **vacuum-packed meats**, a good alternative to the supermarkets is Delta Deli at Riley's Garage [157 D7], or Beef Boys on Tsheko-Tsheko Road [150 A5] – where you can order what you want in advance ready to pick up as you head out of town.

Supermarkets don't sell **alcohol**, so to stock up on beer and wine you'll need to go to one of the liquor stores around town. One of the better ones is Bateman's in Penstone Plaza [156 G1] (⊕ *10.00–18.00 Mon–Fri, 10.00–14.00 Sat*).

The main local **market** [157 B7] is between Tsheko-Tsheko Road and Tsaro Street, where you'll find lots of small stalls and local sellers. It's certainly worth checking out for the odd pile of fruit and vegetables, but also expect for more offbeat foods, like mopane worms in season, and an assorted range of bootleg CDs and secondhand items.

SOUVENIRS, CRAFTS, BOOKS AND CURIOS
There's no shortage of places that sell curios in Maun, and virtually every camp in Botswana has a small curio shop. Thus it pays to shop around, particularly for books and crafts. It's also well worth seeking out individual workshops, or places where the work of local craftspeople is available. If you're just after something to read, check out the secondhand books sold at the French Connection restaurant [156 D3]. And for several things under one roof, try Motsana 'village' [map 161], where there's a curio shop, Textures, and a gallery of local art and photographs.

African Art & Images [156 D1] Maun Airport; ✆686 3584. At this upmarket gift shop cum gallery inside the airport gates, take your pick from high-quality African art, carvings, baskets, jewellery & some beautiful photographs & prints – with correspondingly high price tags.

Botswana Book Centre [157 A7] Pulane Rd; ✆686 0853. This traditional bookshop stocks books, magazines & newspapers, including a range of titles by African writers.

Bushman Craft Shop [156 D1] Maun Airport, ✆686 0025/0339; ⊕ 08.00–17.00 daily. Just inside the airport gates, immediately opposite the main terminal building, this convenient shop sells a very good range of books, postcards, crafts, curios & safari clothes. Barely a minute's walk from the check-in desks, it's perfectly situated to dash out to whilst you're waiting for a plane.

The Craft Centre [156 C2] Power Station, Mophane Av; ✆686 3391. This small workshop sells local crafts including pottery, textiles, paper products & paintings – much of it handmade on the premises.

InOv8 Botswana [map 161] Sir Seretse Khama Rd; ✆680 0094; m 7287 6421; e mauncloth@ gmail.com. From a workshop north of Maun, the former Sibanda's Crafts produces hand-painted fabrics & soft furnishings designed by Amanda Haywood. Sold at Audi Camp & other outlets in town, all are of 100% cotton, printed & painted with natural dyes by local women. Youngsters also make crafts from zinc & recycled materials; look out for earrings featuring tiny baskets.

Jazella's [156 D1] Natlee Centre, Airport Av; ✆686 1900; ⊕ 07.00–18.00 daily. Jam-packed full of jewellery, bags, wall hangings, books & much, much more, Jazella's is just opposite the airport.

Matlapana Baskets [map 161] Sir Seretse Khama Rd; m 7227 1422; e thitakukushonya@ yahoo.com; ⊕ 06.30–18.30 daily. Award-winning master weaver Thitaku Kushonya sells baskets from her workshop about 8km north of Maun, opposite Marina's. Do pay her a visit: her work is excellent, & you'll learn a little of how to tell a low-quality basket from a higher-quality one that's double woven.

Okavango Ceramics [off map 161] Off Sir Seretse Khama Rd; 686 2606; e okavangoceramics@gmail.com; http://botswanatrophies.homestead.com; 08.00–13.00 & 13.30–16.30 Mon–Fri; outside hours by prior appointment only; 19°54.433'S, 23°29.545'E. The company's workshop is some 3km down a side-road next to Marina's, about 8km north of Maun. Hand-painted mugs, bowls, plates & more are made on site, as well as bronze sculptures & a range of eco-friendly toiletries.

Textures [map 161] Motsana 'village', Shorobe Rd. A classy find in a quirky environment, Textures is an Aladdin's cave of curios, jewellery & feminine clothes, well sited next to a popular café.

Wax Apple [156 E2] Airport Av; 686 2606. A useful find near the airport, selling books, safari gear & classy gifts.

CAMPING EQUIPMENT Most visitors bring their own camping equipment, or are booked on trips which include it. For those on budget trips, some of the tour operators hire out their kit for the duration of your trip. However, if you need to buy anything, or you need some of your own kit repaired, then there are a few specialist options.

Jacana Enterprises [156 B3] Mophane Av; 686 1202; e jacana@botsnet.bw; www.jacanaent.com; 08.00–16.00 Mon–Fri, 09.00–13.00 Sat. An unexpected find in an office building, Jacana has safari clothing & camping equipment, good torches & knives, a range of maps (laminated survey maps from around P110 each) & GPS equipment, & lots, lots more. It also has an exhaustive (& somewhat quirky) website!

Kalahari Kanvas [156 C2] Mathiba I Rd; 686 0568; e kalkanvas@botsnet.bw; www.kalaharikanvas.com. From its beginnings in 1986 as a tiny tent-repair company, Kalahari Kanvas has burgeoned into a major manufacturer of tents & equipment for the safari industry. They still offer a tent-repair service & also hire out an amazing range of kit by the day, from a knife, fork & spoon set, to a 2-person, 2.4m x 2.4m dome tent, or a double-canvas bedroll with 75mm-thick mattress, a blanket, 2 pillows & 2 sheets. It's best to book stuff in advance, & deposits are required, proportional to the items hired; credit cards are accepted. Note that all kit must be returned to this office.

PAAM [156 E2] New Mall, Sir Seretse Khama Rd; 686 0992. Despite the name (the acronym stands for Pan African Ammunition Manufacturers), PAAM specialises in the outdoors generally, with fishing gear, camping kit & safari clothing.

Swamp Donkey [156 G1] Penstone Plaza, Sir Seretse Khama Rd. For camping gear including tents, cooking equipment, cool bags, etc: it's all here.

CLOTHES Several of the camping equipment outlets also stock safari gear, and for last-minute safari purchases you could try the Bushman Craft Shop (above), but for basic tops and trousers, you'd probably do better at one of the more general clothing stores: PEP next to Shoprite [157 C7], JB Sports in New Mall [156 E2], or Woolworth's in the Ngami Centre [156 F2]. More specialist than any of these, with a good range of safari clothes, sports clothing and boots, is:

West Sports [157 D7] Riley's Garage, Tsheko-Tsheko Rd; 686 0483

OTHER PRACTICALITIES

These days Maun is, above all for most visitors, a place to restock, refuel and get organised.

BANKS AND MONEY The main **banks** – Stanbic [156 D2] (*Natlee Centre, Mathiba I Rd*), First National [156 F2] (*Ngami Centre*), Barclays [157 B7] (*Tsheko-Tsheko Rd*) and Standard Chartered [157 B7] (*Old Mall*), have ATM machines that accept Visa and, less frequently, MasterCard, so this is usually the easiest, quickest and cheapest way to get pula. Alternatively, with your passport and a little time spent in queues, you can cash travellers' cheques or obtain a manual cash advance on a credit card at any of these three.

Bureaux de change generally offer a quicker service and longer hours. Most conspicuous are the branches of Sunny's, which charges no commission: one next to Riley's [157 D7] (⊕ *08.00–17.30 Mon–Fri, 08.00–13.30 Sat*) and the other by the First National Bank [156 F2] (*Ngami Centre;* ✆ *686 0919;* ⊕ *08.00–18.00 daily*). Better rates may prevail at Open Door by Riley's Garage [157 D7] (✆ *686 3225;* ⊕ *07.30–16.00 Mon–Fri, 08.00–16.00 Sat, 09.00–16.00 Sun*), but this is against a commission of around 4%, so check both and do your sums first.

COMMUNICATIONS

Telephone Local SIM cards can be purchased at various outlets, including the Mascom office [157 C7] (*Old Mall, Tsheko-Tsheko Rd*).

Post and courier The post office [157 B8] is on Tsheko-Tsheko Road, south of Barclays Bank. DHL [156 G1] (✆ *686 1207*) has a branch in Penstone Plaza, on Seretse Khama Road.

Internet Wi-Fi access is increasingly available at individual lodges, but there are dedicated internet cafés in town. Most accessible are the following, though note that connection speeds may vary considerably.

🖳 **Open Door** See *Bureaux de change*, above. P15/30mins.

🖳 **Sunny's** See *Bureaux de change*, above. Offers free internet access to customers using their exchange facilities.

🖳 **Xnaxi** [156 F2] Sir Seretse Khama Rd, opp Engen; ⊕ 08.30–19.30 Mon–Sat, 12.00–18.00 Sun. P4 for 10mins.

GARAGES AND VEHICLE SPARES
There are several fuel stations in Maun. While in theory they take credit cards, don't rely on this; if the machine isn't working, you'll have to pay cash in pula.

If you're passing through and heading off into the bush then Maun is the best place to make sure your 4x4 is in tip-top condition, with plenty of spares. Places that may be able to help are usually open Monday to Friday and Saturday morning, and include:

Auto World [150 A5] Tsheko-Tsheko Rd; ✆ 686 3890. Spares for most major makes of vehicle.

Delta4x4 [off 150 A6] ✆ 686 4572. Just south of Maun Sports Complex on the Ghanzi road, Delta offers vehicle repairs & 4x4 hire.

Kelly Tyres [150 C6] Tawana I Rd. Located between Maun Lodge & the Shell garage.

Lesedi Motors [150 C7] Kwena Rd; ✆ 686 0884; e landrover@lrmaun.co.bw. Specialist in Land Rover parts, servicing & repairs.

Maun Motors Nata Rd; ✆ 686 0138

Motovac [156 B3] Mophane Av; ✆ 686 0872. The local branch of the spares & accessories chain.

Ngami Toyota [150 A5] Tsheko-Tsheko Rd; ✆ 686 0252. Maun's Toyota dealer also has spares

& a bodyshop. They will repair all makes of vehicle, not just Toyotas.

Riley's Garage (Shell) [157 D7] Tsheko-Tsheko Rd; ✆ 686 0203; e parts@rileys.co.bw. In the centre of town, next to the famous old hotel, Riley's has a 24hr fuel station, as well as a workshop, & a shop (Autozone) carrying a range of spares, tyres & batteries.

Trans World Motors [off 150 D7] Francistown Rd; ✆ 686 0656; m 7130 2729, 7211 6012. About 1km beyond Caltex. Offers mechanical repairs, as well as a 24hr breakdown service.

Tyre World [150 C7] ✆ 686 0107

Should the worst happen, and you break down in the bush without back-up, then help is at hand:

Mechto ☎686 1875, 680 0155; m 7130 3788
Premonition m 7299 0663, 7178 2051

You could also try Trans World Motors (above), who advertise a 24-hour breakdown service.

HEALTH Maun's modern Letsholathebe II Memorial Hospital [off 150 D5 and map 161] (*Disaneng Rd;* ☎686 0444) is located to the east of the town. If you're coming from Shorobe or one of the lodges to the north, then continue straight over at the roundabout before the bridge rather than heading into town; it's clearly signposted.
There are also a couple of good private clinics and a dentist:

✚ **Delta Dental Clinic** [157 A8] Moremi III Rd; ☎686 1023/4224
✚ **Delta Medical Centre** [157 C6] Old Mall, 458 Tsheko-Tsheko Rd; ☎686 1411/1236; e deltamedicalcentre@info.bw. There are rumours that this established clinic with its own small hospital may soon be the subject of a takeover.

✚ **Medi-Help Clinic** [156 E2] New Mall, Sir Seretse Khama Rd; ☎686 4084. Near the Engen garage, this is run by South African Dr Chris Carey.

Pharmacies Pharmacies are usually open normal shopping hours, but most have an emergency number for calls out of hours.

✚ **Okavango Pharmacy** [157 C7] Letsego Bldg, Old Mall, Tsheko-Tsheko Rd; emergency m 7170 6435

✚ **Portsway Pharmacy** [157 C6] Old Mall, Tsheko-Tsheko Rd; ☎680 0857; emergency m 7143 5045
✚ **Taurus** [157 C7] Tsheko-Tsheko Rd; ☎686 3340

Opticians It makes sense to bring spare glasses and contact lenses with you, but if you do come unstuck, try:

✚ **Opticals Botswana** [157 C7] Old Mall, Tsheko-Tsheko Rd; ☎686 1742; www.opticalsbotswana.com

PHOTOGRAPHY Your best chance for anything photographic orientated is Maun Photolab [157 B7] (*Tsheko-Tsheko Rd;* ☎686 2236), close to Barclays Bank.

WHAT TO SEE AND DO

Maun is really much more of a place to get organised than a destination in its own right, so few visitors are really looking for activities here. That said, if you have time to kill, here are a few suggestions. You could also visit one or two of the craftsmen listed under *Shopping* above, or take a day trip to Moremi with one of the operators listed on pages 175–9.

IN MAUN With the demise of Maun Educational Park, there's little in town itself to delay visitors, bar a couple of low-key cultural attractions, though exploring the river is a pleasant way to spend an afternoon, and horseriding is an added option. If you've time on your hands, you could check out what's on at the impressive **Maun Sports Complex**, which lies about 2.5km southwest of Riley's Garage on the road towards Ghanzi. It's used for political rallies as well as sports matches, with details published in the local newspaper, *The Ngami Times*.

Nhabe Museum [156 E3] (*Sir Seretse Khama Rd*) More of a gallery than a museum, this small venue has constantly changing exhibits that often showcase the art of local students. A small collection of artefacts includes musical instruments and hunting tools. '*Nhabe*', incidentally, is from the Bushman word for the sound of cattle pulling their feet out of the mud, now more usually rendered as '*ngami*'.

Sexaxa Cultural Village [off map 161] (*Shorobe Rd; contact Ednah on* m *7417 8457;* ⊙ *daily; P100 pp*) For a hint of Botswana's traditional way of life, pay a visit to this cultural village, 18km north of Maun on the Shorobe road; it's clearly signposted to the left. The village is designed to give visitors an idea of Bayei culture, urban style – as against the rural culture depicted at Shandereka Cultural Village near Moremi (page 351). If you're just dropping in, don't hold your breath; it's far better to book.

Thamalakane River Boat trips along the Thamalakane River are a great way to while away an hour or two, keeping an eye out for birds. Costs vary, but P400/ hour for a four-seater boat is a good indication. Contact Afro Trek (page 179) or perhaps Okavango River Lodge (page 164). If **birding** is the primary appeal, it may be worth contacting the local branch of Birdlife Botswana (\ *686 5618;* m *7465 4464;* e *birdlifemaun@botsnet.bw; www.birdlifebotswana.org.bw*) to see if one of their members would be prepared to guide you along the river for an hour or two.

Horseriding Riding for all levels can be organised through Jen Weimann at African Animal Adventure Safaris (page 178). Typically rides are along (and sometimes in!) the Thamalakane and Boro rivers. Hard hats are available. All abilities of rider are also welcome by Ride Botswana (page 179) at Royal Tree Lodge, where you could find yourself aloft among zebra, giraffe and other wildlife.

FURTHER AFIELD
Scenic flights Short flights over the Delta in light aircraft or helicopters are offered by several companies (see *Charter airlines*, pages 152–3). Most people tend to book for 45 minutes then regret it; an hour is a better bet! Rates are usually quoted on a 'per-plane' basis, rather than per person, and vary depending on the company and fuel costs. As an indication, you can expect to pay from around P2,250/hr (US$260) for a two seater, or P3,350/hr (US$385) for a five-seater. Helicopter trips are more expensive at around US$190 per person for 45 minutes, for up to three people, with each person having a window seat and their own headset. Note that all flights are subject to P60 airport tax per passenger, which is not always included in the rates.

Mokoro trips Perennially popular are mokoro trips into the Delta, lasting from one to three days. Typically you'll leave Maun by motorboat at around 08.00, reaching the launch site 15km upstream in about 45 minutes, and returning in the evening by about 17.00. When the river was dry, and vehicle transfers took around two hours each way, a single-day trip hardly seemed worth the effort, but a shorter boat transfer changes the dynamics considerably.

Almost all these trips are run by the same community trust, the OKMCT (see box above), but can be booked only through an affiliated tour operator; you cannot book direct or drive yourself in. However, although the polers, mekoros and areas being offered by the various competing companies in Maun are all exactly the same, prices vary according to the individual company. As an indication, Audi Camp charges P775 (US$90) per person for a day trip, including lunch, with a single supplement of P100 (US$9) per day. For an overnight trip, with two days on the water, expect to pay around P1,230 (US$142) if you're prepared to take all your own food, or P2,250 (US$260) per person with meals. Extending this to two nights/three days will cost around P1,650/P3,000 (US$190/345). Prices at The Old Bridge Backpackers and Okavango River Lodge are slightly lower. A trip very like this, from Island Safari Lodge, was my first view of the Okavango and, whilst it has its limitations, I'd still regard it as remarkably good value.

Moremi Game Reserve Several tour operators offer trips into Moremi, costing from around US$390 per person for a day trip, based on two people sharing, to

US$460 per person for a three-night trip for six people travelling together. Typically such trips include a guide, park fees, camping equipment, meals and transfers, but most exclude drinks.

Lake Ngami About 90km west of Maun, Lake Ngami is very accessible as a half- or full-day trip from Maun if you have your own transport – but do ascertain first whether or not there's water in the lake. For details, see *Chapter 13*, pages 371–3.

Okavango Guiding School (OGS) (↳ *680 0115;* e *ogs@wildguides.org; www. guidetrainingcourses.com*). Visitors looking for a wildlife experience with a difference can spend anything up to a month at OGS. Set up in 2003 to train guides in wildlife and ecology, it is based in the Delta in the NG30 Concession. Skills include poling a mokoro, tracking wildlife, rifle handling and safely approaching big game on foot, with all courses taught by licensed guide trainers. Participants also help benefit one aspiring local guide who receives sponsorship from the school and joins students for the duration of the course. Accommodation is in comfortable, two-man dome tents, with en-suite long-drop toilets and shared bucket showers.

BEYOND MAUN: GETTING ORGANISED

Although the majority of those passing through Maun are pre-booked on an all-inclusive trip, this is also the best place for independent travellers and those without plans to get organised. If it all seems rather overwhelming, there are just a few points to remember.

ORGANISING A TRIP INTO THE NATIONAL PARKS If you are organising your own trip, note that you can no longer go into the national parks without pre-booking your entrance permits, for which you will also need to have confirmed reservations for campsites or other accommodation (unless you plan just a day trip). For details of the system, and who operates the individual campsites, see pages 84–7.

Most of the campsite operators have offices in Maun, and unless you have everything in writing beforehand, you may need to visit more than one of them to confirm your bookings, so do allow plenty of time. With reservations in hand, head to the all-important Department of Wildlife and National Parks (DWNP) to secure your entry permits.

Department of Wildlife & National Parks (DWNP) [157 E5] Audi Dr; ↳686 1265; f 686 1264; ⏱ 07.30–16.30 Mon–Sat, 07.30–12.00 Sun
Kwalate Safaris [156 F2] Above FNB, Ngami Centre, Koro St; ↳686 1448; e kwalatesafari@gmail.com; ⏱ 08.30–17.00 Mon–Fri
SKL [156 C2] Apollo Hse, Mophane Av; ↳686 5365/6; e reservations@sklcamps.co.bw, sklcamps@botsnet.bw; www.sklcamps.com; ⏱ 08.30–17.00 Mon–Fri, 8.00–15.00 Sat, 08.30–13.00 Sun
Xomae Group [156 E2] New Mall, Sir Seretse Khama Rd; ↳686 2221; m 7386 2221; e xomaesites@botsnet.bw; www.xomaesites.com; ⏱ 08.00–17.00 Mon–Sat, 08.00–13.00 Sun

If you'd rather have independent help, then contact one of the travel agents, who can act as a sort of one-stop shop, arranging anything from a scenic flight to setting up your whole trip, including national parks, transport and accommodation. Finally, there are the tour operators and safari companies, whose role is to organise your safari, usually using their own suppliers – which may include their own lodges and aircraft.

TRAVEL AGENTS Maun may seem to the uninitiated to be full of travel agents, but many of the companies you see are in fact tour operators (see below) who own and run camps and safari companies. However, if you look hard there is a handful of normal travel agents who (generally) know the local safari industry well, and can help you choose a trip. They are especially useful if you arrive in Maun without any arrangements and want to book a budget trip immediately. In such cases, booking through one of these agents will cost you exactly the same as booking directly with the camp or safari company.

The caveats to this are, firstly, that none is well prepared for booking a range of the top-end lodges at short notice; there's very little demand for this. Secondly, some will have their own favourite camps or operators – so do ask them to be exhaustive about researching the options for you before you make a decision. Also ask them to make very clear if anyone associated with them has any links with the camps or trips that they're suggesting to you. (This shouldn't necessarily put you off booking – but you ought to know!)

Liquid Giraffe [map 161] Motsana 'village', Shorobe Rd; ☎ 680 1054
Safari Essence ☎ 686 1344; m 7230 9099; e passion@safari-essence.com; www.safari-essence.com. Sister company to Endeavour Safaris.
Tete Travel & Tours [156 E2] New Mall, Sir Seretse Khama Rd; ☎ 686 3239; m 714/ 1908; e tetetravel@botsnet.bw
Time Travel [156 D2] off Mathiba I Rd; ☎ 686 1007; e info@timetravelafrica.com; www.

timetravelafrica.com. This general all-purpose travel agent has moved to new premises next to Hilary's Coffee Shop.
Travel Wild (see advert, 3rd colour insert, page iii) [156 D1] Natlee Centre, Mathiba I Rd; ☎ 686 0822/3; e botswana@travelwildafrica.com; www. travelwildafrica.com. This very good, independent travel agent is a friendly, helpful & efficient one-stop shop for what to do in & around Maun, short trips into the Delta, & longer holidays in Botswana.

TOUR OPERATORS AND SAFARI COMPANIES Looking at the length of this list – which is by no means comprehensive – you'll realise that Maun is the safari capital of Botswana. Listed alphabetically, followed by specialist mobile, horseriding and camping/canoeing operators, these safari companies range from large operators with many camps through to tiny outfits which are little more than a guide and a vehicle. Since prices change regularly, these have not been included – although for an indication of the costs of, say, a mobile safari, see *Budgeting* in *Chapter 4*, page 95.

While many of the larger operators have staff in Maun as well as booking offices overseas, the smaller operations may take days, or even weeks, to answer communications – sometimes because the whole team is out of the office and on safari. This kind of tiny outfit has both advantages and disadvantages, as you'll realise.

Larger safari groups For the sake of completeness, also included here are a few companies that operate from towns other than Maun.

&Beyond [156 C2] off Mathiba I Rd; ☎ 686 1979, reservations ☎ +27 11 809 4300; e safaris@ andbeyond.com; www.andbeyond.com. Formerly Conservation Corporation Africa, &Beyond is a leading company committed to high quality, including good food & impressive standards of

guiding, with a tracker & guide on every vehicle. Of 32 lodges throughout east & southern Africa, they have 4 in Botswana's Okavango Delta: Nxabega, Sandibe, Xudum & Xaranna. They also offer 2 semi-permanent tented camps – Savute Under Canvas & Chobe Under Canvas – & a 10-day 'expedition', taking in the Okavango, Moremi, Chobe & Victoria Falls.
African Bush Camps [156 E2] Airport Av; ☎ +263 9 234307, emergency ☎ +263 772 126986; e info@africanbushcamps.com; www.

africanbushcamps.com. Established by a top Zimbabwean guide, ABC operate a handful of camps throughout northern Botswana: Linyanti Bush Camp, Linyanti Ebony, Saile Tented Camp & Footsteps across the Linyanti, as well as Khwai Tented Camp. ABC also offers scheduled safaris to areas that include Nxai Pan National Park, combining tented & lodge-based accommodation.

Desert & Delta Safaris [156 E3] Cnr Airport Av & Sir Seretse Khama Rd; 686 1559; e info@ desertdelta.com; www.desertdelta.com. This established operator, which recommends that their lodges be booked through a tour operator, runs Chobe Game Lodge, Chobe Savanna Lodge, Savute Safari Lodge, Camp Moremi, Camp Okavango, Xugana Island Lodge, Xakanaxa Camp & Leroo La Tau. A sister company, Safari Air, operates a charter air service, enabling integrated access to each lodge. In 2009, Desert & Delta launched a programme of 11-day guided mobile safaris around Botswana, in co-operation with the affiliated Chobe Explorations. With just 2–6 participants, each trip operates between Victoria Falls or Livingstone & Maun, taking in the Chobe River, Savute, Moremi, the Okavango Delta & Makgadikgadi Pans National Park.

Great Plains Conservation +27 21 434 5208; info@greatplainsconservation.com, www. greatplainsconservation.com. In 2006, Great Plains took over Selinda & Zarafa camps in the Selinda Concession from Linyanti Explorations, & added Selinda Explorers Camp & the Selinda Canoe Trail. They also operate Duba Plains in NG23. The company is very focused on raising the bar in standards of environmental & social responsibility &, while by no means the only one with this remit, is certainly one of the most proactive in marketing its part in 'conservation tourism'.

Ker & Downey Botswana [156 E1] Mathiba I Rd; 686 0375/1226; e info@kerdowney.bw; www.kerdowneybotswana.com. Ker & Downey are 2 of the oldest names in the Delta. Back in 1945, Donald Ker & Syd Downey founded a hunting safari company in Kenya, to be joined in the mid-1950s by Harry Selby – who started their Botswana operations in 1962. Around 1979 they bought Khwai River Lodge as a photographic camp, & in 1985 the photographic company Ker, Downey & Selby was split off from the hunting company, Safari South. Today it's known simply as Ker & Downey Botswana, & runs Okuti, Kanana, Kanana

Mokoro Trail, Shinde, & its neighbouring walking operation, Footsteps across the Delta: all quite different camps & experiences, with varying costs.

Kgori Safaris [156 E2] Pharmacy Hse, New Mall; 686 5788; e mankwe@info.bw. This relative newcomer to Maun's tour operators offers a range of itineraries for 4–14 participants. They also own & run Mankwe Bush Lodge, in NG43, just south of Chobe & east of Moremi, & manage the boat station on the northwest tip of Mboma Island in Moremi.

Kwando Safaris [156 E2] Sir Seretse Khama Rd; 686 1449; e info@kwando.co.bw; www. kwando.co.bw. Based in Maun, Kwando is a small, independent operator running 1st-class camps in Botswana. Lagoon & Lebala are primarily dry-land camps beside the Kwando River in NG14, while Kwara & Little Kwara have a full range of dry & wet activities, on the north side of the Delta. Further south are Nxai Pan Lodge within the national park of the same name, & Tau Pan Lodge in the Central Kalahari Game Reserve. All are different, but all operate game drives with both a tracker & a guide – a real advantage when it comes to tracking predators. Their focus is on enthusiastic wildlife spotting rather than excessive frills in camp, although their camps are of a high standard.

Lodges of Botswana [156 C2] Power Station Bldg, Mophane Av; 686 1154; e info@ lodgesofbotswana.com; www.lodgesofbotswana. com. This Maun-based company is run by the irrepressible Peter Sandenbergh, who was one of the first to see the area's potential for backpacking tourism as well as the more usual upmarket variety. Today they own & run Delta Camp & Oddballs', in NG27B. They have particularly close links with both Delta Air & the Bushman Craft Shop.

Orient-Express Safaris [156 C3] Mophane Av; 686 0302, reservations +27 21 483 1600; e reservations@orient-express-safaris.com; www. orient-express-safaris.co.za. Part of the global group that also runs the famous Venice-Simplon Orient Express train, Orient-Express Safaris have 3 upmarket lodges in Botswana: Savute Elephant Camp, Khwai River Lodge & Eagle Island Camp. Specifications in each are comparable to top hotels, very much belying their 'tent' status.

Sanctuary Retreats 686 2688, reservations +44 (0)20 7190 7728; e sasales@

sanctuaryretreats.com; www.sanctuaryretreats. com. Part of the Abercrombie & Kent group, Sanctuary Retreats operates 4 lodges in Botswana: Chobe Chilwero, Chief's Camp, Stanley's Camp & Baines' Camp, as well as Sussi & Chuma in Livingstone.

Uncharted Africa See page 420.

Under One Botswana Sky [156 C2] Mathiba 1 Rd; ☎686 0023; e reservations@gunns-camp.com; www.underonebotswanasky.com. From its base, near the airport, this is the operation behind Pom Pom Camp, Gunn's Camp & Moremi Crossing in the Delta, as well as Chobe Safari Lodge & Chobe Bush Lodge in Kasane, & Nata Lodge. Safari itineraries can be tailormade to include some or all of the properties.

Wilderness Safaris [156 C2] Mathiba I Rd; ☎686 0086, reservations ☎+27 11 807 1800; enquiry@ wilderness.co.za; www.wilderness-safaris.com. Started by safari guides Colin Bell, Chris MacIntyre (not this book's author!) & Russel Friedman in Botswana in 1983, this has since grown into one of the subcontinent's leading safari organisers – with operations throughout southern Africa. From their office in Maun, across the road from the airport, they also market Botswana's largest selection of safari camps. These are mostly in private reserves & include DumaTau, King's Pool, & Savuti Camp in NG15; Vumbura Plains & Little Vumbura in NG22; Kwetsani, Jacana, Jao, Tubu Tree, Little Tubu & Pelo in NG25; Chitabe & Chitabe Lediba in NG31; Mombo, Little Mombo & Xigera in the Moremi Game Reserve; & Kalahari Plains in the CKGR. Marketed as 'premier' or 'classic', their style, standard & prices vary, yet Wilderness effectively sets the baseline for high-quality camps in Botswana, by which other operators tend to be measured. A third, rather looser group of lodges fall within their 'adventures' brand & are accessible to drive-in guests. Wilderness advises travellers to book their camps through a local tour operator.

Wilderness also own their own flight company, Wilderness Air. In addition, they offer non-participatory mobile safaris, with luxury Discoverer trips & Classic Adventurer trips. These aim to recreate the atmosphere of an unhurried exploratory journey, operating primarily in private concession areas. Departures are guaranteed with a min of 2 guests (max 8).

Mobile safari specialists

Bush Ways Safaris ☎686 3685; e reservations@ bushways.com; www.bushways.com. Established in 1996, Bush Ways operates scheduled mobile safaris lasting 7–18 days as well as tailormade tours. Itineraries cover Chobe, Moremi, Nxai, Makgadikgadi & the CKGR, as well as Victoria Falls & the Caprivi Strip. Travellers can opt for semi-participation or fully serviced camping trips (run even with just 1 participant), or lodge-based safaris, with no hidden costs or 'kitty' requirements. French & German translators are provided on selected safaris. Bush Ways also owns Sango Safari Camp in Moremi, & Chobe Elephant Camp.

Capture Africa ☎686 1200; e hildrene@ captureafrica.net; www.captureafrica.com. Brian & Hildrene Gibson founded their mobile-safari operation in 1997. Theirs is a flexible approach, with different styles of tents to cater for a variety of travellers, but they specialise in tailormade luxury safaris with specialist guides.

Drumbeat Safaris ☎686 3096; e drumbeat@ drumbeatsafaris.com; www.drumbeatsafaris.com. Established in 1996, Drumbeat is still run by its Dutch co-founder Annelies Zonjee, who organises fully inclusive comfortable & luxury mobile safaris throughout northern Botswana, as well as lodge-based safaris & helicopter trips. Mobile safaris are always private (min 2 people) so you won't be sharing – a real plus for families. Guests stay in walk-in tents, usually in private campsites within the parks, & travel in game vehicles, with the equipment & staff either trailed behind or transported separately.

Endeavour Safaris ☎686 1344; e info@ endeavour-safaris.com; www.endeavour-safaris. com. Based on the premise that everyone should have the chance to visit & experience Botswana's wilderness, Mike & Silvia Hill's safari operation caters for a range of budgets, from participation mobile safaris to luxury fly-in lodge options. Where Endeavour really scores, however, is in its safaris for families (with no age restrictions); & for disabled & senior travellers, including guests with mobility issues, or hearing & visual impairments. With this in mind, the company's modified Land Cruiser & mobile camp are maintained & operated by specially trained staff.

Harkness Safaris m 7405 7917; e enquiries@ harkness-safaris.com; www.harkness-safaris. com. Andrew Harkness's safari operation caters

for up to 12 guests in dome or walk-in tents, with en-suite long-drop loos & bucket showers. Trips are tailormade but usually start in Maun & finish in Kasane or Victoria Falls, taking in Moremi, Khwai, & the Savuti & Chobe River areas of Chobe National Park. The CKGR can be included in any itinerary.
Karibu Safaris ✎686 1225; e karibububots@info. bw; www.karibu.co.za. Karibu offers 'comfort' mobile safaris taking 4–17 days, with set departures. Some include Namibia & Botswana; others incorporate lodge accommodation. Tailormade itineraries are possible in the low season.
Letaka Safaris (see advert, 3rd colour insert, page viii)✎680 0363; e info@letakasafaris. com; www.letakasafaris.com. Brothers Brent & Grant Reed set up Letaka in 2000, focusing on set-departure trips in Moremi & Chobe, as well as to Makgadikgadi & Nxai pans. These, including specialist birding & photography trips, are all led by a team of high-quality guides. You'll stay in walk-in tents with gauze windows, solar-powered lights & an en-suite long-drop loo & bucket shower – with hot water brought to your tent on request.
Masson Safaris ✎686 2442; e massonsafaris@ gmail.com; www.massonsafaris.net. This small family operation runs mobile photographic safaris, both scheduled & tailormade, concentrating on game & birdlife, with a general appreciation of Botswana's more remote areas (they're especially keen on the great salt pans, Tsodilo & the Central Kalahari). Ewan Masson, who has been guiding in Botswana for 20 years, leads most trips. Expect walk-in dome tents, complete with linen, washstand, reading light & a private chemical flush loo. Game drives are taken in extended Land Rovers (max 8 guests).
Maun Rest Camp Safaris ✎686 2623/3472; e simonjoyce@info.bw. Based out of Maun Rest Camp (page 164), owners Simon & Joyce, both of whom are qualified guides, run & lead fairly small, low-budget mobile safaris in adapted Toyota Land Cruisers, with a staff member to help with camp chores. Full bedrolls with linen are set up in stand-up-size dome tents, & good, wholesome meals come with plenty of fresh fruit & vegetables. Don't expect glossy brochures or silver service, but do expect comfortable – not luxury – safaris at a very fair price, & a swift & efficient response to any queries. As well as Moremi & Chobe, they cover the Central Kalahari, Nxai Pan, Makgadikgadi, Tsodilo Hills & even Drotsky's Caves.

Penduka Safaris ✎686 4539; e info@ pendukasafaris.com; www.pendukasafaris.com. Started in 1963 by Izak Barnard, Penduka has been run by his son, Willem, since the early 1990s. It operates fully inclusive safaris throughout Botswana, varying in length, but 8–12 nights would be typical, & some are tailormade. All camp duties are undertaken by the staff, who serve excellent meals with fresh fruit & vegetables. Tents are spacious with camp beds & mattresses; vehicles are specially adapted 4x4s with pop-top roof hatches.
Roger Dugmore Safaris ✎686 2427; e rdsafaris@ngami.net; www. rogerdugmoresafaris.com. Owned & run by Roger Dugmore, this small company runs mobile tented safaris & specialised photographic expeditions around Botswana's national parks & wilder areas of the desert & Okavango Delta, plus set-departure trips to Moremi. Safaris are guided by Roger, who likes to take time to get to know each area.
Wilderness Dawning Safaris ✎686 2962; e reservations@wildernessdawning.com; www. wildernessdawning.com. This reliable small operator offers scheduled camping safaris of 10, 11 & 14 days with experienced Batswana guides. These non-participation trips, for 4–10 guests, all incorporate the Victoria Falls, & one includes a couple of nights on the //Kabbo houseboat on the Okavango at Shakawe, but otherwise are spent entirely in the national parks.
Wilmot Safaris ✎686 2615; m 7169 7200; e lloyd@wilmotsafaris.com; www.wilmotsafaris. com. Best known for his Lloyd's Camp in Savuti, Lloyd Wilmot brings a lifetime's knowledge of Botswana's bush to his mobile safari operation. Trips are non-participation, comfortable but not luxurious, with the emphasis placed firmly on the wildlife. He is also planning a new lodge, Samochima, near Shakawe.

Horseriding specialists
African Animal Adventure Safaris
m 7336 6461; e AAASafaris@gmail.com, jen@africananimaladventures.com; www. africananimaladventures.com. In addition to local rides, Jen Weimann offers overnight horseriding trips in the Ngamiland region, perhaps along the Boro River or on the edge of the Delta, as well as further afield to the Makgadikgadi Pans.
African Horseback Safaris ✎686 1523;
e reservations@africanhorseback.com; www.

africanhorseback.com. Specialist horseriding safaris based out of Macatoo Camp on the western side of the Delta, in NG26. See pages 321–2.

Okavango Horse Safaris ☎686 1671; e safaris@okavangohorse.com; www. okavangohorse.com. See pages 336–9.

RAW Botswana See Motswiri, page 254.

Ride Botswana m 7248 4354, 7167 1608; e info@ridebotswana.com; www.ridebotswana. com. As well as riding for all levels at their Maun base at Royal Tree Lodge, Ride Botswana offers horseriding safaris for experienced riders in the Makgadikgadi Pans.

Rides on the Wild Side m 7178 4973; e rides@ ridesonthewildside.com; www.ridesonthewildside. com. Dany Hancock has brought together her experience of mobile & riding safaris to market riding holidays throughout the world. Botswana options include the Okavango Delta (for experienced riders) & – for beginners or the less experienced – the Makgadikgadi Pans, with plenty of opportunity to customise a trip.

Camping, boating, canoeing & budget safaris

Afro Trek ☎686 0177/2574/5110; e sedia@info. bw; www.afrotrek.com. Based at the Sedia Hotel, Afro Trek offers 1–3-day mokoro trips, 4x4 game safaris & short trips in & around Maun. There are also 14-day mobile safaris, to include Victoria Falls, with set-date departures (max 9 people).

Audi Camp Safaris ☎686 0599; e info@ okavangocamp.com; www.okavangocamp.com. The safari operation based out of Audi Camp (page 163) organises budget trips into Moremi & the Delta, from mobile camping safaris to drive-in mokoro trips. They also venture to Nxai Pan & the

Central Kalahari. Typically, trips require 2 people min & include meals, park fees, vehicle, guide & camping equipment, with travellers expected to bring their own drinks & sleeping bags, & muck in with all camp chores. Your own luggage can be stored at base.

Naga Safaris Shorobe Rd; ☎686 2353, 680 0587; m 7163 7250, 7182 5999; e info@african-wildlife-safaris.com; www.nagasafaris.com. Owned & run by local Batswana, this friendly, no-frills outfit, established in 2001, offers mobile camping safaris with their own guides & cooks to Chobe & Moremi, Makgadikgadi & Nxai pans, the Central Kalahari & Victoria Falls, as well as guided day trips to Moremi, & overnight trips into the Delta, Moremi or Nxai Pan. Camping equipment is available for hire.

The Old Bridge Backpackers ☎686 2406; e info@maun-backpackers.com; www.maun-backpackers.com. The local backpackers' place offers a range of trips, from rock-bottom basic to fully inclusive, tailormade options. These include 2-night guided excursions from the camp by motorboat to Chief's Island; mokoro trips on the edge of the Delta, some as far as the Panhandle; & desert trips into the Tsodilo Hills & the Central Kalahari. They also rent out a 4x4 vehicle with driver (P3,500 a day, plus fuel, max 8 people).

Okavango Still ☎686 5547; e info@ okavangostill.com; www.okavangostill.com. Specialist boating safari operators, Okavango Still organises camping trips across the Delta, moving between island campsites on aluminium motorboats. Most trips start from Maun, but the longest – an 8-day 'trans-Okavango' – involves an initial flight to Seronga, on the Panhandle, returning right through the Delta.

THE ROAD NORTH OF MAUN: TO MOREMI AND CHOBE [map 260–1]

FROM MAUN TO MOREMI GAME RESERVE Leave Maun heading northeast, passing the airport turn-off on your left. After about 10km you'll reach a roundabout with a right turn to the hospital, and a left to Shorobe. Take this left turn, passing lodges that include Crocodile Camp and Okavango River Lodge. It's a good tar road, but beware of travelling too fast as you'll find domestic animals on many stretches.

Just under 40km out of Maun you'll pass through the sizeable village of **Shorobe**. The village is 53km south of Moremi Game Reserve's South Gate, and marks the northern limit of the tar road between Maun and Moremi or Kasane. Drive slowly through here as you can usually expect plenty of goats and people wandering on the road. Dotted through the village are a few small shops which sell soft drinks and very basic supplies. Otherwise, the one place that may be worth checking out is Shorobe Baskets, housed in a green thatched building at the northern edge of the village.

From Shorobe, a wide gravel road leads after about 19km to the veterinary control fence, or the 'buffalo fence' as most people know it. In late 2013, work had restarted on regrading this stretch, which was in a dreadful state of repair: deeply scarred with pot-holes and with thick patches of sand.

Just 2km after the vet fence, a left-hand turning is signposted to Moremi Game Reserve, bringing you after a further 32km to the reserve's South Gate. For comments on this road, see the section on South Gate (page 282).

🏠 **Where to stay** The only place to stay that's actually on the road to South Gate is Kaziikini Campsite, although there's a national park campsite at South Gate itself. If you're prepared to drive some 30km out of your way, you could consider Mankwe Bush Lodge (page 352), on the road north to Chobe National Park, but the other lodges in this area, Santawani and Moremi Tented Camp, no longer accept drive-in guests.

⚊ **Kaziikini Campsite** [map 261] (4 rondavels, camping) NG34 Reserve; ✪ 19°35.394'S, 23°48.144'E. About 28km from South Gate, the community-run Kaziikini & adjacent Shandereka Cultural Village are set just off the road. For details, see page 351.

CONTINUING TO CHOBE If you're heading straight to Chobe, follow the directions above for Moremi, but after the buffalo fence continue straight ahead. This leads, after about 24km, to the village of **Sankuyo** [map 261]. There's little to delay the passing motorist here, beyond a shop, a couple of bars and a school, but the village is the base for the Sankuyo Tshwaragano Management Trust, which operates in the small NG33 Concession. As well as Kaziikini campsite and Shandereka Cultural Village (see above), the trust owns Santawani Lodge, about 15km south of Moremi Game Reserve's South Gate (see page 351).

Continuing north from Sankuyo, you'll reach a slightly obscure left turn after 13km. Ignore this and after a total of 30km, you'll come to Mababe Village. From the village, where the road bears northwest, continue for another 3km to a junction. Turning right here will lead after a final 7km to Chobe's Mababe Gate (✪ MABGAT 19°06.182'S, 23°59.119'E).

Had you taken the obscure left turning after Sankuyo (at ✪ MORCUT 19°29.050'S, 23°55.111'E), you would be driving due west along the Moremi cutline before it joins up with the road between Moremi's South and North gates. Veronica Roodt says that this is a legitimate way to access North Gate, but it is not a route that we have driven, so we would welcome any feedback from readers.

🏠 **Where to stay** Two lodges lie close to the road leading north to Chobe: one in the drier NG43, which lies to the east of Sankuyo; the second in the neighbouring NG41, which shares its northern and western boundaries with Chobe National Park. For details of both the lodges and the reserves, see pages 351–2.

🏠 **Mankwe Bush Lodge** [map 261] (8 tents, camping) NG43 Reserve. On the edge of the concession, Mankwe is to the west of the road, about 7km north of Sankuyo.

🏠 **Mogotlho Safari Lodge** [map 261] (13 tents) NG41 Reserve. Set on the Khwai River near Mababe Village, Mogotlho is a further 20km north of Mankwe.

8

Kasane and the Northeast

KASANE

The administrative centre of Chobe District, Kasane is on the surface just a small town in the northeast corner of Botswana. It lies on the southern bank of the Chobe River, a few kilometres from its confluence with the Zambezi – where the borders of Zambia, Zimbabwe, Namibia and Botswana meet at a point. Thus, while the town is of limited interest in itself, it is an important gateway: to the Chobe National Park; to Victoria Falls in Zimbabwe and Livingstone in Zambia; to the road across Namibia's Caprivi Strip; and to the small charter flights which ferry visitors between the various lodges in northern Botswana.

If you're just passing through the area, it's quite likely that you'll come via Kasane, if only on a transfer bus. And if you've organised your own travelling then you're likely to want to stop here, to refuel and refresh before continuing. But for many people, Kasane is a relaxing place to stay for a couple of days and to take advantage of its proximity to Chobe National Park, affording opportunities of boat cruises and game drives into the park.

GETTING THERE AND AWAY
Self-drive and hitchhiking
To/from Nata and Francistown From Kasane it is about 316km of tarred road to Nata, and 506km to Francistown. For hitchhikers this road is easy by Botswana's standards – make an early start from Francistown and you can expect to reach Kasane by nightfall. For details of the road between Kasane and Nata, see page 203.

To/from Zimbabwe
Kazungula There is an excellent tarred road from Zimbabwe to the Kazungula border (⏲ 06.00–18.00) and across into Botswana. This means that one of Africa's biggest attractions for visitors, Victoria Falls, is a day trip away from Kasane – and, more notably, that Chobe can be visited as a day trip from the Falls.

About 2km after entering Botswana at the substantial immigration office, there's a T-junction. The right turn is for the ferry to Zambia only; left leads you immediately past a disease-control post. Here your vehicle will be driven through a puddle of insecticide and you'll be asked to stamp your shoes on an impregnated mat. You'll also be checked to make sure that you're not importing banned animal products – like fresh meat, milk, bones or skins (all part of Botswana's zealous efforts to protect their national herd from diseases). Less than 2km later there's a right turn to Kasane, while straight on leads to Nata and Francistown. This is about 12km east of Kasane town.

If you're on an organised trip, it's very easy to have a road transfer arranged for you between Kasane and Victoria Falls town. It'll take about two hours, and cost in

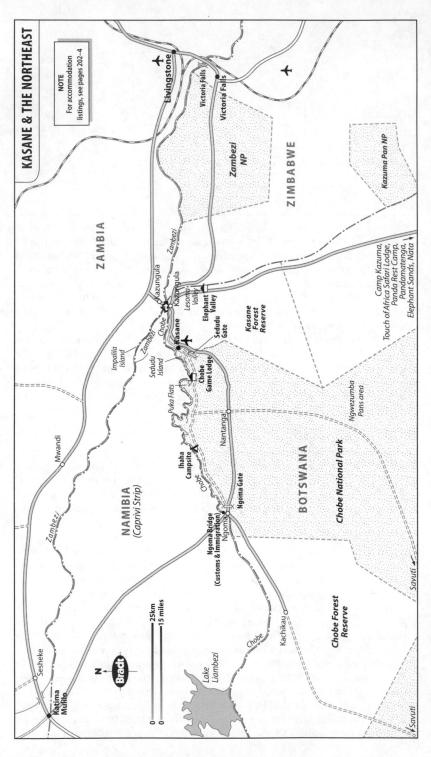

KASANE & THE NORTHEAST

NOTE
For accommodation
listings, see pages 202–4

ZAMBIA

Livingstone

Victoria Falls

Victoria Falls

Zambezi NP

ZIMBABWE

Kazuma Pan NP

Zambezi

Kazungula

Kazungula

Chobe

Lesoma Valley

Elephant Valley

Kasane

Sedudu Gate

Kasane Forest Reserve

Camp Kazuma,
Touch of Africa Safari Lodge,
Panda Rest Camp,
Pandamatenga,
Elephant Sands, Nata

Impalila Island

Zambezi

Sedudu Island

Chobe Game Lodge

Puka Flats

Ngwezumba Pans area

Nantanga

Mwandi

NAMIBIA
(Caprivi Strip)

Zambezi

Ihaha Campsite

Chobe

BOTSWANA

Chobe National Park

Ngoma Gate

Savuti

Ngoma Bridge
(Customs & Immigration)

Ngoma

Sesheke

N

Bradt

25km
15 miles

0
0

Kasika

Lake
Liambezi

Chobe

Kachikau

Chobe Forest Reserve

Katima Mulilo

Savuti

the region of US$70 per person, one-way. Note, however, that a visa for Zimbabwe will set you back a further US$55.

Pandamatenga About 93km south of Kasane, and 223km from Nata, this is one of the country's few arable-farming areas. It's easily distinguished by the prominent grain silos, which tower over the surrounding sorghum and maize fields. The small border post with Zimbabwe (⊕ *08.00–17.00*) is less than 50km from Robins Camp, deep in the heart of Zimbabwe's Hwange National Park, so it can be a convenient way to drive between Chobe and Hwange.

To/from Zambia While transfers from Livingstone airport are easily arranged and relatively inexpensive (about US$70 per person one way, based on three passengers), the Zambian government charges US$50 per person for a visa. Thus, unless you're rushing through, it's well worth an overnight stop in Livingstone, giving you the opportunity to visit Victoria Falls before heading on to Kasane. The journey from Livingstone to the border takes about 50 minutes along a straight, tarred road of about 65km, running parallel to the Zambezi.

Kazungula About 2km from the disease-control post mentioned above is a substantial vehicle ferry over the Zambezi (⊕ *06.00–17.30*) to the village of Kazungula in Zambia. It gets very busy on both sides of the river, with large lorries, local traffic and numerous pedestrians jostling to board, so allow an absolute minimum of two hours and plenty of patience to get through all the paperwork and for the short crossing. This is particularly important in the afternoon, if you want to be sure of crossing that night. The chaos is generally greater on the Zambian side, where access to the harbour, hampered by narrow gates, is frequently gridlocked, while in Botswana the lorries tend to form an orderly – if very long – queue; one evening we counted a tailback of more than 60 trucks stretching for 1.5km!

Foot passengers can get to the border by combi from opposite the bus station in Kasane (P3.50), or can organise a transfer from P40 per person. They are ferried across the river free of charge, but vehicle fares are based on size; expect to pay about US$30 for a Land Cruiser. Those taking a car into Zambia will be liable for tax and insurance, costing around US$20, in addition to any customs fees payable.

The idea of a road bridge across the Zambezi at this point has been mooted for many years, but it looks as though it is finally taking hold. Although work is expected to start in 2014, completion of the bridge is likely to take many years, so there's still plenty of time to experience the colour – and hassle – that make the ferry crossing so interesting.

If you want to hitch across to Zambia, then try standing where the Zimbabwean and Zambian roads fork, hitching on both of them. The disease-control post makes a perfect hitchhiking spot to get into Kasane or to head for Nata, as vehicles have to stop here anyway.

Sesheke Heading west on the Zambian side, it's about 130km to the small town of Sesheke, the gateway to Zambia's Western Province. The tar road crosses the Zambezi at a superb new bridge, currently one of only six to span the width of the Zambezi anywhere along its length (the others are at Chirundu, Tete, Livingstone and Katima Mulilo, with a footbridge at Chinyingi mission) – although another is under construction in Mozambique, and work on the latest bridge, at Kazungula, is scheduled to start in 2014. Sesheke can also be reached painlessly on good tar roads via Ngoma and Namibia.

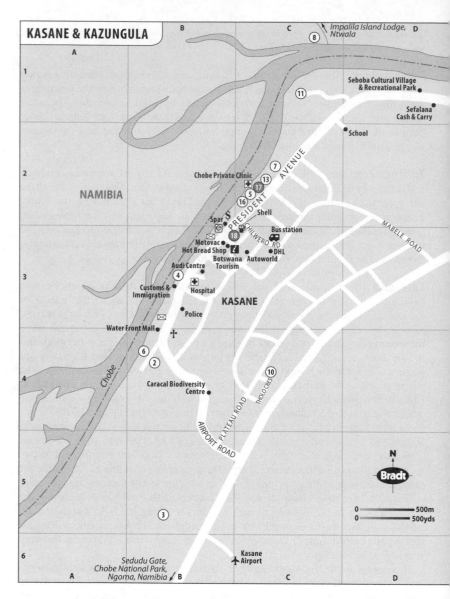

KASANE & KAZUNGULA

Impalila Island Lodge, Ntwala

Seboba Cultural Village & Recreational Park

Sefalana Cash & Carry

School

NAMIBIA

Chobe Private Clinic

PRESIDENT AVENUE

MABELE ROAD

Spar

Shell

Bus station

CHILWERO RD

DHL

Motovac

Hot Bread Shop

Botswana Tourism

Autoworld

Audi Centre

Customs & Immigration

Hospital

KASANE

Police

Water Front Mall

Chobe

Caracal Biodiversity Centre

AIRPORT ROAD

PLATEAU ROAD

THOLO CRES

N

Bradt

0   500m
0   500yds

Sedudu Gate, Chobe National Park, Ngoma, Namibia

Kasane Airport

To/from Namibia Ngoma (see page 216) is the location for a bridge across the Chobe, and a border with Namibia (⏱ *06.00–18.00*). It's about 51km from the centre of Kasane by good tar road, or rather more if you take the scenic riverside route (4x4 essential) through Chobe National Park. From Ngoma, it's a further 69km of good tar to the main town of Namibia's Caprivi Strip, Katima Mulilo.

By bus Kasane's new bus station [184 C3] is situated on Chilwero Road, behind the Shell garage in the centre of town. Buses leave Kasane for Francistown every day at 07.00, around 11.30 and 13.00 (*5hrs; P120*). If you want to get to Maun, take this bus, then change at Nata (*P65*) onto a bus coming from Francistown. To get your

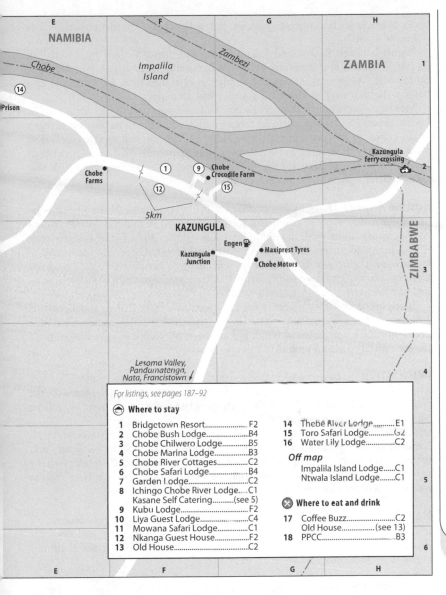

For listings, see pages 187–92

Where to stay

1	Bridgetown Resort	F2
2	Chobe Bush Lodge	B4
3	Chobe Chilwero Lodge	B5
4	Chobe Marina Lodge	B3
5	Chobe River Cottages	C2
6	Chobe Safari Lodge	B4
7	Garden Lodge	C2
8	Ichingo Chobe River Lodge	C1
	Kasane Self Catering	(see 5)
9	Kubu Lodge	F2
10	Liya Guest Lodge	C4
11	Mowana Safari Lodge	C1
12	Nkanga Guest House	F2
13	Old House	C2
14	Thebe River Lodge	E1
15	Toro Safari Lodge	G2
16	Water Lily Lodge	C2

Off map

Impalila Island Lodge	C1
Ntwala Island Lodge	C1

Where to eat and drink

17	Coffee Buzz	C2
	Old House	(see 13)
18	PPCC	B3

ticket, you'll need to arrive at least half an hour early. Operators include Pure White (240 5195; m 7145 5610). There are other buses later in the day, but these don't depart until they are full.

Regular minibuses and small combis ply between Kasane and Nata, linking on to both Francistown and Maun, with fares on a par with the larger buses.

To get to Kazungula for the ferry across to Zambia, or to cross into Zimbabwe, pick up a combi opposite the bus rank; the fare is around is P3.50.

By air Kasane (airline code BBK) is traditionally a busy gateway for the light aircraft that taxi visitors around the camps of northern Botswana, but its scheduled traffic is gradually beginning to pick up, too, with regular international as well as domestic flights.

Flights between Kasane and Johannesburg are operated daily by SA Airlink (↘ 390 5740), and four times a week by Air Botswana (↘ 625 0161), via Gaborone, on Monday, Wednesday, Friday and Sunday in each direction. Air Botswana also has two flights a week to Maun, on Tuesday and Thursday.

Most travellers coming through Kasane will also pass through Victoria Falls or Livingstone, so find it best to use the frequent flights to/from those airports to reach either Harare or Johannesburg. Do note, however, that you will need to pay US$50 for a visa in both Zambia and Zimbabwe. The 90-minute road transfer between Kasane and Victoria Falls or Livingstone costs around US$70 per person, or you could charter a plane – albeit at exceptionally high cost.

Kasane Airport [184 C6] This small, neat and very organised little airport is set on a ridge just a couple of kilometres west of the town. To find it, follow President Avenue nearly to its western end, then – just before Chobe Safari Lodge – turn left up the good tarred Airport Road. After 1.4km you'll meet the main road to Ngoma at a T-junction. Turn right here and less than 1km further you'll see a left turning clearly signposted to the airport. A transfer from town will cost around P40 per person.

There are desks at the airport for Air Botswana, SA Airlink and Botswana Tourism, and an office for Avis car rental, as well as toilets and a snack bar, but little else. Plans for a new terminal building have been mooted for some time, though progress so far has been limited to a new car park.

ORIENTATION Kasane is a fairly linear town, spread out along President Avenue, which shadows the Chobe River as it meanders from east to west, forming the boundary with Namibia. Most of the visitors' lodges stand on the river's southern bank, accessed by short side-roads.

A second tar road runs parallel to the town and the river to reach the border with Namibia at Ngoma. This actually cuts inland through the Chobe National Park, though isn't usually of interest for game viewing. Another tar road, which offers the only 2WD access to the rest of Botswana, heads southwards towards Nata and the rest of the Eastern Corridor area.

Maps There are few good maps of Kasane or its environs, perhaps because it's relatively easy to find your way about. For Chobe National Park, you need the excellent Shell map, by Veronica Roodt (see *Maps*, page 100). This is usually available from the shop at Chobe Safari Lodge.

Tourist information Botswana Tourism [184 B3] has recently opened an office near the bus station in Kasane (*Madiba Shopping Centre;* ↘ 625 0555; e *kasane@ botswanatourism.co.bw;* ⊕ *07.30–18.00 Mon–Fri, 09.00–14.00 Sat*), with a second desk at the airport (↘ 625 2210/1). There's certainly plenty of scope for browsing along shelves packed with leaflets and brochures.

GETTING AROUND Most visitors to the Kasane area will either have their own transport, or they'll be visiting as part of an organised trip with an all-inclusive package – so the general lack of transport won't be a problem. If you're backpacking or want to explore alone, there are a few minibuses that ply up and down the main road from opposite the new bus station. These are particularly useful for those staying at the eastern end of the town or in Kazungula. There are also several taxis, which tend to congregate near the supermarkets.

Car hire For self-drive car hire just about the only choice is Avis (\ *625 0144;* e *aviskse@botsnet.bw; www.avis.co.za;* ⏰ *08.00–13.00 & 14.00–17.00 Mon–Fri*), which operates out of the airport and accepts Visa, MasterCard and Amex. Note that it'll usually be cheaper to make a reservation and pay outside Botswana (indeed, outside of Africa), rather than turn up here and take the rate at the counter. For an indication of rates, see pages 83–4. For fuel, there's a Shell garage in the centre of town (⏰ *24hrs*), and another at the Kazungula junction.

Many hotels will arrange transfers to Kasane from Victoria Falls or Livingstone, for which you can expect to pay US$50–100 per person, excluding any visa costs, depending on numbers and whether or not you want a guide.

WHERE TO STAY For such a small town, Kasane has a surprising proliferation of accommodation options for all tastes and budgets, from top-class hotels to small lodges, B&Bs, and a range of campsites. Shared by almost all, though, is that all-important riverside location. All are usually open year round, unless otherwise stated.

When planning where to stay in this area, you should also consider the lodges inside the national park (see *Chapter 9*, pages 217–20), on the eastern side of the Chobe Forest Reserve, near Ngoma (pages 221–2) and in the Lesoma Valley (page 202). If you're just passing through Kasane, then it might make sense to choose to stay in one of the lodges outside the national park, as listed below, since they tend to be a little cheaper than those in the park, and you may also save a few days' park fees. However, if you're visiting the Kasane area specifically to see northern Chobe, and can afford to use one of the lodges in the park or near Ngoma, then you might be better there.

Lodges and hotels

⌂ **Chobe Chilwero Lodge** [184 B5]
(15 chalets) Contact Sanctuary Retreats (page 176). The erstwhile delightful small bush lodge of Chobe Chilwero, now owned by A&K under their highly exclusive Sanctuary Retreats brand, affords something of the atmosphere of a British country house in the bush. Set high above the river, looking out over the Chobe's floodplains from behind a relatively discreet electric fence, it boasts impressive standards of construction & design, with tasteful décor & many beautiful African artefacts that create something of the feel of an ethnological museum.

An imposing entrance hall leads through to the elegant lounge, where a small library has an excellent selection of books, magazines & games, & a discreetly covered TV. Much effort goes into the food here, with treats like breadsticks & truffles made at the lodge. The service is impeccable – but friendly – & the wine cellar extensive. Large, solidly built guest bungalows topped with thatch & cooled by AC are inviting in their own right, from canopied beds to free-standing baths,

indoor & outdoor showers, & private terraces with hammocks overlooking landscaped gardens. Those who can't live without the outside world will welcome the iPad made available for each chalet, with Wi-Fi throughout the lodge, & even a business centre. More hedonistic beings will head for the beautifully landscaped pool (with showers, toilets & sunbeds) or the seriously stylish spa (at extra cost), with its spa bath, hydrotherapy, plunge pool, & treatment rooms – one of them at tree height – offering Africology & Thalgo products. And then there's the classy shop…

Game drives are conducted by knowledgeable, enthusiastic guides in high-quality 4x4s, taking a max of 6 guests, although the lodge's location effectively limits these to the eastern part of Chobe's riverfront. Afternoon boat cruises are also offered in small, single-decker boats – or their own dbl decker, which is also used for lunches & teas. Fishing trips, & day trips to Victoria Falls in Zimbabwe, are available at additional cost.

Chobe Chilwero is a luxurious lodge with excellent views in an accessible spot on the edge of

Chobe, & makes an ideal 2–3-day excursion from Victoria Falls or Livingstone, but is not isolated enough to offer a real wilderness experience. *From US$650 pp to US$1,055/1,583pp sharing/sgl low–high season, inc FB, most drinks, activities, park fees, laundry; exc premium wines, spa, transfers*.

⌂ **Bridgetown Resort** [185 F2] (26 rooms, 10 suites) 📞625 1341; e info@bridgetownbw.com; www.bridgetownbw.com. You can hardly miss this rather ugly building on the Kazungula Rd. It was originally built as a block of smart apartments, but then changed to a 'resort'. Yet only its suites get a decent view of the river; most other rooms face the road, or the back of the suites. And the reception when we visited was in an underground car park. There are plans for a restaurant, bar, pool, in-room spa treatments, activity centre & curio shop, but as it stands, the site is fundamentally flawed. 🝆

⌂ **Chobe Marina Lodge** [184 B3] (60 rooms) 📞625 2221; e res1@chobemarinalodge.com; www.chobemarinalodge.com. There's no mistaking this upmarket resort, with its deep-red & ochre buildings that feel instantly at one with its luxuriant gardens. Built across a narrow creek, with extensive tree shade, it was opened in 2002 in direct competition with Mowana Safari Resort & Spa. The spacious tiled & thatched entrance opens on to dark wooden decking, from where walkways fan out to restaurants & the bar, a curio shop, in-house tour company, private jetty, & a large infinity pool with its own bar overlooking lawns along the river.

Rooms, including 1 adapted for paraplegics, range from individual chalets at the back, each incorporating 2 separate rooms, to rather small river-facing 'suites' with dbl beds, & – best value by far – the surprisingly spacious studios, closer to the river, which can interconnect to form a suite with a lounge & small kitchenette. All have tiled floors, TV, AC, fan & safe, & private balcony; & once the latest refurbishment is complete, all will have a bath & separate shower.

The hotel has 2 dining options: informal eating above the pool, or the 1st-floor Commissioners restaurant, where à-la-carte or buffet meals are served in air-conditioned comfort or on a balcony overlooking the river. There's free Wi-Fi in the central area & a 100-seat conference room, but if relaxation is more your thing, try a massage in the Kwa Maningi spa.

Activities, here as elsewhere, focus on the river, with well-guided river cruises in intimate 16-seater boats, fishing trips, & of course game drives. Returning by river to the rhythm & vitality of traditional dancers performing above the jetty is an occasional highlight not to be missed. 🝆

⌂ **Mowana Safari Resort & Spa** [184 C1] (114 rooms) 📞625 0300; e resmowana@cresta.co.bw; www.mowanasafarilodge.net; central reservations 📞391 2431; e reservations@cresta.co.bw. The Botswana flagship of the Cresta group, Mowana was conceived on a grand scale. Well designed, airy & spacious, it makes imaginative use of wooden decking, with an old baobab tree at its heart. Double & twin en-suite rooms, incorporating 4 suites, 16 family rooms & 2 rooms for paraplegics, are attractively finished with river views, & offer everything that you'd expect from a top international hotel, including remote-control AC, fan, phone, fridge, TV & safe.

Overlooking the river are 2 restaurants & 2 bars. The main restaurant has both an à-la-carte menu, & a set-price buffet. Above it, the open-sided upstairs bar/lounge catches the breeze, with a warming wood fire for winter evenings. Less formal is the outside bar & restaurant located above a large, modern pool with separate children's pool. Guests will also appreciate the smart curio shop, an internet room & free Wi-Fi in all central areas & some rooms. But talk of the town is an extensive new riverside spa, whose 4 treatment rooms, sauna, jacuzzi & serene infinity pool share a lovely setting; even the gym has a certain appeal!

For the business visitor there are conference facilities for up to 100 people, but most are more interested in the game drives & boat cruises (US$35 & park fees) that venture into Chobe National Park from the hotel's own jetty. In case that's not enough, there's also a tennis court & a 9-hole golf course, as well as evenings of traditional African culture. 🝆

⌂ **Chobe Bush Lodge** [184 B4] (42 rooms) President Av; 📞625 0336; e reservations@chobebushlodge; www.chobebushlodge.com. Opening in early 2014, this 2-storey sister to Chobe Safari Lodge (see below) lies just across the road. It's constructed in similar style, with exactly the same activities (& prices), & accommodation on a par with Safari Lodge's 'safari' rooms, but instead of the river frontage it offers viewing platforms overlooking Chobe National Park. Bush Lodge has its own pool, bar, shop & restaurant serving à-la-carte lunches & set dinners, & has Wi-Fi in the lounge area, but for a change of scene (& to use their amenities) guests are welcome across the road, too. **$$$$** *exc b/fast (US$16–26 pp).*

🏠 **Garden Lodge** [184 C2] (8 rooms) 714 President Av; ☎ 625 0051; **m** 7164 6064; **e** reservations@oshaughnessys.org; www. thegardenlodge.com. This small, friendly lodge, 5km from the national park, is relaxed, personal & well designed, a welcome change from the more corporate style of the larger lodges. Unobtrusively tucked behind secure gates, it has a tranquil setting with attractive gardens. From the lofty central area, combining lounge & dining room, & uniquely flanked by a semi-covered pool, a shaded terrace looks across an expanse of lawn towards the river. Upstairs, a rustic wooden bar is an ideal spot for chilling out. En-suite twin or dbl rooms are bright, light & cool: kitted out in natural fabrics, with cane chairs & coir carpets, AC, ceiling fans & kettle. Each looks towards the river from its own balcony, or from a terrace leading on to the lawn. A 2-storey family chalet lacks a fan or river views, but is completely detached with a private veranda. In addition to game drives & boat cruises from its own jetty, the lodge offers boat hire & day trips to Victoria Falls **$$$$** *US$250/365 pp sharing/sgl DBB May–Nov, US$195/290 Dec–Apr, inc local transfers. No children under 4.*

🏠 **Chobe Safari Lodge** [184 B4] (81 rooms, 8 rondavels, camping) President Av; ☎ 625 0336; **e** reservations@chobesafarilodge; www. chobesafarilodge.com. On a spacious site overlooking the river, on the western fringes of town, Chobe Safari Lodge is the oldest of Kasane's camps. Its wide lawns, well shaded by mature trees, attract warthogs & families of banded mongoose, as well as vervet monkeys & numerous birds. Although it is the closest lodge to the national park for boat trips, this proximity makes little difference if you're driving, since the entrance to the park is several kilometres by road.

The impressive reception, lobby, lounge, activity centre & restaurant shelter under a huge, open-sided thatched structure whose heavy rafters are an occasional playground for vervet monkeys. In front, a sparkling crescent-shaped pool is surrounded by loungers & tables beneath the trees, making this an attractive lunch venue; the

burgers are said to be excellent & buffets at lunch & dinner (US$27/33) are hugely popular. Other facilities include a very well-stocked shop, a health & beauty centre, Wi-Fi access in the central area, & 2 bars, with the Sedudu bar at the campsite a favourite place for sundowners.

There's a good choice of accommodation, in 2 price bands. At the top end, the modern 'river' rooms & slightly larger, predominantly dark-wood 'safari' rooms have twin or dbl beds, en-suite shower & bath, AC/fan, TV, safe, kettle & phone, plus a balcony or veranda overlooking lawns to the river. 'Standard' rooms, & the lodge's original rondavels, now have AC, TV & safes, too, as well as braai stands. For a party of 4, the family rooms are particularly good value. Meanwhile, the campsite by the river changes little, though it has acquired a few pre-erected tents over the years. It is still popular with overlanders, but note that independent campers may not pre-book.

Game drives (US$39 pp, plus park fees) depart daily at 06.00 & 15.00, while well-guided boat cruises (US$33) leave at 15.00. For something a little more intimate you can explore the river between 07.00 & 14.00 in a small motorboat with a driver (US$57 pp/2hrs), or go fishing (US$44 pp/hr inc tackle). Numerous other excursions include Victoria Falls (US$199 with a guide, exc visa), & a Namibian village walk (US$39). **$$$–$$$$** *exc b/fast (US$16–26 pp). Camping US$14/11 adult/child.*

🏠 **Kubu Lodge** [185 F2] (11 chalets, camping) ☎ 625 0312; **m** 7126 5000; **e** kubu@botsnet. bw; www.kubulodge.net. About 9km from the centre of Kasane, Kubu stands on a sloping site beside the river, clearly signposted from the main road. Batswana-owned & run, the lodge (whose name means 'hippo' in Setswana) is friendly & personable, & immaculately kept.

Kubu's square thatched chalets are substantial wooden buildings raised off the ground with steps up to a veranda at the front, set under shady trees in lush green lawns sloping down to the river. Each is well furnished with rugs on the wooden floors, wood & metal furniture & a dbl & sgl bed – or 3 sgls. Mosquito nets, screened windows & a fan keep the bugs at bay, there's a compact en-suite bathroom, & a coffee machine provides a touch of luxury.

Overlooking the river, a solid wooden building with screened windows houses the restaurant, with tables spilling out on to the veranda & a cosy mezzanine area above. A buffet lunch is around P115, & the set dinner, changed daily, P225. Lower down are a braai area & boma, then a swimming pool surrounded by lawns. A large shop offers a variety of curios, cards & a few books.

A few mins' walk from the lodge, Kubu's campsite is popular with private campers, though its 8 large dusty pitches, each with a braai stand, offer limited shade at the end of the dry season, when the trees are bare. Toilets & hot showers are clean & functional, & there's a small plunge pool (campers may not use the lodge pool). Part of the campsite slopes down to the river so though the road is lit, it's wise to take a torch if you eat at the restaurant in the evening.

Game drives & boat cruises run morning & afternoon, & fishing trips can be organised too. While the jetty at the lodge is used for cruises up the confluence of the Chobe & Zambezi, visitors heading for the Chobe River in the national park are transferred by road to a jetty in Kasane. The extensive grounds feature a marked nature trail, with helpful notes & a map on hand. **$$$** *Camping P87 pp. No children under 4.* ⊙ *Closed mid-Jan–Feb.*

🏠 **Water Lily Lodge** [184 C2] (10 rooms) President Av; 📞625 1775/2709; e waterlily@ botsnet.bw; www.janalatours.com. Owned by Monica Kgaile, 'quite a character' according to one local, Water Lily Lodge was opened in 2004. From the outside it looks like a giant cream-washed rondavel, & effectively that's what it is, albeit built around a central fountain. Nicely presented en-suite rooms overlook the river, with doors onto the garden or a small balcony. Inside are twin beds & mosquito nets, plus AC, TV, safe, desk & kettle.

Meals can be taken in the attractive restaurant or outside on a thatched terrace alongside a convivial bar & a small, kidney-shaped pool. The à-la-carte menu focuses on fresh fish (inc excellent bream), steaks & chicken dishes at around P75, with lighter lunches from P45. Boat cruises, game drives & day trips to Victoria Falls are all on offer through their own tour company. **$$** *exc b/fast (P80 pp).*

Guesthouses, B&Bs and self-catering

🏠 **Chobe River Cottages** [184 C2] (6 rooms) President Av; 📞625 2863; m 7566 3152;

e bookings@choberivercottages.com; www.choberivercottages.com. Opened in March 2013, this secure set-up is smart & airy, with modern apartment-style rooms adorned with evocative aerial photographs. Stroll past the small free-form pool (with separate baby pool), & the warthogs pulling at the grass beyond, & you'll come to a high viewing deck above the river, where a jetty is being built for boat trips.

From the large kitchenette off the lounge area (which would put many a home kitchen to shame) to the twin or dbl bedrooms with AC & ceiling fans, it's all exceptionally well equipped & thought out. There's a sofa bed in the lounge for an extra couple of guests, & the veranda even has a giant mosi-net curtain so you can sit out in privacy & comfort after dinner cooked on your own BBQ. If you don't fancy self-catering (& Spar is just a short walk away for supplies), then Coffee Buzz is on hand for b/fast, with several more options for lunch or an evening meal. **$$$** *exc b/fast.*

🏠 **Kasane Self Catering** [184 C2] (2 cottages) President Av; 📞625 0114; m 7553 2117; e trish@ chobeselfcatering.com; www.chobeselfcatering.com. Under the same ownership as Chobe River Cottages, & almost adjacent, these 2 cottages have an entirely different style & atmosphere. Each has a leafy porch & chairs looking out to the tranquil, verdant gardens of Trish Williams' home, a haven for birds (inc several endemics) that showcases her profession as a landscape gardener. In the bedrooms – a twin & a dbl – handmade patchwork quilts lend a homely touch to dark-wood traditional furniture, yet there's AC to keep the temperature down, a kitchenette with all that you could need for self-catering, & a private BBQ area. Here, as at Chobe River Cottages, there are safes, secure parking & free Wi-Fi, though there's also a friendly dog. The same practical comments apply, too, & guests may use the neighbouring pool & riverside viewing deck. **$$** *exc b/fast.*

🏠 **Liya Guest Lodge** [184 C4] (5 rooms) 📞625 2376; e liyaglo@botsnet.bw. This unremarkable but clean guesthouse on a suburban street above Kasane is conveniently close to the airport. Twin & dbl rooms all have AC, TV, a kettle, fridge & their own bathroom, with 3 rooms en suite, & there's a small lounge with TV. Lunch & dinner are available on request (P80), or guests may use the kitchen. **$$**

🏠 **Nkanga Guest House** [185 F2] (10 rooms) 📞625 0177; m 7349 8383; e nkanga@botsnet.

bw. Recommended by reader Jon Williamson, Nkanga has expanded from a small B&B to a substantial guesthouse – yet it remains pleasant, modestly decorated & absolutely spotless: a good place to lay your head. It's set well back from a fairly busy road, within a secure compound, where 4 older rooms are in the main house, & newer ones (at the same price) in an adjacent block. All are en suite with AC, TV, mosi nets, a kettle & fridge. There's a lounge with sofa & TV, too, & they'll advise on activities in & around Kasane. **$$** *exc b/fast (P70).*

⌂ **The Old House** [184 C2] (10 rooms) 718 President Av; ☎ 625 2562; e reservations@ oldhousekasane.com; www.oldhousekasane.com. This popular restaurant now offers B&B in modern but unpretentious twin, dbl or family rooms with AC & en-suite showers. The complex is wheelchair-accessible, as is one of the rooms. For amenities, there's free Wi-Fi, secure parking, a plunge pool & a very good gift shop – & of course the relaxed, pub-style bar & restaurant. The normal range of activities can be organised, as can sunset river cruises, fishing trips & more, & it's also the base for Gecko canoe trips. **$$**

Chalets and camping
As well as these 2 options, there are excellent campsites at both Chobe Safari Lodge & Kubu Lodge. Note that many of the campsites in Kasane will not accept advance bookings from individual campers (as against overland groups), so in high season it's a good idea to arrive early.

⌂ **Thebe River Lodge** [185 E1] (31 rooms, camping) ☎ 625 0995; e reservations@ theberiversafaris.com; www.theberiversafaris. com. This friendly, family-owned site is well run, with much of the atmosphere of a popular backpackers' lodge. Located about 5km from the centre of town, it's the base for Thebe River Safaris (page 195) & was almost entirely rebuilt in 2008, complete with an extensive reception area. Simple,

clean, modern rooms are all en suite, with twin beds (plus 1 family room), mosi nets, tea & coffee facilities, & ceiling fan. Most are built in a thatched block around a courtyard, but some – in a row behind – are rather dark.

The campsite is usually occupied by overlanders or travellers taking a trip with Thebe – whose activities are some of the most affordable in Kasane. Bookings are not accepted from independent campers, who take pot luck, & in high season the site may be full. Each of the campsite pitches has its own shaded gazebo & braai stand. Nearer to the river are a large bar, restaurant & small pool. Transfers/day trips can be arranged to & from Victoria Falls & Livingstone. **$$$** *exc b/fast (P78-90). Camping P105 pp.*

⌂ **Toro Safari Lodge** [185 G2] (37 chalets, camping) ☎ 625 2694; m 7458 4254; e torolodge@botsnet.bw; www.torolodge.co.bw. Opened in 2004, Toro lies just 600m from the turn-off towards Kasane from Kazungula. Despite its riverside location, this modern complex, with its orange-painted square chalets in neat rows, seems devoid of personality, a perspective that isn't enhanced by the 'Enclave' (think 'H' block) of rooms. Each of the small thatched chalets is approached through screened doors from a brick veranda. Inside, they're carpeted, with a fan, AC, TV, kettle & en-suite shower, & some – very close together – have riverfront views. Behind these a level, grassy campsite incorporates 24 neat pitches with power points, a fireplace & – a big bonus – private ablution facilities, including hot showers. Shade, in the form of immature trees, is growing rapidly. The lodge hosts several overland groups, but independent campers are welcome too. In the wide-fronted central area, open to the river, solid wood furniture gives an air of permanence to the bar & dining area, while next to the pool is a second bar. Activities include boat cruises (from the jetty at Garden Lodge) & game drives; fishing can also be organised. **$$$** *Camping P113 pp.*

✗ **WHERE TO EAT** Between them, Kasane's hotels and lodges offer a range of restaurants, some of them very good, and most visitors choose to eat in their place of accommodation.

For something more relaxed, seek out the Old House, while for a more local flavour, there's the restaurant at Water Lily Lodge. If you're after somewhere a bit different consider PPCC next to the fuel station. And if you're craving fast food, Kasane can oblige in the form of KFC, close to Spar.

✗ **Coffee Buzz** [184 C2] 721 President Av; m 7131 8956; www.thecoffeebuzz.co.za; ⏰ 07.00–14.00 daily. Bettina Kelly's pleasant, fan-cooled café does a good b/fast, as well as coffee & cakes, milkshakes & a range of lunch dishes. The menu, dubbed 'German-African' cuisine, includes 2 daily specials – 1 vegetarian & 1 non-veg: perhaps Moroccan chickpea soup & garlic bread, or fish & chips. Guests may relax in the small garden & use the pool, & it's worth checking out Bettina's colourful mosaics, too. $$

✗ **The Old House** [184 C2] President Av; ☎625 2562; ⏰ 06.30–21.30 daily. The reincarnation of this old favourite has been a boon for Kasane. It's a fun place, very friendly & relaxed, with pub-style tables & sports TV for the latest on the rugby field. Food – focusing on the likes of burgers, steaks & pizzas – is served under cover or on a wooden deck facing the garden, where you can let off steam playing volleyball or wander down to the river. $$

✗ **PPCC** [184 B3] Next to the Shell garage; ☎625 2237; m 7272 8318; ⏰ 09.00–22.00 daily. PPCC stands for Pizza Plus Coffee & Curry, but that's only the half of it; also on the menu are burgers, pizzas, Chinese dishes & even a full English b/fast. The restaurant & bar are relatively formal, but there's a small, shaded terrace set back from the road, & we understand that the food is good. A take-away service is handy for anyone self-catering. $$

SHOPPING

Food and drink Most accessible for travellers are the town's two **supermarkets**: Spar, which is close to Barclays Bank [184 B2], and Choppies at Water Front Mall [184 B3] (*both* ⏰ *07.30–19.00 Mon–Fri, 07.30–18.00 Sat, 08.00–17.00 Sun*). (A second branch of Choppies is under construction at Kazungula Junction [185 F3]. Both have pretty well everything you'll need for a camping trip.

More specialist is the Butchery at Water Front Mall [184 B3] (⏰ *07.00–18.00 daily*), which in addition to very good vacuum-packed steaks offers handy 'braai boxes' (instant BBQs), a range of sauces, and some good fresh fruit and veg. Do note, though, that if you're heading south towards Nata, you cannot take fresh red meat across the veterinary fence.

For good **bread**, as well as pies and take-away meals, try the very popular Hot Bread Shop [184 B3] (⏰ *07.30–19.00 Mon–Fri, 07.30–13.00 Sat/Sun*) behind the Shell garage, where there's also a small **market**.

While supermarkets themselves are not licensed to sell **alcohol**, Spar has its own off-licence, Tops (⏰ *10.00–19.00 Mon–Fri, 10.00–18.00 Sat*), on the parade in front of the supermarket, while at the Water Front Mall there's the Jacaranda Bottle Store with similar hours.

For large-scale shopping expeditions, including beer and wine, try **Sefalana Cash & Carry** [184 D1] (⏰ *08.00–17.00 Mon–Fri, 08.00–14.30 Sat*), just east of the turn-off to Thebe River Safaris. Not far from here is **Chobe Farms** [185 E2], where a wide variety of seasonal fruit and vegetables is available direct from the grower.

Crafts, gifts and books These are the domain of the gift shops at the various hotels along the river, with the two at Chobe Safari Lodge [184 B4] among the best.

It's also worth checking out the various craft shops in the parade behind Spar [184 B2], and the mosaics at Coffee Buzz [184 C2] – where a new art and curio shop, Buzzadi Trading, is in the offing. For locally made baskets and other crafts, try the shop at the new Seboba Cultural Village [184 D1], or:

Gecko Gift Shop [184 C2] Old House, President Av; ⏰ 08.00–17.00 daily. This colourful Aladdin's cave of gifts & jewellery is found at the Old House – so you can combine browsing with a spot of lunch or a drink.

Chobe Women's Arts & Crafts Centre [184 B4] Airport Rd; ⏰ 08.00–17.00 daily. Soon to move into new premises at the Caracal Biodiversity Centre, this is a co-operative of 30 or so women who get together to make traditional baskets & to teach their skills to others. The plan is for the women to work *in situ*, so that visitors can watch them weave, & perhaps meet the person who created 'their' basket. Until the building is complete, there is a temporary display of their work at the Caracal Centre itself.

Clothes and equipment Several shops in the Spar complex opposite the Shell garage [184 C3] sell everyday tops, trousers and shoes, so there's likely to be something that will fit the bill. For items of safari clothing, you'll probably do better at the shops in the larger hotels.

OTHER PRACTICALITIES

Banks and bureaux de change Kasane is an obvious spot for changing money and has a couple of banks plus several ATMs, of which the most reliable is FNB at Water Front Mall [184 B3]. I still have memories of changing money at Barclays [184 B2] (⊕ KASANE 17°47.97'S, 25°9.015'E) in 1988 when it occupied a small, picturesque thatched rondavel; now its home is a modern, architect-designed building opposite the Shell garage. Neither ATM accepts MasterCard, but you can get cash against a card in the banks.

If you're planning to change cash, it's normally considerably quicker to go to one of the town's bureaux de change, where rates are only slightly lower than at the bank, queues are shorter, and opening hours are considerably longer. While considering how much cash to change, note that park fees at the Sedudu Gate are most easily paid in either pula or US dollars, so bear this in mind if you're intending to drive yourself through the national parks.

$ **Cape to Cairo** [184 B2] Opp Spar; ⊕ 08.30–17.00 Mon–Fri, 08.30–16.30 Sat. Also offers an internet service.
$ **Open Door Bureau de Change** [184 B3] Water Front Mall; ☏ 625 2088; ⊕ 07.30–10.00

Mon–Fri, 08.30–16.00 Sat, 09.00–16.00 Sun. Internet P15/30mins.
$ **River Ride** [184 B3] Audi Centre; ☏ 625 1156; ⊕ 08.00–16.00 Mon–Fri, 08.30–13.00 Sat

Communications
Post and courier Kasane boasts two **post offices**, of which the main Chobe Post Office [184 B3] (⊕ *09.00–17.15 Mon–Fri, 09.00–12.15 Sat*) is close to Barclays Bank, opposite the Shell garage. A second, smaller office [184 B3] (⊕ *08.00–16.00 Mon–Fri, 08.00–11.00 Sat*) is further west, just down from Water Front Mall. You can also get stamps at Kasane Computers, in the Audi Centre [184 B3].

DHL [184 C3] Opposite the bus station; ☏ 625 0069

Internet There are several internet cafés in the town, including the main post office, typically charging P10 for 15 minutes, or P15 for 30 minutes. Most reliable are the two bureaux de change (above), and:

🖳 **Kasane Computers** [184 B3] Audi Centre; ☏ 625 2312; www.kasanecomputers.com; ⊕ 08.00–17.00 Mon–Fri, 08.00–13.00 Sat. P5/10mins. They'll also download your digital

photos on to CD & hold them for up to 2mths – a great back-up in case of memory-card disasters. They have a second office at Kazungula Junction.

Telephone Local SIM cards can in theory be purchased at many outlets, including Chobe Post Office, but most efficient is the Mascom office tucked almost out of sight next to Choppies at Water Front Mall [184 B3], and open normal shopping hours.

Health Kasane's **hospital** [184 B3] (☏ *625 0222/0333*) is on the main road towards Chobe Safari Lodge. The town also offers a couple of private clinics, along with a dentist and a pharmacy.

⊞ **Chobe Private Clinic** [184 C2] President Av; ☏ 625 1555

✚ **Pharma Africa** [184 B3] Audi Centre; ☏ 625 1502, emergency m 7322 8502; ⊕ 08.30–17.00 Mon–Fri, 09.00–13.00 Sat

Photography To download photos to CD, try Kasane Computers (see *Internet*, above), who also sell memory sticks and CDs. For camera memory cards, batteries and binoculars, try Chobe Photo Lab [184 B3] (*Audi Centre;* ☏ *625 0254/1050*).

Vehicle repairs and equipment If you must break down, then Kasane's not a bad place to do so, as it's used as a supply base by some of the safari operators and has both several garages and branches of two well-known parts suppliers. Certainly if you're heading across Chobe and Moremi you should make sure your vehicle's in tip-top shape before you head off. Both parts outfits are located next to the Shell garage (⊕ *08.00–17.00 Mon–Fri, 08.00–13.00 Sat, 09.00–12.00 Sun*).

Autoworld [184 C3] ☏ 316 3840. Behind the Shell garage. Sells spares for all major makes, including Land Rover, Nissan & Toyota. Also has a workshop out towards Kazungula.
Chobe Motors [185 G3] Kazungula; ☏ 625 0673/4. At junction with the Nata road, opposite Engen garage.

Maxiprest Tyres [185 G3] Kazungula; ☏ 625 1032. Also opposite Engen garage.
Motovac [184 B3] ☏ 625 0848. Another well-known chain, also behind the Shell garage, offering a similar range of parts.

WHAT TO SEE AND DO
Tour operators, safari companies and travel agents Because overland truck companies that are not officially registered in Botswana can't use their own vehicles in the park, there's a strong market in Kasane for day trips into Chobe. Most of the hotels and lodges organise these for their own guests, but some welcome outsiders too, and there are also several independent companies. There is also a handful of mobile safari operators based in Kasane.

For those all-important national parks bookings, make your way to Chobe National Park's Sedudu Gate (page 198).

African Odyssey Chobe Marina Lodge; ☏ 625 2270; m 7449 2506; e odyssey@info.bw; www.wildhorizons.co.za. Offers game drives, river cruises, fishing & various guided trips & walks.
Bushtracks Botswana ☏ 625 0840; e reservations@bushtracksafrica.com; www.gotothevictoriafalls.com. A satellite of Bushtracks in Livingstone, Bushtracks Botswana offers transfers in & around Chobe, including a private boat crossing of the Zambezi River, plus game drives & boat cruises in Chobe National Park, & day trips to Livingstone & Victoria Falls.
Chobe Tours & Safaris ☏ 625 0880; e info@kalahari-tours.net; www.kalaharichobe.com.

Formerly known as Kalahari Tours, this is the place for day trips & a range of short camping safaris into Chobe National Park.
Gavin Blair Safaris m 7562 2440; e gbs@gavinblairsafaris.com; www.gavinblairsafaris.com. This small, personal outfit leads tailormade safaris throughout Botswana, Zimbabwe & Namibia, all guided by Gavin himself, who has 30 years' guiding experience. Options include lodge, fly-in, walking & canoeing safaris.
Janala Tours & Safaris ☏ 625 1775/2709; e janala@botsnet.bw; www.janalatours.com. This tour company linked to Water Lily Lodge offers

some of the more affordable trips into the national park, as well as safaris further afield.

Kazuma Trails +263 13 40857; m 7136 3653, 7192 4703; e info@mobile-safaris.com; www.mobile-safaris.com. Owned & run by one of Zimbabwe's top guides & his wife, David & Antonette Carson, Kazuma offers mobile safaris to all Botswana's major wildlife hotspots. Led by David or another high-quality guide, there are participation safaris, using dome tents with a toilet & shower between 4 guests; 'semi-luxury' using larger dome tents; & 'luxury' with en-suite walk-in tents. Tailormade safaris are possible, but you'll need to book well ahead if you want to request David as a guide.

Pangolin Photo Safaris (see advert, page 204) 625 1244; m 7642 9758; e info@pangolinphoto.com; www.pangolinphoto.com. The ultimate tour company for photoholics, Pangolin uses adapted vehicles & boats kitted out with long-lens DSLR cameras mounted on swivelling tripods.

Puku Safaris 625 0753; m 7375 2047, 7479 6707; e pukusafaris@botsnet.bw; www.pukusafarisbotswana.com. Game drives, boat cruises, & transfers to Victoria Falls.

SGS Africa 625 0259/1754; e reservations@sgsafrica.com; www.sgsafrica.com. Safari and Guides Services Africa organises customised & scheduled mobile safaris of different styles throughout Botswana, with lodge-based itineraries a further option.

SM Travel & Tours m 7143 5525; e smtours6@gmail.com. Locally run & well recommended, SM can organise transfers & tours in & around Kasane, & trips to Victoria Falls, with or without a guide.

Thebe River Safaris 625 0995; e reservations@theberiversafaris.co.za; www.theberiversafaris.co.za. As well as a popular campsite & backpackers' lodge, Thebe organises its own realistically priced activities into the national parks. It is also the base for a mobile-safari operation that runs tailormade & set trips around northern Botswana & into Zambia. It's run by Jan, Annatjie, Jannie & Louis van Wyk, & sister Franci, who pitch trips as 'budget, middle or luxury' – depending on how much effort/cash you are willing to expend. Thebe also arranges boats, vehicles & guides for game drives/boat trips in the park.

In Kasane Until recently, attractions in Kasane itself were limited to a couple of low-key wildlife operations, but the opening of a new cultural village is set to raise the bar considerably. Rather quirky is a large hollow **baobab tree**, with a locking door, which stands behind the present police station, and was used as a prison in the early 1900s.

Seboba Cultural Village and Recreational Park [184 D1] (⊕ 06.00–22.00), Scheduled to open in 2014, and beautifully sited above a short stretch of rapids on the Chobe River, Seboba is an ambitious community project that has received considerable funding from Botswana's tourist office, with a view to involving the community in the tourism sector and fostering their traditional heritage. Essentially the park is split into two: a cultural village, and a lovely riverside boardwalk – but it also houses a large auditorium that will accommodate up to 165 people for performances of dance, music and drama. A bar and tables behind the traditional rows of seating will allow a more relaxed view of the stage. The whole site is wheelchair accessible.

The cultural village incorporates traditional homesteads from four different tribes hailing from the Chobe area: the Banambiya, the Basubiya, the Basarwa and the Batawana. Here it is planned to have a traditional *kgotla*, or meeting place, with each tribe in turn nominating a chief for group discussions, and perhaps visits from a witch doctor and other key members of the community.

In the centre of the site, a high mound gives a tantalising vantage point over the rapids, while almost back at ground level, a partially raised 1km walkway runs parallel to the river, with a couple of small observation 'hides' that are likely to prove popular among photographers as well as those just taking in the view. At the

8

end of the walkway, you're rewarded with a shaded picnic site set up with benches, tables and barbecue stands, as well as toilets. For the visitor, one of the unspoken advantages of the site is the opportunity to go for a walk – something that is all too rare while on safari!

To round off a visit, it is planned for the large curio shop to showcase the work of local basket weavers and other artisans, thus encouraging the development of traditional skills among future generations. For now, talk of adding to the facilities with a caged swimming area in the river, and walks on the islands, is just a pipedream.

Caracal Biodiversity Centre [184 B4] (*Airport Rd;* \ *624 2391;* e *caracal@ botsnet.bw; www.caracal.info;* ⊕ *09.00–17.00 daily; P35 pp*) Formerly known as Chobe Snake Park, the centre is part of the NGO known as CARACAL (the Centre for Conservation of African Resources: Animals, Communities and Land use; *www.caracal.info*). It hosts a collection of indigenous fauna, ranging from mambas, cobras and boomslangs to the greater numbers of harmless snakes, as well as other reptiles, not to mention frogs, birds, butterflies, insects and banded mongooses. These last are the subject of a research project into why the animals are contracting TB. Caracal is also home to the Chobe Women's Arts & Crafts Centre (page 192), which will soon occupy an imposing thatched building that's clearly visible at the entrance to the centre.

BATTLE FOR AN ISLAND

The precise boundary between Namibia and Botswana in this area has been defined to follow the deepest channel of the Chobe River – a definition which works well for most river boundaries. However, the Chobe splits into many streams, whose strengths and depths seem to gradually alter over the years.

Sedudu Island (or Kasikili Island, as it's called in Namibia) is a very low, flat island which covers about 3.5km^2 when the waters are low, but shrinks to a much smaller size when it is flooded. It's used mainly for grazing cattle.

Both Botswana and Namibia have claimed that the island belongs to them. In the 1990s it was occupied by the Botswana Defence Force (BDF) who built several watchtowers on it – chunky structures towering over the island's grassy plains, and cunningly disguised with variegated military-pattern netting. In early 1995, both Botswana and Namibia agreed to put the issue before the International Court of Justice (ICJ) in The Hague, and in February 1996 they both agreed to abide by its eventual judgment.

Botswana argued that the northern channel was the main river channel, while Namibia maintained that southern channel was the larger one. Finally, in December 1999, the ICJ pronounced that the border should 'follow the line of the deepest soundings in the northern channel of the Chobe River around Kasikili-Sedudu Island'.

That said, the court also diplomatically ruled that 'in the two channels around Kasikili-Sedudu Island, the nationals of, and vessels flying the flags of, the Republic of Botswana and the Republic of Namibia shall enjoy equal national treatment'.

For visitors, this means that game-viewing boats from both countries are allowed on both sides of this tiny, troublesome patch of floodplain!

Chobe Crocodile Farm [185 F2] (⏲ *08.30–12.30 & 14.30–16.00 Mon–Sat; P40/20 adult/child*) Kasane's crocodile farm, down a quiet lane close to Kubu Lodge, is a particularly good place to take children, with tours during which you can see the eggs, hatchlings and larger creatures.

Birdwatching The local branch of Birdlife Botswana (*www.birdlifebotswana.org. bw*) can organise birdwatching excursions with a qualified guide lasting an hour or longer. If you're interested, contact The Old House (page 191).

Canoeing New to Kasane from the brains behind The Old House (page 191) are canoeing trips on the Chobe River. Typically you'll be on the water for two–three hours, costing P200 per person. But do remember that you'll be sharing your space with both hippos and crocs, so make sure that your guide has given serious thought to the safety aspects of such a trip.

Fishing Several of the tour operators run fishing trips on the Chobe River, primarily in search of bream. Expect to pay upwards of US$165 per person for three hours.

Chobe National Park (⏲ *Apr–Sep 06.00–18.30, Oct–Mar 05.30–19.00; P120/day, vehicle P50/day*) Visitors to Kasane can easily explore the park from a game-drive vehicle or from the river – with the latter being one of the region's top attractions. Excursions can be organised either through your lodge, or directly with one of a handful of small local safari operators (see pages 194–5), or – for game drives – you can drive yourself. Costs for boat cruises and game drives vary considerably according to the operator, the style and the number of participants, but average around US$30–40 per person for each activity, plus park fees.

River trips Boat cruises range from ten-seater motorboats to double-storey boats taking 40 or more people on a champagne breakfast – and most last around three hours. The game viewing from the river can be surprisingly good, especially in the later afternoon during the latter half of the dry season. Large numbers of elephants are virtually guaranteed, and often whole herds will cross the river from one side to the other.

Some of the lodges/operators will send you out on a private little boat with a driver and a coolbox. The small boat gives you a lot more flexibility in what you concentrate on, and how long you stop somewhere, as it's just a question of requesting what you want to do from your driver/guide. It's certainly my favourite way to see the Chobe riverfront area, and probably remains one of my favourite safari experiences in Africa. It can be magical.

Because of the number of lodges in the area, the river can become quite full of boats at times, so if you want a quieter experience, try and arrange for a boat at the crack of dawn. Most of the cruises don't leave until 09.00, so you'll have the river almost to yourself for a few hours – apart from the occasional Namibian fisherman in a mokoro (there's no fishing allowed in the national park from Botswana).

Game drives Organised game drives generally head west straight into the national park, and then cover the game-drive roads and loops around the riverfront area (see *Chapter 9* for more details of these areas). If you're organising a trip with a local company, remember to compare the various options available, asking how long the drive is, and how much of that time it takes to get to the park gate and back.

Typically trips last about three hours, though generally the lodges further east will spend more of this getting to and from the park than those further west. Either way you're going to find yourself mostly around the eastern side of the riverfront area, where traffic densities are relatively high.

The national park allows driving only in daylight hours, but several lodges now advertise 'night drives'. Note that these are conducted outside the park, in areas where quantities of big game are much more limited.

National park permits Self-drivers should note that the Sedudu Gate into Chobe National Park (↖ 625 0235) is one of the few places in the country where independent visitors can pay park fees for any of Botswana's national parks. As a result, some hefty queues can be anticipated, especially between June and October, so allow plenty of time, or – if an early start is important – pay your fees the night before. These can be paid in pula, US dollars, sterling, rand or by Visa or MasterCard – though the credit-card machines don't always work, and the rate of exchange against sterling in particular can be awry, so payment in pula or US dollars is generally the most efficient and cost-effective. For those planning to camp, there's a handy kiosk here manned by staff from SKL, who run the Savute and Linyanti campsites within Chobe National Park. For more details, see pages 86–7.

Technically, independent drivers are not allowed into the park until after 10.00, allowing the tour operators to get in first, though it's hard to ascertain if this is enforced. In practice, access times probably depend on how busy the gate is on a given morning.

Further afield Most of the lodges and tour operators in Kasane can organise trips further afield, including mokoro trips, village walks across the river in Namibia, and excursions to Victoria Falls in Zambia or Zimbabwe – the latter with or without a guide.

Rather less well known is a **memorial** in the Lesoma Valley which was built to commemorate the members of the Botswana Defence Force (BDF) who were massacred by Zimbabwean soldiers on 27 February 1978 (see box opposite). It lies close to Lesoma Valley Lodge (page 202) (✪ LESOMA 17°54.528'S, 25°13.470'E).

AROUND KASANE

Although technically on Namibian soil, there are several lodges on the northern side of the Chobe River that use Kasane as a base. Many of their visitors come through Kasane, and their activities feature trips on the river beside the park.

Two of these – Chobe Savanna Lodge and King's Den – stand on land directly opposite the national park, hence I'll cover them, along with the *Zambezi Queen* houseboat, in *Chapter 9, Chobe National Park*, pages 28–30. Three others, and a trio of 'safari' boats, lie northeast of Kasane, on Impalila Island, so are discussed below. For more details of the Impalila area, and the rest of Namibia's Caprivi Strip, see one of my other guidebooks: *Namibia: The Bradt Travel Guide*.

IMPALILA ISLAND AREA Around Kazungula is the confluence of the Chobe and the Zambezi. The Zambezi flows relentlessly to the sea but, depending on their relative heights, the Chobe either contributes to that, or may even reverse its flow and draw water from the Zambezi. Trapped between the two rivers is a triangle of land, of about 700km², which is a mixture of floodplains, islands and channels that link the two rivers.

BOTSWANA DEFENCE FORCE　　*Tricia Hayne*

Many, if not most, young boys in Botswana, when asked what they'd like to do when they grow up, will respond that they'd like to join the army. If that shows the esteem in which the Botswana Defence Force is held, it gives no indication of the short history that underpins the organisation.

In 1966, when Botswana gained independence from Britain, the country had no military presence. Money was tight, and the best that the government could muster was a paramilitary unit within the police force. At the time, this seemed all that was necessary.

However, despite Botswana's stability, the capacity of this small force was soon swamped by the knock-on effect of anti-colonial struggles along its eastern, southern and western borders. The increasingly violent conflict in Rhodesia saw both refugees and freedom fighters seeking a safe haven in Botswana, but the Rhodesian security forces were swift to follow their dissident population, and the fighting spilled indiscriminately on to Botswana's soil. At the same time, the country's western borders were threatened by similar cross-border skirmishes from South West Africa (now Namibia), then suffering under the apartheid regime of South Africa. To compound the problem, security forces in South Africa itself were crossing into Botswana in their hunt for anti-apartheid activists. Thus, Botswana – and its citizens – were threatened on every side, and the police force was increasingly unable to cope.

It was against this background in 1977 that the Botswana Defence Force was formed. Initially a body of just 600 men, incorporating the police paramilitary unit, it fell under the command of the deputy police commissioner, with Seretse Khama Ian Khama (now Botswana's president), as his deputy. By the end of the 1980s, Khama himself was in command of the army.

The new force was soon to come under intense pressure. Only a few months later, on 27 February 1978, reports were received of a Rhodesian military presence just inside Botswana's northeastern border, near Kasane, apparently intent on flushing out anti-government guerrillas from Rhodesia. The BDF responded, only to drive straight into an ambush. In total, 15 members of the force were killed in the incident – the first of the BDF's soldiers to die in action.

Today the BDF is over 12,000 strong, with many of its officers trained in the USA. In addition to internal responsibilities, the force is involved in international peacekeeping duties as part of SADC and UN forces.

This swampy, riverine area is home to several thousand people of Namibian nationality, mostly members of Zambia's Lozi tribe. (The main local languages here are Lozi and Subia.) Most have a seasonal lifestyle, living next to the river channels, fishing and farming maize, sorghum, pumpkins and keeping cattle. They move with the water levels, transferring on to higher, drier ground as the waters rise.

The largest island in this area, Impalila Island, is at the far eastern tip of Namibia, home to around 2,500 people living in some 25 small villages. It gained notoriety during the 1980s as a military base for the South African Defence Forces (SADF), as it was strategically positioned within sight of Botswana, Zambia and Zimbabwe. It still boasts a 1,300m-long runway (⊕ 17°46.48'S, 025°11.23'E) of compressed gravel, used today by charter airlines to bring visitors to the lodges, but the barracks are now a combined school, serving most of the older children in the area.

The **customs and immigration post** on the island (⏱ *07.30–17.00*) is fairly laid-back and informal as borders go, but remember that, if you transfer to the island from Kasane, you'll have to clear customs and immigration for both Botswana and Namibia on arrival and departure.

Flora and fauna
The area's ecosystems are similar to those in the upper reaches of the Okavango Delta: deep-water channels lined by wide reedbeds and rafts of papyrus. Some of the larger islands are still forested with baobabs, water figs, knobthorne, umbrella thorn, mopane, pod mahogany, star chestnut and sickle-leafed albizia, while jackalberry and Chobe waterberry overhang the rivers, festooned with creepers and vines.

Large mammals are scarce here, and most that do occur swim over from Chobe. Elephants and buffalo sometimes swim over to Namibia, and even lions have been known to take to the river in search of the tasty-but-dim domestic cattle kept there.

Even when there are no large mammals here, the birdlife is spectacular. Large flocks of white-faced ducks congregate on islands in the rivers, African skimmers nest on exposed sandbanks, and both reed cormorants and darters are seen fishing or perching while they dry their feathers. Kingfishers are numerous, from the giant to the tiny pygmy, as are herons and egrets. However, the area's most unusual bird is the unassuming rock pratincole with its black, white and grey body, which perches on rocks within the rapids and hawks for insects in the spray.

🏠 Where to stay
Visitors to the island arrive either by air at the small airstrip, or by boat from Kasane. Supplies for the lodges are normally brought in by boat from Kasane or Katima Mulilo. Because of their location, none of the lodges here can organise game drives in Chobe; they're limited to boat trips. Prices are quoted in US or Namibian dollars.

🏠 **Ichingo Chobe River Lodge** [184 C1] (8 Meru tents) m 7130 2439 (on island), +27 79 871 7603 (reservations); e info@ichobezi.co.za; www.ichobezi.co.za. Ichingo was the brainchild of Dawn & Ralph Oxenham, who since 1996 have run the lodge themselves. Occupying a secluded site on the south side of Impalila Island, it overlooks the quiet backwaters of some of the Chobe River's rapids, a world away from busy Kasane just across the water. It makes a super base for river trips & game viewing from boats along the Chobe River, & offers some excellent birdwatching too.

Guests stay in walk-in Meru tents, each set high above the flood levels – important in a location where the rise & fall of water is up to 2m. En-suite showers are at the back under thatch, & there's a balcony at the front, with views of the water & surrounding vegetation, dominated by the water-tolerant waterberry trees (*Syzygium guineese*), & the orange-fruited mangosteen (*Garcinia livingstonei*). In the evening a generator ensures a steady power supply, backed up by battery lights in each tent. Meals are taken around a large, solid wooden table in the thatched dining area/bar/lounge that fronts on to the river.

Activities are run individually, with a guide allocated to each tent for the duration of the guests' stay. Not surprisingly, the river is the main focus, with game viewing, birdwatching & fishing from motorboats, & fly-fishing in the rapids, as well as island walks through local villages to a giant baobab. Unusually for a bush lodge, the camp actively welcomes children of all ages, even when not accompanied by adults, as craft activities can usually be organised for them. *N$2,850–4,000 pp sharing, inc FB, most drinks, activities, boat transfer from Kasane Immigration Post.* ⏱ *All year.*

🚤 **'Safari' boats** m 7130 2439; e info@ ichobezi.co.za; www.ichobezi.co.za. For those seeking to spend longer on the river, Ichingo (see above) has 3 luxury 'safari' boats: the 8-berth *Ichobezi Moli* & *Ichobezi Mukwae*, & the newly acquired 10-berth *Pride of the Zambezi*, which cruise on the Zambezi & Chobe rivers, as well as into the contiguous wetlands of Namibia's Caprivi Strip. As Namibian-registered vessels, they are permitted to cruise the waters of the Chobe when the national park is closed & all Botswana-registered vessels must leave, so offer a unique opportunity to watch game & experience the tranquillity of the river after dark & at sunrise.

With its crew of 5, of whom 3 are trained guides, each boat is considered an extension of the lodge, with small groups & personal attention. Each en-suite cabin has huge picture windows, so guests can sit & watch wildlife from their rooms or up on deck. This is the chance for total relaxation with a drink, or in the on-board plunge pool, but for more involvement tender boats are available for fishing or birdwatching with an experienced guide. *N$3,000–4,700 pp sharing, inc FB, most drinks, activities, boat transfer from Kasane Immigration Post.* ⊕ *All year.*

🏠 **Impalila Island Lodge** [off 184 C1] (8 chalets) An African Anthology, South Africa; ☎ +27 11 781 1661; e sales@anthology.co.za; www.anthology.co.za; lodge m 0813 639173. Situated on the northwest side of Impalila Island, overlooking the Zambezi's Mambova Rapids, Impalila Island Lodge has in many ways brought the island to people's attention.

Accommodation is in raised-up wooden chalets, each with twin beds or a king-size dbl. It is fairly luxurious, with much made of polished local mukwa wood, with its natural variegated yellow & brown colours. The chalets have a square design, enclosing a bathroom in one corner, giving blissfully warm showers from instant water heaters. Below the high thatch ceilings are fans for warmer days, & mosquito nets. Large dbl doors open one corner of the room on to a wide wooden veranda, overlooking the rapids. These doors have an optional mosquito-net screen for when it's hot, though are more usually glass: being next to the river can be quite cold on winter mornings.

The main part of the lodge is a large thatched bar/dining area & comfortable lounge built around a huge baobab. This is open to the breeze, though can be sheltered when cold. The wooden pool deck has reclining loungers, umbrellas, & a great view of the river. Impalila's food is excellent & candle-lit 3-course meals around the baobab make a memorable scene.

Activities include guided motorboat trips on the Zambezi & Chobe: the Zambezi mainly for birdwatching & fishing, while longer boat trips on the Chobe offer remarkable game viewing on the edge of the national park. There are nature walks on the island, & superb fishing (especially for tigerfish, best caught on a fly-rod), with guides who are experienced enough to take both experts & beginners out to try their luck.

Since the design stage, the team at Impalila has worked in a low-key but positive way to involve the local community. Currently the lodge pays into a 'community development fund' that is utilised by the community for various projects – the clinic, the school, measures to encourage preservation of wildlife & to conserve the local environment – & administered jointly with the local chief. The lodge has been actively involved in setting up the Impalila conservancy, which protects local wildlife. The lodge also makes a US$40 per guest donation to a community development fund. Because of their excellent approach, don't miss the visits that the lodge organises to local villages, as they can be very rewarding. (Note that Impalila has a super sister lodge, Susuwe Island Lodge, in Namibia's Caprivi Strip. It's on an island in the Kwando River, just northeast from the Kwando Concession in Botswana, & is also a 1st-rate spot with an equally progressive approach to community involvement.)

This is a stylish, well-run lodge ideal for fishing, birding, walking or just relaxing, with the added bonus of game viewing from the river in Chobe. *US$335–395 pp sharing, inc FB, most drinks, laundry & activities; 30% sgl supp't.* ⊕ *All year.*

🏠 **Ntwala Island Lodge** [off 184 C1] (4 suites) Ntwala Island; m 0816 735652; reservations as for Impalila Island Lodge (above). The secluded & ultra-exclusive camp operated by Impalila is situated on a cluster of islands within the Mambova Rapids, linked together by floating walkways. Each chalet has all that you would expect – & more – in the way of luxury, & comes complete with indoor & outdoor showers, its own sand-fringed plunge pool & deck with hammock, & a private sala extending over the water. Facing the rapids, the central building continues the theme, with guests coming together for evening meals. Guests in each suite are allocated a personal guide & their own boat, ready to explore the quiet backwaters, indulge in a spot of tigerfishing, or take in a sunset cruise on the Chobe River. *US$415–595 pp sharing, inc FB, most drinks, laundry & activities; 30% sgl supp't.* ⊕ *All year.*

LESOMA VALLEY Some 20km from Kasane, the tranquil Lesoma Valley (map 207) (also spelled Lehsoma or Lisoma) lies to the east of the main Kasane–Nata road. For those seeking a budget option away from the bustle of Kasane, this area could be worth considering.

Where to stay

Elephant Valley Lodge (20 tents)
620 0054; e elephantvalley_gm@yahoo.com; www.evlodge.com; ✪ ELEVAL 17°51.193'S, 25°14.585'E. Looking across to Kasane Forest Reserve, Elephant Valley Lodge is set in secluded surroundings about 17km from Kasane. It's easy to reach from the Kazungula–Nata road: just drive south until you get to the *1st* telegraph wire that crosses the road, then turn immediately left down a straight, sand track to the lodge. For those who don't have a 4x4, the lodge can arrange to pick up guests from the Engen garage by the Kazungula junction.

After years of exclusive use by an American operator, the lodge now accepts independent travellers as well. A low, dark reception area, with a curio shop & internet facility, leads through to the main bar, lounge & separate restaurant, all under thatch with an open deck. A short walk brings you to a good bird hide (which doubles as a romantic dining spot) overlooking a waterhole, where elephant & buffalo are regularly seen. Simple, en-suite, walk-in tents, on concrete plinths, are well spaced on a shaded grassy site, some around a good-sized pool. Each has twin beds, a desk, kettle, safe, fan & electric points. Special rates can often be organised through Jollyboys or Fawlty Towers in Livingstone.

While the location is an attraction in itself, game drives & boat cruises can be organised in Chobe NP too, a drive of about ½hr. *US$470/611 pp sharing/sgl May–Oct, US$365 pp Nov–Apr, inc FB, activities; exc drinks.* ⊕ *All year.*

Liya Campsite (8 chalets, camping) 625 2376; e liyaglo@botsnet.bw. Linked to the guest lodge of the same name in Kasane is this campsite with pre-erected tents & chalets, 4 of which are en suite. It lies about 25km from Kasane. Take the main road towards Nata, then turn left at the *2nd*

telegraph wire that crosses the road, signposted to Lisoma village. Once in the village, turn right, & ask for the campsite. Pitches have water points & braai stands, with power provided by generator. Meals are available on request. **$$** *Tent P237/361 sgl/dbl; camping P93 pp.* ⊕ *All year.*

Lesoma Valley Lodge (10 rooms, camping) m 7152 5450; e lesomavalley@brobemail. co.bw; www.lesomavalleylodge.com; LESOMA 17°54.528'S, 25°13.470'E. Tucked away 2km down a narrow track, some 12km from the Engen garage at the Kasane turn-off, this small lodge opened in 2006 almost next to the military monument (see page 199). Thatched, ochre-painted rondavels with terracotta-tiled floors are neatly kept, their dbl or twin beds spread with ethnic print covers; some rooms can sleep 3 & there's also a family chalet. In addition to a tiled bathroom, each has AC, a kettle & TV. There's a bar & restaurant, & a pleasant pool with a narrow terrace. A campsite, scheduled for completion in early 2014, will have 25 pitches, each with a braai stand & its own ablution block. Competitively priced at the lower end of the range, the lodge caters primarily for the South African self-drive market. **$$$** ⊕ *All year.*

Senyati Safari Camp (7 chalets, camping) m 7188 1306; e senyatisafaricamp@gmail.com; www.senyatisafaricampbotswana.com; ✪ SENYAT 17°52.331'S, 25°14.167'E. Some 10km from the Engen garage at Kazungula, & well signposted from the tar road, Senyati has both private camping pitches, each with its own toilet, shower, braai & electricity point, & rustic thatched chalets. The bar is open from 17.00 daily, & there's free Wi-Fi throughout. An interesting new addition is a subterranean bunker positioned at the camp's waterhole, offering some great ground-level photographic opportunities of wildlife coming down to drink. **$$** *exc b/fast; camping P160 pp.* ⊕ *All year.*

SOUTH OF KASANE

Kasane is ideally situated for those driving into Botswana's national parks. The road south to Maun via Chobe and Moremi is covered in *Chapter 9, Chobe National Park*. For Kasane to Nata, read on.

KASANE TO NATA The long, straight, tarred A3 road from Kasane to Nata covers some 316km. For self-drivers it is effectively the gateway from Kasane to the Makgadikgadi Pans and the Central Kalahari Game Reserve, as well as south to Francistown and Gaborone. Between Kasane and Pandamatenga was until recently a minefield of pot-holes, but repairs have now been largely completed and it's once again a very good surface. That said, aside from the occasional stopping area, the road is relatively narrow, so it's not ideal if you're looking for a picnic spot.

Though the journey is not terribly interesting scenically, the road forms a corridor between the unfenced Chobe National Park and Hwange National Park over the border in Zimbabwe. As a result, the area sees a fair amount of wildlife, especially elephants, throughout the year – which for drivers means exercising considerable caution. As with most roads in rural Africa, driving at night is asking for trouble – especially as grey elephants are well camouflaged against the grey tarmac.

At the Ngwasha veterinary checkpoint, about 64km north of Nata, you can expect stringent checks for prohibited goods, specifically any form of red meat. Staff regularly confiscate meat from self-drive vehicles, so unless you're prepared to cook it at the roadside, it's not worth taking the risk. You may also be asked to get out of your vehicle and sanitise not only the shoes you're wearing but also those in your luggage in a foot trough, so it's worth keeping all footwear easily accessible.

Where to stay Places to stay along this road [off map 207] are listed below from north to south. Most are geared to those stopping overnight rather than being destinations in their own right, and most have camping facilities – the exception being Camp Kuzuma. As the northern part of the road is sandwiched between Chobe and Hwange national parks, the area benefits from the wildlife that roams freely between the two. Thus, at least during the dry season, you could see a fair amount of game, including elephant, giraffe, zebra, tsessebe, sable and possibly wild dog.

For details of places to stay in Nata, see pages 432–4.

Camp Kuzuma (5 suites) m 7223 4449, 7586 1842; e info@campkuzuma-bw.com; www. campkuzuma-bw.com; ✪ CAMKUZ 18°20.409'S, 25°29.203'E. The newest camp in this area, founded in late 2011, is situated in its own concession just inside the Kazuma Forest Reserve. To find it, turn left off the main road about 65km from Kazungula, down the gravel-&-sand Kuzuma cutline towards the Zimbabwean border, & after about 3km you'll arrive at the camp. In stark contrast to other accommodation options in this region, it looks & feels more like a lodge in the Okavango Delta.

The elevated main area overlooks a large waterhole frequented by elephant; there's a pool & deck at the front; & inside are a well-stocked cocktail & cigar bar, coffee machines, open-plan lounge & dining area. It's all very light, stylish & breezy. Well-spaced canvas suites are accessed along elevated wooden walkways. King-size beds (which can be converted to twins) form the centrepiece, with bedside tables & 2 wing chairs. Canvas flaps can be rolled down over mesh windows when the wind picks up. Concrete floors are covered with antelope & cow skins, which keep off the chill in the cooler months. A stone partition at the head of the bed separates the bedroom from the bathroom, with twin washbasins, twin indoor showers, an outdoor shower & a claw-footed Victorian bathtub – & of course a flush loo.

A spa will appeal to those looking for a little pampering, while activities include guided walks & morning, evening & night game drives; we're told that there have been decent lion, leopard & wild dog sightings in the area. Further afield, sunset cruises & day trips to Chobe National Park & Victoria Falls can be arranged. *From US$525 pp sharing, inc FB, local drinks, activities, laundry, transfers.* ☉ *Mar–20 Dec.*

Touch of Africa Safari Lodge (9 chalets, camping) m 7165 6340, 7438 9191; e touchofafrica@botsnet.bw; www.touchofafrica. tv; ✪ TOASL 18°30.163'S, 25°36.256'E. Some 100km south of Kasane, & 5km north of the turning to Pandamatenga, this small lodge is adjacent to Kazuma Forest Reserve on the east of the road. Lawns dotted with lemon trees surround the buildings & a small pool. Power is supplied by generator. Visitors can pitch a tent, or opt for the more comfortable (& pricier) en-suite thatched chalets, painted a deep orange & kitted out with ceiling fans, mosquito nets, & tables & chairs on shaded verandas. B/fast & dinner from an à-la-carte menu are served in the central dining area, which encompasses a bar & lounge. Both self-drive or guided game drives (the latter P160 pp) & guided walks (P180 pp) can be organised. **$$** *exc b/fast (P55); camping P50 pp.* ⊕ *All year.*

🏠 **Panda Rest Camp** (7 chalets, camping) m 7162 2268; e pandarestcamp@yahoo.com; ✪ PANDAR 18°32.186'S, 25°37.461'E. Run by safari guide Chris Burnie & his wife, this quiet camp has a spacious, grassy site east of the road, 5km south of Touch of Africa & close to the Pandamatenga turn-off. In addition to a campsite, there are twin & dbl en-suite chalets, all cooled by AC. The restaurant, separate from a large bar, serves b/fast, lunch & dinner. Although the place caters primarily for self-drivers, it offers both walks & drives. A popular option is a game drive culminating in a bush dinner overlooking a waterhole, followed by a night drive back to camp (P250 pp). **$$** *exc b/fast; camping P70 pp.* ⊕ *All year.*

𝝠 **Elephant Sands** (14 chalets, camping) e bookings@elephantsandsbotswana.com; www.elephantsands.com; ✪ ELESAN 19°44.935'S, 26°04.265'E. Just 7km south of the vet fence, & 53km north of Nata, this simple but welcoming campsite about 0.5km west of the road is clearly signposted. Its popularity extends to both independent campers & overlanders, who pitch in together & share rustic but clean open-air ablutions. That said, there's plenty of space, & a new ablution block has just been completed. If you don't fancy camping, there are en-suite rondavels, each with an unusual semicircular bathroom with open-air shower. There are also a couple of block-built family chalets under thatch, each sleeping 4 people. The lack of electricity means an absence of AC or fans. Recent sightings of elephants, cats & even wild dogs mean that visitors must stay within the confines of the camp – though that's no hardship with a large restaurant area, a separate bar, & a sunken boma surrounded by bush. **$$** *exc b/fast; camping P85 pp.* ⊕ *All year.*

9

Chobe National Park and Forest Reserve

Chobe National Park takes its name from the Chobe River, which forms its northern boundary, and protects about 10,700km² of the northern Kalahari. Its vegetation varies from the lush floodplains beside the Chobe River to the scorched area around the Ghoha Hills, dense forests of cathedral mopane to endless kilometres of mixed, broadleaf woodlands. And then there's the beauty of the newly flowing Savuti Marsh. This is classic big-game country, where herds of buffalo and elephant attain legendary proportions, matched only by some exceptionally large prides of lion.

Much of the park is devoid of water in the dry season, and most of it is inaccessible, so this chapter concentrates on the four main areas of Chobe that are accessible: the Chobe riverfront, Ngwezumba Pans, Savuti and the Linyanti. It also covers the Chobe Forest Reserve, a populated enclave almost surrounded by the park.

BACKGROUND INFORMATION

HISTORY The Chobe's original inhabitants were the Bushmen, followed by the Hambukushu, Bayei and Basubiya. The 1850s saw David Livingstone pass through the area, on his way to seeing the Victoria Falls, and a succession of big-game hunters seeking trophies and ivory. The area was first protected as a game reserve in 1961, and then proclaimed a national park in 1968, which was none too early.

Despite this distant trophy-hunting past, the game density in some areas of the park remains remarkable, ensuring the park's continued popularity. Simply driving a few kilometres along the Chobe riverfront in the dry season is demonstration enough, as you'll be forced to halt frequently to allow game to wander slowly across the road, or to watch herds coming down to drink from the river.

However, perhaps more than any of Botswana's parks, Chobe has felt the impact of tourism. In the 1980s, park fees were low and the few basic campsites were full. Rubbish became a problem, solitary game viewing was almost impossible and the animals became habituated to people. While Chobe has never been busy by east African standards, its three or four basic public campsites and simple network of game-viewing roads couldn't cope with so many visitors.

Fortunately, around 1987, the government started to implement a policy of 'high-cost, low-density' tourism. Park fees went up and the numbers of visitors dropped. The situation has now changed. With regular increases in these park fees the flood of visitors through the park has turned into more of a moderate flow. Once again, most of the park feels like a wilderness area. Even the 'honey pot' of the northern Chobe riverfront area isn't quite as busy, though the proximity of Kasane's lodges and campsites ensures that it's never going to be that quiet either.

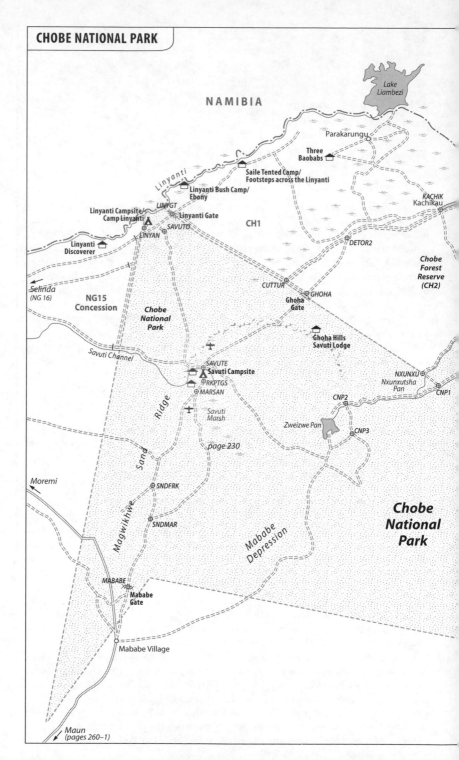

CHOBE NATIONAL PARK

NAMIBIA

Lake Liambezi

Parakarungu

Three Baobabs

Saile Tented Camp/
Footsteps across the Linyanti

Linyanti

Linyanti Bush Camp/
Ebony

LINYGT

KACHIK
Kachikau

Linyanti Campsite/
Camp Linyanti

Linyanti Gate

CH1

LINYAN

SAVUTO

Linyanti
Discoverer

DETOR2

Chobe
Forest
Reserve
(CH2)

Selinda
(NG 16)

NG15
Concession

CUTTUR

GHOHA

Chobe
National
Park

Ghoha
Gate

Ghoha Hills
Savuti Lodge

Savuti Channel

SAVUTE
Savuti Campsite

NXUNXU
Nxunxutsha
Pan

CNP1

RKPTGS

MARSAN

CNP2

Zweizwe Pan

CNP3

Savuti
Marsh

page 230

Chobe
National
Park

Moremi

SNDFRK

Mababe
Depression

SNDMAR

MABABE
Mababe
Gate

Mababe Village

Maun
(pages 260–1)

206

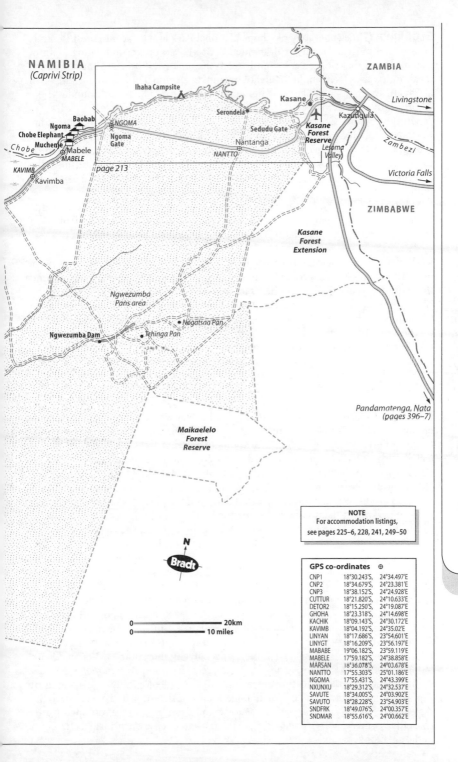

NAMIBIA
(Caprivi Strip)

ZAMBIA

Livingstone

Ihaha Campsite

Kasane

Serondela

Kazungula

Baobab

NGOMA

Sedudu Gate

Kasane
Forest
Reserve

Zambezi

Ngoma
Chobe Elephant

Ngoma
Gate

Nantanga

Muchenje

Chobe

Mabele
MABELE

NANTTO

Lesoma
Valley

Victoria Falls

KAVIMB

Kavimba

page 213

ZIMBABWE

Kasane
Forest
Extension

Ngwezumba
Pans area

Nogatsaa Pan

Ngwezumba Dam

Tchinga Pan

Pandamatenga, Nata
(pages 396–7)

Maikaelelo
Forest
Reserve

N

Bradt

NOTE
For accommodation listings,
see pages 225–6, 228, 241, 249–50

GPS co-ordinates ⊕		
CNP1	18°30.243'S,	24°34.497'E
CNP2	18°34.679'S,	24°23.381'E
CNP3	18°38.152'S,	24°24.928'E
CUTTUR	18°21.820'S,	24°10.633'E
DETOR2	18°15.250'S,	24°19.087'E
GHOHA	18°23.318'S,	24°14.698'E
KACHIK	18°09.143'S,	24°30.172'E
KAVIMB	18°04.192'S,	24°35.02'E
LINYAN	18°17.686'S,	23°54.601'E
LINYGT	18°16.209'S,	23°56.197'E
MABABE	19°06.182'S,	23°59.119'E
MABELE	17°59.182'S,	24°38.858'E
MARSAN	18°36.078'S,	24°03.678'E
NANTTO	17°55.303'S,	25°01.186'E
NGOMA	17°55.431'S,	24°43.399'E
NXUNXU	18°29.312'S,	24°32.537'E
SAVUTE	18°34.005'S,	24°03.902'E
SAVUTO	18°28.228'S,	23°54.903'E
SNDFRK	18°49.076'S,	24°00.357'E
SNDMAR	18°55.616'S,	24°00.662'E

0   20km
0   10 miles

GEOGRAPHY The geography of Chobe National Park and adjacent Forest Reserve, and indeed most of northern Botswana, is one based on an undulating plain of Kalahari sand that slopes very slightly from the northwest down to the southeast. Its altitude varies from about 950m at Linyanti, to around 930m at Ihaha and 942m at Savuti. In many ways its most defining feature is its northwest boundary: the Chobe–Linyanti river system.

On the ground, Chobe's geographical features are subtle rather than striking. Various vegetated sand dunes and sand ridges occur, including the large Magwikhwe Sand Ridge. Natural pans are dotted throughout the park, reaching their highest densities around the Nogatsaa and Tchinga areas, and also the Zweizwe area east of Savuti. Only occasional rounded hills break the Kalahari's flatness.

Whilst the region is bounded by great rivers, within this area there are only dry, or at least very seasonal, watercourses. The Savuti Channel is the most famous of these – and until 2009 that hadn't flowed since 1982.

GEOLOGY See *Geological history* (pages 45–53) in *Chapter 3* for a comprehensive overview of Botswana's geological past. Here it's enough to note that by around three million years ago the Kalahari's longitudinal dunes had formed, channelling rivers south and east into the Limpopo. Then, around two million years ago, a tectonic shift blocked this drainage, leaving the rivers feeding a superlake in the heart of Botswana – Lake Makgadikgadi. Geologists think that the level of this fluctuated in time, but that it reached as far as the Savuti area. Compelling evidence for this are the great sand ridges in the area and the presence of smooth, wave-washed pebbles and boulders – for example those found on the southern side of the Ghoha Hills.

FLORA AND FAUNA Trying to describe Chobe as a whole without any comment or subdivisions would be very misleading. Unlike some of Africa's national parks, Chobe is best considered as a handful of totally different areas, each with a different feel, slightly different vegetation and distinct populations of animals.

Later in this chapter, I'll treat separately the wildlife highlights of the **Chobe riverfront**; the variation to be found around the **Ngwezumba Pans**; the unique situation around **Savuti**; and the isolated corner of the park that reaches northwest to the **Linyanti**. In passing, I'll also mention the circumstances of the populated Chobe Forest Reserve enclave. Meanwhile, here I'll try to give a brief overview, and cover some of the species which are found throughout the park.

Flora In general, across the whole park you'll find many similarities. Near any of the permanent rivers the vegetation is varied, with a large number of tree and bush species. It's classic riparian forest – as occurs throughout southern Africa.

Away from water, Chobe has fairly thick and sometimes thorny bush with relatively few open areas. Much of this is Kalahari sandveld, often with a high proportion of acacias and species that love deep sand, like the silver terminalia (*Terminalia sericea*). Some of Chobe, especially in the south, is covered with mopane woodland, containing almost exclusively *Colophospermum mopane*.

The main exceptions to this are a few areas of (geologically) recent alluvial deposits, like Savuti Marsh, which look totally different. Here you'll find the skeletons of various acacias and leadwoods (*Combretum imberbe*) on open plains covered in couch grass (*Cynodon dactylon*) – the latter being the principal attraction to the area for zebra.

Fauna Most of Chobe's wildlife is found across the whole park. Occasional elephants and buffalo are seen everywhere, but the large herds generally follow a highly seasonal pattern of migrations. These are principally dictated by the availability of water.

As the dry season progresses, all the small clay pans in the bush (and particularly the mopane woodlands) dry up. Then the elephants and buffalo start to form larger herds and migrate to the permanent waters of the Chobe and Linyanti rivers. These gather in their thousands by the rivers, having come from as far away as Zimbabwe's Hwange National Park. Then, as soon as it rains and the small pans in the bush start to fill with rainwater, the animals move away again and disperse.

Many of the park's animals will follow a smaller-scale, less noticeable version of this type of seasonal migration to the water, and this is what makes the game viewing in Chobe so remarkable towards the middle and end of the dry season.

At any time of year, Chobe's big game includes blue wildebeest, Burchell's zebra, impala, kudu, tssesebe, giraffe, impala, common duiker, steenbok, warthog, baboon and vervet monkey throughout the park. Eland, sable and roan antelope also range across the park, but are relatively scarce, just as they are elsewhere in southern Africa.

Lion and spotted hyena are very common, and are generally the dominant predators, whilst leopard, cheetah and wild dog all occur, though are seen much less frequently. Both side-striped and black-backed jackal are present – though the former are found more in the north of the park, and the latter in the south. Brown hyena probably occur, though rarely, in the drier parts of the south, though they don't seem to co-exist happily with a high density of lion or spotted hyena.

Cape and bat-eared fox are found here, though again the Cape fox prefers the drier south. I once had a particularly good sighting of a whole family of bat-eared foxes in the middle of the open plains on Savuti Marsh, early in the morning on a cold September day. There are a variety of mongooses found here; the most often seen of these are probably the banded and dwarf species, both of which are social, and very entertaining to watch.

Serval, caracal, aardwolf and aardvark are found all over the park, though are only occasionally seen due to their largely nocturnal habits. Pangolin are found here too, though they're very rarely seen.

If you have the chance to take any night drives in areas adjoining the park (no night drives are allowed inside the park) then you've a good chance to spot scrub

AN UNEASY ALLIANCE

Co-operative relationships between mammals and birds are unusual, but the honey badger enjoys two. Its association with the greater honeyguide is well known. This small bird uses a distinctive song to lure the honey badger to a bee's nest, whereupon it feasts on the grubs after the badger has ransacked the nest and had its fill of honey.

Less well known is the honey badger's association with the pale chanting goshawk. This relationship is of no benefit to the badger, since the goshawk – or sometimes a pair of them – simply follows the bigger predator around as it digs and forages for prey, and pounces on any rodent or reptile that slips past. The badger may have the last laugh though, since goshawk eggs and nestlings are among its 59 different prey species that have been recorded in the Kalahari.

hares, spring hares, lesser bushbabies, porcupines, genets (small-spotted and large-spotted), civets, African wildcats and honey badgers.

Though white and black rhino would occur here naturally, as they should throughout northern Botswana, it's likely that by the early 1990s they had all been wiped out through poaching. There were then occasional reports of individual sightings – but a viable breeding population had been destroyed. The return of white rhino to Botswana was initiated in 2001, when a number of white rhino were reintroduced into the Moremi Game Reserve. Although numbers remain small, they are increasing, and are gradually spreading out – with wandering rhinos now occasionally turning up in Chobe and even Magkadikgadi. Black rhino, too, have been reintroduced, though they are very rarely seen.

Birdlife Over 450 species of birds have been seen in Chobe – too many to even try to list here. Therefore I'll cover the birding highlights in the separate sections concerning the specific areas within the park. Note that the summer migrants generally arrive around October and leave again in March.

WHEN TO VISIT Noting the general comments made under *Planning and Preparation*, pages 67–74, you'll generally find a wider variety of bird species here in the wet season, many of which will be in their breeding plumage.

The movement of the animals is rather more complex. Most of Chobe's larger herbivores migrate with the seasons, to find water to drink and pastures new. These movements are, to a large extent, predictable, so bear them in mind as you plan your trip to maximise your chances of good game viewing.

Like most of Africa's game migrations, the principle behind this one is simple. The animals stay close to the permanent sources of water during the driest months, then they disperse into the forests and (especially) the open grasslands at the start of the rains to take advantage of the fresh grazing and browsing. In northern Botswana, this means that game becomes more and more prolific near the permanent watercourses – the Chobe, the Linyanti, and the edges of the Okavango – as the dry season wears on. Then as soon as the rains come, many animals head south and east into the interior's forests and plains (especially the Makgadikgadi area and Nxai Pan). This gives the vegetation beside the rivers a little time to recover, so that when the dry season returns the animals will again find some grazing near the water.

The finer details of this are more complex, and slightly different for each species. Zebra, for example, have been the focus of a research project which tracked them using radio transmitters and a microlight aircraft, based in Savuti. This study suggested that they spend the rainy summer, from November to about February, in the Mababe Depression – venturing south to Nxai Pan, and then following the Boteti River down to around Tsoe, before heading across to the Gweta area and back north to Nxai Pan.

In March and April they pass through Savuti for a few months, where they foal. This makes a particularly good foaling ground as rich alluvial deposits from the old Savuti Channel have left the area with mineral-rich soil supporting particularly nutritious grasses. A few months later, as dryness begins to bite around July, they move again towards the Linyanti for the dry season. Finally in late October and November, they return to the Mababe area as the rains begin and the grasses start to sprout.

Similarly, Sommerlatte (see *Appendix 3, Further information*) studied elephant movements in the park in the mid-1970s. Though clearly movements have changed since then, he found that the highest wet-season concentrations were around the Ghoha Hills, the eastern side of the Mababe Depression, and the mouth of the Ngwezumba River (the Nogatsaa/Tchinga pans area).

For the visitor, this means that the game in the dry season is best in the river areas. In the wet season, and just afterwards, the interior pans are definitely worth a visit. Savuti is unusual in that, remarkably, it has good game all year, but is especially interesting around April/May and November.

GETTING ORGANISED

As with most of Botswana's wilder areas, there are basically three ways to visit Chobe: on a fly-in trip, staying at the lodges and camps; on a mobile-safari trip, organised by a local safari operator; and on a self-drive trip with all your own equipment and food.

Only self-drive visitors really need to do much of their own planning, and they should take everything they'll need to live on (including supplies of water) between Maun and Kasane. Chobe is often combined with Moremi on such a trip – which, taken at a relaxed pace, typically takes about ten days. You should stock up on food, fuel and supplies before you leave. There are a few small local shops in the villages of the Chobe Forest Reserve, but otherwise there's nothing available on the whole route, and certainly no fuel.

Although it's only about 300km between Maun and Kasane across Chobe, a lot of the driving is in second gear and permanent 4x4, so prepare for fuel consumption that's perhaps two or three times your normal tar-road consumption. In addition to long-range fuel tanks, it's wise to carry at least one if not two additional jerrycans of fuel.

The park entrance gates are open 06.00–18.30 from April to September, and 05.30–19.00 from October to March. Park rules prohibit cars on the roads between sunset and sunrise, and it would be extremely foolish to attempt to drive after dark anyway, so be careful to plan your journey to give plenty of time. The speed limit in the park is 40km/h, though you'll be very unlikely ever to get near this on the deep sand tracks which are the park's roads.

ORIENTATION Though the maps make Chobe National Park look complex, it's really very simple. In the northeast corner is Kasane, and in the southwest corner the road leaves for Maun and Moremi. Most visitors drive in on one side, and exit the other – and in the middle all roads lead to Savuti. There are concessions and camps around the national park, particularly along the Linyanti River, but in terms of orientation, work on this basis!

North of Savuti there's a 'direct' road that links it to Kasane via the Chobe Forest Reserve and the Chobe riverfront area. Then there's an indirect route that travels to Kasane via the Nogatsaa Pans area in the forested heart of the park. Most visitors choose one of these routes; see *Driving from Kasane to Savuti* on pages 222–6 for a discussion of their relative merits in various seasons. In all the above I use the word 'road' loosely – to mean two adjacent tyre tracks in the sand. You need a high-clearance 4x4 for a trip to Chobe, and lots of time.

Maps There is really only one map of Chobe that is worthwhile for normal navigation and that's the Shell map of Chobe National Park, by Veronica Roodt. The main map itself is fairly small, but it has a good inset of the game-viewing tracks of the Chobe riverfront area, and also aerial photograph backdrops for first-rate insets of the area around Savuti and Nogatsaa. Veronica's map of Savuti is especially good for navigation!

BOOKING AND PARK FEES If you're flying into organised camps, then your park fees will probably already be included in the price of your safari. If you're driving into Chobe then you'll need to have booked all your campsites and paid your park fees in advance; you can no longer just turn up and pay park fees at the gate. See pages 84–7 for details of how this works, and a scale of the fees. You'll then need to carry confirmation of your campsite bookings and the park permit itself, ready to present at the park gates before you can enter.

CHOBE RIVERFRONT

Perhaps the park's greatest attraction is its northern boundary, the Chobe River. In the dry season animals converge on this stretch of water from the whole of northern Botswana. Elephant and buffalo, especially, form into huge herds for which the park is famous. In November 1853 David Livingstone passed through the area and described the river:

> though the river is from thirteen to fifteen feet in depth at its lowest ebb, and broad
> enough to allow a steamer to ply upon it, the suddenness of the bending would
> prevent navigation; but should the country ever become civilised, the Chobe would be
> a convenient natural canal.

Fortunately that kind of civilisation hasn't reached the Chobe yet – there are no canal boats to be seen – and today's traveller must make do with 4x4s or the small motorboats that weave along the river, amongst channels still ruled by hippos.

FLORA AND FAUNA HIGHLIGHTS The Chobe River meanders through occasional low, flat islands and floating mats of papyrus and reeds. These islands, and beside the river, are always lush and green – and hence attract high densities of game. Beside this the bleached-white riverbank rises up just a few metres, and instantly becomes dry and dusty. Standing on top of this are skeletons of dead trees, sometimes draped by a covering of woolly caper-bushes.

In several areas this bank has been eroded away, perhaps originally where small seasonal streams have joined the main river or hippo tracks out of the water have become widened by general animal use to access the floodplains. Here there are often mineral licks, and you'll see herds of animals in the dry season coming down to eat the soil as well as drink from the river.

Flora On the bank beside the river the vegetation contains many of the usual plants found in riparian forest in the subcontinent. Yet despite this it has a very distinctive appearance, different from that of any other African river – and this difference is perhaps largely due to the sheer volumes of game, and especially elephants, that visit it during the dry season.

The main tree species found in this riverine forest include Natal mahogany (*Trichilia emetica*) – which isn't found in the rest of Botswana – plus Rhodesian teak (*Baikiaea plurijuga*), large feverberry (*Croton megalobotryus*), umbrella thorn (*Acacia tortilis*), knobthorn (*Acacia negrescens*), raintree (*Lonchocarpus capassa*), African mangosteen (*Garcinia livingstonei*), bird plum (*Berchemia discolor*), jackalberry (*Diospyros mespiliformis*) and the odd sausage tree (*Kigelia africana*).

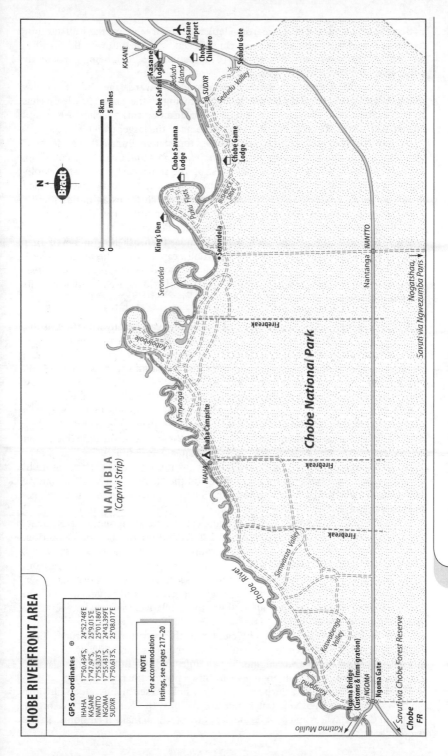

CHOBE RIVERFRONT AREA

GPS co-ordinates ⊕

IHAHA	17°50.434'S,	24°52.748'E
KASANE	17°47.97'S,	25°9.015'E
NANTTO	17°55.333'S,	25°01.186'E
NGOMA	17°55.431'S,	24°43.399'E
SUDXR	17°50.613'S,	25°08.017'E

NOTE
For accommodation
listings, see pages 217–20

0 _____ 8km
0 _____ 5 miles

N

Bradt

KASANE

Kasane Airport

Kasane

Chobe Safari Lodge

Sedudu (Island)

Chobe Chilwero

Sedudu Gate

⊕ SUDXR

Sedudu Valley

Chobe Savanna Lodge

Chobe Game Lodge

Puku Flats

King's Den

BUSHBUCK DRIVE

●Serondela

Serondela

NAMIBIA
(Caprivi Strip)

Kabolebole

Firebreak

N'tinyanga

Chobe National Park

▲ Ihaha Campsite

IHAHA

Firebreak

Nantanga *NANTTO*

Nogatshaa,
Savuti via Ngwezumba Pans ▼

Firebreak

Simwanza Valley

Chobe River

Kaswabenga Valley

Kangumu

Ngoma Bridge
(Customs & Imm gration)

✕ NGOMA

Ngoma Gate

Savuti via Chobe Forest Reserve

Chobe
FR

Katima Mulilo ◄────

Because of the intense pressure from elephants, you'll often see the still-standing remains of dead trees which have been ring-barked by elephants, with the termite-resistant skeletons, probably leadwoods (*Combretum imberbe*), being particularly noticeable.

These riverside forests can seem quite denuded towards the end of the dry season, which many naturally blame on heavy grazing by the game. Clearly this has an impact here, but commercial logging took place along this riverside before and during World War II and also took its toll of some of the larger trees.

Despite this, several different types of bushes thrive here. Buffalo thorn (*Ziziphus mucronata*) and knobbly combretum (*Combretum mossambicense*) are common, though Chobe's most distinctive bush must be the remarkably successful woolly caper-bush (*Capparis tomentosa*). This sometimes grows into a dense, tangled shrub, but equally often you'll find it as a creeper which forms an untidy mantle covering an old termite mound. Sometimes you'll even find it covering the crown of dead trees, or draped continuously over a series of bushes.

If you're out game viewing with a local guide, then ask him or her if they know of any local medicinal uses for the woolly caper-bush. The plant has very strong antiseptic qualities, and both Palgrave and Roodt (see *Appendix 3, Further information*) report that this is one of the trees most widely used in Africa for its magico-medicinal properties.

Fauna The game densities along the Chobe riverfront vary greatly with the seasons, but towards the end of the dry season it is certainly one of Africa's most prolific areas for game. It is an ideal destination for visitors seeking big game. Elsewhere in the dry season you'll find fascination in termites or ground squirrels, but here you can find huge herds of buffalo, relaxed prides of lion, and perhaps Africa's highest concentration of elephant – huge herds which are the hallmark of the area.

One of the main attractions of the boat trips on the Chobe is that large family groups of elephants will troop down to the river to drink and bathe, affording spectacular viewing and photography. You'll find these here at any time of day, but they're especially common in the late afternoon, just before sunset.

When it's very dry you'll also find elephants swimming across the river at night to raid the relatively verdant crops and farms on the Namibian side, often coming back to Botswana during the day when the villagers feel more confident to emerge and scare them.

If you are not floating but driving, then be careful. Read my specific comments on driving near elephants, pages 223 and 226–7, and err on the side of caution. Most of Chobe's elephants are in family groups containing mothers with calves. They can be sensitive to any perceived threat, so keep a respectful distance from them. This can be especially difficult when you see licensed guides driving closer, but you should still keep your distance. Their experience, and general coolness in case of elephant aggression, will allow them to do relatively safely what would be dangerous for you to attempt.

If you find your car surrounded by elephants, then try to relax. Virtually all of Chobe's elephants have seen lots of vehicles before, and so are unlikely to get too upset. Don't panic or rev your engine; just sit quiet and still until the animals have passed. Ideally switch off your engine – but this is not for the faint-hearted.

The riverfront itself offers the best chance in Chobe to see hippos, crocodiles and the odd sunbathing leguvaan (water monitor). Whilst there, also look out for the delightful Cape clawless and spotted-necked otters, which make their homes in the riverbank.

above **Elephant**
(*Loxodonta africana*)
(VS/SS) page 493

right **Nile crocodile**
(*Crocodylus niloticus*)
(AVZ) page 491

below **Hippopotamus**
(*Hippopotamus amphibius*)
(TH) page 494

left	**Lion cub** (*Panthera leo*) (NH) page 477
below left	**Cheetah** (*Acynonix jubatus*) (JG) page 480
below right	**Caracal** (*Felis caracal*) (CM) page 481
bottom	**Leopard** (*Panthera pardus*) (TL) page 477

above **Wild dog (*Lycaon pictus*)**
(JG) page 481

right **Serval (*Felis serval*)**
(JG) page 481

below left **Spotted hyena (*Crocuta crocuta*)**
(MD/SS) page 483

below right **Bat-eared fox (*Otocyon megalotis*)**
(JG) page 483

above   **Buffalo (*Syncerus caffer caffer*)**
(AVZ) page 494

left   **Sable antelope (*Hippotragus niger*)**
(TH) page 485

below left   **Waterbuck (*Kobus ellipsiprymnus*)**
(AVZ) page 487

below right   **Male kudu (*Tragelaphus strepciseros*)**
(CM) page 488

above   **Plains zebra (*Equus quagga*)**
(JG) page 495

right   **Gemsbok *(Oryx gazella)***
(JG) page 486

below   **Tsessebe (*Damaliscus lunatus*)**
(CM) page 488

above   Darter or snakebird (*Anhinga anhinga*) roosting (AVZ)

left   Carmine bee eater (*Merops nubicoides*) (O/SS)

below left   Pied kingfisher (*Ceryle rudis*) (CM)

bottom left Spoonbill (*Platalea leucorodia*) (CM)

below   Yellow-billed hornbill (*Tockus leucomelas*) (JMS/SS)

above left   Pale chanting goshawk
(*Accipiter gentiles spp*) (CM)

above right   African fish eagle (*Haliaeetus vocifer*) (JG)

right   Secretary bird (*Sagittarius serpentarius*) (JG)

below left   Pel's fishing owl (*Scotopelia peli*) (TH)

below right   Little bee eater (*Merops pusillus*) (JG)

above   **Banded mongoose (*Mungos mungo*)**
(JC/SS) page 496

left   **Warthog (*Phacocoerus africanus*)**
(JC/SS) page 495

below   **Painted reed frog (*Hyperolius argus*)**
(MI)

bottom   **Meerkat (*Suricata suricatta*)**
(JG) page 497

Perhaps the riverfront's most talked-about antelope is the Chobe bushbuck. This is a localised race, or perhaps a subspecies, of the bushbuck (*Tragelaphus scriptus* or, if a subspecies, then *ornata*) which has wide distribution within sub-Saharan Africa, from the edge of rainforests to the edges of the Kalahari and throughout the eastern side of southern Africa. Their colouration exhibits a lot of regional variation, and there is certainly a distinctive race which occurs only in this Chobe riverfront area – with brighter coloration and clearer markings than are found in the rest of southern Africa.

Bushbuck are small, attractive antelope which usually occur singly or in pairs. Only the males have horns, which are short and spiralled. They are well camouflaged, with a red-brown colouration, like the soil, and a covering of white spots that blend into the shadows of the riverside's thick vegetation. They will freeze if disturbed, and there are reliable reports of lions and hyena passing within 10m of a plainly visible bushbuck and not noticing it. Only if disturbed will they bolt for cover as a last resort.

Another antelope often noted here is the puku (*Kobus vardonii*) – which some sources claim is rarely seen. This is true, but only if you've never been to Zambia, where puku are arguably the most common antelope. South of the Chobe they probably occur only in this Chobe riverfront area, and especially around the aptly named 'Puku Flats' peninsula of the floodplain.

The red lechwe (*Kobus leche*) is another water-loving antelope that is resident here, and is easily confused with the puku at first glance. Look closely and you'll see that the lechwe's underparts are much lighter, their coats seem less shaggy, and the males' horns larger. Also notice that when they run, lechwe tend to hold their heads close to the ground, while puku normally run with their heads held much higher. This makes identifying them from a distance easier – and soon you'll realise that red lechwe are usually the most common antelope on Chobe's floodplains.

Waterbuck and reedbuck are also usually found in wetter areas, and so seen around Chobe riverfront and Linyanti but not elsewhere in Chobe. Roan are also found here, but are fairly scarce, as befits an antelope that is sought after by private game areas and is expensive to buy. Finally, the beautiful sable antelope are common nowhere, but I've seen large and relaxed herds here on several occasions. Being specialist grazers, they are more commonly found in the wooded south of the riverfront, though as sable and roan usually drink during the middle of the day, you will quite often see a small herd near the riverfront road, between Ngoma and Kasane.

Birdlife From a boat on the main river in the park you're likely to spot numerous beautiful kingfishers (pied, giant, some malachite and the occasional half-collared), with the pied seeming to be particularly numerous, perching on reeds by the river, or hovering to hold their eyes static above the river's surface. You'll also see plenty of reed cormorants and darters, various bee-eaters, hamerkops, wire-tailed swallows, a high density of fish eagles and even African skimmers (November–March only; the best place to see them is probably near Hippo Pools, beside Watercart Drive).

The fringes of the islands and floodplain are particularly good for birding, being home to many storks, herons, geese, egrets and a wide variety of plovers (blacksmiths, long-toed, crowned, wattled and, of special interest, white-crowned). Particularly unusual and worth seeking are rufous-bellied and white-backed night herons, slaty egrets, brown firefinches and wattled cranes.

For a totally distinct environment attracting several different species, head downstream and out of the park, to the shallow rapids dotted with rocks, which are adjacent to Impalila Island on the Chobe and Zambezi rivers. (The Chobe's are the Kasane Rapids, whilst those on the Zambezi are known as the Mambova Rapids.) In the dense waterside vegetation before the rapids look out for the shy finfoot, whilst around the rapids themselves there's a thriving population of rock pratincoles.

If you have the chance to explore the Kasai Channel (which connects the Zambezi and Chobe rivers), then do so. Technically you'll need to cross into Namibia, so this trip is probably easiest to undertake from one of the lodges on Impalila Island (see pages 200–1). Here you'll find small lagoons beside the main channel covered in waterlilies, and bird species that include the uncommon lesser and purple gallinules, lesser jacanas and moorhens, pygmy geese and African rails. On the edge of these, in the adjacent reeds and papyrus beds you'll probably hear (if not see) chirping cisticolas, greater swamp warblers and swamp boubous.

Back inside the park, in the band of forest beside the river, you'll find many drier-country species, including coucals (Senegal and coppery-tailed), oxpeckers, sunbirds (you can find coppery sunbirds here), rollers (look out for the racket-tailed), hornbills, flycatchers, weavers, shrikes and francolins. Large flocks of helmeted guineafowl seem particularly visible, and are especially fond of loitering along the tracks in front of vehicles. Or so it seems!

There's a tremendously wide range of raptors here, from the ubiquitous fish eagles perching on dead trees overlooking the river, through to the huge martial eagles patrolling the drier woodlands. Other resident eagles include the uncommon western banded snake eagle, black-breasted and brown snake eagles, bateleur, tawny, long-crested, Ayres' and African hawk eagle. These are joined in the summer by migrant eagles, including steppe and Wahlberg's eagles, and all year by many species of falcons, goshawks, harriers, kites and even the rarely seen bat hawk.

ORIENTATION The southern bank of the Chobe River is slightly raised above the river, perhaps 3–4m high. Below this is a fairly level floodplain of short green grass and reeds, through which the river follows a very meandering course, roughly west to east, with many switchbacks, loops and adjacent old lagoons.

High on the bank is the main riverfront track, which is wide but for the most part sandy. This leads from the Kasane to the Ngoma Gate fairly directly. Looping off from this are game-viewing tracks. Most of those on the north side drop down to the floodplains, and then loop around by the river. Those few heading off south usually follow straight firebreaks into the dry woodlands that make up the bulk of Chobe behind the thin band of riparian forest.

You can't get lost, provided that you don't cross to the south of the main road. Head east and you'll reach Kasane, west and you'll find Ngoma.

The game densities are generally at their best between Kasane and Ihaha, although the density of vehicles is also high here. When you head west past Ihaha, towards Ngoma, you'll find an increasing number of Namibians herding cattle on the floodplain areas across the Chobe River. Game densities in the forest reserve are significantly lower than those in the park, but you do have better chances of spotting some less common species like sable and roan antelope.

For details of the roads between Kasane and Savuti, see pages 222–6.

Ngoma border post (⊕ *06.00–18.00*) At the westernmost point of the Chobe riverfront is the Ngoma Gate (✪ NGOMA 17°55.719'S, 24°43.665'E), which marks the boundary between Chobe National Park and Chobe Forest Reserve. Turning northwest towards the river at this point brings you to the border post at Ngoma,

At several checkpoints in Botswana, particularly near rivers, notices are posted warning of the problems posed by the invasive waterweed, *Salvinia molesta*. Known locally as *mosthimbambo*, and more widely by its common names, giant salvinia or Kariba weed, it was first identified in the Zambezi River over 50 years ago. Since then it has become widespread throughout the southern part of the continent, migrating to the Chobe River in the 1980s.

A native of Brazil, Kariba weed is a water fern that was at one time sold for ornamental use in aquariums and garden ponds. With an exceptionally fast rate of reproduction, the plant spread rapidly from these relatively narrow confines into larger bodies of warm, relatively sluggish water. As the plant multiplies, its originally flat green leaves die back and fold together, forming an impenetrable mat that can be as much as a metre deep. The implications for waterways such as the rivers of Botswana are considerable. Not only do the matted plants create an obstruction, impacting on boat traffic and blocking irrigation pipes and water supplies, they also create an ideal breeding ground for mosquitoes and other insects. The impact on the environment is no less devastating, with indigenous plants affected by loss of light and oxygen, an effect that is compounded as decaying plants sink to the riverbed and adversely affect the development of fish and other river wildlife.

Control of such a virulent plant has proved extremely difficult. While it can be sprayed, this is rarely fully effective, and the chemicals used are in themselves harmful to the environment. Rather more successful has been the introduction of a weevil imported from Australia, *Cyrtobagus salviniae*, whose adults and larvae feed on and damage the plants under the right circumstances.

The problem is by no means confined to Africa. Kariba weed is on the environmental hit-list of countries across the globe, from New Zealand to the US, where both sales and ownership of the plant are now banned. In Botswana, however, the challenge is to prevent serious damage to the country's aquatic ecosystem. With this in mind, the authorities have introduced strict measures, which include controlling the boats allowed on the country's waterways, and decontamination of those that are licensed.

where on the Botswana side is a mid-1990s building perched high above the river by a venerable old baobab, complete with picnic benches. On the other side of the river, Namibia has a more imposing office next to the tarred bridge, about 2km further on. Both are efficient, pleasant and generally quiet. As with many borders, don't be alarmed if you see the odd soldier wandering around with a gun, and don't even think about taking any pictures near the bridge without permission.

From the border, it's signposted 57km to Kasane, 65km to Kazungula, 115km to Savuti and 362km to Nata. Over in Namibia, the conversion of the 69km stretch of gravel road between the Ngoma border and Katima Mulilo has now been completed, meaning that you can now drive from Kasane into Namibia and right across the Caprivi Strip on a good tar road.

WHERE TO STAY Many people visit the Chobe riverfront whilst staying in or around Kasane (see pages 187–91 and 200–2), or possibly from a base at Ngoma (see pages 221–2). Generally the options inside the park are more expensive, but they have better locations. Within northern Chobe, there are only two permanent choices: the basic public campsite at Ihaha or the stylish Chobe Game Lodge. There is also a mobile operation, while the river itself hosts a recently refurbished riverboat, the *Zambezi Queen*. On the opposite side – technically in Namibia – are two further lodges, which I've included as they are primarily used to visit Chobe – though note that one of these, King's Den, has been closed for some time.

Å Ihaha Campsite [map 213] (10 pitches) Contact Kwalate Safaris, page 174; ⊕ IHAHA 17°50.484'S, 24°52.748'E. About 35km west of the Sedudu Gate, Ihaha is the only campsite for private visitors within northern Chobe. If you're taking the riverfront road from Kasane you'll come to a signpost close to 3 sharp turns in the road, which effectively form a square around the gate.

For all the imposing entrance, Ihaha has changed little under privatisation. Large pitches run parallel to the river, some with almost unlimited views across to the Namibian plains, though not all have good tree shade. It's not terribly pretty, but the ground is firm & sandy underfoot, & it's a great spot to while away the hours watching the abundance of waterbirds by the river, or herds of impala & zebra grazing among the cattle on the other side. Two modern ablution blocks, with hot water courtesy of solar panels, are reasonably clean, & each pitch comes with a water supply & BBQ – of sorts. *US$40 pp, exc park fees, bed levy.* ⊕ *All year.*

⌂ Chobe Game Lodge [map 213] (43 rooms, 4 suites) Contact Desert & Delta Safaris, page 176; ⊕ CHOBGL 17°50.850'S, 25°05.083'E. Opened in 1972, about 9km from the park's Sedudu Gate, this is the largest lodge in any of Botswana's national parks. In some ways it seems like just another luxury hotel, yet its design is unusual, with tribal antiques in almost Moorish surroundings, which blend together very well.

Each of the comfortable rooms is set slightly into the bank with a barrel-vaulted ceiling & French windows on to a balcony or small veranda overlooking the river, about 60m away. The style is colonial: red-tiled floors are dotted with rugs, the furniture is solid Rhodesian teak with wicker chairs, & punkah-punkah ceiling fans (together with AC), keep the everything cool. En-suite bathrooms have a bath with shower attachment, but plans are in hand to add a separate shower. Large suites come equally well furnished but with a lounge as well as a bedroom, a shower separate

SERONDELA

For years the only campsite in northern Chobe was at Serondela, sprawling along the riverside about 17km west of Kasane. The local animals had all lost their fear of man. Hence all the dangerous big game seemed to make a point of regularly sauntering through camp. Ignorant tourists had, over the years, fed some animals and the baboons, particularly, became a menace – aggressive, adept at stealing food if you turned your back for a second, and even able to open zips on unguarded tents.

On one occasion a lone male bounded on to the tailgate of my 4x4, snatching a packet of biscuits in its jaws from a food box, and sprinted off – all in a matter of seconds whilst I and a companion were a few steps away at the front of the vehicle. Before leaping up into the back it knew that we'd seen it and were coming back to chase it, but also knew that it was faster and so continued. It was obviously very well practised at this sort of smash-and-grab raid.

Further, Serondela was relatively close to the eastern side of the park, so it added considerably to the density of traffic in the peak dawn and dusk time for game viewing. So for several reasons the site was closed in the late 1990s and superseded by the new Ihaha site. Today it is used only by safari groups as a tranquil picnic site.

from the bathroom, & a small, private infinity pool. When Elizabeth Taylor & Richard Burton chose this as a romantic place in which to be re-married & spend their honeymoon in 1975, it was something of a PR coup!

The completion of a wide riverside walkway in 2012, entirely accessible by wheelchair, has transformed the lodge. Now it's possible to take a stroll, then enjoy a drink or a meal at one of several intimate seating areas along the walkway, with one eye on the plains below. The food is good, with a buffet for b/fast & lunch, & a more leisurely à-la-carte dinner served by candlelight. In the main building, a rather womblike bar downstairs contrasts with the more masculine upstairs bar, complete with full-size billiard table & a terrace overlooking the river. A library with TV & computers (there's free Wi-Fi in the central areas), an attractive, free-form pool, a beauty salon with a gym (fortunately with AC), a small treatment room, & a well-stocked curio shop add to the facilities.

Activities, led by an all-female guiding team, are very flexible: you can take as many as you have the time & energy for. Game drives in open-sided 4x4s typically go out 3 times a day – early or late morning & late afternoon – for about 3hrs, or you can take out a small boat with a driver/guide, usually in the late morning or the early afternoon. Guests may also tour behind the scenes & discover how the lodge gained its high level eco credentials; it's fascinating! *US$873pp/1,135 sharing/sgl Jul–Oct, US$573 pp Apr–Jun & Nov, US$495 pp Dec–Mar, fully inc.* ⊕ *All year.*

⋏ **Chobe Under Canvas** (5 tents) Contact &Beyond, page 175. Effectively a mobile camp, Chobe Under Canvas moves between private campsites along the Chobe riverfront (although never with guests on site). Guests are collected from Kasane airport, with a 1hr transfer to the camp. Those with their own vehicle can leave it in Kasane, & transfer from there; no self-drivers are allowed into camp. Accommodation is in en-suite twin or dbl tents, with battery-powered lamps, an open-air bucket shower (hot water on request) & a separate toilet. Communal tents offer space for drinks, dining or just relaxing with a book. With game drives in the morning & afternoon, & boat cruises along the river, there's plenty to keep guests occupied until a traditional bush dinner,

served under the stars. *US$435–700 pp sharing, inc FB, most drinks, activities, laundry. No children under 12.* ⊕ *Feb–Dec.*

⌂ **Chobe Savanna Lodge** [map 213] (13 chalets) Contact Desert & Delta Safaris, page 176; ✪ CHOBSL 17°49.838'S, 25°03.198'E. The smaller sister lodge of Chobe Game Lodge stands on a private concession of land on the Namibian side of the river, facing west out over the Puku Flats. Recently refurbished, it focuses on a dbl-storey thatch-&-timber building, which has superb views across the river & its floodplains. Inside is a lounge, library & dining room, whilst outside is an open boma for evening fires, a plunge pool & a wooden sundeck.

The brick-&-thatch suites all have en-suite facilities with separate showers & baths, AC, overhead fans, minibars & tea/coffee-making facilities. It's a stylish spot, designed carefully with lots of rich dark earthy browns.

Activities here major on game viewing & fishing by motorboat, as well as sunset cruises. Nature walks along the river & trips to one of the local villages are also offered. *US$580/755 sharing/sgl Jul–Oct, US$385 pp Nov–Mar & Jun, fully inc.* ⊕ *Jun–Mar.*

⌂ **King's Den** [map 213] The former Namib Sun hotel overlooking Chobe National Park from Kasikili (Sedudu) Island is currently being rebuilt, apparently to a very high standard. Note that it is nearer to the park than any of Impalila Island's lodges.

🛥 ***Zambezi Queen*** (14 suites) 📞 +27 (0)21 438 0032; ℮ info@zambeziqueen.com; www. zambeziqueen.com. Formerly owned by King's Den, this prestigious 45m riverboat had a serious makeover in 2009 to emerge polished & kitted out in 5-star luxury. Up on deck there's a pool & various areas for relaxing in the shade or soaking up the sun, & at night a telescope beckons guests to explore the heavens. In the lounge areas, AC assures cool comfort, while from the adjacent restaurant you can spot animals at dusk as they approach the water. A well-stocked bar is popular, too! There's mosquito screening throughout, including in the individual suites which feature sliding doors to private balconies.

Cruises last either 2 or 3 nights, departing from Kasane on Mon, Wed & Fri. During the trip, expect to watch game or birds on the Chobe River from deck or from smaller boats, or – for rather a lot of effort – from a 4x4 within Chobe National Park. Fishing (in season) for tigerfish or bream, & visiting a local village, are further options. *2 nights* *(dep Mon & Wed) R8,900–13,000 pp sharing; 3 nights (dep Fri) R13,350–19,500; prices in South African rand. ⊕ All year.*

WHAT TO SEE AND DO Game viewing and birdwatching are the main activities on the Chobe riverfront; walking and night drives are not allowed. Most visitors explore along the floodplains beside the river, which offers relatively easy game viewing, even without a guide.

If you're driving yourself and have a little time to spare, don't ignore the roads away from the river on the western side of this riverfront section, particularly the Kaswabenga and Simwanza Valley roads, as well as the firebreaks marked on Veronica Roodt's maps of Chobe. The landscape here is broken country with rocky hillsides and gullies: classic leopard country and very different from anything else you're likely to see in Chobe. You'll often find surprisingly good concentrations of game here in October, despite its apparent distance from the river, because the game tends to rest in the shade of the forest on its way to and from the water.

THE CAPRIVI STRIP

As you look across the Chobe River – and indeed the Linyanti – from Botswana you're looking into Namibia's Caprivi Strip, but how did the land come to belong to Namibia in the first place? On the map, the Caprivi Strip appears to be a strange appendage of Namibia rather than a part of it. It forms a strategic corridor of land, linking Namibia to Zimbabwe and Zambia, but seems somehow detached from the rest of the country. The region's history explains why.

When Germany annexed South West Africa (now Namibia) in 1884, it prompted British fears that they might try to link up with the Boers, in the Transvaal, thus driving a wedge between these territories and cutting off the Cape from Rhodesia. Out of fear, the British negotiated an alliance with Khama, a powerful Tswana king, and proclaimed the Protectorate of Bechuanaland – the forerunner of modern Botswana. At that time, this included the present-day Caprivi Strip. Geographically this made sense if the main reason for Britain's claim was to block Germany's expansion into central Africa.

Meanwhile, off Africa's east coast, Germany laid claim to Zanzibar. This was the end game of the colonial 'scramble for Africa', which set the stage for the Berlin Conference of July 1890. Then these two colonial powers sat down in Europe to reorganise their African possessions with strokes of a pen.

Britain agreed to sever the Caprivi from Bechuanaland and give control of it to Germany, to add to their province of South West Africa. Germany hoped to use it to access the Zambezi's trade routes to the east, and named it after the German Chancellor of the time, Count George Leo von Caprivi. In return for this (and also the territory of Heligoland in the North Sea), Germany ceded control of Zanzibar to Britain, and agreed to redefine South West Africa's eastern border with Britain's Bechuanaland.

At the end of World War I the Caprivi was re-incorporated into Bechuanaland, but in 1929 it was again returned to South West Africa, then under South African rule. Hence it became part of Namibia.

CHOBE FOREST RESERVE

Chobe Forest Reserve is an enclave largely surrounded by Chobe National Park. To the northwest of it are seasonal marshes, Lake Liambezi and, eventually, Namibia.

The reserve, and the area to the north of it – concessions known as CH1 and CH2 – have long been designated respectively for photographic safaris and community-managed hunting, but with a ban on commercial hunting coming into force in January 2014, this is set to change. The photographic area in CH1, beside the Linyanti River, is the location of Linyanti Bush Camp and its two sister camps, as well as Three Baobabs away from the river. However, as the flora and fauna here are essentially the same as in the Linyanti Concession, we have included the camps in that section (pages 249–50).

Most visitors simply pass through the southern corner of CH2 between Kasane and Savuti, but for those visiting the riverfront, the lodges near Ngoma are well worth consideration. See *Western route: via the riverfront*, page 224, for details of this drive.

WHERE TO STAY [map 206] Chobe's game-drive loops become quieter as you move from the Kasane area west to Ngoma. There are now four lodges here in the forest reserve, so think of them as alternatives to those in the Kasane area, as well as potentially convenient stopovers. All are set high on a ridge overlooking the Chobe River floodplain and are normally reached by road from Kasane, taking about an hour for the transfer.

Chobe Elephant Camp (11 chalets) 686 3763; e reservations@ chobeelephantcamp. com; www.chobeelephantcamp.com; CHOBEC 17°56.840'S, 24°42.055'E. The newest arrival in this area opened in Nov 2013. With a view to mitigating the effects of a harsh climate & the impact on the environment, the entire lodge has been constructed of sandbags – while a pool helps guests to cool off in the heat. Rather rustic-looking chalets, including a family suite, combine with modern styling in the lounge, dining & bar areas to create something of a farmhouse effect: understated & relaxed. As well as game drives & boat cruises, guests can take part in cultural visits to a local village. *US$385 pp Apr–Jun; US$495/650 Jul–Oct pp sharing/sgl, US$325 pp Dec–Mar, inc FB, local drinks, activities (inc boat cruise for 2-night stay), park fees, laundry, transfer from Kasane. Self-drive US$310–390/545 pp sharing/sgl inc FB, local drinks* All year.

Muchenje Safari Lodge (10 chalets) 620 0013–15; m 7164 6017; e info@muchenje.com; www.muchenje.com; MUCHEN 17°57.115'S, 24°42.361'E. Perched on the escarpment overlooking the floodplain, Muchenje was built in 1996 by Matt & Lorna Smith, who have owned & run it ever since. It's a comfortable, traditional lodge with a strong sense of hospitality & a good team of staff. To get there, follow the signs from the T-junction at Ngoma

towards Mabele & Savuti; the turning to Muchenje is just 3km along on your right.

Well-spaced thatched chalets are comfortably furnished with a dbl or twin beds surrounded by a walk-in mosquito net. Each has a modern en suite shower & toilet, ceiling fan, electric lights, & a veranda-with-a-view. Discreetly tucked away is a honeymoon (or family) chalet – it sleeps up to 4 – with a 2nd storey, a large bath tub, & an absolutely private veranda set to one side.

At the heart of the lodge, a wide, solid, stone building under a high thatched roof forms a crescent above the plain, making the most of the setting. Here you'll find a large table for communal dining, a lovely curved central bar with plenty of seating, & a small clothes/curio shop. Above the bar is a game-viewing platform which, along with a small pool, shares that impressive view. And in the evening, bush dinners can be arranged in their private boma.

Activities at Muchenje are many & varied; if you want to be busy all day, you can be! Game drives into the national park use an area that tends to be more private than around Kasane, as less traffic reaches this far west. Bush walks (with armed guides) in the forest reserve are also offered, as is birdwatching on the river. Those staying 2 nights or more – which includes most guests – can opt for a full-day safari taking in a midday boat cruise along the Chobe

9

(thus avoiding the afternoon 'boat rush'), followed by a picnic lunch in the bush & a game drive back through the park. In 2014, the lodge hopes to have its own jetty in the Ihaha area, thus avoiding the extra drive as far as Kasane. Fishing is available with advance notice only, & at extra cost, as it is arranged through a separate company. And if you'd like to visit a local village, your guide will introduce you to his family & show you round. *US$465/660 Apr–Jun pp sharing/sgl, US$645/870 Jul–Oct, US$395 pp Nov–Mar, inc FB, local drinks, activities, laundry, Kasane transfers.* ⊕ *All year.*

🏠 **Ngoma Safari Lodge** (see advert, 3rd colour insert, page viii) (8 chalets) ☎ +263 13 43211–20, 43201; e aatreservations@saflodge.co.zw; www.africaalbidatourism.com; ⊕ NGOMSL 17°56.513′S, 24°42.558′E. More or less adjacent to Muchenje, Ngoma opened in 2011. As if anchored to an old baobab, its dining tables, bar, umbrella-shaded terrace, rock-style pool & firepit are all strategically placed on different levels to make the most of panoramic views over the floodplain below. It's light, airy & stylish (don't miss the beaded chandeliers!), yet retains a strong sense of place combined with more than a hint of tradition. As for practicalities, there's Wi-Fi in the central area, & a spotting scope helps you to keep an eye on the game in the distance.

Well spaced along the ridge are split-level chalets, which soak up the view from individual patios with sunloungers, & tiny plunge pools that are the envy of the local elephant population. There are outside showers, too, while inside are contemporary bathrooms with twin basins, a bath & separate loo. On a lower level, the beds – lit by good lights & enveloped by mosquito nets – face the plains through full-length glazed windows, & cool drinks, tea & coffee, & biscotti are on hand to help while away the afternoon. Although the room nearest the central area has no steps, so is more suited to those with limited mobility, note that the paths are quite rough. Two further rooms can be converted into triples.

Typically, guests spend their 1st day on a short game drive to the river below the lodge, with their 2nd full-day trip taking in a game drive through Chobe National Park, lunch, & a cruise on the Chobe River. *US$895/1,119 pp sharing/sgl Jul–Nov, US$577 pp Dec–Jun, inc FB, most drinks, activities, laundry, Kasane/Kazungula transfers. No children under 10.* ⊕ *All year.*

🏠 **Baobab Safari Lodge** (8 chalets) ⊕ BAOBAB 17°56.615′S, 24°43.319′E. About 3km inside the Chobe Forest Reserve, this stone-built camp is currently privately run, with no walk-in guests accepted. The rather dark central building combines dining & lounge areas. Behind & alongside sit individual chalets with pitched canvas roofs, each with twin beds & an en-suite bathroom. As you would expect, activities focus on game drives in the national park.

LIAMBEZI AREA

This large, shallow lake is located between the Linyanti and Chobe rivers. When full, it covers some 10,000ha, although since 1985 it has been much drier, and frequently something of a dustbowl – until the exceptional rains of 2009. Thus for many years, people and cattle have populated its bed rather than hippos and crocodile.

Lake Liambezi's main source of water used to be the Linyanti River. However, even in recent years of good rain it failed to fill the lake after filtering through the Linyanti Swamps (which themselves are very dry). Even despite good water levels in the Kwando-Linyanti system in the 2001–12 rainy season, it didn't break through as far as Liambezi. As a result there has been a trend towards less and less water in the lake and the marshes around it, and more villages. By 2014, however, for the first time in many years Lake Liambezi had a few inches of water in it, due to good rains, a recovery of the Bukalo Channel from the northeast, and possibly some flow-back from the Chobe River.

DRIVING FROM KASANE TO SAVUTI

There are two routes through Chobe National Park between Kasane (⊕ KASANE 17°47.97′S, 25°9.015′E) and Savuti. Certainly the shorter, and probably the more

DRIVING NEAR ELEPHANTS: AVOIDING PROBLEMS

Elephants are the only animals that pose a real danger to vehicles. Everything else will get out of your way, or at least not actively go after you, but if you treat elephants wrongly there's a chance that you might have problems.

To put this in perspective, most drivers who are new to Africa will naturally (and wisely) treat elephants with enormous respect, keeping their distance – simply out of fear. Also in the more popular areas of Chobe or Moremi, where the elephants are habituated to vehicles, you'd have to really annoy an already grumpy elephant for it to give you trouble.

To give specific advice is difficult, as every elephant is different. Each is an individual, with real moods and feelings – and there's no substitute for years of experience to tell you what mood they're in. However, a few basics are worth noting.

Firstly, keep your eyes open and don't drive too fast. Surprising an elephant on the road is utterly terrifying, and dangerous for both you and the elephant. Always drive slowly in the bush.

Secondly, think of each animal as having an invisible 'comfort zone' around it (some experts talk of three concentric zones: the fright, flight, and fight zones – each with a smaller radius, and each more dangerous). If you actively approach then you breach that zone, and will upset it. So don't approach too closely: keep your distance. How close depends entirely on the elephants and the area. More relaxed elephants having a good day will allow you to get within 25m of them, bad-tempered ones that aren't used to cars may charge at 250m! You can often approach more closely in open areas than in thick bush. That said, if your vehicle is stationary and a relaxed, peaceful elephant approaches you, then you should not have problems if you simply stay still.

Thirdly, never beep your horn or flash your lights at an elephant (you shouldn't be driving yourself at night anyhow!). Either is guaranteed to annoy it. If there's an elephant in your way, just sit back, relax and wait; elephants always have right of way in Africa! The more sound and fury – like wheelspins and engine revving – the more likely that the elephant will assume that you are attacking it, and this is especially the case with a breeding herd.

Finally, look carefully at the elephant(s):

- Are there any small calves around in the herd? If so expect the older females to be easily annoyed and very protective – keep your distance.
- Are there any males in musth around? These are fairly easy to spot because of a heavy secretion from penis and temporal glands and a very musty smell. Generally these will be on their own, unless they are with a cow on heat. Such males will be excitable; you must spot them and give them a wide berth.
- Are there any elephants with a lot of seepage from their temporal glands, on the sides of their heads? If so, expect them to be stressed and easily irritable – beware. This is likely to have a long-term cause – perhaps lack of good water, predator pressure or something as random as toothache – but whatever the cause, that animal is under stress, and so should be given an extra-wide berth.

beautiful, is the western route, which is about 172km from Kasane to Savuti, via the Chobe Forest Reserve, and can take in the Chobe riverfront drive (above) if you have time. The alternative is the eastern route, which is about 207km long. This stays within the park and passes through the Nogatsaa Pans area.

Note that in the wet season, you're recommended to use the western route. Firstly, it's probably slightly more frequented by vehicles. Secondly, you'll find it particularly easy to get stuck in the clay soils found around the pans (both Zweizwe and Nogatsaa/Tchinga). That said, if you do brave the pans route, the birding can be particularly good at that time of year.

Don't imagine that the western route is always easy at that time. Most of this is fairly thick sand and you'll often be crossing fossil dunes with woodland on the crests and scrub or grasslands in the valleys. Veronica Roodt (see *Appendix 3, Further information*) reports that there's a patch where water sometimes gathers just south of the Ghoha Hills. So beware of problems there after heavy rains.

EASTERN ROUTE: VIA THE PANS For the eastern route, you need to take the fast tar road from Kasane to Ngoma, away from the river. About 18km beyond the Sedudu Gate into the park, you'll reach a crossroads (✿ NANTTO 17°55.303'S, 25°01.186'E). A right turn, north, would take you to the riverfront road in the Serondela area. Left, signposted to Nogatsaa 50km, and Photha 78km, leads you on to the only road south through Chobe National Park, and within 1km to the Nantanga Pans.

About 35km later there is a left turn to the complex of roads around Nogatsaa airstrip, Ngwezumba Dam and the old Nogatsaa and Tchinga campsites. Continue straight and after about 22km you'll pass another left, leading back to the same area. Shortly after this the road begins to follow the dry bed of the Ngwezumba River.

Around 22km from this (at ✿ CNP1 18°30.243'S, 24°34.497'E) you pass a small track on the right, which leads after almost 4km to Nxunxutsha Pan (✿ NXUNXU 18°29.312'S, 24°32.537'E), which is the southernmost point of the Chobe Forest Reserve.

About 60km later, after the second Nogatsaa turn-off, this road takes a more southerly direction and leaves the riverbed behind (✿ CNP2 18°34.679'S, 24°23.381'E). About 7km later the road splits it (✿ CNP3 18°38.152'S, 24°24.928'E), with the right turn leading southwest through the pans. About 11km later the road turns west and finally northwest towards Savuti. This track enters Savuti by the south side of Qumxhwaa Hill (Quarry Hill) and joins the western route from Kasane just north of the channel.

At this final split in the pans route, there is an alternative left fork (which is not recommended as a route) which leads south for a few kilometres before passing Chosoroga Pan. One spur from this used to swing west around the pan and join into the roads on the south side of Savuti Marsh (from where you bear north and slightly west to reach the centre of Savuti). Another track apparently heads down directly from this pan to Mababe Village. I'm unsure of the current state of either of these tracks, so I would welcome news on either (preferably accompanied by details and GPS co-ordinates if they're navigable).

The total distance from Kasane to Savuti along the eastern route is about 207km, and it takes five or six hours to drive in the dry season. An advantage is the possibility of a midway stop at the Ngwezumba Pans (page 227), although scenically this route lacks the beauty of the Chobe River.

WESTERN ROUTE: VIA THE RIVERFRONT Taking the western route you have a choice of ways to start. If you're in a hurry, or starting late in the day, then drive the

57km to Ngoma from Kasane on the tar. Alternatively, and much more enjoyably, meander along the riverfront road (see *Chobe riverfront*, pages 212–22), which passes Serondela and Ihaha before joining up with the end of the tar road at Ngoma near the border post (see pages 216–17). Both routes are a little over 50km, but whereas the tar road will take about an hour (the speed limit is 80km/h), the river route will take several, depending on how much you stop to watch animals or take photographs.

Whichever route you take, you'll reach the park gate at Ngoma, where you may be required to sign the register and possibly also to walk across a disinfectant mat while the wheels of your vehicle are sprayed to prevent the spread of any disease. Then you should take a left turn, heading roughly southwest, and signposted as the B334 to Mabele (12km), Kachikau (37km), Parakarungu (67km) and Savuti (110km). This is now tarred all the way to Kachikau, making the first part of the journey – through the **Chobe Forest Reserve** (see pages 221–2) – very straightforward.

After about 11.5km you'll pass a big baobab and a large sign proclaiming **Mabele**. You'll still be able to see the Chobe floodplain off to the right, but with little game on it. Mabele General Dealer (✪ MABELE 17°59.182'S, 24°38.858'E), on the right before the soccer pitch, is the best shop in town, though it's still very limited. The vegetation is mostly acacia species here, with lots of umbrella thorn (*Acacia tortilis*), but the scenery becomes less inspiring.

Some 25km from Ngoma you come to **Kavimba**, whose landmark two baobabs stand guard on each side of the road (✪ KAVIMB 18°04.192'S, 24°35.020'E). This is the location of the Kachempati Basket Weavers Cooperative (〰 625 0339; ☉ 08.00–17.00 *daily*) – so if you're interested, it may be worth asking around for their craft shop. Then a little over 10km later you'll reach the sprawling town of **Kachikau** (marked on some maps as Kachekabwe), where you can buy a limited range of drinks and foodstuffs. There's also a forestry camp here, and the smart, well-built Liswaani Community School. In the centre of town (✪ KACHIK 18°09.143'S, 24°30.172'E) there's a right turning signposted to Setau, a small settlement in the communal area to the north of the forest reserve, near Lake Liambezi.

Just beyond Kachikau, some 92km from Kasane, the tar road comes to an abrupt halt, reverting almost instantly to deep, sandy tracks. Having passed a bottle store and Chobe Craft Centre on the left, this leads almost immediately to the turn-off point for those driving themselves to Three Baobabs, about an hour's drive west of this road (for details, see page 250.). The country around here is rolling vegetated dunes, which means lots of corrugations and deep, deep sand. Plenty of leadwood trees are around, so beware of punctures (especially if you've reduced the pressure in your tyres for the sand). The long, strong, leadwood spines will cause punctures in even the sturdiest of 4x4 tyres.

Continuing southwest, the next 40km towards the national park are, quite simply, challenging. The final 16km or so can be particularly hard going, with many a vehicle getting bogged down in the sand. To avoid this, you can take a right fork towards Linyanti, as indicated by the signpost at ✪ DETOR2 18°15.250'S, 24°19.087'E, rather than the left fork (signposted to Savuti). This leads to a point on the cutline (✪ CUTTUR 18°21.82'S, 24°10.633'E) which is about 7.7km northwest of the gate. Thus you just need to turn left along the cutline to return to the main track, and turn right to the gate. Although you'll still encounter plenty of sand on this route, it's not as thick as the more direct alternative. (For anyone heading in the opposite direction, from Savuti to Kasane, you would simply turn left up the cutline

If you get into a hair-raising situation with elephants, then you've probably not kept your distance. The key was prevention, and you failed. Now you must keep cool, with your logic ruling your fear. A few words here are inadequate – you need experience – but I'll outline some basics.

If you are unexpectedly surrounded by peaceful elephants when your vehicle is stationary and switched off, don't panic. Don't even start the engine, as that would startle them. Just sit there and enjoy it; there's no real cause for concern. Only when they've passed and are a distance away should you start up. When you do start: never start and move off simultaneously, which will be interpreted as the vehicle being very aggressive. Instead start up quietly, wait a little and then move.

More often a situation occurs when one from the herd will be upset with you. In that case you've approached too closely. (The key was to keep your distance – remember?) Then an annoyed elephant will usually first mock charge. This normally first involves a lot of ear flapping, head shaking and loud trumpeting – mock charges are often preceded by 'displacement activities', and the animals often show uncertainty about charging. The individual then runs towards you with ears spread out, head held high, and trumpeting loudly. This is terrifying, especially if you're not used to it. But be impressed, not surprised; elephants weigh up to 6,000kg and have had several million years to refine this into a really frightening spectacle.

However terrifying, if you stand your ground then almost all such encounters will end with the elephant stopping in its tracks. It will then move away at an

immediately after exiting the gate, and then take a right turn (⊕ CUTTUR) just after the end of a band of mopane trees.)

Either way, about 80km from Ngoma you'll arrive at the impressive Ghoha Gate (⊕ GHOHA 18°23.025'S, 24°14.732'E), which marks the end of the forest reserve, and the start of Chobe National Park. If you were to turn right here, then this (very rough and bumpy) cutline would lead you to a spot on the Linyanti River just east of Linyanti Campsite, and to the various camps run by African Bush Camps (generally the right side is better when it's wet; the left better in the dry season).

Savuti, however, is a further 28km to the southwest, so you'll need to sign in at the gate, and produce your park-entry permit and camp reservations. (Don't forget that park permits must now be bought in advance; fees are no longer accepted at the park gate.)

As you enter the national park you'll see the Ghoha Hills on your left in the distance. A few kilometres later you'll pass the first of the hills, which is dotted with baobab trees, and now topped with the new Ghoha Hills Savuti Lodge. The road inside the park is generally less sandy and better than that which is outside, although it does cross the northern edge of the Magwikhwe Sand Ridge just south of the hills.

About 25km after the entrance gate you'll pass a sharp-angled right turn which leads to Savuti airstrip, and a couple of kilometres further on you'll reach a new bridge over the now-flowing Savuti Channel, almost next to Savuti Campsite. Although this route is shorter (about 172km in total) and arguably more spectacular than the eastern route described above, the southern section in particular is generally more difficult and time-consuming to drive.

angle, with its head held high and turned, its back arched, its tail raised, and the occasional head-shake. Often you'll find the 'teenagers' of the herd doing this – testing you and showing off a bit.

However, if you flee or back off rapidly during such a mock charge, the elephant will probably chase your vehicle, perhaps turning a mock charge into a full charge (see below). So, before you move, make very certain that you have a swift escape route, and that you can drive faster than the elephant can run. (In deep sand, you can forget this.)

As a fairly desperate measure, not normally needed, if the elephant is really getting too close, then increasing the revs of your engine – commensurate with the threat – will encourage the animal to stop and back down. Don't beep your horn, don't rev up and down, but do steadily press your accelerator further down as the elephant gets closer. (I've never needed to do this; it's overkill for most mock charges.)

However, if you're really unfortunate then you'll come across an upset or traumatised animal, or one that really perceives you as a threat and that makes a full charge. This is rare – expected only from injured elephants, cows protecting calves, males in musth and the like. Then the individual will fold its ears back, put its head down, and run full speed at your vehicle. I'm pleased that I've never faced one of these, but if you do then your only option is to drive as fast as you can. If you can't get away then I'd try revving, as above, matching its threat with your engine's noise. But I'd also start praying – this is a seriously dangerous place to be.

NGWEZUMBA PANS

About 70km south of the Chobe River lies a large complex of clay pans surrounded by grassland plains, mopane woodlands and combretum thickets. There are well over a dozen individual pans: Noghatsau, Gxlaigxlarara, Tutlha, Tambiko, Kabunga, Cwikamba and Poha, to name but a few, and all hold water after the rains. This makes them a natural focus during the first few months of the year, when the animals tend to stay away from the permanent waters of the Linyanti and Chobe rivers.

If any of the water pumps here are working consistently then it also ensures the pans are excellent during the dry season too. However, if visiting in the heart of the dry season then ask the scouts at Savuti or Nantanga if the pumps are working before you head this way.

FLORA AND FAUNA HIGHLIGHTS With water there, the pans are excellent in the dry season. Early in the dry season they're quite likely to hold water anyway – so taking the eastern route certainly makes sense around May–August. Once the natural water dries up, the pumps are vital. With water in the late dry season you can expect herds of Chobe's game interacting; it's a place to just sit and watch for hours.

Curiously, perhaps the area's most notable game doesn't need permanent water and so is found here all year. This area is perhaps the only place in Botswana where oribi antelope occur naturally. These small, elegant grazers are orange-red above, white underneath, have a dark circular scent gland under their ears and a short bush tail with a black tip. Only the males, which are very territorial, have short, straight horns. They are usually seen in pairs, or small groups, feeding in the open grasslands during the morning or late afternoon. If startled they will often emit a shrill whistle before bounding off at a rapid rate with a very jerky motion.

This is also the only area of Chobe where you've any real chance of spotting gemsbok (or oryx). This is the dominant large antelope species in the parks south of here, but it's relatively unusual to see them in Chobe. These pans, together with the complex around Zweizwe, are probably the park's best place to spot roan antelope, which never thrive in areas of dense game but seem to do well around here.

For birdwatchers, the pans, and especially the larger ones like Kwikamba Pan, can be superb during the rains. Expect a whole variety of aquatic birds passing through including Egyptian and spur-winged geese, lesser moorhen, red-knobbed coot, red-billed and Hottentot teal, African pochard, dabchick and even the occasional dwarf bittern. The large grassland plains here also attract grassland species such as yellow-throated sandgrouse, harlequin quail, croaking cisticola and, occasionally, Stanley's bustard.

 WHERE TO STAY There used to be two campsites here, at Nogatsaa – which was a great place for watching the game coming to bathe and drink – and the very basic Tchinga (alias 'Tshinga' and 'Tjinga'), but both are now strictly closed to private visitors. There are certainly HATAB camping facilities in the area (see page 82 for an explanation), so you ought to have no problems visiting with a mobile safari run by a licensed Botswana tour operator.

GHOHA HILLS

Most people pass through the Ghoha Gate on their way to Savuti with scarcely a glance at the two hills that give this area its name. That's not unreasonable, given the game-rich areas further south, yet the hills are notable for providing the only high ground for some distance – and also offer a vantage point for a new lodge.

Many years ago the area was inhabited by the Basubiya, and rocks by the turning to the lodge indicate that there was once a well here. The predominant vegetation is Zambezi teak, scattered across deep tracts of Kalahari sand. The thickets provide a perfect hiding place for steenbok, and offer good camouflage for giraffe, which in turn are stalked by waiting lion, but the game is very skittish.

GETTING THERE Most visitors fly in to Savuti airstrip, followed by a 40-minute transfer to the lodge, but it's possible be transferred by road from Kasane. If you're driving yourself, you'll find a well-marked turning to the left just 7km from the Ghoha Gate; from here, it's a further 1.8km, culminating in an unexpectedly steep and rocky track.

 WHERE TO STAY

⌂ **Ghoha Hills Savuti Lodge** [map 207] (11 chalets) ☏319 0662, 620 0001, reservations ☏+27 (0)82 579 5249; ℮ reservations@ghohahills.com; www.ghohahills.com; ⊕ GHOHAL 18°26.175'S, 24°13.122'E. Opened in Jun 2012, this smart new lodge is perched on a hill above the plains, facing east to catch the sunrise. Entirely Batswana owned, it is set in its own private concession within the national park, with an exclusive 60km network of game-viewing tracks. From a viewing deck at the lodge, you can observe 2 waterholes, one of them overlooked by a well-shaded hide which makes a perfect spot for a sundowner. Most guests, however, spend their time on a full-day game drive to the Savuti Marsh, taking in some rock paintings *en route*. The journey takes at least an hour each way, so exploring the area around camp is often restricted to the evening of arrival or the early morning. Thus, while the lodge is quite a way from the marsh, it may best be considered as a satellite from there, rather than as a destination in its own right. Boat trips on the Linyanti can be taken at additional cost, & walks are planned for the future.

High standards have been set for the buildings here. As if marching up the hill, huge en-suite tented chalets, including 2 family suites, have either twin beds or a king-size dbl. In front, a giant gauze panel feels like a living cinema screen with the plains as backdrop, & at the back are a separate toilet & shower. Inclusion of a foot massage in the rates is a bonus – with additional massage at extra charge. It's unfortunate that the access road runs behind the chalets, slightly compromising privacy on the verandas & even in the rooms themselves. Crowning the hill is an extensive central area, like a big thatched tithe barn, stylishly set on several levels with apron decks looking over the plains. Well-prepared meals are usually served at private tables, but if guests wish to eat together, or with their guide, this can be arranged. Below, a pool is set among the rocks & there's a warming firepit for winter evenings – or stargazing. *US$450/585 pp sharing/sgl mid-Jan–Mar, US$650/845 Apr–Jun & mid-Dec–mid-Jan, US$795/985 Jul–Oct, inc FB, local drinks, activities, laundry, park fees; exc transfers. No children under 6.* ⊕ *All year.*

SAVUTI

Unlike most game-viewing areas, Savuti isn't just about animals. Its game can be great, but that's only half the story. To understand the rest, and discover some of its spirit, you must dig into its history – from the geological past, to the first humans and then the European hunters, 'explorers' and conservationists – and learn of the reputation of some of its famous characters. Savuti seems to have more stories linked with it than all the other game areas in Botswana combined. So seek these out before you come, as only then will you really appreciate why Savuti has a legendary quality about it.

HISTORY The key to the area's attraction is the mysterious Savuti Channel, which is often dry (as it was for a large part of the last 30 years) but sometimes – as now – inexplicably flows. Its journey starts in a lagoon at the southern tip of the Linyanti Swamps. When it flows, it meanders a little south and then eastwards until it enters the national park.

Continuing east, it flows through a wide gap in the Magwikhwe Sand Ridge (in former times, its flow probably formed this gap); this is the place usually referred to as Savuti. From here the channel turns abruptly south, and spills out into the Mababe Depression, a huge flat area which was once the bed of an ancient lake (see pages 45–6 for more details), and formed the flat expanse of the Savuti Marsh.

At its peak, with the channel and marsh full, it must have been like a huge drinking trough over 100km long, penetrating the heart of the dust-dry northern Kalahari. It's no surprise that it attracted huge quantities of game and, in turn, whatever people were around at the time.

San/Bushmen The early hunter-gatherers certainly had settlements here, evidenced by at least five sites in the hills around Savuti containing rock art. Archaeologists link these paintings with those in the Tsodilo Hills, and with the traditions of people of the Okavango.

A few of these sites are known to the guides at some of the lodges here, so if you are staying at one then request for your guide to take you to see them. Despite park regulations about walking, at least one of these sites now has a clear signpost to it. However, you need to think very carefully before trying this on your own – given not only the park's rules, but also the high density of lion, leopard, buffalo and elephant in the area.

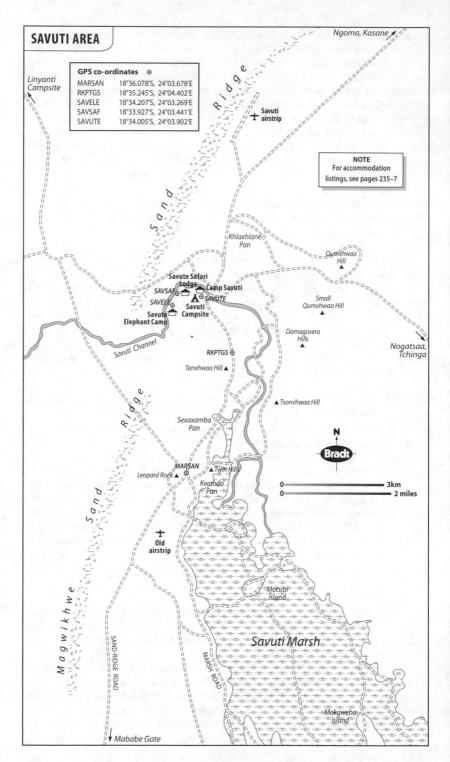

SAVUTI AREA

Linyanti Campsite

GPS co-ordinates ⊕

MARSAN	18°36.078'S, 24°03.678'E
RKPTGS	18°35.245'S, 24°04.402'E
SAVELE	18°34.207'S, 24°03.269'E
SAVSAF	18°33.927'S, 24°03.441'E
SAVUTE	18°34.005'S, 24°03.902'E

Ngoma, Kasane

Savuti airstrip

NOTE
For accommodation
listings, see pages 235–7

Khlaxhlane Pan

Qumxhwaa Hill ▲

Savute Safari Lodge
SAVSAF ⊕
SAVELE ⊕
Savute Elephant Camp ▲
▲ **Camp Savuti**
⊕ SAVUTE
Savuti Campsite

Small Qumxhwaa Hill ▲

Savuti Channel

RKPTGS ⊕

Damagosera Hills ▲

Nogatsaa, Tchinga

Tanxhwaa Hill ▲

▲ *Tsonxhwaa Hill*

Sexaxamba Pan

N

Bradt

MARSAN ⊕
Leopard Rock ▲ ▲ *Twin Hills*

Kwando Pan

0		3km
0		2 miles

✚ **Old airstrip**

S a n d   *R i d g e*

M a g w i k h w e   *S a n d*   *R i d g e*

SAND-RIDGE ROAD

MARSH ROAD

Motsibi Island

Savuti Marsh

Mokgweba Island

↓ *Mababe Gate*

Early explorers There are many reports of this area from the early European explorers – fascinating if only to look back and see what they recorded of Savuti. In June 1851 when Livingstone passed through here the marsh was a 'dismal swamp' some 16km long, fed by both the Mababe (now called Khwai) River, which spilled over from the Okavango system, and also by the 'strongly flowing' Savuti Channel.

Chapman also crossed the channel around 1853, when he recorded it as dry. When the great white hunter, Frederick Courtney Selous, came in 1874, the channel was full and flowing into the marsh. However, when Selous came back in 1879 he noted that the channel had partially dried out, and no longer fed the marsh. Mike Main, in his excellent book on the Kalahari (see *Appendix 3, Further information*), concludes that sometime in the 1880s the channel dried up.

Modern history The channel seems to have remained dry until a heavy rainy season, 1957–58, when it began to flow strongly once again. This continued until 1966, when it dried up once more. It then flowed from 1967 to 1981, when it seemed permanent and enhanced the area's reputation as a top game destination.

In the 1970s Lloyd Wilmot started a camp here, Lloyd's Camp, which was to put both Lloyd and Savuti on the map. Lloyd is, in fact, the son of one of the Okavango's famous crocodile hunters, Bobby Wilmot, and has many sisters, most with strong connections in the area. A safari here was always offbeat. Lloyd built up a reputation for empathy with the game, and a total lack of fear for his own safety when dealing with it. Everyone who visited came away with stories of remarkable animal encounters, and Savuti's reputation grew.

However, the channel's flow was gradually reducing and, in 1982, it ceased to flow completely. Gradually the water shrank into a few remaining pools, and then they dried up too. With them went the fish, hippos, crocodiles and all the other creatures that had lived there. During this time Lloyd was frequently photographed kneeling or lying in front of a thirsty elephant, excavating sand from a hole in the bottom of the channel until he reached water. This sad time was well chronicled in a video, *The Stolen River*, by Dereck and Beverly Joubert. It's also one of the main subjects of Clive Walker's book, *Savuti: the Vanishing River* (see *Appendix 3, Further information*).

Nobody really knows why it stopped, as nobody understood why it started again after almost 80 years of dryness. Explanations range from changes in the paths used by the Linyanti's hippos to tectonic shifts; see Mike Main's book, *Kalahari*, for a more detailed discussion. That the channel has been once more flowing since 2009 is thus of considerable note.

Even with the channel dry, Savuti remains a classic area for game. Experts observe that the soil here is especially good, and the grazing particularly rich. Furthermore, there are now several permanent waterholes in the area. The oldest, near the centre of Savuti, is pumped by the national park, while two others are in front of the two lodges in the area. A further two are towards the bottom of the marsh, on opposite sides of it – and these try to attract the game, and especially the elephants, away from the centre of Savuti which has been so heavily impacted by game over the years.

ORIENTATION The (normally dry) Savuti Channel starts from the Zibadianja Lagoon, at the southern tip of the Linyanti Swamps, and flows through the Linyanti Reserve, before entering the national park about 35km away. Heading east, it cuts through a wide gap in the Magwikhwe Sand Ridge, around which are a number of low, rounded hills – the Gubatsaa Hills. This area, about 54km due east of the lagoon, is known as Savuti – and until 2009, had been dry for much of the past 30 years. From here, the channel spreads out into the Mababe Depression, forming a large marshy area covering about 110km², and known as the Savuti Marsh.

Maps There are numerous small, winding sand roads around Savuti, relatively few landmarks and very few signs on the tracks. It's easy to become disoriented. If you want to explore the area in detail, you should have with you Veronica Roodt's excellent Chobe map (see *Appendix 3, Further information*), and preferably also a GPS.

FLORA AND FAUNA HIGHLIGHTS

Flora Savuti's habitat is a mostly undistinguished thick thorny scrub, with camelthorn (*Acacia erioloba*) and silver terminalia (*Terminalia sericea*) making up much of it, though there are also large areas of mopane (*Colophospermum mopane*). You'll also find substantial stands of shaving-brush combretum (*Combretum mossambicense*) and Kalahari appleleaf (*Lonchocarpus nelsii*), and it's perhaps the most westerly area where you can find the lovely paper-bark albezia (*Albezia tanganyicensis*). Dotted all over the drier parts of the area are landmark baobab trees (*Adansonia digitata*); their ability to survive being ring-barked is essential to survival here.

The main contrast to these wooded areas is the Savuti Marsh. Here, the dry areas of the marsh are covered with a variety of perennial grasses that stand above the (geologically) recent alluvial deposits of the channel. These grasses are tolerant of the slightly higher salinity levels present, and some are particularly nutritious and a great attraction for the game when there's moisture about. With the recent floods, part of the marsh is once more under water, with an attendant change in the vegetation in those areas.

Here you'll also see the skeletons of dead trees, still standing in the flat grasslands and newly flooded marsh areas. These were mostly camelthorns, umbrella thorns (*Acacia tortilis*) and leadwoods (*Combretum imberbe*) which are thought to have seeded and grown up between the 1880s and the 1950s, when the marsh was dry. Then when it flooded in the late 1950s they were drowned – though the hard, termite-resistant wood still stands.

On the southern side of the marsh you can see the bush gradually starting to invade the grasslands again, with the distinctive, low 'round mounds' of candle-pod acacia (*Acacia hebeclada*) leading the aggressors.

Fauna At the heart of the park, Savuti sees most of the park's species (see pages 209–10), with the normal exception of the Chobe bushbuck and the water-loving species – though with the return of the water, reedbuck and waterbuck may well make their way back

Whereas when the channel was dry, much of the interest was concentrated around the three remaining waterholes, now there is plenty of water to be found. Either way, there is invariably a lot of game. Lion are frequently found lying around, and big herds will pause as they approach, or wait until their thirst overcomes their fear.

Savuti's elephants are notable for a number of old bulls that live in the area permanently, and are often individuals known to guides who have spent a lot of time in the area. These are augmented by large breeding herds which pass through. Whenever it's dry you can be sure that there's action and jostling for drinking positions at waterholes and along the channel.

In recent years, at least one of the local lion prides has grown so large that they will kill elephants to satisfy their hunger – traumatising the local elephants in the process. (The Khwai River area in Moremi has a similar phenomenon.)

Spotted hyena have always been numerous and very noticeable at Savuti. In the late 1980s and early '90s they would appear at the campsite, skulking around the bins, as soon as the sun set. After dark, and when people had gone to sleep, they'd pick up anything that they could carry, and eat anything small enough to crunch up – including, I was once assured, a glass lens from a 35mm camera! My aluminium camping cooker was stolen by a hyena once at Savuti, and still bears the scars of its strong jaw.

S M Cooper (see *Appendix 3, Further information*) studied the clan sizes here in 1986–88, and found that there were five territorial clans in the area, and a number of transient animals passing through. The clans each averaged about 18 adult females, six males, five of unknown sex and ten cubs under two years of age – so around 39 members of each clan. They tend to prey on reliable, low-density resident game species like impala and warthog throughout the year, and augment this by feasting on the herds as they pass through the area, especially the new-born zebra foals.

Despite the presence of so many lion and hyena, leopards also do well here, perhaps helped by the presence of the rocky kopjes which make a perfect habitat for them. Daryl and Sharna Balfour have some lovely shots of leopard at Savuti in their book on Chobe (see *Appendix 3, Further information*).

Once, when driving with one of Lloyd's guides (who shall remain nameless), we realised that there was an early-morning commotion in the air, and followed this to a young female leopard that had *just* killed an impala. The guide knew that she had a cub nearby to feed. However, our vehicle's approach had, unwittingly, frightened the leopard off her kill, and soon after we arrived so did a hyena – which proceeded to claim the prize.

Such was the maverick nature of Lloyd's Camp that this guide simply jumped out of the cab, grabbed the hindquarters of the impala, and started upon a tug of war with the hyena for the carcass. Spurred on by this, and the realisation that the cub would otherwise miss a meal, I joined in. Eventually we won the carcass and hauled it up on to a low branch hoping that the leopard would reclaim it.

BABY HUEY

One of Savuti's more famous residents was an elephant named Baby Huey, who had become very relaxed around people. He'd also picked up a liking for oranges, after foolish visitors fed him. Gradually he came to associate people with food. When I first visited Savuti in 1998, this was a problem.

Nobody drives around at night, but on that trip we were woken at 05.00 one morning by a vehicle driving up to our tent. The couple inside it had seen our fire burning, and come to seek sanctuary. It seems that they, and their small son, had been sleeping in the back (the pick-up section) of their 4x4 when Baby Huey had passed by. Smelling oranges, he'd used his tusk on the front cab like a can-opener on a tin, and then delved inside for a snack.

The couple were completely traumatised, and left Chobe at first light. Two days later Baby Huey was shot – and camping visitors are still banned from bringing citrus fruit into the park. And all because people were naive enough to feed the animals.

But nature, once upset, isn't so easily put right. As we pulled back from the scene the hyena returned, stretched up on its hind legs, and plucked the impala from the branch with ease. Others swiftly joined it, devouring it within minutes. The leopard had already given up and disappeared, perhaps in disgust.

In the wet season there are still movements of buffalo, zebra and wildebeest which come on to the marsh to graze, though the huge herds of buffalo that used to come when the channel last flowed have now stopped coming. In his guide to Botswana (see *Appendix 3, Further information*) in 1968, Alec Campbell describes the scene on the marsh at that time:

> Here the Savuti Channel carries water from the Linyanti … forming a marsh about a meter deep. From June to December huge herds of buffalo visit the marsh to feed in the surrounding scrub mopane and one can see as many as 6,000 daily. Out on the flats which surround it on the southern and western sides are herds of bull elephants, wildebeest, impala, giraffe, tsessebe and sometimes large numbers of zebra. Lion are also quite common.
>
> Cow elephants with their young spend much time in the taller mophane to the east of the marsh but come down to drink in the afternoon. Hippopotami and waterbuck are to be seen in the Channel especially near the mouth where it enters the marsh.

Numbers now probably don't match what was seen then, though April–May is still the prime time for zebra and wildebeest herds to pass through, usually foaling as they go. The precise timing of this is heavily dependent upon the local rainfall patterns.

The dry season can witness large numbers of tsessebe move on to the marsh area to graze. Occasionally, at the end of the dry season, oryx have been known to appear at the south end of the marsh, but they are very uncommon this far north.

HITCHING A RIDE

The kori bustard (*Ardeotis kori*) is one of the world's heaviest flying birds, weighing up to 17kg, and – despite a wingspan of 2.8m – it is a reluctant flyer, needing a good run-up to get airborne. On the ground, these stately birds strike conspicuous figures, and are often seen around the pans, either picking their way hesitantly across the grassland in pairs, one at least 100m from its partner, or resting in the midday shade of an acacia.

Kori bustards often associate with game herds, whose trampling hooves disturb the locusts, beetles, reptiles and other small creatures on which they feed. In turn, they sometimes provide a similar service for the carmine bee-eater (*Merops nubicoides*). This dazzling bird arrives from central Africa in October, and spreads out across the grassland in large flocks. Its usual hunting technique is to hawk for insects – particularly bees – in acrobatic sorties from a fixed perch, such as an anthill or bush, and return to the perch to dispatch and swallow the catch. In open grassland, where fixed perches are in short supply, a kori bustard provides an ideal mobile alternative.

In fact the bustard goes one better than a bush by actively stirring up food for the bee-eater, which snaps up whatever it can catch around the bigger bird's feet before settling again on its back. Bee-eaters are not known to try this trick from the backs of mammals, yet the bustard remains surprisingly tolerant of its passengers, and sometimes two or more of them will hitch a ride.

Always you'll find groups of giraffe in the acacia woodlands on the edge of the marsh and all over the area.

Finally, if you're anywhere around the hills in the area, then P C Viljoen (see *Appendix 3, Further information*) notes that several klipspringer were spotted here on the Qumxhwaa Hill (Quarry Hill) in 1978 and 1979. This has since been confirmed by several reliable sources – including Tricia and Bob Hayne in 2005. Their existence here is remarkable, as the nearest other significant klipspringer population is probably in Zimbabwe's Hwange National Park, about 130km to the east.

Birdlife The list of bird species found in Savuti runs to over 300 species, but some of the more unusual include the Marico flycatcher, crimson boubou, capped wheatears, pennant-winged nightjars (only during the summer, October–January; look especially on the roads at dusk) and Bradfield's hornbill.

In addition, when you're in areas of acacia woodland then keep a lookout for racket-tailed rollers and the spectacular displays of the male broad-tailed paradise whydahs in breeding plumage (February–April).

On Savuti's open areas you'll find the occasional secretary birds, Stanley's bustard, and plenty of the larger kori bustards. The Balfours' coffee-table book on Chobe (see *Appendix 3, Further information*) has a wonderful picture of a carmine bee-eater using the back of a kori bustard as a perch from which to hawk around for insects. Kori bustards are Africa's heaviest flying birds, but heavier still is the flightless ostrich, which can sometimes be seen here. During the summer, Abdim's and white storks congregate in numbers on the marsh.

GETTING THERE It's a day's drive from either Kasane or Maun to Savuti, so most guests at the lodges fly in to Savuti's airstrip (which can take planes as large as a DC3). Visitors to the campsite usually arrive driving their own fully equipped 4x4s, complete with all their supplies. For details, see *Driving from Kasane to Savuti*, pages 222–7, and *Driving from North Gate (Khwai) to Savuti, Chobe NP*, page 271.

WHERE TO STAY Savuti's two luxury camps, its campsite and a new mid-range lodge are all close to each other. All face on to the Savuti Channel, and all are near the new bridge over the channel, just to the north of the marsh. Note that the small Savuti Camp, though on the Savuti Channel, is in the private Linyanti Concession west of Savuti: nowhere near the marsh, nor in the area that has, historically, been known as 'Savuti'. For details, see *Chapter 10*, page 248.

Stay in the area for long and you'll hear of the legendary Lloyd Wilmot and his famous Lloyd's Camp. This became something of an institution here, but has sadly now closed. (Lloyd visits occasionally, but now runs a mobile safari operation.) Despite this, you'll still find books and websites that haven't caught on to this. Allan's Camp and Savuti South were opened here (by Gametrackers) and subsequently closed – only to be combined and rebuilt as Savute Elephant Camp (see below). The current options for visitors are:

Savute Elephant Camp [map 230]
(12 chalets) Contact Orient-Express Safaris, page 176; ✪ SAVELE 18°34.207'S, 24°3.269'E. Situated close to the Safari Lodge, this was the first of Orient-Express Safaris camps that I visited following their reconstruction, & I was amazed at its scale. 'Tents' is far too flimsy a word for the

elegant rooms here, each built on a large, raised platform of wooden decking about 18m x 6m. At the front, safari chairs & a comfy day bed face west over the river from quite a height; behind them is a huge shaded tent lined with cream canvas. Inside, on the polished wooden floor, stylish soft furnishings in muted neutral colours offset twin

9

¾ size beds (or a dbl) under a 4-poster mosquito net. AC/heating units flanking the beds augment a ceiling fan, which, like the room's lights, can be used day & night. There's no shortage of space for the solid furnishings, including a sofa & a writing desk, not to mention an intercom system in case of emergency. Behind the wooden headboard is a wardrobe & storage for suitcases, &, in the middle, a dressing room with twin basins, several large mirrors & acres of hardwood surround. Through polished hardwood doors you'll find a separate flush toilet, & a very private outside shower (easily big enough for shared showers).

Lawns under acacia trees link the rooms with the camp's airy bar, lounge & dining room, an open-sided barn-like construction that leads down to a terrace, & down again to a large swimming pool overlooking the Savuti Channel: a far cry from the dry years when, at the height of the dry season, stressed elephants argue over precious gulps of muddy water below you. There's a spotting scope on the terrace, & free Wi-Fi throughout, while discreetly tucked away is a library with a guest computer & satellite TV. Locally made baskets can be bought in the curio shop.

The lodge emphasises the quality of its food, served à la carte on the terrace or in the dining area, with traditional evenings held in the boma. It's very similar indeed to its sister camp, Khwai River Lodge (see page 269), with which it shares a professionalism marked by friendly service. Activities concentrate on 4x4 game drives during the day (night drives, & driving off-road, are not allowed in Chobe). Visits can be arranged to local Bushman paintings on request. *US$788–1,750 pp sharing, inc FB, activities, drinks, laundry.* ☼ *All year.*

🛖 **Savute Safari Lodge** [map 230] (12 chalets) Contact Desert & Delta Safaris, page 176; ✥ SAVSAF 18°33.927'S, 24°3.441'E. Savute Safari Lodge opened in 1999, right next to the site of the old Lloyd's Camp, so the local wildlife is exceptionally relaxed with people – to the point that lions have occasionally been found sleeping on the paths between rooms. (There's a discreet electric fence around the lodge &, as with most wildlife camps in Botswana, guests are always escorted by the staff if walking around the camp after dark.)

Here, as at the Elephant Lodge, most visitors arrive by plane.

Giraffe statues welcome visitors to the lounge, where a hi-tech fireplace takes centre stage among the sofas & bar. With glazed windows & sliding doors, it's both contemporary & rather angular. Above, a library looks over the trees, ideal for an hour or so's birdwatching. In the dining area, a huge wrought-iron candelabra hangs over tiled floors & light wooden tables & chairs, although lunch & dinner are usually served on a lower terrace with a firepit & a view of the river, where elephants congregate in the afternoons. Sharing the view is a shaded pool, surrounded by loungers. A curio shop has a reasonable range of handicrafts, jewellery, books & clothing.

Facing the river are large, light, airy chalets, similarly in size to those at Elephant Camp, but mostly of wooden construction, with a high thatched roof over slightly raised, polished decking. Glass sliding doors backed by mesh mosquito screens form one entire wall, affording a spectacular view for 8 of the rooms, though matching windows in the modern white-tiled bathrooms can be unnerving, until you realise that you're not overlooked. Soft neutral décor blends with contemporary design & furnishings, including a comfortable 2-seater couch & armchair, & chic lamps. Twin or dbl beds with quality linen are surrounded by a (cleverly designed) walk-in mosquito net, below a ceiling fan; there's no AC, but the design of the chalets helps to moderate the excesses of the climate. On the veranda are safari chairs & roll-down blinds to cover the windows. Electricity during the day is from a generator, backed up by battery power at night. When Hilary Bradt & Janice Booth visited, they were woken by the yelps of wild dog which had made a kill directly under their chalet. They watched as the dogs were joined by a cohort of hyena, who challenged the dogs for their booty – dim shapes wheeling & criss-crossing in the moonlight.

Activities are limited to morning & evening game drives & the occasional wander to see a Bushman painting. The young guides here when I last visited were keen on nature & enthusiastic about finding it. With notice at the time of booking, private guides can be arranged for a whole day. *US$495 pp Jan–Mar & Dec, US$573 pp Apr–Jun & Nov, US$873/1,135 pp sharing/sgl Jul–Oct, fully inc.* ☼ *All year.*

🏕 **Savuti Campsite** [map 230] (14 pitches) ☏620 0218; contact SKL, page 174; ✥ SAVUTE

18°34.005'S, 24°03.902'E. Savuti's newly privatised campsite now has an impressive office & entrance gate, but remains a wonderful place to camp. The site is unfenced, but an ingenious circular wall surrounding the ablution block is designed to be elephant-proof. Smaller animals like cats can easily get out over the wall, but not easily get in. The toilets, showers & laundry areas themselves, with solar-heated water & electric light, are certainly cleaner than of yore.

Many of the numbered pitches sit under old camelthorn trees (with pitch No 1 being particularly good), but shade is very limited in the wet season, when the trees have no leaves. Each has its own braai stand, & a water tap ingeniously encased in concrete to prevent elephants from pulling the pipes to access the clean water (they would often make such an effort for clean water, rather than drinking from the dirty waterhole!). The size of the site, & the distance between the pitches, is such that some campers even drive to the ablution block after dark. Others opt for the proximity & shade offered by the reserve pitches closer to the block. Visibility is good, with not too much undergrowth around, though the ground can be very dusty & there may be the low whine of a water pump or a generator in the background.

New to the site is a shop (🕐 08.00–12.00 & 17.00–19.00) stocking biscuits, tinned goods, beer, wine, basic toiletries & sometimes firewood – oh, & boot polish! Don't rely on it, though; it makes sense to bring in everything you need. Game drives can be organised through Camp Savuti (below) at US$85–95, depending on the season.

Alongside the elephants for which Savuti is famed, the camp has almost nightly visits from spotted hyenas which, I once discovered, can carry away a full rucksack at high speed, despite being pursued. They will steal & eat anything, from a camera lens to a bar of soap, so leave nothing outside. Then sit back after dinner, turn off your lights, & shield your eyes from the fire. Now, when your vision has adjusted to the dark, shine around a powerful torch. With a little patience you should be able to pick out the ghostly green eyes of hyena, just beyond your firelight. (But beware of shining a torch accidentally at a passing elephant. They don't like this at all!) If you do have any hyena problems, remember that they will push their luck, but are essentially cowardly animals. Chase them & they will always run, sometimes dropping their spoils. Just be very careful of what else you might run into during the chase! *US$50 pp, exc park fees, bed levy.* 🕐 *All year.*

🏠 **Camp Savuti** [map 230] (5 tents) Contact SKL, page 174. This relatively traditional camp was opened on a large, sandy site next to the main campsite in 2010. Set up on wooden platforms, its smart Meru-style tents have verandas overlook the Savuti Channel. With twin/dbl beds, AC, en-suite corner baths, flush toilets & open-air showers, they're fairly large & well finished – but note that one of the chalets is literally adjacent to one of the campsite pitches, so not as exclusive as you might expect. Steps lead up to the chalets & to the open-fronted central area, whose pole-walled sides under a canvas roof help to keep it airy & cool. With decorative ropework & handmade baskets, it's attractively designed, combining a large bar & dining area at the back with plenty of seating. By the river, a new deck provides the option for dining under the stars. There are early-morning & afternoon game drives, but as these may be shared with campers, they're not as private as you might expect. *US$450 Apr–Jun & Nov pp sharing, US$540 Jul–Oct, US$420 Dec–Mar, inc FB, local drinks, activities, laundry, park fees, airstrip transfer.* 🕐 *All year.*

🏕 **Savute Under Canvas** (5 tents) Contact &Beyond, page 175. Like its sister operation, Chobe Under Canvas (see page 219), this is a mobile camp which operates from private campsites, but here within the Savuti area. It boasts exactly the same style of accommodation, facilities & activities. *US$435–700 pp sharing, inc FB, most drinks, activities, laundry. No children under 12.* 🕐 *Feb–Dec.*

WHAT TO SEE AND DO Game viewing and birdwatching are the main activities at Savuti, and there's always something going on – especially now that the channel is flowing again!

Driving at night is not allowed, though often the wildlife will come quite close enough if you just stay in your campsite/lodge and keep looking around you.

DRIVING SOUTH FROM SAVUTI

TO THE MABABE GATE From Savuti campsite, it's a drive of about 66km along the direct route south to the Mababe Gate, though you can add another 7km if you take the scenic marsh road. About 5km south of the campsite, just before the hill known as Leopard Rock, the track splits two ways. This junction (✦ MARSAN 18°36.078'S, 24°03.678'E) is shown very clearly on Veronica Roodt's Chobe map. Along this short stretch, you'll see a couple of signs pointing to the left stating 'rock paintings'.

At the junction, the left-hand track is the **marsh road**, signposted to Savuti Marsh; it's more scenic but becomes very rutted and bumpy in parts following the western side of the marsh itself. This is fine during the dry season, and you'll have great views of the marsh. It's often a particularly good area for giraffe due to the high number of acacia trees around. However, it's a bad route to choose during the rainy season, as you will almost certainly get stuck.

The right fork is the **sand-ridge road**, which heads west of the marsh, and is the more direct route towards the Mababe Gate and Maun. Taking this you will come to another fork after about 25km (✦ SNDFRK 18°49.076'S, 24°00.357'E), where you bear left. The road is named for the Magwikhwe Sand Ridge, which you'll cross about 26km south of Savuti. Don't expect this to be too obvious, as the ridge is little more than a wide, vegetated sand dune. You will climb slightly to get on to it, and drop slightly to come off – and in between the driving is more difficult than normal as your vehicle's tyres will sink deeper into the sand.

Both roads meet up again at ✦ SNDMAR 18°55.616'S, 24°00.662'E, about 20km north of the Mababe Gate: the sand-ridge road takes 37km to reach this from the junction, and the marsh road about 44km. A sign here reads: Khwai 45km, North Gate 54km and Maun 133km. Around here the road becomes more difficult during the rains. In contrast to Savuti's relatively lush vegetation, there is little ground cover, and only low stunted mopane trees to protect the soil from the extremes of the elements. The road's fine earth is hard-baked when dry, and very slippery when wet.

On reaching the Mababe Gate (✦ MABABE 19°06.182'S, 23°59.119'E; ✎ *620 0219*), you sign out of (or into) Chobe National Park, by presenting your park permit.

CONTINUING TO MOREMI GAME RESERVE AND NORTH GATE From the Mababe Gate, a wide new gravel road leads all the way to North Gate, passing through Khwai Village on the way. While this is much faster than the old route, it misses out on the stunningly beautiful valley of the Khwai River (see pages 265–7) where, after the unrelenting dryness of southern Chobe in the dry season, the lily-covered waterways and shady glades under huge spreading umbrella thorns (*Acacia tortilis*) are completely magical.

The new road is not difficult to find, but there are a couple of junctions that can be confusing. Almost immediately south of the Mababe Gate, the road forks, with a green block indicating Moremi to the right; straight on is for Maun directly. Continuing towards Moremi, you'll come after 4km to another green block (✦ TOKHW 19°07.719'S, 23°58.078'E). Ignore the signpost right to Khwai, but continue straight ahead for a further 3.5km. At the T-junction, turn right on to the new transit road between Mababe Village and North Gate.

The new road crosses NG18, the Khwai Community Development Trust concession, so you cannot drive off route without a permit. Close to the board proclaiming the trust's ownership, you'll see a signpost to the left to their two Magotho campsites, but otherwise it's an uneventful drive to the Khwai River. You will, though, come to a turning north along this road (at ⊕ SEROTO 19°04.317'S, 23°50.071'E), signposted to Seronga. Beware of this, as it would lead you astray through private concessions towards Selinda.

Continuing to North Gate, the road turns sharply to the left then comes to a new steel bridge. From here, it's a further 6.5km to North Gate (⊕ NOGATE 19°10.394'S, 23°45.092'E). First, though, you'll go over (or around) another river, pass through Khwai Village, and finally cross a pole bridge over the Khwai River.

CONTINUING TO MAUN Going straight on at the Mababe Gate fork will lead you much more directly and quickly to Maun, reaching Mababe Village (also known as Kudumane) on the new gravel road, after about 10km. Here you'll take a right turn, passing through Sankuyo, the veterinary fence, and then Shorobe, before a final stretch on the tar to Maun. (See page 282 for the latter part of this route – and if you have a GPS then set it for ⊕ MAUN at 19°58.508'S, 23°25.647'E to keep you in roughly the right direction!)

If your destination is Maun, then don't imagine that travelling through the edge of Moremi (on the direct road from North Gate to South Gate) is a quick option. It'll take a good six or seven hours to reach Maun this way. You'll have some slow, heavy driving across the sand ridge, and will be liable for an extra set of park fees for Moremi (even if you have already paid some for the same day in Chobe). However, if you have pre-arranged a few nights in Moremi, then do take this road and don't miss the chance to stop off. It offers a completely different experience.

 Where to stay There are three clear accommodation options along the route towards Maun: two lodges and a community campsite. Close to Mababe Village you'll spot a right turn to **Mogotlho Safari Lodge** (page 352), then a little over 20km further south there's another right turn to **Mankwe Bush Lodge** (page 352). Further south again, **Kaziikini campsite** (page 350), and Shandereka traditional village, lie some 4km east of the road, in the direction of South Gate.

LINYANTI

The Linyanti River acts as a magnet for game during the dry season, just as its continuation, the Chobe, does further north. Although a few kilometres of the river fall within Chobe National Park, this section tends to be dominated by some very thick reedbeds and vegetation, so can be a disappointing area for wildlife. In addition, reaching this area requires a considerable side-track from the established Moremi–Savuti–Ihaha route across Chobe, so it has tended to get few visitors in the past.

East of the park along the river is the CH1 photographic concession, which is the location of Linyanti Bushcamp and its sister camps (pages 249–50). To the west is NG15, the Linyanti Concession (pages 244–8), which has several good camps, the nearest of which is Linyanti Tented Camp. And in the middle, within the national park, are Linyanti Campsite and the new Camp Linyanti. Visitors driving themselves are restricted to the national park area and CH1; access to the camps within the Linyanti Concession is permitted only on a fly-in safari.

Note that despite there being a track marked on the maps from Seronga towards the Linyanti, this is not a practical one to use to get here from the west. First, neither private self-drive vehicles nor mobile operators are allowed to drive through the private concessions between the Linyanti and Okavango. Second, you cannot at present cross the Selinda Spillway. And third, even with a GPS, navigation would be a complete nightmare!

FLORA AND FAUNA HIGHLIGHTS This area has a very similar ecosystem to that of the Chobe riverfront (pages 212–16), although the vegetation beside the water here seems to have many more large trees and to be in a more natural state. Because Chobe's Linyanti riverfront is sandwiched between two private concession areas, it's a relatively limited size for game drives. You'll usually see large numbers of elephant at the end of the dry season, but this small stretch of the park is seldom quite as rewarding as the Chobe riverfront area, where the game is much more 'tame'. The presence to the east of an area where hunting was until recently still practised probably hasn't helped to relax the game, although things have improved considerably in that area. West of Linyanti is the private Linyanti Reserve, which is an excellent area with a long stretch of beautiful riverfront and some very good game (see pages 244–8).

GETTING THERE AND AWAY Linyanti Campsite and Camp Linyanti (and therefore Linyanti Bushcamp and its sister camps) can be approached along deep, sandy tracks either from Savuti (about 40km) or along the cutline from the Ghoha Gate (totalling 43km). If you're coming from Kasane, follow the directions for Savuti (see *Driving from Kasane to Savuti*, pages 222–6) until you reach the cutline, where instead of turning left for the Ghoha Gate, you turn right towards the Linyanti River. From here it's a slow-going 28km to the Linyanti Gate (⊕ LINYGT 18°16.209'S, 23°56.197'E), where – if it's manned – you'll need to present your permit before proceeding to the campsite, just 5km to the southwest.

From Savuti, drive over the new bridge across the Savuti Channel and on to its north bank, and then turn left, heading northwest. Within 1km or so, you'll approach a T-junction, and take a left heading westwards. This crosses the sand ridge (though you may not notice this!) and about 3km later there are two left turnings. Ignore these. Follow the road around to the right, heading in a more northerly direction.

The first few kilometres of this drive is relatively easy, but after this there's about 30km of trickier driving – very deep sand and tougher going, especially one 3km stretch that will test your driving skills (and your vehicle) to the maximum. The scenery is gently rolling dunes, with many flatter areas of low mopane. Visiting one October, I found large numbers of elephants on the road north. Towards the river there was also a pall of dust and woodsmoke hanging over the woods, which was clearly coming from fires raging across the river in Namibia, though in the same month a few years later, the air was clear.

If you're doing this journey in reverse, note that the roads around Linyanti campsite are very, very confusing to navigate, so be particularly vigilant in finding the right track south. You'll find the correct turning south at ⊕ SAVUTO 18°18.228'S, 23°54.903'E, where there's a motley collection of signs at a clear crossroads. Driving through in October 2013, we inadvertently took the cutline road south from Linyanti, ending up at the Savuti Channel before we realised our mistake. Be warned!

 WHERE TO STAY Until recently, drive-in guests to this area of Chobe National Park were limited to camping with their own equipment at the national parks' Linyanti Campsite, but with privatisation has come the introduction of a new permanent camp, Camp Linyanti.

ᴧ Linyanti Campsite [map 206] (5 pitches) Contact SKL, page 174; ✪ LINYAN 18°17.686'S, 23°54.601'E. About 40km from Savuti, this is a beautiful little site, close to the river & very quiet, with an acceptable standard of cleanliness. Its pitches share a small ablution block , but there's no drinking water – although filtering & treating river water to drink would be possible in an emergency. Activities can be organised through Camp Linyanti, below. *US$50 pp sharing, exc park fees, bed levy.* 🕐 *All year.*

⌂ Camp Linyanti [map 206] (5 tents) Contact SKL, page 174. Opened next to the campsite in June 2013, this new venture is something of a disappointment. Right on the river, the main area with expanses of wooden decking is well placed to make the best of the picturesque setting. In its tented rondavels, though, there's scarcely room to squeeze around the dbl or twin beds (with no view), yet sharing the space are a largish chest, an en-suite corner bathtub & an outside shower. It's all very cramped. *US$450 Apr–Jun & Nov, US$540 Jul–Oct, US$420 pp sharing Dec–Mar, inc FB, local drinks, activities, laundry, park fees; exc transfers.* 🕐 *All year.*

WHAT TO SEE AND DO Game drives, walks, mokoro excursions and boat trips can be organised at Camp Linyanti for all visitors – campers and lodge guests alike. With only 7km of riverfront accessible, driving opportunities used to be limited, but new game-drive routes have recently been opened in this corner of the park. Next to the riverbank, there are plenty of reedbeds which can be a delight for birdwatchers, and the water is home to countless hippo. I've come across the occasional person who absolutely adores this section of the park.

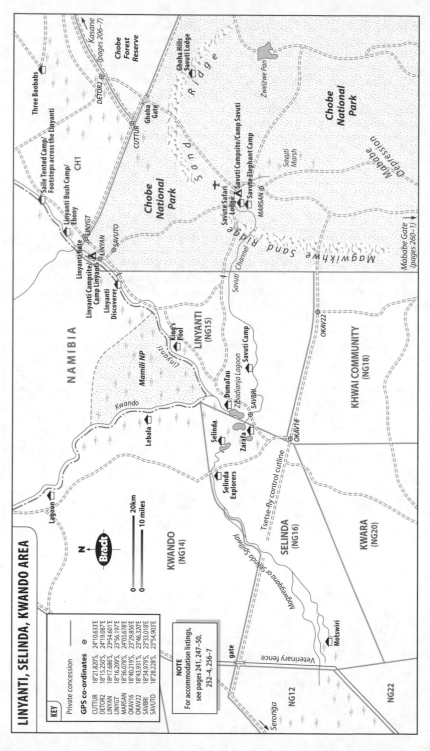

LINYANTI, SELINDA, KWANDO AREA

KEY

Private concession

GPS co-ordinates ⊕

CUTTUR	18°21.820'S,	24°10.633'E
DETOR2	18°15.250'S,	24°19.087'E
LINYAN	18°17.686'S,	23°54.601'E
LINYGT	18°16.209'S,	23°56.197'E
MARSAN	18°36.078'S,	24°03.678'E
OKAV16	18°40.219'S,	23°29.856'E
OKAV22	18°43.931'S,	23°46.320'E
SAVBRI	18°34.979'S,	23°33.018'E
SAVUTO	18°28.228'S,	23°54.903'E

NOTE
For accommodation listings, see pages 241, 247–50, 252–4, 256–7

N

Bradt

20km
10 miles

0
0

NAMIBIA

Chobe Forest Reserve

Three Baobabs

Kosane (pages 206–7)

DETOR2

Saile Tented Camp/
Footsteps across the Linyanti

Linyanti Bush Camp/
Ebony

CH1

Ghoha Hills
Savuti Lodge

Ghoha
Gate

CUTTUR

Sand Ridge

Zweizwe Pan

Chobe
National
Park

Savuti Campsite/Camp Savuti

Savuti
Marsh

Savute Elephant Camp

Savute Safari
Lodge

MARSAN

Chobe
National
Park

Mababe
Depression

Mababe Gate
(pages 260–1)

LINYGT

LINYAN

SAVUTO

Linyanti Gate

Linyanti Campsite/
Camp Linyanti

Linyanti
Discoverer

Chobe
National
Park

Magwikhwe Sand Ridge

Savuti Channel

King's
Pool

Linyanti

Mamili NP

LINYANTI
(NG15)

DumaTau

Zibadianja Lagoon

Savuti Camp

SAVBRI

OKAV16

OKAV22

KHWAI COMMUNITY
(NG18)

Kwando

Lebala

Selinda

Zarafa

Selinda
Explorers

Magwegqana or Selinda Spillway

Tsetse-fly control cutline

SELINDA
(NG16)

KWARA
(NG20)

KWANDO
(NG14)

Lagoon

Motswiri

Veterinary fence

gate

Seronga

NG12

NG22

10

Linyanti, Selinda and Kwando Reserves

Almost parallel to the Okavango, the Kwando River flows south from Angola across the Caprivi Strip and into Botswana. Like the Okavango, it starts spreading out over the Kalahari's sands, forming the Linyanti Swamps. Also like the Okavango, in wetter years this is a delta, complete with a myriad of waterways linking lagoons: a refuge for much wildlife. It's a wild area, much of which is on the Namibian side of the border, in the Mamili National Park, where it's difficult to access. A faultline channels the outflow from these swamps into the Linyanti River, which flows northeast into Lake Liambezi, and thence into Chobe.

Both the Kwando and the Linyanti rivers are permanent, so for the animals in Chobe and northern Botswana they are valuable sources of water. Like the Chobe and Okavango, they have become the ultimate destination for migrations from the drier areas across northern Botswana – and also sought-after safari destinations, especially in the dry season.

In recent years this area, between the Chobe National Park and the Okavango Delta, has been split into three large concessions – Kwando in the north, Linyanti in the east, and Selinda in the middle. In some ways these are similar, as each encompasses a large area of mopane woodlands and smaller, more prized sections of riparian forest and open floodplains on old river channels. Look at the locations of the camps and you'll realise that much of the interest lies in these floodplains and riparian forests – diverse habitats rich in species.

Away from the actual water, two fossil channels are also worthy of attention: the Savuti Channel and the Selinda Spillway. Both offer contrasting and interesting wildlife spectacles.

BACKGROUND INFORMATION

HISTORY The Kwando River has its headwaters in Angola, from where it flows south across Namibia's Caprivi Strip, forming one boundary between Namibia and Botswana. Progressing over the Kalahari's sands, it is thought that once – around one or two million years ago – it continued southeast, probably through the course of the present-day Savuti Channel, into the Mababe Depression to swell the vast Lake Makgadikgadi (see *Chapter 3* for more on the geological history of the region). Then, at some point in the last million years, tectonic shifts raised up a faultline running northwest which effectively 'captured' this river, and diverted it along the fault to flow into the Chobe and Zambezi rivers, thus creating what we now call the Linyanti River.

Around the same time, a parallel fault – the Thamalakane Fault – is also thought to have halted the Okavango's course, trapping it and ultimately silting it up to form an inland delta. As the gradients in this part of the northern Kalahari are very small indeed (1:4,000 is typical of the gradient in the Okavango Delta) the routes taken by these watercourses are very susceptible to the tiniest tilts in the earth's surface. As an aside, these faults probably mark the most southerly extent of Africa's Great Rift Valley.

Like the trapped Okavango, silting gradually allowed the Kwando/Linyanti river to spread out into a small inland delta, forming what we call the Linyanti Marshes today.

There is one further geographical feature of note in this area: an ancient river course known as the Magwegqana (spelled in various ways) or Selinda Spillway. This splits off from around the Okavango's Panhandle area, and heads northeast, entering the Linyanti River system just north of the Zibadianja Lagoon. This doesn't seem to be the obvious product of any local faultlines – although it does roughly follow the line of the Linyanti–Gumare Fault. It's either some form of overflow from the Okavango Delta, or perhaps an ancient river course, or both. Either way it's highly visible from the air, and on the ground offers a rich and open environment for game.

GEOGRAPHY The geography of the various parts of this area follows on directly from its geological history, and can easily be divided into four types of environment.

Firstly, there are the Linyanti Swamps, composed of river channels, lagoons, reedbeds and banks of papyrus. Secondly, adjacent to these is a narrow belt of riparian forest that lines these waterways – on the northern edge of the Linyanti Reserve, and the eastern edge of Kwando.

Thirdly there are two intermittent rivers, the Selinda Spillway and the Savuti Channel. Although both were dry for a number of years, both have flooded annually since 2009. There are similarities as well as differences between them, most notably the sheer width of the spillway as it approaches the Linyanti Swamp compared with the relatively narrow Savuti Channel.

Finally, and common to all the concessions, are large areas of dry woodland dominated by large stands of mopane trees, which cover most of the three areas but are usually of least interest to the visitor on safari.

LINYANTI CONCESSION (NG15)

The Linyanti Concession covers 1,250km² of the northern Kalahari, dominated by large areas of mopane woodlands. However, its northern edge is bounded by the waters of the Linyanti River, complete with a string of lagoons and marshes. Adjacent to this is a narrow band of highly varied riparian forests which is the focus of most safari activities.

Cutting from west to east, through the centre of the concession, is the bed of the Savuti Channel. A dry sand river during the 1990s and early 2000s, where a number of waterholes would attract game during the dry season, the channel started flowing again for the first time in 2008. As the water has returned hot dusty conditions have been replaced by lush, riverine woodland along the banks.

GETTING ORGANISED
Getting there and away Getting to any of the camps in the Linyanti Concession is simple: you fly. Wilderness Safaris (who run all four camps) include light-aircraft

flights in their trips into these camps, and it's very easy to fly here from Maun, Kasane, or another camp in northern Botswana.

There are two main airstrips in the concession: one on the river's floodplain near King's Pool (see pages 246–8; ✪ KINAIR 18°26.734'S, 23°41.095'E), and another cleared from the bush between DumaTau and Savuti Camp (see page 248; ✪ DUMAIR 18°31.948'S, 23°39.264'E).

All these camps work on the basis that the logistics are worked out well in advance. Everybody who arrives has a prior reservation (most made months earlier) and everyone arrives and leaves by light aircraft. No self-driving visitors are allowed into these camps, even by prior arrangement. So if you just drive in, you can expect to be escorted off the property and pointed in the direction of a public road!

When to visit Note the general comments made under *Planning and Preparation*, pages 67–74, and then also the specific comments made for the Chobe riverfront, on pages 212–16 – because the Linyanti's riverfront has broadly the same kind of game movements as that area. In short: game concentrates around here when it needs the water, and spreads out when it can easily drink elsewhere.

This means that the game will be better when it's drier, although you'll find a wider variety of bird species here in the wet season, many of them in their breeding plumage.

FLORA AND FAUNA Until recently the Linyanti Reserve was technically a 'multi-purpose concession', where both photographic safaris and hunting were allowed. Although commercial hunting was outlawed throughout Botswana in 2014, Wilderness Safaris, the company currently running the reserve, has always focused exclusively on photographic tourism, thus helping to reduce the negative impacts that hunting has on the animal populations.

Flora As with the animals, in many ways the vegetation here is very similar to that of the Chobe riverfront area, though it generally seems in much better condition. It's thicker, older and more lush – though perhaps that is simply the result of much less logging by humans and slightly less pressure from the animals.

In the dry season there is usually at least 1km of open ground between the slightly raised riverbank, dotted with mature riparian forest, and the actual waters of the Linyanti. Most of this is open grassland (making a conveniently smooth runway for King's Pool), and this will flood occasionally at times of very high water in the river system. In this area you'll find some smaller bushes, like russet bush-willows (*Combretum hereoense*) and Kalahari star apples (*Diospyros lycoides*) – the latter also known as toothbrush bushes after a surprisingly effective use for their thinner branches. (You may also hear this called the blue bush.)

Beyond the floodplain, and up the riverbank, you'll find classic riparian forest with plenty of tall species like knobthorn (*Acacia negrescens*), raintree (*Lonchocarpus capassa*), leadwood (*Combretum imberbe*), jackalberry (*Diospyros mespiliformis*), African mangosteen (*Garcinia livingstonei*) and some marvellous spreading sycamore figs (*Ficus sycomorus*). There are some woolly caper-bushes (*Capparis tomentosa*) in the lower vegetation, but fewer of them than you'll notice beside the Chobe.

Inland, far from the river, is dominated by mopane (*Colophospermum mopane*), though there are also mixed areas, notable for their Kalahari appleleaf (*Lonchocarpus nelsii*), wild seringa (*Burkea africana*), and others in the areas of deeper sand, like old watercourses. Baobabs (*Adansonia digitata*) are dotted around sporadically.

10

The area around Savuti Camp is very much like this dry woodland, interlaced with sandy fossil riverbeds, whilst along the narrow Savuti Channel itself you'll find more open grassland.

Fauna All year round you're likely to see impala, kudu, giraffe, reedbuck, steenbok, warthog, baboon and vervet monkeys throughout the area. Lion and spotted hyena are common, and generally the dominant predators, whilst leopard are often seen in the riparian forest and can be the highlight of night drives.

Cheetah occur, but not very frequently, and may have moved out of the area. Wild dog usually stay near their dens from around June to September (with July and August being the most reliable time for them), and then range widely over most of northern Botswana. Wild dog sightings on the reserve were reportedly consistent in 2012, with two packs being spotted regularly, one of which is believed to have denned between Savuti and Duma Tau. (As an aside, dens in wild areas like this are not easily located, even when wild dogs have a presence in the vicinity.)

Blue wildebeest and Burchell's zebra are present all year, although around May they will arrive in larger numbers, remaining within reach of the water until just before the rains begin in around November–December, when they head off southeast towards Savuti Marsh. Elephants and buffalo follow a similar pattern, with small groups around all year, often only bulls, but with much larger breeding herds arriving in June–July and staying until December. During this time you'll regularly find very large herds of both buffalo and elephant, hundreds strong.

Tsessebe occur, but are uncommon. In very dry years sable and roan start appearing around September–October. Eland are very rare here, and gemsbok don't occur this far north.

Waterbuck are permanent residents, especially towards the northeast of the concession. This is one of relatively few areas of Botswana where they're found. Keep a lookout around King's Pool and Linyanti Discoverer Camp, particularly at the interface between the mopane woodlands of the interior and the riparian forest by the river. Sitatunga are occasionally sighted from boat trips on the river.

Side-striped and black-backed jackal are around, the latter reaching the extreme northern edge of its distribution here (so it isn't common). Bat-eared fox are regularly seen; the area around King's Pool airstrip seems to be a particular favourite. Mongooses, especially banded and dwarf, are always around.

Serval, caracal, African wildcat and aardwolf occur. Before the channel started flowing in 2009, Savuti Camp had a notably excellent record of sightings for these, especially serval. Sightings have since been less frequent, but they still sometimes occur. Aardvark are occasionally seen, with one local expert reporting that they used to be spotted frequently in the riverine forest near the Zibadianja Lagoon. Also close to the lagoon, I've had reports in August 2012 of two pangolins at Mophane Bridge.

When you're out on night drives, you've also got a chance to see scrub hares, spring hares, lesser bushbabies, porcupines, genets (small-spotted and large-spotted), civets and honey badgers.

Birdlife In the riparian woodlands, birds of particular interest include wood owls, swamp boubous, brown firefinches, white-rumped babblers and collared sunbirds. Of particular note is the beautiful Schalow's lourie, a local race of the Knysna lourie found in this region.

There are numerous summer migrants, including carmine bee-eaters that nest here. There are several colonies in the area, including one between King's Pool and DumaTau, where there used to be a hide. Carmines tend to arrive around September and leave by March–April. Some appear to have learned to follow vehicles down the Savuti Channel, catching the crickets that jump away from the moving wheels. Others use the kori bustards, which frequent the channel, as moving perches.

Other summer visitors include the thick-billed cuckoo and the narina trogon, although one expert on the area's birdlife, Mark Tennant, comments that the latter may be resident.

The raptors are well represented. Bateleur and fish eagles are probably the most numerous, but you're also likely to spot African hawk, and tawny, martial and black-breasted snake eagles. Gymnogenes are relatively common. When the first rains come in December, migrants like Wahlberg's and steppe eagles seem notably attracted to the first flush of green in the Savuti Channel – hence December to February can be a particularly good time here.

Throughout the year, western banded snake eagles are also sometimes seen, though they're not common, along with giant eagle owls, bat hawks (look out on the edge of the forest, by the river, in the evening) and the occasional Pel's fishing owl.

On the water there's a host of different species, though some of the marshes and lagoons within the Linyanti Concession can be difficult to access. (For mokoro and boat trips, consider the camps operated by African Bush Camps in the CIII concession, below.) Some of the more unusual residents include slaty and black egret, rufous-bellied heron, painted snipe, long-toed plover, African rail and wattled crane. African skimmers usually nest here in September, with Zibadianja Lagoon, amongst others, being a favourite spot for them.

WHERE TO STAY All four camps within the Linyanti Reserve are owned by Wilderness Safaris (see page 177). They range from the substantial comfort of King's Pool to the much more simple bushcamp style of Linyanti Discoverer Camp, and are listed here from north to south. All cater exclusively for fly-in visitors and none will accept visitors who want to drive in.

⚤ **Linyanti Discoverer Camp** [map 242] (5 chalets) About 10km southwest of Chobe's Linyanti Campsite (see page 241), & not to be confused with Linyanti Bush Camp, this started life as the very rustic Linyanti Tented Camp. Used predominantly by set-departure fly-in groups, & normally accepting only 8 guests at a time, it's an old-style safari camp, far from the interior-designer chic found elsewhere. The tents have recently been replaced by wood-framed, canvas-walled chalets, but it still offers modest comforts in place of plush luxuries. Each chalet has basic, functional features such as a wardrobe, bedside table with reading lamp & dressing table with mirror & all have an en-suite hot shower, washbasin & toilet. Together with the dining & bar area, which nestles beneath an open & slightly elevated timber-&-canvas structure, they all overlook the Linyanti River. Activities are limited

to 4x4 game drives in the camp's concession & day trips further afield. *Rates quoted only as part of a group trip.* ⊕ *All year.*

⌂ **King's Pool** [map 242] (9 chalets) ✪ KINGSP 18°26.276'S, 23°42.415'E. Luxury is the keyword here – for King's Pool is one of Botswana's top 3 or 4 lodges & one of Wilderness's flagship camps. It overlooks the Linyanti River & the swamps beyond from a position in the very centre of the reserve, almost 19km northeast of DumaTau & a similar distance from Linyanti Discover Camp.

Each of the well-spaced rooms, which include a 2-bedroom family unit, is effectively like an individual villa, on high wooden decking under a thatched roof. Extensive & stylish, they're pole framed with canvas-&-gauze wall panels, & a soundly constructed bathroom, with separate toilet. Leather armchairs, nice fabrics in neutral colours, & a large bed under a mosquito net

10

give a solid, conservative feel. Big folding doors lead to a deck with a small plunge pool & a sala – think exclusive thatched gazebo with day bed – overlooking the Linyanti River. You could justifiably just chill here & watch game on the river – & many visitors do – though for the energetic, each room comes supplied with an exercise mat & weights. The central area, while not particularly cosy, is well appointed with leather chairs & extensive decking, whilst outside there's an open-air boma for meals under the stars. On the edge of camp there's a swimming pool &, separately, a hide for game viewing (though it's questionable if this offers better game viewing or birdwatching than is already possible from the balconies of the chalets).

Activities are mainly 4x4 game drives & night drives. These concentrate on the riverine forest areas beside the water &, when dry, the wide grassy floodplains between the river's water & the high bank. Short walks are also possible, & when the water levels are high enough (eg: around Apr–Aug) there's a dbl-decker boat for gentle river cruises – with sleepouts on board a further option.

A couple of small game hides allow guests to get close to wildlife, especially elephants, hippo & waterbirds. Both double as a lovely setting for lunch, with one great option for dinner à deux. *US$1,242/1,463 pp sharing/sgl Jan–Mar, US$1,403/1,624 Apr–May, Nov–Dec; US$2,105/2,326 Jun–Oct, inc FB, most drinks, activities, park fees, laundry; exc transfers. ⊕ All year.*

🏠 **DumaTau** [map 242] (10 tents) ⊕ DUMATA 18°32.217'S, 23°33.917'E. At the western end of the Linyanti, overlooking the Zibadianja Lagoon from its southeastern shore, DumaTau is just east of the source of the Savuti Channel. Its location between 2 elephant corridors means that pachyderm sightings are almost guaranteed, especially in the dry season (Jun–Oct), & the camp's elevated design permits elephants to get very close without any awareness of spectators just metres away. Indeed, a colleague visiting in 2012 was welcomed to tea in camp by a group of elephant cows & their calves.

The camp was rebuilt completely in 2012. Its luxurious en-suite tents, 2 designed for families, are raised on wooden platforms, & have hot showers (both indoors & outside) washbasins & flush toilets. There is a central dining room, bar & lounge, & a small plunge pool for afternoon dips.

Activities centre around 4x4 game drives, & night drives which visit the riverine forest beside the Linyanti, as well as the drier areas along the upper reaches of the Savuti Channel & the mopane forest between. Short walks are sometimes possible, & when water levels are high, a boat can be used on the lagoon & in nearby waterways. An added bonus is a hide, known as 'Zib', sometimes used for coffee or sundowners, but also for sleep-outs (best arranged in advance); a guide will sleep in a tent not too far away. *US$983/1,251 pp sharing/sgl Apr–May, US$1,413/1,681 Jun–Oct, inc FB, most drinks, activities, park fees & laundry; exc transfers. ⊕ All year.*

🏠 **Savuti Camp** [map 242] (7 tents) ⊕ SAVUTI 18°35.834'S, 23°40.412'E. Savuti Camp stands beside the Savuti Channel, about 42km due west of the Savuti Marsh – the area within the Chobe National Park that's commonly known as 'Savuti' (see pages 229–37). It's about 13km as the eagle flies from Zibadianja Lagoon.

The camp's Meru-style tents, 1 designed for families, are raised up on individual wooden decks with a veranda, under the cool shade of a large thatched roof. All have en-suite showers, toilets & washbasins with hot & cold water. Raised wooden walkways lead to a dining room & bar/lounge area under a thatched roof, a star deck & small plunge pool.

Activities concentrate on 4x4 game drives by day & night, although walks are also possible, & there are several elevated hides to visit. Until the heavy rainfall of 2008–09, the waterhole in front of the camp was the only source of water in the dry season for miles around. Hence the camp had a justified reputation for lion & elephant – & witnessed a surprisingly high concentration of serval on night drives. Since then, however, the Savute Channel has become a permanent body of water supporting a diverse range of species: aquatic, terrestrial & avian. It is impossible to say how long this wetland oasis will last as so much depends on each year's rains, but as long as the channel continues to flow, Savuti will be a great camp from which to witness the action taking place along its banks. *US$736 pp sharing mid-Jan–Mar, US$832 Apr–May & Nov–mid-Dec, US$947 mid-Dec–mid-Jan, US$1,291 Jun–Oct inc FB, most drinks, activities, park fees & laundry; exc transfers. ⊕ All year.*

LINYANTI AND SAILE ENCLAVE (CH1)

Just to the east of Chobe National Park's Linyanti Gate, this concession shares a very similar environment to that of the Linyanti Reserve, although the riverside camps here all offer water-based activities as well as game drives. Along the river, African Bush Camps (page 175) operates three very open camps: Linyanti Bush Camp, Linyanti Ebony and the simpler Saile Tented Camp, which also hosts specialist walking safaris. Away from the river is the intimate Three Baobabs camp. For Linyanti Campsite and the attendant Camp Linyanti, both sharing a river frontage but within Chobe National Park, see *Chapter 9*, page 241.

GETTING THERE Whereas camps within the Linyanti Reserve are exclusively for fly-in guests, those in CH1 can also be accessed by self-drivers – although all guests must have a prior reservation; you cannot just turn up here.

By air Guests arriving by air at one of African Bush Camps' properties are flown to Saile airstrip, from where it's a pleasant half-hour game drive to Linyanti Bush Camp and Linyanti Ebony.

By road Self-drivers can approach the Linyanti River camps from one of two directions, both involving significant stretches of deep sand. From Savuti, take the direct route to Linyanti as described in *Chapter 9* under *Linyanti, Getting there and away*, page 240. Approaching from Kasane, the best option is to drive towards Chobe National Park's Ghoha Gate, as described under *Driving from Kasane to Savuti*, on pages 224–6, but then to turn right along the cutline; this is outside the park, so you don't need to pay park fees. Some 36km from the Ghoha Gate you'll reach the Linyanti Gate, where you turn right. From here, it's just over 4km northeast along the river to Linyanti Bushcamp. For access to Three Baobabs, see below.

WHERE TO STAY

Linyanti Bush Camp [map 242] (6 tents)
⊕ LINYBC 18°14.804'S, 23°57.514'E. This fundamentally traditional camp on the edge of the Linyanti Marshes opened in 2007. It's comfortable & attractive, but the setting is almost entirely unmanicured, imparting a strong sense of the bush. Its walk-in tents are large & well equipped, with sisal floor rugs, twin ¾ beds or a king-size dbl, a homely sofa & a writing desk. En suite are a basin, solar-heated shower & flush toilet, & lighting is supplied by paraffin lamps & low-voltage electric appliances.

The camp has a deliciously cool splash pool surrounded by a stockade to keep out elephants, but its old logpile hide, a relic of hunting days, now does service as a backdrop for traditional dinners. Typically you'll enjoy an early-morning b/fast round the campfire, or dine at a long table in the open-sided canvas shelter, where comfortable chairs invite relaxation.

Activities – day & night game drives, mokoro excursions & walking – are led by top-class guides & are very flexible; guests are welcome to do 3 activities a day if they wish. When the water is high enough, usually around Dec–Aug, a shaded pontoon boat makes for leisurely cruising along the channels. From 2014, a helicopter will be based here, with a ½hr flight included in the rates for both Bush Camp & Linyanti Ebony. This is likely to take the form of a flight across the marshes, followed by a picnic & a game drive back to camp. *US$495 pp Jan–Mar & Dec, US$695 pp Apr–Jun & Nov, US$895/1,070 pp sharing/sgl Jul–Oct, inc FB, most drinks, activities, park fees, laundry; exc transfers. No children under 7. ☉ All year.*

Linyanti Ebony [map 242] (4 tents)
Adjacent to Linyanti Bush Camp, but newer & slightly more contemporary in style, Ebony works as a stand-alone camp that's ideal for small groups or families. With this in mind, its elevated family

10

tent, sleeping up to 5 in 2 interconnecting en-suite rooms, is reached from the main area along a wooden walkway that incorporates a small splash pool. Sand paths lead to the other tents, each on low wooden decking. The mess tent is open to the front, its deck shaded beneath a mature ebony tree, & with a traditional firepit facing the marsh. Activities follow an identical format to those at its sister camp, but with its own vehicles & guides. *Rates as Linyanti Bush Camp.* ⊕ *All year.*

⌂ **Saile Tented Camp/Footsteps across the Linyanti** [map 242] (6 tents) ⊕ SAILE 19° 09.826'S, 23°45.783'E. Considerably simpler than its siblings, Saile is about ½hr's drive east of Linyanti Bush Camp & has an exceptionally beautiful outlook across open water dotted with reeds. Saile's small, en-suite walk-in tents have comfortable beds, & a flush toilet & bucket shower under the stars. Solar or battery-powered lights are provided, but the rest of the camp is lit by paraffin lamps; batteries can be charged only at Linyanti Bush Camp. Meals are prepared fresh over an open fire in front of the guests.

Activities are as at its sister camps, although helicopters trips here are at extra charge (US$70/30mins pp). Saile also hosts specialist walking safaris, dubbed Footsteps across the Linyanti, offering the chance to explore on foot with an armed guide. Most walkers come for 2 or 3 nights, & an average level of fitness is required – although it's definitely not a route march. When walkers are in camp, they have exclusive use of the place; walking & 'ordinary' safari visitors are never mixed. *US$495 pp Apr–Jun & Nov, US$630/805 pp sharing/sgl inc FB, drinks, activities. No children under 10, unless camp booked for exclusive use or for Young Explorers safari.* ⊕ *Apr–Oct.*

⌂ **Three Baobabs** [map 242] (4 tents) Contact Garden Lodge (page 188); ⊕ THBAOB 18°07.267'S, 24°17.781'E. Opened in 2009 to provide a bushcamp for the Garden Lodge's many fans, Three Baobabs is set in what feels like open farmland, a tranquil spot where the only sounds are from the birds & the wind in the trees. Many visitors are driven in from Kasane, although the camp is fully accessible to self-drive vehicles. If you're driving yourself, you will be given directions at the time of reservation, but expect the journey to take around 2½hrs from Kasane: up to 1½hrs on the tar road to Kachikau, then a final hour's haul through the bush. Unusually, both German & English are spoken.

Two of the '3 baobabs' stand guard by a simple wooden L-shaped structure under a canvas roof. It's breezy, light & low key, with squashy leather armchairs, & lit by paraffin lanterns & candles. In front, meals are cooked on an open fire, overlooking a small waterhole. Sand paths lead guests to their circular tents, widely spaced on wooden decking & with oodles of space for dbl or twin beds & a couple of smart lockable chests. Hot water is brought for tea & coffee, & hot-water bottles are provided for the winter months. A few steps across the deck, you'll find a private, pole-walled bathroom, with outdoor covered bath & shower, & separate flush toilet.

Activities comprise sundowner drives, full-day game drives to Savuti, & bush walks. It's also possible to visit the village of Parakarungu, which has a primary school & hospital. *US$495/650 pp sharing/sgl inc FB, activities, laundry; exc drinks, park fees. DBB rates available. No children under 12.* ⊕ *Apr–mid-Jan.*

SELINDA CONCESSION (NG16)

Selinda covers a long swathe of 1,350km², including a large section of the Magwegqana or Selinda Spillway, the often-dry waterway that links the Okavango to the Linyanti Swamps. However, after a period of close on 30 years, the Spillway is again flowing all the way from the Okavango Delta to the marshes of the Kwando and Linyanti, transforming the landscape into a mosaic of savannah and wetland.

Most of the reserve's camps are in the far east of the concession, in a very open area where small tree-islands stand amidst large dry plains. The western side of the concession is largely thick combretum and mopane forest; here, the old Motswiri Camp, once used for hunting, has been totally refurbished for photographic safaris.

FLORA AND FAUNA

Flora The area around Selinda and Zarafa camps is the wide mouth of the Magwegqana or Selinda Spillway – which is largely composed of open floodplains dotted with small palm islands. The spillway floods only very rarely, as now, but when it does it clears, or kills off, many small trees and bushes on the plains, leaving only flat marshes and grasslands behind.

Until 2009, these areas were gradually being colonised by 'pioneer species' of invading bushes, among them the wild sage (*Pechuel-loeschea leubnitziae*), which covered large areas of the spillway with its aromatic grey-green foliage, and the candle-pod acacia (*Acacia hebeclada*). With the return of the water, these plants are likely to be cleared.

Dotted around this area are small, slightly raised 'islands' of trees. These have been here for decades, and can survive the periodic flooding – though see the comments on pages 51–3 if you're curious as to how such 'islands' are formed. The trees found on these tree-islands are typical in many ways of those in the riparian forests, though with the addition of lots of real fan palms (*Hyphaene petersianna*). Some are tall trees, many are only bush-sized, but all help to make Selinda's environment a particularly attractive one. Amongst the other tree species here, African mangosteens (*Garcinia livingstonei*) seem particularly common and lush, their branches all apparently flung outwards, as if a green bomb had exploded inside.

Fauna As in the Linyanti and Kwando reserves, there's a population of resident game here, which is swelled from about June onwards by the arrival of large numbers of game which move into the reserve for its proximity to the permanent waters of Zibadianja Lagoon and the Kwando–Linyanti river system.

Permanent game includes impala, red lechwe (on the east side near the lagoon), kudu, tsessebe, giraffe, reedbuck, steenbok, warthog, baboon and vervet monkeys. Lion and spotted hyena are common, whilst leopard are seen more rarely, usually around the larger tree-islands. The very open country is certainly good for cheetah, and though I've never seen them myself, I do get regular reports of them here.

Selinda certainly is one of the best reserves for wild dog; the pack known locally as the 'Selinda pack' have denned at various locations in the area every year for some time now. Although wild dog do range over the whole of northern Botswana, if you want any chance of seeing them then you'll need a place where your guide can drive off-road, to stick with them as they hunt, and where there's lots of dry, open grassland with not too many trees, so that the driving is relatively free of obstacles. This narrows your choice down to a few of the private reserves, but would certainly include Selinda, Mombo, Vumbura, Linyanti and the southern side of Kwando. I don't wish to imply here that you won't see dogs elsewhere; you will. However, if I were going out specifically to look for dogs, then I'd start in these areas. On my last visit I followed them hunting on one occasion for over an hour. Following them at speed across the open ground, they would frequently run through the small palm-islands to try and flush out any game hiding there. At the same time we'd drive around the islands, and wait for them to come out on the other side again.

Herds of wildebeest and zebra arrive around May, staying here until just around November–December. Elephants and buffalo follow a similar pattern with individuals being seen all year, and larger breeding herds arriving around June–July and staying until December. Eland, sable and roan occur, but none of them is common.

Side-striped jackal, bat-eared fox and various mongooses are resident, as are the more nocturnal serval, caracal, African wildcat and aardwolf. Night drives will

10

usually locate scrub hares, spring hares, lesser bushbabies, genets (small-spotted and large-spotted), civets, sometimes honey badgers or porcupines, and – rarely – aardvark.

Birdlife Virtually all of the birds typical of riparian woodlands in the neighbouring Linyanti and Kwando reserves (see pages 246–7 and 256) also occur in the tree-islands of Selinda. In addition to this, the reserve is noted for good sightings of collared palm thrush, plus species of open grasslands like ostriches, secretary birds, kori bustards, red-crested korhaans, various sandgrouse and both common and (from November to March) harlequin quails. The family of coursers is well represented here – with the uncommon bronze-winged and three-banded varieties occurring as well as the more widespread Temminck's and double-banded coursers.

During Botswana's summer months the birding is at its best, with all the European and central African migrants in residence. Then, black coucal, carmine bee-eaters, and flocks of Abdim's and white storks can be seen, whilst raptor concentrations are always good.

GETTING THERE AND AWAY Now that the spillway is flowing, the Selinda Reserve is effectively cut off from Maun and Kasane by rivers, so all visitors arrive by air, rendering redundant the detailed directions for self-drivers that appeared in earlier editions of this guide. The flight takes about an hour from Maun or Kasane, and is very easily organised by the camp or your tour operator. There's an airstrip situated halfway between the Selinda and Zarafa camps, less than 5km from either of them.

WHERE TO STAY All the camps in the Selinda Concession, except Motswiri, are now run by Great Plains Conservation (page 176), but the pioneer here was Linyanti Explorations.

Linyanti Explorations started in Botswana in 1976 as the small, owner-run operation which founded Chobe Chilwero (selling it in 1999), and they solidified their reputation with the superb, simple camps of the Selinda Reserve. Over the years, as ownership of Botswana's safari camps became concentrated into fewer companies, and many of those camps have opted to prioritise luxury, Linyanti Explorations dared to be different. It stayed simple, concentrating on its wildlife and guiding – and hence was always a firm favourite of mine!

In 2006 the company was bought by Great Plains Conservation, which is backed by Dereck and Beverly Joubert, famous wildlife film-makers and photographers. They stopped the (controlled) hunting that took place in the west of the reserve, and spent a lot of money upgrading and rebuilding the two camps. They also refurbished Motswiri Camp (page 254), a former hunting camp which stands in a lovely spot beside the Selinda Spillway in the far west of the concession – and is now leased to RAW Botswana, who specialise in riding and walking safaris. (I was lucky enough to drive from Selinda to Motswiri during the high flood of 2006. Then the spillway flooded completely, nearly linking the Linyanti and Okavango systems for the first time in many years; three years later, in 2009, the link was made.)

More recently, the company added Selinda Explorers camp to their portfolio. Two simple tented camps in the western section of the reserve, Lechwe Island and Ketumetse Trails camps, have been demolished. In their place, Great Plains has introduced the Selinda Canoe Trail, which traverses the reserve from west to east.

Like most of Botswana's high-quality camps, bookings for all these must be made in advance and virtually everyone flies in. Great Plains encourages travellers to book through good overseas tour operators that specialise in Africa.

🏕 **Selinda Camp** [map 242] (9 tents) Contact Great Plains, above; ⊕ SELIND 18°31.897'S, 23°31.354'E. Standing on the edge of the Selinda Spillway, this is the reserve's main camp. It was extensively refurbished in 2007, with further changes during 2009. Substantial walk-in tents, including one for families, are constructed on raised wooden decks under thatched canopies. Each has comfortable twin or dbl beds, & an en-suite bathroom with shower, washbasin & flush toilet at the back, as well as an egg-shaped stand-alone bath. The tents are decked out with furniture from all over Africa, including colonial-style desks & lamps made from Maasai gourds. Electricity for fans, water heaters, etc is provided by solar power.

The camp's main building is now a towering thatched structure, its horseshoe shape containing a bar (often self-service) & a comfy lounge, with many of the pieces painted by wildlife artist Keith Joubert. Meals are served both indoors & under the stars, where the candlelit dinners are marvellously atmospheric. There's also a reading area, an artefacts store, & a walk-in wine cellar. Outside is a small plunge pool for when it's hot, & a boma area with central campfire for cool mornings & evenings.

The team remain enthusiastic about their activities, which concentrate on 4x4 game drives in the morning & afternoon/evening. The former can start very early in the morning (a good sign of commitment to their game spotting!), the latter eventually becoming spotlit night drives. In addition, short walks can be organised, often as part of a drive, & during the winter months canoeing & boating are on offer. Hides across the reserve offer good spots to relax during an afternoon siesta. *US$950/1,283 pp sharing/sgl Apr–mid-Jun, US$1,415/2,123 mid-Jun–Oct, inc FB, most drinks, activities, park fees, laundry; exc transfers.* ⊕ *All year.*

🏕 **Selinda Explorers** [map 242] (4 tents) ⊕ SELEXP 18°30.686'S, 23° 25.913'E. About 90mins' drive west of Selinda & Zarafa, on the banks of the Selinda Spillway, this is the most recent addition to the concession. It is designed very much in the style of a classic mobile camp, albeit in a static setting, with canvas the fabric of choice & an open-sided main area shaded by large jackalberry trees. Uniquely for northern Botswana, Selinda Explorers may be reserved only as a whole, so is ideal for a large group of friends or a family. The atmosphere really comes to life as the sun goes down, when the camp is lit entirely by paraffin lanterns & a campfire. Although there's no electricity, cameras & other devices can be charged through an inverter system powered by the game-drive vehicle batteries.

Guests stay in large, Meru-style tents, with more than enough space to stand up & walk around in. Each is simple but well decorated with twin beds, or a dbl, & some nice touches such as a decanter of port or cognac on a night stand. The bathroom is open to the night sky, with canvas walls for privacy. There's no running water, but hot & cold water are delivered to your tent on request, & the 'flush toilet' has an external tank, filled regularly with water from the spillway.

Although game drives are an option, activities focus on getting out of the vehicle & into the bush on foot, or exploring the spillway by canoe, always accompanied by experienced armed guides. *US$572 pp Mar, US$618 Apr–14 Jun & Nov–19 Dec, US$850 15 Jun–Oct, inc FB, most drinks, activities, park fees, laundry; exc transfers.* ⊕ *Mar–Oct.*

🏕 **Selinda Canoe Trail** High wet-season rainfall across southern Africa from about 2008 to 2011 resulted in increased water levels that have been almost unprecedented in the last 30 years. As a result, the waters of the Selinda Spillway have been ideal for canoeists, leading Great Plains to set up a canoe & walking safari, with weekly departures Jun–Aug.

The 4-night trip, for 2–8 participants, starts midway along the spillway, running east to Selinda & Zarafa camps for about 45km, with stops to explore the banks on foot. Usually, 2 participants share a Canadian canoe, although these can accommodate 3 people if fitness is an issue. At night, fly-camps are set up along the riverbank, with a cook on hand to prepare the evening meal. Starting or ending the trip with a night at Selinda or Zarafa is encouraged. *4-night safari US$2,660/3,590 pp sharing/sgl, inc FB, most drinks, activities, park fees, laundry; exc transfers.* ⊕ *Jun–Aug.*

🏕 **Zarafa** [map 242] (4 tents) ⊕ ZARAFA 18°35.17.54'S, 23°31.54.36'E. Once Botswana's smallest permanent camp, the former Zibadianja Camp was renamed in 2009 to reflect a complete rebuild, taking it right upmarket. The new camp, constructed along a well-vegetated forest about 2km southeast of the original, overlooks the

10

floodplains of the Zibadianja Lagoon. It remains tiny, but the huge tents (each almost 100m²), top service & food put this in the bracket of one of Botswana's best camps. Set among the trees, each tent (more like a marquee in style) is an individual suite with a large deck, a separate lounge with comfortable chairs, & its own plunge pool. Both indoor & outdoor showers are complemented by a copper bath, & there's even a copper-hooded fire for warmth in the winter months. Conversely, there's a unique cooling system above each of the beds for the warmer months.

Mirroring the style of the suites is the main dining & lounge area, with an expansive deck for outdoor dining. Power for the whole camp is derived entirely from solar panels – claimed to be an African first for such a luxury camp.

Activities at Zarafa, & the team's enthusiasm for them, mirror those at Selinda, with the addition of a motorised pontoon which traverses the lagoon in front of camp. The guiding when I last visited was up to its usual high standards. *US$1,550/2,093 pp sharing/sgl Apr– mid-Jun, US$2,250/3,375 mid-Jun–Oct, inc FB, most drinks, activities, park fees, laundry; exc transfers.* ☺ *All year.*

✗ **Motswiri** [map 242] (5 tents) ☏ 686 0244; www.rawbotswana.com; ✪ MOTSWI 18°46.00'S, 23°02.5'E. In the face of increasing levels of luxury in much of Botswana, Motswiri is refreshingly simple. It lies about 70km or 4hrs' drive from Zarafa, on the far western side of the reserve, which has until recently been virtually unvisited for photographic safaris.

The camp, set under leadwood trees, benefits from fantastic views over the Selinda Spillway. Its split-level tented main area, all chunky wood with rustic chairs & tables, allows comfortable, sheltered dining even during the rains. A sandy path leads past a small pool with a deck & sunloungers to the Meru-style tents, which are modified slightly with proper wood-framed doors & timber poles. Inside are a dbl or twin beds (which one of my colleagues commented was the most comfortable he had ever slept in!), hessian floor covering, & an en-suite bathroom with both indoor & open-air showers & plenty of hot water. Lighting via a battery system allows for charging of batteries too.

Motswiri focuses almost exclusively on horseriding & walking safaris, while – when water levels permit – boating & a spot of fishing are a great way to occupy an afternoon. Motswiri also has the use of a small, semi-permanent fly-camp which guests can either walk or ride to, spending a night or two exploring this section of the spillway by boat, on horseback & on foot. *From US$495 pp low season to US$750/1,125 pp sharing/sgl high season, inc FB, most drinks, activities, park fees.* ☺ *All year.*

KWANDO CONCESSION (NG14)

On the northern edge of Botswana, bordering Namibia across the Kwando River, the Kwando Concession covers an enormous 2,320km² of very wild bush. It's one of Botswana's larger wildlife concessions. Beside its eastern boundary, formed by the river, is a narrow belt of riverine forest. In the south this opens out into some large tree-islands and open floodplains. There are two photographic camps on this productive eastern side.

The vast western part of the concession includes huge tracts of thick mopane woodland. Here, far from the river, there is a seasonal hunting camp.

GETTING ORGANISED

Getting there and away Like most of Botswana's private concessions, Kwando is reached by a short flight from Maun, Kasane or one of Botswana's other camps. There are two main airstrips in the concession: one near Lagoon, and the other near Lebala. Both the camps here work out their logistics well in advance. Trips are always pre-arranged, and they don't welcome drop-in visitors, nor ever really get any.

Thus virtually nobody would consider self-driving into these camps, even by prior arrangement. However, if you did then you'd pre-arrange your visit with the camps and take the transit route north through Selinda. It's about 14km in a straight line from Selinda to Lebala, and a further 30km by road from there to Lagoon.

When to visit Game viewing revolves around the reserve's riverfront on the Kwando River and its adjacent riverine forest. Thus note the comments made under *Planning and Preparation*, pages 67–74, and also the specific comments made for the Chobe riverfront area, on pages 212–16. The Kwando's riverfront has broadly similar game movements to the Chobe or Linyanti riverfronts. In short: game concentrates around here when it needs the water, and spreads away again when it can easily drink elsewhere.

This means that the game viewing improves as the land dries out. Then buffalo and elephants move into this area from the west and south and zebra and wildebeest move in from the great plains of the Chobe. Later, when it rains, so the animals will move away – although birdwatchers will find more of interest in the wet season when there's a greater variety of bird species, many in breeding plumage.

FLORA AND FAUNA

Flora Kwando's environment and ecosystems are similar to those of the Linyanti and Selinda reserves. The north of the reserve is most like the Linyanti Reserve, in that it's dominated by the presence of the river, which runs on its eastern border in a roughly straight line. Adjacent to this is a band of riverine forest, characteristically rich in its variety of trees. These include African mangosteen (*Garcinia livingstonei*) – which remind me of a bomb exploding, as all the stems grow out straight from the top – jackalberry (*Diospyros mespiliformis*), sausage tree (*Kigelia africana*), leadwood (*Combretum imberbe*) and knobthorn (*Acacia nigrescens*).

As you move further south in the reserve, around Lebala Camp, you're getting into the northern side of the Magwegqana or Selinda Spillway, and here the riverine forest opens out, becoming a mosaic of open areas covered in low bushes and grasses. These open areas are often dominated by wild sage (*Pechuel-loeschea leubnitziae*) and interspersed with patches of forest, which become smaller and more island-like as you move further south.

These forest patches and islands contain many of the same riverine tree species, and you'll also find marula trees (*Sclerocarya birrea*), occasional baobabs (*Adansonia digitata*) and increasing numbers of real fan palms (*Hyphaene petersiana*), plus many camelthorns (*Acacia erioloba*) and the invasive candle-pod acacia (*Acacia hebeclada*).

Further south still, the land becomes even more open as you approach the reserve's southern boundary and the Selinda Reserve.

Fauna Like the Linyanti and Selinda, Kwando's resident game is augmented in about June by migrant game which arrives here from the drier areas south and west, attracted by the permanent waters of the Kwando River.

Common species found here include impala, red lechwe, kudu, tsessebe, giraffe, steenbok, warthog, baboon and vervet monkeys. Roan, sable and common duiker also occur, but not frequently. Lion, leopard and spotted hyena are common, whilst cheetah are rarely seen. Hippo and crocodiles frequent the river, along with the playful spotted-necked otters.

Herds of wildebeest and zebra are resident from about May to December. Elephants and buffalo follow a similar pattern with individuals around all year, and larger breeding herds arriving around June–July and staying until December. These large herds are particularly common near the river during the dry season, and the elephants seem to have a penchant for aggression if approached too closely. When one of the camp's guides was driving, he would refer to them nonchalantly as 'cheeky' animals; but driving myself through the area once I found it much more nerve-racking. They reacted completely differently from the relatively passive elephants found in the busier parts of Chobe and Moremi.

Kwando is also a good reserve for seeing wild dog, especially in the south of the reserve around Lebala, helped by Kwando Safari's policy of actively 'tracking' animals across the bush, and having both a tracker and a driver/guide on each of its vehicles.

Highlights of the night drives here include Selous' mongoose, genets and aardwolf – along with more usual sightings of scrub hares, spring hares, bushbabies, genets, civets, honey badgers and porcupines.

Birdlife The birdlife here is almost identical to that of the Linyanti Reserve (see pages 246–7), with plenty of variety. I particularly remember a huge colony of carmine bee-eaters that we seemed to have discovered by accident when stopping on a drive for a 'sundowner' drink.

Sacred and hadeda ibis are particularly common in the waterways, whilst rarer residents include slaty and black egrets, and rufous-bellied herons.

WHERE TO STAY Both the camps here are owned and run by Kwando Safaris, based in Maun (see page 176).

Lagoon [map 242] (8 tents) ⊕ LAGOON 18°12.980'S, 24°24.790'E. Overlooking the Kwando River, Lagoon is the smaller & more northerly of Kwando's 2 camps in the riparian forest belt. It stands amidst tall, mature forest that includes some fine marula (*Sclerocarya birrea caffra*) & jackalberry (*Diospyros mespiliformis*) trees.

The whole camp was rebuilt in early 2011 & is now in fantastic shape. Large chalets set on stilts along the river are designed to maximise the views from both the veranda & each area of the interior. The front walls are made entirely of gauze, & this, together with a ceiling fan over the bed, ensures that everything is light & breezy. In the split-level interiors, there's a comfortable seating area at the front, a dbl or twin beds set higher up, & an en-suite bathroom with a stand-alone tub & outdoor shower.

The food at Lagoon is good, served in a thatched dining room facing the river. The bar is largely self-service, & an extensive curio shop has local handicrafts & some useful books. The lounge area has comfortable armchairs, a small library & various board games. Game frequently wanders into camp & on one visit an old bull elephant came within touching distance of the dining room as we ate brunch, in search of some tasty morsels in the tree above. It was very relaxed, apparently oblivious to the general fuss that it was causing.

Lagoon Camp has a plunge pool for the hotter months, but its main activities are 4x4 game drives & boating excursions, usually one early in the morning (after coffee & biscuits), & the second in late afternoon, which usually turns into a night drive as the light fades. With a tracker accompanying every drive, & a maximum of 6 people per vehicle, there's a willingness to drive cross-country & actively track coveted game, such as big cats & wild dogs. The guides are enthusiastic about their big game, & sometimes positively zealous in their tracking of it. For gentle sundowner cruises there is a 2-storey floating pontoon-type boat on the river, & if you're keen on fishing, you can try your hand at spinning for tigerfish & bream.

Lagoon's atmosphere is laid-back, friendly & not at all regimented – mealtimes are usually adjusted around game-viewing times, rather than vice versa. A slight minus is that the tents are quite close together (although all have canvas blinds that can be closed). *From US$550 pp low season to US$1,132/1,432 pp sharing/sgl high season, inc FB, most drinks, activities, park fees.* ⊕ *All year.*

Lebala [map 242] (8 tents) ⊕ LEBALA 18°24.760'S, 23°32.540'E. Lebala is in a very different location; the name means 'open space', which is appropriate as there are lots of plains around it. It's just 14km from Selinda, & yet 26km (measured in a straight line) from Lagoon – so it's no surprise that its environment is close in character to that of Selinda, but quite different to the area around Lagoon.

The camp's substantial & custom-designed tents, rebuilt in 2008, are on raised decking made of polished Zimbabwe teak. Sliding doors lead to a very large bedroom, with 2 ¾-size beds & solid but simple teak furniture. Screened 'shadecloth' walls mean that wildlife can be watched from your room, with curtains & blinds to control the level of light. Outside is a large private veranda for sitting out, with a few chairs & a table. Canvas room-divisions separate the bedroom from the 'entrance hall', where there is a spot to put suitcases, a hat-&-coat stand, a large wardrobe & a writing desk. The large bathroom has a stand-alone claw-footed bath, his & hers washbasins & a separate toilet, while outside is a dbl shower. (Hot water comes very efficiently from individual gas geysers.)

Teak walkways wind from the tents to a thatched dining area, where good meals are served. Adjacent is a comfy lounge & bar area, with a modest library of books, & one side open to the plains around. There's a campfire for the cooler months, & a plunge pool for the warmer ones.

Activities concentrate on 4x4 game drives & walking. As at Lagoon, the guides always drive with a tracker & will actively seek the game. Last time I visited, I arose late one morning, only to learn that wild dog had sprinted through camp just before sunrise. *From US$550 pp low season to US$1,132/1,432 pp sharing/sgl high season, inc FB, most drinks, activities, park fees.* ⊕ *All year.*

11

The Okavango Delta – Moremi Game Reserve

Much of what is covered in this section – especially concerning flora and fauna, and when to visit – is applicable to the Okavango as a whole. Therefore I've covered this information here in detail, and made reference to it elsewhere where appropriate. The map of the Delta on pages 260–1 relates to the whole area.

Remember that Moremi and its surrounding reserves are separated only by lines on a map; their ecosystems blend together seamlessly. Birds and animals move without hindrance across almost the whole of the Okavango, Linyanti and Chobe regions. Thus all the country covered in *Chapters 11–15* is really one continuous area dedicated to wildlife. The enormous size of this, and the diversity of ecosystems that it contains, are two of the main reasons why the wildlife of northern Botswana is so spectacular.

Although seasonal flooding is the lifeblood of the Okavango Delta, between 2009 and 2011 the area experienced the biggest floods in over 20 years. Normally seasonal or even dry rivers are flowing, roads and dykes have been swamped, and camps have found themselves under water. Even in the south and east of the Delta, the Gomoti has flooded all the way to Shorobe and there is contiguous water between the Gomoti, Santantadibe, Thamalakane and Boro systems. All this in turn impacts on the wildlife, and is a tremendous boost to the area's ecology. For the visitor, minor inconveniences are offset by a greater concentration of game on the islands, and increased opportunities for water-based activities.

BACKGROUND INFORMATION

HISTORY In his *Travels and Researches in South Africa* (see *Appendix 3, Further information*), David Livingstone recounts what he was told by the local people near Lake Ngami in 1849 about the origin of a river there:

> While ascending in this way the beautifully-wooded river, we came to a large stream flowing into it. This was the Tamunak'le. I enquired whence it came. 'Oh, from a country full of rivers – so many no one can tell their number – and full of large trees.'

However, within 100 years of Europeans finding this 'country full of rivers', its environment and wildlife were under threat. In an exceedingly far-sighted move, the Batawana people proclaimed Moremi as a game reserve in 1962, in order to combat the rapid depletion of the area's game and the problems of cattle encroachment.

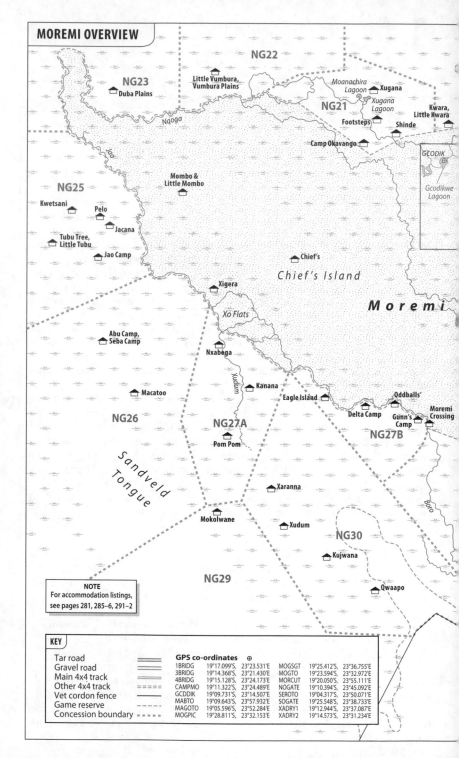

MOREMI OVERVIEW

NG22

NG23
Duba Plains

Little Vumbura,
Vumbura Plains

Moanachira
Lagoon Xugana

NG21
Xugana
Lagoon

Kwara,
Little Kwara

Footsteps
Shinde

Camp Okavango

GCODIK

Ngoga

Jao

Gcodikwe
Lagoon

NG25

Mombo &
Little Mombo

Kwetsani

Pelo
Jacana

Tubu Tree,
Little Tubu
Jao Camp

Chief's

Chief's Island

Xigera

M o r e m i

Xo Flats

Abu Camp,
Seba Camp

Nxabega

Xudum

Macatoo

Kanana

Eagle Island

Oddballs'

Delta Camp

Gunn's
Camp

Moremi
Crossing

NG26

NG27A

NG27B

Pom Pom

S a n d v e l d

T o n g u e

Xaranna

Boro

Mokolwane

Xudum

NG30

Kujwana

NG29

Qwaapo

NOTE
For accommodation listings,
see pages 281, 285–6, 291–2

KEY

Tar road	
Gravel road	
Main 4x4 track	
Other 4x4 track	
Vet cordon fence	
Game reserve	
Concession boundary	

GPS co-ordinates ⊕

1BRIDG	19°17.099'S, 23°23.531'E	MOGSGT	19°25.412'S, 23°36.755'E
3BRIDG	19°14.368'S, 23°21.430'E	MOGTO	19°23.594'S, 23°32.972'E
4BRIDG	19°15.128'S, 23°24.173'E	MORCUT	19°20.050'S, 23°55.111'E
CAMPMO	19°11.322'S, 23°24.489'E	NOGATE	19°10.394'S, 23°45.092'E
GCDDIK	19°09.731'S, 23°14.507'E	SEROTO	19°04.317'S, 23°50.071'E
MABTO	19°09.643'S, 23°57.932'E	SOGATE	19°25.548'S, 23°38.733'E
MAGOTO	19°05.596'S, 23°52.284'E	XADRY1	19°12.944'S, 23°37.087'E
MOGPIC	19°28.811'S, 23°32.153'E	XADRY2	19°14.573'S, 23°31.234'E

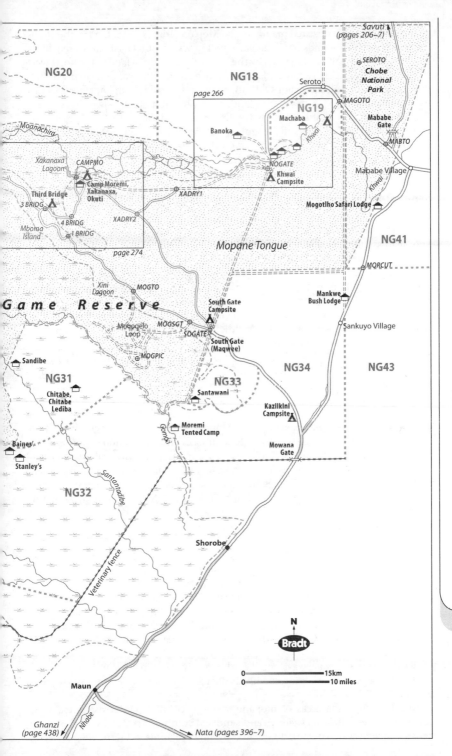

NG20

Moanachira

Xakanaxa
Lagoon

Third Bridge

3 BRIDG

Mboma
Island

CAMPMO

Camp Moremi,
Xakanaxa,
Okuti

4 BRIDG

1 BRIDG

XADRY2

XADRY1

page 274

NG18

page 266

Banoka

NGATE

NG19

Machaba

Khwai
Campsite

Khwai

Savuti
(pages 206-7)

SEROTO

Chobe
National
Park

MAGOTO

Mababe
Gate

MABTO

Mababe Village

Mogotlho Safari Lodge

NG41

Mopane Tongue

MORCUT

Xini
Lagoon

MOGTO

South Gate
Campsite

Mankwe
Bush Lodge

Game   Reserve

Moqpgelo
Loop

MOGSGT

SOGATE

South Gate
(Maqwee)

Sankuyo Village

MOGPIC

NG34

NG43

Sandibe

NG31

Chitabe,
Chitabe
Lediba

Santawani

NG33

Kazilkini
Campsite

Baines

Stanley's

Gomoti

Moremi
Tented Camp

Mowana
Gate

NG32

Santantadibe

Veterinary fence

Shorobe

N

Bradt

0   15km
0   10 miles

Maun

Nhabe

Ghanzi
(page 438)

Nata (pages 396-7)

Initially Moremi consisted mainly of the Mopane Tongue area; then in the 1970s the royal hunting grounds of Chief Moremi, known as Chief's Island, were added. In 1992 the reserve was augmented by the addition of a strip of land in the northwest corner of the reserve, between the Jao and Nqoga rivers. This was done to make sure that it represented all the major Okavango habitats, including the northern Delta's papyrus swamps and permanent wetlands which had not previously been covered.

As an aside, this is often cited as the first reserve in Africa that was created by native Africans. This is true, and recognises that the native inhabitants were the prime movers here, rather than the colonial authorities. However, beware of ignoring the fact that Africa's original inhabitants seemed to co-exist with the wildlife all over the continent without needing any 'reserves', until Europeans started arriving.

GEOGRAPHY Moremi Game Reserve protects the central and eastern areas of the Okavango Delta. It forms a protected nucleus for the many wildlife reserves/concessions in the region. Physically Moremi is very flat, encompassing extensive floodplains, some seasonal, others permanent, numerous waterways and two main land masses: the Mopane Tongue and Chief's Island.

Its area is defined in some places by rivers, although their names and actual courses are anything but easy to follow on the ground. Its northern boundary roughly follows the Nqoga–Khwai river system, whilst its southern boundary is defined in sequence by the Jao, Boro and Gomoti rivers.

It's worth noting that since the middle of the last century it seems that the western side of the Delta (specifically the Thaoge River system) has gradually been drying up. As this has happened, an increasing amount of water is entering the Moanachira–Khwai river system, on the eastern side of Chief's Island – helping to raise water levels around the Khwai River area, and increase the incidence of flooding on the roads there.

FLORA AND FAUNA The ecosystems of Moremi Reserve are amongst the richest and most diverse in Africa. Thanks to generally effective protection over the years, they have also been relatively undisturbed by man. Now with wildlife tourism thriving around the park as well as in the private concessions, we can be really optimistic about its future. The regime of conservation supported by money from benign tourism is gaining ground. One such success story is the reintroduction of rhino into Moremi: the first to be sent back into the wild areas of northern Botswana since poaching wiped them out.

Flora There are over 1,000 species of plants recognised in Moremi, yet large tracts of the reserve are dominated by just one: mopane (*Colophospermum mopane*). This covers the aptly named Mopane Tongue and parts of Chief's Island. Because the park has had effective protection for years, and the soils are relatively rich but badly drained, much of this forest is beautiful, tall 'cathedral' mopane – so called for the gracefully arching branches which resemble the high arches of a Gothic cathedral. You'll often find large areas here where there are virtually no other species of trees represented.

Beside the many waterways you'll find extensive floodplains, and some lovely stretches of classic riparian forest with its characteristically wide range of tree and bush species.

Laced through the areas of mopane you'll also find open areas dotted with camelthorn trees (*Acacia erioloba*), and sandveld communities following the sandy beds of ancient watercourses, dominated by silver terminalia (*Terminalia sericea*), wild seringa (*Burkea africana*) and Kalahari appleleaf (*Lonchocarpus nelsii*). You'll find much, much more detail on this vegetation in Veronica Roodt's essential *Trees and Shrubs of the Okavango Delta* (see *Appendix 3, Further information* for details).

Fauna Moremi protects as dense and diverse a population of animals and birds as you'd expect to find in one of Africa's best wildlife reserves. With the reintroduction of rhino, you can see all the big five, and a lot more besides.

Elephant and buffalo occur here year-round in large numbers, and you're likely to see blue wildebeest, Burchell's zebra, impala, kudu, tsessebe, red lechwe, waterbuck, reedbuck, giraffe, common duiker, bushbuck, steenbok, warthog, baboon and vervet monkey throughout the park. Eland, sable and roan antelope also range across the park but are less common, as they are elsewhere in Africa. Sitatunga live deep in the swamps.

Lion, leopard, cheetah and spotted hyena all have thriving populations here. Moremi is central to wild dog, which range widely across most of northern Botswana.

Both side-striped and black-backed jackal occur, though the latter are more common. Brown hyena probably occur, but relatively rarely and only in the drier areas with lower densities of the other large predators. Similarly, bat-eared fox are found, though not so commonly as in Botswana's drier areas. There is a wide variety of mongooses to be found, including the banded, dwarf, slender, large grey, water and Selous' mongoose. Meanwhile in the water, Cape, clawless and spotted-necked otters are often glimpsed though seldom seen clearly.

Serval, caracal, aardwolf and aardvark are found all over the park, though are only occasionally seen due to their largely nocturnal habits. Pangolin are also found here, and seem to be slightly less rare than in other areas of their range.

Although night drives aren't allowed within the reserve itself, some of the camps near North Gate will finish their afternoon drives outside the park, and hence do short night drives back to camp. Then you have a chance to see scrub hares, spring hares, lesser bushbabies, porcupines, genets (small-spotted and large-spotted), civets, African wildcats and honey badgers. Black-and-white striped polecats are also nocturnal, though very seldom seen.

Until 2001 rhino had been absent due to poaching, though in November of that year the first white rhino were reintroduced into the Mombo Concession, in northeast Moremi, with black rhino following a couple of years later. Although they're now free to roam, several have remained on Chief's Island.

Birdlife Moremi boasts over 400 bird species, a great variety, which are often patchily distributed in association with particular habitats; though visiting any area, the sheer number of different species represented will strike you as amazing.

Although there are no birds that are truly endemic to Botswana, the Okavango is a hugely important wetland for many species, amongst which are a number of rarities worth noting. Top of the Okavango's list of 'specialities' is the slaty egret. Expect to find this in shallow, reedy backwaters and pans. Besides the Okavango, this rare egret is only resident in the quieter corners of the Chobe and Linyanti rivers, and the Bangweulu Wetlands in Zambia. To identify it look for its overall slate-grey colouring, except for its lower legs and feet which are yellow, as are its eyes and some of its face, while the front of its neck is a rufous red. (The less uncommon black egret lacks the yellow on the legs and face, or the rufous neck.)

Much easier to spot are magnificent wattled cranes which can be seen in the Delta fairly readily, usually in pairs or small groups wandering about wet grasslands or shallow floodplains in search of fish and small amphibians and reptiles.

For keen birdwatchers, other specials here include brown firefinch, lesser jacana, coppery-tailed coucal, Bradfield's hornbill, pink-throated longclaw and the inconspicuous chirping cisticola.

WHEN AND HOW TO VISIT See *When to go* in *Chapter 4* for more general comments on the whole of northern Botswana, and note that the best times to visit are dependent upon how you intend to visit, exactly which camps you are visiting, and why.

Flying in If you're flying into a camp in Moremi or the Delta then the season won't make much difference to the access. The Okavango's camps used to close down during January and February, but now most keep open throughout the year, despite being much quieter during the green season (December to March).

In terms of vehicle access to the various game-viewing areas from your camp, the rains are often less of a concern than the flood, the peak of which usually lags behind the rains by several months (depending on how far up the Delta you are). However, generally there will be the most dry land from about August to January.

Driving in If you're driving yourself into Moremi, it's important to understand that only a restricted area of the reserve will be accessible to you, and the wet season will make this access even more difficult. As the rains continue, their cumulative effect is to make many of the roads on the Mopane Tongue much more difficult to pass, while it simply submerges others. Thus only the experienced and well equipped need even think about driving anywhere through Moremi between about January and April.

Most visitors who drive themselves come to Moremi in the dry season, between around May and October. Then the tracks become increasingly less difficult to navigate, although even then there are always watercourses to cross. As with all national parks, the speed limit in the park is 40km/h, with no vehicles allowed on the roads between sunset and sunrise.

Flora and fauna The flora and the birdlife are definitely more spectacular during the rains. Then the vegetation goes wild, migrant birds arrive, and many of the residents appear in their full breeding plumage. So this is a great time for birders and those interested in the plants and flowers.

The story with the animals is more complex. In most of Moremi there is water throughout the year. Higher water levels here simply means less land area available for animals that aren't amphibious. However, around the edges of the Delta, animal densities are hugely affected by the migration towards the water from the dry central areas of the country.

Thus game viewing generally gets better the later in the dry season that you go … although this trend is probably less pronounced in the centre of the Delta than it is at the edges.

Activities The water levels will affect the activities that you can do whilst here. In some areas mokoro trips are possible only for a few months every year, when water levels are high enough. Similarly, the game drives from a few of the camps are generally possible only when water levels are low enough.

Costs The cost of some camps in the Okavango varies with the season. This depends very much on the company owning/marketing the camps, but in general you can expect July–October to be the period of highest cost, December–March to be the time of lowest cost, and November, April, May and June to be pitched somewhere in the middle.

GETTING ORGANISED

Orientation
Moremi Game Reserve covers a large tract of the centre of the Okavango Delta, and a wide corridor stretching east to link that with Chobe National Park.

At the heart of Moremi is a long, permanent island, Chief's Island, oriented from southeast to northwest. At about 60km long and around 10km wide this is the largest island in the Delta, and it's usually cut off from the mainland by waterways and floodplains. Within the eastern side of Moremi is a triangular peninsula of dry land covered (mostly) in mopane trees, known as the Mopane Tongue.

Between and around Chief's Island and the Mopane Tongue, Moremi is a mosaic of rivers, lagoons, floodplains and small islands which slowly and gradually change with the passage of time.

Maps
Once again, Veronica Roodt's definitive map of Moremi Game Reserve (see *Maps and navigation* in *Chapter 4*, pages 100–1) can't be recommended too highly for visitors to Moremi, and is essential for anyone planning a self-drive trip there.

Booking and park fees
If you're flying into an organised camp, then park fees will probably already be included in the price that you've paid. If you're driving in you'll need to have booked all your campsites and paid all your park fees in advance; see pages 84–5 for details of how to go about this, and a scale of the fees. On arrival at the park gate, you'll need to present your confirmation documents confirming that you have pre-booked your campsites, and paid your park fees, before you are allowed to proceed.

Opening hours
(⊕ *Apr–Sep 06.00–18.30, Oct–Mar 05.30–19.00*) As with other national parks, Moremi's opening hours vary with the season, roughly corresponding to 'dusk 'til dawn'. You're not allowed to drive in the park outside of these hours.

THE MOPANE TONGUE

Within eastern Moremi, the dry triangle of the Mopane Tongue juts into the Delta from the east, between the Khwai and Mogogelo rivers. Each side of this is about 40km long, and roughly marking the corners are the campsites of South Gate (Maqwee), North Gate (Khwai) and Xakanaxa – a reminder that this is the only area of Moremi that is accessible for visitors driving themselves.

Aside from the riverine forest which lines its edges, most of the interior of this peninsula is covered in forests of mopane, including many stretches of very mature and beautiful forests.

KHWAI RIVER AND NORTH GATE (KHWAI)
Near the northeastern edge of Moremi, the northernmost waterways of the Okavango gradually narrow to form the Khwai River, which is spanned by a wooden pole bridge. The tracks beside the river and around the floodplains are often stunning in their beauty, and prolific in their wildlife. It's a spectacular area, and especially so if approached from the dusty heartlands of Chobe during the dry season.

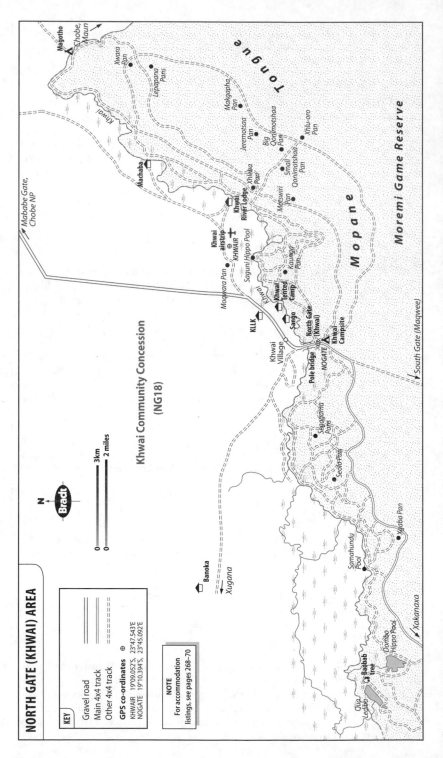

NORTH GATE (KHWAI) AREA

KEY

Gravel road
Main 4x4 track
Other 4x4 track

GPS co-ordinates ⊕
KHWAIR 19°09.052'S, 23°47.543'E
NOGATE 19°10.394'S, 23°45.092'E

NOTE
For accommodation
listings, see pages 268–70

N

Bradt

0 ___ 3km
0 ___ 2 miles

**Khwai Community Concession
(NG18)**

Moremi Game Reserve

Mopane Tongue

Magotho
Chobe, Maun
Xwara Pan
Lepapana Pans
Makgapha Pan
Jeremotsaa Pan
Big Oonimotshaa Pan
Qonimotshaa Pan
Xhu-oro Pan
Small Oonimotshaa Pan
Xhl̄aba Pan
Khwai River Lodge
Motswiri Pan
Kaungti Pan
Machaba
Khwai airstrip ⊕ KHWAIR
Saguni Hippo Pool
Moqwara Pan
Khwai Tented Camp
Sango Camp
North Gate (Khwai)
KLLK
Khwai Campsite
Khwai Village
Pole bridge
⊕ NOGATE
Sagagama Pans
Seolo Pan
Banoka
Xugana
Samahundu Pool
Xgaba Pan
Dombo Hippo Pool
Baobab tree
Oga Lediba
Xakanaxa
South Gate (Maqwee)
Mababe Gate, Chobe NP

266

While this stretch of the Khwai River falls within the community-run NG19 concession (see *Chapter 12*, page 297), I have included it here as it falls naturally between Chobe and Moremi, and thus – especially for self-drivers – it feels more logical. Most of the lodges here conduct their activities along the river, although some do occasionally go into Moremi.

Flora and fauna highlights

Flora All along the edge of the Khwai's floodplain you'll find some of the region's most beautiful, mature riverine forest. Stunning trees, tall and old, abound, including a large number of camelthorn (*Acacia erioloba*) and some almost pure stands of leadwood (*Combretum imberbe*). There are also patches of acacia woodlands, usually standing on sandy patches of ground between the river valley and the mopane woodlands of the Tongue's interior.

Fauna The Khwai area seldom fails to deliver some very impressive wildlife spectacles when visited in the dry season. This is perhaps to be expected, as it marks the boundary of the Okavango's waters that flow east and north – and so is the closest drinking water for large numbers of thirsty animals in southern Chobe during the late dry season.

Of particular note are the lion prides. In 1999 one was so large that it had started taking down small elephants – a practice which visibly worried the area's large elephant herds.

I've had some particularly good leopard sightings here, seeing the cats lounging around in shady trees during the day, usually on the edge of the riverine forest. Mixed areas of broken woodlands and open areas is classic leopard territory, and because it's been protected for so long, many of the residents are very relaxed in the presence of game-viewing vehicles. Well suited to this environment, too, are wild dogs, which denned close to the river in 2013 and were regularly seen with their pups on game drives. Other prolific predators include spotted hyena, which also had a den nearby in 2013.

As well as the almost ubiquitous impala, you're likely to spot kudu and waterbuck in this environment, and you probably have a better chance than in most places of seeing the normally elusive roan antelope, which come down to the river to drink regularly.

Birdlife Khwai's birdlife is varied, like the habitats found here, though with only a narrow channel of water in the dry season, you'll usually have to search elsewhere for large numbers of the more aquatic species. That said, even in the dry season you will find storks (saddle-billed and marabou) and wattled cranes pacing around the open areas in search of fish, frogs and reptiles to eat.

Khwai does have a reputation, especially towards the end of the dry season, for having a very high density of raptors – with which I can concur. I've been closer to a martial eagle here than anywhere else, and had a lovely sighting of a marsh harrier hunting, and both bateleur eagles and giant eagle owls seem particularly common. So as you drive along, keep glancing into the sky and checking the tops of trees for the distinctive outline of a perched raptor.

Orientation It's easy to orient yourself here – although with the opening of the new transit road, most self-drivers pass through this area, glimpsing the Khwai River only from the bridge. The Okavango's waters approach from the west down the Khwai River. To the west they're flanked by floodplains, loops, meanders and lagoons, but gradually travelling east this valley narrows and concentrates the river water into a small channel.

Central to the whole area is the bridge at North Gate (now more commonly called Khwai), which spans the channel. South of this is Moremi Game Reserve, and north are the small settlement of Khwai Village, the community-controlled concessions of NG18 and NG19 (see pages 297–8), and the area's airstrip. Access to the reserve is through the village of Khwai.

Although the lodges along the river are technically inside the NG19 concession, I've included them in this chapter as they lie between Chobe National Park and North Gate, and their focus is essentially on the area that borders the Khwai River, opposite Moremi.

Getting organised There are a few small shops in Khwai Village, a welcome sight if you've been driving for several days and supplies are running low. Most sell just a few cans and soft drinks, but ask around and you might find potatoes and other fresh vegetables, and even fresh bread. There are also baskets for sale.

In the centre of the village is the office of the Khwai Development Trust (\ 686 2361–2/2385, 680 1211; e khwai@botsnet.bw; www.khwaitrust.org; ⏲ 07.30–16.30 Mon–Fri, 08.00–12.30 Sat). This is where you can book their campsites, or organise an escort to join you if you wish to explore off the main road within their concession. There's no cost for the guide (except for a tip), but the self-drive fee is P70 per person per day.

Getting there

By air Virtually all visitors to the lodges arrive at the airstrip (✈ KHWAIR 19°09.052'S, 23°47.543'E), which is close to Khwai River Lodge. This is a short hop from Kasane, Maun or any of the other airstrips in the region. There are no facilities at the airstrip; it's just a flattish section of low grass with a windsock next to it.

By road If you're driving into the Khwai area from Savuti, Xakanaxa, South Gate or Maun, see the directions given under *Getting away from North Gate*, pages 271–3, and simply follow them in reverse – or check out the individual 'getting away' sections for these places.

🏠 **Where to stay** The erstwhile three lodges here were at one time reduced to one, Khwai River Lodge, but since then accommodation in this area has burgeoned. All the lodges listed here lie on the north side of the river, overlooking Moremi Game Reserve, so are technically in the NG19 concession (see *Chapter 12*, page 297), as is the simple guesthouse. The national park's campsite is across the river.

Note that all the lodges and the campsite must be pre-booked; you are likely to be turned away if you simply roll up.

🏠 **Machaba Camp** [map 266] (10 tents) \ 686 3700, reservations \ +27 82 579 5249; e enquiries@machabacamp.com; www. machabacamp.com; ✈ MACHAB 19°07.371'S, 23°48.820'E. Delightfully positioned on a wide, shallow stretch of the river frequented by elephants & hippos, Machaba opened in March 2013 on the site of the old Machaba Camp. It's a welcoming, hospitable camp that strikes a good

balance: comfortable & attractive while still at one with the environment.

At the heart of Machaba, 2 open-fronted tented wings spread from the entrance. One is furnished with armchairs & sofas, its tables dotted with books, magazines & sweets, its walls adorned with maps. In the other, tables set with white linen are backed by a buffet. And in front, directors' chairs surround a warming firepit by the river. It's the kind of place that invites conversation.

The attention to detail runs through to the spacious tents, reached along sandy paths beneath shady trees, & accessible by those with limited mobility. Spacious & uncluttered, these are a twist on the traditional safari camp, their floors dotted with rugs, their metal basins in pairs beneath hanging mirrors, & their en-suite 'bucket' showers boasting hot running water. In 2 family tents, a central lounge separates 2 bedrooms which share a bathroom & outside shower. In-room massage is offered at extra cost by the resident therapist.

At the far end of the site is a secluded circular pool, a real draw during the heat of the day to cool off or to lounge with a book; no doubt elephants would be attracted too, should the river ever dry out! Even the curio tent (including baskets made by the staff) is appealing rather than simply functional. Game drives are the backbone of activities here, but walking safaris are an option, & mokoro trips when the water is high enough. The guiding is both good & personable. And if you'd like to see behind the scenes, just ask. *US$575/920 pp sharing/sgl Apr–Jun & mid-Dec–mid-Jan, US$765/1,225 Jul–Oct, US$415/664 Nov–mid-Dec & mid-Jan–Mar, inc FB, activities, most drinks, park fees, laundry.* ⊕ *All year.*

🏠 **Khwai River Lodge** [map 266] (15 chalets) Contact Orient-Express Safaris, page 176; ✤ KHWAIL 19°08.860'S, 23°48.019'E. I've very fond memories of the original Khwai River Lodge, with understated little bungalows amongst the leadwood trees on the edge of the floodplain. It was one of the Okavango's oldest lodges, & full of character. Now all that remains is the basic structure of its old office, which has been transformed into a gym & spa (fortunately with AC!). Around this, an opulent lodge was built in the late 1990s to the same design as that used for Savute Elephant Camp (see pages 235–6) – & with similarly excellent levels of service.

Set among neat grassy lawns, the central area is slightly raised on a timber platform & topped by an enormous thatched roof. A fireplace forms the focus of the lounge, with comfy couches & a small library. There's a bar to one side, & to the other a dining area where candles illuminate wooden tables for stylish table d'hôte dinners. In front, a wide area of decking sports a telescope for scanning the shallow river valley, while a second

sits on a raised observation deck – a good spot for a private dinner. On a lower level are a firepit, for convivial evening drinks, & a huge swimming pool. For keeping tabs on the outside world there's an internet lounge with a satellite TV & a computer for guests' use, & Wi-Fi throughout. Activities focus on early-morning & late-afternoon game drives, with night drives after dinner if requested.

The lodge's large (18m x 6m) tented rooms – far too opulent to be called tents – are built on high timber platforms under thatch, & well spread out along the river valley. From a wide veranda, with a hammock & wicker chairs overlooking the river, glass sliding doors reveal polished wooden floors, rugs & good-quality wooden furniture with muted fabrics. 4-poster-style mosquito netting surrounds the twin ¾-size beds, usually pushed together, as well as bedside tables & battery-powered lamps. Above, an AC unit fights a valiant if sometimes losing battle to keep the room cool. Separate rooms at the back of the room house the toilet & 2-person shower, while a suite also has an outside shower & private plunge pool. *US$788–1,750 pp sharing low–high season, inc FB, local drinks, activities (exc spa), laundry.* ⊕ *All year.*

🏠 **Khwai Tented Camp** [map 266] (6 tents, family cottage) Contact African Bush Camps, page 175; ✤ KHWAIT 19°09.208'S, 23°46.291'E. Set in a grove of feverberry trees some 1.5km from Khwai Village, Khwai Tented Camp opened in 2008, but moved in 2012 to this new location on a tributary of the Khwai River. Small & intimate, it combines the rustic simplicity of an old-style safari camp with a smattering of creature comforts. Its relatively small (& some very low!) walk-in tents have twin beds, solar-powered lights & a large safe, plus an en-suite flush toilet & open-air bucket shower, for which hot water is brought in on request. The tented communal area, finished with a long refectory-style table & homely seating, is a convivial place to relax over a meal or a drink – while in front the firepit on a raised deck adds another focus.

At the far end of the site, a stone-built thatched cottage sits well back from the river, with plenty of space for children to play in the daytime (always remembering that the camp is unfenced, & wild animals do wander through). Along 2 sides is a large shaded deck with a dining table & chairs & a braai area, so self-catering could be an option – though note that there's no fridge. Inside is effectively one large room, with a curtain separating the living/kitchen area, which incorporates twin beds, from a dbl bed & the bathroom (with bath, basin, flush toilet & shower).

Activities are fairly flexible, from walking safaris & 4x4 game drives (day & night), to mokoro trips when the water is high enough, & visits to Khwai Village, which benefits from the camp in many ways. Most visitors arrive by air, self-drivers are welcome on the same basis – which includes doing all activities with the camp's staff. *US$495–630 inc FB, local drinks & activities. No children under 7 except in family cottage. ⊕ All year.*

⌂ **Sango Safari Camp** [map 266]
(6 tents) Contact Bush Ways Safaris, page 177; e reservations@sangosafaricamp.com; www. sangosafaricamp.com; ⊕ SANGO 19°09.826'S, 23°45.771'E. Opened in 2010, Sango is that rare find: an old-fashioned camp that focuses on safaris rather than frills. It's set back from a shallow section of the river, just a short drive from Khwai Village. Self-drivers (who must pre-book all meals & activities), should turn off the road almost opposite KLLK Guesthouse (⊕ 19°09.578'S, 23°45.594'E), from where a track leads to the camp.

Colourful cushions enliven the airy mess tent, which is open to the view. Guests stay in traditional tents, set on low varnished wooden decks with a small veranda, & well spread out along sandy paths. Each has neat twin beds with bedside tables & lights surrounded by mosquito netting, & an en-suite toilet & outside bucket shower. Day & night game drives are at the heart of Sango's activities, but there are also nature walks with an armed guide, & mokoro trips on a tributary of the Khwai when water levels permit. Baskets woven in the village are on sale, & village tours may include the opportunity to watch the weavers at work. *US$430–650 pp sharing/sgl Apr–Jun & Nov, US$540–760 Jul–Oct, US$295 pp Dec–Mar (US$395 20 Dec–4 Jan), inc FB, activities, most drinks, park fees, laundry; exc transfers. Self-drive rates available; exc activities, park fees. ⊕ All year.*

⌂ **KLLK Guesthouse** [map 266] (4 chalets) m 7350 8245; e kllkguesthouse@gmail.com. On the edge of Khwai Village as you're coming in from Mababe, this simple but friendly guesthouse is owned by Constance Mpeya. Beautifully painted

colourful murals adorn the front of each of its en-suite chalets; we particularly liked the *trompe l'oeil* effect of one painted as a wooden kraal. Meals can be arranged with advance notice. *P300 pp.*

⋏ **Khwai (North Gate) Campsite** [map 266] (10 pitches) ☎ 683 0082; contact SKL, page 174; ⊕ NOGATE 19°10.394'S, 23°45.092'E. Khwai is situated on a lovely site to the south of the Khwai River, immediately on your left as you enter Moremi at North Gate. Recently privatised (& with a hefty resultant price hike), its pitches are dotted amidst tall woodlands, some along the river, where fireflies put on a mesmerising display as night falls, & the grunts of hippos form the bass notes to the general cacophony from baboons & francolins. There are good, clean ablution facilities, & each site has a braai stand of some description with a firepit & waste bin. In the past, monkeys here could be a menace, openly stealing from our vehicle as we stood close by, though it was hard not to laugh at their brazen theft.

Look out for especially impressive specimens of sickle-leaved albizia (*Albizia harveyi*). Their fine leaves & flattened seedpods might look like acacias, but trees of the Albizia family don't have thorns. You'll also find a few huge sycamore figs (*Ficus sycomorus*), easily spotted because of their yellow-orange bark & a tendency for parts of their wide trunks to form buttresses. Old Africa hands will avoid camping directly under a fig tree, though, as their fruits are sought after by everything from baboons & bats to elephants – any of which can make for a messy tent in the morning, & a very disturbed night's sleep. *US$50 pp, exc bed levy & park fees. ⊕ All year.*

⋏ **Magotho Campsite** [map 266] (10 pitches) Contact Khwai Development Trust, page 268. Reached from a turning south off the main transit road between Mababe & North Gate (at ⊕ MAGOTO 19°05.596'S, 23°52.284'E), these 2 campsites – Magotho 1 & 2 (sometimes spelled Mogotho) – are set beneath mature camelthorn trees. Neither has any facilities at all, so you will need to bring everything with you, including all water, & take everything out. Note that the trust's other 2 campsites, Sable Alley & Matswere, are reserved for operators & not open to the public. *P240 pp. ⊕ All year.*

What to see and do Wherever you stay, however you travel, your activities during the day will be almost exclusively game drives, as walking and night drives are forbidden by park rules, and the Khwai is too shallow and narrow for safe boating.

Game-viewing roads and loops spread out on both sides of North Gate, to the west and east. Most stick close to the Khwai River, either exploring the river's floodplain or the adjacent band of riverine forest. You'll need Veronica Roodt's map of Moremi (see page 100) to get the best from these, as they're not shown on the main map of Botswana.

One particularly attractive loop, almost 14km west of North Gate and signposted 'Hippo Pool', leads to a large, shallow lake where hippos wallow in the permanent water. At one end of the pool is a tall bird hide, giving the opportunity to leave the vehicle and spend unlimited time in the heat of the day observing the waterbirds that congregate here, including Egyptian and spur-winged geese, knob-billed and white-faced ducks and woolly-necked storks. (Quite unexpectedly, a toilet has been built at the base of the hide, which suggests that this is well frequented by safari groups.)

If you're visiting in the wet season, then consider taking one of the long drives that loop away from the river east of North Gate – like Sepanyana Road. These give you access to some of the pans in the mopane area, which might prove more productive for game at that time.

Getting away from North Gate

Driving from North Gate (Khwai) to Savuti, Chobe NP This route used to be very confusing, but the opening of a new gravel road running parallel to the old sand tracks near the Khwai River has simplified it considerably. On the downside, the route no longer takes you along the stunningly beautiful Khwai River, which is now largely the preserve of the lodges dotted along its banks (see pages 268–9).

From the park entrance at North Gate (⊕ NOGATE 19°10.394'S, 23°45.092'E), cross the pole bridge over the Khwai River, and follow the road through Khwai Village, then over (or around) another small river to a new steel bridge (⊕ STEELB 19°07.564'S, 23°45.840'E). A little over 2km from here, the road turns sharply to the right, then continues uninterrupted all the way to Mababe Village. For the Mababe Gate into Chobe National Park, turn left about 35.5km from North Gate (⊕ MABTO 19°09.643'S, 23°57.932'E), then follow that road for about 7.5km. At the gate, stop and sign in before continuing roughly north towards Savuti.

About 20km north of the Mababe Gate, the road splits. Both forks lead to Savuti. The right fork is the **marsh road**, which is more scenic, but can be very rutted and bumpy during the dry season, with great views of the marsh. It is certainly going to be the worse of the two during the rainy season, when you'd be wise to take the left fork, the more direct if less interesting, **sand-ridge road**. This stays closer to the Magwikhwe Sand Ridge, climbing on to it at one point.

After about 37km on the sand-ridge road, or 44km on the marsh road, these routes converge (⊕ MARSAN 18°36.078'S, 24°03.678'E) beside Leopard Hill Rock, which is about 5km south of the heart of Savuti.

Driving from North Gate (Khwai) to Xakanaxa This route is really very straightforward – although the introduction of a new 'dry' route to avoid the oft-flooded sections on the old road has changed things a little in recent years. Start from the park's entrance at North Gate and follow the road southwest towards South Gate for about 1km. Here you'll find a substantial right turn signposted to Xakanaxa, heading in a more westerly direction. Following this for about 44km would lead straight to Xakanaxa, mainly through old, established mopane woodlands. This route, however, has been frequently closed since the unusually high floods of 2009, so if you're planning to take it, do ask advice from the staff at the gate before you set off.

11

Fortunately there is now a more circuitous but considerably more predictable route that bears away from the original one at ⊕ XADRY1 19°12.944'S, 23°37.087'E, continuing southwest for 12km before joining up with the main route from South Gate at ⊕ XADRY2 19°14.573'S, 23°31.234'E. From here, it's a further 11km or so northwest to the new Xakanaxa Gate (⊕ XAKGT 19°11.865'S, 23°25.865'E). Drivers with reservations at the campsite or one of the lodges should sign in here before proceeding, but if you're camping at Third Bridge, their paperwork is handled at the campsite.

The real joy of this journey – and especially along the old route – comes from the numerous side-loops which detour to the right of the road. If you feel lost, remember that heading west and south will generally keep you going in the right direction. Heading north will go deeper into the detours and usually bring you back to the Khwai River.

Driving from North Gate to South Gate and Maun This is a very straight-forward route, on a very straight road. From North Gate's campsite you simply follow a substantial track for about 30km, which heads southwest, directly towards South Gate (⊕ SOGATE 19°25.548'S, 23°38.733'E).

To continue to Maun, see *Driving from South Gate to Maun*, page 282. Alternatively, and thus avoiding park fees, you could follow the first part of the instructions under *Driving from North Gate (Khwai) to Savuti, Chobe NP*, page

NEGOTIATING THE ROADS AROUND XAKANAXA

While the new road has done much to alleviate the problems of getting from North Gate to Xakanaxa, tracks along the old route, and indeed off road, can get pretty waterlogged. When I drove this route in 1999, most of the loops were fine. A few – often those marked as 'seasonal roads' on Veronica Roodt's map of Moremi – were tricky and required one to cross quite deep water in the vehicle. The scenery on the road around Qua Lediba (*lediba* is the local word for 'lagoon'), particularly looking out west towards the Xuku floodplain, was very beautiful as we meandered between the dappled light of the forest and open lagoons.

However, west of Qua Lediba, the road became progressively more difficult, with deeper and deeper stretches of water to cross. Several times we forded water across the road, until one large pool stopped us. Forest to the left and lagoon to the right. There was no easy way around. The track was flat sand; solid not slippery. Vehicle tracks had been this way recently – a good sign.

As we considered our next move, two large trucks, run by a mobile-safari operator, approached and drove across, showing us the depth; we crossed safely. We avoided the next pool, but in a third the vehicle lurched alarmingly to the right – my passenger falling across me as I drove. The Land Rover didn't blink though and pulled us through. Nerve-racking when alone, such puddles are more fun with a party of two vehicles, as then one can pull the other out of difficulty if necessary.

Back on the main road, heading west we found a drift, where the road had been washed away. Various alternatives circled off left, finding shallower, but more slippery, places to cross. The water at the main road was deeper, but the substrate was more solid. On the whole, a safer bet.

271. Instead of turning off for the Mababe Gate, continue on the gravel road as far as Mababe Village, where you turn south on to the road to Sankuyo, Shorobe and ultimately to Maun.

TIP OF THE TONGUE: XAKANAXA AND BEYOND One corner of the Mopane Tongue's triangular peninsula juts towards the centre of Moremi, and at the end of the tip is Xakanaxa Lagoon. Beyond it, on three sides, is the Delta's maze of channels, floodplains, lagoons and islands. A few of the larger, closer islands, such as Goaxhlo and the large Mboma Island, are accessible via simple pole bridges. Beyond this, Moremi becomes inaccessible without a boat: that's the realm of the small, fly-in safari camps.

The patchwork of environments found here is typical of the inner reaches of the Delta. It's also phenomenally beautiful, and one of the most reliably good areas for wildlife on the subcontinent. Expect extraordinary densities of game and birdlife and, as it's been protected for years, the animals are generally very relaxed.

For the self-driving visitor, the game and scenery here are as good as they get in Botswana – don't miss this area.

Flora and fauna highlights Picking out the wildlife highlights for an area like this, and trying to point out what's special, is virtually impossible. There's usually something special around every corner. It's not that you'll see different things here than you will elsewhere in Moremi, or even Botswana; it's just that you'll see them all in a very small area.

Orientation The main route from North Gate to Xakanaxa roughly follows the northern edge of the Mopane Tongue. Similarly, the main road from South Gate to Third Bridge roughly follows the southern edge of the Tongue. This section covers the area around and between Xakanaxa and Third Bridge.

In Veronica Roodt's map of Moremi (see page 100) there are some detailed insets of the road layouts around this area, so make sure that you buy a copy of this before you get here. You'll also find plenty of useful references and background information on the reverse of the map.

Getting there
By air Virtually all lodge visitors arrive and leave via Xakanaxa airstrip, which is easily linked with any of the other airstrips in the region.

By road For details of self-drive access, see *Driving from South Gate (Maqwee) to Xakanaxa* (pages 271–2) and *Driving from North Gate (Khwai) to Xakanaxa* (page 282).

Where to stay
There are three camps and one campsite, all clustered around the Xakanaxa Lagoon, a huge open lagoon which is fed by the Moanachira River. This can be traced upstream, passing close to Camp Okavango, Shinde and Xugana, allowing these isolated water-based camps to be used as 'satellites' for sojourns of a few days into the Delta, linked by a boat journey of a few hours. A second campsite lies a little further away, at Third Bridge. All these options must be pre-booked; you cannot just turn up, even at the campsites.

Note that because of the particularly high game densities here, and the relaxed, fearless nature of the animals, even walking around within camp can be an experience at times. Lion, hyena, leopard, buffalo, wild dogs and elephants all

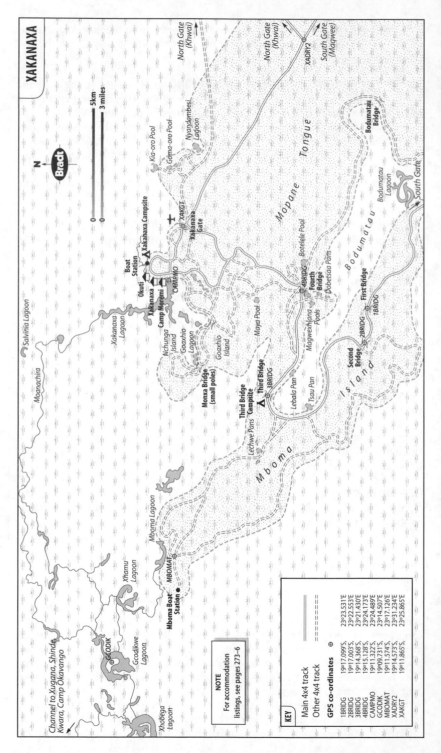

XAKANAXA

NOTE

For accommodation
listings, see pages 273–6

KEY

| Main 4x4 track | ———— |
| Other 4x4 track | ==== |

GPS co-ordinates ⊕

1BRIDG	19°17.099'S,	23°33.531'E
2BRIDG	19°17.003'S,	23°22.553'E
3BRIDG	19°14.368'S,	23°21.430'E
4BRIDG	19°15.128'S,	23°24.173'E
CAMPMO	19°11.322'S,	23°24.489'E
GCODIK	19°09.731'S,	23°14.507'E
MBOMAT	19°11.574'S,	23°17.126'E
XADRY2	19°14.573'S,	23°31.234'E
XAKGT	19°11.865'S,	23°25.865'E

Channel to Xugana, Shinde,
Kwara, Camp Okavango

5km

3 miles

N Bradt

North Gate (Khwai)

North Gate (Khwai)

South Gate (Maqwee)

XADRY2

Mopane Tongue

Nyandambesi Lagoon

Goma-oro Pool

Kia-oro Pool

Xakanaxa Campsite

Xakanaxa Gate

XAKGT

Boat Station

Okuti

Xakanaxa Camp Moremi

CAMPMO

Botelele Pool

4BRIDG

Fourth Bridge

Dobetsaa Pans

Nchunga Island

Goaxhio Lagoon

Goaxhio Island

Maya Pool

Monxa Bridge (small poles)

Magwekhana Pools

3BRIDG

Third Bridge

Third Bridge Campsite

Lebala Pan

Tsau Pan

2BRIDG

Second Bridge

First Bridge

1BRIDG

Bodumatau Bridge

Bodumatau Lagoon

Bodumatau

Island

South Gate

Lechwe Pans

Mboma

Salvinia Lagoon

Moanachira

Xakanaxa Lagoon

Mboma Lagoon

Xhamu Lagoon

Gcodikwe Lagoon

Gcodik

Xhobega Lagoon

MBOMAT

MBOMAT

Mboma Boat Station

wander through the camps and campsites very frequently – so be careful when you are walking around, especially after dark.

⌂ **Camp Moremi** [map 274] (11 tents) Contact Desert & Delta Safaris, page 176; ✪ CAMPM 19°11.322'S, 23°24.489'E. The established & well-kept Camp Moremi is the furthest southwest of the 3 camps here, set under huge old trees where natural papyrus & ferns nod over lawns cropped short by hippos. A lot of other animals venture into camp, too, though elephants are kept at bay by discreet strands of electrified wire around the perimeter.

A large, square wooden construction, somewhat akin to a treehouse, comprises the camp's central area, cooled by punkah-punkah fans & partially open to the breeze. Clever use of space upstairs has created a dining area, some comfy sofas & a small library, as well as a rather modern bar. Beneath is a good curio shop, & nearby a shaded boma hosts b/fast, brunch & high tea. A high observation platform affords a super view over the lagoon. Tucked to one side is a small pool raised up on a wooden deck, with umbrella-shaded sunbeds.

The camp's rooms, refurbished in 2012, feel almost like suites. Raised up on teak platforms, each has a proper door (which must be kept locked because of kleptomaniac monkeys & baboons) that opens into a small hall with a writing desk. To one side is a modern tiled bathroom with flush toilet & glass-screened shower; to the other, a tented bedroom with dbl or twin beds & wooden furniture on sisal matting, as well as a table-top fan & a tea station. From here, glass doors slide to reveal a deck with chairs overlooking the bush. Raised up quite high at the end of the camp, the 'honeymoon' suite is imaginatively built around the 5 trunks of a marvellous old jackalberry tree.

Activities concentrate on morning & afternoon game drives, & motorboat trips around the lagoons & waterways. As Camp Okavango & Xugana (pages 303–5) are owned by the same company, it's a good idea to combine several nights at one of these with Camp Moremi (or Xakanaxa, below), sticking to game drives here, & switching to motorboat & mokoro trips there. *US$495 pp Jan–Mar & Dec, US$573 pp Apr–Jun & Nov, US$873/1,135 pp sharing/sgl Jul–Oct, fully inc.* ☺ *Closed mid-Jan–mid-Feb.*

⌂ **Xakanaxa** [map 274] (12 tents) Contact Desert & Delta Safaris, page 176; www.xakanaxa-

camp.com; ✪ XAKANA 19°10.973'S, 23°24.567'E. Less than 1km northeast of Camp Moremi, Xakanaxa was for years run by Bob & Flo Flaxman, & latterly by Tim & Lettie Letlhakane, who remain in charge under new owners Desert & Delta. It's a classic old camp, solidly built among natural vegetation overlooking the lagoon, & with plenty of tree shade. Lighting is largely provided by candles & paraffin storm lanterns (but there's a generator in the day, & batteries can be charged.)

Refurbishment in 2014 is not expected to impact on Xakanaxa's intrinsic character. The camp's raised, thatched dining area is memorable for a long, 18-seater table, made from reclaimed old railway sleepers, & lit by candlelight from a handmade wrought-iron candelabra. There's a separate lounge/bar, a circular area built out over the water with a central fire, & another apron with a plunge pool. A second, much larger & more secluded pool nestles behind the curio shop.

Meru-style tents stand on wooden decks, with verandas facing the lagoon & solid wooden dbl or twin beds, where you'll find a carefully chosen reference book. At the back, screened by reeds, are a hot shower, handbasin & flush toilet. The whole is covered by a large canvas roof with an innovative 'irrigation' system designed to cool the air inside.

The camp is surrounded by a high, but discreet, 3-strand electric fence, designed purely to keep out elephants, which can be destructive to the trees as well as dangerous. Xakanaxa is better than most camps in Botswana at catering for families & children, & the whole site is wheelchair accessible. Activities focus on 4x4 game drives & boat trips on to the lagoon, as well as short mokoro excursions from one of the islands. *US$495 pp Jan–Mar & Dec, US$573 pp Apr–Jun & Nov, US$873/1,135 pp sharing/sgl Jul–Oct, fully inc.* ☺ *All year.*

⌂ **Okuti** [map 274] (7 rooms) Contact Ker & Downey Botswana, page 176. Sandwiched between Xakanaxa & the boat station, Okuti occupies quite a tight spot overlooking the lagoon, among shady trees. Although opened in the early 1980s, it was completely rebuilt in 2007. The result is something of a triumph of design over space – all vaulted ceilings & soft curves, with walls daubed a rich earthy red. The scene is set by a domed entrance, opening on to a series of raised wooden decks, linked by walkways. In the centre, the lounge, bar & library with an extensive circular deck are partially open to the lagoon, under a high roof that has something of the feel of an enormous wagon. From here, the walkways are punctuated with reed-lined 'tunnels', each opening to reveal a huge en-suite bedroom, & on through mesh sliding doors to a private veranda over the lagoon – & an outdoor shower. In 2 family chalets, the bathroom is shared by 2 bedrooms, while the honeymoon suite boasts an outdoor bath. A curio shop offers locally made baskets, & below it all is a pool, surrounded by rough wooden stakes in the style of a rural *kraal*. Activities concentrate on 4x4 game drives & motorboat trips on the lagoon. *US$495 pp Jan, Mar & Dec, US$666 Apr–Jun & Nov; US$850/1,088 pp sharing/sgl Jul–Oct, inc FB, local drinks, activities, laundry; exc transfers.* ☺ *Mar–early Jan.*

⋏ Xakanaxa Campsite [map 274] (8 pitches) Contact Kwalate Safaris, page 174; ✪ XAKCMP 19°11.026'S, 23°24.986'E. Lying to the east of Okuti, Xakanaxa Campsite stretches along this tip of the Mopane Tongue, almost adjacent to Xakanaxa Boat Station. On arrival, campers should sign in at the smart new Xakanaxa Gate (✪ XAKGT 19°11.865'S, 23°25.865'E) which is 3km southeast of the campsite. The site's roughly marked pitches, some only just off the dirt road (though there's no traffic to speak of), blend into one long camping area lining the river. There's a new ablution block which is reasonably well maintained, & water taps are dotted around the site, with a motley selection of tables, benches & braai stands of varying quality.

I've always loved these sites, & on my last visit one September the purple hanging flowers of the Kalahari appleleaf (*Lonchocarpus nelsii*) were in full force, reminding me of small jacaranda trees. However, as with Third Bridge, this is an area of particularly dense game, so always remain vigilant as you move about the campsite, making sure that you keep your eyes open for animals at all times. *US$40 pp, exc park fees, bed levy.* ☺ *All year.*

⋏ Third Bridge Campsite [map 274] (10 pitches, 4 en-suite tents) Contact Xomae

Group, page 174; ✪ 3BRIDG 19°14.368'S, 23°21.430'E. Third Bridge is about 8km in a straight line from Xakanaxa Campsite, although by road it's about 18km, depending on the route used. Despite their relative proximity, if you're camping in the area for 4–5 nights, then ideally try to split your time between the 2 sites. Third Bridge is well located for visiting Mboma Island, & is a more open site, with plenty of tree shade. Sadly, though, with privatisation its inherent character as a wilderness destination has been compromised. It used to be my favourite site in Moremi; now – with an ostentatious new gate to greet you on the 'dry' route from Xakanaxa, a clutch of staff houses & 2 large ablution blocks – it's lost its old allure.

That said, the old pole bridge has missed out on the upgrade, & is slowly sinking into the mud. You'll see that the water's crystal-clear as it passes over the sandy bottom of the narrow waterway, & people used to bathe here often, but despite the apparently impenetrable stands of papyrus, there have been regular attacks by crocodiles; hence the plethora of notices warning you against swimming.

The site itself is sprawling, with pitches spread out across 2 almost distinct areas. It's notable for some attractive large feverberry trees (*Croton megalobotrys*) & a particularly fine sausage tree (*Kigelia africana*). Third Bridge is also well known for a troop of very cheeky baboons, who have developed stealing food into a form of sport – & they usually win. So what's good practice anywhere is absolutely vital here: lock everything away when you're not using it, & make sure any rubbish is securely fastened in the cage provided. When we last stayed, there wasn't a baboon in sight, but don't bank on it.

Cold drinks can be bought here (as can baskets), but otherwise you'll need to be fully equipped, including with firewood. Motorboat (*P504/hr for 4 people*) & mokoro (*P400/2 people*) trips can be organised – though by comparison with the boat station at Mboma, the mokoro rates seem very high. *Camping P300 pp, tent P550/770 pp sharing/sgl, all exc park fees & bed levy.* ☺ *All year.*

What to see and do Until recently, self-drive visitors here conducted their own game drives, or perhaps took a boat trip for a few hours from one of the lodges. Now, more organised water activities are available for independent visitors too.

Self-drive There's a lot of exploring to do in this area, which is veined with game-viewing loops and tracks. So take your time – and be aware that after heavy flooding some previously navigable tracks might be impassable. Drive around slowly, and stop frequently. There are a number of specific areas that you might aim for, or just end up at.

Floodplain roads The network of tracks to the west of the main track between Xakanaxa and Third Bridge is probably the most rewarding in Moremi for game. Many are also very beautiful, lined with glassy pools that attract considerable numbers of both game and birdlife.

Goaxhlo Island and Pan Also known as Dead Tree Island, you'll recognise it by the number of skeletal trees that surround the pan of open water. Like those at Savuti, these were killed by drowning – when the channels changed and inundated the area. Most are mopane trees, and because of their resistance to termites, and semi-submerged state, they're decomposing very, very slowly indeed. This is quite an eerie sight, and photographers will find plenty to inspire them, especially if there are any animals present. Keep a particular look-out for the graceful pink spoonbills which breed here.

Dobetsaa Pans Take a left in a southerly direction, perhaps 1km after crossing Fourth Bridge on the way to Third Bridge, and you'll find a short loop leading down past a few very scenic pans. Veronica Roodt comments that this is 'one of the few places in Moremi where the African skimmer can be seen'. But even without the skimmers it's a good birdwatching spot with some very open pans.

Mboma Island West of Third Bridge is a large, long island, circled by a loop road which stretches for about 50km around it. There's a spur to this at the north end, and a short cut back to Third Bridge halfway round. It's worth spending a day here, as Mboma's environments are varied and beautiful, though different from the floodplain loops nearer to Xakanaxa. I've had great sightings of cheetah on the northern side of the island, and the south is said to be a popular haunt of buffalo herds.

Boat trips I'd strongly recommend that you take at least one trip by boat or mokoro on to the lagoons and waterways of Moremi. It's certainly worth the cost, unless you're due to be going on to a camp with water-based activities. But remember that boat fuel is costly to buy and transport, and that you're in a very remote location, so these trips aren't cheap.

Two boat stations in the immediate vicinity hold the exclusive rights to take boats on to the lagoon, although effectively there are three operators involved. This exclusivity is in part to help prevent the spread of *Salvinia molesta*, or Kariba weed, an invasive plant that is posing a serious threat to Botswana's waterways. You'll need a hat, suncream and drinks, but little else except, of course, a camera. It is reasonably safe to leave a vehicle parked at either place.

All the drivers are qualified guides, in as much as they can name the various birds and plants that you'll see, but their understanding of what you want may not tie up with yours. For this reason, do explain your objectives clearly before you set out, or you may find yourself being driven at breakneck speed from one side of the lagoon to the other, watching a hastily named bird rise up in fright at the approaching roar of the engine, or veering away from the occasional pod of hippo. And do ask questions – your driver may well know the answers.

There's little or no shade on most of the boats, so the best times to venture on to the lagoon are early morning, or in late afternoon, culminating in sunset over the lake. A couple of hours is really the ideal; less than that and it'll seem rushed so you'll miss out on the gentle beauty of the place. In theory there's no need to book, but the number of boats is limited so it makes sense to give them advance warning – and at Mboma, if the polers are running a camping trip, there may be no-one available to take day visitors out on a mokoro.

Xakanaxa Boat Station [map 274] Ngami Marine; ✆ 686 0364; e nm@info.bw; ⊕ dawn– dusk; ✪ XAKABT 19°13.98'S, 23°22.247'E. Literally adjacent to the campsite at Xakanaxa, this enterprise – signposted as Okavango Boating – offers trips on to the lagoon from 4 boats, including a dbl decker (P666/US$76 per hr for up to 16 people), a 12-seater (P572/hr) & an 8-seater (P520/hr). If you ask around at the campsite, you may well find someone to share a boat, thus cutting costs.

A little further along the lagoon, east of the campsite, a second outfit (*Impala Tours & Safaris;* ✆ *686 3440;* m *7233 5544;* e *impalatours@ botsnet.bw; www.impalatoursafaris.com*) offers similar trips but with a smaller range of boats, all at P540 (US$62)/hr.

Mboma Boat Station [map 274] Contact Kgori Safaris, page 176. The more established of Moremi's boat stations is at the far northwest tip

of Mboma Island, about 1hr's drive (15km) from Third Bridge, or 3hrs (63km) from South Gate. The turn-off from the main loop road is at ✪ MBOMAT 19°1.574'S, 23°17.126'E, with the station about 1.5km west of there.

A 9-seater motorboat & driver can be hired for P935/US$107 per hr, or P3,890/US$447 for a full day. For a more leisurely trip, you can go out on a mokoro with an experienced poler (P290/US$33 per hr for 2 people, or P1,190/US$137 per day. Cold drinks, including water & beer, are available here but nothing else.

The longer trips usually leave at around 08.00 & return at about 15.00, sometimes stopping for lunch (bring your own) on one of the islands on the lagoon. With advance notice you can arrange to stay overnight on one of the islands – either catering for yourself or with them providing all the food & equipment.

Overnight camping trips Camping one one of the islands can be organised in advance through Kgori Safaris, who own Mboma Boat Station, or at Xakanaxa Boat Station to three nearby islands: Gcodikwe 1, Gcodikwe 2 and Xhobega. These are in the area of the Gcodikwe and Xhobega lagoons, just northwest of Mboma Island; see below for a description of the Gcodikwe Lagoon with its heronries. Transport is either by motorboat or – from Mboma – by mokoro; if you're going from Xakanaxa, expect the boat trip to take around 1½ hours. Such trips can be fully catered (expect to pay around P1,550 per person/night including boat transfer), or you can bring in all your own equipment and food.

Gcodikwe Lagoon Gcodikwe Lagoon (✪ GCODIK 19°09.731'S, 23°14.507'E) is one of the Okavango's largest and most famous lagoons. Reachable only by boat, it is a huge, almost circular oxbow lagoon that has several large tree-islands in it. Xakanaxa is 18km away, or about 90 minutes by boat. It is perhaps best visited from one of the lodges just outside of the park, the best being Kwara (6km northeast), Shinde (11km northwest) or Camp Okavango (15km west) – though you can double all these 'straight-line' distances to allow for meandering through the waterways.

The 'islands' are made up mainly of water-fig trees and a little papyrus growing in shallow water. Over the millennia these have accumulated a mass of bird guano and detritus under them to raise their levels and grow. Now they're large, but still isolated from any predators that are not aquatic. Hence they've become a vital breeding ground for the Okavango's waterbirds. That said, there is evidence that the heronry is much smaller than it used to be. One reason for this is considered to be elephant, which come here to feed in the early summer, which causes considerable disruption to the breeding birds.

Traditionally, thousands of birds have come to this heronry to breed, including herons, egrets, storks, ibises, cormorants and many others. Most of the nest-building activity starts around August, and breeding seems to be timed so that the chicks hatch around October and November, when water levels are low and thus the birds find fish easier to catch. Certainly when I last visited in late February, there were only a few birds around.

Watch carefully and you'll see that the larger, more robust species like marabou and yellow-billed storks tend to nest in the canopy of the trees, while the smaller, more vulnerable species can be found within the trees. Also keep an eye out for water snakes and leguvaans, which come here in search of chicks.

Getting away from the Mopane Tongue

Driving from Xakanaxa to North Gate (Khwai) It's about 44km to drive directly from Xakanaxa to North Gate; just head east from the Xakanaxa Gate (⊕ XAKGT 19°11.865'S, 23°25.865'E). However, ask advice from the camp's office before you set off as if this road is blocked by high water levels, you will need to take the 'dry' route to the south. For details, see pages 271–2.

Driving from Xakanaxa to South Gate (Maqwee) Many would travel from Xakanaxa to South Gate via Third Bridge, using the route described in the next section, as the scenery's more varied and, in the dry season, I'd expect the game to be better – especially around the Mboma Island area.

However, the most direct route is along a track that heads southeast from near the western end of Xakanaxa's airstrip, taking about 42km to reach South Gate. The route is generally good, even when it's wet, apart from a number of clay pans which can be sticky.

Driving from Third Bridge to South Gate (Maqwee) I always find the tracks around Mboma Island confusing, but to reach South Gate you set off west on to Mboma Island from Third Bridge. Keep bearing left when the road forks and after 3–4km you'll be travelling south. The road then bends east, south and even west until you reach another pole bridge which is known, rather unimaginatively, as Second Bridge (⊕ 2BRIDG 19°17.003'S, 23°22.553'E).

Crossing this, you'll then head southeast towards another pole bridge referred to as (surprise!) First Bridge (⊕ 1BRIDG 19°17.099'S, 23°23.531'E). From here it's an uncomplicated drive southeast to South Gate, with most of the trip through mopane woodlands – which in turn conceal any number of elephants.

If time is on your side, consider a detour off the main track. There's a short, easy loop off to the south of the road, about 12km before the gate; it's clearly marked on Veronica Roodt's map of Moremi (page 100). Characterised by flat, open plains, dotted with anthills and small pans, this is a great place to look out for storks, with large numbers of marabou in particular when we visited at the end of the dry season. Don't worry if you miss the connection with the main road at the picturesque Xini Lagoon, which isn't at all clear on the ground when it's dry; the track links up almost seamlessly with the main road to South Gate, and the woodland landscape, just a couple of kilometres further on.

Very close to here, at ⊕ MOGTO 19°23.594'S, 23°32.972'E, is a turning towards a new and promising series of tracks, signposted to Mogogelo Hippo Pool and Black Pools. The loops here are clearly marked, running around and across floodplains,

11

shallow pans and areas of woodland. An added and unexpected bonus in the heat of the day is a picnic site (⊕ MOGPIC 19°28.811'S, 23°32.155'E), with benches and tables set out in a beautiful shady grove of trees looking out onto a floodplain. If exploring at the end of the dry season, when most of the pools had dried up, was somewhat disappointing, Veronica Roodt claims that the area supports 'vast numbers of game'. Certainly all the signs were there, imprinted in the mud across numerous shallow depressions – and at the neighbouring Xini Lagoon, the scene was like something out of a picture book of African wildlife. If you follow the loops in an easterly direction, you can rejoin the main track about 4km west of South Gate at ⊕ MOGSGT 19°25.412'S, 23°36.755'E.

SOUTH GATE (MAQWEE) South Gate (⊕ SOGATE 19°25.548'S, 23°38.733'E), also known as Maqwee Gate, is usually treated as a transit stop by most visitors as it's in the midst of fairly unexciting mopane forest, with a small campsite sheltered among the trees.

Having described it as unexciting, this may just be my failure to really get to know the area well. I've only stayed here for three individual nights, one during each of three different trips (always at the start or the end of a trip across Chobe and Moremi). However on one of those occasions, just as I was getting up, about half a dozen wild dogs gently jogged through the camp and into the forest. I don't think our roof tent has ever been packed away so rapidly – but try as we might, tracking them was a waste of time, with park rules forbidding off-road driving in Moremi!

On another trip I found a whole pack of wild dogs lounging on the road a few kilometres south of South Gate, in the NG33/34 concession area. They posed for photographs just a few metres from my vehicle for 20 minutes or so – totally unconcerned with our presence. So perhaps, especially in the earlier months of the year, South Gate warrants a closer look and more than just an overnight stop.

Flora and fauna highlights

Flora Around South Gate the trees are almost all mopane (*Colophospermum mopane*), with their distinctive butterfly-shaped leaves. Tall, undamaged specimens can reach 18m in height, when they're known as 'cathedral' mopane for their gracefully arching branches. In neighbouring areas, where the nutrients are not as plentiful or the trees have been damaged by elephants, this same species grows much lower – and is known as 'stunted mopane'. In both you'll find their leaves hanging down and tending to fold together during the heat of the day, leaving little shade underneath.

This tremendously successful tree is one of the commonest species in the hot, dry areas of the subcontinent. It's notable for its tolerance of poorly drained, alkaline soils – and often occurs in areas where there's a lot of clay. Driving in mopane country during the rainy season usually involves negotiating lots of sticky, clay-filled mud-holes.

For the camper, the mopane wood is a dark-reddish colour, hard, heavy and termite-resistant. Thus even long-dead pieces won't have been completely eaten by termites. It burns exceedingly well, smelling sweetly and producing lots of heat. You're no longer allowed collect firewood in Moremi, but it's worth seeking out outside the park. (Turn each piece over, looking under it carefully for snakes and scorpions, before picking it up.)

Fauna With relatively dense forests this area can seem devoid of wildlife. But don't be mistaken; it isn't. Because the soil in mopane forest areas is often very poorly drained, it's dotted with small pans – temporary shallow ponds – during and shortly after the rains. This allows most of the big-game species to leave the over-populated areas beside the watercourses and disappear into these huge areas of forests.

Elephant, zebra, impala, kudu, tsessebe, common duiker, bushbuck, steenbok, eland, roan warthog, baboon and vervet monkey can all be found here, as can lion, leopard, cheetah, spotted hyena, wild dog and many of the smaller mammals. But you will have to look much harder here for them than on the open floodplains and beside the watercourses where they congregate during the dry season.

What you are guaranteed to see at any time of year are lots of bush squirrels (*Paraxerus cepapi*), which are so common in mopane woodlands that they're often known as 'mopane squirrels'. See *Appendix 1, Wildlife guide*, page 500, for more details.

Birdlife The high density of small rodents in mopane woodlands, especially bush squirrels, means that it's a good place for small raptors which hunt from perches (rather than the air). These include barn owls, smaller hawks and kestrels, and even martial eagles.

Meanwhile two species here are very common. The small, black-and-white Arnot's chat appears in pairs or small groups, often hopping about the ground or lower branches in search of small insects – memorably described by a friend on first sight as 'little flying zebras'. There's also the red-billed hornbill, which seems to be everywhere with its heavy flap flap-flap ... glide... flap-flap-flap ... glide ... style of flight. Remember Rowan Atkinson's performance as the hornbill in Walt Disney's *The Lion King* and you'll never be able to watch one again without smiling.

Orientation Navigating around South Gate is very straightforward, with just five clear roads: one to Maun via the veterinary checkpoint; another to North Gate; one to Third Bridge, which stays close to the southern side of the Mopane Tongue; and a fourth to Xakanaxa which cuts through the heart of the Tongue. The fifth, now closed to self drivers, leads to Santawani Lodge (see *Chapter 12*, page 351). There are now several game-drive loops quite close to the gate in Moremi; for details, see *Driving from Third Bridge to South Gate (Maqwee)*, page 279.

Getting there For directions to South Gate, see *Driving from Xakanaxa to South Gate (Maqwee)*, *Driving from North Gate to South Gate and Maun* and *Driving from Third Bridge to South Gate (Maqwee)* on pages 279, 272 and 279.

Where to stay There's only one place to stay:

⚐ South Gate (Maqwee) Campsite [map 207] (10 pitches) Contact Kwalate Safaris, page 174. Immediately next to the park gate, where campers should book in, this campsite stands among shady mopane trees, with the constant buzz of cicadas for company. Pitches around the edge of the site are both larger & more private than the others, but each has its own table & benches. The site boasts the new ablution blocks that have been installed across many of Botswana's parks, with solar-heated water – though the old facilities remain as a reminder of how it used to be! *US$40 pp, exc park fees, bed levy.* ☉ *All year.*

Getting away from South Gate
Driving from South Gate (Maqwee) to Third Bridge Take the most westerly exit from the campsite and the route is very easy. After about 24km you'll pass a right turn, marked by an old green cement block. One side of this notes that

Mboma and Third Bridge are off to the left. There are no indications where the right turn goes, though it actually leads around the east side of the Bodumatau Lagoon.

Keeping on the main road (to the left), you'll then pass, in order, First Bridge (⊕ 1BRIDG 19°17.099'S, 23°23.531'E) and Second Bridge (⊕ 2BRIDG 19°17.003'S, 23°22.553'E), before finally reaching the campsite at Third Bridge (⊕ 3BRIDG 19°14.368'S, 23°21.430'E). Note that when we last drove this route, in late 2013, Second Bridge was impassable, and the Third Bridge has partially collapsed, though it was still possible to drive across.

Driving from South Gate (Maqwee) to Xakanaxa The more scenic route is to follow the directions to Third Bridge, above, then continue southwest to Fourth Bridge (⊕ 4BRIDG 19°15.128'S, 23°24.173'E) and thence to Xakanaka. Even if the bridge is in poor repair, it's possible to drive to the side of it in the dry season. From there proceed broadly north east to the Xakanaxa Gate (⊕ XAKGT 19°11.865'S, 23°25.865'E), where you turn west for the campsite and lodges. You can navigate through this labyrinth of game-viewing loops using Veronica Roodt's map, or by sticking to the main track, setting your GPS for Xakanaxa, and then keeping slightly east of the direct-line direction.

However, if it's late in the dry season and you've plenty of time, then you may want to take a detour around the Bodumatau Lagoon, which avoids Third Bridge completely. (This track is marked as 'seasonal' on most maps, and is much less reliable than the main track, especially when wet.) In that case, take the right turn at the green concrete block that is about 24km from South Gate. It's 16km to the Bodumatau Bridge from here, then a further 13km to Fourth Bridge. One local operator refers to the first part of this road after the green concrete block as 'Elephant Alley', for its winding road through dense mopane is often frequented by elephants. Drive carefully.

Alternatively, there's a shorter, alternative route marked on the Shell map. Head towards North Gate from South Gate for about 300m, then turn left for 10km to the Kudu Flats, where you bear left again and follow the road all the way to Xakanaka. The final part of this ties up with the 'dry' route from North Gate to Xakanaka.

Driving from South Gate to North Gate (Khwai) A very direct, straight road leads about 30km north-northeast from South Gate to North Gate (⊕ NOGATE 19°10.394'S, 23°45.092'E). There are no game-viewing loops off this road.

Driving from South Gate to Maun Leaving the park from South Gate, after a few hundred metres there's a well-signposted fork. For Maun, take the main fork to the left, along a wide but badly rutted gravel road that is painfully slow-going. The right fork leads to Santawani Lodge in NG33 (page 351) and the wild-dog research station near Chitabe (page 348), but this road is now closed to self-drivers.

Heading towards Maun, to the right lies the NG33 concession, whilst to the left is an area managed by the community, NG34. Both are good wildlife areas, but because the land and the wildlife are managed, technically the road you are on is a 'transit route', and you are not allowed to stop and camp. The nearest place to camp is the community-run Kaziikini site (page 350).

After a further 17km you'll reach the sizeable village of **Shorobe** (see pages 179–80). Roadside vendors sell cold drinks, and there's a craft studio on the east side of the road, but little else to tempt the passing traveller. From here the road to Maun is tarred, passing the University of Botswana. The total journey from South Gate to the Engen garage, which is the first fuel station in Maun, is about 90km.

THE PRIVATE AREAS OF MOREMI (NG28)

Aside from the Mopane Tongue, the only way to access any of the rest of Moremi is from one of the small private safari camps with access only by air. There are three main camps within Moremi: Mombo and Chief's Camp at the north end of Chief's Island, and Xigera right on the western edge. These are described below.

However, there are a number of camps, such as those in NG19 near North Gate (pages 268–70), which stand just outside the edge of the park, but conduct some of their activities within the park. These include the camps in NG21 (Camp Okavango, Shinde and Xugana – pages 303–5) and the old camps along the south end of the Boro River in NG27B (Oddballs' Camp, Delta Camp, Gunn's Camp and Eagle Island – pages 331–2).

Because these two areas are very different I'll subdivide this concession into two sections: one covering Xigera's area, and the other concentrating on Mombo and Chief's Camp.

XIGERA If you had to stick a pin on the map in the centre of the Delta, you'd probably put it near to here. The Xigera (pronounced 'keejera') area is within the boundaries of Moremi Reserve, near its western border and technically in Moremi's only private concession area, NG28.

Concession history Look at an old map of the Delta and you'll realise that the western boundary of Moremi used to be further east than it is now. Then the Xigera and Mombo areas were part of the NG28 concession and outside the park. Xigera was originally built in 1986 by Hennie and Angela Rawlinson, two well-known Maun residents, at a place that Hennie called 'Paradise Island'.

Then in 1992 Moremi was expanded westwards and northwards. This was done in order to bring under its protection all the major Okavango habitats, as until then none of the northern Delta's papyrus swamps or permanent wetlands had been included. This expansion swallowed up NG28, including the Xigera and Mombo areas. Thus these camps now occupy prime sites within Moremi Game Reserve.

In 1998, the Rawlinsons renewed the lease for another 15 years and shortly after, the camp was completely demolished, and rebuilt from scratch a short distance away. Now, however, the lease is wholly owned by Wilderness Safaris (see page 177).

Flora and fauna The area around Xigera is one of the Delta's few truly deep-water experiences. (Jedibe, when it was open, used to deserve this accolade. It really was surrounded by apparently endless papyrus swamps, with only the odd island. Camp Okavango, Kwara, Xugana and Shinde could also lay claim to have deep-water experiences to some extent.)

Here at Xigera you're very close to the Jao River, which feeds the Boro and is one of the Okavango's major waterways.

Flora Spending nearly all of your time on the water, you're probably going to be particularly aware of the aquatic grasses and sedges. Of these the graceful, feathery papyri (*Cyperus papyrus*) are perhaps the most striking, and certainly one of the most interesting (see box below).

In shallower sections you'll also find large areas of common reeds (*Phragmites australis*) and the tall miscanthus grass (*Miscanthus junceus*). There are also a few lovely stands of pure water fern (*Thelypteris interrupta*) on the edges of some of the channels and lagoons.

PAPYRUS

The graceful, feathery papyrus is a giant sedge which dominates large areas of the Okavango. It grows in areas of permanent swamp in thick floating mats, unmistakable for its feather-duster heads that sway in the breeze. At first it's perhaps surprising that such vigorous, lush, emerald-green vegetation thrives here with apparently few nutrients available from the clear water or the poor Kalahari sands beneath.

The secret lies in a number of remarkable adaptations. Firstly, papyri have nitrogenous bacteria between their scale-leaves which 'fix' nitrogen from the air into a form that the plants can use. Secondly, they photosynthesise using a special 'carbon-4' pathway, thus making more efficient use of the sun's energy than most plants.

With these adaptations, plus water and sunshine, papyri are amongst the fastest-growing plants in the world. You'll quickly see another factor that helps them here if you cut a stem of papyrus (preferably a dying one!). Observe that although thick and strong, it's very light. So the plant is committing relatively little energy or materials to raise such a tall, strong stem.

In fact papyri store most of their energy in long, thick rhizomes which form part of the tangled floating mat. From this base, their shoots can rise up to about 2.5m high, and yet typically have a life cycle of only three months. Within this they grow swiftly to maturity, flower and die – leaving a tangle of brown, dead stems near water level. The nutrients from these old stems are withdrawn back into the rhizome, ready to power the birth of another shoot. This rapid recycling of nutrients is another of the keys to the plant's lush, vigorous growth.

On the islands you'll find the normal trees of the Delta, including a good number of confetti trees (*Gynmosporia senegalensis*). The English name for these comes from the small, scented white flowers which come out around May–June, and then fall underneath the tree in large enough quantities to be scooped up.

Fauna This area isn't a bad one for big game, though that's not why I'd go to Xigera. If you're staying at Xigera then remember that the bridge across the channel, linking the camp on one island with the main vehicle track to the airstrip on the other, isn't only used by people. Many other animals find it convenient, especially at night. Spotted hyenas cross it almost religiously every night, lion regularly and leopard occasionally too. Monkeys and baboons play on it during the day. Look underneath at the fish in the clear water and you may even see the odd spotted-necked otter fishing for bream.

On the larger island elephants are often in evidence, and when I was last here the floodplain beyond my tent's veranda was dotted with lechwe. Elephant are often around, sometimes in substantial herds of 50 or so, and on game drives you've a good chance of spotting impala and tsessebe.

As you'd expect for the environment, the Xigera area has one of the highest densities of sitatunga antelope in the Delta. These lovely creatures are notoriously difficult to spot, but gliding around silently in a mokoro probably offers you the best chance possible – just keep yours eyes wide open and your mouth tightly shut!

On one occasion here recently, an eminent guide was leading a number of mekoro, trying to get as close as possible to a sitatunga. When the antelope made a break to get away, it jumped directly over one of the mekoro.

Birdlife Given the environment of large areas of permanent papyrus and swamp vegetation, plus some islands, this is a good camp for seeking the more water-dependent birds in the Delta.

Notable amongst these are the African skimmers, which usually arrive at Xigera Lagoon around September or October. About 20 pairs of these incredible birds have been noted here in recent years; if they're new to you then take a few moments to watch one of them through binoculars. You'll see it using the most amazing flying skills to place its lower mandible in the lagoon at a fixed depth, and steadily scythe through the water. Then periodically you see the bill snap shut with its catch of an unfortunate small fish. This is compulsive viewing, even if you never normally look at anything smaller than a lion; an incredible fishing technique.

Whilst floating around you can expect to see assorted kingfishers, herons, egrets and other waterbirds. Included in this list, if you're lucky, will be purple (but not lesser) gallinules, lesser jacanas, moorhens, lesser moorhens and green-backed herons. It should be a good area for bitterns (including the dwarf and little), though I've never seen one here.

Other unusual birds that enthusiastic ornithologists should look out for include chirping cisticolas, tawny-flanked prinias and palm swifts, all of which are regularly sighted here.

When to visit Because the focus at Xigera is more on the environment and birdlife than game per se, this area can be visited any time of the year.

Getting there and away Only pre-booked guests may visit this area, flying in to Xigera's own airstrip (⊕ XIGAIR 19°23.155'S, 22°44.618'E). Note that there's no practical dry-land access from here to Mombo, Chief's Camp or the nearby Nxabega, and that driving in isn't an option.

Where to stay Although there are two camps here, one – Xigera Mokoro Trails – is predominantly visited as part of a set mobile itinerary. For most visitors, Xigera is the only option. Both camps are run by Wilderness Safaris (see page 177).

Xigera [map 206] (10 tents) ⊕ XIGERA 19°23.647'S, 23°45.535'E. Sited on Paradise Island, Xigera opened in 2000. If you've never been to the Delta, then simply conjure up an image of a luxurious safari camp in the heart of the swamps, enveloped by a green, tropical lushness: you've probably come close to visualising Xigera.

Xigera's tents are widely spread out on one fringe of the island along 800m of raised boardwalks that stretch as far as a small lagoon that seems to attract good game. Constructed of part wood, part canvas, each is raised on a wooden deck a few metres above the island floor. The front, with 2 large sliding doors & huge gauze windows, is easy to open up for good views & airflow, the latter assisted by an efficient, free-standing, antique-style electric fan. The camp is fully solar powered, with constant 220V electricity supplied to the chalets, & a backup generator.

Inside, along with dbl or twin beds enclosed in a walk-in mosquito net, are a writing desk, large trunk & easy chairs. Behind the bed is a bamboo screen & towel rack, a dressing table, twin basins, an inside flush toilet & separate shower. Through the tent's rear door is a blissful outdoor shower. One of the tents is designed for families, with 2 tents linked by an internal passage.

Overlooking a perennial channel, & the footbridge across it, is the camp's comfortable thatched dining room, bar & exceedingly cosy lounge. Close by, the camp has a good-size curio shop selling materials, jewellery, postcards, film, T-shirts & a few hats. There's also a small plunge pool, filled with water pumped from the Delta. This may seem superfluous in such an environment, though clearly litigious-minded visitors aren't encouraged to find 'safe' places to swim in the Delta itself.

LIFE IN PAPYRUS SWAMPS

Papyrus swamps are in many ways a difficult habitat. Below the waterline, little light penetrates the floating mat of dead, tangled stems and rhizomes. The constant decomposition of dead papyrus stems means much organic debris, and water which is acidic and low in oxygen. With no light, there's no chance for algae or any other higher plantlife.

Above the waterline the stems form a dense, tangled mass. The stems themselves are fibrous, difficult to digest and very nutrient-poor. Combined with a floating base that can't support any weight, this makes life here almost impossible for most larger animals. Only the specially adapted sitatunga antelope is at home here.

For animals as small as rats and mice, the situation isn't so bad. They don't generally stay in the papyrus beds, but they are light enough to make forays there, supported by the floating mat and individual stems. Greater cane rats are the largest of these, growing up to about 80cm on a diet of papyrus shoots, reeds and other vegetation. Although they swim well, they normally live in small family groups in burrows on permanent dry land, leaving these at night to forage in the reedbeds and papyrus.

A few birds also use the papyrus for shelter and nesting, including several species of weavers, the red-shouldered widow and red bishop bird – which will tear the feathery umbels of the papyrus as material to weave their intricate nests. Many more will come into papyrus areas to hunt for fish or insects, and there will be very few trips here when you won't see at least a few malachite and pied kingfishers.

Like Jao, Xigera feels like one of the Delta's most tropical, slow & romantic camps. It offers a great water experience, though I'd suggest that most visitors spend only 2 nights here, rather than 3 or 4 that might be the norm at a camp with more emphasis on game activities.

US$736/924 pp sharing/sgl Jan–Mar, US$832/ US$1,020 Apr–May, Nov–Dec; US$1,291/1,479 Jun–Oct, inc FB, most drinks, activities, park fees & laundry; exc transfers. No children under 6. ⊕ All year.

Activities Motorboat trips and mokoro excursions have always been the main activities from Xigera, but their team has located a good area for game drives, and has come up with a way of stationing vehicles on the larger islands there. So usually, water levels permitting, it's now possible to drive there too.

Thus from about May until October, whilst the water is high, you boat to the game-drive vehicles, and then drive from there. Then it's possible to do motorboat trips as well as mokoro trips directly from the camp.

However, between about November and May, the water level is lower and it's then possible to keep the vehicles near camp and drive directly from there, though the motorboats have to be stationed in deeper water a short distance north of camp, and are reached by mokoro.

A recent change of regulations means that catch-and-release fishing is now permitted, except during the closed season of January and February. Xigera keeps a limited supply of basic angling gear.

Because the camp is within Moremi Game Reserve, night drives and off-road driving are not allowed. Short walks are conducted, but the guides are not allowed to carry rifles.

MOMBO AND CHIEF'S CAMP Mombo and Chief's share a concession within Moremi, but they are about 25km apart – which is a long way in the Okavango. Hence, unless they want to cross paths, you'll never normally see vehicles from one camp in the other camp.

Concession history
Since the mid-1980s the rights to run Mombo were owned by Jao Safaris (now defunct). They subleased this to many safari companies including Ker & Downey, Bonadventure (who were one of the main tour agencies when I first visited Maun in 1987) and, lastly, Wilderness Safaris. During this time, and especially in the last few years, it gained a first-class reputation for game.

When Jao Safaris' lease expired in 1998, there was clearly going to be very stiff competition for this area. Because it was recognised as such a prime area, the Land Board (ie: the government body responsible) allowed for two sites to be put up for tender, at opposite ends of the concession. Some 29 companies entered. There was tremendous competition: the best proposal and overall management plan would win.

Eventually two bids were accepted, one from Wilderness Safaris and another from A&K (whose Botswana operation has recently become Sanctuary Retreats). Each needed to promise the government the highest possible revenue, as well as the best (that is, most sustainable and productive) management plan.

To achieve this, they both arrived at the obvious solution: each built one of the country's most upmarket camps, and attached an appropriately high price tag to it. It was the only way to make financial sense with such high concession fees.

Thus the new, much more luxurious Mombo came into being, near the old Mombo site, and Chief's Camp was built south of that, on the northwestern side of Chief's Island. The tender process had maximised the government's revenues, and pushed part of the area's tourism a step further upmarket.

Flora and fauna highlights
Flora The environments found here aren't unique in the Delta, but they are old, established, and have long been protected – and so are basically pristine and undisturbed.

Perhaps the most interesting, and certainly the most photogenic, habitats here are the shallow floodplains which surround the northern end of Chief's Island. (It's such a distinctive landscape that an image of it has remained deeply ingrained in my mind since my first visit here, in the mid-1990s.)

Looking at the whole Delta, you'll realise that this area is very close to the permanent swamps at the base of the Panhandle. Because of this, the floods here are more regular and predictable than they are lower down the Delta. This regular seasonal flooding has created a very photogenic environment of short-grass plains, amongst which are a number of tiny islands fringed by dense, feathery stands of wild date palms (*Phoenix reclinata*). For me, this is the quintessential Delta landscape – and it's sufficiently open to be excellent for game viewing.

(Away from the Okavango Delta, the only place that I've seen which is similar to this in southern Africa is the Busanga Plains of northern Kafue, in Zambia. Again, these are consistently flooded every year, and have very little disturbance.)

Go back on to the dry land of Chief's Island and you'll find a range of more familiar landscapes and floral communities. Mopane woodlands are dominant across much of the island, with some areas of impressive, tall 'cathedral' mopane (*Colophospermum mopane*), often a popular retreat for game during wetter months.

Running through this you'll find lines of Kalahari sandveld, reflecting the locations of old, long-dry watercourses. Here you will see sand-loving species like

11

the silver cluster-leaf (*Terminalia sericea*), the Kalahari appleleaf (*Lonchocarpus nelsii*), perhaps some camelthorn (*Acacia erioloba*) and umbrella thorns (*Acacias tortilis*), and the odd leadwood tree (*Combretum imberbe*).

Where the land meets the water, there are bands of classic riverine forest including fine specimens of raintree (*Lonchocarpus capassa*), sausage tree (*Kigelia africana*), jackalberry (*Diospyros mespiliformis*), African mangosteen (*Garcinia livingstonei*), figs (mostly *Ficus sycomorus*) and some wild date palms (*Phoenix reclinata*). Throughout the area's forests you'll occasionally find huge old baobab trees (*Adansonia digitata*) – which probably have lived long enough to see the environment change around them!

Fauna   The game in this area is at least as dense as anywhere else in the Okavango (or indeed the subcontinent), and because the area's a private one, the game viewing is just about the best you'll find in southern Africa. It's dense, varied, and good sightings of predators are virtually guaranteed.

See *Flora and fauna* at the start of this chapter for more extensive comments on Moremi as a whole; in this particular area impala, tsessebe, zebra and giraffe are usually the most numerous of the larger herbivores – although warthogs are remarkably common. (So numerous that they have become a major prey species for both lion and leopard.) Elephant and buffalo are resident here in good numbers, with more individual animals seen during the rains, and generally larger herds recorded as the dry season progresses.

Herds of red lechwe are common in the flooded areas when the water's high, but they rarely venture into the drier parts of the reserve. Kudu and wildebeest also occur, as do the occasional reedbuck and steenbok; sable and roan are usually never seen here.

Though the majority of the Delta's usual line-up of nocturnal animals do occur, without taking night drives most are difficult to spot. The exception seems to be honey badgers, porcupines and spring hares, which are sometimes seen around the camps at night. In 2013 Mombo was also regularly visited by a civet after dinner.

The area has a justified, first-class reputation for excellent predator sightings. Spotted hyena are probably the most successful large carnivore in the area, though lion are also common – as they are in many areas of the Delta.

However, it seems that a recent demise in the dominance of the lion and a rise in the fortunes of the hyena has turned the tables on the once-thriving cheetah population here. Despite the sprinkling of slightly raised date palm islands and termite hills that make ideal look-out posts, they are rarely seen now. This is really just a small-scale example of the constant ebb and flow of power struggles in the animal kingdom.

There are good numbers of leopard around – although their appearances during the day are relatively limited. Originally Mombo, and this area, built its reputation on some of Africa's best sightings of wild dog – largely because of a very large and successful pack of about 40 dogs that denned here for several years in the mid-1990s. With this pack in residence, visitors were virtually guaranteed amazing sightings, and the area's dry open floodplains proved marvellous for following the animals as they hunted.

Now, however, that pack has broken up, as is the usual process when the alpha female dies. Thus while wild dog sightings are as good as in most areas in the eastern Delta, they're no better as there's no sizeable pack in regular residence – although a lone wild dog that was left behind when the others departed seems to hang around with the jackals – a very unusual sighting.

Until the middle of the 20th century, the white rhino was common in northern Botswana, while the less populous black rhino was still holding its own in the area around the Kwando and Chobe rivers. However, protection was inadequate, and with illegal hunting spurred on by the value of rhinoceros horns on the world market, the animals' presence was increasingly threatened. By 1992, the area's population of black rhino had been wiped out, declared 'locally extinct', and white rhino numbers were down to a critical 19. The future looked bleak.

In response, an anti-poaching operation was set up by the Department of Wildlife and National Parks, backed by the Botswana Defence Force. As a result, the remaining white rhino were removed to wildlife sanctuaries so that they could be protected until the time came when they could safely be released back into the wild.

Then, in 2001, in a collaborative venture between Wilderness Safaris (*www.wilderness-safaris.com*), the Department of Wildlife and National Parks, and the Botswana government, the Botswana Rhino Relocation and Reintroduction Project was born. Under its auspices, four white rhino were reintroduced on to Chief's Island on 9 November 2001: two females and two males. Over the next two years, a further 16 animals were reintroduced, and as this founder population settled, so the first calf was born. Despite setbacks, the project has paid off, and a healthy population of white rhino is now firmly established both in the Moremi Game Reserve and elsewhere in the Delta.

Next it was the turn of the black rhino. Almost two years after the project started, in November 2003, four black rhinos were released to roam in the Delta for the first time in well over a decade. This population has also bred but remains small, with sightings very rare. Future reintroductions of animals from either South Africa or Zimbabwe are expected to bolster this breeding nucleus and help build up numbers here as a meaningful conservation initiative.

As both species gain ground, and without being constrained by fences, some are moving away. With the aid of tracking devices, these migrations are being carefully monitored. While for security reasons the location of individual animals is not divulged, it is known that a small group of white rhinos has wandered quite widely and established itself in the Makgadikgadi Pans National Park – where Desert and Delta Safaris has played an active role in introducing an additional animal and monitoring the population. Such movements have prompted the establishment of the Botswana Rhino Ecology Project, with a view to gaining a greater understanding of the distances travelled by both species of rhino, the importance of individual habitats, and their preferred choice of vegetation. In turn, this will provide key information for those engaged in similar projects in the future.

Poaching, though, remains a serious issue. According to Wilderness Safaris, over 700 rhino were killed for their horns in South Africa in 2013 alone. Greater protection for the rhinos in Botswana, although by no means watertight, has ensured that the Delta's new rhino population has suffered considerably less, with just two animals poached – in 2003 – but vigilance remains crucial.

The Okavango Delta – Moremi Game Reserve   THE PRIVATE AREAS OF MOREMI (NG28)

11

Finally, a real good-news story for this area, and the Delta as a whole. Both black and white rhino used to occur here naturally, but by the early 1990s they had been exterminated by poaching. At last, in 2001, the first white rhino were brought back into this area. Over the next few years more were released onto Chief's Island and they have been breeding well. With the success of the white rhino reintroduction, the focus shifted in 2003 to returning the black rhino to the Okavango Delta as well. See box, *Return of the rhino*, page 289 – but note that although both species are present, sightings of them are not common.

Birdlife At the heart of the Delta, and with a large and diverse area of dry land and floodplains, this area of Moremi gets periodic visits from virtually all of the birds in the Delta, so singling out a few to mention here is inevitably a flawed process.

However, top of the list for a special mention are the vultures, attracted by the game densities and predator activity. Most numerous are the white-backed, hooded and lappet-faced vultures – though you'll also find a surprising number of white-headed vultures. Palm-nut vultures occur, too (usually frequenting the real fan palms), though they're not common.

Also attracted by the game are both kinds of oxpecker – though yellow-billed (which feed on the backs of hippos) seem more common than the red-billed variety.

As happens everywhere in the Delta, when the waters recede, isolated pools of fish are left behind. As these gradually dry up the fish become more and more concentrated, attracting the most amazing numbers of predatory birds. Pick the right day (usually one between about May and October) and the right pool, and you'll be entertained for hours by large concentrations of pelicans, saddle-billed storks, marabou storks, black egrets, grey and Goliath herons to name but a few. It's an amazing sight. In other receding pools you'll find congregations of pelicans or, in those which aren't so frantic, painted snipes can be seen if you look hard (or have a good guide!).

The short-grass floodplains here suit wattled cranes, which are often found in numbers, and on the drier plains watch for secretary birds and kori bustards. The latter occasionally have carmine bee-eaters using their backs as perches. In plains with longer grass you may be able to spot an African crake, while ostriches are very rarely seen (perhaps because there are too many large predators).

On the water look for pygmy geese and dwarf jacanas in the quieter areas, along with many species of more common waterbirds. There's often a good number of the relatively rare slaty egrets about too.

When to visit Because the focus here is firmly on game viewing, the dry season is the obvious time to visit. That's when the game is at its most visible and most dense. That said, from July to October the camps (especially Mombo) have substantial 'high-season supplements', which can make the costs at other times of the year seem very attractive.

If you decide to come at a less popular, and cheaper, time then remember that Chief's Island is a large, permanent island with its own large, permanent population of game. Thus you'll still see some first-rate game even if the game viewing isn't quite as good as it would have been during October.

Getting there and away Only pre-booked guests flying in visit this area, as there is no practical dry-land access to Chief's Island. Driving here isn't an option. Each camp has its own airstrip on Chief's Island; Mombo's airstrip is at ✪ MOMBOA 19°12.680'S, 22°47.510'E.

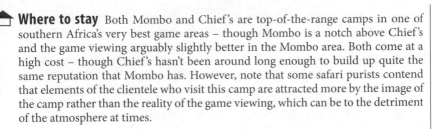

Where to stay Both Mombo and Chief's are top-of-the-range camps in one of southern Africa's very best game areas – though Mombo is a notch above Chief's and the game viewing arguably slightly better in the Mombo area. Both come at a high cost – though Chief's hasn't been around long enough to build up quite the same reputation that Mombo has. However, note that some safari purists contend that elements of the clientele who visit this camp are attracted more by the image of the camp rather than the reality of the game viewing, which can be to the detriment of the atmosphere at times.

Mombo Camp [map 206] (9 tents) Contact Wilderness Safaris, page 177. This is the flagship Wilderness Safaris' camp in Botswana – one of their 4 'premier' camps (the others are Jao, page 315; Vumbura Plains, page 310; & King's Pool, page 247) & is one of the most expensive photographic camps in Botswana.

It all stands on wooden decking raised high off the ground. A long polished wooden table for candlelit dinners sits in the main dining area under a high thatched roof, with one side open to the decking via roll-down grass blinds. A couple of smaller areas, one of them al fresco, extend the dining options.

The adjacent lounge/bar overlooks wide floodplains & is furnished comfortably with wooden coffee tables & colonial leather chairs. Glass-fronted cases display a well-stocked small library, & easy chairs are set around a wooden Pygmy bed, imported from the Congo, which doubles as a table. Behind is a large boma where traditional dinners are sometimes served, while in front on the decking is a campfire, surrounded by deckchairs, for after-dinner drinks. Near to the small plunge pool some loungers cluster in a patch of shade.

Mombo's 'tents' – 5 to the east of the main area, & 4 to the west – are very large. Made of canvas supported by wooden poles, they're connected by raised wooden walkways, with the furthest, aptly labelled the 'Mombo Lounge', close to a small lounge that is used for private dinners. (It also has a second plunge pool, a firedeck – & even a gym!) Each tent's large wooden door opens to reveal a dbl or twin beds enveloped by walk-in mosquito nets, bedside tables with lamps, a sofa, coffee table & writing desk, plus a minibar hidden in an old travel trunk, while underfoot is polished parquet. Mombo is predominantly powered by solar energy, allowing for both overhead & free-standing fans. The bathroom has a dbl indoor shower (2 shower heads & lots of space), as well as an open-air shower, plus free-standing twin sinks

(the plumbing disguised by wooden latticework), a rather magnificent mirror, & a separate loo.

The gauzed doors at the front of each tent open on to a decked balcony, where a table, chairs & a lounger are shaded from the sun by the canvas roof. On one side is a thatched sala, or small gazebo, with a mattress & cushions, which makes a nice shady spot from which to watch game. That said, the area underneath the decking of the chalets themselves seems to be a popular evening spot for buffalo. *US$1,783/2,378 pp sharing/sgl 11 Jan–Mar, US$2,012/2,607 Apr, May, Nov–19 Dec, US$2,577/3,172 Jun–Oct, US$2,293/2,888 20 Dec–10 Jan, inc FB, most drinks, activities, park fees, laundry; exc transfers.* ☺ *All year.*

Little Mombo [map 206] (3 tents) Continuing along the decking, past Mombo's 'lounge' tent, is its tiny sister camp. Although adjacent to the main camp, Little Mombo operates as a separate entity. Its tents have the same design as those of its neighbour, & its main lounge/dining/bar area is similarly furnished, though smaller. Little Mombo has its own outdoor boma, small pool & communal sala – as well as individual ones for the rooms. *US$1,783/2,378 pp sharing/ sgl 11 Jan–Mar, US$2,012/2,607 Apr, May, Nov–19 Dec, US$2,577/3,172 Jun–Oct, US$2,293/2,888 20 Dec–10 Jan, inc FB, most drinks, activities, park fees, laundry; exc transfers.* ☺ *All year.*

Chief's Camp [map 206] (12 tents) Contact Sanctuary Retreats, page 176. About 25km from Mombo, just off the western side of Chief's Island, this is the pride of Sanctuary Retreats' operations in Botswana.

Chief's main area is raised on decking where its high thatch roof covers a large, open-plan area. This is dotted with expensive ethnic curios & the odd bookshelf, where there is a varied mix of interesting reading. Adjacent to this you'll find the lounge & a well-stocked bar, with wooden coffee table & weaved 'sea-grass' sofa, & a dining room with a number of tables. Here guests tend to dine

11

with their own guide, who is generally allotted to you when you arrive (you usually stick with the same guide & take all your drives with him/her). When last visited, Chief's food was good & imaginative, & accompanied with an impressive selection of wine.

Outside this dining/lounge area, an expanse of wooden decking acts as a veranda, where you can sit in the shade of large jackalberry (*Diospyros mespiliformis*) & marula (*Sclerocarya birrea*) trees. An 8m-long swimming pool is surrounded by loungers & a small sala. Those with a passion for shopping might seek out the efficient shop stocked with books, T-shirts & some stylish curios.

Chief's secluded tents, slightly raised off the ground on decking, are reached from a simple bush path, lit at night by electric hurricane lamps. Tents 1–7 are on the eastern side of the main area, the others on the west. All have private verandas overlooking the plains (which usually flood around Jun–Aug, when the water may come all the way up to the lodge). Each tent has a wooden door & polished wood floor. The décor is stylish & partly modern, partly ethnic – including masks made by the Teke people of Cameroon – but it's not at all rustic. Beside the twin or dbl beds, adjustable aluminium lamps stand on bedside tables. There's a solid wardrobe with roll-down canvas door, a couple of chairs & tables, a free-standing lamp & a ceiling fan, powered by 24hr electricity (110/220V). The bathroom is adjacent to the main body of the tent, but feels different. It has proper partition walls & a brick shower cubicle with glass door, opposite which is a large glass mirror. On one side is a door leading out to a small open-air shower. The toilet is behind a wooden door, & there are twin washbasins, both with individual mirrors – completing the impression that this is the bathroom of a plush hotel rather than a safari camp.

Set at the far end of the tents is Chief's dedicated spa – one of only 3 in the Delta. Small but well equipped, it offers treatments including massages, facials, manicures, body scrubs & wraps – all of which can be experienced from a deck overlooking the floodplain. *US$1,160 pp Jan–14 Jun, Nov–20 Dec; US$1,950/US$2,925 pp sharing/sgl 15–30 Jun, Sep–Oct, 21 Dec–5 Jan, US$2250/3,375 Jul–Aug, inc FB, most drinks, activities, park fees, laundry; exc transfers. ⊕ All year.*

Activities Game drives are the main activity at Mombo and Chief's camps, though both are constricted to some extent by the park's rules. Night drives, fishing and off-road driving are not allowed – though the camps have been campaigning to have these rules relaxed.

Chief's Camp also offers mokoro trips, subject to water levels. When the floods arrive, up to 70% of Chief's Camp's network of roads becomes covered in water, and mokoro trips can start off right at the lodge.

12

The Okavango Delta – Private Reserves around Moremi

In his book, *Lake Ngami and the River Okavango*, the Victorian-era explorer and trader Charles John Andersson wrote:

> On every side as far as the eye could see, lay stretched a sea of fresh water, in many places concealed from sight by a covering of reeds and rushes of every shade and hue; whilst numerous islands, spread over its whole surface, and adorned with rich vegetation, gave to the whole an indescribably beautiful appearance.

For modern visitors the Okavango Delta has lost none of its beauty. However, finding reliable information on the various areas from brochures can be as challenging as Andersson's expedition. This chapter aims to demystify these areas, and to identify some of the strengths and weaknesses of the areas and their camps.

It aims to cover all of the private reserves around the Okavango and the main camps within these. But before you read any of my comments, here are a few general observations on the chapter:

- I've covered the reserves in the order of their concession numbers, from NG12 to NG43.
- There are virtually no fences between these areas, so the game flows freely between them, and won't always be where I suggest it is.
- Remember that differences in environment and game can be as great within a reserve as they are between one reserve and its neighbour. Despite this, some trends are evident, which I've tried to draw out.
- The marketing leaflets of the reserves usually claim that every animal/bird is found in their particular areas – particularly the 'sexy' ones like wild dogs and Pel's fishing owls! There is some truth in this, in that virtually all the animals/birds do occur in all the reserves. However, I've tried to get behind the spin with a realistic assessment of what you're most likely to see, and where you're most likely to see it. I've tried to make my comments reflect realistic probabilities, but they can't be definitive.
- I've made comments largely from my own first-hand experience, informed when in these areas by guides and experts. Occasionally, I have used reliable local sources. That said, I have not spent a year in each reserve, so my observations have been snapshots from the times that I've visited, augmented by comments from travellers sent by my travel company. They don't pretend to be comprehensive, systematic surveys, but I do believe that they're broadly representative.

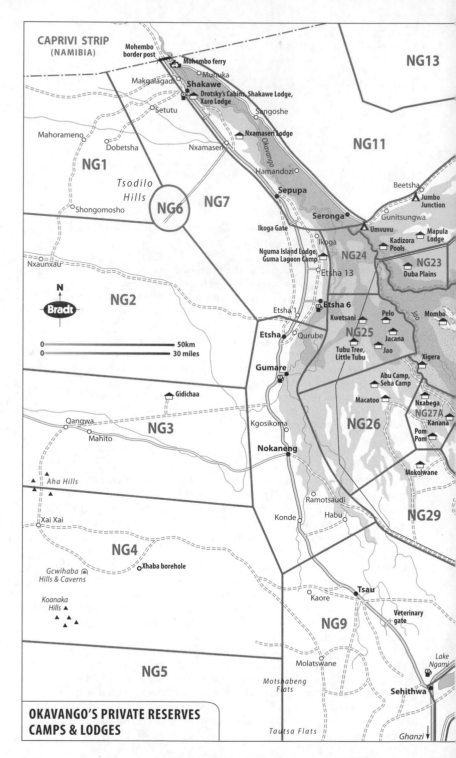

OKAVANGO'S PRIVATE RESERVES
CAMPS & LODGES

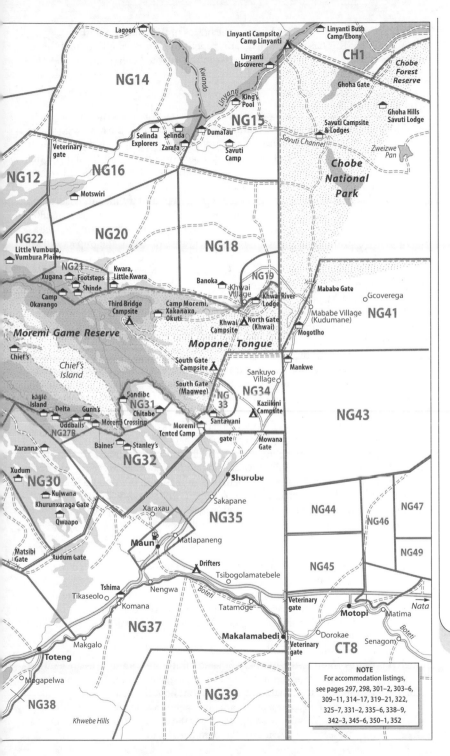

Lagoon

Linyanti Campsite/
Camp Linyanti

Linyanti Bush
Camp/Ebony

Linyanti
Discoverer

CH1

NG14

*Chobe
Forest
Reserve*

Ghoha Gate

King's
Pool

NG15

Ghoha Hills
Savuti Lodge

Selinda
Explorers

Selinda
Zarafa

DumaTau

Savuti Campsite
& Lodges

Savuti Channel

Veterinary
gate

Savuti
Camp

*Žweizwe
Pan*

NG12

NG16

*Chobe
National
Park*

Motswiri

NG22

NG20

NG18

Little Vumbura,
Vumbura Plains

NG21

NG19

Mababe Gate

Gcoverega

Xugana

Footsteps

Kwara,
Little Kwara

Banoka

Khwai
Village

Khwai River
Lodge

Mababe Village
(Kudumane)

NG41

Shinde

Camp
Okavango

Third Bridge
Campsite

Camp Moremi,
Xakanaxa,
Okuti

North Gate
(Khwai)

Mogotlho

Khwai
Campsite

Moremi Game Reserve

*Chief's
Island*

Mopane Tongue

Chief's

South Gate
Campsite

Mankwe

Eagle
Island

Sondibe

Sankuyo
Village

NG34

Delta

Gunn's

NG31

Chitabe

South Gate
(Magwee)

NG
33

Kaziikini
Campsite

Oddballs'

Moremi Crossing

NG27B

Moremi
Tented Camp

Santawani

NG43

Xaranna

Baines'

Stanley's

gate

Mowana
Gate

NG32

Xudum

NG30

Kujwana

Shorobe

Khurunxaraga Gate

Qwaapo

Sakapane

NG44

NG47

Xaraxau

NG46

Matsibi
Gate

Xudum Gate

NG35

NG49

Maun

Matlapaneng

Drifters

NG45

Tshima

Nengwa

Tsibogolamatebele

Tikaseolo

Komana

Boteti

Tatamoge

Veterinary
gate

Nata

Motopi

Matima

NG37

Makgalo

Makalamabedi

Dorakae

Senagom

Boteti

Toteng

Veterinary
gate

CT8

Mogapelwa

NG38

NG39

Khwebe Hills

NOTE
For accommodation listings,
see pages 297, 298, 301–2, 303–6,
309–11, 314–17, 319–21, 322,
325–7, 331–2, 335–6, 338–9,
342–3, 345–6, 350–1, 352

- Under each reserve I've tried to cover the basics of the wildlife and the practicalities. This has necessitated some repetition, but it's a reflection of the fact that there are more similarities between the various reserves in the Delta than there are differences.

MAPULA (NG12)

Outside the buffalo fence, north of Vumbura and Duba Plains, the Magwegqana or Selinda Spillway starts in an environment similar to southeast Vumbura – though generally NG12's islands are bigger and its vegetation more established. In the south are good game viewing and extensive mopane woodlands; last time I was in the area, two cheetah left Vumbura heading north to hunt in NG12.

Several villages stand on this concession's northern boundary, including Seronga, Beetsha (Betsaa), Eretsha (Eretsa), Gunotsoga (Ganitsuga) and Gudigwa. In 2003 the area received its first visitors, thanks to an exciting project to create the Delta's first upmarket, community-run 'cultural camp', Gudigwa. Sadly, the impact of two bushfires in 2003 took its toll, however, and although the camp was re-opened in 2006, a further fire and irresolvable issues with the community mean it has now shut down with little hope of re-opening.

More positively, Mapula Lodge – which opened at about the same time – is set to be refurbished in 2014. Despite a few hiccoughs along the way, it has considerable potential. Another new lodge within this area, Kadizora Pools, is expected to open in mid-2014.

Anyone familiar with recent community-company partnerships in NG12 could be forgiven for feeling a little despondent regarding their lack of success. There is, however, a new community cultural centre, **Dinga Village** (*www.dingavillage.com*), taking shape near the village of Gunitsungwa (Ganitsuga), on the border between NG11 and NG12, which is showing great promise. The village brings together various elements of the five tribes found in this region to demonstrate how they live and work in the Delta. At its heart is the grass-roofed 'Dumela Hut', which has been constructed using local methods from locally sourced materials. This is where visitors are entertained with traditional dancing and will be able to see art and craft exhibitions. Access to the village is by road, boat and air. Little Vumbura (page 310) offers its guests a helicopter excursion to visit Dinga, while those with a lower budget can organise a trip with Sepupa Swamp Stop (page 365), travelling by boat. Alongside the cultural and community side of things, there are plans for crocodile and elephant research centres to be based here, as well as a lion–livestock conflict study.

FLORA AND FAUNA HIGHLIGHTS The NG12 concession is bisected by the Okavango's main buffalo fence, which is punctuated by gates to allow access, but is reasonably effective in controlling the flow of larger game from one side to the other. Gudigwa – currently closed – lies in the north of the concession, so used to conduct game drives in that area alone. Mapula, however, is just north of the buffalo fence, so is able to operate on both sides.

Wildlife on both sides of the fence reflects the variety of habitat in this area, though it is more prolific to the south. Zebra and giraffe are common, as are a range of antelope, from red lechwe and waterbuck to impala, wildebeest and kudu. These in turn attract the predators, including leopard and lion, but also wild dog, which den here regularly. Buffalo and elephant are permanent residents. The birdlife, too, is exceptionally varied. This is a good place to spot the endangered wattled crane, as well as carmine bee-eaters, and the African paradise flycatcher.

GETTING THERE AND AWAY Visitors to all lodges in NG12 arrive by air. The trip takes 40 minutes from Maun, and costs around US$225 per person each way.

WHERE TO STAY

Mapula Lodge [map 294] (9 chalets) \686 3369; e mapulalodge@info.bw; www.mapulalodge.com; ⊕ MAPULA 18°51.265'S, 22°44.823'E. Occupying a stunning position on the edge of seasonal floodplains, Mapula Lodge overlooks a permanent lagoon complete with a large contingent of resident hippos. Batswana owned & run, it has a relaxed, homely atmosphere, with many of its staff drawn from nearby villages. A comfortable open-sided lounge & dining area under thatch extends to a large deck in the shade of an ancient African ebony, & beyond to a sunlounger placed enticingly at the end of a long jetty. More loungers around a small pool are an inviting spot to relax in the afternoon, while the bush bar comes into its own as the sun dips below the horizon.

Full refurbishment planned for early 2014 should see the spacious, solidly built chalets replaced with canvas-&-wood structures to create a cooler environment. They will, though, remain raised up on private decks fronting the lagoon, & will retain their entirely meshed fronts from bedroom, bathroom & (very good) outside shower.

Activities focus on day & night game drives on both sides of the buffalo fence (the range covered depending on flood levels, but drives can be quite long), as well as boat trips (when water levels permit), mokoro excursions & guided walks. Often, vehicles go out with a guide & tracker.

Mapula went through a rough patch around late 2011 & a subsequent change in ownership also took some time to turn things around. Now, things are improving & – with a new manager in late 2013 & a full refurbishment in hand – the lodge appears to be receiving the commitment it deserves. This is good news, not least because Mapula is that increasingly elusive entity in Botswana: an independent lodge not owned by one of the larger safari companies. *US$620 Apr–Jun & Nov pp sharing, US$620 Jul–Oct, US$440 Dec–Mar, inc FB, local drinks, activities, laundry. No children under 8.* ⊕ *All year.*

Kadizora Pools [map 294] (12 rooms) reservations \0861 010200; m 7264 7810; e okavangoplains@gmail.com, sales@anthology.co.za; www.africananthology.co.za; ⊕ 18°53.350'S, 22°35.366'E. Scheduled to open in 2014, Kadizora will lie some 15km northwest of Duba Plains. *US$400 pp.*

KHWAI DEVELOPMENT TRUST (NG18 AND NG19)

On the southern edge of the small NG19 concession, where hunting has long been illegal, you'll find a collection of lodges benefiting from the beautiful frontage along the Khwai River. For the sake of continuity, I've described these in *Chapter 11* under North Gate, on pages 265–7.

The larger NG18 area, which stretches north to the Linyanti concession, east of Kwara and west of Chobe, is owned and managed by the small community of Khwai Village. Here the people have formed the Khwai Development Trust, funded at least in part by auctioning off their hunting quota to various hunting organisations. The only time that I've been here was when driving on the 'transit route' between Moremi and the Linyanti and Selinda reserves, a route that is no longer passable. The interior of this concession appeared to be fairly monotonous mopane, but there were signs of game around. Note that a P70 concession fee per person is now payable by anyone who plans to drive around (as against through) the area, and that you must have a community escort with you at all times. These escorts are there simply to show you the routes; they have no guiding qualifications, and are not paid – though a tip is normally expected.

FLORA AND FAUNA HIGHLIGHTS This was for many years a hunting concession, so the game here is still quite skittish, albeit becoming gradually more habituated to

12

vehicles. Wild dog pass through the area frequently and there are good numbers of leopard and lion. Elephants and particularly zebra seem to be prolific too.

GETTING THERE AND AWAY Most guests at Banoka arrive by air into a new airstrip built in 2012. From there it's just a ten-minute drive to camp. Driving yourself in a well-equipped 4x4 is also an option, but only for those with plenty of experience of driving in the bush.

WHERE TO STAY New to this concession is Banoka Bush Camp, owned by Wilderness Safaris (page 177). The community operates four campsites within the concession, but only two – Magotho 1 and 2 – may be used by independent campers. As both are accessed from the road between Chobe and North Gate, I have included them with the riverside lodges in that section, in *Chapter 11*.

In late 2013 there were plans afoot for the semi-permanent Khwai Bedouin Camp (*www.africanluxuryhideaways.com*) to move from here to a permanent location and be reconstructed as a lodge, but at the time of going to press, details were yet to be finalised.

Banoka Bush Camp [map 295] (10 tents) ⊕ BANOKA 19°07.607'S, 23°39.678'E. Overlooking a deep, lily-lined lagoon connected to the Khwai River, Banoka – named after the Banoka people, or river Bushmen – opened in late 2010. It's about 2hrs' drive west of Khwai, but most guests arrive by air. It's rather more laid-back than most Wilderness camps, though still very comfortable with friendly & attentive staff.

The open main area, set on stilts overlooking the river, is vast – so even when camp is full (& note that Banoka is sometimes used for groups), you can be as social or as reclusive as you wish. Fortunate, as Banoka is sometimes used for groups. There's a well-stocked bar, & plenty of seating areas to chill out with a drink. A protruding deck over the water hosts the dining area, where well-prepared meals may be taken communally or in individual groups. And there's the bonus of an excellent swimming-pool area.

Sandy pathways lead to the tents, which are also raised on stilts. From each veranda, timber-framed, mesh swing doors open to reveal twin beds, or a dbl, with a large 'floating' headboard separating the bedroom from his & hers washbasins, a shower, & a wardrobe with a safe. The toilet is in a separate cubicle, with a door.

Early in the season, around April/May, the mopane around the lodge is quite dense, so game drives can be quite uneventful at first, but a short distance away the landscape opens up into wide pans & some attractive riverine scenery. Walking in these more open areas is a real treat, & there are also mokoro trips on offer. The guiding is good.

Banoka combines well with other contemporary 'bushcamps' such as Kalahari Plains Camp (page 450) or Linyanti Bush Camp (page 249), which share a simple design & subtle style combined with great views & understated luxury. *US$732/940 Jun–Oct pp sharing/sgl, US$586/794 Nov–May, inc FB, most drinks, activities, park fees, laundry; exc transfers.* ⊕ *All year.*

KWARA (NG20)

The Kwara Concession covers a huge 1,750km², in the middle of the Delta's northern edge. It's bounded to the north by Selinda, to the west by Vumbura and to the east by NG18.

On the south side, near to Kwara camp itself, the reserve is adjacent to Moremi Game Reserve and the small enclave of NG21 (which includes Camp Okavango, Xugana and Shinde). This location gives Kwara access to the shallow floodplains and deep-water areas on the north side of the Delta, as well as a huge, dry game-viewing area to the north of that.

CONCESSION HISTORY Kwara has been an established safari camp since the mid-1990s. It was initially privately owned and run, before being operated first by Bird Safaris, then by Ker & Downey, with the marketing taken on by Wilderness Safaris. In 1999 the camp was taken over by the Kwando Safaris team, who bought the rights to the concession in 2008.

FLORA AND FAUNA HIGHLIGHTS Kwara Reserve is very large, and covers a wide spectrum of environments from deep-water lagoons and thick papyrus to dry-country scrub and mopane. Therefore, trying to describe here any dominant species of plants or animals is at best inconclusive, and at worst completely misleading.

These are a few general notes on what you're likely to find here, plus observations of what I found most interesting on my last visit.

Flora South of the camp lie the permanent swamps; a true deep-water environment. You'll find large stands of both papyrus and phragmites reeds, often with waterberry and water-fig trees dotted amongst them. Look down in some of the deeper main channels and you'll find the water opaque, heavy with sediment.

However, in most of the lagoons and the slower channels you'll be able to see right to the Kalahari sand at the bottom, and any water creatures or plants there. Amongst the mass of weeds, ask your guide to point out the delicate web of stems belonging to one of the Okavango's many species of bladderwort (*Utricularia* species). These usually form a submerged tangle of green, hair-like stems with tiny, thin leaves. Dotted amongst these are numerous small 'bladders' which, when touched by a small invertebrate like a mosquito larva, can suck the animal in and capture it. The bladder then digests the animal, and in the process gets valuable nitrogen, which is in very short supply in the mineral-impoverished waters of the Okavango.

Much easier to locate, floating on the surface of the lagoons, you'll find the fan-shaped, serrated leaves of the water chestnut (*Trapa natans*). This is often found on the edges of the lagoons, and is interesting not so much for its white flowers, but for the horned seedpod which it forms. The barbs on this will latch on to the fur or skin

---

THE WATERLILIES

The two main species of waterlily in the Okavango are the day-lilies (*Nymphaea nouchali caerulea*) and the night-lilies (*Nymphaea lotus*), which are sometimes called lotus lilies. The day-lilies are more common, and the species are fairly easy to tell apart.

The large floating leaves of day-lilies have smooth edges. As you might expect, the flowers open in mid/early morning, and close in the afternoon; they start off as a delicate shade of violet-purple (earning them the name of 'blue lily'), with only the centre having a yellowish tinge. These last for about five days, gradually turning whiter as they age, before the stem twists and drags the pollinated seed-head under water. There it matures until the seeds are eventually released, complete with air-filled bladders to help them float and disperse better.

Night-lilies are similar but have much darker green leaves, sharply serrated at the edge. The flowers have creamy white petals, edged with yellow, and a strongly yellow centre; these flowers often lie very flat on the surface, facing directly upwards. They open in the late afternoon and close in the early morning, relying for their pollination on night-flying insects.

of animals, as an aid to dispersing its seed. Their large size suggests that the area's numerous hippo are involved.

Move away from the water, north of camp, and you'll start entering the drier parts of the Kwara Reserve. You'll see that between the dry and wet, there's a transition zone where the bush is a mixture of ancient tree-islands surrounded by plains that were once flooded. The tree-islands were once more distinct, and surrounded by true floodplains, but as this area has dried out, the vegetation on the plains has grown and blurred the distinction between plains and tree-islands. Similarly, the salt deposits that are often found at the heart of the tree-islands have dissipated.

Like many areas on the edges of the Delta, this is in the extremely slow process of change. This zone was once wet, and now its landscapes and vegetation are very, very gradually reverting to landforms and vegetation of the drier areas – a process that will take millennia to complete. Here you'll find most of the Delta's usual species of trees, from African mangosteens to jackalberries, and both real fan and wild date palms. Plus a few species more often seen in the drier areas of Chobe, like Kalahari appleleaf (*Lonchocarpus nelsii*) and silver cluster-leaf (*Terminalia sericea*).

Fauna In the drier areas, Kwara's dominant antelopes appear to be tsessebe and impala, with very healthy populations of reedbuck, kudu and giraffe. You'll also find wildebeest, zebra, bushbuck, warthog and steenbok, plus a liberal sprinkling of elephant and the odd herd of buffalo. On the floodplains around camp, lechwe are also common, whilst deep in the papyrus there are sitatunga, though these are not often seen.

All the big cats – lion, leopard and cheetah – are around, and given the open nature of some of the environment and Kwando Safaris' policy of tracking game as actively as possible, it is a good area for wild dog. My last very short visit here was in February, which is usually a very difficult time for spotting predators. But despite the thick, green vegetation the guide and spotter managed to locate a pack of wild dogs as they killed an impala, having tracked them for several miles across the bush.

When I first visited this area in 1976, it was still in the grip of hunting, with dismal game viewing and a bleak outlook. The few game drives I went on yielded remarkably little. Antelope would flee at 500m, and we had almost no sightings of big game. Inevitably, the first people who tried to run photographic safaris here, Wilderness Safaris, couldn't make a go of the place, and it changed hands several times. Since then, the wildlife situation has changed immeasurably and for the last five or six years photographic camps have been run successfully in the area by Kwando Safaris. This is an interesting reflection of what's been happening in northern Botswana in the past ten to 15 years, in that the more interesting areas that had been used for hunting have now been supplanted by photographic camps. At the same time, the hunting safari operations have been pushed to operate in more marginal areas with environments that are of less interest to photographic visitors.

Birdlife As with the range of animals, the birdlife is inevitably varied. About 6.5km southwest of Kwara is Gcodikwe Lagoon. This is within Moremi Game Reserve, but Kwara is the nearest camp to it, so makes a good base for visits here. See the more comprehensive notes on pages 278–9 of *Chapter 11* about Gcodikwe, but note that within a boat ride you'll find one of the region's most important breeding colonies of storks, egrets, herons and spoonbills. It is at its busiest between September and November, but there are always a few birds there.

Elsewhere in Kwara you'll find a good range of the usual species found in and around the Delta. The more common residents include reed cormorants, darters, African and lesser jacanas, malachite, pied and giant kingfishers, pygmy geese, fish eagles and marsh harriers. Meanwhile the coucals are particularly well represented, with Senegal, coppery-tailed and (in summer) even black coucals all seen. More unusual sightings include fulvous duck, swamp boubous, black and slaty egrets, black-crowned and white-backed night herons, and the occasional migrant osprey.

In the drier areas north of the permanent waterways, some of the more common residents include blacksmith plover, red-billed francolins, double-banded sandgrouse, lilac-breasted rollers, yellow-billed hornbills, Meyer's parrots, fiery-necked nightjars, palm swifts, white-rumped babblers, red-eyed and Cape turtle doves, black-crowned tchagras, Heuglin's robins and black-breasted snake eagles. More unusual sightings might include western banded snake eagles, Dickinson's kestrels (often perching on palm trees), red-necked falcons, bat hawks, swallow-tailed bee-eaters, red-billed helmet shrikes, brown-throated weavers and wattled cranes.

WHEN TO VISIT As with much of the Delta, the big game here is usually more prolific during the dry season; and although many of the birds breed between December and March, Gcodikwe is generally at its most spectacular before then. That said, visiting in February still allowed me some first-class game viewing, including wild dog, as noted above. So don't write off the green season as a universally lousy time for game: it just takes a bit more tracking down then.

GETTING THERE AND AWAY Technically Kwara could be reached by boat from Camp Okavango, Camp Moremi, Xugana or Shinde, but in practice virtually all visitors arrive by air to the small airstrip a short distance from camp. Like most camps in the Okavango, you can't just drop in here, and even if you could the camp wouldn't welcome you. It's essential to pre-book your visit.

WHERE TO STAY Kwara and the newer Little Kwara are both owned by Kwando Safaris (see page 176) and often linked with its sister camps in NG14, Lebala and Lagoon (see pages 256–7).

⌂ **Kwara** [map 295] (8 tents) ✆ KWARAC
19°06.473'S, 23°15.867'E. Kwara stands on a small tree-island amidst floodplains. Most of its large tents, measuring 3.5m x 7m x about 2m high, are raised on teak decks with good views over the surrounding plains & lagoons. Lined in a light-green canvas that makes them much brighter than a normal tent, they have large windows of traditional insect-proof mesh. The wardrobe, luggage rack, bedside tables, chairs & beds are all of solid teak, standing on a polished floor dotted with rugs. The bathroom, in a separate part of the tent, includes twin washbasins, a flush toilet, & an inventively designed large shower that's enclosed but surrounded by a screen that's partially open to the outside. The honeymoon suite (No 8) also has a free-standing bath.

Slightly raised up on decking beneath a large jackalberry tree (*Diospyros mespiliformis*), Kwara's thatched bar-lounge & dining area is cosy & comfortable. It overlooks a shallow lagoon that often attracts good numbers of game. The camp's food is good & the bar well stocked, as you'd expect from a high-quality camp. Nearby there's a substantial swimming pool set into wooden decking & lined by sunloungers, & a raised look-out hide where you can spend the middle of the day reading or taking in the view. There's also a gift shop. Kwara shares a fairly informal approach with its sister camps, Lagoon & Lebala, which are all designed slightly differently as part of a real effort by Kwando Safaris to ensure that the camps have their own individuality. While each aims to provide a very comfortable camp, the accent is firmly on the activities & the guiding rather

12

than ever more creature comforts. *US$918/1,218 pp sharing/sgl Jul–Oct, US$600/800 Apr–Jun & Nov; US$515 pp rest of year, inc FB, activities, park fees.* ⊕ *All year.*

🏠 **Little Kwara** [map 295] (5 tents) Although Little Kwara is only 2km or so from Kwara, it is constructed very differently. Built in 2006 on a tree-island, its tents are raised on high wooden decks, with canvas walls & ceilings into which large mosquito-gauze windows have been set, all with roll-down flaps. Polished wooden flooring, twin ¾ or king-size beds, & some solid & slightly contemporary furniture set the tone, while behind a large bedhead is the dressing area. Each tent has its own en-suite bathroom complete with bath,

& indoor & partially covered outdoor shower. To the front, a large sliding door of gauze leads to a private veranda set amidst the trees.

Sandy paths lead to the spacious main lounge overlooking the lagoon, & a well-stocked bar area where guests can help themselves. Low wicker tables, trendy sofas & proper armchairs with comfy cushions all add to the sense of a tastefully designed camp. To the side is a restaurant area, & there's also a curio shop.

Activities are of the same high standard as those at Kwara, with trackers as well as guides on every vehicle. *US$1,132/1,432 pp sharing/sgl Jul–Oct; US$734/934 Apr–Jun & Nov; US$550 pp rest of year, inc FB, activities, park fees.* ⊕ *All year.*

ACTIVITIES Kwara is big on activities, and has a wider range available through the year than many camps in the Delta. Game drives and night drives are the norm, and the camp boasts that there are never more than six guests on a vehicle with a guide and tracker. Together with very knowledgeable guides, this makes the game-viewing experience here amongst the best in the Delta, and certainly better in the green season than most dry-land camps. Much of this is due to their willingness to actively track the game, heading off-road and into the bush at the slightest sign of something interesting.

On the water, the varied terrain means that motorboat and mokoro trips are possible all year, and the camp also has a double-decker pontoon-type boat. Climbing on top of this in the papyrus-lined channels is magical, and will give you a completely different view of the waterscape.

XUGANA, CAMP OKAVANGO AND SHINDE (NG21)

This concession is relatively small by Botswana's standards, but shares a long southern boundary with Moremi Reserve, and is entirely devoted to photographic safaris. To the north, NG21 adjoins the Kwara and Vumbura concessions.

Within the reserve, the activities are primarily water-based, although Shinde also offers game drives, and its sister camp, Footsteps across the Delta, specialises in walking safaris.

FLORA AND FAUNA HIGHLIGHTS NG21 is adjacent, and in many ways very similar, to the southern parts of the neighbouring Kwara Reserve, NG20. Thus read my comments on the flora and fauna there (pages 299–300) for a complete picture. That said, a greater proportion of NG21 reserve is permanent swamp, as it has several large, permanent rivers flowing through it. The Moanachira passes through, heading east to feed the Gcodikwe Lagoon, before flowing into the Xakanaxa Lagoon. This in turn forms the source of the Khwai River that eventually reaches to the far eastern corner of the Delta.

A less clear channel, the Mborogha, flows southeast almost to Chief's Island where it ultimately feeds into the Gomoti and Santandibe rivers, both important watercourses of the lower Delta (though in the last few decades there seems to have been a change of flow between these two major rivers, from the Mborogha to the Moanachira).

In *Okavango: Jewel of the Kalahari* (see *Appendix 3, Further information*), Karen Ross notes that the eastern rivers, the Moanachira and Mborogha, carry far more water today than they did 100 years ago. So with all these waters concentrated into NG21 it's perhaps not surprising that it's an area where you'll find plenty of deep-water lagoons and channels.

Most of the NG21 Reserve has too much water to be one of the Delta's prime game-viewing areas, but in the dry area around Shinde you'll still find good numbers of game, including impala, red lechwe, tsessebe and giraffe. Lone bull elephants are around for most of the year, whilst the breeding herds migrate here from the dry interior towards the end of the dry season.

Kudu, sable and buffalo are infrequently seen. Sitatunga, while common in the areas of thick papyrus, are rarely sighted – though one of the guides at Shinde seems to be particularly adept at spotting them from motorboats and mokoros. NG21 is also a good place to look for water-based mammals like the very common hippo and the more elusive spotted-necked otters.

The dominant predators are lion and hyena, with leopard and wild dog also found here. In 2013, a pack of seven dogs was regularly spotted around Shinde and Footsteps, and was thought to have denned on the concession.

WHEN TO VISIT Whilst game viewing under the clouds of the green season can be quite rewarding, the attraction of sitting on a boat or a mokoro is more elusive. To appreciate the magic of boating through the Okavango, most people need at least dryness and preferably a blue sky and tropical sun.

Last time I visited Camp Moremi during the green season, the weather one morning was glorious. This prompted the enthusiastic manager to ask me why Expert Africa sends relatively few visitors to the Okavango between January and March. 'It's almost empty of visitors and often the weather's superb,' he beamed. Later that day the clouds drew in and it rained on and off for 36 hours, foiling any ideas I had about photography for the rest of my stay. Hence I'd advise that water-based camps like Xugana and Camp Okavango are best visited during the dry season.

GETTING THERE AND AWAY All guests pre-arrange their trips here, and fly into the camps' own airstrips, which are all situated near by. Camp Okavango's (⊕ CAMPOA 19°07.720'S, 23°05.930'E) is a short walk behind the camp, and from the air you'll realise that it takes up most of the very small island on which the camp is situated!

Shinde's airstrip (⊕ SHINDA 19°07.070'S, 23°09.180'E) is a five-minute drive northeast of the camp. Xugana's (⊕ XUGAIR 19°02.200'S, 23°05.710'E), too, is very close and northwest of the camp.

Guests heading for Footsteps arrive at Shinde by plane, then have a leisurely 1½-hour transfer. This involves a game drive, followed by a short river crossing by mokoro, and a final game drive to the camp.

WHERE TO STAY Of the three camps in this area, the two water camps, Camp Okavango and Xugana, are both owned and marketed by Desert & Delta Safaris (see page 176). The third camp, Shinde, is run by Ker & Downey Botswana (see page 176).

Xugana Island Lodge [map 295]
(8 chalets) ⊕ XUGANA 19°04.097'S, 23°06.014'E. Though it's been periodically reinvented, with the

latest refurbishment in 2008, Xugana is one of the Delta's older camps; it is said that it may have been started as a hunting camp as early as the

1960s, probably by Henry Selby (of the hunting company Ker, Downey & Selby). Subsequently, in the early 1980s, it was bought by a local businessman, David Hartley, as a private family retreat. This eventually became more commercial &, along with its sister camp, Tsaro Elephant Lodge (now closed), was marketed under the banner of Hartley's Safaris until they were bought by Desert & Delta Safaris in 2000.

One of the few things that hasn't changed about Xugana over the years is its location on the banks of a forested island beside a large, deep lagoon: a spectacular site, fitting for a camp that concentrates entirely on water-based activities. It's about 7.5km north of Camp Okavango (yet the most direct route by boat covers about 16.8km of waterways). For many years Xugana used the lagoon itself as a swimming pool, suspending a crocodile-proof wire cage in the lagoon for bathers to cool off in. Whilst environmentally admirable, some of the camp's less enlightened guests found this pool's occasional murkiness off-putting, so a new swimming pool was built amongst the landscaped lawns at the centre of camp. These are dotted with natural vegetation, with everything protected from hungry elephants by an electric fence. (What remains of the old swimming pool is now a floating deck, used for the odd alfresco dinner.)

The camp's open-sided lounge, bar & dining areas under thatch are set back slightly from the jetty, facing the water. In good weather, most meals are taken on the spacious deck overlooking the lagoon, shaded by fig & leadwood trees, & with a fireplace perched above the water. A good small curio shop sports a fair selection of local books & wildlife guides, plus T-shirts, handicrafts & postcards.

Xugana's chalets are built of reed & thatch, raised up on wooden decking, with twin beds or a dbl under a large, walk-in mosquito net. Each has a ceiling fan under its high ceiling, operated by the camp's generator during the day. There's a 12V lighting system in the rooms for use at night. The bathrooms are en suite with a walk-in hot shower, flush toilet & washbasin, & outside, facing the lagoon, is a private wooden deck with a pair of canvas safari chairs. Water is heated by solar power. *US$873/1,135 pp sharing/sgl Jul–Oct, US$495 pp Jan–Mar; US$573 pp Apr–Jun &Nov, fully inc.* ☺ *All year.*

⌂ **Camp Okavango** [map 295] (11 tents, 1 suite) ✪ CAMPOK 19°08.118'S, 23°06.035'E. On the south side of this concession, Camp Okavango stands on the west side of Nxaragha Island amidst floodplains, lagoons & waterways. It's a measure of the meandering geography of the Delta's waterways that although its sister camp, Camp Moremi, is only about 33km away as the egret flies, the most direct route by boat (coincidentally, via the Gcodikwe Lagoon) is slightly over 60km.

'Camp O', as it's usually known, was started by an American woman, Jessie Niel, in the early 1980s, & was swiftly followed by Camp Moremi. She ran & marketed them as a pair under the banner of Desert & Delta Safaris until, in the mid-1990s, the operation was taken over by a group called Chobe Holdings, associated with Chobe Game Lodge & AfroVentures – though the name was kept.

The camp is quite large by Okavango standards, & its spacious thatched dining, lounge & bar area reflect this. All open out on to a large area of lawn, which is often the venue for meals outside – usually accompanied by lots of candles & flaming torches. For seclusion during the day, there's a raised viewing hide that's been built into a sausage tree (*Kigelia africana*) & 3 knobthorn trees (*Acacia nigrescens*) near the end of the jetty. It's a good spot to relax with comfy chairs, & the view over the papyrus & reeds might interest patient birdwatchers. The plunge pool, sundeck or the sprinkling of hammocks around camp, however, are probably better venues for relaxation.

Sand paths – a pleasant change from the usual acres of hardwood walkways – link the main areas with large Meru-style tents, raised up on individual wooden platforms. These are very comfortably furnished, with twin or dbl beds, crisp linen, a teak wardrobe, luggage rack, dressing table, bedside pedestals & canvas safari chairs. You'll also find rugs on the floor & co-ordinated linens & blinds to cover the mesh windows. Each has an en-suite bathroom with a hot shower, washbasin & flush toilet. Following a recent refurbishment, gone are the tent flaps in favour of glazed aluminium sliding doors, thus affording extra light.

The camp also has the 'Okavango Suite', the old house of the camp's original owner. It's a unique, open-plan bungalow that's clearly been built to a personal specification. At its centre is a lounge with old-style settees, with a wooden room-divider. On one side of this is a large bedroom, dominated by a bed shrouded in mosquito netting. On the other is a dining room built for entertaining (though even just 2 guests staying in the suite can arrange to have dinner served here). It's all floored, panelled & furnished in wood. However, the suite's *pièce de résistance* is down a few steps from the bedroom: a black bathroom suite lit by recessed lighting in a room lined with black tiles & mirrors. Urban Gothic, circa 1970, in the heart of the Okavango. It's wonderful!

Although the camp focuses on boat & mokoro trips, bush walks on the islands are possible, though see my comments on walking trips in Botswana (pages 142–5) before you set off. Camps like this which concentrate on water activities tend to have a slower pace than those which also offer game drives; you'll have more time just to relax. As befits this, the tents also have their own tea/coffee-making facilities & even towelling robes.

The camp's curio shop is notable for a fine collection of baskets, all made by the staff, with the proceeds going to them. There are also a few books, T-shirts & film. *US$873/1,135 pp sharing/sgl Jul–Oct, US$495 pp Jan–Mar; US$573 pp Apr–Jun & Nov, fully inc.* ☺ *All year.*

🏠 **Shinde** [map 295] (8 tents) Contact Ker & Downey Botswana, page 176. The long-established Shinde – owned by Ker & Downey since the early 1980s – stands in a tree-shaded spot in the heart of NG21, about 6km east of Camp Okavango, 12km west of Kwara & 8km southeast of Xugana. It's a well-run camp, with a long-serving team of staff & a very flexible approach. The camp is set on a picturesque channel that feeds the Moanachira River, so with land-based as well as water activities, there's plenty of choice; if you have the energy to do 3 activities in a day, then that can be accommodated.

Shinde's lounge & dining areas are built on several levels, rising towards an unusual bowed canvas roof that's a little like an old ox-wagon. Down below, guests can help themselves to drinks from the bar, & peruse the collection of baskets made by the staff, before gathering round the firepit before dinner. Set well away, beyond a discreet electric wire fence designed to deter elephants from coming into camp, is a sheltered pool with sunloungers & views across the plains.

Sharing the view are traditional, walk-in tents with mesh windows, protected by large shadecloths that also shelter a porch with a couple of comfy chairs. Approached along open, sandy paths, most are at ground level, but 3 – including the 'honeymoon suite' – are built on raised wooden platforms. Inside, twin beds (or a king-size dbl) dominate the tents, their crisp white linen offset by the warm ochres & oranges of cushions, gossamer-light curtains & throws. Bedside lights are efficient, Moroccan-style rugs dot the wooden floors, & there's plenty of hot water for the en-suite shower & basins. Large mirrors & a separate flush toilet are an added bonus.

Families or groups of up to 6 seeking a more exclusive set-up can book the 3 tents that together form Shinde Enclave, which comes with a dedicated waiter & guide, & has its own bar, firepit, dining area & lounge, & a small deck overlooking an expanse of papyrus & reeds dotted with palm islands. *US$495 pp Mar & Dec, US$695 pp May–Jun & Nov, US$950/1,265 pp sharing/sgl Jul–Oct, inc FB, most drinks, activities, park fees, laundry; exc transfers. No children under 10.* ☺ *Mar–early Jan.*

🏕 **Footsteps across the Delta** [map 295] (3 tents) In operation since 1998, Footsteps is – along with Selinda Explorers & Footsteps across the Linyanti (pages 253 & 250) – one of the few operations in the Delta that take walking safaris really seriously. It's an intimate, semi-permanent camp, moving between sites every couple of years, & the standard of guiding is excellent.

As with any good walking safari, numbers are small; Footsteps takes a maximum of 6 guests at a time. Its small, twin-bedded tents, lit by battery-powered lanterns, have an en-suite flushing toilet, canvas basins on the porch, & a private but separate bucket shower. It's all very rustic, with dinner usually eaten under the stars & wildlife regularly roaming through. Yet despite the camp's remote location & rudimentary facilities, the standard of food is good, with plenty of fresh fruit & vegetables, newly baked bread each day, & a well-stocked bar. If you'd like to take a look 'backstage', they're very happy to show guests around.

The days largely revolve around walking (always with an armed guide & back-up guide), but it's very flexible. Typically you can expect 2 walks each day: one of 3–4hrs in the early morning, & a second, shorter walk combined with a game drive in the late afternoon, allowing you to explore further afield. Mokoro trips & fishing are also possible when the water is high enough.

12

Footsteps is one of the bases for Ker & Downey's Young Explorers safari (see page 73), for which the camp is always booked exclusively. Otherwise children are not accepted here. *US$495 pp Mar–* *Jun & Nov, US$630/795 pp sharing/sgl Jul–Oct, inc FB, drinks, activities, laundry; exc transfers. No children under 16.* ⊕ *Mar–Nov.*

ACTIVITIES Xugana, Camp Okavango and Shinde all operate motorboat excursions to explore the lagoons, plus mokoro trips to visit the areas of shallower water nearby. Often the mokoro trips are combined with walking on the islands, though these are usually led by an unarmed guide, so read my comments on walking (pages 142–5) before you depart. Note that if you're keen to visit Gcodikwe Lagoon then Camp Okavango or Shinde are much nearer to it than Xugana.

Both water activities are primarily for birdwatching and for learning about the general environment rather than for game viewing, though it's also possible to go fishing (for bream and tigerfish normally) from the motorboats.

In addition to these water activities, Shinde also has permanent access to dry land and so can offer 4x4 game drives and night drives (a maximum of seven guests per vehicle), and walks accompanied by an armed guide and tracker. However, those serious about walking would be better off spending a few nights at their specialist sister camp, Footsteps across the Delta.

VUMBURA AND DUBA PLAINS (NG22 AND NG23)

Immediately north of Moremi's Mombo Concession, the Vumbura and Duba Plains reserves (NG22 and 23) share many similarities of game and landscape with Mombo. This northern area of the Delta is one of my favourites, but because of the similarity between Vumbura and Duba, if you are planning a trip to this area then it's best to include only one of them in your itinerary.

Vumbura is a varied reserve, and the areas through which you drive are often very pretty. Much of its landscape consists of wide-open plains with tiny islands – almost a cliché of the Okavango. Vumbura's game is notably diverse, so most visitors will see a wide range of antelope and have a good chance to spot the less common predators.

Duba Plains, to the west of Vumbura, is visually similar but with larger open plains. It doesn't quite have Vumbura's diversity of game, though this is improving, but instead is the long-standing venue for battles between large herds of buffalo and sizeable prides of lion. Thus, it will often provide a very impressive spectacle of big game, particularly during the drier months of April to October. In the wet season (November to March), when the buffalo are fitter from eating the lush grass, the lions focus more on lechwe and warthog.

Both camps can access water activities, Vumbura for the whole year, although the areas aren't quite so picturesque as, say, the Jao Flats.

CONCESSION HISTORY Until around 1997 this was a hunting area, but then Wilderness Safaris started Vumbura, Little Vumbura and Duba Plains camps.

For several years there were two small, seasonal hunting camps running in the northeast of the Vumbura Concession (one of which was on the site of Kaporota). These had closed by 2001 and both are now used solely for photographic safaris.

In 2012 Duba Plains split from Wilderness Safaris and is now owned and managed by Great Plains Conservation, along with its sister camps in the Selinda Reserve (pages 250–4). Dereck and Beverly Joubert, the wildlife photographers, are closely involved with this venture, while Vumbura and Little Vumbura are still very much a part of Wilderness Safaris.

As is increasingly the case with reserves in Botswana, both Duba and Vumbura have an element of local community involvement. Five local villages – Seronga, Eretsha, Beetsha, Gudigwa and Gunitsungwa – have some control over the concession, and derive considerable benefit from its success. Most of the staff for the camps come from these villages too, so there's a flow of revenue from these camps back to the communities by way of wages (see *The anatomy of a community partnership*, below, and comments on NG12 on page 296).

THE ANATOMY OF A COMMUNITY PARTNERSHIP

Though 'community-based natural resource management' is recognised as one of the main strategies for achieving sustainable development in the rural areas of Botswana, really good examples of it are few and far between. Wilderness Safaris have a strong track record with successful community projects in other countries, like Damaraland Camp in Namibia, and here in Botswana their flagship community project is the Vumbura and Duba concessions. The camps in these private reserves or concessions started in 1997 when the safari company and their partners made an agreement with the community to which the government had given management of concession areas NG22 and NG23. Great Plains continues to liaise and work with the local communities in much the same way that Wilderness still do.

The community, in this case, consists of five villages to the north of the Okavango Delta: Seronga, Eretsha, Beetsha, Gudigwa and Gunitsungwa. The villagers had to set up a trust, with a fully constituted board to represent all the villages and people of the area in their dealings with the government, the Land Board and the safari companies. The ten-person board is made up of two elected people from each of the five villages. Wilderness Safaris/ Great Plains Conservation pay a six-figure US-dollar lease fee each year to the board (this is a lot of money in rural Botswana). The board decides how to use that money for the benefit of the community. Further, as part of the deal, the two safari companies have to employ at least 118 people from the villages (though they actually ended up giving jobs to around 150), and to deliver on a number of community projects. These projects have resulted in the setting up and supporting of a number of secondary cottage industries in the villages, like basket weaving and vegetable gardens; in addition they have sponsored an inter-village soccer tournament; helped with transport problems; and set up village shops, mortuaries, etc.

Perhaps the most difficult issue about this kind of agreement for any safari company is the short duration of the leases; the community can swap their safari company after the first year if it wishes to, then again after the second year, the fifth year and the tenth year. Given the huge investment in infrastructure and the long-term nature of the marketing, this is difficult for most safari companies to contemplate. Duba certainly had a few paperwork issues during the changeover, though most seem to have been ironed out now. Yet 16 years into the project, the safari companies are slowly starting to reap the benefits of a stable, long-term relationship with the community as their partner. Equally, guests to these camps know that their safari is actively benefiting both the communities in the area, and thus, in turn, the local wildlife.

12

FLORA AND FAUNA HIGHLIGHTS Both these reserves are broadly similar in character, although Duba Plains (as you might expect) has more extensive open plains, whereas the plains at Vumbura are often partially flooded, and they're broken up by more islands, including many small palm islands.

Flora Much of these concessions consist of very beautiful, open floodplains dotted with islands, many of which are tiny. The vegetation of the larger islands is dominated by many of the Okavango's usual tree species, including raintree (*Lonchocarpus capassa*), leadwood (*Combretum imberbe*), African mangosteen (*Garcenia livingstonei*), jackalberry (*Diospyros mespiliformis*), sausage tree (*Kigelia africana*) and sycamore fig (*Ficus sycomorus*).

You'll also find knobthorn trees (*Acacia nigrescens*), although relatively few of them, and some particularly large, wonderful specimens of feverberry trees (*Croton megalobotrys*), named after the anti-malarial properties of the seeds and the bark. (These properties had been known to local African residents for centuries, but were brought to the attention of a wider audience by an article in the medical journal, *The Lancet*, in 1899. Apparently there has still not been any detailed research on these medicinal properties.)

Amongst the main bushes that you'll find here are the Kalahari star apple (*Diospyros lycioides lycioides*), which is often also called the blue bush, for its overall bluish tinge, or the 'toothbrush bush', as its roots can be peeled and used as a toothbrush. (Veronica Roodt reports that on using it 'at first my mouth burned and I became extremely worried when my whole mouth turned yellow. The result, however, was remarkable – white teeth and fresh breath.') Another very common bush in this area is the evergreen magic gwarri bush (*Euclea divinorum*), also sometimes known as the 'toothbrush bush' for the use of its branches. Both these bushes produce dyes that are used in Botswana to colour palm leaves for weaving baskets.

In the northeast of Vumbura there are some fine acacia woodlands, whilst as you travel west from Vumbura into Duba you'll find more and larger open floodplains, slightly less thick wooded islands, and more clusters of the wild date palm (*Phoenix reclinata*).

As well as the drier areas, there are many small channels near the Vumbura camps, and some open, lightly reeded lagoons. The channels are lined intermittently with a mixture of papyrus and common reeds, and periodically open out on to floodplain areas. Scenically the areas near these camps don't quite match up to the sheer beauty of the Jao Flats, as there are very few feathery real fan palms or lily-covered lagoons.

Fauna When I last visited, I was very impressed by the varied line-up of antelope that I saw in the Vumbura Reserve in a few days. Unlike many of the areas further from the heart of the Delta, there wasn't just a high density of one or two species, to the virtual exclusion of the rest.

Species that you can expect to see here include tsessebe, impala, lechwe, kudu, zebra, wildebeest, giraffe, warthog and steenbok. Sable are seen fairly often, especially near the airstrip. Waterbuck are common; Vumbura is one of the few places within northern Botswana where you'll find good numbers of them. Duiker, reedbuck and bushbuck are seen infrequently, whilst roan antelope are rare, though have been seen occasionally in the late dry season. I know of just one (February) sighting of sitatunga in Vumbura.

Wild dogs had denned here for several years running prior to my visit, and I was lucky enough to be able to watch a beautiful pack with pups at its den, situated in the mopane woodlands on the east side of the Vumbura. However, in a thick band of mopane woodlands it wasn't possible to follow them when they moved off.

Cheetah are also resident, though, like the rest of the smaller game, they will move through the buffalo fence and out into the huge NG12, to the north. In the dry season, when many of the open floodplains are dry, it's a classic open environment that is perfect for cheetah, rather like Mombo and parts of Selinda, so it's a particularly good area in which to seek them.

Leopard are occasionally seen on night drives. Lion and spotted hyena are both relatively common. Both black-backed and side-striped jackals occur here, though the black-backed are seen much more regularly.

Moving westwards, Duba Plains is noted not only for its huge open plains, but also for having some of the best concentrations of buffalo in Botswana. Particularly large herds are found here during the dry season. These can easily number over a thousand animals, and inevitably they attract a very high concentration of lion – which in the Duba Plains area is very much the dominant predator. The converse of this is that Duba doesn't have quite the same balance of species, or the diversity, that you'll usually find in Vumbura, zebra, cheetah and impala being the notable absentees. That said, giraffe have recently returned to Duba, and there are very good populations of lechwe, reedbuck, bushbuck, waterbuck and kudu. And the area is curiously popular with warthogs!

Spotted hyena are flourishing, despite the sizeable prides of lions, and side-striped jackals are seen fairly frequently, but black-backed are largely absent.

Birdlife The birdlife here is as varied as you'll find in any area of the Delta with a good mix of dry and wet environments. Certainly in one afternoon of very casual bird spotting on the river from Vumbura you can expect to find a range of kingfishers (malachite, pied and giant), jacanas, several species of egrets (including slaty), black-winged stilts, open-bill storks and reed cormorants. In addition, the open floodplains with short grass seemed to attract very good numbers of various waders plus saddle-billed storks, glossy and sacred ibises, spoonbills and – relatively unusually – pelicans. Visiting in 2013, we were particularly impressed by the quality of birdlife, when as well as large numbers of these species we spotted less common birds such as the pink- (or rosy-) throated longclaw, wattled crane and Stanley's bustard. Pel's fishing owls can also be found here, and in October 2006 and again in 2010 (albeit just for a day!), the waterlogged plains of Duba Plains played host to a very unusual treat in the Delta, flamingos.

WHEN TO VISIT As elsewhere in the Delta the big game is more diverse and prolific during the dry season, although the birdlife is generally better between December and March. Driving around the reserve can be more difficult then, as there's a lot of water around and many roads are submerged, but to counter this problem Duba Plains have modified their vehicles to be higher off the ground.

GETTING THERE AND AWAY All the camps here accept only pre-booked guests who fly in. Driving isn't possible without permission – and permission is never given (though it would be only a few hours' drive from Seronga, if you knew the way!). Note that each camp has its own separate airstrip. Vumbura's (VUMAIR) is at ✪ 18°57.504'S, 22°49.063'E, and Duba's (OMDOP) at ✪ 19°01.039'S, 22°41.059'E.

WHERE TO STAY The two Vumbura camps are marketed by Wilderness Safaris (page 177): Little Vumbura as a 'classic' camp, and Vumbura Plains one of their 'premier'

12

camps. Duba Plains – similar in style to Little Vumbura – is now marketed by Great Plains Conservation (page 176), who are planning to revamp it in due course.

⌂ **Little Vumbura** [map 295] (6 tents) Although less than 2km from its larger sister camp, Little Vumbura (✪ LVUMBU 19°00.070'S, 22°51.710'E) feels quite separate, perhaps because it's on a small island & always approached by boat. Little Vumbura has a small dining area & a comfy lounge/bar section. All is under canvas on decking about a metre off the ground, & attached, via a 50m jetty, to the launch area for the boats.

Over the dining room/bar stands a large waterberry tree (*Syzygium cordatum*), & the open sides of the canvas structure (which can be rolled down) are shaded by dense surrounding stands of wild date palms, a couple of fig trees (*Ficus sycomorus*) & an assortment of jackalberry trees (*Diospyros mespiliformis*). This all leaves you with the very comfortable feeling that the camp's been built from within the vegetation, & you're cocooned in a small, tropical hideaway.

The walk-in tents, 1 designed for families, are comfortable, with wickerwork shelves, wardrobe & furniture. They stand on low platforms & have an en-suite shower, washbasin & toilet inside. A few paces away outside is a much more natural open-air shower, with a view of the surrounding floodplains.

Aside from the main area, there's also a small curio shop (with books, materials, local baskets & African curios for sale), a plunge pool & a wonderful open hexagonal section of decking (with a firepit in the middle) which extends into the reeds & is used for dinner, drinks & stargazing.

Originally, this little camp accepted just 8 people & was certainly one of Wilderness's hottest properties in Botswana. Now, to capitalise on this, Little Vumbura has been enlarged to take up to 12 people, while the main Vumbura Plains has been slimmed down in size. *US$983/1,251 pp sharing/ sgl Apr–May, US$1,413/1,681 Jun–Oct, inc FB, activities, park fees, laundry & most drinks; exc transfers.* ⊕ *All year.*

⌂ **Vumbura Plains** [map 295] (7 rooms north, 7 rooms south) This new camp falls into the 'seriously posh' bracket: a boutique lodge in the bush, split across 2 sites: Vumbura Plains North, which incorporates 2 family rooms, & Vumbura Plains South. Although these are linked by a walkway, they have separate central areas &

management, so feel like 2 camps, softening what could otherwise be a slightly corporate effect.

Contemporary in design, each of its large, square rooms (emphatically not tents) of quality light wood has a big open area with voluminous white net curtains which slide on ceiling rails to act as room dividers. Mundane things like wardrobes & hanging spaces are cleverly concealed along one side. In one quarter of the room, a square sunken lounge with low seating & soft cushions is a great place for unwinding after a game drive or early in the evening. In another, a tall post with a free-standing shower looks down on a concrete slab – with a shower curtain for privacy. And outside another shower beckons. Each room also boasts its own sizeable private deck with plunge pool & little sala, lit by soft spots. It's all quite unexpected & very different from a typical safari camp – & is already proving popular with the American market, & the moneyed glitterati.

For families, Vumbura Plains has a big plus. It was one of the first camps in Botswana to have 2 private family suites, with a completely separate en-suite room for children (from 6). Linking the 2 rooms is a private deck with 3 enclosed sides, which means that – unusually – children can safely be slightly independent of their parents.

The central area of each camp, linked to the rooms by wooden walkways, focuses on a wooden platform, sheltered by a roof held up on poles & set beneath indigenous trees overlooking the plains. When it's raining or blowing a gale, wooden slatted blinds protect guests from the worst of the elements, but during the dry season, this makes for dining or relaxing almost al fresco, with a cool through breeze. As everywhere else, the décor here is contemporary & quite fun: with shaggy, long-pile rugs, plenty of comfortable, soft sofas & modern *objets d'art*.

The stylish mode of the camp extends to meals as well: food is served to the table, & there is a choice of carefully designed dishes, rather than the usual safari camp buffet. Expect sparkling cutlery for your food, & crystal glasses to hold your choice of the wines of the day (which usually come from South Africa). A cappuccino maker is on hand throughout the day, & the bar is particularly well stocked.

As you'd expect from a Wilderness camp, the service is friendly & staff try very hard to meet the high standards set by the camp. Activities include the usual 4x4 Land Rover safaris, walking & boats/mekoro trips. There's also a well-stocked curio shop between the camps – & shared by guests at both.

On my last visit, I found that camps like this, Mombo & King's Pool attract some of the company's more ambitious & keen guides, who certainly rank amongst the best in the company. *US$1,403/1,719 pp sharing/sgl Apr–May, US$2,105/2,421 Jun–Oct, inc FB, activities, park fees, laundry & most drinks; exc transfers.* ☺ *All year.*

⌂ **Duba Plains** [map 294] (6 tents) Of all the 'usual' fly-in camps in the Delta, Duba Plains is one of the most northern. It is north of Moremi Game Reserve, a 5min flight west of Vumbura.

Duba is a fairly small camp with the main dining area built on raised decking under a high thatched roof, around a large jackalberry tree. The cosy lounge/bar area is adjacent, on a slightly lower level, with armchairs & a couple of sofas around a wicker coffee table. A new star deck extends off the lounge area, & judicious use of sapling screens lends it a pleasant rustic feel. The thatched guest toilet is nearby, & beyond is another area of raised decking. On one side of this is a swimming pool, opposite is an observation deck with chairs, tables & loungers. This commands a good view over the plains, & is often used for brunch or supper. To the side of this is a quiet sala (a small gazebo), with a couple of wicker chairs & a bench. It's perfect for relaxing in the afternoon. About 150m from the main lounge is a small hide for birdwatchers, with a copy of *Newman's Birds of Southern Africa* for those 'hard to identify' species.

Duba's bright, airy tents are linked by bush paths, & raised on decks to give good views of the plains. Each has a small veranda with a table & 2 chairs, & a wooden door. Inside, wood has been used extensively for simple, tasteful décor. The headboard at the back of dbl or twin beds extends into twin washbasins, & there's a small wardrobe & laundry basket. The tent has mosquito-proof gauze, so mosquito nets are not usually provided. Inside at the back is a flush toilet & a shower, beyond which a door opens on to raised decking where an outdoor shower has a great view of the plains.

Because of its location near the Panhandle, Duba is one of the first camps in the main Delta to be flooded. From about May to the end of August the shallow-water plains around it usually have enough water for mokoro trips. *US$990/1,337 pp sharing/sgl 11 Jan–Mar, US$1,125/1,519 Apr–14 June & Nov–19 Dec, US$1,495/2,243 15 Jun–Oct, US$1,225/1,838 20 Dec–10 Jan, inc FB, most drinks, activities, park fees, laundry; exc transfers.* ☺ *All year.*

ACTIVITIES The Vumbura camps have year-round access to deep permanent water, and so boat trips are possible all year, with opportunities to fish if you wish. Boating at Duba Plains, however, is dependent on water levels. There are also mokoro excursions, 4x4 game drives and night drives (though night drives may sometimes be restricted when flood levels are very high, from May to August). Short walks are also offered by these camps, though I would generally go to a specialist walking camp if I wanted to do much walking.

COMMUNITY AREA (NG24)

Currently this is the only one of the Delta's photography-specific areas (ie: hunting is not allowed) which has no proper safari operation in it. Until about 1999 this was the location for Jedibe Camp, which had long been run by Wilderness Safaris and was one of their earliest camps in the Delta.

I visited Jedibe in about 1996. It was located deep within a maze of deep-water channels and papyrus, and the main activity there was exploring on motorboats. This was superb fun (although motorboats are probably the most expensive activity to run for any camp, given their thirst for fuel!) as the boats could reach some stunning areas of the most beautiful floodplains, as well as exploring the papyrus-

12

lined channels of the main rivers. Mokoro trips, incorporating walks on the islands, were also possible but usually of secondary interest.

However, in 1999 Jedibe's lease came up for tender – which means a re-opening of negotiations between the government, the community (the Okavango Jakotsha Community Trust) and anyone who is interested in taking responsibility for the area's lease.

Since Jedibe was built, many new mixed land-and-water camps had come into existence in the Delta, and proven very successful. Furthermore their range of game drives and water activities was wider than Jedibe's options. This left Jedibe looking less commercially attractive, with a very specific, limited niche as a deep-water camp in permanent papyrus, running mainly (inherently costly) motorboats. Jedibe's northerly location, far from Maun, meant expensive transport links and running costs too.

These factors all made Jedibe less commercially attractive, at a time when the local community was expecting to get more for the concession. Eventually no agreement could be made.

If you do visit this area, then don't go for the animals. Although there are animals on the islands, this is a deep-water area and you should treat any game sightings as a bonus. Instead come for the bird and water-life. Expect lots of deep, fast-flowing channels and endless banks of papyrus, which periodically open out on to spectacular floodplains.

 WHERE TO STAY The small Makwena Camp on the edge of the reserve, accessed from Etsha 6 on the Panhandle road, folded some time ago, and despite an application to build a 12-room lodge on the site, with a further tented camp at nearby Majamboroka, neither has yet materialised.

JAO, KWETSANI, JACANA, TUBU AND PELO (NG25)

Close to the Panhandle, west of Moremi, NG25 is a particularly beautiful concession covering about 600km² of the upper Okavango Delta. Most of this is a fairly wet environment, with extensive floodplains, especially around the Jao Flats, though there is a substantial drier section, where Tubu Tree Camp is situated, to the west of the reserve. The annual flood generally reaches this reserve around April or May, instantly expanding the area of the floodplains.

FLORA AND FAUNA HIGHLIGHTS The area around Jao and Jacana feels very much like most people's image of the Okavango: watery and terribly picturesque. It's a lovely environment, one that is mirrored at Kwetsani when the flood arrives. Whilst the game diversity in the area might not quite match some of the areas further east yet, lechwe and lion are generally common and those alone will keep most people entertained. That said, visiting on one occasion in April, we didn't see a single lion.

The birding is also good, with enough diversity of habitat to mean that you'll find most Delta species here if you look hard enough. I've had great luck in the past here with gallinules and pink-throated longclaws.

Hundu Island, the area around Tubu Tree Camp on the western side of the concession, is much drier and totally different from the eastern part of the reserve where the three older camps are situated. In particular, this area now has a firm reputation as a good place to see leopard, and in 2013 we also saw an unusually large number of sitatunga.

Flora The reserve's most memorable area must be the beautiful Jao Flats, a series of huge open floodplains, dotted with tiny islands that are often only a few metres across. These vast floodplains are covered in a mix of very sparse vegetation, much of which is the aptly named hippo grass (*Vossia cuspidata*), which has round, slender leaves, pointing periodically out of the water by up to a metre. Often these have a tiny flower spike on top, reminiscent of a minute papyrus head.

Much taller and denser are the stands of tall common reeds (*Miscanthus junceus*), and even areas of the attractive bulrush (*Typha capensis*). The latter have distinctive velvety seedheads and edible roots (which taste a little like chewing gum or sugarcane!). As you'd expect in such a watery area, the deeper parts have thick stands of papyrus.

There's usually plenty of open, shallow water around, and in the slow-flowing channels look out for water lettuce plants (*Ottelia ulvifolia*) underwater, with its wavy leaves, long trailing stems and delicate, trumpet-shaped flower held above the surface by a single air bladder.

The many small islands in the area are often little more than bases for the emergence of a ring of bushy wild date palms (*Phoenix reclinata*), and perhaps the odd real fan palm (*Hyphaene petersiana*), springing up through the centre of the low canopy, perhaps around a termite mound.

Also look out for the wild dagga plant (*Leonotis nepetifolia*), with its bright-red flowers, like baubles from a Christmas tree. These will remain standing long after they turn brown and die. There are also thickets of the uncommon magic gwarri bush (*Euclea divinorum*), which is believed by some local people to have wood with supernatural powers. Above these you'll find rain trees (*Lonchocarpus capassa*), woodland waterberry trees (*Syzygium guineense*) and the occasional bird plum or motsentsela (*Berchemia discolor*).

Some of the bushes on the larger islands are more typical of drier areas, including the Kalahari appleleaf (*Lonchocarpus nelsii*) and the Kalahari star apple (*Diospyros lycioides lycioides*), with its bluish tinge which sometimes gives it the name of 'blue bush'. Ask your guide and s/he may show you how its twigs can be used as a toothbrush!

Similarly these larger islands have bands of acacias, including the umbrella thorn (*Acacia tortilis*). These become more prevalent as you move further east in the reserve, where you find larger islands, with thicker belts of acacia bush and areas of mopane also.

Fauna Most of the reserve around the Jao Flats is a superb area for lion and lechwe, which are both fairly common. The lechwe occur in large herds and will frequently startle; listen to them splash as they run across the flooded grasslands. The lion are certainly the dominant predator, with a number of prides in the area.

Other game is usually present in lower densities, but in the eastern section you can expect to spot blue wildebeest, zebra, small groups of tsessebe and elephants. Kwetsani, in particular, is noted for the increasingly relaxed bushbuck which seem to frequent its island. Sable and roan are virtually never seen here, but the large areas of papyrus are home to sitatunga, though as ever these take a lot of effort to see.

Lone male buffalo will pass through, especially from June onwards, and later in the dry season larger breeding herds move across the reserve. Elephants have a broadly similar pattern, and their herds get larger as the dry season progresses.

Cheetah aren't usually seen on the eastern side of the reserve until the waters have receded a long way, which means around October. Then they'll move west again as the waters rise in February. Hyena are seen occasionally but infrequently throughout the reserve and the year, while sightings of leopard are becoming relatively common. Sightings of wild dog are very unusual, but again, things are improving.

The western area of the reserve, accessed from Tubu Tree and Little Tubu, is a much drier habitat where you can expect giraffe, kudu, tsessebe and impala in the mixed acacia woodlands. Leopard are now increasingly common here on Hunda Island and, with the exception of some of the more skittish males, really very relaxed with vehicles.

Like most of the reserves around the Okavango, Jao Reserve was previously used for hunting, although questions were raised about whether the hunting here was ethical. It is alleged that leopard were baited and snared in numbers, and hyena shot. This would have enabled the lion prides to grow with little competition, thus satisfying the demand for lion trophies – and explaining the once very high numbers of lion and relative scarcity of other predators.

All commercial hunting has now been stopped in Botswana, and the animal populations are slowly returning to a more natural balance.

Birdlife This is a good reserve for birdwatching, particularly for some of the less common water-based species. During a few gentle boat rides on the eastern side of the reserve, I had good sightings of many of the commoner waterbirds, plus lesser jacanas, lesser moorhens, purple and green-backed herons, slaty egrets, white-faced whistling ducks, lesser moorhens, and both purple and lesser gallinules. (Both of the gallinules were seen in small lagoons close to Kwetsani.) The number of waterbirds peaks during September and October, notably in the channels between Jacana and Jao, while between October and November, wattled cranes are here in good numbers, too. Very occasionally, visitors are treated to the sight of African skimmers, too.

Meanwhile driving in the drier areas we came across a similarly good range, and noted several flocks of Meyer's parrots, Dickenson's kestrels nesting at the top of an old palm tree, wattled starlings and a tree full of open-bill storks. Then, again near Kwetsani, we found some very uncommon pink-throated longclaws (a big tick!) in a wide marshy plain where they seem to be resident.

Though not too unusual, African snipes can be found here. Listen carefully around dusk, as the sun sets and darkness falls. Then, during the breeding season, the birds fly high and zoom back to the ground. Their fanned-out tail feathers make a noise like a percussion instrument – called 'drumming'.

The western side of this reserve, around Tubu Tree, should have a wider range of raptors than the east (Jao, Kwetsani and Jacana), simply because it's drier.

WHEN TO VISIT For the water activities, any time is fine as long as it doesn't rain. Hence from April to November would be my choice of time to visit. However, if you're on a serious game-viewing trip then it's better to come towards the end of the dry season where this area's diversity of species does pick up, with dry-country species like cheetah being seen here periodically.

GETTING THERE AND AWAY As with most camps, flying in here is the only option, and is almost always booked in advance. Driving in is totally impractical.

WHERE TO STAY All six camps in the Jao Reserve are marketed by Wilderness Safaris (see page 177). They range from the opulence of Jao to the relative simplicity of Pelo. All cater exclusively for fly-in visitors.

⌂ Jao Camp [map 294] (9 rooms) ⊕ JAOCAM 19°18.431'S, 22°36.071'E. Imagine what Tarzan would have built if he'd had a few million dollars & some chic Italian designers, & you're close to imagining Jao Camp. Standing on the southeast side of the Jao Reserve, Jao is one of Wilderness Safaris' flagship 'premier' camps (the others being Mombo, Vumbura Plains & King's Pool, which were designed by the same architect).

Approaching Jao by boat, you navigate through gentle waterways surrounded by reeds before coming to the large, 2-storey main building. It's about 30m long & 8–10m wide, with designer-inspired scraggy thatch & hints of an Indonesian longhouse. Upstairs is the dining room, where everybody usually eats around a long elegant table (handcrafted on site, apparently, using Zimbabwean rosewood); a spacious lounge with comfy leather sofas, a chess table & stylish lamps; there's a long outside balcony where b/fast is sometimes served.

Down a magnificent flight of stairs there's a small library, a snug, a well-stocked wine cellar (set to include French & Italian vintages from 2014) & a curio shop. A few paces away from this you'll find 2 circular swimming pools & a few sunloungers amidst the palms.

The rooms at Jao are probably the most luxurious & spacious in the Okavango region. All are on stilts, accessed by raised wooden walkways. They have one long side, facing the nearby channel, & scraggy thatch to match the central longhouse. Their position gives lots of privacy, though also makes the walk from the farthest rooms as much as 600m from the centre (less fit visitors can request chalets closer to the centre). At the side of the chalet, through a large, swivelling door, is a lounge with huge coffee table, big comfy settee, a fridge, minibar & tea/coffee station. This is only a third of the open-plan room, which also has twin beds or a dbl under a walk-in mosquito net, with air filtered by a state-of-the-art cooling system over the bed. The chalets are effectively insect-proofed, though one long side of the room is made of gauzed or glass doors which can all be opened & folded back, concertina-style. This opens up the front of the chalet on to the wide balcony outside. All of the floors are held together with wooden dowels & studs rather than nails or screws & beautifully finished with 'adzed' edges to the light, wooden floorboards.

A slight partition (plus a roll-down reed blind) divides the main bedroom & lounge from a dressing area with a wardrobe (containing a lockable safe), an old-style claw-footed bath, & 2 conical sinks placed centrally: a stylish use of space. Another partition separates this from a shower room, & there's a sliding door to the toilet. Outside is an open-air shower, surrounded by circular clay walls & with a view over the channel.

To one end of the full-length veranda is a sala, a small outside gazebo under a shady thatched roof, with a mattress & cushions. This makes a lovely perch for relaxing in the afternoon, raised far off the ground in the heart of the date-palm forest, overlooking the channel. Jao even has probably the best spa in the Delta, offering a wide range of treatments, including ones specifically for children.

In short, the camp is visually stunning & exceedingly comfortable. For private luxury in the Delta, it's superb. It's an obvious choice for honeymoon couples, & despite its opulence it is surprisingly good for children. Yet it's a large camp where guests tend to stay in their rooms rather than mix socially, so it doesn't have quite the intimacy or sociable feel of some of the smaller camps. *US$1,242/1,543 pp sharing/sgl 11 Jan–Mar, US$1,403/1,704 April, May, Nov–19 Dec, US$2,105/2,406 Jun–Oct, US$1,598/1,899 20 Dec–10 Jan inc FB, most drinks, activities, park fees, laundry; exc transfers.* ⊕ *All year.*

⌂ Kwetsani [map 294] (5 tents) ⊕ KWETSA 19°14.594'S, 22°32.200'E. Kwetsani faces east, towards the rising sun, from a long, narrow island about 10km northwest of Jao, its larger, more opulent neighbour. (This can take 40mins if the roads are dry, or 1hr by boat.)

The main lounge/dining room area at Kwetsani is slightly raised & stands under a high thatched roof, with one side open, overlooking an open plain. There's a dining table under part of this, a trendy metal fireplace in the centre (handy when it's cool in the morning), & an open lounge area with comfy chairs, a leather sofa & a small bookshelf. Nearby is a well-stocked bar, complete with a jackalberry, *Diospyros mespiliformis*, growing up through it.

The wooden decking floor extends from under the thatch on to a wide veranda, which has been built around a huge sycamore fig (*Ficus sycomorus*), a marula (*Sclerocarya birrea caffra*) & a sausage tree (*Kigelia africana*). There's usually a spotting scope standing on the deck. Nearby is a guest washroom/toilet, which not only has a tree growing up through it, but also has half of its wall cut away to give a view. Down a sloping walkway, almost on the level of the surrounding plains, a few sunloungers, umbrellas & chairs surround a small splash-pool (about 5m x 3m). On the other side of the lounge is a viewing platform about 3m up from the main deck – though the view from the rooms is usually as good.

The chalets are all raised off the ground, & linked by wooden walkways. Two are south of the main area; 3 are on the north side. Each has twin beds, or a dbl, under a large mosquito net, with a fan above it. Behind the substantial wooden bedhead is a large mirror, twin washbasins & a small wardrobe with shelves. On either side of this, separate doors lead into small rooms, one containing an indoor shower, the other a toilet.

There is also a reed-walled outdoor shower on the balcony, along with several easy chairs & a table. Kwetsani is a lovely camp which, perhaps helped by its small size, had a very relaxed & positive atmosphere when I last visited. *US$736/991 pp sharing/sgl 11 Jan–Mar, US$832/1,087 Apr, May, Nov–19 Dec, US$1,291/1,546 Jun–Oct, US$947/1,202 20 Dec–10 Jan, inc FB, most drinks, activities, park fees, laundry; exc transfers.* ⊕ *All year.*

🏠 **Jacana Camp** [map 294] (5 tents) ✦ JACANA 19°16.766'S, 22°36.619'E. Although less than 4km north of Jao, Jacana is a 35min boat ride away. It stands on an island in the very beautiful Jao Flats area, & as at Jao, the density of date palms lends the feeling of a tropical island. In the last few years, water levels in the Delta have been quite high, & the area around Jacana is now permanently flooded. Consequently the camp is best for mokoro excursions, while game drives entail a 20min boat ride to reach their vehicles.

Jacana started life as a base for mokoro excursions for small escorted-group itineraries across Chobe & Moremi, then it was upgraded to one of Wilderness's 'classic' camps, though it's still much smaller than most in the Delta. The dining/bar area is a simple 2-storey structure under thatch with roll-down screens around its side. Downstairs are a neat, well-stocked bar & a small lounge/reading area with easy chairs & a sofa. Upstairs is the dining area, with a polished wooden floor & a large dining table. Behind this is a thatched

hut, which they call a *hustshi*, & a few hammocks. Meals are sometimes eaten outside, near the firepit, which reminds me of eating in a traditional African kraal.

Rebuilt in 2012, the tents are raised slightly on decking to offer more space & style. From the small veranda, with directors' chairs & a table, doors slide open to reveal a dbl or twin beds beneath a large walk-in mosquito net, itself beneath a ceiling fan. Two comfortable wicker chairs & a writing table invite relaxation, while practicalities are served by a basic wardrobe, some shelves, & a tea/coffee station. Another sliding door leads to a spacious, largely open-plan bathroom. A large metal-framed mirror hangs over dbl basins set into a wooden surface, & head-height wooden poles serve to section off the shower & adjacent toilet slightly.

One of Jacana's most entertaining features is the guest toilet, which features an impressive cement-moulded bowl, a pulley made in 'Heath Robinson' style to flush the toilet, & a great view. In similar vein, a painted concrete hippo & crocodile pay tribute to the builder's imagination. They may not sound fun, but they are.

The camp is a really good option at any time of the year for those wanting water-based activities, & is pretty good value for a couple of nights, especially towards the end of the dry season. *US$736 mid-Jan–Mar, Nov–19 Dec pp sharing, US$814 Apr–May, US$1,234 Jun–Oct, US$916 20 Dec–mid-Jan, inc FB, activities, most drinks, park fees, laundry; exc transfers.* ⊕ *All year.*

🏠 **Pelo Camp** [map 294] (5 tents) Set in the centre of the concession, Pelo is the simplest camp in the reserve, focusing on mokoro excursions, as well as boating & fishing.

Tented in construction, Pelo incorporates a dining & lounge area set beneath jackalberry, wild date palms & mahogany trees, alongside an outdoor 'boma' area & a viewing platform on an old anthill. Its small rooms are also of canvas, with a covered porch to the front, & twin or dbl beds separated by a curtain from a flush toilet & a basin with running water. In front of the tent, a bucket shower is well placed to take advantage of the views over the floodplain.

Pelo should appeal most to the more adventurous traveller who is happier without latter-day frills. It is not a place for those in search of dry-land activities: it opens when the flood arrives & closes when the waters recede. That said, there is talk of opening up a short game-drive road on the island across the water from camp. This will also act as an access road to the airstrip, when water levels permit. However, it's important to realise that as Pelo is situated on an island, all activities must finish before dark; no boats are permitted on the water after sunset. On the other hand, the camp takes advantage of its westerly facing firepit & has sundowner drinks ready for your return to camp. *US$404/602 pp sharing/sgl Apr–May, US$594/792 Jun–Oct.* ⊕ *Apr–Oct.*

⌂ **Tubu Tree Camp** [map 294] (8 tents) West of the other camps in the concession, & another of Wilderness Safaris 'classic' camps, Tubu Tree opened in 2002 & was completely renovated in mid-2013.

It now has the feel of a large treehouse, elevated on wooden walkways that link the tents to the main area, & with great views over seasonal floodplains.

To one side is a large, simply furnished dining area; to the other, a relaxing, open-sided lounge with comfy sofas & chairs & some interesting reference books. A viewing scope enables guests to focus on the comings & goings of wildlife on the floodplains. From a quirky bar, built around the trees & with a top carved from a sausage tree, a walkway leads down to a small plunge pool & sundeck with loungers. Beyond, a firepit is the venue for evening get-togethers.

Tubu's tents – 2 of them designed for families – stand on wooden decks, each with a veranda & a couple of directors' chairs affording super vistas over the floodplains. Double or twin beds, a writing desk & a couple of soft chairs furnish the bedroom, while a divider behind the bed separates this from the en-suite shower, toilet & washbasin, plus a separate outside shower.

Tubu has access to large areas of dry mopane & acacia woodlands. From around Apr–Sep, & perhaps later, mokoro trips & fishing ought to be possible, but for the rest of the year activities are generally limited to game drives & walks on Hunda Island. That said, they can access different launch points for the mekoro which can extend their seasonal use. *US$903/1,158 pp sharing/sgl 11 Jan–Mar, US$983/1,238 April, May, Nov–19 Dec, US$1,413/1,668 Jun–Oct, US$1,107/1,362 20 Dec–10 Jan, inc FB, most drinks, activities, park fees, laundry; exc transfers.* ⊕ *All year.*

⌂ **Little Tubu** [map 294] (3 tents) Situated adjacent to Tubu Tree (above), & with a similar 'treehouse' feel, the much smaller Little Tubu was opened in 2013, & affords a more intimate & exclusive option than its bigger sister. Shaded beneath a riverine canopy & overlooking the floodplain, the elevated dining area & bar, & a raised pool, are well placed to watch the abundant wildlife. Sharing the views are Little Tubu's spacious en-suite tents, with his & hers outdoor showers (including some of the best water-pressure anywhere in the Delta!), a covered veranda, & great views enjoyed from its dbl or twin beds. *US$903/1,158 pp sharing/sgl 11 Jan–Mar, US$983/1,238 April, May Nov–19 Dec, US$1,413/1,668 Jun–Oct, US$1,107/1,362 20 Dec–10 Jan, inc FB, most drinks, activities, park fees, laundry; exc transfers.* ⊕ *All year.*

ACTIVITIES I would visit Jao and Kwetsani primarily for their water activities – trips by boat and mokoro – which are generally offered all year (though motorboats at Kwetsani may be restricted by water levels around October–January). That said, day and night game drives (and sometimes short walks on the islands) are also possible nearby, and will make a bonus for your stay.

Jacana is also best regarded as a water-based camp, with motorboat and mokoro trips all year, as well as game drives near camp when the water levels are not in high flood. Game drives, offered by all the camps except Pelo, are usually taken on Hunda Island, which is reached by a short boat ride. Closer to camp, Kwetsani offers slightly better game viewing than the other two.

Pelo is also all about the water – in fact, because of concession limits it has no vehicle of its own. Even if game drives become a small part of the activities here in the future, they will not replace the emphasis on exploration by boat or mokoro of some of the Okavango's most iconic landscape.

Tubu Tree is quite the opposite: a dry-land camp for game drives which can also arrange mokoro trips when the flood levels are high. A couple of nights at Jacana or

Pelo, and a few at Tubu Tree, make a relatively inexpensive combination, at least by the standards of the Delta.

The comfortable game drives in this reserve tend to be in vehicles with three rows of three seats, of which the centre seats are often left empty. When I last went walking, the guide was a capable, experienced walking guide who gave an appropriate pre-departure safety briefing and clearly knew how to use the rifle that he carried. He also escorted the mokoro trip, which I was pleased to see eschewed the easier hippo trails in favour of a more difficult, but much safer, route through a shallow floodplain. Though he's now left this reserve, I hope that the standards of safe practice which he set will remain.

ABU, SEBA AND MACATOO (NG26)

At this large concession west of Moremi, the focus has for several years been more on the activities than the environment. Abu Camp is the only place in the Delta for riding elephants, and Macatoo Camp is one of the Delta's two centres for horseriding. A third hunting camp, the relatively famous Selby's, has been closed (hunting is no longer carried out on the concession), but the recent introduction of a new lodge by Elephant Back Safaris has broadened the appeal of the concession to include more conventional safaris.

FLORA AND FAUNA HIGHLIGHTS The finer details of the wildlife in this concession tend to be eclipsed by the experience of the horses that you ride, or the elephants that you're with – hence I will make only relatively sketchy comments here on the wild fauna in this area.

However, you will find here most of the Delta's usual big game, including elephant, buffalo, giraffe, blue wildebeest, kudu, tsessebe, red lechwe, impala, zebra, reedbuck, steenbok, warthog, baboons and vervet monkeys. Lion and spotted hyena are the dominant predators, with occasional appearances by leopards and wild dogs.

That said, like NG25 to the north, and NG29 and 30 to the south, I don't think that the variation and density of game are quite up to the levels of, say, central Moremi or some of the areas on the north side of the Delta. However, rest assured that you'll still see plenty of game when visiting here.

WHEN TO VISIT Because the focus of a trip here is for most people the experience of horseriding or the interactions with elephants, it's fine as long as you avoid the rains. So visit anytime from late April or May to the middle or end of December.

GETTING THERE AND AWAY The only option for these camps is to make advanced bookings and fly in. There's an airstrip near Abu Camp which is used by this and Seba Camp, while Macatoo has a second airstrip. Driving here is not possible.

ELEPHANT-BACK SAFARIS (*Elephant Back Safaris;* \ *686 1260;* e *ebs@info.bw; www.abucamp.com*) This is the original elephant-back safari operation, set up in 1990 by Randall Jay Moore, one of the Delta's more colourful characters, and sold in 2008 to a European investment company. The concept has since been emulated by several camps in various parts of southern Africa. (Grey Matters, in NG32, is the Okavango's only other place which offers interactions with non-wild elephants; see pages 346–7). Some claim it's simply the ultimate in amazing safari experiences; others detest the whole idea of riding on trained elephants. If you can afford it (it's the Delta's most expensive place to visit), you can make up your own mind.

The camp was named after its lead elephant, Abu (see box, page 320), who was brought to Africa from the USA by his trainer, Randall Moore.

The experience Activities are flexible, depending on both the guests and the elephants, but will usually include either a morning elephant ride or a whole-day excursion, travelling with the elephants to a shady spot for a long picnic lunch, and then back with them in the late afternoon. Alternatively 4x4s and, depending on water levels, mekoro or motorboats are always available.

Riding on an elephant involves using a large, custom-made saddle. Although comfortable, in many ways this feels more detached than walking beside them. When you're riding, the other game is largely unaware of your human presence, but the real fascination of these trips is not the other game that you see, or even the ride. It is the experience of being so close to the elephants: being able to walk beside them as they plod along and being comfortable with them at close quarters, effectively as one of the herd, rather than viewing them from afar.

Safety issues In common with most safari camps throughout Africa, all visitors at Abu Camp are required to sign an indemnity form which, basically, absolves the camp from any responsibility for your safety whilst participating in a trip. And as when visiting any camp in the bush, you accept that you're taking on certain risks to do with Africa's animals and their unpredictability that you wouldn't face sitting on the couch at home.

The only difference here is that being in such close proximity to such huge, strong animals does present a greater risk than most normal photographic safaris. Although, the camp prides itself on a very good safety record, and no client has ever been injured by one of the elephants in 19 years of operation, it is important to remember that elephants are unpredictable and can react in unpredictable ways. In extreme cases, the consequence can be fatal.

🏠 **The camps** Elephant Back Safaris operate two accommodation options within this concession, each offering something different, but each very luxurious. The original camp, and the only one to offer elephant-back safaris, is Abu Camp. The other camp, Seba, is more akin to a regular safari lodge in the Okavango Delta – and is good for children.

🏠 **Abu Camp** [map 294] (6 tents) When Ker & Downey was involved with this operation, Abu Camp stood on the site that today is occupied by Nxabega (page 326). Today's Abu Camp, the original elephant-riding camp founded 17 years ago, also overlooks a lagoon but is now nestled in a grove of hardwood trees. A full rebuild in 2011 resulted in an immaculately designed lodge with a price tag to match – this is one of Botswana's most expensive camps.

Raised up on teak decking, with a shaded veranda & canvas chairs, Abu's tents are among the most luxurious rooms in the Delta: all slightly different, but all very stylish. Beds are antique 'sleigh-style' or 4-posters. Beautifully polished teak floors are dotted with matching rugs. Spacious en-suite bathrooms feature a stand-alone shower, flush toilet, twin washbasins – & a sliding door from the shower to a claw-foot bath on the veranda. And each tent has a small study area with a writing table & cabinets featuring old books, local artefacts & a selection of southern African rocks.

The dining area, set on an expanse of tiered teak decking punctuated by jackalberry trees (*Diospyros mespiliformis*) & sycamore figs (*Ficus sycomorus*), stands in front of the main lounge, which has comfy chairs & a small library. The food is good & the service attentive, as you'd expect of a camp which regularly hosts the world's glitterati as guests. Pictures, ornaments & carvings of elephants (& especially of Abu) are all over the camp.

12

Elephant-back trips take a maximum of 12 visitors (6 riders & 6 walkers), & last 3–5 nights: Tue–Fri or Sat–Tue. *US$1,783/2,378 pp sharing/sgl 11 Jan–Mar, US$2,012/2,607 Apr, May, Nov–19 Dec, US$2,577/3,172 Jun–Oct, US$2,293/2,888 20 Dec–10 Jan, inc FB, drinks, activities & laundry.* ⊕ *All year.*

⌂ **Seba Camp** [map 294] (8 tents) Named after one of the original elephants in the herd, Seba Camp is also the base for research into the

ABU CAMP'S ELEPHANTS

Abu Camp was named for a large bull with matching tusks, born around 1960. Probably from east Africa or the Kruger Park, Abu was taken when small to the United States, where he was used for rides at a wildlife park in Grand Prairie, Texas. He was returned to Africa in 1988, to feature in the movie *Circles in a Forest*, and moved to Botswana in 1990, where Randall Moore described him as exceptionally calm, intelligent and gentle. He appeared in many later films, including *White Hunter Black Heart* and *The Power of One*. He died in 2002, but his name lives on in 'Baby Abu', born in 2006.

At present, there are about a dozen trained elephants at the camp. Some of Abu's older elephants came from zoos in the USA, whilst many of the younger ones were orphans from South Africa's Kruger National Park and several were born at the camp. Under a long-term research programme that commenced in 2002, a number of Abu's residents have successfully been released into the wild, although some – such as Pula and Seba – are still seen around camp. Notable among the current Abu herd are:

CATHY The herd's largest adult cow was born around 1960, captured in Murchison Falls National Park, Uganda, when young, and taken to a zoo outside Toronto. In 1988, she returned to Africa with Abu, coming to Botswana in 1990. Gentle and temperamentally stable, she is the matriarch of the herd, and considered the most comfortable of the elephants to ride.

SHIRHENI Born around 1986 and orphaned in Kruger, Shirheni moved to the camp in 1989. She lost her first calf, but her next three – Pula (now released into the wild, but regularly seen), Abu and Warona – have thrived, and she has proved to be a calm and doting mother.

ABU Known to all as 'Baby Abu', Abu was born in 2006, an energetic young bull who entertains guests with his efforts to keep up with the herd and mimic their conduct during the rides.

KITIMETSE Her name means 'I'm lost' and she was found at the end of 1999 after she had been injured by a crocodile and abandoned by her own wild herd. Her wounds were treated at Abu Camp where she was accepted by the other elephants. Having mated with the first Abu elephant to be released into the wild, she gave birth to Lorato in 2008.

LORATO Daughter of Kitimetse, Lorato was born in 2009, just before Valentine's Day: hence her name, which is a derivation of the word 'love'.

NALEDI The latest addition to the Abu herd – whose name means 'star' – was born to Kitimetse on a starlit night in November 2013.

interaction between wild elephants & those released into the wild. It's an upmarket camp, with en-suite tents secluded among riverine vegetation overlooking a lagoon. Unusually for the Delta, there is no age limit here, & 2 family rooms, with 2 interconnecting en-suite bedrooms & their own plunge pools, are ideal for those with younger children. All the rooms are equipped with solid wood furniture, their décor reflecting individual Batswana ethnic groups. Central to the camp are a tasteful & comfortable living & dining area, & a pool. Guests can take day & night game drives, & mokoro trips when the water is sufficiently high. *US$736/991 pp sharing/sgl 11 Jan–Mar, US$814/1,069 Apr, May, Nov–19 Dec, US$1,234/1,489 Jun–Oct, US$916/1,171 20 Dec–10 Jan. No children under 6. ⊕ All year.*

RIDING SAFARIS Contact African Horseback Safaris, page 178. These riding safaris were established by British rider Sarah-Jane Gullick, who set up the operation in 1994, originally with Ker & Downey Safaris (based out of a camp called Macateer Camp). Today, the operation has been taken over by John Sobey.

The general comments on Okavango Horse Safaris (pages 336–8) about the fascinating experience of riding through the Okavango apply equally well to this operation. Suffice to say that once you step into the saddle, most of the Okavango's resident game will treat you and your horse as a single, composite four-legged herbivore. So antelope will relax around you, and predators will give you pause for thought!

Below is some basic information for these trips. Contact African Horseback Safaris if you need more precise details as they've a lot of information about their trips that they can send.

The horses The horses are a variety of thoroughbreds, Namibian Hanovarians, Arabs and Kalahari–Arab crossbreeds ranging from 14 to 18 hands (140–180cm) high.

Tack and clothes Good-quality English- and Western-style trail saddles are supplied, each with its own water bottle. Guests may borrow half chaps; long leather boots are impractical.

African Horseback Safaris does not supply hard hats or safety helmets; you must bring your own. They suggest that riders wear their riding clothes and boots on the plane, and bring their hat and wash bag as hand luggage, in case luggage gets delayed.

Information about you
Riding ability These safaris are for experienced riders aged 12 years and over. Riders over 60 need to be 'riding fit' and strong. Trips usually involve about four to six hours in the saddle each day. Thus riders need to feel competent about keeping up with the group, and capable of riding at all paces, rising to the trot and controlling their horse at the canter. They may also be required to gallop out of trouble, so these trips do not take beginners. For safety reasons, if they think that your riding is not up to standard, you won't be allowed to ride here.

Weight limits There's a weight limit of 15 stone (210lb or 95kg) per person, above which they can sometimes make special arrangements for advanced riders.

About the trips African Horseback Safaris offers a range of safaris from three to ten nights, giving plenty of scope. Following arrival in camp, each trip starts with an introductory talk on the safari, and a safety briefing. While safaris were once timed

12

to start and finish on Tuesdays and Fridays, guests are now welcome to choose the dates that best suit their itinerary.

The riding groups have a maximum of six to eight guests. Trips normally incorporate not only riding but also the occasional game drive, walk and night drive, while the more adventurous may opt to spend a night in the 'treehouse', sleeping high up in the tree canopy under the African night sky. Boating, canoeing and fishing are also possible sometimes, depending on water levels.

Safety Two guides accompany each riding safari, carrying a first-aid kit, rifle, radio and GPS.

The riding camp

⋏ Macatoo Camp [map 294] (7 tents) Renovated in 2013, Macatoo is comfortable but simple &, as with most camps, the service is of a good standard. Each of its large tents has twin beds, & an en-suite shower & toilet, while new to the camp are the 'honeymoon suite', with a bath on a raised platform & a large private deck, & a 'friends & family suite' with 2 tents linked by a walkway & viewing deck above ground level. Dinner is usually a stylish 3-course affair, served by candlelight, with high-quality food freshly prepared. There is a furnished mess tent, a small splash pool & a daily laundry service.

The costs From January to March, and 16 November to the end of December, rates are £445 per person per night, including all meals, drinks and activities. This rises to £500 between April and 15 July and 1–15 November, while in the high season (16 July to the end of October) the cost is £560 per person. Note that prices are quoted in pounds sterling, rather than the more normal US dollars.

Air transfers to/from Maun are £180 per person, one way. Macatoo use a cement airstrip, which is 45 minutes' drive from camp.

POM POM, KANANA AND NXABEGA (NG27A)

This large, strictly photographic concession is now effectively split between three safari companies: Ker & Downey Botswana (who run Kanana), &Beyond (who run Nxabega) and Under One Botswana Sky (who own Pom Pom).

CONCESSION HISTORY By the early 1970s there were a number of camps throughout the Delta, most of which accepted either hunting or photographic guests. One of the bigger companies involved here was Safari South, who ran many camps including Khwai River Lodge, Four Rivers Camp (near the present Kwara), Queenie, Splash, Jedibe, Machaba, Mombo, Pom Pom and Shinde.

Around 1985 Ker & Downey was split from Safari South, as a wholly owned subsidiary, to differentiate the photographic camps from those used for hunting. Ker & Downey then had four photographic camps in the Delta: Shinde, Mombo, Jedibe and Machaba.

A company called Jao Safaris owned Mombo at that time. Various contracts changed, which resulted in Ker & Downey leaving Mombo and Jedibe. (These were eventually taken up by Wilderness Safaris, in 1989.) Meanwhile, the government had designated NG27 for photographic use only, and Ker & Downey took over the running of Pom Pom, which had been another old hunting camp run by Safari South.

From 1985 Pom Pom was the only major camp here, but in 1990 they started a 'partnership' with Randall Jay Moore. Moore brought trained African elephants over from the USA to start Elephant Back Safaris (see page 319), and Ker & Downey built Abu Camp (pages 319–20), on the site that Nxabega now occupies, in the north of the reserve. In 1993 I was very excited to visit Pom Pom – and to get here I took my first flight over the Delta! It was then one of Botswana's most upmarket camps, and the rest of the clientele during my stay were from America. The combination of Pom Pom and then Abu Camp was a winning one; business was good for them. (Note that throughout this time there were also a few simple bushcamps in the area, used by various operators.) However, the following year Randall Moore tendered for, and obtained, his own concession next door: NG26. This upset the apple cart, as he then built the camp that is today known as Abu Camp – thus taking away a highly profitable chunk of business from Ker & Downey.

NG27 Concession has always been subdivided. First AfroVentures (who subsequently merged with CC Africa, now &Beyond) built Nxabega Camp on the site of the old Abu Camp, in the north. Then in 2000 Ker & Downey opened their own new camp, Kanana.

In 2001, Wilderness Safaris took over the marketing and management of Pom Pom, building a completely new small camp here, but keeping the name and location of the 'old' Pom Pom. Since then, it has again changed hands, and is now under the same ownership as Chobe Safari Lodge in Kasane.

FLORA AND FAUNA HIGHLIGHTS Travelling from south to north, the landscapes, flora and fauna change very slowly, but there are slight differences between the various parts of the reserve. Bear in mind whilst reading this that the similarities between the different areas are much greater than their contrasts.

Flora The NG27 Concession is in the heart of the Delta and contains most of the typical Delta environments: thickets and stands of riverine forest; more open areas of invasive bushes; and occasional floodplains.

The area around Pom Pom is very open and pretty, notable for many tiny islands amidst wide open floodplains, which are often submerged between May and September. These distinct islands are often covered, or at least fringed, by real fan (*Hyphaene petersiana*) and wild date palms (*Phoenix reclinata*), and between them are large marshy floodplains. There are quite a few baobabs in the area, and the forest patches are fairly sparse.

Moving northeast to the area of Kanana, there are fewer flat, open plains and more areas colonised by expanses of wild sage. Around these are larger islands and woodland patches with plenty of the Delta's usual riverine tree species: sausage trees (*Kigelia africana*), jackalberries (*Diospyros mespiliformis*), knobthorns (*Acacia nigrescens*), the occasional marula (*Sclerocarya birrea caffra*) and the odd raintree (*Lonchocarpus capassa*). (The raintree, also sometimes called the appleleaf, gets it name from the droplets which are secreted by froghopper insects as they suck the sap from the leaves. This keeps the soil beneath the tree moist, and in exceptional cases can even form pools.)

Further northwest, around Nxabega, the forests become more in evidence with large, dense lines of broadleaf forests and patches of acacia. Mixed with these are a few open plains, fringed by real fan palms (*Hyphaene petersiana*) and stands of riverine trees. In the midst of the larger floodplains you'll see occasional islands crowned with an African mangosteen (*Garcinia livingstonei*), or perhaps a large sycamore fig (*Ficus sycomorus*), growing out of an old termite mound perhaps surrounded by a few russet bush-willow bushes (*Combretum hereroense*). Some of the Nxabega's floodplains have thick coverings of hippo grass (*Vossia cuspidata*) that turn a lovely shade of orange-red around September.

12

Fauna The variety of game in NG27 certainly seems wider to me than that found in areas further south and west – though I feel that it's not as wide as some of the reserves on the northeast side of the Delta. Tsessebe, impala, wildebeest, lechwe, steenbok, baboon and zebra are all common and seen very regularly. Giraffe do particularly well here, they're very relaxed amongst the many acacia thickets, and there is a good number of resident elephants.

Lion and spotted hyena are the commonest large predators, though the mixed woodland is a perfect habitat for leopard that are numerous, though only seen occasionally. Cheetah are seen only rarely, when the reserve is at its driest (October to March); they're not at all common. Wild dog pass through periodically (as they do through most areas of northern Botswana) though not frequently. Both black-backed and side-striped jackal are common.

As with most of the Delta there's always plenty of smaller animals, too widespread to be worthy of particular comment … though I recall a great sighting of an entertaining troop of dwarf mongooses here once!

Birdlife The birding is good and very varied in this concession. Kanana has immediate access to the deep Xudum channel that is lined with a mixture of water figs, huge floating mats of graceful papyrus and anchored sections of miscanthus grass (*Miscanthus junceus*). Amongst the birdlife, there's a notable profusion of squacco herons. However, what is really interesting is the Kanana heronry (⊕ KANHER 19.30'02S, 22.51'10E), discovered only in 2001. Like the heronry at Gcodikwe, the shallow floodplain is dotted with tree-islands, primarily of water-fig trees interspersed with papyrus and waterberry. Protected in some measure from predators, these in turn attract countless waterbirds during the breeding season, which starts in July and reaches its peak between September and December.

When found, many birds were breeding here, including yellow-billed, marabou and open-billed storks, darters, cormorants, herons and egrets, while a survey by Birdlife Botswana in 2011 confirmed the presence of vulnerable pink-backed pelicans from mid-July. How such a large heronry went 'unnoticed' for so long is a

THE LIZARD

There's a tale of a slightly fussy, older woman coming to stay on her own in a tented safari camp. Over lunch she complained about a lizard in her room, but was told this was nothing to worry about – and it'd probably vanish of its own accord soon.

That afternoon after lunch, whilst most of the camp was having a siesta, she wandered out in search of one of the staff. 'That lizard is still in my room,' she proclaimed, with agitation, to one of the managers that she found in the dining room. He then explained that this was really nothing to worry about, as lizards often came in and out of the rooms. In fact, he elaborated, 'it's very good as they're a natural way of keeping the mosquito population down.' So, she could go back and sleep, relaxed in the knowledge that it wouldn't do her any harm at all.

Off she went, but 20 minutes later she was back again. She couldn't sleep, claiming that the lizard was making too much noise. Unimpressed, but determined to satisfy the guest, the manager took her back to the room – only to be completely embarrassed to find a huge monitor lizard thrashing about, trying to find a way out of the tent.

complete puzzle, but the survey concludes that it is 'the most dynamic and vibrant heronry that we have ever visited in Botswana'. However fascinating, visitors must remember the problems that disturbances can cause to the birds; don't encourage your guide to approach too close to the heronry.

Nxabega doesn't have the heronry, though one recent September over 500 open-billed storks and about 1,000 squacco herons were seen gathering to roost just a little west of Nxabega. It does, however, have a couple of very old pole bridges across small waterways in its reserve. These prove particularly attractive perching places for waterbirds that can then be seen while driving. (This is an advantage if, like me, you prefer a stationary base from which to use a camera and tripod, rather than a rocking boat.) There are lots of hamerkops, small herons, egrets (including a good number of slaty), black crakes and bee-eaters. Kingfishers are well represented; here I've got closer to photographing a diminutive malachite kingfisher than I ever have whilst on a boat.

Read the marketing literature for almost any camp in the Delta and you'll realise that claims for sightings of 'the elusive Pel's fishing owl' are a tedious marketing cliché. Every camp simultaneously trumpets their rarity, and yet claims you'll see one whilst staying there. That said, when I last visited Nxabega, one such owl was making predictable, regular appearances on one of the old bridges, and the guides advised that three pairs were regularly seen in different locations in the area. Meanwhile, I'm reliably informed that in 2002 a pair of Pel's fishing owls were seen in, and said to be nesting in, trees about 100m from camp.

Having said all that about the resident birds that associate with water, you'll find an equally good variety of drier-country birds in this reserve. On my last visit, amongst the eagles, I spotted tawny, bateleur, Wahlberg's and, most remarkably, a martial eagle battling with a large monitor lizard on the ground beside our vehicle, near Pom Pom. (We found both locked in combat, but at a stalemate. Eventually they disentangled themselves and the great lizard made a hasty retreat under a bush.)

Finally, on a more domestic note, the staff at Nxabega seem to have 'tamed' a pair of wild yellow-billed hornbills sufficiently for them to come along to afternoon tea on most days.

WHEN TO VISIT The area is lightly less seasonal than those further south and west, though there's still a big difference between the game densities through the seasons: they're a lot better when it's drier. As usual, the birding is as good as it gets during the wetter time of the year (December to around March).

GETTING THERE AND AWAY All of these camps work only with guests flying in, usually having made their bookings months before they travel. Driving here is not possible without permission, and is anyway totally impractical.

WHERE TO STAY The camps are totally different from one another, perhaps because they're run in different ways by different companies.

🏠 **Kanana** [map 294] (8 tents) Contact Ker & Downey Botswana, page 176; ✈ KANANA 19°32.577'S, 22°51.731'E. Opened in 2000 & rebuilt in 2009, Kanana is a few kilometres from the site of a basic old bushcamp known as Khurunxaragha Camp (once used by Wilderness for their mobile safaris, & located near the present airfield). It stands at roughly the centre of NG27, & overlooks the reedbeds of the Xudum River. This gives the camp access to a permanent, deep-water channel for boating all year.

Accommodation is in very comfortable tents spread out to the left of the main area. These are separated by about 20m, so even the furthest

12

room isn't miles from the centre of camp. Inside, the teak floor is covered with various rugs, & the tents are well furnished with a wooden wardrobe, luggage rack, dressing table & chairs, & plenty of thoughtful touches. Teak bedside tables have electric lights powered by solar-powered batteries – the camp's generator is usually switched on only during the day. Twin or dbl beds have good-quality cotton sheets & down pillows with blankets. A canvas divider separates the sleeping space from the en-suite flush toilet, washbasin & (very efficient) shower. Outside on the shaded veranda, to the front & side of the tents, there's a table & comfy chairs, & all the tents face the river from under a cover of riverine trees – jackalberries, knobthorns & sausage trees. These, & the plunge pool, are linked by sandy paths, illuminated at night by electric lanterns,.

Kanana's main area is a U-shaped wooden building with a large tree in the centre & a long dining room, several small lounge areas (one with a small library), a bar &, down nearer the water, a 'sandpit' for fires.

Though the comfortable game-drive vehicles have been carefully thought out, with canvas pockets for binoculars & lots of space, the camp's strongest suit is its mokoro trips, often including short island walks. It's particularly convenient that when water levels are good, these can be launched directly from the side of the lodge's main area, & into the reedbeds which surround the Xudum River. There are also boat trips, including fishing for bream or catfish. A real highlight, especially around Sep–Dec when many species of birds are breeding, is a boat trip to the heronry. As with most camps, Kanana works on the basis of one long safari activity after b/fast, then siesta time after lunch, & another activity following afternoon tea, before dinner. Sometimes a late-night drive is possible after dinner. *US$495 pp Mar & Dec, US$666 Apr–Jun & Nov, US$850/1,088 pp sharing/ sgl Jul–Oct, inc FB, drinks, activities, laundry; exc transfers.* ⊕ *Mar–Dec.*

🏕 **Kanana Mokoro Trail** [map 294] (2 tents) Contact Ker & Downey Botswana, page 176. This simple island camp, 40mins by mokoro from Kanana, is the base for a 2-night trip exploring the area by mokoro or on foot. With bucket showers & long-drop toilets, it's by no means luxurious, but each tent has its own private facilities, as well as solar-powered lighting. The complement of

staff includes 2 guides & a chef, so this is a good opportunity to get a deeper understanding of the Delta with a fair degree of comfort. *US$495 pp Mar–Jun, US$630/795 pp sharing/sgl Jul–Oct, inc FB, drinks, activities, laundry; exc transfers. No children under 16.* ⊕ *Mar–Oct.*

🏠 **Nxabega Okavango Tented Camp** [map 294] (9 tents) Contact &Beyond, page 175; ⊕ NXABEG 19°29.081'S, 22°47.634'E. Built on the site of the original Abu Camp, Nxabega is the most northerly of the camps in NG27, occupying an area of 70km². It's about an hour's drive north of Kanana (though only around 12km as the birds fly!) & 11km south-southeast of Xigera, which is in Moremi. However, for most of the year Xigera is inaccessible by land from Nxabega because of the Boro River.

Nxabega's main building is constructed on a grand scale around a huge jackalberry tree, from local timber & reeds, with a high shaggy thatched roof. Inside, it is swish but understated, with clean lines & teak-panelled walls. The large dining area stands under 2 electric candelabras. Nearby in the lounge are 2 separate groups of luxurious settees. Heavy glass-topped coffee tables rest on game-skin patchworks, supporting the odd picture book, cigar boxes & a backgammon set. It's comfortably done with style & the odd striking African artefact (sadly of west rather than southern African origin). The bar is almost hidden, but stocked exceedingly comprehensively with obscure liqueurs, imported spirits & good wines. (Unlimited house wine, beers & soft drinks are normally included in the rate, but if you want to drink their cellar of vintage wines dry, they'll charge extra!)

The large, high-quality tents are raised on wooden platforms about a metre above the ground, with verandas overlooking the floodplain. All are well spread out, with a discreet 30–40m between them – from No 1 on the far right to the honeymoon suite, past the large swimming pool on the left. Inside, on sisal mats laid on a smooth wooden floor, twin or dbl beds are draped with quality cotton sheets, down duvets & assorted pillows. Each tent is well furnished with chairs, a dressing table, luggage rack, wardrobe & bedside lamps (powered by a solar-powered battery system). At the back of each is a small en-suite bathroom with a flush toilet, hot shower (heated by a gas geyser) & a washbasin.

Activities include 4x4 game drives, mokoro excursions & boat trips, with good catch-&-release

fishing possible on the Boro River. Nxabega has been constructed with care & generally seems to be run with a higher complement of staff than most lodges (average 2 staff per guest). This gives it an air of quality. The food is particularly good, but what I appreciated more was the flexibility that visitors have over everything, from the timings of b/fast & lunch, to the scheduling of activities. These are seldom regimented, & the staff make real efforts to organise activities to suit you. If you've ever wanted to do a late-night drive after dinner to look for aardvarks, or a midday boating trip … Nxabega is a good choice! *US$570–1,200 pp sharing, low–high season, inc FB, local drinks, activities, laundry.* ⊕ *All year.*

🏠 **Pom Pom** [map 294] (9 tents) 📞686 4436; m 7132 4404; e reservations@pompomcamp.com; www.pompomcamp.com; ⊕ POMPOM 19°35.072'S, 22°50.560'E. One of the original upmarket camps in the Delta, opened in 1985 by Ker & Downey, Pom Pom was rebuilt by Wilderness in 2001, then brought under the same umbrella as Chobe Safari Lodge in Kasane (see page 189) in 2005. Although it is barely 5km southwest of Kanana, a game drive between the 2 camps would take 45mins.

The camp's Meru-style tents under thatch stand on the ground at the edge of an island overlooking a small, permanent lagoon. Furnished with twin or dbl beds (there's also 1 family unit), a wicker chair, wooden dresser & wardrobe, they each have an en-suite bathroom, behind a wall & partially open to the stars.

A central area under thatch brings together the dining area, bar & a curio shop; there's also a small pool. Activities include day & night drives, mokoro trips & short walks. There is the opportunity to fish, or watch game & birdlife, from a boat at all times, but only when water levels are very high can you take a boating excursion. (The main flood hits here around May, often filling the dry lagoon in a day. The area's highest water levels usually occur around Jun–Aug.) While children over 8 are welcome, families with children aged 8–12 will be taken on game drives in a private vehicle, at an additional US$220–50 per day, depending on the time of year. *US$860/995 pp sharing/sgl Jul–Oct, US$590/710 Apr–Jun & Nov, US$460 Dec–Mar, inc FB, most drinks, activities, park fees, laundry; exc transfers. No children under 8.* ⊕ *All year.*

DELTA, ODDBALLS', GUNN'S AND EAGLE ISLAND (NG27B)

Between NG30, NG32 and Moremi stands a fairly small photographic reserve, just off the southwest side of Chief's Island. This was the first area of the Okavango where tourism really took off in volume, and it's now very interesting to see it making the transition to smaller numbers of visitors, and more upmarket camps.

CONCESSION HISTORY A short history of the Delta and Oddballs' camps is an interesting illustration of the transition between different types of tourism mentioned above. It started shortly after Lodges of Botswana bought Delta Camp in 1983. During their first year they not only catered to upmarket visitors, but also used the camp as a base for the mokoro trips of more budget-conscious travellers.

This mix didn't work in one camp, and so in 1984 they built a separate lower-budget camp at the other end of their island. The nickname of their first manager was 'Oddball', and so this became – tongue in cheek – Oddball's Palm Island Luxury Lodge. Oddball's marketing was astute and well targeted, portraying a relaxed, hippie hangout where spaced-out campers could find paradise on their own island in the Delta. This became a buzzing base for budget mokoro trips in the heart of the Delta – *the* backpacker's place in the Delta, known in hostels from Nairobi to Cape Town, and beyond.

It was very successful. At first they just had showers, toilets and a (fridge-less) bar; campers brought all their own food and kit. It grew fast, eventually encompassing a shop for campers and food, as well as chilled drinks from a fully fledged bar.

When business peaked during the late 1980s and early 1990s, they had up to 120 visitors *per day* flying in, some camping for a night in the camp and others heading

12

out on mokoro trips. Then there were no limits on how many visitors the camp could accept. The camp had a rule that every visitor had to stay at Oddball's for at least one night.

Then two things happened which changed this business. First, in July 1989 the government raised its national park fees from P10 per person per week to P30 per person per day, and then to P70 per day. Mokoro trips from Oddball's had always been to Moremi, and this increased their prices dramatically.

Second, there had long been a process of tendering for camps, whereby safari operators bid for leases to operate safari camps. In 1996 the government introduced new leases to camps in many of the Delta's reserves, insisting that safari companies not only produce large cheques for rental and royalties (per visitor), but also a 'management plan' for the reserves. These became effective in January 1997.

In drawing up these detailed management plans, the safari companies were forced to look not only at their game and environmental policies, and the sustainability of them, but also how they trained their staff, and what they were doing to help the wider community in the area. This process raised the issues of sustainability, responsible tourism and community development – and placed them in the centre of the government's decision-making process. Thus, it made them important to the safari operators.

Oddball's had started a programme of training their polers as early as 1988. Like all camps, it now insists that all of its polers have a qualification as a professional mokoro guide. The government requires that standards like these are now applied across the board for all the camps in the region.

By 1997 Oddball's alone had about 35 mokoro guides working for them. They were able to renew their leases on Oddball's and its smaller, upmarket sister camp, Delta Camp. However, the government had made a hard bargain: they had to reduce the number of visitors to a maximum combined total of 60 people at any one time. That was 40 guests at Oddball's and 20 at Delta Camp, a fraction of past numbers.

Immediately prices had to be increased in order to cover their costs from a much smaller base of visitors. In December 1999 both camps were extensively renovated; economics dictated that they had to move more upmarket, charging more, to stay in business. The camp on the Oddball's site was rebuilt in much greater style, as a fully fledged upmarket camp that could command high prices. Then the names of the two camps were switched. This newly built camp on the site of Oddball's old site is now known as Delta Camp, whilst the older camp which was once known as Delta Camp became Oddballs' (with the apostrophe moved to reflect a change of emphasis).

Thus the 1980s camp has become an upmarket camp for the next century, whilst the original budget camp has been totally rebuilt and refurbished as a new luxurious camp, to standards which are now much higher than they were.

This is a textbook example of what has happened right across Botswana. Pressure from the government, using park fees and the concessions as tools of implementation, has led to lower numbers of visitors to Botswana's wild areas, and hence to more costly safaris and more upmarket lodges. For their money visitors now get a much more exclusive experience, with mokoro guides who have more training and better skills than before – and are paid better as the result.

In summary: the environment benefits, the local people benefit, Botswana's finances benefit, and even the visitors get a better experience – that is, those who can still afford to visit!

GEOGRAPHY NOTE As with the whole Delta, the floods in this area are variable and unpredictable, in both duration and timing. The flood usually arrives between

March and May, and remains for an average of four months. However, hydrologists note that since the late 1980s, there was a measured decrease in the amount of water flowing down the Boro River. In the 1994–95 period of water inflow, it was estimated that the lower Boro River received little over half of its long-term average. That water flow then gradually decreased, until – due to heavy rainfall in Angola – water levels rose again, and by 2009 were back to those of the 1980s. The flood levels continued to be very impressive through 2010 and 2011, before starting to return to more normal levels in 2012 and 2013.

Changes in water levels could also be explained by postulating that the western side of the Delta is gradually rising relative to the eastern side. Hence the Thaoge is gradually flooding less, and the Khwai is flooding more. The Boro is fairly central to the Delta, and derives its flow from the Nqoga River (the source of the Khwai River). However, it breaks from this at a very sharp, acute angle, and hence some experts suggest that it should be considered as being influenced the same way as the rivers on the western side of the Delta.

Having said all this, some say that changes in water flows could be caused simply by a hippo changing its regular path in the higher reaches of the Delta! Whatever the cause, this reduced flow isn't necessarily good or bad for the visitor; but it is a help in understanding some of the gradual changes which are happening (over decades) to the area's vegetation.

FLORA AND FAUNA HIGHLIGHTS The Boro River and its associated floodplains dominate this reserve. A land survey in 1996 estimated that only about 4% of the whole reserve was permanent swampland, but 75% was classed as seasonally inundated swamp and grasslands. The remainder is dry land: riverine forests and grasslands on the islands. So this is a very seasonal environment, which changes annually with the floods.

Flora As noted above, there is relatively little permanent swamp here. Small patches of papyrus are found though, usually in photogenic little clumps beside the main Boro River. Look carefully and you'll also find areas of common reeds (*Phragmites australis*), Miscanthus grass (*Miscanthus junceus*), bulrushes (*Typha capensis*) and a number of floating-leafed, emergent and submerged species.

Perhaps the major feature of the area is some splendid, mature patches of riverine forests that line sections of the Boro River. Here you'll find lots of real fan palms (*Hyphaene petersiana*), often in beautiful dense stands. There's also a scattering of all the 'usual suspects' that you'd expect in riverine forest in the region, including leadwoods (*Combretum imberbe*), jackalberries (*Diospyros mespiliformis*), knobthorns (*Acacia negrescens*), sausage trees (*Kigelia africana*), large fever-berries (*Croton megalobotrys*), woodland waterberries (*Syzygium guineense*) and occasional baobab trees (*Adansonia digitata*). However, perhaps the area's most unusual flora are the huge strangler figs (*Ficus* species, probably *thonningii*, *natalensis* or *fischeri*). There are several specimens here enveloping large leadwood trees – an amazing sight.

On the larger island, and particularly on Chief's Island (in Moremi, but visited from these camps), you'll find permanently dry forest areas. These vary from mopane woodlands in areas of clay soil, to areas of acacias where there's more sand.

In the deepest areas of sand you'll find *Terminalia sericea*, the source of the best wood from which to craft traditional mokoro poles.

Adjacent to the river are large areas of very shallow floodplains. A wide variety of grasses, sedges and herbs are found in these areas with various species of *Eragrostis*, *Imperata*, *Panicum*, *Aristida* and *Cymbopogen* being common. More than 200 plant

12

species have been recorded here, though the floodplains are very often dotted with a sparse covering of *Imperata cylindrica,* sometimes known as 'silver spike', with long, rigid leaf spikes growing from a rhizome, some with a small 'spikelet' at the end.

Fauna None of the camps in this reserve conducts game drives, so a visit here is usually much more about the ambience of the Delta than about spotting game. Come for the experience, let any game sightings be a bonus, and you'll have a good trip.

That said, there are good game densities in the area, and especially on the adjacent Chief's Island. Even from a mokoro you're likely to see hippopotami and crocodiles in the water. Elephants are frequently seen in the drier months, from May to October, wandering through the floodplains; from December to April they are around in smaller numbers.

When out walking on the islands there is a chance of much more game. The area's dominant antelope is the red lechwe, but you will also find tsessebe, impala, zebra, kudu, reedbuck, giraffe, warthog and buffalo. As the area becomes drier with time, blue wildebeest are being seen more often. Roan, sable and waterbuck remain absent from this area. When the flood is at its height, sitatunga are occasionally seen. With the recent reintroduction of rhino to Chief's Island, there's a very slim chance that you could bump into one of them.

The most common predators are lion, spotted hyena and jackals. Leopard are rarely seen, but they will be relatively common as the riverine forest suits them perfectly. Wild dogs and cheetah also occur, but are rare sightings. There was even a report from this area of a brown hyena sighting, though this is certainly a rarity here.

Birdlife Birding is an important feature of all the trips here; you'll probably spend much of your time exploring the area from a mokoro. As mentioned above, the water levels can vary hugely – in October 2002 they dropped by 15cm in just three weeks. So expect the channels and the birdlife to vary greatly through the seasons.

When water levels are lowest, around November to February, you may find skimmers on some exposed sandbanks. Meanwhile knob-billed ducks, long-toed and blacksmith plovers, and saddle-billed storks are amongst a whole host of permanent residents. As levels rise, red-winged pratincoles gather in large flocks, and there is always a good variety of kingfishers, from giant and pied to the tiny pygmy and malachite. Woodland kingfishers – insectivorous birds which are usually seen hunting for insects in the riverine forest – appear for the summer around the end of October. They arrive with a variety of migrants, including carmine bee-eaters, aerobatic yellow-billed kites, and paradise flycatchers, the males of which have the most spectacular tails. I've a reliable report of black coucals in front of Delta Camp, but haven't seen them there myself.

Much of the Boro's channel usually sees the annual catfish run (see box, page 362), and this area is no exception. If you're lucky enough to catch this then you can spot 30 species or more in a 100m stretch of waterway. Pelicans, skimmers and a wide variety of herons, egrets, storks, stilts, snipes and cormorants all appear in quantity then, to take advantage of the abundant food.

WHEN TO VISIT Though open all year, these camps rely primarily on mokoro trips and so are certainly at their best when the sun is shining and the sky blue, ie: between April and November. If you're camping out then it makes for a better trip if it's not too cold at night, thus my favourite months for visiting here would be around May–early June (though those months can be cold, too) and September–October time.

GETTING THERE AND AWAY Although years ago safari operators used to offer boat transfers up the Boro River from Maun to here, now flying in is really the only way. There are several airstrips, including Delta airstrip (⊕ DELAIR 19°31.840'S, 23°05.430'E), which is closest to both Oddballs' and Delta Camp, and, about 4km southwest from there, Xaxaba airstip (⊕ XAXAIR 19°33.220'S, 23°03.510'E).

WHERE TO STAY Of the camps in this reserve, Delta and Oddballs' are run by Lodges of Botswana (page 176); Gunn's Camp and Moremi Crossing (formerly Gunn's Bush Camp) from their base in Maun, Under One Botswana Sky (page 177); and Eagle Island Camp, Khwai River Lodge and Savute Elephant Camp by Orient-Express (page 176).

🏠 **Delta Camp** [map 295] (7 chalets) Owned & run by Lodges of Botswana since 1983, this camp overlooks the Boro River. In 2001 it was completely rebuilt on the site of the old Oddball's Camp, & renamed Delta Camp. Its reed-&-thatch chalets have open verandas looking northeast into Moremi. All have an en-suite bathroom, including a shower, toilet & washbasin.

Activities centre around mokoro trips, with your guide poling the mokoro & leading walks on the islands. With a little advanced notice, it's possible to go on day trips with picnic lunches. *US$450 pp sharing Dec–Mar, US$650 Apr–Jun & Nov, US$785 pp Jul–Oct, inc FB, drinks, activities & park fees; 30% sgl suppt. Maun–Delta airstrip flights US$163 each way, strict 20kg luggage allowance.* ☺ *All year.*

🏠 **Oddballs' Palm Island Luxury Lodge** [map 295] (14 dome tents) Southeast of Delta Camp, but beside the same Boro River, Oddballs' is still thought of as a destination in the Okavango for budget travellers, even though it's *much* more expensive than it was.

For your money, you now have your own 2.4m x 2.4m (3-person) dome tent which stands on a raised wooden deck, surmounted by a roll of reeds for shade. Outside is a view over the Delta; inside are a dbl or twin beds; & on its veranda are a small table & stools.

Unlike the backpackers' camp of old, a stay here now includes all meals & activities. It usually includes a first & last night at Oddballs' itself, with the intervening nights camping out on the islands. All your camping kit & food is provided (drinks are not – you buy these separately), but you do your own cooking whilst you're on the mokoro trail. *US$260 pp sharing Dec–Mar, US$320 Apr–Jun & Nov, US$395 pp Jul–Oct, inc FB, activities, & park fees; exc P200 pp wilderness camping fee for mokoro trail. Other details as Delta Camp.* ☺ *All year.*

🏠 **Oddballs' Enclave** [map 295] (5 tents) An upmarket off-shoot of Oddballs', with 'mini-Meru' walk-in tents, all en suite, & its own bar, lounge & dining areas. *US$420 pp sharing Dec–Mar, US$450 Apr, May & Nov, US$540 pp pp Jun–Oct, inc FB, activities, & park fees.* ☺ *All year.*

🏠 **Gunn's Camp** [map 295] (8 tents) Situated on the Boro River, overlooking Moremi Game Reserve, Gunn's was founded & run for years by the brusque Mike Gunn. It used to be accessed as often by motorboat as by plane from Maun, & in the 1980s it ran week-long 'fitness in the wilderness' courses which, amongst other things, taught you how to punt your own mokoro.

Since then it has been taken more upmarket, with twin-bedded Meru tents, enlivened by colourful fabrics & teak furniture. All have en-suite bathrooms with flush toilets, stand-alone bathtubs & outdoor showers; a small outside sitting area with comfy chairs; & electric lighting – run from a generator, with battery back-up. The central dining/bar area is wood & thatch, with an excellent upper seating area overlooking the river & floodplains, & a small swimming pool & a campfire.

Activities are organised in the morning & evening, usually involving mokoro trips & perhaps including a walk on one of the islands. With prior notice, overnight mokoro trips can be arranged, camping on an island with dinner around a campfire & a walk the following morning. And when the channels are deep enough, motorboat trips along the Boro are possible. *US$650/785 pp sharing/sgl Jul–Oct, US$495 Apr–Jun, US$375 Nov–Mar inc FB, most drinks, activities & park fees. No sgl suppt for 3 nights or more. Maun–Gunn's Camp flight US$160 each way; strict 20kg luggage allowance.* ☺ *All year.*

🏠 **Moremi Crossing** [map 295] (16 tents) 📞686 0023; e reservations@moremicrossing.com;

12

www.moremicrossing.com. The former bushcamp at Gunn's has been completely refurbished & renamed, drawing a line under the camping options of yore. Accommodation is in en-suite Meru-style tents, shaded by African ebony, sycamore fig & palm trees. Meals are served in a thatched central area, which houses a bar & curio shop. This is fronted by a crescent-shaped deck that overlooks the permanent Boro channel & Chief's Island, & there's a swimming pool tucked behind. The camp aims to be 100% eco-friendly, with solar power & modern disposal technology. Activities combine mokoro trips with walks on the islands, as well as motorboat cruises & camping on nearby islands. As an alternative to the flight into camp, it's possible to take a boat trip from Maun as an optional extra. *US$520/655 pp sharing/sgl Jul–Oct, US$465 Apr–Jun, US$335 Nov–Mar inc FB, most drinks, activities & park fees, inc FB, most drinks, activities, park fees, laundry; exc transfers. No sgl suppt 3 nights or more. No children under 8.* ⊕ *All year.*

🏠 **Eagle Island Camp** [map 295] (12 tented rooms) One of the Delta's first photographic camps was built here at Xaxaba Island (unless you're fluent in one of the local Khoisan languages & used to the various clicks, this is usually pronounced 'Kakaaba', with 'Ka' as in 'cat'). It was known as Xaxaba Camp &, at one point, was bought by Lloyd Wilmot (of 'Lloyd's Camp, Savuti' fame) before it was run for many years by Gametrackers, now known as Orient-Express Safaris. There's still a bushcamp, known as Baboon Camp, used by wildlife researchers, on the same spot today, but the main camp nearby is this reserve's plushest: Eagle Island.

As you might expect, it's built to basically the same design & specification as its sister camps,

Khwai River Lodge (page 269) & Savute Elephant Camp (pages 235–6). This means large, opulent tented rooms built to high-quality standards on timber platforms under thatched roofs, each with a wide veranda at the front & an outside lounge with a hammock. They're well spread out & linked by well-lit pathways. Inside, each tent is fully furnished with polished wooden floors, rugs & luxurious furniture. The twin ¾-size beds, which are usually pushed together, have high-quality cotton bedding, bedside tables & twin lamps, not to mention the accoutrements of a top hotel such as minibars & safes. The beds are surrounded by mosquito netting & surmounted by 2 AC units (yes, really – & there's a ceiling fan!). And there's 110/220V power augmented by 24hr battery electricity. At the back, each tent has a separate toilet room with his & hers basins, a large shower room, & acres of polished wood. For relaxation in camp, there's a library of books & videos, tea- & coffee-making facilities, & a heated pool next to the lagoon.

Eagle Island is primarily a camp for water-based activities – mainly mokoro trips & guided walks on the islands, plus motorboat trips during high-water periods (usually Jun–Sep). For most of the year there's also a large 14-seater 'sundowner cruiser' which can slowly coast along the main channels. Helicopter safaris – a great way to see the scenery & animals from a different perspective – are also on offer. And on very rare occasions, when it's been so dry here that there's not enough water for good mokoro trips, the camp has organised game drives. *US$788–1,750 pp sharing, inc FB, activities, drinks, laundry.* ⊕ *All year.*

ACTIVITIES Though these camps differ slightly in their activities, they are essentially water-camps from which you take guided mokoro trips along the Boro River, and out on to its associated floodplains.

Most also offer walking trips on the islands – just as camps here have for decades. These generally use the bush-wise local mokoro guides, whose local knowledge can be excellent (even if their communication skills in English are more variable). They will almost never be carrying any firearms for protection, so see my general comments under *Walking in the bush* in *Chapter 6*, for a further discussion of the safety issues raised by this approach.

A final note of warning from a cost perspective. The government has introduced a 'wilderness camping fee' for visitors camping overnight within Moremi Game Reserve as part of a mokoro trip. The fee, P200 per person per day, is payable in cash on arrival, and cannot be prepaid.

XIGERA, MOMBO AND CHIEF'S CAMP (NG28)

Although technically in the NG28 concession, on the north and west side of Chief's Island, Xigera, Mombo and Chief's Camp were effectively swallowed up by Moremi Game Reserve in 1992. Thus these three private camps and their satellites are covered in *Chapter 11, The Okavango Delta – Moremi Game Reserve*, pages 283–92.

GUBANARE, XUDUM, XARANNA AND OHS (NG29 AND NG30)

Together these equally large concessions cover a total of about 2,500km² on the southern edge of the Delta, sandwiched between southern Moremi and the Sandvelt Tongue. They're designated as 'multi-use' concessions, and so separate parts of each are used for hunting and for photographic trips. All pay a lease fee to the local community for their use of the land.

I've only described the non-hunting camps here, which are split between two operations: a specialist horseriding operation run by Okavango Horse Safaris, and two new photographic camps run by &Beyond. The reserves are so large that horseriders and safari campers are most unlikely to come across one another. Travellers should realise that these areas don't have the best game densities, but they are perfect for keen birdwatchers, and there are relatively frequent sightings of lion.

FLORA AND FAUNA HIGHLIGHTS Visiting one September, I concentrated my time in the area around Gubanare, which is in the far northern corner of the concession, close to Moremi Game Reserve – and probably its most productive area for wildlife. There the land was relatively dry, with only a few areas of floodplain, which is probably fairly typical of these areas towards the southwest edge of the Delta. Because of this location, the annual flood hits these areas relatively late – typically around the end of May or June. Then good water levels last until around the end of October or November.

Further south, around Xudum, there have been extensive changes in water levels over the last decade, which has impacted significantly on the wildlife in this area. A recent visit, in February, found the birding at its best here.

Flora Across the reserve there are lots of large, open plains covered in tall grass and interspersed with dry established thorny thickets and expanses of turpentine grass, (*Cymbopogon* sp). Tall and with sharp barbs, it is widely used for thatching. Among these are dense stands of leadwood trees (*Combretum imberbe*) and knobthorns (*Acacia nigrescens*). The latter are so numerous that their beautiful, creamy flowers combine to form a powerful perfume.

Perhaps as the result of fires in the past, there are large areas of chest-high wild sage, amidst occasional 'islands', typical of the Delta, where termite mounds are dotted among African mangosteens, raintrees, marulas, sausage trees and jackalberrys. Amongst the larger stands of trees are umbrella thorns (*Acacia tortilis*) and real fan palms (*Hyphaene petersiana*). But these islands of forest are relatively infrequent and quite poorly defined.

In the far north, the concession has a short boundary with Moremi: the Boro River, which is one of the Delta's best-known channels and is lined in parts by mature riverine forest.

Overall the mixed environment contains a wide variation of tree and plant species, though it doesn't have the beauty of some of the more mature, established forests or floodplain areas.

12

Fauna There's a good range of species here, typical of the Delta, though game densities are probably not as high as further north. They are certainly highly seasonal with animals proving scarce during the rains, and then numbers improving as the land dries out in the dry season. In the deeper waters around the Boro River, there's no shortage of hippos or crocodiles.

In the north, the dominant antelope is probably tsessebe (in one study of the Delta these made up 70% of all lion kills), though impala are also fairly common, occurring frequently in small groups. Family groups of giraffe and small numbers of zebra and wildebeest are also seen in the drier areas, along with kudu and steenbok, but rising water levels around the Xudum River over the past decade have impacted on the wildlife in this area. Populations of red lechwe and reedbuck have swollen, while those of the plains game such as zebra and wildebeest have declined. Roan, eland and gemsbok are seen very rarely, and generally only in the drier areas on the south side of the NG29 concession.

Between about December and June elephants occur in small family groups (this is typical of their behaviour in the whole region when food is plentiful). Then they tend to be most frequently found in the mopane scrub areas in the south of the concession. Later in the year, as the land dries up, they gradually coalesce into larger herds, hundreds strong, which move north and east, nearer to the heart of the Delta. Buffalo tend to occur in large herds that move through the concession in the dry season; smaller groups are seldom seen.

Of the predators, lion are by far the most common in these concessions, although numbers have reduced as the plains game moved away. Typically the prides are relatively small nowadays, but the largest – comprising seven lionesses – is seen fairly regularly. Leopard are also permanent residents and, though generally shy, are increasingly seen around the new camps. I didn't see any spotted hyena on my last visit, though they're almost certainly around. Cheetah are very scarce, and generally only seen in the driest of months, around October to December. Then the grass is shorter, and there's more dry land, and so less pressure from lion. At other times of the year the cheetah tend to move away from the water, south and west out of the concession.

Birdlife The varied habitat leads to good birdwatching, and explorations both of the Boro River area and further south can be excellent. Along the river, very large flocks of red-winged pratincoles congregate on the exposed sandbanks, where the grass is cropped short thanks to the grazing lechwe. May witnesses the biggest pratincole colonies, which first appear as the Boro River begins to rise. Before that, while the sandbanks are exposed, you'll sometimes find African skimmers around. Old favourites include saddle-billed storks, knob-billed ducks, night herons, long-toed plovers and spurwing geese. Look out, too, for the endangered lesser jacana among the more common African jacanas, and the rufous-bellied heron. With luck, you might even spot the rare blue-grey flycatcher.

In the area's drier grasslands black-bellied khorans are highly visible, with their eye-catching courtship displays. The wild sage areas here are often burned and, immediately after this, wattled cranes arrive in numbers to dig up snails and other creatures that are exposed by fires.

Raptors which are frequently seen include various vultures, bateleur, fish and tawny eagles, both the black-chested and brown snake eagles, and the occasional martial eagle. The opportunist yellow-billed kites and steppe eagles usually start arriving for the summer in late August, and whilst the smaller raptors are more scarce, black-shouldered kites are often spotted (and easily recognised because they hover in mid-flight). Trees on the islands also shelter both eagle owls and the occasional Pel's fishing owl, its tawny plumage unmistakable against the dark foliage.

WHEN TO VISIT These areas on the edge of the Delta have more seasonal variation than areas further north, so the game really is significantly better later in the dry season than earlier. As with anywhere in the Delta, the wetter times of the year are better for birdwatching.

Geography note Be aware that the western side of the Delta (from the Thaoge into Lake Ngami) has been drying up since the middle of the last century. As a result of this (or vice versa) an increasing amount of Okavango's water is finding its way into the Muanachira/Khwai system, on the eastern side of Chief's Island.

Thus the floodplains of the west are gradually drying out and being invaded by flora used to drier conditions, whilst the drier areas of the Khwai River, and areas like Sandibe, are gradually becoming wetter.

GETTING THERE AND AWAY Access to all the camps is by light aircraft, using Pom Pom airstrip in the neighbouring concession, followed by a 45-minute drive to Xaranna, or about 1½ hours to Xudum (which may also involve a boat trip). However, road transfers from here to the riding camps is possible only between about June and September; the alternatives are a helicopter transfer, or a four-hour road/boat trip from Maun. Guests must have a prior reservation. No self-driving visitors are allowed into these areas, though in case of emergency, it's sometimes possible to access the camps by road – though it's a dusty, bumpy six hours from Maun.

🏠 **TRADITIONAL SAFARI CAMPS** Following many years when the camps in this concession were caught in some form of legal limbo, two new lodges were opened in 2008 by &Beyond (see page 175). Both are located in the south of the concession, so share a similar area in terms of wildlife and activities, and both have a similar commitment to high standards. Their high ratio of staff to guests allows considerably greater flexibility in choice of activities than is often the case. Rates are identical, so the choice for the visitor comes down more to one of style than substance.

🏠 **Xaranna Okavango Delta Camp** [map 295] (9 tented chalets) ✪ XARAN 19°42.734'S, E 022°53.176'E. Spread out among mature jackalberry & sycamore fig trees, Xaranna Camp faces east across a permanent water channel, & occupies a super birding spot. It can offer mokoro trips from camp throughout the year, as well as fishing, bush walks & game drives, with trips by motorboat an added option in the winter months, usually Apr–Sep. There's considerable emphasis on flexibility, which is a big bonus for guests.

Themed using light wood offset by green & white fabrics, with splashes of pink, the camp has the strong imprint of a designer at work. The wide, open-fronted central area, under green canvas raised on heavy poles, is divided neatly into sections at different levels. At one end is a circular boma-style area & firepit, while at the other is a comfortable lounge, with squashy chairs & sofas, all in the hallmark green & white; there's even a green-covered Scrabble set! A good library of brown-paper-wrapped books contrasts with other volumes bound in pink & green, & monochrome photos are used to dramatic effect both on walls or under glass as tables or counters. In the centre are green plastic chairs for dining, set round long tables with more than a hint of the staff canteen, while more comfortable chairs invite guests to relax with a drink. The theme continues on to the deck, & even on to the jetty where a family of white-painted hippos is in residence. A curio shop offers a range of items, from the lodge's own sarongs to beaded jewellery, baskets, candles & a few field guides, as well as clothing essentials & even binoculars. There's a guest computer & Wi-Fi in the main area.

12

To each side of the main building lie spacious tented chalets, with gauze panels & coloured blinds. From the private bar at the entrance to the 5m private pool at the back, it's clear that these are far removed from the standard safari tent. In the middle is a good-sized bedroom, its twin beds (or a king-size) under walk-in mosi nets affording a view across the channel. To one side, sharing the view, the bathroom features twin basins, a separate toilet, a free-standing bath, & showers inside & out. A narrow deck runs around the front, linking a sheltered circular day bed to the pool. It's clear that plenty of thought has gone into kitting out these rooms. As well as AC, there are fans on each side of the bed, attached to the bedposts. Camp-style hanging wardrobes contain everything from toiletries to a hairdryer & torch, & for those in need of activity, each room has its own 'gym in a basket', offering the potential for a workout after all those game drives. There's even a couch in the bathroom, with stylish sarongs as well as bathrobes & slippers. Access is by sliding doors front & back, but the problem of retaining heat in winter was still being addressed when we visited. An inverter system means that lights & fans operate at night, while a generator powers appliance (inc AC) during the day.

For those who put style & service high on their agenda, this – & its sister camp, Xudum – should be serious contenders. *US$750–1,550 pp sharing, low–high season, inc FB, local drinks, safari activities, laundry. Children 6–12 join activities at manager's discretion.* ⊕ *All year.*

🛖 **Xudum Okavango Delta Lodge** [map 295] (9 chalets) ✪ XUDUM 19°38.003'S, 022°53.998'E. Built a short distance from the older camp of the same name, Xudum is on a long, thin, wooded island towards the middle of the NG29 concession. Situated just ½hr by boat from Xaranna, or 1½hrs by road, the camp has its own airstrip – & its own helicopter, 1 of only 2 kept in the Delta. As well as offering an alternative means of transfer (max 2 people & luggage), the chopper is available for scenic trips, when it flies low, with earphones for on-board communication. Scenic 45min helicopter trips to Chief's Island are available at additional cost. More conventionally, day & night drives &

mokoro trips are on offer throughout the year, with boat cruises & walking safaris in winter only, when the grass is low & the water levels up. The flexibility at Xaranna extends to this lodge, too, with early-afternoon activities available if requested, in addition to those during the morning & late afternoon.

First impressions are monochrome & deceptively low-key. Off-white plastic canteen chairs are drawn up to functional tables; tyres hanging from the roof & stacked beer cans make handy occasional tables. But make no mistake: the style guru at Xaranna is behind the set up here, too. Flat roofs & square areas of thatch combine to create less a sense of continuity than one of unstudied homeliness. The open-plan kitchen adds a surprisingly homely touch, too, with many guests enjoying the chance to get involved. Comfy black sofas, outsize black-&-white photos & individual tables for dining make this a place to relax, rather than stand on ceremony. A curio shop holds a similar stock to that at Xaranna.

Xudum doesn't have rooms: it has suites. Spacious, stylish suites with AC, fans & good lighting. Constructed of wood with sliding meshed doors, each has a thatched upstairs sala to catch the breeze (& wonderful for alfresco nights), extensive ground-level decking with a second, circular day bed tucked in the shade, & a 5m plunge pool with adjacent outside shower, all overlooking the plains. Inside, dark-wood panelling offset by brown textured blinds & mosquito nets around the king-size or twin beds lend something of the air of a 5-star hotel, with wide steps leading down to a grand bathroom, where a free-standing bath takes centre stage. (There's also a huge open-plan shower, & a separate toilet.) Mostly it avoids being ostentatious, though the dbl-length basin is a design idea too far. Individual touches include sarongs, a personal 'gym', & a cocktail shaker for the minibar, & in-room massage is available. The chalets, reached along sandy paths through the bush, are generally well spread out, 3 to one side, 6 to the other. That said, some have been built closer together, making them ideal for friends or families. For absolute privacy, choose numbers 1 or 9, out on the end. *Rates & children as for Xaranna, above.*

RIDING SAFARIS Contact Okavango Horse Safaris (OHS), page 179. Provided that you are a competent rider, seeing the Okavango from horseback can be totally magical. From the point of view of most of the rest of the Delta's animals, once you step into the saddle you become part of a four-legged herbivore (albeit a strangely shaped one). Thus generally they relax around you, so you can ride with herds of antelope without disturbing them, and see the place from a kudu's-eye view. The palm islands, grassy floodplains, mopane forests and clear streams all ensure that the ground under you is always changing. Your horse will wade from island to island, where the going is normally quite good and firm along the edges – allowing the ride to move on at a trot and canter.

Having said all this, just as the herbivores perceive you as an antelope, so will the predators. Hence the emphasis on safety that a horseriding operation must have in this environment: it's not unusual to have to gallop to safety from a pride of lion – usually with the guide at the rear, gun in hand.

Perhaps unlike most of the other camps in this book (except African Horseback Safaris, pages 321–2), the precise details of Okavango Horse Safaris' camps are really much less important than the arrangements made for the riding activities. Thus here I'll cover briefly the basics of these safaris, before mentioning the camps and costs. However, it's worth pointing out that the revamped Mokolwane Camp is now geared to a more general audience, with a broader range of activities than just riding, such as bird walks, game drives and mokoro excursions.

The horses OHS advises that they use Pure Arab, Anglo Arab, American saddle bred, part- and full-thoroughbred, Kalahari and Kalahari-cross horses. All are between 14 and 17 hands high, well schooled and responsive, and have fairly even temperaments.

Tack and clothes The tack used is English style, of a high quality and kept in good condition. An assortment of leather saddles is used, including well-known makes such as Barnsby, Ideal and Symonds, and each has a seat-saver for comfort. All horses go in snaffle bridles.

OHS produces specific 'clothes lists' for their trips, but they can do laundry in their camp. Like all operations, the air transfers dictate that you stick to a strict weight limit (excess can be left in Maun). Note that proper riding clothes, and clothes of bush colours, are important here. A limited assortment of half chaps and riding gloves is kept in the camp for guests' use, but it is strongly recommended that riders bring and wear their own hats.

Information about you To book a place on one of their trips, OHS will ask you for your age, weight, height and riding experience – as well as the more usual questions of your preference in drinks, specialised dietary requirements, allergies etc. They'll also require you to fill out an indemnity form in camp before beginning your trip, a practice which is now widespread in camps throughout southern Africa.

Riding ability You must be able to ride well. This isn't a place to learn to ride, or to come if you feel at all nervous on a horse. This means being able to 'post to the trot' for ten minutes at a time, being comfortable at all paces, and being able to gallop out of trouble. It is a great advantage if you are fit and a proficient rider. A separate programme can be organised for non-riding partners, on request.

Weight limit The maximum weight for any rider is 14½ stone (200lb or 90kg), and OHS insist that potential riders may be required to step on a pair of scales! That said, for heavier riders an alternative programme of shorter rides, game drives and walks is possible, but this must be discussed with OHS when you arrange your trip.

12

About the trips Having established that you can cope with the rigours of a riding safari, you have a choice between five-day, seven-day and ten-day safaris, although two–four-night breaks are available on request. The longer trips are normally scheduled in advance on set dates throughout the year. While this does lack flexibility, it means that you are with a group of people and can get to know each other. Generally, the best time to go is in the latter half of the dry season, between August and October.

On all trips there's a demonstration and talk at the beginning of the safari on how to handle big-game situations, as well as a familiarisation session with the tack. After that, expect to spend between four and six hours in the saddle each day, broken by refreshment stops. Typically this means that you'll have some picnic breakfasts and lunches, and also ten-minute walks every couple of hours spent in the saddle. (This acts to rest the rider by giving him/her the chance to use different muscles, and it also helps to relieve the horse from the constant pressure of a rider's weight.)

Although the focus here is firmly on horseriding, alternative activities are often possible during afternoons which are not 'day rides'. These can include game drives, birdwatching walks, mokoro rides and night drives.

Safety Riding in big-game country can be difficult, especially when a horse looks very much like an antelope to a hungry lion. Thus safety is a big issue; it's at the root of why this isn't a place for inexperienced riders. An extremely experienced guide, usually PJ or Barney, accompanies every ride, and they do carry a .375 rifle in case of emergency.

These riding itineraries take a maximum of eight riders at once (again, for safety reasons). They will accept children, though these must be strong, competent riders (a Pony Club test pass is insisted upon). The cost for a child is the same as for an adult.

The riding camps These aim to be comfortable and simple, and all are staffed. Three meals a day are prepared, with vehicle-supported picnic lunches and bush breakfasts. As with most camps, they emphasise fairly healthy food with fresh vegetables and salads, and bake fresh bread each day. Dinner is often a three-course affair, usually served by candlelight at a dining table beside the campfire. Lighting and power for charging of cameras is supplied by a solar system.

The camps are spread out over a considerable distance, with Kujwana – the company's base, where the horses are stabled – in the centre, almost 20km southeast of Mokolwane, and 11.5km northwest of Qwaapo Fly-camp. All of which goes to emphasise what a large amount of ground these horseriding safaris can cover.

Kujwana Camp [map 295] (6 tents)
✪ KUJWAN 19°44.370'S, 22°57.115'E. Kujwana is the company's base, & this is where the horses are stabled. It is situated on the Xudum River, on a hippo-shaped island of mature trees about 8.5km southeast of Xudum lodge.

At the heart of the camp, overlooking the river, is a raised treehouse complete with a bar & separate dining area. Lined up one side of this main area are Meru-style tents, each on a raised deck with a shaded veranda & twin or dbl beds, & a flush toilet & hot-water shower en suite. Laundry is done every day except when the camp is on the move. The camp has 220v solar power, so it's possible to recharge camera batteries.

Mokolwane Camp [map 294] (5 tents)
www.mokolwane.com; ✪ MOKOLW 19°37.137'S, 22°49.277'E. Mokolwane is the most northern of the OHS camps, barely 5km southwest of Pom Pom in the adjoining NG27A reserve. It is situated among mature trees on a small island, facing east across open plains & a tributary of the Matsebi River. In winter, when the river is full, access is by water only. Following complete reconstruction

in 2009, it eschews the increasingly elaborate offerings of other establishments in favour of a more traditional approach.

While the camp is in part a satellite of Kujwana, this is no longer its sole focus. As well as riding (limited here to 3hr sessions, which must be pre-booked), guests can choose from mokoro trips, game drives & walking, including overnight walking safaris. Central to the camp is an open-sided green canvas-roofed dining area, built on 2m stilts beneath a mature African ebony overlooking the plain, & with drop-down sides to keep out the worst of the elements. A levelled-off termite mound under a neighbouring sycamore fig forms a convenient bar area. Sharing the view, & the height, are canvas 'treehouses', spaced out on either side along sand paths. Their sides are of half-height canvas, with drop-down clear plastic screens for extra protection.

Each is accessed by wooden steps, & has twin beds (or there's 1 dbl) under mosquito nets, & an en-suite bathroom at the back that's open to the skies, with flush toilet, basin & shower; water is heated by a gas geyser.

⌂ **Qwaapo Fly-camp** [map 295] (6 tents) ⊕ QWAAPO 19°47.553'S, 23°02.666'E. Another east-facing camp, this one on the river of the same name, Qwaapo is on the southeast side of the reserve in an area of mopane woodland & floodplains. Accommodation is in simple, Meru-style tents, each with a shaded veranda overlooking the river & en-suite bathroom. This includes a long-drop toilet & a bucket shower (that's the type where the bucket is filled with hot water & raised on a pulley for you by the camp staff!). Single stretcher-type beds are supplied with bedrolls, cotton sheets, duvets & towels.

The costs Unusually for Botswana, but in common with the other riding camps, prices here are quoted in pounds sterling rather than US dollars. From December to March, riding trips cost £480 per person sharing per night, including full board, drinks, guiding, riding, game drives, walks and mokoro trips, and a concession fee of US$14 per person per night). From April to mid-July and during November, the cost is £520 per person sharing per night, rising to £600 between mid-July and the end of October. Visitors who want single accommodation should add 50% to these costs, though this is usually waived if you're prepared to share a tent with another visitor.

The flight between Maun and the camps costs £165 per person return, or £255 to include a 12-minute scenic helicopter flight on either arrival or departure. In addition, a bed levy of £5 per person is charged at Mokolwane towards a fund to enable children of some of the staff to attend university.

CHITABE AND SANDIBE (NG31)

NG31 Reserve covers a relatively small 360km² of the eastern Okavango Delta. However, it's a superb location which looks on a map like a bite out of the southern side of Moremi Game Reserve – between Chief's Island and the Mopane Tongue. Sandibe and Chitabe share this reserve, though generally keep to their own sides of it. Sandibe has about 160km² on the northern side, and Chitabe (with the adjacent Chitabe Lediba) occupies the southern 200km². The two camps are relatively close, about 12km apart, and they share an airstrip.

The reserve is particularly interesting as it's experiencing a period of change. The Gomoti River, which forms the northern and eastern border of the reserve, was dry from about 1984, but began to flow again in 1999, spilling on to the seasonal floodplains and dramatically increasing the amount of water in this area. Previously only about 5% of Sandibe's area had water on it; now it's closer to 50% permanent water. Around Chitabe, however, only around 10% of the area is permanently flooded, with a further 56% flooding seasonally; the rest is dry throughout the year.

FLORA AND FAUNA HIGHLIGHTS NG31 is a varied reserve: there are quite marked differences between the northern sides (east and west) and also between these two and Chitabe's area further south, even if the list of species which occur in both are broadly the same. There is a complex mix of environments in this reserve; what follows here is very much a simplification.

The most striking difference is that the northwest of the reserve is a wetter environment than the rest. Just north of this reserve, in Moremi, the Mboroga River flows south between the dry-land areas of Chief's Island and the Mopane Tongue. Forming a number of large lagoons, it splits into two channels. One branch, the Gomoti River, then forms part of this reserve's northern boundary, and all of its eastern side. The other branch, the Santantadibe River, is a deep, wide channel that leads to lots of lagoons and runs down this reserve's southwestern side.

Flora Sandibe overlooks the permanent Santantadibe River from within this watery area, in the reserve's northwestern corner. Around it there are plenty of open-water areas and floodplains, fringed by belts of riverine vegetation with a high proportion of real fan palms (*Hyphaene petersiana*). The islands here can be large and continuous, and on the larger of these you will find occasional baobab trees growing – an indication that they've been dry islands for a long time.

The northeastern side of the reserve, around the location of the airstrip, is a spit of dry land where the habitats seem to occur in belts. There are belts of thick mopane forest interspersed with belts of dry 'acacia thornveld', where you'll find mixed stands of camelthorn trees (*Acacia erioloba*), umbrella thorns (*Acacia tortillis*) and the very similar, but thornless, sickle bush (*Dichrostachys cinerea africana*); also buffalo thorn (*Ziziphus mucronata*), with its two types of thorn, which snag on any passing animal (and on clothing) and have earned it the Afrikaans name *wag-'n-bietjie*, meaning 'wait-a-bit'.

There are also bands of lower, more 'scrubby' vegetation, including classic species of deep Kalahari sand like the silver cluster-leaf (*Terminalia sericea*), and some very striking areas forested with large numbers of dead leadwood trees (*Combretum imberbe*). These trees, with their hard, termite-resistant, wood were killed by flooding when the water levels in the area changed – but will probably stand for many years, looking from the air like a river of dead trees .

Moving to the south side of the reserve, nearer to where Chitabe stands, you will find a lot of mixed forest areas with classic riverine species of trees like the large feverberry (*Croton megalobotrys*), sausage tree (*Kigelia africana*) and jackalberry (*Diospyros mespiliformis*).

Around here there are some smaller islands surrounded by shallow floodplains covered with hippo grass (*Vossia cuspida*). The deeper channels are mostly lined by phragmites reeds (*Phragmites australis*) and miscanthus grass (*Miscanthus junceus*). These are permanent channels which don't dry up, and seem to have relatively little seasonal variation; they simply spread out on to wider floodplains when the flood finally arrives (around May or June usually).

At the southern end of the reserve is a belt of soil with a high clay content, providing the perfect substrate for large stands of mopane trees (*Colophospermum mopane*), which sometimes seem so uniform that it almost appears to be a monoculture.

Fauna This reserve has a wide range of game species, dominated by impala, tsessebe, kudu and, on the floodplains, red lechwe. Zebra are fairly numerous, blue wildebeest less so, and giraffe are very common in the bands of acacia thornveld (35 were observed together at one point on the airstrip). Reedbuck, duiker and steenbok are often seen, whilst eland and roan are found only rarely (usually towards the south of the reserve); sable seem to be totally absent.

The sightings here of buffalo and elephants seem to follow the same broad patterns. Throughout the year there are small resident herds of both around, plus odd old bulls and small bachelor groups. However, from around June to October large breeding herds pass through. Then buffalo herds can number well over a thousand, and herds of a hundred elephants are not unknown.

The key to understanding this is to realise that when there has been rainfall, usually starting around November–December, the big herds move into the large swathes of mopane forest between the Okavango and the Kwando–Linyanti river system; that is, into the interior forests of Kwando (NG14), Linyanti (NG15), Selinda (NG16), Khwai Community (NG18) and Kwara (NG20). Whilst there, their water needs are sustained by the seasonal clay pans which hold water. However, when these pans start to dry up, around May or June, they move back to the areas of permanent water, including this reserve.

The reserve has plenty of lion including, when I last visited, a resident 17-strong pride. Recently they seem to have concentrated mainly on hunting buffalo, though that may have been just the natural response to having a lot of mouths to feed.

Leopard are common here, with the mixed woodlands and floodplains being an ideal habitat for them. I've had one of my best leopard sightings in Botswana near Chitabe, and hence tend to regard it as one of the country's best camps for leopard.

Cheetah stay here throughout the year, and are most frequently seen in the drier, more open eastern side of the reserve. Their populations are perhaps helped by relatively low numbers of spotted hyena.

The reserve seems to have made a name for itself for wild dog. This may partially be due to the involvement in the reserve's management of Dave Hamman, who took many of the photographs for the book *Running Wild* (see *Appendix 3, Further information*), about the 'Mombo' pack of wild dogs in Moremi.

There certainly is a healthy population of dogs here. They seem to like the marginal floodplains, and will flush the antelopes through plains and islands to catch them. A few years ago there were three dens in the concession, though these are usually moved from one year to the next … so the situation is relatively unpredictable from year to year. Having said this, I'd probably choose a more open and less wooded area than Chitabe if I were specifically hoping to track down some wild dogs.

Finally, on a more unusual note, this reserve seems to have had a very high incidence of pangolin sightings: they have recorded about six sightings in the last two years. (Most camps would count themselves lucky with one such sighting, as these are very rare animals.) Many of these sightings have been on full-moon night-drives, when the pangolin has been seen foraging around in the open. Aardvarks and aardwolves are also frequently seen here at night. Perhaps this, and the pangolin sightings, is really a reflection of the camps' enthusiasm for (or at least willingness to organise) serious late-night game drives, rather than a higher density of these animals in this area per se.

Birdlife A recent survey counted 386 species in this immediate area. In general, Sandibe is the better location for waterbirds, although this is by no means exclusive. Along with many more common species, Okavango 'specials' like the Pel's fishing owl, wattled crane, slaty egret (thought to be the world's rarest heron), black coucal and black egret have been recorded.

Chitabe has a wider variation of dry-country birds, with its most common raptor being the bateleur eagle, though there are also good numbers of many other eagles including martial, brown snake, black snake, tawny and western banded snake eagles. Marsh harriers are found in the wetter areas, along with the inevitable fish

12

eagles and even the uncommon migrant European marsh harriers. Look out for bat hawks in the late evening. Less spectacular, though almost equally uncommon, brown firefinches can certainly be found here.

WHEN TO VISIT As with the rest of the Okavango, the big game here is more diverse and prolific during the dry season, although the birdlife is generally better between December and March. That said, NG31 really is in the heart of the Okavango where the water is basically permanent, and so these differences aren't as great here as you'll find in some of the more outlying, western areas of the Delta.

GETTING THERE AND AWAY All visitors to these camps pre-book their time and fly to the camps. NG31's main airstrip (⊕ CHITAA 19°27.952'S, 23°22.443'E) is about 7km north of Chitabe and 8km east of Sandibe. This is barely 60km from Maun, making it one of the closest of the Delta's airstrips for camps. However, this doesn't usually affect the price of a trip. Wilderness Safaris, for example, usually charge a set rate for a package including time at its camps and flights to/from them. This price doesn't vary with the position of the camp within the Delta.

🏠 **WHERE TO STAY** There are just three choices, all very good, if very different. Chitabe and Chitabe Lediba are run by Wilderness Safaris (see page 177), as part of a joint venture with Flamingo Investments which has resulted in a very loyal staff: many have been at these two camps for ten years or more. Sandibe is run by &Beyond (see page 175).

Unusually for the Delta, both Sandibe and Chitabe Lediba welcome children. At Sandibe they're even given a workbook to keep them busy whilst teaching them about the area, and the camp staff are adept at ensuring that they don't disrupt the activities or ambience for the other guests. At Chitabe Lediba there are currently two family rooms – where two twin-bedded rooms share an interconnecting bathroom; a second is under consideration. That said, Chitabe Lediba limits children to those aged six or over, unless the whole camp is taken over, and those travelling with under 12s must book a private vehicle.

🏠 **Chitabe Camp** [map 295] (8 tents) Chitabe is set facing southwest across a channel on an old, established tree-island. It first opened in 1997, but since then has been considerably revamped, taking the camp more upmarket. In accordance with Wilderness's current policy, the entire site has step-free access throughout.

The whole camp is raised up on wooden decking under typical tall, shard trees of riverine forests, including jackalberries (*Diospyros mespiliformis*), knobthorns (*Acacia nigrescens*) & sausage trees (*Kigelia africana*). 2m-high walkways lead between the tents & the lounge & dining areas which form the centre of the camp. Here you'll find a large central area with a bar on one side, under thatch, & a separate dining area. Scattered around the open areas of decking are tables & chairs, & a walkway leads from here down to a largish plunge pool (about 8m x 3m).

Chalets at this old favourite were completely rebuilt & enlarged in 2009. Gone are the traditional if appealing old tents, to emerge as a fully fledged luxury camp under canvas. In the words of the architect, the effect is 'overstated camping'. The designers have gone minimalist, but have taken great pains to iron out the little annoyances of many upmarket safari tents. Thus, glazed sliding doors with mesh sides lead indoors, where there are opening windows as well as gauzed panels, to maximise the flow of air. Mosquito nets run right round bedside tables & lamps as well as the twin or king-size beds; basins are designed to use, not just for show; & in a unique piece of design the bathroom (with twin basins, a dbl wardrobe & separate loo) can be separated from the bedroom by doors that are cleverly designed to slide into the bedhead. A second, outdoor shower, enables you to watch the stars as you refresh. The new tents are lined with a sand-coloured canvas that sets the tone for the neutral décor. Interior design ranges from an African theme in some, to a copper theme in others, with a third take embracing traditional 'campaign' furniture. *US$903/1,171 pp sharing/ sgl mid-Jan–Mar, US$983/1,251 Apr–May & Nov– 19 Dec, US$1,413/1,681 Jun–Oct, US$1,107/1,375 19 Dec–mid-Jan, inc FB, most drinks, activities, park fees, laundry; exc transfers.* ⊕ *All year.*

🏠 **Chitabe Lediba** [map 295] (5 tents) This smaller version of Chitabe Camp, formerly Chitabe Trails, lies just a few hundred metres away, on the other side of the same island. While the central area is very similar in design & style to that at Chitabe, with a pool & curio shop, here the tents are built on low platforms, & they're linked by lower walkways. Each tent has a solid door leading from the deck into the bedroom, where twin beds, or a dbl, are surrounded by mosquito netting under a fan, & there's a table & wicker chairs. The en-suite bathroom is part of the tent, with a shower cubicle, washbasin & flush toilet; there's also a (much nicer) outdoor shower off the deck. Ideal for families, couples or friends travelling together are 2 units in which 2 twin-bedded rooms are linked by a shared en-suite bathroom, with a dining table on the front deck. It's worth noting, though, that the second room has no view.

Chitabe Lediba's tents were upgraded in 2010 to match those of Chitabe Camp, but this remains a very relaxed, if now smart, camp, & one of my favourite camps in the Delta. I often prefer the Delta's smaller, more intimate camps & the experience that I had here on my last visit was magical. *Rates as Chitabe, above.* ⊕ *All year.*

🏠 **Sandibe Okavango Safari Lodge** [map 295] (15 chalets) Set in a band of thick riverine vegetation facing the Santantadibe River,

Sandibe originally opened in 1998, but is now being completely rebuilt & should re-open in July 2014. Gone will be the permanent concrete buildings, to be replaced by largely wooden structures on elevated decks – with inspiration for the curving roofs drawn from pangolins & weaverbird nests. The aim is to create a luxurious, but more 'sustainable & environmentally efficient' camp.

The main lodge will house an indoor & outdoor dining area, as well as the bar & lounge. As at its sister camp, Nxabega, Sandibe will have a well-stocked wine cellar. Though unlimited good house wine is included as part of your stay, the vintage wines & more esoteric, imported spirits cost extra. And although no mention has been made, there's almost certainly going to be a curio shop.

The first phase will incorporate 8 rooms, with the remainder to follow in September. All will be larger, well spread out on sizeable wooden decks linked to the central area by elevated walkways rather than the original sandy pathways. Each will feature its own separate sundeck with private plunge pool & sunloungers – while on the opposite side, a day bed & private dining area occupy the main deck. Through sliding doors at the front, plans show an open-plan room with a dbl or twin beds facing the river, & a walk-in dressing room to the rear. To one side will be a small lounge, separated from the rest of the room by a double-sided fireplace. Opposite will be the bathroom with his & hers handbasins, & indoor & outdoor showers, while the toilet will be in a private cubicle at the back.

Like Nxabega, Sandibe is likely to retain a large enough staff complement to be better than most camps at tailoring its activities to what guests want & when they want it. *US$910–1,550 pp sharing low–high season, inc FB, drinks, laundry, all activities.* ⊕ *All year.*

ACTIVITIES The camps differ little in their activities. All three are essentially dry-land camps, which concentrate on day and evening game drives, plus – during the dry season, when the grass is low – occasional guided walks.

STANLEY'S, BAINES' AND BUDGET MOKORO TRIPS (NG32)

This 'multi-purpose area', covering over 1,500km², is controlled by the local communities – and perhaps because of this operations continue to change and evolve more than they do in most of the Okavango's private areas. In the last few years, two permanent sister camps have been operating in one section of the reserve: Stanley's Camp and Baines' Camp. The Grey Matters elephant project also works in the same area. A second, quite separate, part of the reserve is used mainly for budget mokoro trips by many operators from Maun. Because these are such distinct operations, I've described them separately.

FLORA AND FAUNA HIGHLIGHTS

Flora NG32 is the concession on the other side of the buffalo fence from the relatively populated areas around Maun. It's at the southern end of the Delta, relying on the Boro and Santantadibe rivers for flooding – and last in line to receive the water. In a dry year, the floods can be very low and patchy.

This means that there are relatively few short-grass plains which are regularly flooded, but significant patches of floodplains which are only intermittently wet. These provide an ideal base for a profusion of the invasive wild sage (*Pechuel-loeschea leubnitziae*), which covers large open areas with its aromatic grey-green foliage. Where they've had slightly longer to become established, you'll find the distinctive rounded outlines of candle pod acacia bushes (*Acacia hebeclada*) starting to appear in these areas – as one of the first shrubs to move in it usually indicates that an area has been dry for many years. In some of these open areas where the recent floods haven't reached you'll find a profusion of termite mounds.

Aside from this, driving around NG32 near Stanley's the vegetation seems to occur in strips, including linear expanses of riverine forest where the major tree species are leadwoods (*Combretum imberbe*), jackalberries (*Diospyros mespiliformis*), marula (*Sclerocarya birrea*) and sausage trees (*Kigelia africana*). There are relatively few areas of deep, deep sand here and not that many acacia glades, but there are some quite dense – and very attractive – concentrations of real fan palms (*Hyphaene petersiana*).

When visiting with a mokoro poler, you'll see a very different side to the area. Unless the flood has been very high, you'll probably be poling within the vicinity of the Boro or the Santantadibe. This is at the very shallowest end of the Delta, so expect large areas of miscanthus grass (*Miscantusus junceus*) and common reeds (*Phragmites australis*), plus the occasional floodplains of hippo grass (*Vossia cuspidata*).

If you do actually pole up the Boro, then you'll find the environment generally gets more interesting as you continue. After a few days, you'll leave behind some of the more boring stretches of reeds, and start finding wider floodplains around you, and more lagoons. Wherever you pole, the islands on which you stop will often be classic little palm islands fringed with palms and the riverine forest.

Fauna The game densities generally get better as you head further north in the area. Impala are probably the commonest antelope, with tsessebe a close second and red lechwe certainly dominating any areas which are flooded. Kudu, giraffe, zebra, reedbuck, warthog and occasionally wildebeest are all found here; sable, roan and waterbuck are not. Elephant and buffalo occur singly during the wetter parts of the year, and pass through in larger herds as the dry season reaches its end.

When the flood is at its height, there may be the occasional sitatunga around, but apart from a few places on the rivers, there aren't enough papyrus reedbeds to support them.

Lion are around in good numbers, and while leopard occur, they're not frequently spotted. Wild dog pass though, and sightings of them seem to increase between about October and December. However, the open wide plains where you could follow them are limited in the concession.

Cheetah are certainly around and often seen in the drier areas – on one drive here during a fairly brief visit one of this book's contributors spent a magical 25 minutes with a male cheetah as he strolled from termite mound to termite mound searching for the perfect vantage point.

Birdlife NG32 is a classic edge-of-the-Delta reserve that has a good mix of dry-country and shallow-water bird species. The most common species include red-eyed, mourning and Cape turtle doves, which all greet the morning with a variety of gentle coos. Identify the last by their lyrical exhortations to 'work harder, work harder'.

Other birds frequently seen here include long-tailed shrikes, red-billed quelea, buffalo weavers, lilac-breasted rollers, blacksmith plovers and long-tailed and glossy starlings. Crimson-breasted shrikes provide startling flashes of red; Meyer's parrots can often be seen as a flash of colour flying at speed.

In more open areas you'll find red-billed and Swainson's francolins, flocks of helmeted guinea fowl, kori bustards and occasional ostriches. Sandgrouse are common in acacia groves, as are yellow-billed hornbills, whilst their red-billed cousins prefer the reserve's mopane woodlands.

The floodplains support a varied cast of waders and waterbirds, including the occasional wattled cranes. This is a good reserve for raptors: bateleur eagles, black-breasted and brown snake eagles are especially common, and Gabar goshawks are frequently seen.

WHEN TO VISIT Like most of the areas on the edge of the Delta, the game densities are better during the dry season than during the rains. So whilst from June to October is the best time to visit for game, the birdwatching is usually more interesting during the rains, from around December to March.

GETTING THERE AND AWAY For those staying at Stanley's and Baines' camps, access is by air to the nearby airstrip; you're not allowed to drive yourself.

WHERE TO STAY Both lodges within this part of the concession are operated by Sanctuary Retreats (see page 176).

Stanley's Camp [map 295] (8 safari tents) Originally built by a maverick local character, Alistair Rankin (the subject of a number of local bush myths – some involving mokoro trips, buffalo & uncomfortable nights spent in trees), Stanley's was completely rebuilt by Sanctuary Retreats at the turn of the century, with its central areas fully refurbished in 2011.

The open-plan dining/lounge area sits under a large canvas tent (think of a 'big top' circus), on slightly raised wooden decking. Wildlife photos printed on oversize canvases stand out from the cream walls, with the odd woven basket or wooden carving. The sitting area takes centre stage with a couple of comfy sofas & a few leather chairs around a rather lovely, almost rustic coffee table. The 'library' is a slightly eccentric collection of novels, magazines & reference books. To the rear are the bar, & a small curio shop that also showcases baskets made by the staff. A short

wooden walkway leads to a small pool with sunloungers, a couple of umbrellas & unobstructed views of the floodplains.

Most meals are social affairs, taken with everybody eating together at a long table. That said, if you're staying for a few days then you can request a picnic lunch, so that you can stay out in the bush all day. After dinner in the evening, everybody usually retires for drinks & a chat to a small firepit, outside in front of the big top.

The camp's tents, all raised on wooden platforms, are to one side of the main area, connected by bush tracks. A covered deck extends from the front of each tent, with a couple of armchairs, a small table & a hammock for that all-important midday siesta. Inside all is fairly cosy but comfortable, with rugs on the smooth wooden floors, twin beds with electric lights mounted on the headboard, a desk with drawers & a chair, a couple of bedside tables & an old-style wooden wardrobe, & a fan. Each tent has its own en-suite toilet & shower, complete with a wooden dresser with sink & mirror, & the usual complimentary toiletries. *From US$630 pp low season to US$1,190/1,785 pp sharing/sgl high season, inc FB, local drinks, activities, park fees, laundry; exc transfers & elephant trips with Grey Matters (extra US$264–466 pp per activity). High season 15 Jun–31 Oct.* ⊕ *All year.*

🏠 **Baines' Camp** [map 295] (5 rooms) Named after the Victorian painter Sir Thomas Baines, this relatively new camp is rather funky in design. Linked by raised wooden walkways, the rooms are unusual in that their solid walls are built out of recycled drink cans, wire mesh & hessian, & covered in plastic containing – why? – elephant dung! And so that guests can see how it's constructed, a section of wall in the main area is left with just cans & wire mesh. Distressed frames surround old pictures on the walls, lampshades are of ostrich eggshell, & there's an easel in each room where guests can paint. Rather more contemporary are 'star beds', which are set 4-poster style under mosquito nets, & can be rolled out on to the decking under the stars. *From US$755 pp low season to US$1,450/2,175 pp sharing/sgl high season; see Stanley's (above) for details.* ⊕ *All year.*

ACTIVITIES AT STANLEY'S AND BAINES' CAMPS Activities at both camps usually revolve around 4x4 game drives and night drives, though it's normally possible to take mokoro trips for at least a few months a year – typically around June to September. The water's not consistently deep enough to run motorboat trips from Stanley's, but they are sometimes an option at Baines'.

Elephant activities (⊕ *closed 15 Jan–15 Feb*) Aside from the standard game drives and water-based trips, many guests will pay the extra US$264 per person (or US$466 July–15 October) to spend a morning with Doug and Sandi Groves and their elephants at Grey Matters (see box opposite).

These activities normally consist of about four hours in the morning – a leisurely foraging walk with the camp's elephants, which allows you to get used to observing and interacting with them at close quarters. You'll be encouraged to touch and walk with the elephants as they forage – and to view them as individuals. Riding the elephants is not part of these trips. At the end there's usually a picnic lunch in the bush.

The maximum number of guests at any one time is ten. Do note that the elephants take 'annual leave' between 15 January and 15 February, so this activity is not possible then.

BUDGET MOKORO TRIPS NG32 is the end destination for virtually all of the one- to four-day mokoro trips offered from Maun, through the Okavango Kopano Mokoro Community Trust (OKMCT). These must be booked through a private tour operator in Maun, who will organise a road transfer into the Delta; you cannot just turn up. For full details of how to choose a trip, and what to expect, see page 173.

These trips aren't really about game, although you may see some. Relax, take a bird book and a pair of binoculars, and enjoy the experience of being poled along the waterways, and seeing some of the birdlife, and water-life, close up. My first trip into the Delta was like this – and it was enchanting. Subsequently I've seen more interesting areas of the Delta, and infinitely better game, but it's still hard to beat the sheer joy that you'll get from floating around on a mokoro in such an amazing environment for the first time.

From my experience, mokoro trips are much more fun when the sun's shining and the sky is blue; grey skies and (even worse) rain do take the edge off it. Thus best avoid January and February if you have a choice – and ideally come between about April and the end of October.

GREY MATTERS

Doug Groves started out working with elephants in American zoos, including Washington Park Zoo and San Diego Wild Animal Park. Subsequently, in 1987, he came to Africa as the trainer of four elephants who were being returned from the US to South Africa for a film, *Circles in a Forest* – the first of many filming projects for him. As an aside, the main elephant involved in this was Abu, who now leads the herd at Abu Camp (NG26; see pages 318–19), the Okavango's only other operation that offers visitors time in the company of elephants which are not wild.

In 1994, Randall Moore and Ker & Downey went their separate ways – and almost simultaneously Ker & Downey invited Doug to Botswana, to set up and run an elephant-based tourism project. Now Grey Matters isn't linked to Ker & Downey, and instead works closely with both Stanley's and Baines' camps.

The project now has several elephants, but at its heart are the first three, all orphans from culling programmes:

JABU is short for Jabulani, which means 'happiness'; he was born in about 1986 and orphaned at the age of two by a cull in the Kruger National Park, South Africa. He is described as a proud bull who enjoys leading this small herd – playful, dependable, and the most independent and confident member of the herd. He now stands about 2.9m tall at the shoulder.

THEMBI, a smaller female, is about the same age as Jabu, and was also orphaned by a cull in the Kruger. She's said to be smart and very social, and loves being the centre of attention. Originally a very insecure calf, she's gradually becoming much more confident.

MORULA came to Doug in 1994 as a maladjusted 17 year old, lacking confidence and with a troubled background. Doug comments that she started off being exceedingly submissive to him and the other elephants, but then vented frustrations on trees. He adds that she's gradually become more secure and relaxed here.

Grey Matters is also the base for Living With Elephants (↖686 3198; e contact@ livingwithelephants.org; www.livingwithelephants.org). This not-for-profit organisation was started by Doug and Sandi Groves in 1999, aiming to secure the future of their trio of elephants, and to work through various projects towards a more harmonious relationship between Botswana's elephant and human populations.

Projects undertaken include their 'Outreach programme' whereby children from Maun and nearby villages spend two days at Grey Matters, interacting with the elephants and learning about them through hands-on experience and discussions.

12

See my comments on walking (pages 141–5) before you set off on foot with your poler in search of big game – as none of these trips is likely to be led by someone that I'd describe as a professional walking guide, and none of the polers carry any guns.

SANKUYO TSHWARAGANO MANAGEMENT TRUST (NG33 & NG34)

NG34 covers an area of about 900km², and you drive through the eastern side of this when you leave the Moremi Reserve's South Gate and head towards Maun. It's an area with good game, and is easily accessible (by 4x4) from Maun. Thus, and very unusually for the region, it's a private concession through which you can drive yourself – although note that you should not steer off the main gravel roads.

BACKGROUND INFORMATION NG34 is run for the benefit of the local community, through the Sankuyo Tshwaragano Management Trust – and it's a reserve which sees more frequent changes than most. Until about 2001 it was the location for Gomoti Camp; shortly after that closed, Starling's Camp was built here. Then that morphed into Moremi Tented Camp, which at the time of research was between leaseholders.

Meanwhile there's long been an intermittent presence here of animal researchers, many of whom seem to have subsequently written books. Naturalist and lion researcher Peter Katz was here for several years at a camp some 2km from Starling's. His book, *Prides*, was published in 2000, and more recently the three children staying with him and his partner wrote *The Lion Children* (see *Further information*).

Before that, John 'Tico' McNutt began a wild-dog research unit here in 1989, co-authoring *Running Wild: Dispelling the Myths of the African Wild Dog* (see *Further information*). The project has broadened and developed since then, and now – as the Botswana Predator Conservation Trust (*www.bpctrust.org*) – conducts research into leopard, lion, cheetah and spotted hyena, as well as wild dog.

FLORA AND FAUNA HIGHLIGHTS Look on a map of the reserve's vegetation and you might be struck by the amount of mopane woodlands here – which generally isn't a huge attraction for safari-goers. However, drive on the ground and you'll realise that most of the area around the Gomoti River, where Moremi Tented Camp and its safaris are concentrated, is a much prettier combination of big open floodplains with occasional islands.

Like much of the Delta around eastern Moremi, the flood patterns here do seem to have changed recently. When Tico McNutt first came in 1989, the Mogogelo River, near Santawani, still had water in it; since then this has dried up – and despite the high floods of 2009 it is still not flowing. Yet these indications are mixed. Observe the Gomoti River, which flows seasonally, and seems to have been flooding further and better during the last few years; since 2009 it has flowed beyond Shorobe, and continues to do so.

With something as complex as the changes in water flows and levels in the Delta, everyone has a slightly different opinion. Perhaps one of the most pertinent comments on this was, allegedly, from local wit Willy Philips, who commented that 'the only reliable water in the Okavango is the water in the toilets'.

Flora As mentioned above, much of NG34 is quite thick, and relatively unproductive, mopane woodlands. However, the western side of the reserve, adjoining the Gomoti River and some of its floodplains, is much more interesting.

Even driving on the main road south from South Gate to Maun you'll get a flavour of this, as you pass through some superb stretches of open acacia savannah – where you'll find very good populations of giraffe, if you're not speeding through too fast. The dominant species here is camelthorn (*Acacia erioloba*), though you'll also find a few umbrella thorns (*Acacia tortilis*) and the odd old leadwood (*Combretum imberbe*) mixed amongst them. It's classic mature Kalahari sandveld –

and matches many people's image of Africa. These areas run like veins through the reserve, marking out the areas of deepest sand.

Around the Gomoti River, things are different. Here you'll find plenty of lovely areas of old riverine forest, containing all the usual species including sausage trees (*Kigelia africana*), marula trees (*Sclerocarya birrea*), jackalberries (*Diospyros mespiliformis*), African mangosteens (*Garcinia livingstonei*) and sycamore figs (*Ficus sycomorus*). You'll also find knobthorns (*Acacia negrescens*), which are immediately obvious around September and October for their creamy-white flowers and almost sickly-sweet perfume. Occasionally you'll find small islands, or patches, of these standing together.

The floodplains here come in two broadly different varieties. Those plains that still regularly flood are usually covered with short grass – a photogenic environment that's easy for game viewing. The others, which have been dry for a number of years, have often been largely covered with wild sage (*Pechuel-loeschea leubnitziae*). This classic 'pioneer species' can quickly take a hold when a floodplain dries out; it thrives in areas that have recently been disturbed. Other, slower-growing species of shrubs and trees will eventually germinate and take over these areas, though not for some years yet.

Amidst all of these plains, you'll find islands, large and small. These have riverine trees and shrubs on them, including a scattering of real fan palms (*Hyphaene petersiana*) and a notably high density of knobthorn trees (*Acacia negrescens*).

Fauna I haven't spent a lot of time in this area though my first memory of it was a good one. In May 1993, I'd been driving myself through Chobe and Moremi with a friend. It had been a good trip, though we were disappointed not to have seen any wild dogs. By the time we left South Gate, in the heat of midday, we had given up trying to spot animals. We were in NG34, but didn't think of this as a wildlife reserve.

After about 14km along the main track, we slowed down to find our way blocked by a large pack of very lazy wild dogs wandering about the road, and lounging by the side of it, yet showing little interest in our vehicle. They posed for photographs, as harmless as lapdogs, for about 30 minutes until they finally wandered off – thus providing us with one of the best game sightings of our whole trip. Only now, knowing how long researchers spend following the dogs in this area, do I understand why these dogs were so totally relaxed with our vehicle.

The commonest antelope here is probably the impala, a favourite prey of wild dogs, although you'll also find good numbers of tsessebe, kudu, giraffe and warthog. Elephant are fairly common and, like buffalo, often move through here in the dry season in large herds. Roan are seen occasionally, while a real treat is the small herds of sable which appear fairly regularly in front of camp and near the Gomoti River.

Of the predators, lion are dominant although the area certainly has a permanent presence of wild dogs also. Leopard and cheetah both occur, but aren't seen often. The landscape should suit leopard; I guess that after a few more years leopard will become less shy here, showing themselves a bit more.

Birdlife The birdlife reflects the variety that you'll find anywhere in the Delta, and obviously depends heavily on the water levels. One checklist for NG33 and NG34 lists 208 species, but doesn't even pretend to be exhaustive.

However, the more common birds which are most frequently seen on the Gomoti floodplain and in the area around Moremi Tented Camp and Kaziikini include the long-tailed and glossy starlings (from which the former Starling's Camp took its name), plus red-eyed, Cape turtle and mourning doves; blacksmith and crowned plovers; long-tailed and crimson-breasted shrikes; red-billed queleas;

buffalo weavers; lilac-breasted rollers; and white-backed and hooded vultures. Wattled cranes and paradise flycatchers or whydahs are also spotted periodically.

Meanwhile in the acacia woodlands, along with the ever-present doves, you're likely to find kori bustards; large flocks of helmeted guinea fowl; red-billed and Swainson's francolins; red- and yellow-billed hornbills; Meyer's parrots; double-banded, Burchell's, Namaqua and yellow-throated sandgrouse; plus the occasional Gabar goshawk, bateleur and ostrich.

WHEN TO VISIT Big-game animals are more prolific here during the dry season, as with the rest of the Okavango – although the birdlife is generally better between December and March. Because NG34 is on the southwest side of the Delta, the flood reaches it last. Also note that NG34 contains some of the closest dry-season watering points for the game that spreads out towards Nxai and Makgadikgadi during the rains. Around this, there is a much higher density of game in the dry season than the wet. That said, quite a lot of the reserve is mopane woodlands, a favourite location for animals during the rains and early dry season – so expect it to have some game around all year.

GETTING THERE AND AWAY Those arriving by air come into the Santawani airstrip, which is about 10km due south of South Gate, in NG33. If you're driving yourself, you can follow one of the main routes through NG34 between Maun and Moremi Game Reserve or Chobe National Park, but driving off these routes is no longer permitted without an escort. The campsite is along the road towards Moremi's South Gate. For details of these routes, see the directions in *Chapter 7* under *From Maun to Moremi Game Reserve*, pages 179–80.

WHERE TO STAY With Moremi Tented Camp currently not available, accommodation in this reserve is very limited. If you find yourself travelling between South Gate and Maun and need a space for the night, your best option is Kaziikini Campsite, which lies right on this road (opposite the cultural village of Shandereka). Alternatively you could divert about 30km towards Mankwe Bush Lodge in NG43 (page 352).

Ⓧ Kaziikini Campsite [map 295] (4 rondavels, 2 tents, camping) 680 0664; e santawanistmt@ botsnet.bw; www.kaziikinicampsite.com; ✪ KAZIIK 19°35.425'S, 23°48.190'E. Some 28km from South Gate, Kaziikini occupies a lovely wooded setting just off the road. Its 14 camping pitches (2 with power) are large, shady & well kept, each with its own water tap & rubbish bin. The open-air central ablution block, however, had come under attack by hyenas when we stayed in October 2013, & even when up to scratch, its mixed-sex facilities offer little privacy. The ablutions are currently shared by small, twin-bedded rondavels, but there are plans to make these en suite, like the 2 pre-erected tents.

There's a bar here (⏲ 08.00–13.00, 14.00–17.00; *evening by arrangement*), but if you're after a meal in the restaurant, you'll need to order at least a ½ day in advance, & ideally at the time of reservation (lunch/dinner US$18/25). Locally made baskets can be purchased in reception. At a push you could use Kaziikini as a base for driving into Moremi or Chobe, but within the reserve itself, self-drive game drives can be conducted at P10 pp: you supply the vehicle, they supply a community escort (not a professional guide). Alternatively, you can take a full-day's guided game drive in their vehicle, with lunch (US$128 pp locally, or US$170 pp into Moremi, inc park fees, min 4 people).

Kaziikini is a pleasant spot to regroup & watch some of Botswana's more common birds, but given its location, it feels overpriced & not a place to linger. *Camping US$24 pp, tent rondavel/tent US$57/75 pp sharing/sgl, exc b/fast (US$9–13).* ⏲ *All year.*

Moremi Tented Camp [map 295] (8 tents) In 2013, the former Starling's Camp was between leaseholders, awaiting a new partner to work with the trust. I haven't been here for several years, but if it's kept the feel of the old Starling's Camp, then you can expect walk-in Meru-style tents built on solid plinths, with en-suite flush toilets & hot showers. They were clean, comfortable & functional. Lighting around the camp at night was by paraffin lamps, whilst inside the tents small lights were powered by a 12V battery system. The camp's main area, simple & tented, is built on a big wooden deck with a great view over the Gomoti River & its floodplain into NG32. This stands under a huge marula tree (*Sclerocarya birrea*), around which a few smaller knobthorns (*Acacia nigrescens*) are clustered. Expect activities to focus on game drives & – in season – mokoro trips.

SHANDEREKA CULTURAL VILLAGE (*US$17 pp, min 5 people*) Opposite Kaziikini Campsite, this cultural village under the same ownership is set up for visitors to learn about the rural culture of the Bayei people. A typical two-hour trip will cover such things as hunting techniques, local medicine and traditional dancing.

SANTAWANI PARTNERSHIP (NG33)

The small NG33 reserve is really an enclave that has been cut out of NG34. It borders Moremi, and in character is very similar to the area around South Gate and parts of NG34. However, with no major watercourse or other focal point, it hasn't proved an easy area in which to run a stand-alone operation, and the old Santawani Safari Lodge – one of the Delta's older photographic camps – finally fell into disuse.

In 2002, together with the Sankuyo Tshwaragano Management Trust, the lodge was re-opened, but soon this was struggling, too. Then, in 2009, the Santawani Partnership was established between the community trust and Lodges of Botswana, only for another change in partner to be in the offing for 2014. The partnership leases and manages the NG33 concession, and any lodges within it: currently just Santawani Lodge; Sankuyo Bush Camp in the east of the reserve is at present closed.

GETTING THERE AND AWAY Until 2009, many visitors to Santawani were self-drivers, but all that changed when the new partnership came into force. Access to the lodge is now exclusively by air into Santawani airstrip (✪ STWAIR 19°30.621'S, 23°37.372'E).

WHERE TO STAY

⌂ **Santawani Lodge** [map 295] (6 chalets) ✪ SANTAW S19°30.966'S, 23°37.807'E. Upgraded in 2009, this community-owned lodge has for a while been leased exclusively by an American tour group for their travellers. Its square, brick-built chalets with thatched roofs, metal-framed windows & solid wooden doors sit like neat doll's houses in mixed woodland. In front there's a small paved patio, with a couple of directors' chairs. Inside, twin beds with mosi nets & bedside lights are cooled by an electric fan – essential given the lack of through breeze – & an en-suite shower/toilet at the rear.

The open dining room/bar & separate lounge area boast no frills, with sand floors, bare tables & basic chairs. The staff, though, are friendly & welcoming, & it's all very relaxed. In front of the lodge, a small waterhole is said to attract high numbers of game, including a visit by a large pride of lion just before we visited one Oct. Boat cruises & mokoro trips can be arranged. ⊕ *All year.*

MABABE (NG41) AND MANKWE (NG43)

These two concessions, characterised by open savannah and scattered with large camelthorn (*Acacia erioloba*) trees, lie to the east of the Delta. NG41 is a community concession that shares its northern and western boundaries with Chobe National Park. On its southern border is NG43, which is really a huge (3,460km²) patch of the Kalahari, east of Moremi's South Gate and south of Chobe's Mababe Gate.

This is not an area where there's easy or prolific game viewing. I include it here because it is the base for two small bush lodges, under the same ownership, which may prove very convenient stops between Maun and either Moremi or Chobe. In time, as the areas under wildlife protection effectively expand, it may even become more of a game-viewing destination in its own right. Should you wish to explore NG41, note that there is a P60 concession fee payable, and that you must have a community escort guide with you in your vehicle to show you the various game-drive routes (and make sure you don't go off road). There is no charge for this – the escorts are not qualified guides – but they will in all likelihood expect a tip.

GETTING THERE AND AWAY Virtually all visitors travelling directly between Maun and Chobe will pass through sections of both NG43 and NG41, even if they aren't aware of it. Mankwe Bush Lodge (✪ MANKWE 19°22.030'S, 23°53.510'E) is situated in the northwest corner of NG43, just north of Sankuyo Village.

To reach Mankwe from Maun, head towards Chobe's Mababe Gate (that is, follow the directions to Sankuyo in *The road north of Maun: to Moremi and Chobe*, at the end of *Chapter 7*, pages 179–80). The turning to the lodge is clearly marked, 7km north of Sankuyo Village. Mogotlho Safari Lodge (✪ MOGOT 19°13.109'S, 23°57.365'E), in NG41, is about 20km north of Mankwe Bush Lodge – or some 10km before Mababe Village.

WHERE TO STAY

Mankwe Bush Lodge [map 295] (8 tents, camping) Contact Kgori Safaris, page 176; ✪ MANKWE 19°21.769'S, 23°53.775'E. Some 2km east of the road, Mankwe is set among mopane trees well away from any other lodge. It was opened in 2001 & remains well maintained & very well run. Several levels of wooden decking support the attractive thatched lounge & bar, dining tent, curio shop, outside boma & campfire, & small pool with sunloungers. Overlooking the surrounding bush, fairly large Meru-style tents set on wooden decks are simple but pleasantly furnished, with twin beds, battery-powered lights & an en-suite flush toilet, basin & gas-fired shower.

About 1.5km from the lodge are 6 private campsites, half under camelthorn trees & half under mopane trees. Each pitch has its own flush toilet, bucket shower & washbasin. Firewood is available, but otherwise you'll need to be fully equipped, with all your own drinking water as well as food & fuel. That said, with a couple of hours' notice, campers may eat at the lodge (3-course dinner P210).

If you're just stopping for a day or two on the way to Chobe, Mankwe can organise 3–4hr game drives, including afternoon drives with a sundowner, in NG43 itself (P145 pp, based on 4 people), while full-day drives (P620 pp) are usually into the Khwai River area. Guided bush walks & night drives are further

options, along with 4x4 trails across the NG43 concession, accompanied by a local guide.

Alternatively, you can use Mankwe as a base for mobile safaris into Moremi Game Reserve, often combined with overnight trips into the Delta from Mboma Boat Station (page 278), which is run by the same company. Based on 4 passengers, a full-day drive in Moremi or Chobe will cost P940 pp, while an overnight boat trip from Mboma is P4,445 pp (self-drivers P3,650 pp), including food & equipment, but excluding park fees. *From P2,950 pp sharing, inc FB & activities in NG43; P1,620 pp sharing B&B. Camping P150 pp. Transfers extra.* ☺ *All year.*

Mogotlho Safari Lodge [map 295] (13 tents) ☎ 686 0968; e mogotlho@info.bw; www. mogotlhosafarilodge.co.za; ✪ 19°13.840'S, 23°58.696'E. Opened as a hunting camp in 2000, Mogotlho switched allegiances to a photographic lodge in 2008. It lies 2.5km east of the road, in NG41, its large central deck with a firepit occupying a lovely spot above the Khwai River, shaded by camelthorn (*Acacia erioloba*) trees. Behind, the lounge & dining area seem rather dark, & somewhat spartan en-suite tents on low concrete plinths are set well away from the river, so without a view. Day & night game drives, & bush walks, are centred on the area around the Khwai River. *P1,782/2,227 pp sharing/sgl DBB; 2,770/3,215 FBA, both exc bed levy & P60 concession fee.* ☺ *All year.*

13

The Okavango Panhandle and Northwest Kalahari

If much of the Okavango Delta is the preserve of the privileged few who can afford to fly in to exclusive safari camps, then the Panhandle presents more egalitarian options. Here you'll find the raw edge of Botswana's safari industry, camps on the edge of the Delta run by idiosyncratic owners or local communities – without marketing aids or slick glossy brochures. This is the Okavango's safari scene as it was 20 years ago!

Go west, into the Kalahari, and it's wilder still. Here there's almost nothing organised, yet the amazing Tsodilo Hills have been declared Botswana's first World Heritage Site. Adventurers will want to dig deeper here, reaching the caverns of the Gcwihaba Hills and the remote Aha range.

THE PANHANDLE

Look at a map of the Okavango Delta and you'll see that it's shaped like a frying pan, with the main river flowing down the centre of the handle, from the northwest. Thus this area gets its name.

ORIENTATION The Panhandle's western side is very easy to access with a 2WD, as the road between Sehithwa and Shakawe is tar. Once you leave the main road and the larger settlements, however, a high-clearance 4x4 is essential to cope with the sand in the area.

The track that follows the river on the eastern side is used much less, though it's not intrinsically difficult. Visitors very rarely travel along this track as the only practical access to it is via the ferry that crosses the Okavango at Mohembo, north of Shakawe.

GEOLOGY AND GEOGRAPHY All of this area is in the Kalahari, though here it's dominated by the influence of the Okavango River. This flows south into Botswana from the Angolan Highlands, having crossed Namibia's Caprivi Strip.

Entering Botswana, the river's gradient is very low. However, it is constrained from spreading out by steep riverbanks on either side. Underneath the sand lies a more fundamental constraint: parallel faultlines in the earth's crust that run southeast, about 10–15km apart. Thus the river meanders gradually southeast, between them, forming a series of wide, sweeping curves and the odd oxbow lagoon – but always remaining within the constraints of the banks.

Where the river's meanders kiss the banks at the edge of the floodplain, villages have sprung up: Shakawe, Sepupa and Seronga. The southern extent of the faultlines lies around Seronga, so south of here the river begins to spread wider to form the main body of the Delta.

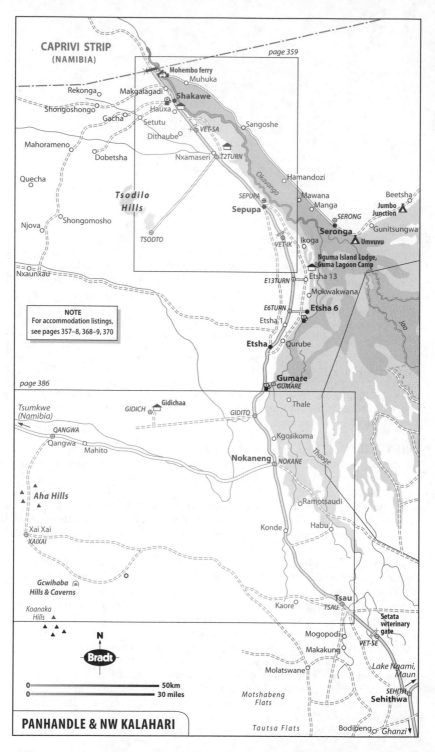

page 359

CAPRIVI STRIP
(NAMIBIA)

Mohembo ferry
Muhuka
Rekonga
Makgalagadi
Shakawe
Shongoshongo
Gacha
Hauxa
Setutu
VET-SA
Sangoshe
Mahorameno
Dithaube
Dobetsha
Nxamaseri
T2TURN
Quecha
Hamandozi
Tsodilo
Hills
Mawana
Manga
Beetsha
SEPUPA
Jumbo
Junction
Sepupa
Njova
Shongomosho
Seronga
SERONG
Gunitsungwa
TSODTO
VET-IK
Ikoga
Umvuvu
Nxaunxau
Nguma Island Lodge,
Guma Lagoon Camp
E13TURN
Etsha 13

NOTE
For accommodation listings,
see pages 357–8, 368–9, 370

Mokwakwana
E6TURN
Etsha 6
Etsha 1
Etsha
Qurube

page 386

Gumare
GUMARE
Tsumkwe
(Namibia)
GIDICH
Gidichaa
GIDITO
Thale
QANGWA
Qangwa
Mahito
Kgosikoma
Nokaneng
NOKANE
Thaoge
Aha Hills
Ramotsaudi
Xai Xai
XAIXAI
Konde
Habu
Gcwihaba
Hills & Caverns
Koanaka
Hills
Tsau
TSAU
Kaore
Setata
veterinary
gate
N
Mogopodi
VET-SE
Bradt
Makakung
Lake Ngami,
Maun
0   50km
0   30 miles
Molatswane
SEHITH
Sehithwa
Motshabeng
Flats
Bodibeng
Ghanzi
Tautsa Flats

PANHANDLE & NW KALAHARI

FLORA AND FAUNA The Panhandle isn't a prime area for game viewing, so don't come here expecting masses of big game or you'll be disappointed. That said, you may catch glimpses of the occasional sitatunga or small herds of lechwe, and you're almost bound to see numerous hippo and crocodile. However, there are some first-class areas for birding, and plenty of areas with deep-water channels and lagoons.

Flora Looking from the Panhandle's banks, often all you can see is a gently swaying mass of feathery papyrus heads. Here, more than anywhere else in the Delta, the environment is polarised: there are deep-water channels, and there are the papyrus beds that surround them.

Occasionally you'll find sections of phragmites reeds and, when the waters are low, open stretches of sandbanks. Sometimes the odd day-lily (*Nymphaea nouchali caerulea*) will take hold in a quiet inlet on the edge of the channel, but mainly the vegetation here is huge expanses of floating papyrus.

Birdlife The birdlife here is as varied as anywhere in the Delta, though getting to actually see the birds that inhabit the papyrus can be tricky. Some of the more sought-after sightings would be painted snipes, rufous-bellied herons, lesser jacanas, chirping cisticolas, brown-throated weavers and coppery-tailed and white-browed coucals. Greater swamp warblers and swamp boubous can often be heard calling from the papyrus, but are less easy to spot.

The Panhandle is a particularly good area for the white-backed night heron. Look out, too, for white-backed ducks (sometimes in large numbers) perching on the sandbanks, as well as long-toed plovers, red-winged pratincoles and, of course, the Panhandle's most acrobatic birding attraction: the African skimmer. These distinctive, black-and-white birds fly south to the Delta between about September and December. They mainly come to breed on the sandbanks of the Panhandle, which are exposed while the water is low. Gathering in small flocks, each pair excavates a shallow depression in the sand where they'll lay their eggs and raise their young.

One of the Delta's most amazing sights is to watch these birds feed. With long, graceful wings they fly fast and low, holding their elongated lower mandible just low enough to cut the water's surface. This is hollow and has sharp edges, shaped to minimise its drag in the water. When this touches a small fish near the surface, it is quickly raised against the upper mandible, trapping the fish firmly. I always marvel at their flying skill, moving their body in all directions whilst their bill traces a constant, steady path through the water.

Note that because African skimmers nest very near the waterline, on low sandbanks, their nests and young are very vulnerable to both predators and to

13

GPS REFERENCES FOR PANHANDLE AND NW KALAHARI MAP (opposite)			
E6TURN	19°06.706'S, 22°16.152'E	SERONG	18°48.771'S, 22°24.988'E
E13TUR	19°00.793'S, 22°17.356'E	T2TURN	18°35.834'S, 21°59.986'E
GIDICH	19°27.273'S, 21°46.273'E	TSAU	20°10.294'S, 22°27.265'E
GIDITO	19°29.983'S, 22°07.150'E	TSGATE	18°47.275'S, 21°44.856'E
GUMARE	19°22.242'S, 22°09.242'E	TSODTO	18° 47.378'S, 21°44.981'E
NOKANE	19°39.694'S, 22°11.184'E	VET-IK	18°50.327'S, 22°13.756'E
QANGWA	19°31.868'S, 21°10.281'E	VET-SA	18°29.256'S, 21°55.142'E
SEHITH	20°28.259'S, 22°42.372'E	VET-SE	20°15.775'S; 22°33.926'E
SEPUPA	18°44.150'S, 22°10.625'E	XAIXAI	19°52.867'S, 21°04.934'E

damage from the wash caused by fast-moving motorboats. So boats operating in these areas should never be driven too fast.

Another spectacular migrant, better seen in the Panhandle than anywhere else in the Delta, is the carmine bee-eater. These come to southern Africa to breed, and stay from about October to March. They nest in large colonies, building their nests underground at the end of tunnels which they excavate into the side of sandy riverbanks. You won't forget the sight of hundreds of these bright carmine-pink birds twittering around a river bank that's holed with nests like a piece of Swiss cheese.

Above the water you'll regularly spot African fish eagles; marsh harriers and even the occasional migrant osprey are also sometimes seen. On the banks beside the waters and papyrus there's a narrow band of thick riverine forest, before the bush becomes that of the dry Kalahari. Here there's a wide variety of different birdlife – typical of any of the riverine areas in this region. Notable sightings would include the tiny brown firefinch, Bradfield's hornbill, the western banded snake eagle and Pel's fishing owl.

GETTING THERE AND AROUND
By vehicle The main road on the west side of the Panhandle is very easy to get along in a 2WD; it's all tar and generally maintained to a high standard – bar the occasional pot-hole. For anywhere else in this area, you really need your own fully equipped 4x4. Do note that fuel supplies along this stretch, and even as far as Maun, can be erratic, so it's important to fill up wherever you can. Even the fuel station at Shakawe is not entirely reliable.

By bus There are several buses per day which ply between Maun and Shakawe, stopping at the main villages on the way. The whole trip takes about seven hours and costs a total of P70. These buses will turn off to the larger centres such as Gumare and Etsha 6, but near the smaller villages they will just pick up and drop passengers on the main road. Most go from Maun to Shakawe in the morning, and back in the afternoon – but ask locally for more precise timings.

By air There are small airstrips dotted around, so if you charter a plane you can get to most places here: Shakawe, Nxamaseri, Nokaneng, Tsau and Guma Lagoon. The Tsodilo Hills have an airstrip, too, but you really need a vehicle whilst you're there to get the most out of it. There are no airstrips anywhere near the Gcwihaba or Aha Hills.

THE EASTERN PANHANDLE Although visitors relatively rarely see the side of the Okavango's Panhandle to the east of the river, those who do usually come for the mokoro trips. These have long been run by the Okavango Polers' Trust, but other companies have now stepped into the market. For travellers who are constrained by a relatively tight budget, this is one of the few options left to see any of the Okavango.

A good gravel road runs down the eastern side of the river from Mohembo to Seronga. Between the two you'll find numerous smaller villages which survive mainly on fishing and, away from the river, a number of tiny 'cattlepost' settlements used by people tending their cattle in the interior of NG11 – which is fairly continuous cattle-ranching country.

Getting there and away
By air Seronga has an airstrip (✪ SERAIR 18°49.180'S, 22°25.020'E) that is by far the easiest and most convenient way for most travellers to access the village. Check

in Maun with an operator such as Audi Camp or The Old Bridge Backpackers for details of the options.

By 4x4 The only practical way to access the eastern side of the Panhandle with a vehicle is to cross the Okavango River on the ferry at Mohembo, in the far north.

There appears on many maps to be another route, which seems to go around the eastern side of the Delta and link into Seronga from the Linyanti area, via the village of Beetsha. However, the tracks on this side have very few users and no signposts. They cross a number of different private concessions, none of which would welcome your visit: straying off designated transit routes will get you into trouble. Meanwhile, when the tracks meet villages they split and vanish. But perhaps the greatest danger is of water blocking the route. It's easy to get dangerously lost in this region and then to run out of fuel, water or supplies. There's no help at hand, so I'd strongly advise against trying to use any of these tracks.

By bus/boat Both Shakawe and Sepupa are fairly easy to access on one of the local buses that run up and down the road to the west of the river, between Shakawe and Sehithwa; getting across to the eastern side of the river is more of a challenge. The once-regular motorboat ferry between Sepupa and Seronga Boat Station (✪ SERBOA 18°49.316'S, 22°24.855'E) has been out of service for many years, but fortunately, Sepupa Swamp Stop (page 365) has stepped in to fill the gap. Passengers pay P2,200 for a small boat, or P2,500 for the larger vessel (carrying up to 16 people), with boats departing from their jetty.

As an alternative, it may be possible to arrange a boat transfer with one of the lodges at Guma Lagoon (pages 368–9), if you're staying there for a period of time. The only other option is to use the vehicle ferry at Mohembo, and then hitch south down the road on the eastern bank.

In the highly unlikely event that you ever need to navigate yourself to Seronga by boat, the turn-off from the main channel towards the boat station is at ✪ SERTUR 18°49.776'S, 22°24.350'E. From Sepupa, the trip east to Seronga, via a variety of winding channels, is downstream and takes 90 minutes, whereas the slower return journey takes a couple of hours.

Seronga Seronga (✪ SERONG 18°48.771'S, 22°24.988'E) is a sizeable village at the eastern base of the Panhandle. It's the regional centre for a number of small settlements to the east of it, along the northern edge of the Delta, as well as a focus for the people who still live in the northern areas of the Delta.

Where to stay There are a couple of options here: one, on the mainland, the second on a nearby island. A third, Mbiroba Camp, run for years by the Okavango Polers' Trust, seems to have disappeared off the radar at the time of research.

⚑ **Umvuvu Camp** [map 354] (camping)
m 7376 9112/3; e umvuvubots@gmail.com;
www.umvuvucamp.com. This relaxed camp
on Xau Island at the base of the Panhandle
is surrounded by riverine forest. It is 15km
southeast of Seronga, with access either by self-
drive vehicle or by boat transfer from Sepupa to
Seronga, which you arrange with Sepupa Swamp
Stop. Walk-in tents have 2 beds with a sheet &

pillow or bring your own. Ablutions are open
air. There's a bar on site, & a cooking area with
braai stand, but you'll need to bring all your own
food & eating utensils. Activities include day or
overnight mokoro trips into the Delta & guided
game walks. *US$110/135/150 pp for 1/2/3 nights
(of which 1 bushcamping).*
⚑ **Jumbo Junction** [map 354] (camping,
2 chalets) m 7264 7810; e okavangoplains@

13

gmail.com; ⊕ JUMBO 18°49.31'S, 22°36.19'E. This new campsite – which also has a couple of chalets – lies some 23km east of Seronga on the northern bank of the lower Selinda Spillway. Fronted by a permanent lagoon, the site takes both overland trucks &, in a separate area, independent campers, & has 4 ablution blocks. Central to the camp is a large thatched bar & restaurant; power is expected to come online by 2014. Activities focus on mokoro trips & island walks, but game drives may be offered when it's dry enough (Oct–Jan). *Chalet US$120 pp, camping US$15 pp.*

THE WESTERN PANHANDLE
Mohembo border Mohembo – almost 16km north of Shakawe – marks the road border at the top of the Panhandle between Botswana and Namibia's Caprivi Strip. Here you'll find a neat customs and immigration area (⊕ MOHEMB 18°15.700'S, 21°45.768'E; ⊕ 06.00–18.00 daily) where the formalities are normally handled promptly and efficiently.

Mohembo ferry For travellers wishing to cross to the eastern bank of the Okavango River, there's a (free) ferry (⊕ 06.00–19.30 daily) a little over 3.5km south of the border. If you're driving from the border, you'll come to a T-junction, where you turn left for the ferry, or right for Shakawe. The ferry usually takes a few vehicles at a time, including the occasional small truck. Expect to find a lot of people waiting around here – some to cross, others to meet those who have crossed, or to buy and sell things.

Shakawe This very large fishing village stands east of the main road on the northern banks of the Panhandle of the Delta, some 16km south of the Mohembo border post, and 281km north of Sehithwa. Driving into the village always used to feel like entering a maze of reed walls, each surrounding a small kraal, as the track split countless ways between the houses. The odd trap of deep sand was enough to stop you for an hour, and thus serve up excellent entertainment to numerous amused locals.

Today, however, Shakawe is a bustling little town, albeit still something of a backwater. Just a stone's throw from the tar road you'll find a significant base for the Botswana Defence Force, as you'd expect in one of the country's more sensitive border areas, and a major police station. If you've the time, take a walk along the river; sometimes there's a mokoro ferry shuttling local people to and from the eastern side of the river, full with their wares to sell or recent purchases to take back home.

Of particular importance to drivers is the filling station close to the entrance to the village when heading north. Barclays Bank (with an ATM) has a presence here, too, as does a branch of Choppies, while other, smaller shops and a post office are largely concentrated within the small shopping centre around the bus stop.

If you fancy a break before driving on, you could try a guided tour of **Krokovango Crocodile Farm** (⊕ KROKO 18°25.817'S, 21°53.682'E; m 7230 6200; ⊕ 08.00–17.00 Mon–Sat; P25/15 adult/child), about 10km south of Shakawe. The farm is in an attractive woodland setting, with crocs at all stages of growth from hatchling to adult. They're at their most active at feeding time, usually at 11.00 on Tuesday and Friday – though the adults are not fed at all between May and July, so the first feed in August could be quite a spectacle!

Getting there and away There are good daily bus services to Maun via the rest of the western Panhandle from the centre of town. Of these, the fastest is the Golden Bridge Express (P89 one way), which leaves at around 08.00 each morning,

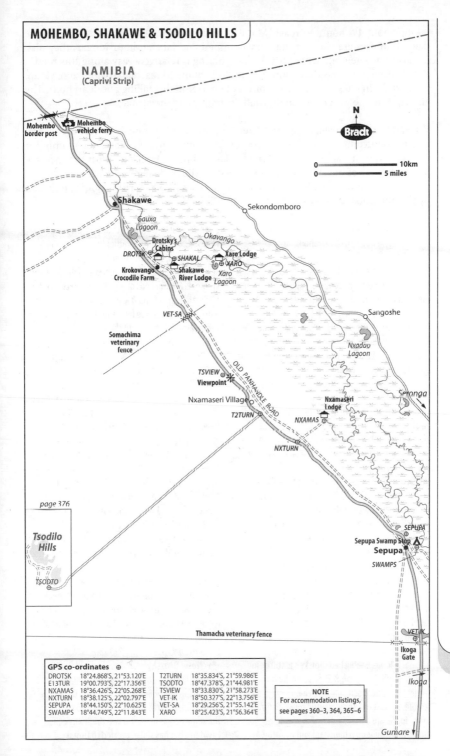

NAMIBIA
(Caprivi Strip)

N
Bradt

0 _____ 10km
0 _____ 5 miles

Mohembo
border post
Mohembo
vehicle ferry

Shakawe

Sekondomboro

Gauxa
Lagoon

Okavango

Drotsky's
Cabins

DROTSK

SHAKAL

Xaro Lodge
XARO

Krokovango
Crocodile Farm

Shakawe
River Lodge

*Xaro
Lagoon*

Sangoshe

VET-SA

Somachima
veterinary
fence

*Nxadau
Lagoon*

TSVIEW
Viewpoint

OLD PANHANDLE ROAD

Seronga

Nxamaseri Village

**Nxamaseri
Lodge**

T2TURN

NXAMAS

NXTURN

page 376

**Tsodilo
Hills**

SEPUPA

Sepupa Swamp Stop
Sepupa

TSODTO

SWAMPS

Thamacha veterinary fence

VET-IK

Ikoga
Gate

13

Ikoga

GPS co-ordinates ⊕			
DROTSK	18°24.868'S, 21°53.120'E	T2TURN	18°35.834'S, 21°59.986'E
E13TUR	19°00.793'S, 22°17.356'E	TSODTO	18°47.378'S, 21°44.981'E
NXAMAS	18°36.426'S, 22°05.268'E	TSVIEW	18°33.830'S, 21°58.273'E
NXTURN	18°38.125'S, 22°02.797'E	VET-IK	18°50.327'S, 22°13.756'E
SEPUPA	18°44.150'S, 22°10.625'E	VET-SA	18°29.256'S, 21°55.142'E
SWAMPS	18°44.749'S, 22°11.843'E	XARO	18°25.423'S, 21°56.364'E

NOTE
For accommodation listings,
see pages 360–3, 364, 365–6

Gumare ▼

taking about 4½ hours to reach Maun. Another service leaves a little later in the day. Minibuses are cheaper but very cramped and take an hour longer; they also depart only when full. Alternatively, hitchhiking is relatively easy along this road.

Self-drivers will need to allow around four hours to reach Shakawe from Maun. And for fly-in guests, there's the option of charter flights taking about an hour. The airstrip is to the west of the main road, just 400m off the tarmac.

🏠 **Where to stay** In Shakawe itself, there's only one real option, but there are several water-based camps on the river about 10km south of town that cater mainly for fishing and birdwatching, while houseboats add further variety. With the increase in the number of travellers along the Caprivi Strip, trade here has picked up so you will often need to book. The options here are listed from north to south, followed by the houseboats.

🏠 **Hawk Guesthouse** (10 rooms) Shakawe;
\ 687 5227; e koyobo2003@yahoo.com;
⊕ 18°21.012'S, 21°50.108'E. To find this welcoming guesthouse, follow the tar road as it goes north through the centre of town to the river, then – having turned away from the river – it's on the left after another 1.5km (& about 300m from the river in the other direction!). En-suite rooms are arranged around a small courtyard within a walled enclosure. It's hardly picturesque, but rooms are clean & come with AC, mosi nets, a kettle & satellite TV. Single rooms have a dbl bed, but dbls are larger & worth the extra P100. There's just about space to pitch a tent here, too, & you'll be allocated a separate toilet & shower. By the pool, there's a shaded restaurant area where b/fast, lunch & dinner are served, so you won't go hungry.
$$ *exc b/fast (P60).*

🏠 **Drotsky's Cabins** [map 359] (3 family chalets, camping) \ 683 0226; m 7212 2971;
e drotsky@botsnet.bw, drotskys@info.bw;
⊕ DROTSK 18°24.868'S, 21°53.120'E. Almost 8km south of Shakawe you'll find a left turn off the tar road. This sandy track will lead you east, crossing the old road up the Panhandle for about 3km to reach Drotsky's Cabins – though note that there are now 2 Drotsky's Cabins (see also below). You should be able to drive this track in a normal 2WD car, though the sand can be very thick, so some driving skill is needed.

The good news for many fans is that the original & long-established Drotsky's is still going strong, & still run by Jan & Eileen Drotsky & their family, who have seen Shakawe change from a remote outpost to a thriving little town. Central to the lodge are a thatched bar & a very large dining area, built on a high bank out over the

river, & decorated with carvings, masks & local maps. (Look out for the rather beautiful wooden top to the bar, too!) The river at this point is several kilometres wide, a network of deep-water channels & large beds of papyrus. It's excellent for birdwatching or fishing – with several boats with a driver/guide for hire by the hour or day, & fishing tackle available too – but there's little game around except for hippos & crocodiles.

Drotsky's simple A-frame chalets are set amongst well-watered lawns under a canopy of thick riverside trees. Colourful shrubs & banana trees have been planted between them, creating the welcoming impression of a green & tropical haven. Built on 2 levels, the chalets have brick walls supporting a tall, steeply angled thatched roof, & sleep 5 people: there's an en-suite dbl room downstairs, with steps up to 3 sgl beds above. Expect mesh on the window, rugs on the tiled floor & a table-top electric fan. Campers enjoy a shaded but sandy campsite with 17 pitches, each with lights, electric points & a firepit – but watch out for the local monkey population! Meals can be arranged with advance notice.

Drotsky's is a genuine old camp, where hospitality hasn't been learned from a manual. If you are willing to take it on its own terms, then it can be a super lodge, & offer you fascinating insights into the area, its history & its ecosystems.
$$$ *exc b/fast; camping P150 pp.*

🏠 **'New' Drotsky's Cabins** [map 359] (10 chalets) Contact via Drotsky's Cabins, above;
⊕ DROTSK 18°24.868'S, 21°53.120'E. Under the same ownership as Drotsky's Cabins, & sharing the same access road, this was originally called Lawdon's but has since reverted to Drotsky's

Cabins. However, to avoid confusion with its elder sibling, we have listed it separately.

Built in 2010 by the Drotsky family, the 'new' Drotsky's is designed like a vast log cabin on high stilts, under a thatched roof, & is approached by an almost palatial series of steps & walkways. Adorned with wrought-iron chandeliers & wood carvings, & with a separate bar under whirling fans, it may sound rather grand, but the effect is homely rather than ostentatious. The log-cabin theme continues in the large, twin-bedded en-suite chalets, also raised up on stilts; space is clearly not an issue here! AC, fans & flat-screen TVs are standard, while old-fashioned armchairs add a touch of traditional comfort, & we loved the ornate ceramic basins. Outside, perfectly manicured lawns sweep around a pool to the river beyond. The main area is entirely wheelchair accessible, as is one of the chalets. For activities, see Drotsky's Cabins, above. **$$$** *exc b/fast.*

🏠 **Shakawe River Lodge** [map 359] (10 chalets, 4 dome tents, camping) ❭684 0403; **m** 7230 6822; **e** info@shakawelodge.com; www. shakawelodge.com; ✪ SHAKAL 18°26.059'S, 21°54.326'E. Known for decades as Shakawe Fishing Camp, this entirely new lodge – opened in 2013 – has risen from humble surroundings. Gone is the simple fishing camp of yore, its expansive river frontage now hosting a stylish yet very open lodge that's all toning neutral colours beneath a topping of smart thatch. From the entrance, you're greeted by a riverside vista of palm trees & papyrus, where basket chairs hang enticingly in the breeze. Sunloungers on a raised pool deck catch the river view, too, as do the smart restaurant & lounge. Most of the twin & king-size dbl en-suite chalets with sliding glass doors are lined up along a rather reedy section of the river, their contemporary décor enhanced by AC, TV & a bar fridge.

Downstream, the shady old riverside campsite has had a makeover, but remains relaxed & unpretentious, with 10 clearly demarcated pitches, its own bar, & spotless if well-worn showers & toilets. Campers are welcome to dine at the lodge, where an à-la-carte menu features a good selection of pizzas. Beside the slipway, look out for the rusting hulk of an old houseboat, a relic of the Angolan war from the late 1970s. Apparently it was used by 32 Battalion of the South African forces, who were stationed in the Caprivi Strip, but

it broke loose & drifted south, & has been gently rusting in Botswana ever since!

The lodge is clearly signposted some 2.5km east of the main road, about 5.5km north of the Somachima Veterinary Fence (✪ VET-SA 18°29.256'S, 21°55.142'E), or 11km south of Shakawe, & is accessible by 2WD. Guests have always come here to fish, especially during the peak season of Jun–Aug, & certainly fishing is still a focus; boats can be hired by the hour or day (from P250/1,200 exc fuel), but birdwatching, as well as day trips to the Tsodilo Hills & Mahango Game Reserve (P800 pp/day, min 4 people) add another dimension. **$$$$$** *Camping P110 pp; pre-erected tent P350.*

🏠 **Xaro Lodge** [map 359] (8 Meru tents) ❭683 0226; **m** 7212 2970; **e** xarolodge@info. bw; ✪ XARO 18°25.423'S, 21°56.364'E. Xaro is about 8.5km downstream from Drotsky's Cabins, its parent camp, & is usually reached from there by a 15min boat trip. It is set in 30ha on an outcrop from the mainland, amidst an old, established grove of knobthorn (*Acacia nigrescens*), mangosteen (*Garcinia livingstonei*) & jackalberry (*Diospyros mespiliformis*) trees, while in the garden you'll find a host of succulents & cacti, banana trees & even a small baobab tree (*Adansonia digitata*). Originally built in the mid-1980s by Hartley's Safaris, Xaro passed through several hands until it was acquired by Jan Drotsky, whose son, Donovan, now runs the camp with his wife, Yolande. Royal, one of the marvellous staff who has been with the family for years, recalls that the lodge has always been used for fishing & birdwatching from motorboats, never from mekoro – & that's still the situation.

The origins of a beautiful, old-style Okavango camp still remain in the thatched, stone dining area with a large table in the centre & various old books on shelves in the walls, but a new bar has been introduced, & the Meru-style tents replaced. With en-suite facilities & sliding doors leading to wooden decks, 2 of these can be accessed with a wheelchair. Activities are as at Drotsky's. **$$$** *exc b/fast.*

🏠 **Samochima Lodge** Contact Wilmot Safaris, page 178. This new lodge next to Shakawe River Lodge is still in the planning stages by Lloyd Wilmot, but may come to fruition in the lifetime of this guide.

Houseboats Moored on the river near Shakawe, several houseboats offer the opportunity to explore the western fringes of the Delta while based on the river itself. It's an entirely different approach, & may well appeal to those seeking a more relaxing trip with less of an emphasis on fishing (although fishing is still an option!). For a general overview, contact Okavango Houseboats (*www.okavangohouseboats.com*), or consider one of the following:

Kabbo (8 cabins) Contact Wilderness Dawning Safaris, page 178. This 2-storey 'floating lodge', moored on the river near Hawk Guesthouse (above), is designed to make the most of its location. On the lower deck, each en-suite cabin has sliding glass doors just above water level, while above are the dining area, bar & – for those who want to brave the African sun – sundecks. Boating & fishing trips (catch & release) are available or – if you tire of the water – there are visits to the Tsodilo Hills, all at US$75 pp (min 2). *US$1,680 up to 8 people, inc FB & 1 water-based activity per day; exc transfers, most drinks.* ⏲ *Apr–Oct.*

Kubu Queen (2 cabins) m 7230 6821/2; e oldafricasafaris@ngami.net; www.kubuqueen. com. From its base at Shakawe, the *Kubu Queen*

THE CATFISH RUN

The amazing phenomenon of the catfish run is unique to the Okavango Delta. It happens every year, between early August and the end of November, though its timing is difficult to predict precisely.

As the water level starts to drop in the northern part of the Panhandle, it is still rising in the southern part of the Delta. The catfish runs start in the north of the Panhandle, where the lowering water levels concentrate the Delta's smaller fish – especially the relatively small churchill (*Petrocephalus catostoma*) and bulldog (*Marcusenius macrolepidotus*) – in the channels and papyrus banks.

The main predatory species involved include the sharp-toothed catfish (*Clarias gariepinus*), a hardy, omnivorous species which grows up to 1.4m in length and 59kg in weight, and the much smaller blunt-toothed catfish (*Clarias ngaensis*). These catfish hunt in packs and a 'run' starts with the catfish swimming upstream inside the papyrus banks. Here they slap their powerful tails on the surface of the water, making a noise like a gunshot, and against the papyrus, to stun the smaller fish, their prey.

Hundreds and sometimes thousands of catfish will work their way upstream like this, making the water 'boil' with their frenzy of activity. All this noise and commotion attracts an eager audience of herons, storks, egrets, fish eagles and other fish-eating birds on the banks, while crocodiles, snakes and tigerfish lurk beyond the papyrus in the deeper channels waiting to snap up anything that escapes into open water.

Although in each run the catfish swim upstream, when it's finished they pause and drift back down, subsequently re-joining other catfish and starting new runs. So as the water levels drop further down in the Delta, the location of the runs moves south also.

These runs occur in many different sizes. There will be several per day in different areas of the Delta, each covering a distance of a few kilometres before fizzling out. A couple may be longer than this, perhaps continuing for as long as two weeks and covering a lot of distance, but these are the exception rather than the rule.

Eventually, signalled by the onset of the rising waters, the catfish will themselves move out on to the floodplains and spawn.

is moored at a different spot each night, with tender boats so that guests can explore the river & its channels, & go fishing (except in the closed season, Jan–Feb). Nature walks on some of the larger islands are a further option. Inside, there's a lounge, bar & dining area. Both cabins have a dbl bed, while a further 2 guests can sleep under the stars on the upper deck, where simple twin beds are set up under mosquito nets. The shower & toilet are shared, but groups are not mixed, so you won't be sharing with strangers. Another alternative for up to 12 people is to camp on one of the islands.

The boat is owned by Greg & Kate Thompson, who have worked in the safari industry in the Okavango for almost 20yrs; Greg is a professional guide. *P2,350 pp, inc FB, fishing, airstrip transfers; exc VAT, drinks, fuel for tender boats.* ⊕ *All year.*

Nxamaseri

Nxamaseri Though the small village of Nxamaseri is not a stop for most visitors, I've included this section because the surrounding area is a very interesting one, offering an insight into the attractions of the Delta that is on a par with most of the reserves further east.

The Nxamaseri Channel is a side-channel of the main Okavango River. When water levels are high, there are plenty of open marshy floodplains covered with an apparently unblemished carpet of grass, and dotted with tiny palm islands. It's very like the Jao Flats, and is one of the Okavango's most beautiful corners.

Like Guma Lagoon, further south, it's fairly easily accessible due to the presence of a lodge. If you want a real Delta experience in the Panhandle, then this should be high on your list of places to visit – though getting here requires either your own vehicle or a flight.

Flora and fauna highlights The Nxamaseri Channel is north of the point where the main Okavango River divides at the base of the Panhandle, and is a stretch of open, clear water up to about 30m wide in places. Beside the edges you'll find stands of papyrus and common reeds, whilst its quieter edges are lined by patches of waterlilies, including many night-lilies (also known as lotus lilies; *Nymphaea lotus*) as well as the more common day-lilies (*Nymphaea nouchali caerulea*). Look out also for the heart-shaped floating leaves, and star-shaped white or yellow flowers of the water gentian (*Nymphoides indica*).

As with the rest of the Panhandle, this isn't a prime area for game viewing. You may catch glimpses of the odd lechwe or the shy sitatunga, and you're almost bound to see hippo and crocodile, but big game is scarce. However, the channel is a super waterway for birdwatching; home to a tremendous variety of waterbirds. Without trying too hard, my sightings included many pygmy geese, greater and lesser jacanas, lesser galinules, colonies of reed cormorants, darters, several species of bee-eater and kingfisher, green-backed herons, a relaxed black crake, numerous red-shouldered widows and even (on a cloudy morning in February) a pair of Pel's fishing owls. Beside the channel are pockets of tall riverine trees and various real fan and wild date palms, whose overhanging branches house colonies of weavers (masked, spotted-backed and brown-throated). Upstream of the lodge, on the main Okavango River, there's a colony of carmine bee-eaters at a location known locally as 'the red cliffs'. This is occupied from around early September to the end of December, but is probably at its best in late September or early October (the best time for most migrant species here). While watching for birds, keep an eye out for the elusive spotted-necked otter (*Lutra maculicollis*), which also frequents these waters.

Getting there Nxamaseri village lies about 37km south of Shakawe, or 19km north of Sepupa. From the north, follow the tar road to the Somachima Veterinary Fence (✪ VET-SA 18°29.256'S, 21°55.142'E), then after 10km you'll pass a slight rise marked by a sign as 'Tsodilo View' (⊕ TSVIEW 18°33.830'S, 21°58.273'E). From here, on a clear day, you should be able to see the Tsodilo Hills to the southwest, but thick vegetation has obscured the view, and sand sprinkled with broken glass makes it a far from attractive place for a break. Less than 3km south of this viewpoint you'll pass a sign to Nxamaseri, which leads to the village of the same name. The turning to Nxamaseri Island Lodge (⊕ NXTURN 18°38.125'S, 22°2.797'E) is clearly signposted almost 9km south of the village turn-off. Advanced reservations are essential; this is not a place to try and drop into unannounced. Most visitors are transferred to the lodge (⊕ NXAMAS 18°36.426'S, 22°5.268'E) from the airstrip, but self-drivers leave their vehicle in the guarded parking spot by the turning, and are transferred by 4x4 vehicle and boat for the final few kilometres.

🏠 Where to stay

🏠 **Nxamaseri Island Lodge** [map 359] (8 chalets) m 713 26619; e info@nxamaseri. com; www.nxamaseri.com. Started as a fishing camp in about 1980, Nxamaseri is now back in the hands of the original owners, PJ & Barney Bestelink (who run Okavango Horse Safaris) & remains a wonderful all-round lodge justifying a stay of at least 2 days. It has been built within a thick & tropical patch of riverine vegetation. All around are knobthorn (*Acacia nigrescens*), waterberry (*Syzygium cordatum*), sycamore fig (*Ficus sycomorus*), mangosteen (*Garcinia livingstonei*), jackalberries (*Diospyros mespiliformis*), sausage trees (*Kigelia africana*) & some of the most wonderfully contorting python vines (*Cocculus hirsutus*) that you'll see anywhere.

Sensitive refurbishment in 2011 means that the strong sense of place has been retained, but with higher standards of accommodation & food. Its wide, thatched lounge/dining area is built around a couple of lofty old jackalberry trees, with an open frontage to the river: it's comfortable & well thought out, but not ornate. Wooden walkways lead to large chalets, & an open 'treehouse'. Most are built of brick beneath high thatched roofs, but both the treehouse & a triple room are predominantly canvas structures. Each chalet has 4-poster-style mosi nets, bedside lights powered by a generator or batteries, an en-suite shower & toilet, & a wooden deck above the river.

It is claimed that fly-fishing in the Delta was pioneered at Nxamaseri, & certainly it remains an attraction for people who fish seriously, but to this have now been added 1st-class boat trips for birdwatching, visits to a local village to watch basket making, & day trips to the Tsodilo Hills. There tends to be less emphasis on mokoro excursions, but these are also possible (& magical) when the water levels are high & there are suitable areas of shallow water nearby. Fly-fishing & lure/spinning fishing with top-quality equipment under expert guidance are possible throughout the year. That said, the very best tigerfishing months are Aug–Nov, while the best times for bream are Mar–Jun. During the first 3 months of the year the rain & new floodwaters are said to disturb the fish, which move out to the floodplains, so fishing in the channels can be more difficult. Nxamaseri's record tigerfish catch is about 10kg, though in a normal season they'd expect to have 10–15 catches over the 6kg mark. Like most Okavango lodges, Nxamaseri operates a 'catch-&-release' system, except for the occasional bream that has been damaged. They have a large, flat, barge-like boat which provides a particularly stable platform for several people fishing, & is also ideal for photography, plus a fleet of aluminium-hulled craft. *US$525/787.50 pp sharing/sgl Jul–Oct; US$415 pp rest of year, inc FB, most activities, fishing tackle, transfers from airstrip/road; exc alcoholic drinks, lost tackle. Day trip to Tsodilo Hills & full-day fishing US$155 pp.* ☺ *All year.*

Sepupa (⊕ SEPUPA 18°44.150'S, 22°10.625'E) Sepupa, sometime spelled 'Sepopa', is 1.7km east of the main road, about 223km north of Sehithwa and perhaps 58km south of Shakawe. Here you'll find a few shops including a bottle stall and a general dealer.

Most visitors, however, are looking for Sepupa Swamp Stop – either to spend the night, or to get a boat across to the eastern side of the river. The lodge is clearly signposted from the main road; just follow the access road to Sepupa Village for 1km until the pot-holed tar runs out, then turn right and continue for a further 2.5km; the track is fine for a 2WD car.

Where to stay For years there was only one option here, but now accommodation has being developed on the tiny Pepere Island, 2.5km long by 1km wide, and there are several houseboats moored close by.

⚑ Sepupa Swamp Stop [map 359] (12 chalets, 5 tents, camping) m 7261 0071, 7137 9326; e res@swampstop.co.bw, carl@ngami.net; www.swampstop.com; ✪ SWAMPS 18°44.749'S, 22°11.843'E. The Swamp Stop was originally just a simple riverside campsite under trees, with a few pre-erected tents for those without their own. Now, the old campsite is still there, with open pitches, power points & lighting, & an ablution block with modern sanitaryware, but there's lots more choice. A 2nd site, at the back, has 8 neatly swept & reed-fenced pitches, each with a BBQ/cooking area, firepit, power & light. Wacky metal doors in a reed enclosure surround the showers & toilets, with handbasins attractively set in an upturned mokoro, & a separate washing-up area. The occasional overlander group gets its own separate area, albeit sharing the same facilities. If you don't have your own kit, there are twin-bedded Meru tents with electric light close to the bar & restaurant, & semi-detached chalets, kitted out with AC, fridge & en-suite bath & shower. It's all very neat, very organised & very clean.

By twin oval pools, the Swamp Stop's riverside bar & restaurant has an upstairs deck with views over the papyrus to the main channel of the Okavango. Down below, you can get b/fast, light meals such as sandwiches & burgers, & mains, from curry to steak – or soak up the views with a beer at the bar.

Although the camp was taken over in 2007, the previous owners marketed it well & positioned it as one of the very few remaining bases for budget safaris into the Delta, & a springboard for getting to Seronga. Now the camp offers the main means of crossing the river, with transfers at P2,200–2,500 per boat – the latter taking up to 16 people. Locally, you can explore the river by motorboat (from P300/hr, but bring your own fishing tackle), or take an overnight mokoro trip to Pepere Island, with excursions to the Tsodilo Hills also on offer. **$$$** exc b/fast; tent P350 dbl; camping P110 pp. ⊕ All year.

⌂ Pepere Island (12 tents, 12 cabins) Contact Sepupa Swamp Stop, above. The new all-inclusive camp at Pepere Island, some 2½hrs by boat from its sister camp, the Swamp Stop, was opened in 2008. It's a simple place, its Meru-style tents set up on wooden decks, & en-suite cabins, with shower & bath, built of timber with reed roofs. Visitors come for the activities – guided mokoro trips, game walks & birding – & the resident wildlife, which includes elephant, zebra, buffalo, red lechwe & sitatunga, as well as hippos & crocs, of course. Of the birds, top attractions are Pel's fishing owl, & the migrant carmine bee-eater. Tent US$240 dbl FB; cabin P850 dbl, exc meals (P300 pp/day).

Houseboats As at Shakawe, there are a few houseboats moored on the river here, affording an entirely different perspective on life in the Delta. Three of these – the Inkwazi, Inyankuni & Madikubu – are operated by Okavango Houseboats (✆ 686 0802, e krause@info.bw; www.okavangohouseboats.com), & cruise between Sepupa & Seronga. If you're prepared to bring all your own food & drinks, you can hire one of these boats outright for P7,280 per day, excluding fuel & transfers, but with a crew available to prepare your meals. Alternatively, you can organise to stay on a full-board basis (P432.20 pp per night, exc drinks).

The boats are accessible by road, but if required, transfers from Seropa to Seronga cost P526.40 pp, while airstrip transfers are P117.60. The use of tender boats for fishing & exploring is included, but mokoro & camping trips, & game flights, cost extra.

⛴ Ngwesi (4 cabins) ✆ +27 (0)12 743 6005; m 0722 02080; e reservations@ okavangoriverboats.com, res@ngwesi.com; www. ngwesi.com. Moored near Shakawe, the dbl-decker Ngwesi has berths in twin & dbl en-suite cabins, while on the upper deck is a glassed-in

13

lounge. Meals can be prepared by the crew (P300 pp/day), or you can opt to self-cater, in which case you must bring all your own food. Either way, there's a cash bar on board for both soft & alcoholic drinks, & ice can be bought on board.

Opportunities for fishing & birding are available in tender boats which can explore the channels away from the main river. *P8,000/day, inc FB fishing, use of tender boats; exc drinks, fishing tackle & permits, transfers; min 2 nights.*

THE DELTA'S WESTERN FRINGES

Ordered from north to south, here's a brief listing of the main landmarks and villages on the road between Sepupa and Sehithwa. If it gets a little repetitive, then take that as a fair reflection of the road, which is long and well surfaced with tarmac. Most of this area has a low, wide verge of groundcover which is often cut – helping to ensure that big game can be seen before it is standing in front of you. But for all this visibility, the scenery is uninteresting.

Although you're travelling at times very close to the western edge of the Okavango Delta, the road passes through apparently undistinguished areas of bush. You may see the occasional animal, but with man and cattle as the dominant species in this area, only birdwatchers are likely to find much of interest on the drive.

SEPUPA TO ETSHA 13 The overall standard of the tar road along the western side of the Delta is generally pretty good, but there are exceptions, so always keep an eye out for pot-holes.

Ikoga Gate About 12km south of the Sepupa turn-off, or 211km north of Sehithwa, you may have to stop at the Ikoga Gate (✪ VET-IK 18°50.327'S, 22°13.756'E), which is a checkpoint on the Thamacha Veterinary Fence.

Ikoga turning About 206km north of Sehithwa, there's another turning east, this time to Ikoga.

Etsha 13 Some 32km south of the Sepupa turn-off, or 191km north of Sehithwa, is a turning (✪ E13TUR 19°00.793'S, 22°17.356'E) which leads slightly over 3km east to Etsha 13. This small village has a few basic shops, but little more. More important for visitors, it marks the access road to Guma Lagoon and Guma Lagoon Camp.

GUMA LAGOON On the western side of the Delta, at the very base of the Panhandle, Guma is a large, papyrus-lined lagoon. It is linked to the Thaoge River, the main eastern finger of the Okavango River system, by a short channel (40 minutes by boat from the camp or the lodge). Both Guma Lagoon and the main Thaoge River are excellent spots for fishing and birdwatching – a combination that, with relatively easy 4x4 access from around Etsha 13, has encouraged two different camps to set up here.

Flora and fauna highlights Guma isn't a place for big game; it's a deep-water environment that offers good birdwatching and fishing.

The vegetation around the lagoon is mainly papyrus, though you'll also find large stands of phragmites reeds. You'll also find the odd waterberry (*Syzygium cordatum*) and water fig (*Ficus verruculosa*), especially in the smaller channels and backwaters.

On the banks, the riverine vegetation is thick and lush. It includes plenty of wild date palms (*Phoenix reclinata*), river beans (*Sesbania sesban*) and potato bushes (*Phyllanthus reticulatus*), which are members of the euphorbia family and are not

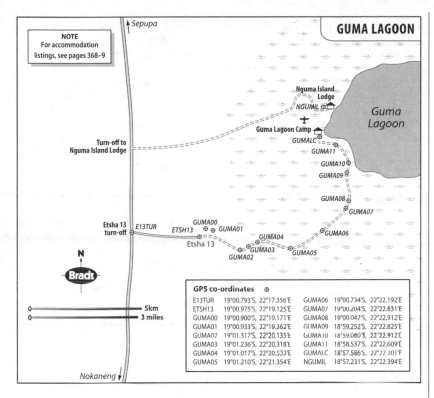

↑ Sepupa

NOTE
For accommodation
listings, see pages 368–9

Nguma Island
Lodge
NGUMIL

Guma
Lagoon

Guma Lagoon Camp
GUMALC

Turn-off to
Nguma Island Lodge

GUMA11

GUMA10

GUMA09

GUMA08

GUMA07

Etsha 13
turn-off E13TUR

GUMA00
ETSH13 GUMA01

GUMA04 GUMA06

Etsha 13

GUMA03 GUMA05

GUMA02

N

Bradt

0 ————— 5km
0 ————— 3 miles

GPS co-ordinates ⊕			
E13TUR	19°00.793'S, 22°17.356'E	GUMA06	19°00.734'S, 22°22.192'E
ETSH13	19°00.975'S, 22°19.125'E	GUMA07	19°00.204'S, 22°22.831'E
GUMA00	19°00.900'S, 22°19.171'E	GUMA08	19°00.047'S, 22°22.912'E
GUMA01	19°00.933'S, 22°19.362'E	GUMA09	18°59.252'S, 22°22.825'E
GUMA02	19°01.317'S, 22°20.135'E	GUMA10	18°59.060'S, 22°22.912'E
GUMA03	19°01.236'S, 22°20.318'E	GUMA11	18°58.537'S, 22°22.609'E
GUMA04	19°01.017'S, 22°20.533'E	GUMALC	18°57.586'S, 22°22.201'E
GUMA05	19°01.210'S, 22°21.354'E	NGUMIL	18°57.231'S, 22°22.394'E

Nokaneng ↓

related to potatoes at all – but smell the air on a warm evening and you'll realise
where their name comes from.

Also keep an eye out for large sour plum (*Ximenia caffra*), water pear (*Syzygium
guineense*), jackalberry trees (*Diospyros mespiliformis*) and the occasional sausage tree
(*Kigelia africana*) – one of which greets you as you enter Guma Lagoon Camp. Further
from the water, you'll often find acacias: camelthorn (*Acacia erioloba*), knobthorn
(*Acacia nigrescens*) and umbrella thorn (*Acacia tortilis*) are the main species here.
There are a few baobabs (*Adansonia digitata*) in the area, but they're not common.

The more common birds include fish eagles, many species of herons, egrets,
warblers, bee-eaters and kingfishers, pygmy geese and greater and lesser jacanas.
Look for red-shouldered widows in the papyrus, and reed cormorants and darters
sunning themselves on perches over the water.

In the riverine forest areas you can find Heuglin's robins (white-browed robin
chats), crested and black-collared barbets, green pigeons, various sunbirds and, in
summer, the spectacular paradise flycatchers in breeding plumage.

Getting there and away Despite their proximity, the two lodges at Guma
Lagoon are normally accessed from two separate points along the main road: Guma
Lagoon Camp (and the lagoon itself) via Etsha 13, and Nguma Island Lodge, from
a well-signposted turning about 3km further north. You'll need a 4x4; if you're
driving a 2WD then with prior notice the lodges can arrange to collect you at a pre-
agreed location, leaving your car somewhere safe whilst you're at the camp.

The actual routes depend on the conditions. Signboards to Nguma Island Lodge
make their access drive of 12km or so relatively straightforward. Although it changes

according to the prevailing conditions, it is usually well marked. Alternatively, Nguma Island Lodge has an airstrip, or you can fly into the small airstrip at Gumare and be collected from there. It may also be possible to fly into Seronga, and be transferred to the lodge by boat from there.

However, the track to Guma Lagoon Camp, although marked with arrows, is very sandy and considerably more circuitous; it's easy to get lost. The first hurdle is finding the right track out of the small village of Etsha 13 (⊕ ETSH13 19°00.975'S, 22°19.125'E). In theory there's a sign saying 'camp' on a telephone pole, but it's none too clear. This will take you through the village on a track going east-southeast. Gradually this turns east, then northeast, and finally north – and the scenery gets prettier, with fewer domestic animals and settlements, and more small date palm islands and open floodplains. The distance varies between 10km and 13km, and you'll need to allow around 45 minutes. As a guide, GPS waypoints for just one possible route are shown on the map on page 367. There are certainly more direct routes than this, as the whole area is criss-crossed with confusing bush tracks. However, many will be seasonal and depend on the water levels, so beware of getting stuck!

⌂ **Where to stay** There are only two choices at this lagoon. Though both have campsites as well as tented rooms, they are each quite different and don't generally work closely together.

⌂ **Guma Lagoon Camp** [map 367] (12 'cabins', camping) ☎687 4626; e info@guma-lagoon.com; www.guma-lagoon.com; ⊕ GUMALC 18°57.586'S, 22°22.201'E. Relaxed, friendly & popular with anglers, Guma Lagoon Camp occupies a picturesque spot with open views across the lagoon. It focuses mainly on self-drive, self-catering visitors, although meals can be provided with advance notice.

Nestling among the trees at the water's edge are smart new en-suite 'cabins', constructed of wood & canvas on raised decks to catch the breeze. With twin/dbl beds, wooden floors, electric lights & a veranda over the lagoon, they're comfortable if not luxurious. At the campsite, each of the 7 pitches has its own toilet, hot shower & braai pit. Guests prepare meals in the fully equipped kitchen, with pots, pans, cutlery, cooking equipment & fridge/freezing facilities, before congregating in the shaded dining/bar area with a deck extending over the lagoon. A small pool is a welcome place to cool off, perhaps after a game of volleyball.

In addition to boating & fishing (boat hire from P295/hr, exc fuel), there is the option of a full-day mokoro trip (P1,065/2 people), or staying overnight on one of the islands (from P1,270 pp, plus P392/day for a luggage mokoro); note that children under 12 may not take part in mokoro excursions. Camping equipment can be hired, & food/drinks organised by the camp with advance notice. Rates exclude transfers (P107 pp) & concession fees. $$$ Camping P134 pp; 4x4 transfer from Etsha 13 P112 pp one way. ⊕ All year.

⌂ **Nguma Island Lodge** [map 367] (8 Meru tents, 5 self-catering tents, camping) ☎683 0159; m 7356 0120; e nguma@dynabyte.bw; www.ngumalodge.com; ⊕ NGUMIS 18°57.231'S, 22°22.394'E. Situated on the northwestern edge of the lagoon, this lodge was opened in 2000, & is owned & run by Geoff & Nookie Randall, who have lived in the area for over 20 years. (Geoff played an important part in pioneering the fibreglass mekoro in the area – & thus is partially responsible for saving an enormous number of the Delta's old trees!)

It's a linear site, neatly divided into two. At one end, where the lodge is based, tents are spread out among the trees along fairly high wooden walkways & raised up on high wooden decking. Inside you'll find comfortable twin beds with percale linen & colourful cushions, chairs, a bedside table & a wrought-iron hanging unit. At the back of each tent is an en-suite shower, toilet & washbasin. Power comes from a generator, with a system of back-up batteries for the lights at night; batteries can be charged in the main area.

Walkways continue to the raised main area, so everything is above water if levels rise to a high flood. Normally the ground beneath is dry, with cool lawns dotted with date palms. A comfortable lounge, dining room & well-stocked bar are housed in a large log cabin. There's a better collection of local baskets & craftwork than in most curio shops, & some are for sale in the small shop.

At the other end of the site, but under the same cool canopy of trees, is the Delta Dawn campsite. As well as camping pitches, there are pre-erected twin tents with linen & towels provided. Ablutions are simple, with wooden-clad showers & toilets, & there are also braai stands & facilities for washing up. The campsite has its own bar & restaurant – with meals by arrangement. (Fishermen should note that there is no freezer space.)

Activities include ½-day, full-day & overnight trips by mokoro, as well as boat trips by the hour (for up to 6 people). Fishing tackle is available for hire, & lures etc for sale. Other options include island walks & birding excursions. *P2,250 pp, inc FB & 1 activity/day, exc drinks, laundry; self-catering tent P950 dbl; camping P140 pp; all exc VAT.* ⊕ *All year.*

What to see and do Precise activities depend on where you're staying, though boat trips are really the main draw. On the whole, the water's deep enough to limit the scope of mekoro for most of the year, and so motorboats are the vehicle of choice. If you're not a devout angler or birdwatcher, then just take a few rods and a pair of binoculars and do a little of both – it's very relaxing.

ETSHA 6 TO SEHITHWA

Etsha 6 About 45km south of the Sepupa turn-off (178km north of Sehithwa) there's a signposted turning (⊕ E6TURN 19°6.706'S, 22°16.152'E) to Etsha 6, which is less than 3km east of the road. For the traveller, it's a reasonable halfway point between the turn-offs to the Gcwihaba Caverns and the Tsodilo Hills, but accommodation is currently lacking.

Fuel is available from a Shell station in the centre of town, though don't rely on it. Opposite is a Co-op which stocks tinned food, soft drinks and basic staples like rice and maize in quantity, though there's very little fresh produce. The post office, with an internet café, is just beyond the fuel station.

Turning right on to the old Panhandle road at the T-junction near here will bring you to the post office, with an internet café. Then, a further kilometre or so along, there's a craft shop run by the Botswana Council of Churches (BCC). Very nice baskets woven on the premises are for sale here, though opening hours seem erratic.

THE ETSHA VILLAGES

In 1969, the war in Angola (which, in many ways, was an extension of the Cold War using African proxies) displaced a large number of mostly Hambukushu people from the Caprivi area into Botswana. There they were accepted as refugees. Initially they were received at Shakawe, but eventually the plan was to move them to a new village called Etsha, south of there.

However, while the refugees were at Shakawe it's said that they naturally split into 13 separate groups. So when they were moved, they naturally split into 13 villages, which spread out along the western edge of the Delta, 1km apart. They were called, somewhat unimaginatively, Etsha 1, Etsha 2, Etsha 3 and so on up to the most northerly, Etsha 13.

Now the old track which links them and runs close to the Delta has been largely superseded by the new tar highway, which takes a more direct route on the east of the old road. However, you'll still find tracks linking the two, one of which is close to Etsha 13, and another close to Etsha 6.

Where to stay Sadly, the guesthouse set up in 2009 by the Botswana Council of Churches (BCC) had hit problems at the end of 2013, and was closed, but we have left the details here in the hope that it will re-open. Further east, the budget Makwena Camp has also been long closed, and plans to develop its site have not materialised.

Botswana Council of Churches Guesthouse (9 rooms) ℡ 637 4200; m 7258 8823; ✪ BCCGH 19°07.504'S, 22°17.612'E. Next to BCC the craft shop, this simple guesthouse remained immaculately swept when we visited in 2013, despite being closed to visitors. On the site of a former mission station, it's across the road from a secondary boarding school – so should you get to stay, expect to hear joyful children's voices throughout the evening. The large compound incorporates en-suite brick-built rooms furnished with just beds & linen (but no towels), electric lights, & a BBQ stand outside. You can get supplies from the Co-op, or ask at the centre & you'll probably find someone who's prepared to cook for you. **$**

Gumare

An ostentatious new 'bus rank' on the main road signals the turn-off to the east for Gumare, which lies about 146km north of Sehithwa, 37km from Nokaneng, and 77km south of Sepupa. There's a Shell fuel station here, too – one of the more reliable places to fill up along this side of the Delta.

Gumare (✪ GUMARE 19°22.242'S, 22°09.242'E) is one of the main towns of the Panhandle area, and has clearly seen considerable investment in recent years. The roads into town are tarred, and as if vying for attention with the bus station, there's a smart branch of Baclays Bank, with a (usually working) ATM, and a very shiny new post office. If you've time to spare, it may be worth seeking out the small craft shop, Ngwao Baskets (⏰ 08.00–16.00 Mon–Fri), on the road into town, where you'll find good local baskets at reasonable prices.

Where to stay Aside from a very good guesthouse in the town itself, there's the rather imposing Sexhebe Guesthouse (m 7177 7750, 7491 1744, 7137 1354), on the main road, just north of the turn-off, but we were unable to raise anyone to show us around during our most recent trip.

Hidden deep in the Kalahari bush a couple of hours' drive to the west of the main road, there's a small bushcamp, Gidichaa (see page 374). The turn-off (✪ GIDITO 19°29.983'S, 22°07.150'E) is 16km south of Gumare, and is clearly marked.

Ramorwa Guest House (9 rooms) ℡ 687 4556; m 7169 4999; e ramorwaguest@botsnet. bw; ✪ RAMORW 19°21.770'S, 22°09.973'E. About 1.3km from the centre of Gumare, & very well signposted, Ramorwa is tucked away down a quiet residential street. Small but comfortable rooms lead off a tree-shaded courtyard, a pleasant place to make use of free Wi-Fi access. With AC, TV & fridge, & a dbl bed under mosi nets, they're well equipped but not fancy. If you can't face the walk into town, you can get traditional or international-style meals here, too. **$$** exc b/fast (P50 pp).

Where to eat Not only does Gumare have a restaurant, it actually offers a selection. Of these the best is rather aptly considered to be Best Food, on the right as you enter the town from the main tar road, while a good alternative is the Rocla Restaurant. If all you're after is food for a picnic, there's also a good bakery in town, and a couple of grocery stores.

Nokaneng

The village of Nokaneng (✪ NOKANE 19°39.694'S, 22°11.184'E), about 114km south of Sepupa, 109km north of Sehithwa, is marked by a radio mast amidst a group of houses. There's little to detain the visitor here except a small grocery shop and a bar.

More significantly for travellers, shortly north of the radio mast is a road heading west signposted '120 to Qangwa' (⊕ QANGTO 19°39.608'S, 22°11.063'E). This leads eventually to the Namibian border, near Tsumkwe, where there's a relatively new border crossing (but check that it's open before you go). Before the border, the village of Qangwa marks the point where you can turn south and access both the Aha Hills area and, eventually, the Gcwihaba Hills and Caverns. See pages 384–93 for more on these areas.

Tsau About 180km south of Sepupa or 43km north of Sehithwa, you'll come across a turning to the village of Tsau (often written 'Tsao'), just to the east of the main road (⊕ TSAU 20°10.294'S, 22°27.265'E). Its prominent radio mast is quite a landmark, too. Here you'll find lots of small houses, though relatively little tree or vegetation cover, and a few small, general shops. Back on the main road, there's a small stall announcing 'tyre fix' – handy in an area where punctures are all too frequent.

Some 10km north of Tsau is a large banner on the side of the road (⊕ GTURN1 20°07.047'S, 22°22.291'E) marking a more southerly turn-off to the Gcwihaba Hills and Caverns.

Setata Veterinary Fence Gate
About 27.5km north of Sehithwa you'll have to stop and pass through the Setata Gate (⊕ VET-SE 20°15.775'S, 22°33.926'E) in the veterinary fence. Here as at other veterinary checkpoints, campers are likely to have their vehicles searched for red meat, which you cannot take across the vet fence.

Sehithwa Coming from the Panhandle, you'll reach a T-junction, where you meet the tarred A3. Turning left will bring you to the turn-off for Sehithwa, and on to Toteng and Maun, while right leads to Ghanzi, some 195km away. Note that the layout of this junction is not entirely clear on the 2008 Shell map.

The village of Sehithwa (⊕ SEHITII 20°28.259'S, 22°42.372'E) itself lies just south of the main A3, about 93km from Maun. There's a useful-looking fuel station close to the turning, but don't rely on it. Fuel supplies are erratic along the entire stretch of road as far as Shakawe, so it makes sense to fill up wherever you can.

Sehithwa is a more substantial settlement than Toteng, with a couple of small guesthouses, of which one – Ditoro Guest Lodge – is 1km or so from the main road. You'll also find a few general shops and liquor stores, and a not inconsiderable police station. Sehithwa and Toteng have a significant Herero population, and you will often pass ladies in the typical Victorian-style full-skirted dress and striking headdress.

LAKE NGAMI
The existence of a great lake within the Kalahari was known to Europeans from early reports of Bekwena and Batawana people, though it wasn't reached by them until the mid 19th century. Livingstone arrived on 1 August 1849, with Cotton, Oswell and Murray, narrowly beating Charles Andersson, who set out specifically to reach it from present-day Namibia.

In his book, *Lake Ngami and the River Okavango* (see *Appendix 3, Further information*), Andersson was hugely disappointed with what he first took to be Lake Ngami. He wrote:

> At last a blue line of great extent appeared in the distance, and I made sure it was the long-sought object; but I was still doomed in my disappointment. It turned out to be merely a large hollow in the rainy season filled with water, but now dry and covered with saline encrustations.

However, he hadn't reached the lake at this stage, and after getting beyond some pans and reedbeds, and over a series of sand ridges, he finally glimpsed the water, and described the moment:

> There, indeed, at no very great distance, lay spread before me an immense sheet of water bounded only by the horizon – the object of my ambition for years, and for which I have abandoned home and friends, and risked my life.

Visiting the lake is certainly easier than it was for those first explorers, though signposting is poor, and at times it can still be very disappointing. Even after the exceptional rains of 2008–09, much of the lakeshore was lined by shoulder-high thistles, so while the lake had plenty of water, it was still far from being an attraction in its own right.

Note that although the lake is very large when full, a high rate of evaporation and a very shallow profile means that the area covered by water can vary enormously.

Getting there and away The lake's bed is surrounded by a triangle of good roads, so approaching it is in theory a matter of turning off one of these and following your nose (or, perhaps better, your compass or GPS). However, it's one of those areas where all roads seem to lead back to where you first started – often enough to Sehithwa – so while you can strike out on your own, there's a simpler way.

About 3.5km north of Sehithwa, on the main road towards Toteng and Maun, there is a clear sign to the lake pointing to the south of the road (⊕ LKNGTO 20°27.021'S, 22°44.427'E). Turn down that track and after continuing straight for about 2km you should get to the lake (⊕ LNGAMI 20°27.812'S, 24°45.247'E).

When to visit The pithy answer to this question is 'whenever it's full of water!' And there lies the rub; it's only worth going if there's water in the lake, but few people will have been there and be able to tell you. Your best chance of getting up-to-date information is probably from operators in Maun, and especially the pilots, because if the lake is just a wide expanse of clay, it's better to save yourself a trip.

The state of this mystical lake varies greatly, depending upon whether the Delta's flood, which has historically been Lake Ngami's main source of water, has been high enough to overflow into the Kunyere River which feeds the lake. The lake was an empty dustbowl for the late 1980s and 1990s, but then filled to a shallow depth during 2000 and 2001, and since 2009 has held a serious amount of water. So ask around to find out what's happening.

If and when it really floods, Lake Ngami comes alive with birdlife, and has been identified as one of Botswana's 'important bird areas' (IBAs). From October, the ducks, geese, waders and other northern migrants arrive, lining the muddy shores until the weather cools towards the end of April. The flamingos, both greater and lesser, don't choose their times so carefully – being found here in their thousands whenever the conditions are right for the algae on which they feed. They appear from the shore as a pink haze settled on the water's surface.

Where to stay There's nowhere official to stay near the lake, but the land is open enough to camp rough – provided that you ask permission first from the nearest local villagers. On my last visit the villagers suggested that I go a few kilometres away from the lake to avoid the mosquitoes. This was a very wise move. You'll need to be self-sufficient, of course; and don't count on finding any drinkable water.

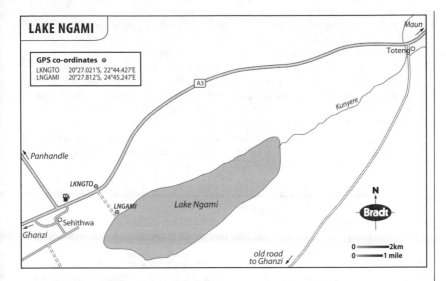

GPS co-ordinates ⊕
LKNGTO   20°27.021'S, 22°44.427'E
LNGAMI   20°27.812'S, 24°45.247'E

LAKE NGAMI

Maun

Toteng

A3

Kunyere

Panhandle

LKNGTO

Lake Ngami

LNGAMI

Sehithwa

Ghanzi

old road
to Ghanzi

N

Bradt

0 ———— 2km
0 ———— 1 mile

What to see and do This is purely a birding destination, though because visitors here are really very rare there are no tracks or pathways (for 4x4s or walkers) designed for birdwatchers. All the tracks have been made to serve the villagers and their many, many cattle. All this makes getting around time-consuming and at times difficult – but if there's water here then it might be worth it.

It's worth noting that Lake Ngami has been incorporated in a new management plan for the Okavango Delta, which proposes developing tourist facilities along the Panhandle and creating a scenic route along this western side as far as the lake. If birdwatching tours start up here, perhaps with the opportunity to take a canoe out on the lake, it could be quite a draw – when the lake is full of water!

TOTENG TO MAUN
Toteng Though a significant dot on the map, Toteng (⊕ TOTENG 20°21.407'S, 22°57.204'E) is little more than a road junction at the centre of a sprinkling of small cattle-farming homesteads. Once it marked the turning southwest to Ghanzi, but now that the new tarred A3 goes via Sehithwa, it's easy not to notice the place at all. If you're looking for the old road to Ghanzi, you'll find it at (⊕ GH2OLD 20°21.407'S, 22°57.204'E), on the west side of the main road.

Despite its apparent insignificance, Toteng has historical importance as a centre for the Batawana; in his *The Guide to Botswana*, Alec Campbell (see *Appendix 3, Further information*) comments that 'When they arrived in Ngamiland in 1795 they settled at Kgwebe and later moved to Toteng.' This was also one of the areas that received an influx of Herero people after their defeat at the battle of Waterberg.

Beyond Toteng, the tar road leads in around 64km to Maun. If you're planning to stop *en route*, there's a delightful small camp, Tshima Bush Camp, about equidistant between Toteng and Maun, though you do need to have a reservation; for details, see *Chapter 7*, page 165.

THE NORTHWEST KALAHARI

This area is Botswana at its most enigmatic. Here you'll find huge tracts of the Kalahari, punctuated only by isolated Bushman settlements. It's an area where you need to have a good 4x4 (or two), and for the most part you must be totally self-sufficient – travelling with all your own food, water, fuel and equipment.

It's not somewhere which will attract visitors for its game viewing or birdwatching, though you will find both game and birds. In fact, it's not an area that attracts many visitors at all. But old Africa hands are drawn here for its isolated ranges of hills. One displays a breathtaking cultural heritage of paintings, another hides a labyrinthine cave system, and a third – well … the Aha Hills are just there. On the map. In the middle of the Kalahari. Waiting to be visited.

For more information on the science and explorations of this area, interested readers are directed to numerous articles in *Botswana Notes and Records*, some of which are noted in *Appendix 3, Further information*.

WHERE TO STAY You can camp at the Tsodilo Hills, the Gcwihaba Caverns and the Aha Hills (see the relevant sections later in this chapter for details), but if you're looking for something that's arguably even more isolated, then there is a small camp a couple of hours' drive west of Gumare that could fit the bill.

Gidichaa [map 354] (4 tents, camping) m 7431 0014; e nick@gidichaa.com; www. gidichaa.com; ✪GIDICH 19°27.273'S, 21°46.273'E. Tucked about as far away as would seem possible in the Kalahari bush, Gidichaa operated as a hunting camp for a couple of years before re-opening for photographic visitors in 2011. To get there, turn off the main tarred road about 16km south of Gumare (✪ GIDITO 19°29.983'S, 22°07.150'E) & follow the cutline due west for almost 38km to another sign; turn right here, & in just under 10km you'll reach the camp.

Gidichaa is set on an unfenced but private 4km² farm, a former cattlepost that sees a fair amount of wildlife – though most of it is very nervous. Its main *raison d'être*, though, is not wildlife. For several years, owner Bernard Horton lived with the Bushmen at Xai Xai, as chronicled in his book, *My Forever Heartache*. His experience led him to employ groups of Bushmen at Gidichaa on a rotating basis, bringing them in from Xai Xai for limited periods to introduce guests to their age-old traditions. During your stay, this is likely to include finding water, making a fire & (for men) hunting,

while women will learn to gather produce from the bush. In the evening, dancing, storytelling & games are on the agenda, set around a fire at the heart of the camp. During down time, there are bush walks led by Bernard & even game drives; it's all relatively unstructured.

The camp itself is simple, lit in the evening with paraffin lanterns, & with en-suite bucket showers (& flush toilets) for each of the walk-in tents. With twin beds or a magnificent dbl, these are raised on 1m stilts with views seemingly forever across the bush. A high circular structure under a big-top-style roof houses a squashy sofa, the kitchen & a dining table, though dinner – often a traditional meal or a braai – is usually taken under the stars. Height comes too, from a tall viewing platform above a waterhole; sit quietly here & you may spot kudu or elephant coming to drink, or Meyer's parrots in the scrubby trees. Close by, a separate campsite with hot bucket showers, toilets, braai stands & firewood will be ready for 2014. *US$380/532–495/693 pp sharing/sgl inc FB & activities; P1,600 pp sharing FB, exc activities; self-catering P420 pp, camping P180 pp. ⊕ All year.*

TSODILO HILLS (✆ *687 8025, 686 1852; admission P50 pp; camping P130 pp/night; ⊕ 07.30–17.30*) Rising to 400m above the bush-covered undulations of the western Kalahari, the Tsodilo Hills consist of four hills, roughly in a line, with names from San folklore: the Male Hill, the Female Hill, the Child Hill and a smaller unnamed kopje. Highest is the Male Hill, rising to 410m above the surrounding bush, and – at over 1,400m in total – often considered to be the highest point in Botswana. The San believe that the most sacred place in the hills is near the top. Their tradition is that the first spirit knelt on this hill to pray after creating the world, and that you can still see the impression of his knees in the rock there.

BOTSWANA

Tailor-made safaris to the Okavango, Linyanti, Kalahari, Chobe and beyond

SAFARI CONSULTANTS

Individually tailored safaris to East and Southern Africa, with expert advice and personal service

Letaka
SAFARIS
SPREAD YOUR WINGS

Affordable Wildlife Adventures
in Botswana, Namibia, Zambia, Zimbabwe & Mozambique.

Wildlife, Birding & Photographic Safaris to Southern & Central Africa's great destinations.

www.letakasafaris.com   Tel: +267 6800363
e-mail: info@letakasafaris.com
Private Bag 206, Maun, Okavango Delta, Botswana

above	Riding safaris are a great, non-intrusive way to see the Okavango's resident game (JG) page 321
left	A walking safari provides the ultimate adrenalin rush, but it's important to stay safe (AVZ) page 74
below	Game drives in the Okavango Delta give guests an exceptional view of wildlife including herds of elephant (JG) page 320

above	During the rains the desolate Makgadikgadi Pans come to life, with migrating herds of zebra and wildebeest (JG) page 410
right	The Central Kalahari Game Reserve is Africa at its most remote (JG) page 439
below right	Waterlily (*Nymphaea nouchali caerulea*) (TH) page 299
far right	Flame lily (*Gloriosa superba*) (TH)
bottom	Once a vast inland lake, the Okavango Delta swells to three times its size during the dry winter months, creating Africa's biggest oasis, a refuge for everything from waterbirds to elephants (JG) page 259

top   **Crossing to Botswana on the Kazungula ferry** (TH) page 183

above   **Luxury lodges in the Linyanti** (CH) page 243

below   **4x4 crossing a river, Okavango Delta** (TH) page 259

above   An extensive knowledge of their environment helps the San to survive in the arid Kalahari (AVZ) page 26

below   Sporadically inhabited for about 60,000 years, the Tsodilo Hills are one of the world's oldest historical sites (TH) page 374

The Female Hill, which covers almost three times the area of the Male, is a little to its north, but reaches only about 300m above the plain. This is where most of the main rock art sites can be seen. Then there's the Child Hill, 2km further north again, and smaller still at only about 40m high. And another 2.2km northwest of the Child is a yet-smaller kopje that is said by the San to be the first wife of the Male Hill, who was then left when he met the Female Hill.

Archaeologists say that the hills have been sporadically inhabited for about 60,000 years – making this one of the world's oldest historical sites. For only about the last millennium has this included Bantu people; for thousands of years prior to that, the San lived here, hunting, using springs in the hills for water, and painting animals (over 2,000 of them) on the rocks.

For both San and Bantu, the Tsodilo Hills were a mystical place, a 'home of very old and very great spirits' who demanded respect from visitors. As told in *The Lost World of the Kalahari* (essential reading before any visit here; see *Appendix 3, Further information*), these spirits created much trouble for some of the first Europeans to visit – and were still doing so as recently as the 1950s. Long ago it must have been, in van der Post's words, 'a great fortress of living bushman culture, a Louvre of the desert filled with treasure'.

The Tsodilo Hills remain a remarkable place, an important national monument which, in 2001, was declared a UNESCO World Heritage Site. Whilst this should help to safeguard the hills for future generations, I can't visit without wondering what it was like when the San were here. What we regard now as the high art of an ancient people is remarkable, but it's very sad that our understanding of it is now devoid of the meaning and spirituality with which it was once imbued.

Visitors are no longer permitted to explore the Tsodilo Hills alone, but it's still worth spending several days searching out the paintings along the marked trails with a guide. However, after several visits over the years, I am left remembering the captivating feeling of spirituality in the hills far more than simply the images of the paintings, however remarkable. I've known this to disturb some visitors profoundly; they were uneasy to the point of wanting to flee the hills, and couldn't wait to get away, whilst others find the hills entrancing and completely magical.

So if you come here, then do so with respect and take your time – don't just come to tick it off your itinerary and leave.

A word of warning
In *The Lost World of the Kalahari*, you can read Laurens van der Post's story of his first visit to the hills: of how his party ignored the advice of their guide, and disturbed the spirits of the hills by hunting warthog and steenbok on their way. Once at the hills, his companion's camera magazines inexplicably kept jamming, his tape recorders stopped working, and bees repeatedly attacked his group – and the problems only ceased when they made a written apology to the spirits.

So perhaps the spirits here are one more reason why you ought to treat the Tsodilo Hills with the very greatest of respect when you visit them.

Folklore and archaeology
The Tsodilo Hills hold a special spiritual significance for the people of the region, and are of immense archaeological value to the wider world for what can be learned about some of our earliest ancestors.

Folklore
The San believe the hills contain the spirits of the dead, and that their powerful gods live in caves within the Female Hill, from where they rule the world. They believe that these gods will cause misfortune to anyone who hunts or causes death near the hills.

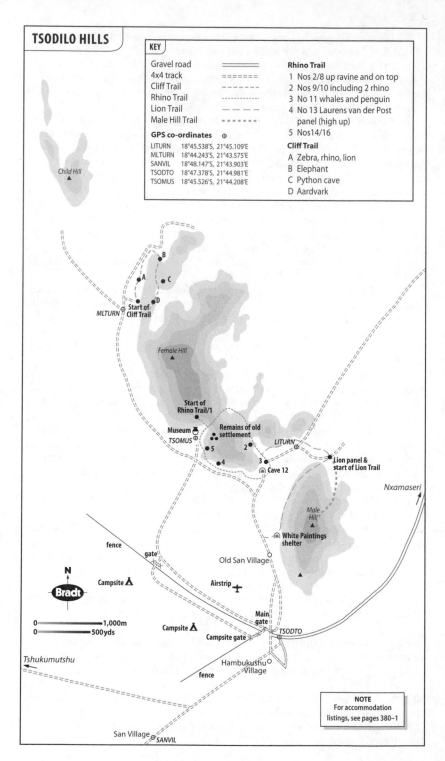

TSODILO HILLS

KEY

Gravel road	————
4x4 track	════════
Cliff Trail	─ ─ ─ ─
Rhino Trail	··········
Lion Trail	— — —
Male Hill Trail	■ ■ ■ ■

GPS co-ordinates ⊕

LITURN	18°45.538'S, 21°45.109'E
MLTURN	18°44.243'S, 21°43.575'E
SANVIL	18°48.147'S, 21°43.903'E
TSODTO	18°47.378'S, 21°44.981'E
TSOMUS	18°45.526'S, 21°44.208'E

Rhino Trail
1 Nos 2/8 up ravine and on top
2 Nos 9/10 including 2 rhino
3 No 11 whales and penguin
4 No 13 Laurens van der Post panel (high up)
5 Nos14/16

Cliff Trail
A Zebra, rhino, lion
B Elephant
C Python cave
D Aardvark

Child Hill ▲

B
A C
D
Start of Cliff Trail
MLTURN ⊕

Female Hill ▲

Start of Rhino Trail/1
Museum
TSOMUS ⊕
5
4
Remains of old settlement
2
3
LITURN ⊕
Cave 12
Lion panel & start of Lion Trail

Nxamaseri ↗

Male Hill ▲

White Paintings shelter

fence
gate
Old San Village

N
Bradt

Campsite ▲

Airstrip ✚

0 ————— 1,000m
0 ————— 500yds

Campsite ▲

Main gate
TSODTO

Campsite gate

Tshukumutshu ←

fence

Hambukushu Village

San Village ⊕ SANVIL

NOTE
For accommodation listings, see pages 380–1

They have many beliefs, all specific to places within the hills. For example, there's a cave on the western side of the Female Hill that contains a permanent source of water and, the San believe, a giant serpent with spiralling horns, like a kudu. If a San guide takes you around the hills, then ask them about legends and stories associated with the places that you visit on the hills.

Meanwhile the Hambukushu people, who also live in the area, believe that God lowered man to earth at the site of the hills, and he landed on the Female Hill. For proof they point to footprints engraved into the rock, high up on the hill. However, modern sceptics claim these are simply natural marks in the rock, or suggest that they might even be the footprints of dinosaurs!

Archaeology Archaeologists think that people (*Homo sapiens* as opposed to *Homo erectus*) have occupied the area for at least 60,000 years. Estimating the age of rock paintings is very difficult, and is usually done by linking a style of painting with nearby artefacts which can be scientifically dated with precision (eg: by carbon-14 dating techniques).

However, the Tsodilo Hills have been the subject of more archaeological research than most of southern Africa's sites – so we do have an idea about the people who lived here. So far, most of the evidence unearthed dates from the Middle Stone Age period. There have been several major excavations, including ones at the Depression Shelter, the Rhino Cave and White Paintings. (See *Appendix 3, Further information* for articles in *Botswana Notes and Records* with more details. There's also a more personal view of a visit to one of these excavations in Mike Main's *Kalahari: Life's Variety in Dune and Delta*.)

Excavations at White Paintings, a site at the base of the Male Hill, indicate habitation going back at least 40,000–50,000 years. For this the archaeological team excavated as deep as 7m below ground level, finding a variety of stone blades and scrapers. It's estimated that over 55% of the raw materials for these tools don't occur in the hills, and must have been brought in from outside. This at least indicates a movement of people, and perhaps early bartering or trading networks.

Excavations at the Depression Shelter certainly indicate that people were using coloured pigments here, probably for painting, more than 19,000 years ago. However, despite what you'll often read, nobody really knows exactly how the artists made their paints. Many things have been suggested, but animal fats and derivatives of plants seem the likely binding agents, probably mixed with pigments obtained largely from ash, various minerals and plant dyes. Iron oxide, in the form of ochre, seems a particularly likely mineral to have been used.

Meanwhile much more recently, about AD800–1000, specularite was being mined here intensively. This mineral was historically used for cosmetic purposes by groups within southern Africa, further emphasising the likelihood of a long-standing trade network that included the people of the Tsodilo.

The paintings The paintings at the Tsodilo Hills chart thousands of years of human habitation, and include some of the world's most important and impressive rock art. Its special nature is augmented by the realisation that these hills are 250km from the nearest other known rock art. They are totally removed from all of southern Africa's other rock paintings. Even within the hills, some of the paintings are located on high, inaccessible cliffs, with commanding views over the landscape. This was surely a deliberate part of the paintings for the people who created them.

Campbell and Coulson, in their excellent book *African Rock Art* (see *Appendix 3, Further information*), assert that the Tsodilo Hills 'contain some 4,000 red finger paintings composed of about 50% animals, 37% geometrics, and 13% highly stylised human figures'.

The paintings belong to several different styles and if you take the time to look closely at them will often amaze you with their detail. Although most of the animals painted are wild, Campbell and Coulson noted that there is a much higher incidence of paintings of domestic stock than at any other similar sites in southern Africa.

The human figures include many schematic men painted with erect penises. It's thought that these could be associated with the trance dance – a traditional dance of the San in which rhythmic breathing often produces an altered state of consciousness.

Geology The Tsodilo Hills are formed from metamorphic rocks that are technically known as micaceous quartzite schists. These started out as shales, probably deposited as mud on the surface of an ancient sea. Great heat and pressure in the earth changed them, and you can see the small crystals of minerals formed during this process if you look carefully.

Tsodilo's schists have particularly high mica and quartz contents, and a coarse-grained surface. Conveniently, this texture means that rocks give a good grip to rubber-soled shoes, so they're relatively easy to clamber around. In many places there are piles of boulders, and you'll often need to hop between these if you want to explore the hills.

There are a few permanent springs of water in the hills, but these are very difficult to find without a local guide. They were certainly important to the early inhabitants of the area though, as they would have been the only water sources for miles around.

Flora and fauna Unlike most destinations for visitors in Botswana, a visit to the Tsodilo Hills really isn't about looking for animals, birds or plants. The focus is much more cultural and historical. That said, don't forget that you are in a very sparsely populated area of the northern Kalahari and there is wildlife around.

On the roads that approach the hills I've been very aware of fresh elephant dung, and fleeting glimpses of occasional fleeing small buck. There are certainly kudu, steenbok and duiker here permanently, as well as leopard and probably spotted hyena.

In his 1934 book *The Mammals of South West Africa* (see *Appendix 3, Further information*), G C Shortridge records that klipspringer were found here at the hills, although I've not come across any reports of them more recently, so it seems unlikely that there is any population of them left now.

Everywhere around the hills you'll find quite a wide variety of birdlife, including the ubiquitous grey hornbills – easily heard as well as seen with their descending call of 'phe, phephee, pheephee, pheeoo, phew, pheeoo-pheeoo' (with thanks to Kenneth Newman – see *Appendix 3, Further information* – for expressing this song so well on paper!).

Look out also for the Tsodilo gecko (*Pachydactylus tsodiloensis*), a small, nocturnal gecko with yellow and brown stripes which is endemic to these hills.

Looking at the vegetation, keep your eyes open for stands of mongongo trees (*Ricinodendron rautanenii*), which occur on the hills and sometimes in pure stands on the Kalahari's sand. These can reach 15–20m in height, and are characterised by smooth, often peeling bark on grey to light-brown stems and compound leaflets a little like the chestnut trees of Europe. After sprays of yellow flowers around October–November, they produce egg-shaped grey-green fruits from February onwards. These can be up to 3.5cm x 2.5cm in size, covered with smooth hairs.

Inside these are mongongo nuts, which can be cracked open to reveal an edible kernel – one of the most important, and celebrated, foods for the San across the Kalahari. Palgrave (see *Appendix 3, Further information*) comments that this is a protected tree in South Africa, and that its light, strong wood is sometimes used as a substitute for imported balsa wood.

Although large animals aren't prolific in this area, there is big game in the bush around the hills, including elephants, so drive carefully when you are in the area.

Getting there and away Access to the Tsodilo Hills was improved immeasurably around 2004 with the construction of a new route from the main Shakawe–Sehithwa road. With a relatively smooth gravel surface, it has cut down driving time during the dry season to about 40 minutes, and in so doing has completely changed the nature of a visit here. After heavy rains, however, the gravel road can become very muddy, so in those conditions you'll need to allow nearer to two hours for the journey. This road is normally accessible by 2WD, but when you arrive at the hills, a high-clearance vehicle may be advisable.

In the past, there were two access routes: both difficult, sandy, 4x4-only routes, taking about 2½–3 bone-shaking hours (mostly in low-range gear) to complete. Both boasted an unusual type of corrugation which made the whole vehicle bounce up and down. Drive faster than about 10km/h and you found your head hitting the ceiling. It was painful, and ensured that getting to the hills was always a long and tedious drive.

Now, however, the bush is gradually reclaiming these old routes, and only the one road in – and out – remains, starting from close to the village of Nxamaseri. The turning off the main road (✪ T2TURN 18°35.834'S, 21°59.986'E) is indicated by a large green signboard that is surprisingly easy to miss, so do keep your eyes open. It's almost 15km south of the Somachima Veterinary Fence (✪ VET-SA 18°29.256'S, 21°55.142'E), or 25km north of the turning to Sepupa. From there the track heads southwest until after 34.4km it reaches a right turning clearly signposted 'Tsodilo 5km' at ✪ TSODTO 18°47.378', 21°44.981'E. This leads after just 0.4km to the main entrance gate to the hills (✪ TSGATE 18°47.275'S, 21°44.856'E), kitted out in the smart green livery of the hills.

Hitchhiking I wouldn't try to walk or hitchhike here, though we know of one intrepid hiker who made it from Maun to the Tsodilo Hills in October 2013. With more animals around than vehicles, and searing daytime temperatures with little shade, his experience must have been unpleasant at best.

By air There's a bush airstrip at the hills, so it's quite possible (albeit at significant cost) to charter a plane to get you here from Maun or elsewhere in the region. However, once on the ground you'll need a 4x4 to get to the base of the hills, and to the start of the various walking trails, which would need to be organised in advance – perhaps with one of the lodges along the Panhandle if you're staying with them.

Approaching from the air you'll appreciate the hills' uniqueness within the desert, though you'll miss the excitement as they're first sighted over the treetops.

Getting organised Access to the hills is now firmly controlled, with all visitors passing through the entrance gate, where you'll pay your entrance fees. Management of the site was recently handed over to the community, and the increase in fees has been significant – but at least it is now the local people who benefit from the extraordinary heritage that is on their doorstep.

Whereas once the hills were a place to explore for yourself, preferably with a local guide, nowadays you must hire a **guide** – either at the entrance gate or by the parking area, where picnic benches are laid out in the shade. The cost varies depending on the trail, so do give yourself plenty of time to investigate each of the paintings as you go; two hours is probably about average, but you may wish to take longer. Some of the guides are truly excellent, while others are less well qualified, so if you're genuinely interested in understanding more about the hills, it may be well to ask a few salient questions before you agree on a guide.

Next to the parking area you'll find a small **museum** (⊕ TSOMUS 18°45.526'S, 21°44.208'E) – currently more a series of contemplative thoughts about the hills than an exhibition of artefacts, but interesting nonetheless. This is where you'll pay for your guide, and can also buy cold drinks, and a small selection of handmade jewellery. A large ablution block contains not just toilets, but showers, too – useful for sluicing off the inevitable dirt that will have accumulated if you've tackled one of the more arduous trails (though there are no towels). For the trails themselves, do wear good, strong shoes or boots, and take a hat, suncream and plenty of water. A walking pole might be a useful extra.

Most visitors spend their time on Female Hill, and may visit the Male. Without a special permit, visitors are not allowed to the Child Hill or the kopje beyond, to which there are no vehicle tracks. Ideally, plan your day to start walking as early as possible – which given that the park gates don't open until 07.30, will not be much before 08.00. Campers, though, can gain a good half an hour on this, which is well worthwhile to avoid walking in the heat of the day.

 Where to stay There is talk of a new tented camp opening at the hills, but for now, your options are limited to camping.

Until recently, there were several individual campsites scattered among the hills, some of them within easy walk of the paintings themselves. Then in June 2013, all these sites were closed, and camping came under the control of the Tsodilo Community Trust. Now there are six new sites, all corralled into one very large

---

GUIDES OF THE FUTURE?

Some years back, before there were any organised guides to the hills, I drove to the San village of Hambukushu – which had been moved from its old location between the hills to a new location (⊕ SANVIL 18°48.147'S, 21°43.903'E) about 3.8km south-southwest of there, well away from the hills. With sign gestures and improvisation, I tried to ask for a guide. The man of the family that I was speaking to eventually sent me off with two of the children, a boy called Xashee, aged 10, and a girl called Tsetsana, aged 16.

At first I thought that I'd been fobbed off with the children, who were silent in the presence of their family. However, as soon as we got into our car to drive back to the hills, it transpired that Tsetsana was on holiday from school, and spoke excellent English. Her brother spoke much less to us, but seemed to know more of the sites with rock art. They bounded up the hills with bare feet, faster than we could in walking boots. They knew their way about very well and although we only followed on the 'standard' trails, we would have missed many of the paintings without their help.

Perhaps these children, or their friends, are among the guides who show people around the hills today.

open area, with a rather over-the-top entrance gate (⊕ *07.00–16.30*) exclusively for campers. You'll find this gate, clearly proclaiming 'Tsodilo Community Trust Campsite', at right angles to the main gate to the hills. If you're camping, you can pay both your camping and entry fees here, and will be told more or less where to pitch your tent. There's also a craft shop to the side of this gate, though when we visited it was firmly closed.

The pitches themselves are only roughly demarcated, and quite far apart, so unless it's busy it's really a question of finding one that you like. Four of them – the Mopororo (⊕ MOPORO 18°47.194'S, 21°44.406'E), Dimbo, Dimbo da diwe and Aininai sites – are only about 1km from the gate, sharing a small modern ablution block that would be fine if the goats would stay out and the local baboon population wasn't so intent in turning on the taps. The pitches themselves have a standpipe for water, and a firepit, so it's all fairly civilised.

Further away, another two further pitches – known as the Quakashu and Dibongo sites – are designated as 'dry': they have no water supply, so you'll need to be entirely self-sufficient (though there's nothing to stop you filling up your water containers on your way past the other pitches).

Wherever you camp, do be aware that you might find cattle around, which one reader has warned us can be fairly aggressive.

Having paid their entry fees along with the camping fee, campers have their own entrance to the hills – a gate in the fence (⊕ CAMPGT 18°46.653'S, 21°43.952'E) that separates the two parts of the site. From the ablution block to the gate it's about 2km, then a further 2.4km from the gate to the parking area. Thus as a camper, you can be at the museum and ready to start on one of the trails slightly earlier than those driving in. There's no great advantage in this except when it's very hot – when the earlier your start, the more pleasant it will be exploring the trails.

The trails Visitors have the option of four trails on the hills: the Rhino Trail, the Cliff Trail, the Lion Trail and the Male Hill Trail. References to other trails, however enticing, are irrelevant: you are no longer permitted to explore beyond these guided routes. The old Divuyu Trail, for example, can be visited only by archaeologists engaged in scientific research.

In theory, guides will tailor your walk as required, taking into account both what you want to see and the level of exertion required. In practice, however, visitors are usually encouraged to take the Rhino Trail, at the north end of the Female Hill, which is the most accessible trail, and features the most well-known paintings.

The notes that follow are from my own and readers' observations. I'm aware they may contain errors as well as omissions, but I hope that they'll spur other readers to explore – and perhaps send me any corrections or additional comments.

Rhino Trail (*P120/guide; approx 2hrs*) This is the only one of the trails that I have walked. In theory it is marked with sequentially numbered posts, though in the lush vegetation of February there were some of these that neither we, nor our young guides, could locate. The original intention was to link these numbers to a series of annotated route plans that were to be written by Alec Campbell, a world-renowned authority on both African rock art and Botswana, and produced by the national museum – but these have been 'in production' for so long that some doubt if they will ever be seen. If you can get hold of one, I'd expect them to be the best guide to the hills.

The trail starts from close to the old Squirrel Valley Campsite (⊕ SQCAMP 18°45.385'S, 21°44.248'E), a short walk from the museum and car park. The numbered posts are clearer at the end of the dry season, and the GPS references here should be a help to make sure you're in roughly the right place, but if your guide doesn't know the trail well, you may still have to search a bit to find the paintings. Note that some of the numbered posts indicate features of archaeological interest, rather than paintings, such as an old waterhole or a place where hunters would have sharpened their spears.

The first marker, **No 1**, sets the scene with a granite rock whose deep grooves suggest that it served for sharpening spears.

Picture 2 (⊕ PICT2 18°45.331'S, 21°44.225'E) is deeper into the ravine and higher up, at an altitude of 1,063m. There's quite a lot of steep rock-hopping to climb up this ravine at the beginning of the trail. It won't be suitable for anyone who is uncomfortable clambering around rocky slopes.

Less than 100m north-northwest of No 2, but higher up again, is **Picture 3** (⊕ PICT3 18°45.291'S, 21°44.239'E), a beautiful silhouette of a rhino that's perhaps 100cm across, with gemsbok below.

By the time you reach **Picture 5**, which includes an impressive giraffe, the trail starts to open out, and you're heading towards the centre of the Female Hill. Here **No 7** marks another spear-sharpening rock on the site of an old San settlement. It's a large, relatively flat and secluded area, where the head of the tribe and his family would have been well protected. Another grooved rock here indicates where tools were sharpened, and the geometric designs painted on the rocks suggest the presence of shaman.

Found under an overhang, **Picture 8** (⊕ PICT8 18°45.150'S, 21°44.576'E) – known as 'the dancing penises' – depicts several men in what is considered to be an initiation ceremony. It lies at an altitude of 1,102m, from where you can see the Male Hill.

Continuing downhill, you'll come to the site of a lower settlement, whose inhabitants' role was to protect the upper settlement from invasion. Here, the white domestic animals of **Picture 9** (⊕ PICT9 18°45.437'S, 21°44.723'E) were created more recently than most of the paintings – around 1,000 years ago. Their chalk-based pigments have survived the elements as they're sheltered beneath a cave overhang. Almost adjacent, the main figures of **Picture 10** consist of two rather beautifully painted rhino, for which the Rhino Trail is named. These are the most famous of Tsodilo's paintings, as they now form the logo of The Botswana Society (see page 114).

Shortly, this trail joins the main track which leads west between the Female and Male hills. Detour to the right of this, and you'll find **Picture 11** (⊕ PICT11 18°45.635'S, 21°44.862'E),which appears to include a penguin and at least one whale. Arguably this is one of the pieces of evidence that indicates that the Bushmen travelled far more widely than is commonly believed, adding weight to Robert Gordon's contention in his *Bushman Myth: The Making of a Namibian Underclass* (see *Further information*, page 504), that our view of the Bushman is often misguided.

This trail then leads around to **No 12** (⊕ CAVE12 18°45.673'S, 21°44.842'E), a large cave at the base of the Female Hill, facing the Male Hill. Known locally as the Makena Cave, it is said to be where a woman who went missing for several months was found, over a thousand years ago. From here there's a short tunnel back to the path, where – if you look up – you'll see an extraordinary rock formation that resembles a three-dimensional map of Africa.

Following the main track north along the west side of Female Hill brings you to **Picture 13** (⊕ PICT13 18°45.627'S, 21°44.436'E). Move closer to the hill here, then look up and slightly back at the hills; there, high up, you'll see what is now known as the 'van der Post panel'. In his inimitable style, Laurens described first seeing this:

Over the scorched leaves of the tops of the bush conforming to a contour nearby, and about a hundred feet up, was a ledge of honey-coloured stone grafted into the blue iron rock. Above the ledge rose a smooth surface of the same warm, soft stone curved like a sea shell as if rising into the blue to form a perfect dome. I had no doubt that I was looking at the wall and part of the ceiling of what had once been a great cave ...

But what held my attention still with the shock of discovery was the painting that looked down at us from the centre of what was left of the wall and dome of the cave. Heavy as were the shadows, and seeing it only darkly against the sharp morning light, it was yet so distinct and filled with fire of its own colour that every detail stood out with a burning clarity. In the focus of the painting, scarlet against the gold of the stone, was an enormous eland bull standing sideways, his massive body charged with masculine power and his noble head looking as if he had only that moment been disturbed in his grazing. He was painted, as only a Bushman, who had a deep identification with an eland, could have painted him.

This footpath, which follows the west side of Female Hill, heads roughly north. Very close to the path, **Picture 14** depicts rhino, warthog and several antelope. Next, less than 400m from the start of the trail, **Picture 15** (✦ PICT15 18°45.556'S, 21°44.361'E) includes lots of very clearly painted giraffe, rhino, gemsbok and other antelope on a wonderfully colourful outcrop of rock.

Finally, just before arriving back at the old Squirrel Valley Campsite, **Picture 16** includes a curious circular design – almost geometrical – that is reminiscent of a shield, the shell of a tortoise or even a wheel; this, like similar earlier paintings, is considered to be a shaman symbol.

Cliff Trail (*P175/guide; approx 3hrs*) This is at the north end of Female Hill, starting near the old Malatso Campsite, which is found by forking right at ✦ MLTURN 18°44.243'S, 21°43.575'E. You'll reach the steep base of the cliffs, about 50m away, where there's a turning circle for vehicles.

The trail circles broadly clockwise around the northern part of Female Hill, before taking a short cut back to near its start over a col.

Reader Jon Williamson walked the Cliff Trail in 2011, and sent us the following report:

The Cliff Trail is fairly similar in appearance to the Rhino Trail, but the path was not as cleared. Some points along the trail were partly obstructed by tree damage caused by elephants. The cliff paintings were as frequent as those found along the Rhino Trail, but not as grandiose: we saw impressions of lion, rhino, zebra, aardvark, elephant and scorpion, as well as some geometric shapes:

zebra	✦ 18°43.917'S, 21°43.734'E
rhino	✦ 18°43.908'S, 21°43.735'E
lion	✦ 18°43.899'S, 21°43.741'E
zebra	✦ 18 43.659'S, 21°43.810'E
elephant	✦ 18°43.669'S, 21°43.880'E
scorpion	✦ 18°43.712'S, 21°43.896'E
ardvaark	✦ 18°44.196'S, 21°43.732'E

The most exciting part of the Cliff Trail was actually just off the trail: a cave (⊕ PYTHCV 18°43.863'S, 21°43.870'E) containing a rock formation shaped like a large snake. Before our trip, we had read that the earliest evidence of practised human rituals was found in a cave in Botswana, so we persuaded our guide to show it to us.

Lion Trail (*P175/guide; approx 2hrs*) This trail stays at ground level, and doesn't include any climbing. It overlaps with some of the Rhino Trail's paintings at the base of the south end of Female Hill, as well as visiting sites on the north side of Male Hill. It starts at the base of the Male Hill, reached by turning off the track between the Male and Female hills at ⊕ LITURN 18°45.538'S, 21°45.109'E.

Male Hill Trail (*P175/guide*) Also known as the Summit Trail, this starts from the same place as the Lion Trail, though eventually goes up and over the top of Male Hill, including some strenuous scrambles.

Around the hills Just south of the entrance gate to the hills is a small settlement, **Hambukushu**, with some corrals for animals. Further away, on the way from the main gate to the San Village, a track heads off right, on a northwest bearing of about 305˚. I've followed this for 7–8km, and it remains a good track, which I believe heads for a place called **Tshukumutshu**. I'd welcome more information on it if readers have gone further.

AHA AND GCWIHABA (*Admission P60 pp; camping P30 pp/night*) Over 150km southwest of the Tsodilo Hills lies an even more remote area, populated by scattered San villages and dotted with a number of hills. This is one of the most remote areas of the Kalahari, and it attracts the most experienced bush travellers simply 'because it's there'. This is expedition territory, best reserved for those who are well equipped and bush-wise.

Most go to visit the Aha Hills, which straddle the border with Namibia, and the nearby Gcwihaba Hills, which contain the well-known Gcwihaba (or Drotsky's) Caverns. These are easily located, not commercialised and fascinating to visit.

In reality, though the Gcwihaba Caverns are the only cave system here that's practical for most visitors to see, there are a number of others in the area which have been unearthed by local scientists in the last few decades. The locations of these are usually kept secret to avoid visitors damaging them or having a serious accident (which would be all too easy).

Geology and geography Turning east from Tsau, you'll soon start to notice the road's gentle decline. It's entering the Gcwihaba Valley, a fossil river valley which may have been an ancient extension of the Okavango Delta. Within this, a group of six low hills protrude above the sand and rise to a maximum of 30m above the surrounding valley. (Compare this with the Male Hill at Tsodilo, which reaches 410m.) About 40–50km northwest of these, the Aha Hills share a very similar geology and appearance.

All of these low hills are made almost exclusively of dolomite marble which, early in its formation, is thought to have been steeply folded, causing many of its strata to stand vertically. It's estimated to be about 800–1,000 million years old.

This rock has been weathered into a very jagged, sharp surface and many loose blocks which aren't always easy underfoot. Underneath, numerous faults and fractures split it. When weathered it appears a grey colour, but if you break it you'll find a pearly-white colour inside. There are occasional bands of muscovite in the marble, and beds of more recent limestone and calcrete.

About 15–20km southwest of the Gcwihaba are the Koanaka Hills. These are similar in geological origin, but essentially inaccessible to visitors. There has been some recent exploration of these (see *Discovery and Exploration of Two New Caves in the Northwest District*, in *Appendix 3, Further information*). One of them – called the 'blue cave' – is Botswana's largest cave complex found to date.

Formation of the caves Like many cave systems in the world, the Gcwihaba Caverns have been formed by the action of acidic groundwater flowing down through the faults in the rock. This gradually dissolves the alkaline limestone over the centuries. Some of this limestone has been redeposited as stalagmites and stalactites.

That said, this simple and quite standard explanation for the cave formation doesn't entirely explain why the cave system is more or less horizontal throughout. (It has northeast and southeast entrances, and appears to have had two levels at different times.) Because of this, Cooke and Baillieul note (see *Appendix 3, Further information*) that from the size of the caves and passages, it seems likely that very large volumes of groundwater must have moved within the rock here – perhaps an underground course of the old Gcwihaba River. This would explain the sheer size of some of the caves.

For that to have been the case, the area's water table must have been much higher for at least one period historically, and probably two. After these levels had subsided, and the caves emptied of water, then stalagmites and stalactites would have been formed gradually by a trickle-through of more moderate volumes of water (eg: rainfall) through faultlines.

History Though people have occupied the area for at least 12,500 years, it doesn't seem as if the caves were used extensively. Excavations in Gcwihaba Caverns (in 1969 by Yellen *et al*; see *Appendix 3, Further information*) did find evidence of charcoal, ostrich eggshell and bone fragments, thought to be the remnants of human occupation, but the finds were limited and there is no rock art here at all.

These caves were first brought to the attention of the outside world in June 1932 when the local !Kung people showed the cave to a farmer from Ghanzi, Martinus Drotsky. Hence for many years this was known as Drotsky's Cave. (As an aside, Martinus was the grandfather of Jan Drotsky, who currently runs Drotsky's Cabins, near Shakawe.)

The local !Kung refer to these hills as '/twihaba' – hence the hills, and main cave and this cave system, are now usually referred to as the Gcwihaba Hills and Caverns respectively (although you'll see this spelled in a variety of ways in various publications).

The hills and caverns were declared a national monument in 1934 and the Director of the Bechuanaland Geological Survey visited the caverns with Drotsky in 1943. The first cave survey was undertaken in 1970 by a school group from Falcon College in Zimbabwe (then Rhodesia). Various scientific explorations and surveys have been done since then, including an expedition in 1991 by the British Schools Exploring Society (now BSES Expeditions).

Nowhere else in this area has had as much time or attention given to it as the Gcwihaba Caverns, though the two sinkholes in the Aha Hills have been surveyed on at least two occasions.

The people The people of the area are mostly Ju/'hoansi Bushmen, together with a few Herero (Mbanderu). Because of the lung disease that swept through this area of the country and the subsequent eradication of cattle here in the late 1990s,

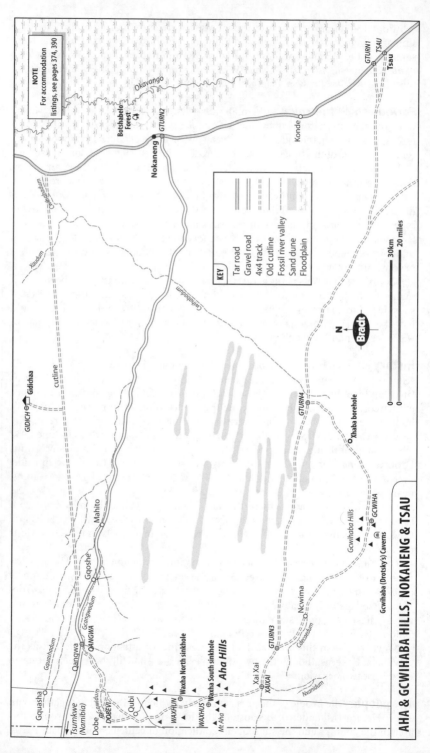

AHA & GCWIHABA HILLS, NOKANENG & TSAU

KEY

Tar road
Gravel road
4x4 track
Old cutline
Fossil river valley
Sand dune
Floodplain

NOTE
For accommodation
listings, see pages 374, 390

Okavango

Botshabelo
Forest

GTURN2

Nokaneng

Konde

GTURN1 TSAU
Tsau

Gqashadum

Xaudum

GIDICH Gidichaa

cutline

Gwihabadum

Gquashadum

Gquashadum

Gcangwadum

Gcangwadum

Tsumkwe
(Namibia)

Gquasha

Qangwa

QANGWA

Dobe

Gcwidum

DOBEYI

Qubi

Gqoshe

Mahito

GTURN4

Xhaba borehole

Aha Hills

WAXHUN

Waxha North sinkhole

WAXHUS

Waxha South sinkhole

Mt Aha

Xai Xai

XAIXAI

Nxanidum

GTURN3

Gckcedum

Ncwima

Gcwihaba Hills

GCWIHA

Gcwihaba (Drotsky's) Caverns

N

Bradt

0   30km
0   20 miles

work patterns have changed. Thus many people are employed by branches of the government, working to clear roads and similar public works.

A particularly detailed and interesting article on the community in the Xai Xai area, with details from a study there, can be found at www.kalaharipeoples.org/documents/Ju-pap.htm.

Flora and fauna Though visits to this part of the Kalahari are usually for caves and culture, there is some wildlife around. As with most places in the Kalahari, this area is at its most beautiful and the flora and fauna are at their most vibrant during and shortly after the summer rains (January to about April).

Flora This classic Kalahari environment is dominated by the silver terminalia (*Terminalia sericea*), identified by the silvery sheen on its blue-grey leaves and the Kalahari appleleaf (*Lonchocarpus nelsii*). You'll also find some bushwillows (*Combretum callinum*) and wild seringa bushes (*Burkea africana*).

Raisin bushes (*Grewia flava*) are here accompanied by sandpaper raisin bushes (*Grewia flavescens*) and the false sandpaper raisin bushes (*Grewia retinervis*). Rub a leaf of either of the latter between your fingers and you'll soon realise how they got their common names.

One tree worth noting here is the Namaqua fig (*Ficus cordata*). This is well known throughout the central highlands of Namibia and down to the Cape – but otherwise unrecorded in Botswana. Here you'll find it growing all over the hills, its roots often flattened against the rocks. Several strong specimens grow around the entrances to the Gcwihaba Caverns, green and thriving even during the dry season, perhaps due to the cooler, moister microclimate in the air of the caves.

Similarly, the mopane aloe (*Aloe littoralis*) is found here and throughout Namibia, but nowhere else in northern or central Botswana. It's a striking plant with a single, vertical stem, succulent leaves with serrated edges and a flower head that branches into pointed spikes of red flowers.

All around the region you'll certainly find the Devil's claw creeper (*Harpogophytum procumbens procumbens*). Recognise it by its pinky-mauve flowers with a hint of yellow in the centre in January to March, and after that its small but wicked oval fruit that has hooks on all sides – like some tiny medieval jousting ball with grappling hooks. (This could be confused with the large Devil's thorn, *Dicerocaryum eriocarpum*, which has a brighter pink flower but a much less elaborate fruit.)

The Devil's claw is found all over the Kalahari, but has recently been in demand from overseas for its medicinal properties. Extracts of this are variously claimed to aid in the treatment of intestinal complaints, arthritis and many other ailments. Hence anywhere near a centre of population is likely to be largely devoid of these plants, but in the more remote areas of the Kalahari you'll often find it beside the sandy track.

GPS REFERENCES FOR AHA & GCWIHABA HILLS MAP (opposite)			
DOBEVI	19°34.830'S, 21°04.428'E	QANGWA	19°31.868'S, 21°10.281'E
GCWIHA	20°01.250'S, 21°21.230'E	TSAU	20°10.294'S, 22°27.265'E
GTURN1	20°07.047'S, 22°22.291'E	WAXHUN	19°43.532'S, 21°03.489'E
GTURN2	19°39.577'S, 22°11.010'E	WAXHUS	19°46.643'S, 21°02.518'E
GTURN3	19°54.286'S, 21°09.418'E	XAIXAI	19°52.867'S, 21°04.934'E
GTURN4	19°57.556'S, 21°44.541'E			

13

Fauna Big game is present throughout this area, but it's relatively scarce especially near to settlements where you're more likely to come into contact with dogs and domestic stock. That said, gemsbok, springbok, eland, steenbok, duiker and kudu all occur in the area. Veronica Roodt reports seeing six very relaxed wild dog near the entrance to Gcwihaba Caverns, and there are also occasional lion, leopard, cheetah and spotted hyena around. Hence there must be a reasonable population of their antelope prey – even if these seem elusive due to the relatively thick vegetation, and lack of waterholes at which they might gather and be more easily spotted.

Given the huge distances that elephant can cover, and the spoor that I've seen near the Tsodilo Hills, I wouldn't be surprised to find lone bulls wandering around during the wet season. Drivers, be warned.

If approaching this area then, whilst looking for big game, don't forget the smaller stuff. Small seasonal pans will fill with a noisy mélange of bullfrogs which have spent the dry season underground, attracted by the water and the number of grasshoppers and crickets around.

There's no better time to see plenty of small reptiles, from the Kalahari serrated tortoise, with its bold, geometric patterns, to the flapnecked chameleon. Around sunset, and for the first few hours after that, listen out for the *click-click* of the barking gecko, sometimes described as like rattling a box of matches. The onomatopoeic name 'Aha' is said to come from the sound made by these often-unseen residents.

Inside the Gcwihaba Caverns is a different story. Some of the earlier scientists to visit the cave noted that leopard inhabited it, and found fresh spoor. Meanwhile, its name derives from the !Kung word for 'hyena's hole'. Whilst I don't know of any more recent visitors who have come across large predators in here, you can't help but notice the bats! These can be noisy and smelly, but are otherwise harmless.

The most common species here is probably the insectivorous Commerson's leaf-nosed bat (*Hipposideros commersoni*). These are the largest insectivorous bats in southern Africa which, although they only grow to a weight of about 120g, can have a wingspan as large as 60cm. These have short, pale fawn-coloured hair all over, and black feet. Males have distinctive tufts of white fur on their shoulders. These are the bats that leave the caves in large numbers at dusk.

Also found in numbers are the tiny Dent's horseshoe bat (*Rhinolophus denti*), which weigh a mere 6g and measure about 7cm long, with a wingspan of 20cm, when fully grown. Horseshoe bats like this are identified because of complex 'nose-leaf' structures on their face between their mouths and their foreheads (used to locate their insect prey using the animal equivalent of radar).

A third common bat here is the Egyptian (also called 'common') slit-faced bat (*Nycteris thebaica*), which is easily identified by its long, rounded ears and the 'split' running down the centre of its face. They fly efficiently but relatively slowly, eat insects, and grow to about 10cm long with a wingspan of about 24cm.

Given the presence of these bats, it's quite likely that they support a small ecosystem of invertebrates in the caves. In similar caves in Namibia, several hundred kilometres to the west of here, scientists have recently also discovered small but highly poisonous spiders. So tread carefully...

Birdlife As with anywhere in the Kalahari, the birds here can either survive without drinking water, or will routinely fly long distances to find it every day. Guineafowl and red-billed francolin are very common, though coqui and crested francolin do also occur. Sandgrouse are common, particularly the namaqua and double-banded species, though you'll also find Burchell's and, occasionally, the yellow-throated varieties. Doves are here too, with Cape turtle, laughing and namaqua species always around.

The area's LBJs ('little brown jobbies', as keen birdwatchers refer to the plethora of smaller, brown birds whose similarities tax their identification skills) include chestnut-backed finchlarks, sabota larks and penduline tits.

Larger and more visible birds, which are easier to spot and identify, include double-banded coursers, and black-bellied and red-crested korhaans. Both of these korhaans show interesting displays during the mating season. You may also come across the world's heaviest flying bird, the kori bustard, and ostriches are not unknown, though they are very uncommon.

Of the raptors, by far the commonest is the pale chanting goshawk, which is usually seen perching atop a bush, small tree or post, surveying the area. When disturbed it'll usually swoop off, flying low, to a similar perch not far away. The very similar, but slightly larger, dark chanting goshawk may also be found here, on the edge of its range. (These are distinguishable in flight, from above, as the pale variety has a white rump, whereas the dark chanting goshawk has a darker colouring and a darker, barred rump.)

Getting organised To get the best out of such an experience, you're probably wisest to come here with an experienced mobile-safari operator who – and this is vital – knows the village and villagers well. They'll also know what's possible, whilst the community benefits in just the same way. Operations who may be able to help include Maun Rest Camp Safaris (see page 178). This will be more costly than trying to do something yourself, but probably much more satisfactory.

The only alternative (since I'm not aware of any landing strips in this area) is to drive yourself, with at least one fully equipped 4x4, and with all your food and water. Although water is usually available at Xai Xai Village, and basic supplies may be found both there and at Qangwa, it's better to bring with you everything that you might need.

As with any tracks in the Kalahari, and especially those that are rarely used, a major danger is fire caused by grass seeds and stems blocking up your vehicle's radiator, or collecting near its exhaust system. If you're driving here, especially during the first few months of the year, you must take steps to prevent this (see *Chapter 6*, page 136).

To explore the caves you'll need several good torches, plus extra batteries and bulbs (a fail-safe emergency back-up is essential, as there's no-one here to help you), and perhaps a lighter or matches. A large ball of string would also be handy to prevent you getting lost.

Getting there and away There are two roads which head west from the main Shakawe–Sehithwa road, the A35, and then loop around and join up with each other around the Aha Hills. Both are very long, very sandy and very hard-going – though of the two, the better is said to be the longer, more northern route – especially after heavy rain. Either way, navigation is reasonably straightforward, and a 4WD remains essential.

The northern route About 300m north of the centre of Nokaneng there's a track heading west (⊕ GTURN2 19°39.577'S, 22°11.010'E). This is the longer of the two routes, but the surface is now gravel, so although it can still be heavy going, it's usually the easier option. From here to Xai Xai, you can expect the drive to take about three–four hours.

From Nokaneng, the road twists and turns quite a lot but after a little over 120km, or around three hours, you'll reach the tiny village of **Qangwa** (⊕ QANGWA 19°31.868'S, 21°10.281'E), sometimes spelled 'Xangwa', or even 'Gcangwa', which supports a small shop.

From Qangwa the gravel road continues west towards Namibia, ultimately to Tsumkwe (⊕ TSUMKW 19°35.507'S, 20°30.184'E). For the hills, take the track that leads southwest for over 10km to another small village, Dobe (⊕ DOBEVI 19°34.830'S, 21°4.428'E). From there the track picks its way through the Aha Hills, heading due south. It passes west of the small group of hills which contain Waxhu North Cave (⊕ WAXHUN 19°43.532'S, 21°3.489'E), and east of the main range of hills, within which is found the Waxhu South Cave (⊕ WAXHUS 19°46.643'S, 21°2.518'E). Finally it reaches the village of **Xai Xai** (⊕ XAIXAI 19°52.867'S, 21°04.934'E) after about 37km.

In some literature you'll find this designated as Nxainxai, CaeCae or, more recently, /Xai/Xai. However you want to spell it, this is one of the largest villages in the area, with a population of about 300–400 Ju/'hoansi San people, and perhaps 50 Herero (Mbanderu) people, who are mostly cattle farmers. The village has a borehole, a small school, a basic health post and a few shops. The airstrip here was being upgraded in 2013.

From Xai Xai the route turns east, becoming the southern route described below which ultimately ends on the main road near Tsau. About 10km east of Xai Xai you pass a clear right turn (⊕ GTURN3 19°54.286'S, 21°9.418'E) to the Gcwihaba Hills and Cave (⊕ GCWIHA 20°01.250'S, 21°21.230'E), a distance of almost 30km.

The southern route A large banner on the side of the road some 10km north of Tsau (⊕ GTURN1 20°07.047'S, 22°22.291'E) clearly marks the correct path to follow for the southern route. This is the shortest route to the hills and caves – but note that it can become a quagmire if there has been very heavy rain in the area.

During the dry season, the first few hours from Tsau are generally fairly easy driving, as the hard, compacted track gently descends into the fossil river valley. However, during the rains a number of wide, shallow pans hold water here, turning it into a series of connected mud-holes and a challenging route even for experienced drivers. After that, the country becomes rolling duneland with thick sand, which is slow going but not as treacherous as the mud.

About 90km from Tsau there's a left turning (⊕ GTURN4 19°57.556'S, 21°44.541'E). This passes the Xhaba borehole, a satellite cattle post of Xai Xai village, after about 26km, and then reaches the hills another 26km later. It's the quickest way to the hills. If you miss this turn-off then continue on to the main turning (⊕ GTURN3 19°54.286'S, 21°9.418'E) used by the northern route, above, and take a left there. This is over 150km from Tsau.

Where to stay There is a rudimentary campsite at the Aha Hills, and three sites at Gcwihaba. Since these are not signposted, it's best to contact the warden, Eric Keharara (m *7375 6518;* e *ekeharara@yahoo.com*), either in advance or when you get to Xai Xai. He can then direct you to the appropriate site – and collect your camping and entry fees.

Note that there is no water (the nearest is at Xai Xai), nor any other facilities, including toilets, so it's vital that you bring everything that you need with you, and take away all of your rubbish (or at least everything that cannot be burned and reduced to ash). Take a spade, so you can bury your waste deeply, and always burn your toilet paper.

Aha Hills About 40–50km northwest of the Gcwihaba Hills, and visible from them, is a range of low, rounded hills: the Aha Hills. These straddle the Botswana–Namibia border, and are among the most remote and little-visited destinations in Botswana.

Like the Gcwihaba Hills, this range is made of dolomite marble that has been split by weathering into numerous faults and fractures. This presents a very jagged surface, with many loose blocks underfoot, and isn't easy to walk on.

The range covers about 245km², most of which is in Botswana, and very little of which has been properly mapped or documented. That said, it's interesting to note that on the Namibian side the range is much easier to reach than the hills in Botswana, being only about 20km from the good, gravel road which links Tsumkwe to Gam.

Exploring the hills In some ways the hills are attractive simply because they're so remote. Even though there are now designated campsites, this is a place that few visitors ever get to.

Clambering around isn't as much fun here as in the Tsodilo Hills, simply because the rock surface is totally different. Instead of large boulders with an even surface and an easy grip, the Aha Hills are made of endless jagged little blocks. So if you do come here, stout walking shoes with strong soles make clambering around a lot easier.

Two sites on the Botswana side have attracted some interest, and both are sinkholes – large holes in the ground. The local people apparently know both simply as 'Waxhu', which means 'house of god'. Both can only be visited using specialist climbing/caving equipment, so don't be tempted to try and climb down. There are no mountain-rescue teams in Botswana!

Waxhu Cave (north; ✪ WAXHUN 19°43.532'S, 21°03.498'E) was first described in 1974 and is about 70m deep.

Waxhu Cave (south; ✪ WAXHUS 19°46.632'S, 21°02.518'E) is also known by some of its recent visitors as 'Independence Cave', because they first visited it on the fifth anniversary of Botswana's independence. This cave is about 50m deep.

Botswana Notes and Records (see *Appendix 3, Further information*) records many more details on these sinkholes, including rough maps of them and information about the various expeditions that have explored them recently.

Gcwihaba Hills and Caverns The low, rounded hills here are not the attraction, but beneath them is a labyrinth of passages and caves, some with enchanting rock formations of stalagmites, stalactites and spectacular 'flowstones' which seem like waterfalls of rock.

Some of these chambers reach up to 10m in height, whilst other passages are so narrow that you'll need to clamber and squeeze through. All were formed by the dissolving and depositing action of acidic water on the limestone of the rocks around, though now the caves are totally dry.

A recent initiative has seen the introduction of a new museum at Gcwhibaba, backed by the Botswana Department of Tourism.

Exploring the caves There are two main entrances to the caves, about 250m apart, each marked with a monument. Although there is a route between them, it's not straightforward or obvious, so getting through may tax your map-reading skills. (You won't be able to rely on your beloved GPS either, as they're useless under the rock ceilings of the caves!) There are lots of dead ends, closed-off passages and caverns to penetrate. If your curiosity flags, then remind yourself of the legend

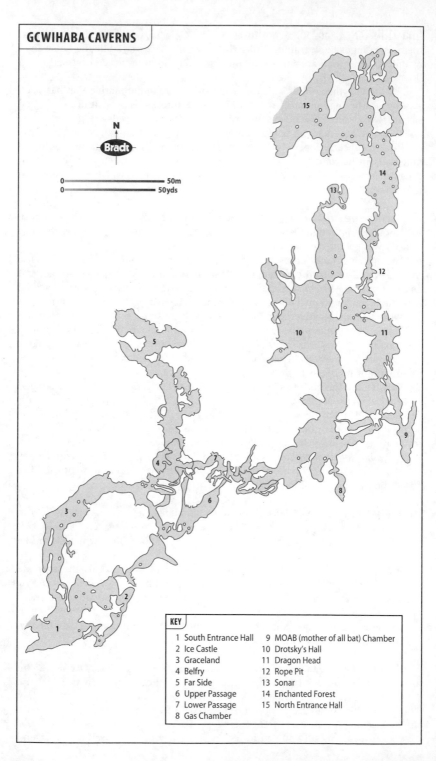

GCWIHABA CAVERNS

N

Bradt

0 ———————— 50m
0 ———————— 50yds

of Hendrik Matthys van Zyl, the wealthy founder of Ghanzi, who is said to have stashed a portion of his fortune here in the late 1800s.

Most of the caves are on one level, though there is a section, slightly nearer to the south entrance than the north, where several of the corridors split into two different levels, one raised several metres above the other. You can expect a considerable amount of bat guano underfoot, but at least the complete lack of natural light means that you shouldn't need to worry about snakes.

Start exploring the caves from the main (north) entrance. Here, on one of the large boulders towards the right of the main entrance hall, you'll find the inscription 'Discovered 1 June 1932, M Drotsky'.

You'll also realise that a string marks a route through the caves. Given how easy it is to get lost in here, this can be very comforting. It starts at the lower entrance, and proceeds down an increasingly steep and narrow passageway. There's a short vertical climb down into what's been christened the 'rope pit', before you emerge up the other side on to a shelf. Then it's a bit of a squeeze before you find yourself in a large chamber.

From here the route basically climbs, though there are lots of side-passages to distract you, and part way through is where there are two different levels to the passages. You'll also come across the chambers with bats in them, deep within the cave complex, before finally emerging from the southern entrance (where there's a ledge that is now used as a roost by a resident barn owl).

14

The Kalahari's Great Salt Pans

The great salt pans lie in the heart of the northern Kalahari, forming an area of empty horizons into which the blinding white expanse of the pans disappears in a shimmering heat-haze. In winter, dust devils whirl across the open plains; in summer many become undulating seas of grasses beneath the turbulence of the stormy skies. It is a harsh, spare landscape, not to everybody's taste, but it offers an isolation as complete as anywhere in southern Africa, and a wealth of hidden treasures for those prepared to make the effort – including Stone Age ruins and prehistoric beaches.

The wildlife is rich, but highly seasonal and nomadic. At times you'll find great concentrations of plains game, with all their attendant predators, and, in good years, spectacular breeding colonies of flamingos crowd the shallow waters of Sua Pan. At other times the stage seems empty. But even then, there is always a cast of smaller Kalahari residents behind the scenes – from coursers and korhaans to mongooses and mole-rats.

BACKGROUND INFORMATION

ORIENTATION The tarred Nata–Maun road bisects this barren region. To the south of this lie the vast, dry depressions of Sua and Ntwetwe, with their scattered 'islands' of granite and fossilised dunes, fringed by grassland and acacia savannah. To its north is the Nxai Pan complex, including Nxai and Kgama-Kgama pans, now grassed over, and Kudiakam Pan, overlooked by the famous Baines' Baobabs.

Much of the region is unfenced ranching country, where wildlife has largely been supplanted by cattle. However, the fauna and flora are protected in a number of reserves. Makgadikgadi Pans National Park extends south of the Nata–Maun road, between the western shore of Ntwetwe Pan and the Boteti River. Nxai Pan National Park adjoins this to the north of the Nata–Maun road, and includes the Nxai Pans complex and Baines' Baobabs. The much smaller Nata Sanctuary, established to protect the seasonal breeding waterbirds of the Nata River delta, is situated in the northeast corner of Sua Pan. Each of these areas has its own distinct attractions and seasonal peculiarities.

GEOGRAPHY The Magkadikgadi Pans consist of an immense expanse of largely flat and featureless terrain in the north of the Kalahari. The pans themselves are located roughly between the diamond town of Orapa in the south, the village of Nata in the northeast and the Boteti rivercourse in the west. This falls away northwards towards the Mababe Depression and the Chobe–Zambezi river catchment system. At its centre lie two huge adjacent salt pans – Sua (to the east) and Ntwetwe (to the west) – which cover an estimated combined area of roughly

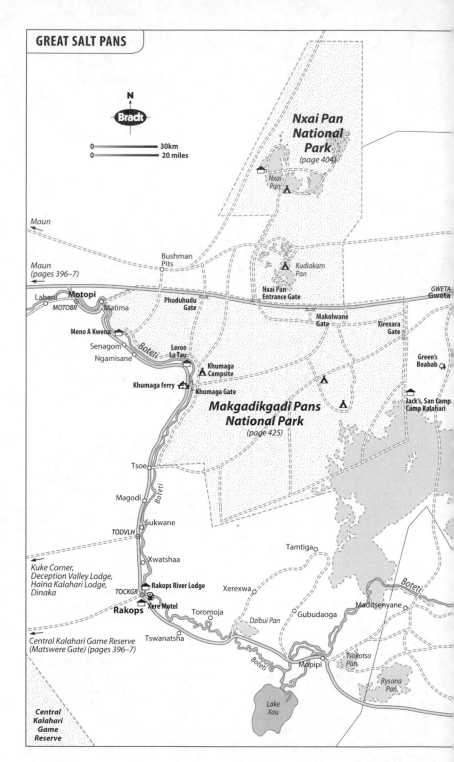

GREAT SALT PANS

N

Bradt

0 ——————— 30km
0 ——————— 20 miles

Nxai Pan National Park (page 404)

Nxai Pan

Maun

Maun (pages 396–7)

Bushman Pits

Kudiakam Pan

Nxai Pan Entrance Gate

GWETA

Labani **Motopi**
MOTOBR
Matima

Phuduhudu Gate

Makolwane Gate

Xirexara Gate

Meno A Kwena

Senagom

Ngamisane

Boteti

Leroo La Tau

Khumaga Campsite

Green's Boabab

Khumaga ferry

Khumaga Gate

Jack's, San Camp Camp Kalahari

Makgadikgadi Pans National Park (page 425)

Tsoe

Boteti

Magodi

TODVLH

Sukwane

Kuke Corner, Deception Valley Lodge, Haina Kalahari Lodge, Dinaka

Xwatshaa

Tamtiga

Boteti

TOCKGR **Rakops River Lodge**

Rakops

Xere Motel

Toromoja

Xerexwa

Gubudaoga

Maditsenyane

Central Kalahari Game Reserve (Matswere Gate) (pages 396–7)

Tswanatsha

Dzibui Pan

Boteti

Tsokotsa Pan

Mopipi

Rysana Pan

Boteti

Lake Xau

Central Kalahari Game Reserve

396

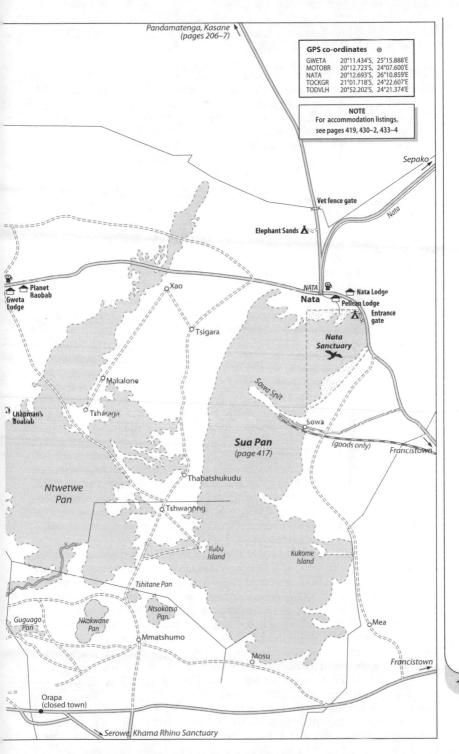

Pandamatenga, Kasane
(pages 206–7)

GPS co-ordinates   ⊕
GWETA   20°11.434'S, 25°15.888'E
MOTOBR   20°12.723'S, 24°07.600'E
NATA   20°12.693'S, 26°10.859'E
TOCKGR   21°01.718'S, 24°22.607'E
TODVLH   20°52.202'S, 24°21.374'E

NOTE
For accommodation listings,
see pages 419, 430–2, 433–4

Sepako

Nata

Vet fence gate

Elephant Sands ⛺

NATA
Nata

Nata

Nata Lodge

Pelican Lodge

Entrance
gate

Planet
Baobab

Gweta
Lodge

Xao

*Nata
Sanctuary*

Tsigara

Makalone

Sowa Spit

Chapman's
Baobab

Tsharaga

Sowa

(goods only)

Francistown

Sua Pan
(page 417)

Thabatshukudu

*Ntwetwe
Pan*

Tshwagong

*Kubu
Island*

*Kukome
Island*

Tshitane Pan

*Guguago
Pan*

*Nkokwane
Pan*

*Ntsokotsa
Pan*

Mea

Mmatshumo

Mosu

Orapa
(closed town)

Francistown

Serowe, Khama Rhino Sanctuary

14

12,000km². Around them are a number of smaller pans, including Nxai Pan to the north and Lake Xau to the south.

GEOLOGY To grasp the complex geology of this area, you really need a broader understanding of the way in which the whole Kalahari was formed (see pages 46–7). In brief, the pans are the desiccated vestiges of the huge superlake which, several million years ago, covered most of central Botswana and moulded the landscape of the entire region. Subsequent climate change, seismic upheavals and the diversion of rivers (the details of which divide geologists) starved this lake of its water supply, shrinking it to today's flat, caustic depressions of grey clay, and withering its surrounding wetlands into arid savannah.

Today the pans receive no more than 400–500mm of rain annually, and have no permanent standing water. After good rains, however, they briefly become shallow lakes again, fed by the seasonal Boteti River from the west – bringing the overspill from the Okavango – and the Nata River from the northeast.

FLORA AND FAUNA The plant and animal life of the region reflects its harsh climate. The plants are hardy and resilient species; the animals comprise either nomadic species that follow the rains in large seasonal movements, or specialised sedentary species adapted to arid Kalahari conditions. Populations fluctuate wildly according to rainfall. Consequently wildlife viewing is a hit-and-miss affair, depending entirely on the time of year and local conditions. However, in the right place at the right time, it can be spectacular, and the wide, open spaces make for excellent visibility.

Flora The flora of the Makgadikgadi Pans region can be graded into a loose series of zones, each determined by the soil in which it grows. At the centre lie the pans themselves: barren, windswept and devoid of any plant life. These sterile, salty dustbowls are surrounded by extensive grasslands which flourish on Kalahari sands, comprising a mixture of salt-tolerant species around the pans, coarse 'finger' grasses across the sandy plains, and nutritious 'sweet grasses' on the margins. The grasslands are punctuated with scattered trees and thickets, consisting primarily of acacia species.

Further from the pans, where the soil has a richer sand and clay mix, this acacia savannah becomes a denser bush, interspersed with other woodland trees, including various combretum and terminalia species. To the north and east, the acacias are replaced by a belt of mopane trees (*Colophospermum mopane*), which flourish on the more heavily clay soils.

To the west, the alluvial soils and hidden water table of the Boteti riverfront support a strip of dense riverine woodland. Here typical Kalahari species, such as camelthorn (*Acacia erioloba*) and blackthorn (*Acacia mellifera*), grow alongside riverine giants such as sycamore figs (*Ficus sycomorus*), sausage trees (*Kigelia africana*) and many of the other riverine species that are usually associated with wetter areas.

Across the region, towering real fan palms (*Hyphaene petersiana*) cluster in elegant, waving stands above the grasslands, forming extensive groves of palm woodland to the west of Ntwetwe Pan. Equally conspicuous are the scattered baobabs, which sprout incongruously around the pans and on isolated rock outcrops, each with centuries of history recorded in its swollen limbs.

Fauna Fossil evidence unearthed on the pans shows that in wetter, prehistoric times, the region supported the whole spectrum of African big game – including abundant elephant, buffalo and rhino. Today, the selection of large mammals is more limited than in the game-rich areas of Moremi and Chobe to the north and west. Rhino had disappeared altogether (though they are once more to be seen in the national park to the west), while elephant and buffalo occur only occasionally, in small numbers on the fringes.

However, the grasslands draw huge herds of grazers, which can, despite recent declines, still rival anything outside Tanzania's Serengeti for sheer numbers. Zebra and wildebeest gather in tens of thousands, supported by smaller numbers of gemsbok, eland and red hartebeest. Movements are unpredictable, but in general the highest concentrations occur in the western Boteti region during the late dry season (August–November) and further north in the Nxai Pan area during the rainy season (December–April).

Hardy springbok are impervious to drought and remain scattered across the grasslands throughout the year. In the Nxai Pans area, the mopane woodland shelters browsers, including impala (which supplant springbok where the bush thickens), kudu, sable and tsessebe. Here, giraffe are common and a few breeding elephant frequent the fringes of the northern pans.

Another pocket of diversity occurs along the Boteti River, where the thicker bush provides cover for grey duiker, bushbuck and waterbuck. Giraffe and elephant also visit this area, while the permanent pools even support a few hippos and crocodiles – emigrants from the Okavango.

A variety of predators prowls the region. Lions generally follow the game, particularly the zebra herds in the Boteti area and the winter springbok in Nxai, but seldom occur on the pans themselves. Cheetah are most often seen around Nxai Pan, while leopard frequent the denser bush of the Boteti waterfront. Spotted hyena keep to the woodland fringes, while the brown hyena – a Kalahari specialist – is found around the pans themselves.

Wild dogs are highly nomadic and, though unusual, can turn up anywhere. Here they are most often seen in the vicinity of Nxai Pan. Smaller predators include bat-eared fox, black-backed jackal, aardwolf, honey badger, African wildcat, small-spotted genet and striped polecat. Yellow mongooses are common on the grasslands, while the slender mongoose prefers acacia thickets.

Without much in the way of fruiting trees, the Makgadikgadi is not a good region for primates – except along the Boteti, where both vervet monkeys and baboons do find food and cover. However, throughout the region the lesser bushbaby, which feeds mostly on insects and acacia gum, thrives in the acacia savannah.

Other mammals of the grasslands include the ubiquitous aardvark and porcupine, and the bizarre spring hare is particularly abundant. Most smaller mammals are nocturnal, allowing them to avoid the high daytime temperatures, when a larger surface area to body ratio quickly causes overheating. On this principle a variety of rodents make their home in burrows and emerge at night, including the desert pygmy mouse, hairy-footed gerbil and Damara mole-rat (see box, page 443).

The black-tailed tree rat avoids the burning sun by hiding in tree holes, and protects the entrance to its lair with a scruffy 'nest' of twigs. At night this species can be seen scampering through the branches of a camelthorn, using its prehensile tail for added agility.

One exception to the nocturnal rule is the ground squirrel, an animal of the deep Kalahari that occurs in the sandy south of the region. This highly sociable rodent can forage in the full glare of the sun by using its tail as a parasol to cast protective shade.

Reptiles and amphibians Further down the evolutionary scale, a variety of reptiles and amphibians thrive in Makgadikgadi's arid expanses, though most pass

14

unseen by the visitor. Acacias, with their deeply fissured bark and abundance of insect prey, provide havens for skinks and geckos above the open grassland. At ground level, the ground agama ambushes termites from a hollow at the foot of a shady bush, while the legless Kalahari burrowing skink swims just below the surface of the sand in search of beetle larvae, and is often found drowned when pans fill up overnight. In sandier areas, barking geckos emerge from their burrows on summer evenings and fill the Kalahari night with their bizarre territorial clicking calls.

Perhaps the highlight of Makgadikgadi's smaller animals is one that few have either heard of or seen: the Makgadikgadi spiny agama (*Agama makarikarica*). This is a small species of the agama family – a lizard – that's endemic to Makgadikgadi. It feeds on termites and beetles, and lives in tunnels at the base of bushes.

The acacia woodland is home to a broad cross-section of typical bushveld reptiles, including monitor lizards (both water and rock), flapneck chameleons and leopard tortoises. Snakes encountered at ground level include black mamba, snouted cobra, African egg-eater, mole snake and the ubiquitous puff adder, while arboreal species such as boomslang and spotted bush snake hunt chameleons and birds' eggs among the thorny tangle.

HIGH-RISE LIVING

The towers of mud built by termites, known as termitaria, are often the only points of elevation for miles across the Makgadikgadi grasslands. Not all termites build mounds – harvester termites (Hodotermitidae), which are common on Kalahari sands, leave little evidence of their underground tunnels above the surface – but those that do, the Macrotermitidae species, are responsible for one of the true wonders of nature.

Communicating entirely through pheromones, millions of blind worker termites can raise several tons of soil – particle by particle – into an enormous structure over 3m high. Below the mound lies the nest, where separate chambers house brood galleries, food stores, fungus combs (where termites cultivate a fungus that can break down plant cellulose) and the queen's royal cell. The queen produces up to 30,000 eggs a day, which means – since she lives for many years – that the millions of inhabitants of the colony are all brothers and sisters.

The whole structure is prevented from overheating by a miraculous air-conditioning system. Warm air rises from the nest chambers, up a central chimney, into thin-walled ventilation flues near the surface (you can feel the warmth by placing your hand just inside one of the upper vents). Here it is cooled and replenished with oxygen, before circulating back down through separate passages into cavities below the nest chambers. Finally, before returning to the nest, it passes through specially constructed cooling veins, kept damp by the termites. In this way, termites maintain the 100% humidity and constant temperature of 29–31°C required for successful production of eggs and young. (These conditions are exploited by monitor lizards, who seal their eggs inside termitaria for safe incubation.)

After the rains, when conditions are right, the queen produces a reproductive caste of winged males and females – known as imagos – who leave the colonies in huge swarms to mate, disperse and establish new nests. Mass termite 'emergences' are one of the bonanzas of the bush, offering a seasonal feast to everything from frogs and spiders to kites, falcons and tawny eagles.

To survive this harsh habitat, many frogs aestivate below ground during the dry season. Giant bullfrogs emerge from their mud cocoons after seasonal rains to take over temporary pans in a frenzy of breeding. These frogs are so aggressive that they have even been observed snapping at lions. The much smaller rain-frogs of the *Breviceps* genus, like the bushveld rain-frog, *Breviceps adspersus*, have toughened feet, evolved for digging their burrows. They also appear with the rains, and gather at the surface during termite emergences, cramming in as many of the hapless insects as time will allow.

Invertebrates The Kalahari teems with invertebrate life. Good years bring swarms of locusts and mass migrations of butterflies to the grasslands, while countless termites demolish and carry away the dead vegetable matter that carpets the ground. Termites are fundamental to the ecology of the region. Not only do they recycle and enrich the soil, but they are also a vital prey species for everything from eagles and aardvarks to skinks and spiders.

There are 14 genera of termites, each of which has a different mode of foraging: harvester termites (Hototermitidae) nest in underground burrows, while Odontoterme termites construct the enormous raised mounds that can be seen for miles across the grasslands – each one a miracle of air conditioning.

Among a multitude of other insects are the wingless tenebrioid beetles, which scuttle rapidly across open ground on long legs and squirt a noxious fluid at attackers. More visible are the chunkier dung beetles, which swarm on strong wings to fresh animal dung, then roll it away and bury it as 'brood balls' in which their eggs are laid and their larvae mature.

On hot summer days, thickets throb with the stridulating calls of cicadas, the adults having only two weeks of life in which to mate and deposit their eggs, after up to 17 years' underground larval development.

Termites and other insects feed a host of invertebrate predators. Sand divers (Ammoxennidae) are small, fast moving spiders that paralyse termites with their venom and bury themselves if disturbed. Golden orbweb spiders (Nephiladae) string their super-strong webs between thorn bushes to ensnare flying insects.

Contrary to popular belief, sun-spiders, or solifuges (Solifugae), are not venomous, but pursue insects at high speed across the ground and despatch them audibly with powerful mandibles. You'll often see these large arachnids running across the ground at night near campfires. Though frightening at first, they're totally harmless and don't bite people!

Not so harmless are the resident scorpions, which detect the vibrations of prey through their body hairs. As a rough rule of thumb for the nervous, species with larger pincers and slimmer tails have less powerful venom than those with smaller pincers and larger tails.

Red velvet mites are parasites on larger invertebrates and often gather in sandy areas in the early morning after rain showers, looking like tiny scarlet cushions. Another tiny parasite, the voracious tampan tick, lurks in the sand beneath camelthorn trees and, chemically alerted by an exhalation of its victim's CO_2, emerges to drain the blood from any unsuspecting mammal that fancies a nap in the shade.

Birdlife The great salt pans region offers several distinct habitats for birds. The open grasslands support typical ground-nesting, arid country species such as coursers, korhaans, sandgrouse, chats, larks and pipits. Both the world's largest bird – the ostrich – and the world's largest flying bird, the kori bustard, strike conspicuous figures in this featureless terrain, while greater kestrels, pale-chanting goshawks, marsh owls and the statuesque secretary bird are among the more common resident predators.

Any isolated stands of trees are beacons for birds: red-necked falcons breed in fan palms, while baobabs provide roosts for owls and breeding sites for hornbills and rollers. Elsewhere, typical arid woodland residents dominate the thicker scrub, including red-billed francolin, grey lourie, fork-tailed drongo, pied babbler, glossy starling, white-browed sparrow weaver and a wide variety of shrikes, barbets, flycatchers, robins, sunbirds, warblers, waxbills and whydahs.

Eagles, including martial and bateleur, roam the skies. Smaller predators such as gabar goshawk and pearl-spotted owl hunt the thorn scrub, and vultures follow the herds across the region, hoping for casualties.

In summer the resident bird population is swelled by a huge influx of migrants drawn to the seasonal bonanza of seeds and insects. Some are non-breeding visitors that come from as far afield as Europe and central Africa. White storks (from Europe) and Abdim's storks (from east Africa) arrive wheeling on thermals to stalk the savannah; carmine and European bee-eaters hawk their insect prey just above the grass; shrikes, including red-backed and lesser grey, claim prominent territories on thorn bushes from where they ambush hapless lizards and grasshoppers.

Other more local breeding visitors include seed-eaters such as wattled starlings, doves, finchlarks, canaries – and the prolific red-billed quelea, whose flocks reach swarm proportions. Migrant raptors are lured by the brief abundance of prey, with many different species – including western red-footed falcons, steppe buzzards, yellow-billed kites and tawny eagles – congregating at mass termite emergences (see page 400).

After good rains, when Ntwetwe and Sua Pans turn briefly into glassy lakes, waterbirds arrive in their thousands. The shallow, saline conditions are ideal for both greater and lesser flamingos, which construct their clay nests under the blazing Kalahari sun and filter-feed on algae and brine shrimps. Meanwhile pelicans, darters, cormorants and ducks flock to the brackish waters of the Nata River delta, in the northeast of Sua Pan. Here, waders such as stilts, sandpipers and avocets forage along the shoreline, while jacanas, pied kingfishers, weavers and bishops frequent the reed beds.

GETTING ORGANISED

Once you leave one of the few main roads in this area, you generally need to be in a self-sufficient 4x4 vehicle. Bringing along all your food and water is always a good idea, as whilst you will find water in some places, there is very little in the way of shops. The few small towns around the pans (see pages 432–7) are good sources of fuel, but in some case supplies may be limited.

If you're venturing off across Makgadikgadi, then you really should take at least two vehicles and have a GPS and a compass; an environment of flat salt without any landmarks at all can be very disorienting, especially during a windstorm. In such a situation, breaking through the pan's crust and getting stuck can create a life-threatening situation.

MAPS The usual 'suspect' – Veronica Roodt's *Shell Tourist Map of Botswana* (page 100) – covers this area well, with a variety of useful GPS points.

If you plan on exploring a lot of the pans, then you should also get hold of a copy of the excellent *African Adventurer's Guide to Botswana*, by Mike Main (see

Appendix 3, Further information). This has a number of carefully described routes through the area, as well as much interesting general information. However, do be aware that tracks can change, so always be vigilant.

BOOKING AND PARK FEES If you want to stay in either of the national parks then you must book ahead for a campsite. See *Chapter 4*, pages 84–7, for details and fees for these national parks.

Similarly Jack's Camp, San Camp and Camp Kalahari should be booked in advance, and it is also advisable to reserve the campsite at Nata Sanctuary. That said, most of Sua and Ntwetwe pans fall outside the control of the authorities, so independent travellers can camp anywhere that appeals – though do first read the notes on safety on pages 137–8.

NXAI PAN NATIONAL PARK

Nxai Pan National Park lies to the north of the Nata–Maun road at the northern fringe of the ancient Lake Makgadikgadi basin. It is contiguous with Makgadikgadi Pans National Park, to the south of this same road. Nxai is probably the easiest area of the pans to drive yourself into, and from December to around July will also have the best game. Add in the spectacular sight of Baines' Baobabs to make a super destination for a three- to four-day self-drive trip.

Note that Nxai is usually pronounced to rhyme with 'high', unless you're familiar with the clicks of the Khoisan languages, in which case the correct pronunciation of the 'x' is actually a palatal click (ie: press tongue against the roof of your mouth, and then move down).

BACKGROUND INFORMATION

Geography The park covers an area of 2,658km², comprising Nxai Pan itself, Kgama-Kgama Pan complex to the northeast, and the Kudiakam Pan complex (including Baines' Baobabs) to the south. The baobabs were added to the original park in 1992.

The pans themselves are ancient salt lakes, ringed to the south and west with thick fossil dunes of wind-blown Kalahari sand. Today they are completely grassed over, but scattered across their surfaces are smaller pans or waterholes that fill up during the rainy season. Two of these are artificially maintained by the park authorities to provide surface water throughout the year, but the watercourses that once fed the area from the northeast have long since dried up.

The park's general topography is flat and featureless, with the famous baobabs being the most striking landmarks, and one of the higher points of elevation. To the north and east the soils become increasingly clayey, supporting the encroachment of mopane woodland and integrating with the dense mopane woodlands of the Chobe–Zambezi river catchment system.

Flora and fauna highlights

Flora The open grassland that covers the pans consists of many palatable 'sweet' grasses (eg: *Themeda* sp), which sustain the large herd of grazers that invade the area in summer. These grasslands are studded with 'islands' of acacias, consisting mostly of candle-pod acacia (*Acacia hebeclada*). This is easily recognised from around October to March, as its seedpods stand upright, like candles. Other very common species here are the umbrella thorn (*Acacia tortilis*) and bastard umbrella thorn (*Acacia leuderitzii*).

14

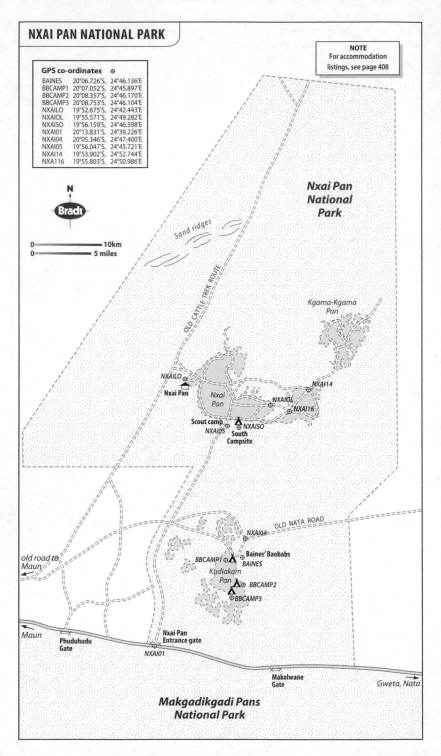

NXAI PAN NATIONAL PARK

NOTE
For accommodation
listings, see page 408

GPS co-ordinates ⊕

BAINES	20°06.726'S,	24°46.136'E
BBCAMP1	20°07.052'S,	24°45.897'E
BBCAMP2	20°08.357'S,	24°46.170'E
BBCAMP3	20°08.753'S,	24°46.104'E
NXAILO	19°52.675'S,	24°42.443'E
NXAIOL	19°55.571'S,	24°49.282'E
NXAISO	19°56.159'S,	24°46.598'E
NXAI01	20°13.831'S,	24°39.226'E
NXAI04	20°05.346'S,	24°47.400'E
NXAI05	19°56.047'S,	24°45.721'E
NXAI14	19°53.902'S,	24°52.744'E
NXA116	19°55.803'S,	24°50.986'E

N

Bradt

0 ————— 10km
0 ————— 5 miles

Sand ridges

*Nxai Pan
National
Park*

OLD CATTLE TREK ROUTE

*Kgama-Kgama
Pan*

NXAILO ⊕
Nxai Pan

*Nxai
Pan*

NXAI14

NXAIOL ⊕
NXAI16

Scout camp
NXAI05 ⊕ NXAISO
**South
Campsite**

OLD NATA ROAD

NXAI04 ⊕

*old road to
Maun*

BBCAMP1 ⊕ **Baines' Baobabs**
BAINES

*Kudiakam
Pan* ⊕ BBCAMP2

⊕ BBCAMP3

Maun

**Phuduhudu
Gate**

**Nxai Pan
Entrance gate**
NXAI01

**Makolwane
Gate**

Gweta, Nata

*Makgadikgadi Pans
National Park*

During the rains, the pans sprout a profusion of wild flowers, including the spectacular brunsvigia lily (*Brunsvigia radulosa*), which brings a splash of red to the summer landscape.

Around and between the pans the vegetation differs according to soil type. Acacias are the dominant trees on sandy soils, with stands of silver clusterleaf (*Terminalia sericea*), and – particularly in disturbed areas – dense thickets of sickle bush (*Dichrostachys cineria*). Mopane (*Colophospermum mopane*) dominates the richer clayey soils to the north and east, carpeting the dusty ground with its golden butterfly leaves and bursting into a flush of green with the rains. Elsewhere, mixed sand and clay support various combretum species, with their wind-borne winged pods, while a richer selection of shrubs thrive on the lime-rich calcrete ridges, including the trumpet thorn (*Catophractes alexandrii*), Western rhigozum (*Rhigozum brevispinosum*) and purple-pod terminalia (*Terminalia prunoides*). Visit South Camp to see some fine examples of these.

Of all the area's trees, the best known must be the great baobabs (*Adansonia digitata*) – in particular the famous Baines' Baobabs that overlook Kudiakam Pan, which were painted by the renowned Victorian explorer and artist Thomas Baines on 22 May 1862, and have changed little in the 155 years since. They are not the only baobabs around, but they're certainly the most celebrated.

Fauna From December to April, Nxai Pan is a breeding ground for large herbivores. Game viewing can be spectacular at the start of this season, when thousands of animals are dropping their young and predators are drawn to the easy pickings. After good rains the lush green grasslands teem with huge concentrations of Burchell's zebra, blue wildebeest and springbok (here at the northeastern limit of their range), while healthy numbers of other grazers include gemsbok, eland and red hartebeest.

Large giraffe herds, sometimes over 40 strong, move across the pans between the acacia 'islands', which they prune into characteristic hourglass shapes. The mopane woodland, mainly to the north of Nxai Pan, shelters browsers such as impala and kudu, which often venture out on to the pans for the permanent waterholes and rich mineral salts. The impala is a versatile species, being able to adapt its diet to graze or browse, according to what is on offer, and Nxai Pan is one of the few areas where impala and springbok occur side by side – their habitats elsewhere generally being mutually exclusive.

In summer, small herds of breeding elephant can sometimes be seen around Kgama-Kgama Pan in the northeast of the park, while lone bulls disperse across the area at other times – generally on the fringes of the mopane. Other visitors from the north include the occasional tsessebe, at about the southern limit of their appearance in the Kalahari. In winter the great herds disperse from the pans, leaving few grazers except the hardy springbok, and a few timid steenbok that find shelter in the thickets.

Predators are well represented on Nxai Pan. Lion can be heard throughout the year: in summer they follow the zebra and wildebeest herds; during the dry season they remain to hunt springbok around the few permanent waterholes. The springbok herds also draw cheetah: Nxai Pan offers perfect open terrain for this coursing predator, and has a good reputation for sightings. Meanwhile wandering packs of wild dog occasionally turn up in pursuit of the same quarry.

Spotted hyena can sometimes be heard at night, especially when there are large concentrations of game around, while the more elusive brown hyena hunts and scavenges for smaller prey items around the pans. Black-backed jackal and honey badger are both versatile smaller predators that occur throughout the area, the latter sometimes foraging in association with the pale-chanting goshawk.

Aardwolf and bat-eared fox snap up harvester termites on the open grasslands. The former is strictly nocturnal and seldom seen; the latter may still be about at sunrise, foraging in loose family groups with ears cocked to the ground for termite rustlings.

African wildcat and small-spotted genet hunt the acacia bush after dark for small rodents and roosting birds, while by day yellow mongoose comb open sandy areas for scorpions, slender mongoose hunt the acacia scrub, alone or in pairs, and banded mongoose rummage through the woodland in large, sociable colonies.

Other smaller mammals found here include lesser bushbaby, aardvark and porcupine, with spring hare on the grassland and scrub hare in the woodland. By day, tree squirrels are common and noisy inhabitants of the mopane.

Birdlife Nxai Pan's rich avifauna comprises a mixture of grassland, acacia scrub and mopane woodland birds, with a total of 217 species recorded in Hugh Chittenden's *Top Birding Spots of Southern Africa* (see *Appendix 3, Further information*). Each habitat has its own typical residents.

Grassland birds include ant-eating chat, white-browed sparrow weaver, capped wheatear and pale-chanting goshawk. White-browed robin, pied babbler and chinspot batis are found in the acacia scrub. Red-billed hornbill, red-billed francolin and barred owl prefer the mopane.

The distinction between adjacent habitats is reflected in the parallel distributions of similar species. For example, double-banded coursers and northern black

BROOD PARASITES

Cuckoos are not the only cheats of the bird world. Whydahs (Viduidae) are also brood parasites that lay their eggs in other birds' nests. Like cuckoos, each species of whydah exploits a specific host, and all of them choose waxbills (Estrildidae). However, unlike cuckoos, whydahs do not evict the eggs or nestlings of their host, so young whydahs grow up alongside their step-siblings, not instead of them.

To enhance the deception, a whydah's eggs – and there are usually two of them – perfectly mimic the colour of its host's clutch, and, once hatched, the whydah nestlings have exactly the right arrangements of gape spots inside their bills to dupe their step-parents into feeding them. A male whydah can even mimic the song of its host to distract it from the nest while the female goes about her devious business undisturbed. Breeding male whydahs are lively, conspicuous birds, who flaunt extravagant tail plumes in dancing display flights – though outside the breeding season they are indistinguishable from the drab females.

Three species of whydah occur in the pans region, of which the most typical is the shaft-tailed whydah (*Vidua regia*), easily recognised by the long thin tail-plumes of a breeding male, each tipped with a pennant. This species frequents sandy clearings in acacia thickets, often in association with its host, the violet-eared waxbill, and apparently without any animosity between them. The other two species are the pin-tailed whydah (*Vidua macroura*), which parasitises the common waxbill and prefers well-watered areas, and the paradise whydah (*Vidua paradisaea*), which parasitises the melba finch and is a common bird of acacia savannah.

korhaans – both Kalahari specialists – occur only on the open grasslands, while bronze-winged coursers and red-crested korhaans, their close relatives, stick to the surrounding woodlands.

Resident raptors, such as bateleur, martial eagle, tawny eagle and brown snake eagle, are joined in summer by an influx of migrants, including steppe buzzard, western red-footed kestrel and yellow-billed kite. Raptor watching can be superb at this time, with more unusual species such as lesser-spotted eagle and hobby sometimes joining the throng at termite emergences.

Kori bustards, secretary birds and (in summer) white storks hunt the grasslands, and after good rains wattled cranes sometimes appear on the flashes. In spring the air resounds to the breeding displays of larks, including sabota, rufous-naped, red-capped, fawn-coloured, dusky and clapper. During summer the game herds are a focus of bird activity, with carmine and blue-cheeked bee-eaters hawking insects around the feet of springbok, zebra, red-billed and yellow-billed oxpeckers hitching rides on giraffes, and white-backed and lappet-faced vultures dropping from the sky on to carcasses.

Away from the pans, the campsites are a good place to search out the smaller passerines: violet-eared, black-cheeked and blue waxbills occur in the sandy acacia scrub together with melba and scaly-feathered finches, while shaft-tailed and paradise whydahs – brood parasites on waxbills (see box above) – dash about in extravagant breeding finery. Baobabs are always worth checking, since they often provide roosting or nesting sites for rollers, hornbills and various owls.

WHEN TO VISIT The game at Nxai is fairly erratic – it can be excellent, though sometimes it will disappoint. If there have been good rains, then between December and April you have a very good chance of witnessing large herds of springbok, gemsbok, giraffe and migrating zebra, plus a scattering of other species. However, note that this is also the time when the pans are at their most treacherous, and driving at its most muddy.

I last visited in February, during a year of good rains, and we had good general game, with large numbers of zebra, although in two days we didn't see a single large carnivore. Conversely, a recent visitor in April was rewarded with sightings of both cheetah and lion during a one-night stay. Reliable reports suggest that game densities remain more or less constant until around August, when – as the dry season progresses and the waterholes dry up – the game becomes sparser and less dependable. Nxai can be a hot and unrewarding park at the height of October's heat.

GETTING THERE AND AWAY Unless you are staying at the new lodge, in which case you will normally arrive by air, you really need a vehicle to visit Nxai Pan National Park. Whether you have your own or are driven by one of the mobile-safari operators from Maun, you should come with all your fuel, water and food – there are no shops or fuel pumps here.

The route is very easy to find. A brand-new gate on the main road (◈ NXAI01 20°13.831'S, 24°39.226'E), half a kilometre to the east of the old cutline, heralded a new entrance in 2009. This is about 135km from Maun and 157km from Nata, and is very well signposted so you're unlikely to miss it. This is where you need to sign and present your entry permit.

There's one track north here, paralleling the old cutline (which until 2009 was the only access road to the park), and leading after some 36km to the scout post. After driving on sand for around 18km, you'll reach a junction, where a right turn leads to Kudiakam Pan and Baines' Baobabs (see page 410 for directions). Continue straight, bearing north-northeast for a further 18km and you'll reach the scout camp (✛ NXAI05 19°56.047'S, 24°45.721'E), which is at the south end of the main pan, near the waterhole. Nowadays this is fundamentally a base for the staff looking after the campsites but you can also get information here about the state of the roads and ask the guides about game movements within the park.

If you're driving yourself, follow the track round the pan from the scout camp to a junction. Here, turn west towards the Old Cattle Trek Route, pass the sign for the HATAB campsite, and continue for a further kilometre.

🏠 **WHERE TO STAY** In 2009, Nxai Pan's campsites were joined by a smart lodge to the west of the pan, opening up this park to visitors who would not consider camping.

Of the campsites around the pan itself, only the southern one remains open. However, three new sites have recently opened close to the famous Baines' Baobabs, reversing a previous ban on camping in that area.

🏠 **Nxai Pan** [map 404] (8 chalets) Kwando Safaris, page 176; ✛ NXAILO 19°52.675'S, 24°42.443'E. Opened in February 2009, & the first lodge to be built inside the national park, Nxai Pan is located on an area of flat, open grassland, 47km from the new park gate, or 8.3km from the old one. The lodge forms a shallow crescent facing west over a waterhole. A particularly welcoming local team affords a homely atmosphere that is quite a highlight.

At the heart of the lodge is a substantial if narrow thatched building, entirely open on one side, but with roll-down canvas blinds with plastic 'windows' to keep out the worst excesses of the weather. Inside, light wooden furniture lends a somewhat Scandinavian air to the bar, lounge & dining area, which flow almost seamlessly from one end to the other. These look over an extensive wooden deck with a small pool near the bar, & a firepit in front. A telescope situated on the main deck is the perfect opportunity to explore the night sky, with the help of a guide, while a curio shop at the back offers a range of gifts & merchandise.

Flanking the main building, & mirroring it in style, are individual chalets, linked by glossy raised wooden walkways that snake behind the complex. A door at the back of each leads into a long & open room, with twin beds – or a dbl – in the centre, & sliding doors with mesh panels opening on to a wooden deck. At one end, there are inside & outside showers, twin washbasins & a separate toilet, while at the other are a desk, low table & chairs. A family room has a 2nd small twin room attached to the lounge.

Morning or afternoon game drives within the immediate area can be extended to full-day

trips to Kudiakam Pan & Baines' Baobabs, with late-evening drives an option, & overnight trips on the pans planned too. Short informative nature walks are possible, too, since although the lodge is inside the national park, it sits within its own 5ha concession. These are conducted by a Bushman tracker, & are a great opportunity to share in their knowledge, sense of humour & passion for the land. *US$471/671 pp sharing/sgl Apr–Oct, US$554 pp Nov–Mar (US$80 sgl supp't 20 Dec– 4 Jan), inc FB, most drinks, activities & laundry.* ☺ *All year.*

⅄ **South Campsite** [map 404] (10 pitches) Contact Xomae Group, page 174. ✛ NXAISO 19°56.159'S, 24°46.598'E. The closest campsite to the entrance, South Camp is probably the busier site – but it benefits from a lovely location. It's situated in a grove of purple-pod terminalia trees (*Terminalia prunioides*) which cast a good shade, making it relatively cool. There are separate ablution blocks for men & women, each with showers & flush toilets. *P236 pp, exc park fees.* ☺ *All year.*

⅄ **Baines' Baobabs** [map 404] (3 sites) Contact Xomae Group, page 174. There are 3 separate campsites around Baines' Baobabs. The closest one to the famous baobabs themselves, at ✛ BBCAMP1 20°07.052'S, 24°45.897'E, is on an island, separated from the baobabs by a salt pan. The other 2 sites (✛ BBCAMP2 20°08.357'S, 24°46.170'E & ✛ BBCAMP3 20°08.753'S, 24°46.104'E) lie further south along the eastern edge of the pan. Each of the sites is equipped with a long-drop loo & bucket shower, but there is no water, so make sure you bring everything you need for the duration of your stay. *P236 pp, exc park fees.* ☺ *All year.*

WHAT TO SEE AND DO Nxai's a great park for watching the herds of plains game, and is certainly somewhere that you need to be patient. Don't rush around in search of predators; instead take your time and you'll see much more. The waterholes are very open and exposed here, so park a good distance away and you won't disturb the animals drinking.

Finally, note that the night sky here is often phenomenally clear – as it is across the centre of the Kalahari. So if you can bring a star chart as well as your route maps, you'll enjoy it all the more. First on your list should be to identify the Southern Cross, and use it to find due south. When gazing up, try using your binoculars and you'll be amazed how many more stars you can see.

Nxai and Kgama-Kgama pans
These are the main pans of the complex. They're covered with grasses and dotted with clumps of acacias – and have always provided me with the best game viewing in this park.

Getting around In the dry season you'll find most of the roads in the area of the pan are good and hard, a pleasant contrast to the thick sand that you ploughed through to reach here.

When the rains come you'll have to be much more careful as many roads on the pan itself turn very muddy. Then the sand road in will be the easiest section, and the park itself will provide the problems. Make sure your self-sufficient vehicle includes a spade, and always carry some wood with you, both for campfires and for sticking under the wheels when you get stuck.

From Nxai Pan to Kgama-Kgama Pan
The road which leads off east towards Kgama-Kgama Pan runs through dense bush, affording little visibility either side. To reach the pan, head east from the scout post for about 10km, passing South Camp on your right. This should bring you to a junction of the tracks (⊕ NXAI16 19°55.803'S, 24°50.986'E). From here one track (clearly marked on most maps) leads off to loop around to the southeast and then turn north.

However, another track leads off heading north of east, before turning northeast, and after almost 5km reaches another junction (⊕ NXAI14 19°53.902'S, 24°52.744'E).

The alternative, which leads roughly west, across the north end of the small pan to the east of Nxai, heads through an interesting area of mostly mopane woodland, mixed with some denser groves of terminalias, and even in May, some of the pans here retained water. This eventually leads west to North Camp (⊕ NXAINO 19°52.707'S, 24°47.358'E).

Kudiakam Pan and Baines' Baobabs
Sandwiched between Nxai Pan and the main road, Kudiakam is the largest of an interesting complex of pans lying in sparse bush east of the track to Nxai. The game here doesn't usually match Nxai's, but the main attraction is an extraordinarily beautiful group of trees known as Baines' Baobabs, which stand at a spectacular site on the eastern edge of the pan. They were immortalised in a painting by Thomas Baines who came here in May 1862 with James Chapman and wrote:

> A lone circuit brought me, with empty pouch, to the clump of baobabs we had seen yesterday from the wagon; five full-sized trees, and two or three younger ones were standing, so that when in leaf their foliage must form one magnificent shade. One gigantic trunk had fallen and lay prostrate but still, losing none of its vitality, bent

14

forth branches and young leaves like the rest ... The general colour or the immense stems was grey and rough: but where the old bark had peeled and curled off, the new (of that peculiar metallic coppery-looking red and yellow which Dr Livingstone was wont so strenuously to object in my pictures) shone through over large portions, giving them, according to light or shade, a red or yellow, grey or a deep purple tone.

The baobabs themselves have changed very little since Baines painted them: the one lying prostrate is still thriving, having lost none of its vitality.

Having thought of the baobabs with reference to a fairly recent Victorian painter, it's perhaps worth reminding ourselves that Baines was far from the first person here. Lawrence Robbins (see *Appendix 3, Further information*) and others have conducted archaeological surveys of this area and discovered extensive remains dating from the Middle Stone Age period, 'especially on the eastern side within a 4km radius of the Baines baobab grove' according to Robbins. Many stone tools were found, plus ostrich eggshell remains, a zebra's tooth and the fossilised bone of a hippopotamus.

This site has been dated to about 105,000–128,000 years old, around which time this was probably a beach location on the edge of the great superlake. This Middle Stone Age period has a special resonance, as this is the period during which we think the first *Homo sapiens* appeared.

Getting there and away The easiest way is to follow the directions to Nxai Pan by turning off the main Maun–Nata road at the new gate (✪ NXAI01 20°13.831'S, 24°39.226'E) into the national park, which is well signposted. After heading north for 18km, you'll find a track off to the east. This track splits very soon, after about 0.9km, and both roads lead to the baobabs.

Dry-season route The right fork heads almost directly for Baines' Baobabs (✪ BAINES 20°06.726'S, 24°46.136'E). It is the more direct route, but it crosses the surface of the pans, so do not try this unless you know what you're doing and are sure they will be dry. (It should be fine after about August, though don't take this as a guarantee!) Even the guides at the main gate mentioned that they always try to take the more northerly wet-season route where possible.

Wet-season route Taking the left fork is more reliable if you're travelling earlier in the year, as it bends around slightly to the north, taking about 14.4km to reach a crossroads at ✪ NXAI04 20°05.346'S, 24°47.400'E. Here you meet the old road between Maun and Nata; this is about 3.6km from the trees themselves. There's a network of small tracks around here, so head straight and then look for tracks off to the right, or turn right and find a track to your left – you can't miss them (✪ BAINES 20°06.726'S, 24°46.136'E).

MAKGADIKGADI PANS

The Sua and Ntwetwe pans that comprise Makgadikgadi cover 12,000km² to the south of the Nata–Maun road. The western side is protected within a national park, while the east is either wilderness or cattle-ranching land. These are amongst the largest salt pans in the world and have few landmarks. So you're left to use the flat, distant horizon as your only line of reference – and even that dissolves into a haze of shimmering mirages in the heat of the afternoon sun. During the rains this desolate area comes to life, with huge migrating herds of zebra, wildebeest, and occasionally (if the pans fill with water) pelicans and millions of flamingos. A couple of odd outcrops of isolated rock in and around the pans add to their sense of mystery, as well as providing excellent vantage points from which to view the endless expanse of silver, grey and blue.

Makgadikgadi Pans National Park lies on the west of the pans, incorporating the western end of Ntwetwe Pan and a larger adjacent area of grassland and acacia woodland. The flora and fauna there are sufficiently different, especially around the Boteti River, to warrant a separate section, towards the end of this chapter, entitled *Makgadikgadi Pans National Park* (pages 424–32).

BACKGROUND INFORMATION This section concentrates on the main salt pans, Sua and Ntwetwe, and the areas of grassland immediately around them which encompass many scattered smaller pans.

Geography and geology
As discussed on page 398, Sua and Ntwetwe lie at the centre of the great prehistoric lake basin that circumscribes the whole region. On top of this is an ancient mantle of windblown Kalahari sands – deposited during the Tertiary period, as the subcontinent was levelled by erosion. Exposed rock is a rarity on the surface of this scrubbed and scoured landscape. However, beneath the sand lie ancient Karoo deposits 300 million years old, comprising basalt larva, sandstone and shales and containing such valuable minerals as gold, silver, copper and nickel.

During the Cretaceous period, 80 million years ago, rifts and buckles in the Earth's crust allowed 'pipes' of molten material – known as kimberlite – to punch their way up from below. Diamonds formed under conditions of massive heat and pressure in these kimberlite pipes. Today they are mined at Orapa, just south of Ntwetwe Pan.

A few isolated outcrops of igneous rock extrude from the surface of the pans, notably Kubu Island and Kukome Island on Sua Pan. Apart from these, and some fossilised barchan (crescent-shaped) dunes to the west, the pans themselves are flat and featureless expanses of dry, sterile salt. However, after good summer rains they are transformed into shimmering lakes, giving a glimpse of what the great superlake must once have been like. The rainwater that pours down on them is augmented in really wet years by seasonal flows from the east: the Nata, Tutume, Semowane and Mosetse rivers. Also, again only in exceptional years, an overspill from the Okavango makes its way to the west side of Ntwetwe, via the Boteti River.

Flora and fauna highlights
The saline conditions of the pans themselves have a strong local influence on their surrounding vegetation. Broadly speaking this becomes richer and more diverse the further you travel from the pan edges, creating a loose concentric series of 'succession' zones, each of which supports a distinctive fauna. These zones effectively chart the gradual demise of the ancient superlake.

Flora
There is no plant life on the surface of the pans, since nothing can tolerate the excessively high concentration of mineral salts, and wind erosion scours the exposed dusty surface, quickly denuding it of any vegetation that tries to take hold. The immediate fringes are carpeted with more-or-less uninterrupted grassland, consisting primarily of *Digitarias* species, which can survive despite the irregular herd movements. Between the pans can also be found patches of prickly salt grass (*Odyssea paucinervis*), a yellowish, spiky species that tolerates high salinity (salt crystals can sometimes be seen on the leaves).

Summer rains bring lush growth to the grasses, which flower in a wind-rippled sea of green. Then you'll also see a scattering of short-lived wild flowers bloom among the grasses, including crimson lilies, acanthus and wild hibiscus (*Hibiscus calyphyllus*). In areas of thicker sand ridges, the runners of the tsama melon (*Citrullus lanatus*) sprawl across the sand, its swollen fruit providing life-sustaining moisture for a myriad of animals, from gerbils to gemsbok. In winter, cropped and shrivelled, the grasses are reduced to a sparse golden mantle over the dusty plains, scattering their seeds to the wind.

Here and there, small hollows in the rolling grassland trap windblown detritus, creating pockets of richer soil that support scattered trees and shrubs. The commonest trees are various acacia species, such as the umbrella thorn (*Acacica tortillis*), which, with their fine leaves for minimising water loss and wicked thorns to deter browsers, are ideally suited to survive this arid environment. The hardy camelthorn (*Acacia erioloba*) thrives in areas of deeper sand, often in an almost lifeless state of disintegration, by tapping deep reserves of groundwater with its long roots.

The shepherd's tree (*Boscia albitrunca*) with its distinct white trunk and dense, invaluable shade, is another versatile pioneer of sandy Kalahari soils. The grasslands are studded with stands of fan palms (*Hyphaenea petersiana*), with their hard, cricket-ball-sized fruit known as vegetable ivory. Thick groves of this elegant tree occur beyond the northwest shores of Ntwetwe Pan and along the Maun–Nata road.

In the far northeast of Sua Pan, the seasonal Nata River spreads out into a small delta formation which is quite different from the rest of the region. Here there's a band of tall dry riverine forest along the banks of the Nata, and a thickening of the ground cover lining the braided channels. Phragmites reeds thrive in the brackish conditions here, and when this delta is in flood the area can seem quite lush.

KALAHARI MELONS

There are at least eight species of the pumpkin family in Botswana, of which the tsama melon (*Citrullus lanatus*) is the most distinctive and frequently seen. It is found throughout the region, and is particularly common after a good rainy season. Then, even after most of the rest of the vegetation is brown and shrivelled, you'll find tempting round melons beside the sandiest of roads – often apparently on their own.

During the dry season these become important sources of moisture for many animals, especially the gemsbok, and are also used by the local people. To get drinking water from one of these, you first cut off the top, like a boiled egg. The centre can then be cut out and eaten. Then take a stick and mash the rest of the pulp whilst it's in the melon, and this can be eaten. Take care not to eat the pips. These are best roasted and pounded, when they make an edible meal that can be cooked with water. Sometimes you'll come across a bitter fruit, which you should not eat as it may cause poisoning.

Another fairly common species is the gemsbok melon (*Citrullus naudianus*), which has similar sprawling tendrils and an oval fruit, covered in blunt fleshy spines. Unlike the tsama melon, this is a perennial plant with a long underground tuber. Inside the fruit is a jelly-like, translucent green which can be eaten raw (again, discarding the pips usually), though it doesn't taste very good. It's slightly more palatable when roasted beside the fire overnight – but I wouldn't recommend that you throw away your muesli or yoghurt before tasting it!

Further from the pans, the grassland gives way to a denser bush. To the east, a mixed sand and clay soil supports a greater variety of woodland trees, including tamboti (*Spirostachys africana*), marula (*Scleroclarya birrea*) and monkey thorn (*Acacia galpinii*), while a belt of mopane woodland (*Colophospermum mopane*) also grows in the more heavily clayey soil around Nata and along the eastern boundary of Sua Pan.

The mighty baobabs (*Adansonia digitata*) are perhaps the region's best-known and most easily identified trees. These grotesque, drought-resistant giants occur scattered around the pans and on isolated rock outcrops such as Kubu Island, where they have stood as landmarks for millennia. The swollen trunks of many are engraved with the signatures of generations of thirsty travellers. Among the baobabs on Kubu some other more unusual species take advantage of this rocky, island niche, including the African star-chestnut (*Sterculia africana*) and common corkwood (*Commiphora pyracanthoides*).

Fauna Large mammals are scarce around the pans. This is partly because of the hostile nature of the terrain, partly because this is cattle ranching country, where wild animals have been marginalised by the activities of people, and partly because of the destructive effect that veterinary control fences have had on animal migration patterns.

There is no doubt that cattle fences to the south (see page 442) have had a significant impact on the populations of herbivores, and especially the blue wildebeest. Now blue wildebeest are seldom seen around Sua Pan and certainly not in the vast herds that built up during the 1950s, when populations are estimated to have peaked at about 250,000.

Today a permanent scattering of springbok inhabit the surrounding grasslands. These hardy and versatile antelope manage without water for long periods, and withstand the harshest daytime temperatures by orientating their white rumps towards the sun to deflect the worst of its ultraviolet rays.

Other large mammals are thin on the ground, being more abundant towards the west of Ntwetwe and the adjacent grazing grounds of Makgadikgadi Pans National Park (see pages 426–8). However, a scrutiny of the pan surface can reveal the tracks of a surprising range of visitors, including rare (perhaps lost?) wandering elephants or giraffe. Zebra and gemsbok are sometimes seen trekking wearily through the heat haze as they cross the pans between grazing areas, while red hartebeest are frequent visitors to the grasslands, where they can subsist on poorer grasses than many species.

The encrusted tracks of lion or cheetah sometimes appear on the pan surface, particularly towards the west, but the comparative lack of large herbivores means that larger predators are scarce, and a wandering lion is apt to be shot by cattle ranchers. More common are the smaller nocturnal carnivores that can survive the harsh conditions and thrive on smaller pickings.

Brown hyena inhabit the area, and a habituated clan of these elusive predators may be observed at close quarters from Jack's Camp, on the western shores of Ntwetwe, where they have been studied by zoologists. Their catholic diet includes tsama melons and ostrich eggs, as well as spring hares, young springbok, smaller mammals and carrion.

Black-backed jackal, bat-eared fox and African wildcat are widespread, while yellow mongoose is common in sandy areas, where it is an accomplished killer of scorpions. At night, a legion of smaller mammals moves out across the grasslands. Spring hares thrive on damaged grassland and are common around villages, where

- Arrange a rendezvous for when you leave the pans, and someone to raise the alarm if you don't arrive. Leave a rough route plan with them.

It's difficult for me to emphasise enough just how dangerous the pans can be. There are periodic deaths of people who visit the area without the proper back-up and preparation, and then get into difficulties. It's different from many areas in Botswana because:

- The sun is merciless on the pan's surface; there's absolutely no shade.
- If you break through the crust of the pans to the wet silt beneath, then getting out is very difficult, even with a second vehicle. Remember: there will be no wood around, no branches to put under the wheels.
- There are so many different tracks on the pans (each diverging vehicle makes a new one), that often there simply isn't a 'right' track which most vehicles take. Thus, it may be weeks or months before someone takes the same route that you do, and passes you.

SUA PAN Sua Pan is the eastern of the two twin pans, and extends roughly southwards from the town of Nata (see pages 432–3) in its northeast corner. On its southern shore is the village of Mosu; to its north lies the Maun–Nata road; to its west it is divided from Ntwetwe Pan by a thin strip of grassland.

Sua (sometimes spelled 'Sowa') is the Setswana word for 'salt', and it is this mineral residue from the vanished superlake that dominates the geology and ecology of the pan. Once, salt was laboriously collected from the pan surface by the San and carried away on donkeys. Today it is mined by Botswana Ash (Botash), a joint enterprise in which the Botswana government is the major shareholder, and taken out by rail. The company supplies sodium carbonate on an industrial scale for use in the manufacture of paper, glass and steel. Their mine is situated along the Sua Spit, a tongue of grassland that extends halfway across the pan from its eastern shore.

The Nata River feeds Sua Pan from the northeast (bringing the rains from Zimbabwe) and, in good years, it floods from December to April with shallow, warm water. Where the fresh water of the river meets the saline pan, a brackish delta of silted reedbeds has formed. In summer, this corner of the pan attracts great concentrations of breeding waterbirds, notably flamingos (see box, page 419). This delta – an area of 230km² – is now protected within the Nata Sanctuary. The flamingos can usually be viewed from the bird hide on the eastern shore, but after heavy rain, access may not be possible.

Evidence of the former lake exists in the form of fossil pebble beaches along the shores of Kubu Island and other granite outcrops around the pan, and fossil diatoms and molluscs on the pan surfaces. These reveal that there was a prolonged wet period about 14,000–17,000 years ago and, more recently, a flood only 1,500 years ago. Near the village of Mosu in the south, an escarpment rises some 40m

GPS REFERENCES FOR SUA PAN MAP (opposite)

KUBU-I	20°53.737'S, 25°49.421'E	TSHWAG	20°48.094'S, 25°45.608'E
KUKOME	20°55.001'S, 26°12.203'E	TSIVET	20°58.620'S, 25°37.178'E
KWADIB	20°54.907'S, 26°16.571'E	TURNM1	21°19.468'S, 25°33.742'E
MMATSH	21°08.590'S, 25°39.214'E	TURNM2	20°55.990'S, 25°40.015'E
THABAT	20°42.606'S, 25°47.476'E		

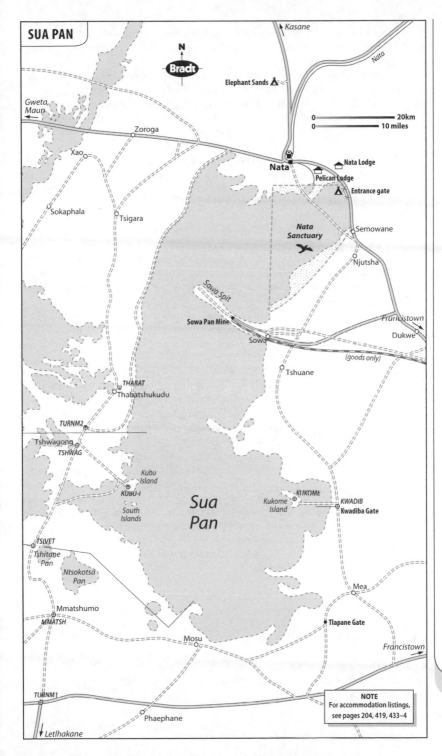

SUA PAN

N
Bradt

↑ *Kasane*

Nata

Elephant Sands

Gweta, Maun

0 ———————— 20km
0 ———————— 10 miles

Zoroga

Xao

Nata
Nata Lodge
Pelican Lodge
Entrance gate

Sokaphala

Tsigara

Nata Sanctuary

Semowane

Njutsha

Sowa Spit

Francistown

Sowa Pan Mine

Sowa

Dukwe

(goods only)

Tshuane

THABAT
Thabatshukudu

TURNM2

Tshwagong
TSHWAG

Kubu Island

KUBU-I

South Islands

Sua Pan

KUKOME

Kukome Island

KWADIB
Kwadiba Gate

TSITVET
Tshitane Pan

Ntsokotsa Pan

Mea

Mmatshumo
MMATSH

Tlapane Gate

Mosu

Francistown

TURNM1

Phaephane

↓ *Letlhakane*

The Kalahari's Great Salt Pans   MAKGADIKGADI PANS

14

NOTE
For accommodation listings,
see pages 204, 419, 433–4

above the edge of the pan, showing the erosive force of the great lake that once washed against these cliffs. Here there is also one of several subterranean springs that emerge around the fringes of the pans.

The pan is a remarkable area, with the occasional spot like Kubu Island that has a magic all of its own. That said, there's a lot more than just Nata Sanctuary and Kubu here – but it does need time to explore it. Read my warning under *Getting around*, above; then get a copy of Mike Main's book (see *Appendix 3, Further information*) and a few good maps, and enjoy it!

🏠 **Where to stay** Most visitors to this area spend the night at one of the variety of options in Nata (see pages 432–4). An alternative would be to camp at Nata Sanctuary (see below). There has been sporadic talk of a new lodge to be built at Sowa for some time now, but this has yet to be substantiated.

Nata Sanctuary (⊕ *All year 07.00–19.00 daily; P55 pp, plus P15 per vehicle, camping P35 pp*) A conservation area was originally established in the northeast corner of Sua Pan with the help of the Kalahari Conservation Society in the 1980s, to protect the important seasonal wetland areas around the Nata Delta. However, although the villagers at Nata were consulted about the plans, the wider community in the area didn't benefit from it.

This area encompassed cattle-grazing land owned by four communities: Nata, Sepako, Maposa and Mmaxotae. In the early 1990s it was realised that without the support of these communities, conservation in the area couldn't be effective. Eventually, as part of a ground-breaking community project, the communities moved about 3,000 head of cattle out of the area, and fencing began. In 1993 Nata Sanctuary was opened to the public, and in the same year it won the prestigious Tourism for Tomorrow award for the southern hemisphere.

Now Nata Sanctuary conserves an ecologically sensitive and important natural environment, and also effectively returns money to the communities for doing so. That said, the fences have become less effective over the years, so you'll probably see the odd cow as you drive around. Consider this an illustration of the increasing difficulties facing wildlife conservation areas in marginal regions of Africa but don't be put off; this is still an excellent area for birding and well worth exploring.

Nata Sanctuary generally makes a very easy place to visit for a day or two, either based in Nata or camping at the sanctuary itself. That said, while the birding is at its best during the rainy season, this is also the time when the roads are likely to be impassable, so if you're intent on spending some time in the sanctuary, then it's wise to check the situation before you set off. Arguably the best time to visit is around April, at the end of the rainy season.

Flora and fauna See above for notes on the general flora and fauna of the pan, but note that a number of mammals have been enclosed (or re-introduced) within the fenced boundaries of this reserve, including gemsbok, springbok, hartebeest, kudu, eland, zebra, reedbuck, jackal, fox, monkey, steenbok, squirrel and spring hare.

Getting there and away The colourfully decorated entrance to Nata Sanctuary is about 17km southeast of Nata, next to the main road to Francistown. It's very well signposted in both directions.

🏠 **Where to stay** Many visitors to the sanctuary stay at one of the lodges in nearby Nata (see pages 432–4), but the sanctuary does have its own campsite.

Of the world's half-dozen or so species of flamingo, two are found within southern Africa: the greater (*Phoenicopterus ruber*) and the lesser (*Phoenicopterus minor*). Both species have wide distributions, from southern Africa north into east Africa and the Red Sea, and are highly nomadic in their habits.

Flamingos are usually found wading in large areas of shallow saline water where they filter feed by holding their specially adapted beaks upside down in the water. The lesser flamingo will walk or swim whilst swinging its head from side to side, mainly taking blue-green algae from the surface of the water. The larger greater flamingo will hold its head submerged while filtering out small organisms (detritus and algae), even stirring the mud with its feet to help the process. Both species are very gregarious and flocks can have millions of birds, though a few hundred is more common.

Only occasionally do flamingos breed in southern Africa, choosing the Makgadikgadi Pans, Namibia's Etosha Pan or even Lake Ngami. When the conditions are right (usually March to June, following the rains) both species build low mud cones in the water and lay one or (rarely) two eggs in a small hollow on the top. These are then incubated by both parents for about a month, until they hatch. After a further week the young birds flock together and start to forage with their parents. Some ten weeks later the young can fly and fend for themselves.

During this time the young are very susceptible to the shallow water in the pans drying out. In 1969, a rescue operation was mounted in Namibia when the main Etosha Pan dried out, necessitating the moving of thousands of chicks to nearby Fischer's Pan, which was still covered in water.

The best way to tell the two species apart is by their beaks: that of the greater flamingo is almost white with a black tip, while the lesser flamingo has a uniformly dark beak. If you are further away then the body of the greater will appear white, while that of the lesser looks smaller and more pink. The best place to see them in Botswana is certainly Sua Pan – although even there they will only appear if the rains have filled some of the pan.

À **Campsite** [map 397] A fire in 2008 destroyed much of the older structure here, but the campsite was rapidly rebuilt, & for a time at least was a really smart facility. Since then it hasn't been looked after very well & is in need of some investment to its main area & bar. That said, just 300m from the sanctuary entrance – so quite close to the road – are a few relatively shady pitches, each with braai stand & picnic table. Ablution blocks, one each for men & women, have flush toilets & showers. There are also the shells of 2 large tented chalets which began construction in 2009 but were never completed. *Camping P35 pp.*

Kubu Island In the southwest of Sua Pan lies an isolated granite outcrop some 10m high and 1km long, known as Kubu Island. It forms the shape of a crescent, and its slopes are terraced with fossil beaches of wave-rounded pebbles, providing startling evidence of the prehistoric lake's former water levels. Crowned with an array of ancient, gnarled baobabs and surrounded on three sides by a vast grey emptiness, Kubu has a unique atmospheric beauty.

At night, with the wind moaning through the baobabs, it is easy to imagine the waves of a great inland sea lapping at its pebble beaches. Many of the island's rocks are white, covered in ancient, fossilised guano from the waterbirds that used to perch here when it was surrounded by the lake. The moonlight reflecting off the pan's white surface gives the place an almost supernatural atmosphere, which is heightened by the mystery of Kubu's former inhabitants. The shoreline is littered with Stone Age tools and arrowheads, while concentric drystone walls on the islands survive from a much more recent village, perhaps around AD 1400–1600, and outside this are a number of stone cairns.

Archaeologists have linked these walls and cairns with the dynasty of Great Zimbabwe, and think that they were probably at the most southwestern tip of that state. In *The Riddle of the Stone Walls* (see *Appendix 3, Further information*), Alec Campbell suggests that they could have been remote 'circumcision camps', to which the boys of the tribe were taken for circumcision and ceremonies leading to adulthood. It is suggested that perhaps ceremonies took place within the walls, and every class that 'graduated' then built a separate cairn.

Campbell also noted that the people of the nearest village, Tshwagong, hold Kubu and the nearby Thithaba Islands as sacred, and men over 16 years of age visit the islands to make contact with God, singing a particular song for rain and leaving offerings on the ground.

Note that Kubu is a national monument, and there are plans to station a warden here to ensure that visitors don't damage anything.

Getting there and away One of the few operators to run trips to this area is Uncharted Africa (see page 422), which offers quadbike excursions here from all their camps. In addition, their Kubu Island safari includes a couple of days at Kubu Island, travelling by quad bike and sleeping under the stars. Alternatively, you can drive yourself.

From the north there are endless possible routes to Kubu Island (⊕ KUBU-I 20°53.737'S, 25°49.421'E), and you can expect it to take about three to four hours from the main Maun–Nata road. Easiest is probably to take one of the many tracks that leave the main road between about 30km and 15km west of Nata. Follow your nose (or, more practically, your GPS) towards Thabatshukudu Village (⊕ THABAT 20°42.606'S, 25°47.476'E), which is about 70–75km south, depending on the track that you take.

From there it's about 10km southwest to the Tshwagong Veterinary Gate, through which any north–south traffic between Sua and Ntwetwe pans passes – so tracks will lead you there. This is about 3km north of the small village of Tshwagong (⊕ TSHWAG 20°48.094'S, 25°45.608'E), from where it's about 14km in a straight line southeast to Kubu Island. (There are several tracks here, so just head southeast and follow your GPS.)

Note that the track that leaves Gweta in a south then southeasterly direction, ending at the Tshwagong Veterinary Gate, passes over several long stretches of Ntwetwe Pan, and so is dangerously muddy during the earlier months of the year.

From the south it's best to start by heading for the village of Mmatshumo (⊕ MMATSH 21°08.590'S, 25°39.214'E). You'll find a number of tracks from the Orapa–Francistown road which will lead you here; the shortest leaves the main road around ⊕ TURNM1 21°19.468'S, 25°33.742'E. From there it's about 23km to Mmatshumo. Heading north from there, there's a good view of the pan to your right after about 5km, before the track bends west and back north to cross the small Tsitane Pan, crossing the veterinary fence at ⊕ TSIVET 20°58.620'S, 25°37.178'E. Then a straight track heading north-northeast brings you to Tshwagong (⊕ TSHWAG 20°48.094'S, 25°45.608'E) after about 20km.

Note that during the dry season you can take a short cut about 7km north of the vet fence, at around ✪ TURNM2 20°55.990'S, 25°40.015'E, which heads east-northeast across the pan to Kubu; but don't try this when the pans are wet!

Other landmarks around Sua Pan
Places detailed here run south from Nata and Nata Sanctuary, then west and north to Kubu Island and beyond. Note that you should never attempt to drive across the pan from the east side to the west, or vice versa, even during the dry season.

Sowa Pan Mine (soda-ash factory) This modern industrial complex seems strangely out of place here, especially as it is easily reached, 40km along a tarred road. The turn-off is about 48km south of Nata on the road to Francistown.

Kukome Island On the eastern shore of Sua Pan, roughly opposite Kubu, Kukome (also spelled 'Kukonje') Island (✪ KUKOME 20°55.001'S, 26°12.203'E) has similar fossil beaches and ancient remains. To reach here, first head for the Kwadiba Veterinary Gate (✪ KWADIB 20°54.907'S, 26°16.571'E) on the east side of Sua Pan, from where a track leads west for about 7km to Kukome Island. (Beware: the GPS point given for the Kwadiba Gate on older editions of the Shell map doesn't seem correct to me.)

Mmatshumo Mmatshumo (✪ MMATSH 21°08.590'S, 25°39.214'E) is a small village on the south side of the pans, between Sua and Ntwetwe pans, as well as an important waypoint when you're navigating yourself around.

South Islands About 7km south of Kubu, far out on the pan, are two other small islands. They too have baobab trees and the larger one, on the east, has a series of rock cairns along its spine.

Thabatshukudu Thabatshukudu (✪ THABAT 20°42.606'S, 25°47.476'E) is another village – notable for the landmark of its colourfully painted general dealer's store – and another useful waypoint when navigating yourself around.

NTWETWE PAN
Ntwetwe Pan is the western twin of Sua, and is of a similar size and general topography, though aligned more east–west. It lies due south of the Nata–Maun road, between Gweta in the north and Orapa and Mopipi in the south. One finger extends to the north of the road, while to the southwest the pan breaks up into several smaller pans, including Lake Xau, just south of Mopipi. The old north–south trading route between Gweta and Mopipi crosses the centre of the pan, and the two famous isolated baobabs (Green's Baobab and Chapman's Baobab) that marked this route for early European explorers – including Livingstone, who left his initials here – still serve as landmarks for today's travellers.

Ntwetwe lacks the famous granite outcrops of Sua; its main points of elevation are fossilised barchan dunes that once crept across the surface of the lake during a dry period and were left stranded when waters rose again. Gabasadi Island is the largest of these. The profiles of the dune islands show steps and lines of vegetation which, like Sua Pan's pebble beaches, are evidence of former higher lake levels.

Stone Age sites are scattered among the smaller pans that form the western shore of Ntwetwe. At Gutsha Pan, near Chapman's Baobab, there is a perennial spring. Here the San once dug pit traps lined with poisoned stakes to trap the plentiful

14

game that came to drink. The remains of these traps, and the calcrete blinds behind which the hunters hid, are still visible today.

🏠 **Where to stay** There are three camps situated on the northwest side of the pan: Jack's Camp, San Camp and Camp Kalahari, in that order of luxury. All are expensive, even by Botswana's standards, and have been extensively refurbished – or, indeed, rebuilt – in the last few years. Though these are the only camps on the pans themselves, you could also visit this area on a day or overnight excursion with Planet Baobab or Gweta Lodge (see pages 434–5). Both offer a cheaper option, aimed at backpackers and people driving along the Nata–Maun road.

Jack's Camp, San Camp, Camp Kalahari and Planet Baobab can be contacted through Uncharted Africa Safari Co (✆ *+27 11 447 1605;* e *reservations@ unchartedafrica.com; www.unchartedafrica.com*), who also operates mobile safaris throughout northern Botswana. Note that, with the exception of Planet Baobab, these camps are usually reached by light aircraft from Maun; a private airstrip (⊕ SANAIR 20°29.504'S, 25°11.054'E) is 20 minutes' drive from camp. They accept self-drive vehicles only in the dry season, and even then all such vehicles must be escorted to the camps from Planet Baobab.

🏠 **Jack's Camp** [map 396] (10 tents) Jack's Camp was the original camp on the pans. When all the other safari operators in Botswana focused on game & the Delta, Jack's dared to offer something totally different – & succeeded in style.

A bushcamp was originally started in this area in the 1960s, by the late Jack Bousfield. After his tragic death in an aircraft accident, his son, Ralph Bousfield, built a camp for visitors here which first opened in 1993. It's set in sparse forest of real fan palms, in grasslands on the edge of Ntwetwe Pan, overlooking Makgadikgadi Pans National Park.

Jack's is furnished in a 'traditional east African 40s safari style'. This means it's very comfortable, with 1st-class attention to detail, but it's not super-luxurious by any means. Jack's green tents are classic Meru-style, built on decks & set in a palm grove. Inside, 7 of the tents have twin beds with individual canopies, while the others have 4-poster dbl beds, all with down pillows & duvets, high-quality linens & even Persian rugs. Each tent has an en-suite bathroom with indoor & outdoor shower, flush toilet & hot water. At night, lighting is by paraffin lamp – much more magical than electricity!

Jack's central 'mess tent' is really a series of grand canvas pavilions. The interior is lined with amber printed cotton, whilst the green of the outside blends with the surrounding bush. This is something of a canvas field museum, sheltering an eclectic selection of items (mostly local) including stone tools, fossils of extinct mega-fauna (like giant zebra), prints, maps, historical etchings, & a fair-size collection of Bushman beadwork. There's also a drinks tent, a library tent, a centralised dining tent & a separate tea tent, its floor scattered with a mass of Persian rugs & cushions, where tea & delicious cakes are usually served before the afternoon activities. Towards the front of camp, with great views, there's an open-sided pool pavilion, where guests can relax & cool off on summer afternoons.

Activities vary with the season. When it's dry, around May–Oct, there's likely to be very little game around. That's fine, as it's not the focus of a trip here. Instead you'll explore the pans in 4x4s, on individual quad bikes & on foot, often with a Bushman tracker. These trips concentrate on the area's smaller wildlife, & also its history & archaeology – often including a visit to Chapman's Baobab, & a part of the pan where old Stone Age flint axe-heads & arrowheads can be just picked up off the surface. (Quite rightly, my guide insisted that they were also to be left there by us!)

During the wet season, around Nov–Apr, the pans can become quagmires. It's often impossible to use the quad bikes, & the 4x4 drives tend to stick to the grasslands on the edges of the pans. However, then there is a much greater density of wildlife around, with many migrant birds &, if you're lucky, large herds of plains game, including zebra & wildebeest. Throughout the year you can have the fascinating experience of interacting with a gang of habituated meerkats & seeing the elusive brown hyena.

Amongst all the camps that I know in Africa, Jack's Camp stands out for its unique style of guiding. Anyone can find you a herd of elephants in Moremi, but to find fascination in a barren salt pan requires a lot more skill. Jack's guides are mostly zoology or biology graduates who come here to combine a few years' guiding with a PhD specialising in some of the local wildlife. Wits comment that they are often British, Oxbridge & good-looking – but this can often mean an informed & very intelligent level of discussion.

As the camp is outside the national park, night drives are possible – when there's often more wildlife around than during the day. Recently, thanks to the lion research that's been done from here, sightings of lion have increased hugely. For a few years, zoologist Glyn Maude was based here, researching brown hyenas. He managed quite successfully to habituate one clan to vehicles, & the guides have continued to monitor the animals, which makes Jack's a great place for sightings of these very shy creatures. Though they occur widely, you'd be very, very lucky to see brown hyena elsewhere! *US$1,490/1,890 pp sharing/sgl 16 Apr–Oct, US$960 pp Nov–15 Apr, inc FB, drinks, activities, laundry, park fees. Flights to/from Maun US$359 pp each way; escorted self-drive from Planet Baobab US$150 per vehicle return (dry season only). MasterCard & Visa accepted.* ⊕ *All year.*

⌂ **San Camp** [map 396] (6 tents) The smaller but no less exclusive satellite of Jack's Camp lies 20 mins' drive away, right on Ntwetwe Pan, & is only open during the dry season. Run by the same team as Jack's, but completely refurbished during 2011, it works in the same way, with similar activities & approach. Like Jack's, it's rustic but stylish & comfortable, its tents – of white rather than green, to reflect the stark landscape – lending something of the air of a circus top. Three linked pavilions, incorporating a central dining area flanked by a library to one side, & a tea tent & 'relaxation area' to the other, are lined in a subtle pinstripe, with dark colonial-style furniture with brass fittings offset by Persian rugs. In addition, a yoga & meditation pavilion is situated right on the edge of the pan. In the individual tents, a veranda with a day bed leads through to a sitting area, then on to the bedroom (2 with 4-poster dbl beds; the rest with twins), dressing room, & bathroom with flush toilet & hot water at the back.

Both Jack's & San Camp are 1st-rate camps offering something totally different to virtually all of the rest of Botswana's camps, though both are expensive. Either makes a great 3- or 4-night stop, best at the very end of a fly-in trip to Botswana. *US$1,170/1,515 pp sharing/sgl, inc FB, drinks, activities, laundry & park fees. Transfers as Jack's Camp, above. No credit cards.* ⊕ *16 Apr–15 Oct.*

⌂ **Camp Kalahari** [map 396] (10 tents) Standing amongst real fan palms & acacias just 5mins from the edge of Ntwetwe Pan, south of Gweta, the former Makgadikgadi Camp was fully rebuilt by Uncharted Africa in 2009. Central to the camp is an ochre-painted building under ridged Kalanga-style thatch with a firepit in front. If this has a distinctly tribal feel, with furniture from Ethiopia & Sudan, the tented rooms hark back to the 1940s, complete with twin or dbl metal-framed beds, paraffin lamps & campaign safari furniture, offset by rich Indian & Moroccan textiles. In 2013, a new pool & deck was added to the camp, bringing this more down-to-earth offering further in line with its pricer sisters. 21st-century creature comforts come in the form of an en-suite bathroom & separate toilet, an alfresco shower, & a solar geyser for hot water. One family tent has 2 rooms linked through the bathroom. In the front, safari furniture sits on a wooden veranda. Batteries can be charged in the main building, but otherwise there's no electricity.

For the equestrians out there, Camp Kalahari also offers horseriding safaris, with 3-, 4- & 5-night options, led by the very experienced David Foot. A 5-night itinerary includes 3 nights at Camp Kalahari & 2 fly-camping. The open pans & sparse vegetation combined with relatively low levels of dangerous game in the area make this ideal riding country.

The style here might be different from the more upmarket Jack's, but the activities (&, effectively, the location) are the same, making this a winning combination for the less well heeled. *US$650/815 pp sharing/sgl 16 Apr–Oct, US$475 Nov–15 Apr, inc FB, drinks, activities, laundry, park fees; riding from US$650 pp sharing per night, depending on numbers, plus US$325 tour leader fee for whole group. Transfers as Jack's Camp, above. No credit cards.* ⊕ *All year.*

14

What to see and do Like Sua Pan, Ntwetwe is an area for experienced Africa hands to explore in their own vehicles – though bear in mind my comments on safety under *Getting around* on pages 415–16. Alternatively, and much safer (albeit very expensive), fly in from Maun to one of the camps for three or four days and explore the pans and surrounding area with expert guides: on foot, by 4x4 or on quad bikes.

Ntwetwe Pan doesn't have anything quite so spectacular as Kubu Island, though it does have a few marvellous old baobabs and an island of its own.

Chapman's Baobab This famous landmark (⊕ CHAPMA 20°29.372'S, 25°14.898'E) was noted by Chapman when he passed with Thomas Baines in 1861. It's a big tree and visible from some distance away. Note that there are endless tracks to the west of here, many made by nearby private safari camps, and so navigation can be especially difficult, rendering a GPS essential.

Green's Baobab Less well known than Chapman's, this tree (⊕ GREENS 20°25.497'S, 25°13.869'E) is close to the only permanent spring in the area, Gutsha Pan, and still bears the inscription 'Green's Expedition 1858–1859' carved into its bark.

Gabasadi Island In the middle of Ntwetwe, to the west of the usual north–south route across the pans, Gabasadi Island is a low mound protruding from the surface of the pan. It's actually a fossilised, crescent-shaped barchan dune, which you'll realise if you climb it.

MAKGADIKGADI PANS NATIONAL PARK

Makgadikgadi Pans National Park covers about 3,900km² in a roughly square-shaped block to the west of the pans. It extends from the western edge of Ntwetwe Pan – one corner of which is incorporated within the park, fragmented into a myriad of smaller pans – westwards to the Boteti River, which marks the park's western boundary. To the north it meets the southern boundary of Nxai Pan National Park, from which it is separated only by the main Maun–Nata road. While for administrative purposes the two parks are often lumped together as Makgadikgadi and Nxai Pans National Park, here they are treated individually, as a reflection of their very different attractions.

BACKGROUND INFORMATION
Geography and geology About one-fifth of the national park consists of salt pan. The rest is rolling grasslands on Kalahari sands, rising here and there into fossilised dunes and low hills of thicker sand which mark prehistoric limits of the great Makgadikgadi superlake. The great breadth of the sandy Boteti watercourse and the riverine woodland that lines its steep banks are evidence of a major river that once carved a channel across central Botswana, carrying the waters of the Okavango into the Makgadikgadi basin.

Until 2008, the Boteti hadn't flooded properly for 16 years, but in early 2009 the water returned and began to advance south again. Today it flows right through to Lake Xau and stays throughout the dry season. That said, in 2013 many locals were predicting that after a couple of years of lower rainfall and floods, the river may gradually revert back to its previous dry-season state in the coming years. Time will tell but for now the transformation is quite something.

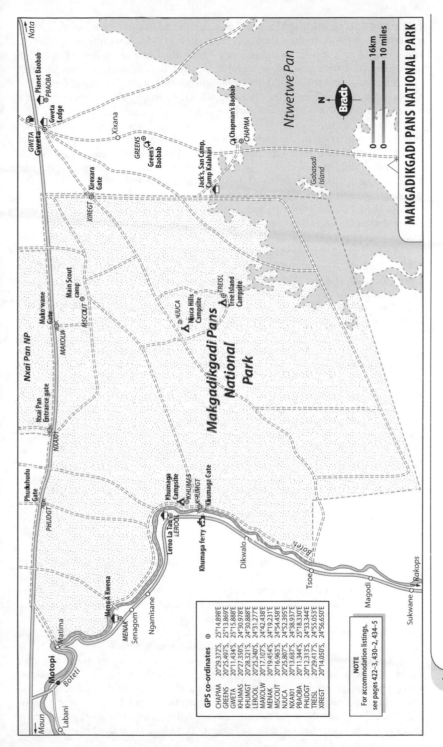

MAKGADIKGADI PANS NATIONAL PARK

GPS co-ordinates ⊕

CHAPMA	20°29.372'S, 25°14.898'E
GREENS	20°25.497'S, 25°13.869'E
GWETA	20°11.434'S, 25°15.888'E
KHUMAS	20°27.350'S, 24°30.978'E
KHUMGT	20°28.321'S, 24°30.888'E
LEROOL	20°25.240'S, 24°31.277'E
MAKOLW	20°17.107'S, 24°42.438'E
MENAK	20°19.454'S, 24°19.231'E
MSCOUT	20°16.963'S, 24°54.458'E
NUJCA	20°25.807'S, 24°52.395'E
NXAI01	20°13.637'S, 24°38.937'E
PBAOBA	20°11.344'S, 25°18.330'E
PHUDGT	20°12.313'S, 24°33.344'E
TREISL	20°29.417'S, 24°55.053'E
XIREGT	20°14.050'S, 24°56.650'E

NOTE
For accommodation listings,
see pages 422–3, 430–2, 434–5

MAKGADIKGADI PANS NATIONAL PARK

14

Flora and fauna highlights Makgadikgadi Pans National Park really contains a spectrum of environments, flora and fauna. Its east side, especially the southeast, is dominated by salt pans and grasslands – very much the same as the rest of Sua and Ntwetwe further east. Its western border, the Boteti River, is lined by thick riverine forest; here the wildlife has more in common with that found beside the Chobe or the Linyanti, or in the Okavango Delta. Between these two very different environments lies the body of the park.

Flora The vegetation on the east side of the park is very similar in pattern to that of the Makgadikgadi Pans (see pages 411–13). Its diversity increases westwards as the saline influence of the pan is left behind; from the bare surface of the pan itself, through rolling grassland and the vegetated dunes of Njuca Hills, into thicker acacia scrub, and eventually to the dense riverine woodland along the banks of the Boteti River. Along the eastern border there are areas of palm-tree woodland, where groves of vegetable ivory palms (*Hyphaene petersiana*) grow among the tracts of tall grassland.

On raised ground between the salt pans, yellowish patches of prickly salt grass (*Odyssea paucinervis*) flourish, contrasting with clumps of the dark succulent *Chenopodiacea* species. Along the pan edges you may also find a cactus-like succulent, *Hoodia lugardii*, which periodically produces striking maroon flowers. The open grasslands are studded with islands of trees and denser vegetation, with such species as the trumpet thorn (*Catophractas alexandri*) and western rhigozum (*Rhigozum brevispinosum*) flowering among the acacia scrub.

Beside the deep sand that normally characterises the Boteti River, camelthorns (*Acacia erioloba*), blackthorns (*Acacia mellifera*) and silver clusterleaf (*Termilalia sericea*) dominate the riverine forest, interspersed with a few other riverine giants such as sycamore figs (*Ficus sycomorus*) and sausage trees (*Kigelia africana*). From the early 1990s until 2009, most of the 'riverbed' itself consisted of a sandy channel carpeted in grasses and punctuated by occasional muddy pools of water. Now though, with the river flowing as far as Lake Xau again, this has all disappeared. Typically, the river flows for a period of 20–40 years, followed by a similar period of seasonal flow only. Thus, if history repeats itself, the Boteti is now likely to flow at least until the 2020s – although reality could see the river revert back to a dry cycle relatively quickly.

Fauna In the wet season, Makgadikgadi Pans National Park boasts good concentrations of grazers that rival those of Nxai Pan to the north, and an aerial view shows the area to be latticed with a dense network of game trails. From about June onwards, herds of Burchell's zebra and blue wildebeest start a westward movement towards the lush grazing around the Boteti River, accompanied by smaller numbers of gemsbok, eland and red hartebeest. (The latter tend to come slightly later, in years when the rains have been exceptionally good.) These herds gradually congregate along the waterfront until, by November, this area becomes jam-packed with game. In attendance are leopard and lion, attracted by the high concentration of prey. You might also be lucky enough to glimpse the elusive white rhino.

In the ecozone between grassland and woodland, browsers such as kudu, bushbuck and grey duiker find a permanent home, while troops of baboons and vervet monkeys forage beneath the trees, and small numbers of giraffe and elephant often occur. The area also supports a small waterbuck population, resident pairs of bushbuck (locals say the same subspecies/race as the Chobe bushbuck) and – now that the Boteti is flowing once more – plenty of hippo. There are also some huge crocodiles, many of which survived for years in the caves along the banks of the riverbed and are now reaping the rewards of their patience.

In peak season, from September to November, the area around the Boteti can offer truly outstanding wildlife watching, and the air is filled with the hiccoughing calls of the milling zebra herds. However, with the arrival of the rains in December–January, the herds disperse. Some head north towards Nxai Pan; others gather in the grazing grounds of the southeast, where their migration route beyond the park to the Central Kalahari is blocked by a veterinary cordon fence. At this time, zebra and gemsbok may often be seen out on the pans in search of the mineral salts that are lacking on the Kalahari grasslands.

A healthy population of large predators, protected in the park from persecution by ranchers, includes lion, cheetah, leopard, spotted and brown hyena. Lion can be common during peak migration, with prides knocking down more zebra than they can consume and (be warned) sometimes wandering inquisitively through the campsites. Cheetah are less common, but may turn up anywhere where there are springbok, while leopard are permanent residents of the denser bush along the Boteti. Spotted hyena, like lion, follow the dry-season herds, while brown hyenas find life more productive (and less competitive) along the park's eastern side.

In the east of the park the campsite at Njuca Hills offers a panoramic base from which to explore the wildlife of the pans and grasslands. Herds of springbok, well adapted to survive the arid and exposed conditions, are common around the pans, while steenbok – usually found in pairs – are also widespread. Nocturnal predators of the pan fringes include brown hyena, aardwolf, bat-eared fox and striped polecat, while black-backed jackal, African wildcat, honey badger and small spotted genet can occur anywhere in the park. Other small mammals include porcupine, aardvark,

THE LIONS OF MAKGADIKGADI

Makgadikgadi is an erratic and uncertain place for lions. With the first rains, huge herds of zebra and wildebeest move out on to the plains to graze on the succulent grasses and drop their young. In the dry months this pulse of life ebbs back to the Boteti River, 50km to the west, leaving the plains largely deserted by large ungulates. The lions have had to adapt to these huge fluctuations and the unpredictability.

For some the solution is simply tracking the herds back to the Boteti for the dry months, where they must dodge the human residents on the west side of the river. Others stay behind amidst the parched grasses, swirling dust devils and spring hares. This is not the place for huge ungainly prides; rather lionesses pair up and wander over large areas, often in excess of 1,000km², in order to find sufficient food. Males typically spread their time between two or more of these small, efficient prides. They can maintain territories of almost double that, walking up to 50km a night to patrol their vast swathes of baked wasteland.

Water is unavailable for up to seven months a year for these lions, so they must gain all their moisture from their prey. Immediately after killing large prey such as gemsbok they snick open the belly and stomach, slurping up the juices before they soak away into the sand. However, large prey is hard to find during the dry season, so they will hunt aardvarks and porcupines, and they increasingly look outside the eastern and western boundaries of the park for sustenance from herds of dopey, slow-moving livestock.

14

spring hare and scrub hare as well as a host of smaller rodents and insectivores (see the general section on pans fauna, pages 413–14).

In sandy areas, ground squirrels (here at the northern limit of their Kalahari range) forage by day in small colonies, holding up their tails as parasols against the fierce sun and dashing for their burrows at any hint of danger. These sociable rodents associate amicably with yellow mongooses, who share their burrow systems and help keep a look-out for predators.

THE CLANS OF THE MAKGADIKGADI

The brown hyena (*Hyaena brunnea*) is one of the three hyena species in southern Africa, the other two being a successful scavenger and hunter, the spotted hyena, and the insectivorous aardwolf. Brown hyena are classed as 'near threatened', with a total population of under 10,000 – of which the Makgadikgadi Pans National Park has about 150 adults.

The brown hyena has evolved to live in desert systems throughout southern Africa, where it occurs at low densities. This shy, nocturnal animal is a solitary forager that can survive independently of permanent surface water. Brown hyenas will eat virtually anything, apart from grass or herbage – and here their diet ranges from old carcasses or ostrich eggs to melons and scorpions.

The Makgadikgadi Brown Hyena Project was established near Jack's Camp in 2003 to improve the management and conservation of this elusive carnivore. This included investigating foraging strategies, scent-marking behaviour, space and resources requirements, and establishing the impact of the Makgadikgadi game fence on the populations of brown hyenas living on both sides of the fence, through changes in food availability and loss of access to the cattle areas. The project followed research in the same area by Glyn Maude as part of his PhD from the University of Bristol.

During the project, Glyn observed that individuals will often cover over 65km in a night when foraging in the Makgadikgadi. Here lion kills are an important source of food. Over the wet season, these are often zebra and wildebeest, whilst over the dry season, when food is more scarce, they can frequently be cattle and other livestock carcasses.

Brown hyenas are not truly solitary animals; they live in clans of between two and ten members. While clans' territories cover 200–1,000km², clan members are rarely seen together since they forage alone, only interacting with other clan members either by a chance meeting while foraging, or at a communal den site. Some brown hyenas, the males in particular, are not part of a clan but are nomadic. Clan members will often be tolerant of an intruder of the opposite sex, but will chase away same-sex intruders.

Brown hyenas are usually almost silent: their vocalisations are minimal. Long-distance communication is by a unique double scent mark deposited on grass stalks. These marks can be made as often as every 150m of foraging, and as well as communicating with other clan members, the scent mark is also a marker for the clan's territory. Defecations are also used as territorial markers and can be found in concentrations in 'latrine sites' which are often located along territorial boundaries. The presence of brown hyenas is more often indicated by their spoor or scent marks, as sightings of the animal in the wild are very uncommon.

Reptiles Perhaps the most bizarre report from this park is of some of the Boteti's larger crocodiles which, when the river drops drastically during the dry season, or dries up completely, retreat into holes in the riverbank that they have dug for themselves. One such lair that I saw was a good 4–5m above the level of water even in May, and would have been completely high and dry by October.

Birdlife The birdlife of Makgadikgadi Pans National Park is largely the same as that elsewhere in the greater Makgadikgadi region (see page 414), with a grading of species according to habitat, and a large summer influx of migrants.

The denser woodland along the Boteti also harbours more cover-loving species such as Myer's parrot, woodland kingfisher, Burchell's coucal and Heuglin's robin, while the return of permanent water has attracted waterbirds such as black-winged stilts, pelicans, cranes and African fish eagles. Many raptors cruise the skies over the park, with gabar goshawks hunting the thickets, secretary birds stalking the savannah, and vultures following the game herds in search of carcasses. In summer, storks, bee-eaters, kites, shrikes and other migrants move in and fan out across the grasslands.

GETTING AROUND If you're driving yourself here then ideally come armed with a copy of the Shell map of Botswana (see page 100 for details), with its wealth of GPS co-ordinates. Then take to heart my caveats in *Getting around*, pages 415–16, and you're ready to explore.

First you'll need to head for one of the scout camps to sign in (though remember that you must have prepaid your park fees; see pages 84–7). The main scout camp (⊕ MSCOUT 20°16.963'S, 24°54.458'E) is inside the park, some 10km south of the Makolwane Gate (⊕ MAKOLW 20°17.107'S, 24°42.438'E, on the Nata–Maun road. This lies about 42km west of Gweta, and about 22km east of the entrance gate to Nxai Pans. Some 34km west of the Makolwane Gate along this road is the new Phuduhudu Gate (⊕ PHUDGT 20°12.313'S, 24°33.344'E), opened in 2009. Both gates are manned.

The alternative scout camp (⊕ KHUMAS 20°27.350'S, 24°30.978'E) is near the Khumaga Gate, on the western side of the park, near the Boteti River. The gate itself – ⊕ KHUMGT 20°28.321'S, 24°30.888'E – is on the other side of the river, and is currently reached via a small but adequate ferry (m *7400 2228; P150 per vehicle*). Finally, there is another new – if little-known – gate, Xirexara (⊕ XIREGT 20°14.050'S, 24°56.650'E), on the eastern side of the park. Note that if you enter the park at any other point – and there are several – then you should go straight to one of the scout posts; meandering through the park without having signed in first is against the rules.

Driving around, you'll find a basic network of sandy tracks that are clearly defined even in the rainy season, when the grass is very high. Moving away from these, though, the tracks are increasingly overgrown and difficult to follow. The more southerly roads, crossing the pans, are particularly hard to locate; arguably they are simply non-existent, washed away with each year's rains. Equally, those around the centre of the eastern side of the park are so numerous that they're totally confusing, complicated by a whole network of tracks used by the camps in the area.

Many visitors enter the park on one side and leave from another – which can make perfect sense. However, with the Boteti River now flowing all the way to Lake Xau, it's as well to check that the ferry is working before committing yourself to entering or leaving the park on the western side at the Khumaga Gate.

14

WHERE TO STAY Both the lodges to the north of this area have spectacular settings on the western bank of the Boteti River, opposite the park. Although the campsite that was once adjacent to Leroo La Tau has now closed, campers have the choice of three campsites within the national park: Khumaga, Njuca Hills and Tree Island. As with all national parks' sites, these must be booked in advance (see pages 86–7). There has been talk for a number of years of a third lodge to be built further south, near Tsoe, but as yet nothing has come of it.

Meno A Kwena Tented Camp [map 425] (8 tents) ☎ 686 0981; e reservations@menoakwena. com; www.menoakwena.com; ✪ MENAK 20°19.454'S, 24°19.231'E (turn off from road ✪ MENATN 20°16.310'S, 24°15.577'E or, slightly further south, MENATS 20°20.538'S, 24°17.848'E). Set on top of a 40m-high bank overlooking a bend in the Boteti River, Meno A Kwena has a highly unusual location for a camp in Botswana, & benefits from regular visits by lion. It's also unusual in that it's independently owned & run by ex-mobile safari operator David Dugmore, who aims to offer a fairly authentic, low-impact safari experience. While the normal mould of 2 activities per day with a rest between is on offer, there's considerable choice. As well as game drives, there are seasonal day trips to Nxai Pan & Makgadikgadi Pans, mobile safaris to the salt pans & a meerkat colony, or – on request – visits to the CKGR (min 3 nights). When the river is flowing, which it has been for the past few years, guests can reach Makgadikgadi Pans National Park after only a short drive & a boat across the river.

Each tent is built inside its own kraal – an enclosure of narrow tree trunks – with views over the river to the national park. Push aside a 'doorway' of half-a-dozen stakes to find a small Meru-style tent, an unusual bucket shower & a separate toilet rondavel. The feel is that of a rather quirky mobile camp, with a bio-oil lamp & a water flask alongside proper twin beds (or 1 dbl) with down duvets,

enlivened by brass dishes & colourful cushions. Outside are 2 safari chairs, a steel day bed, a washbasin on a stand & a couple of safari chests. The camp has solar-power lights, but no other electricity & no running water (except to flush the toilets).

Sand paths through the bush link the rooms to the main central tent. Fronted by a sandy courtyard area, this is of traditional green canvas, complete with guy ropes. The space is split between a fairly large bar, a dining area whose huge dining table is inset with glazed panels displaying local artefacts, & a comfortable lounge area. Overlooking the river & flanked by two small canvas shelters is a rock pool that does service as a plunge pool, while out of sight below is the camp's hide. Across the site, more of those safari chests have been pressed into service as shelves, cupboards, tables & trunks, lending a slightly nomadic feel. The relaxed atmosphere is accentuated by hand-crafted wrought-iron furniture & an eclectic selection of books; it's the sort of place where someone might pick up a guitar & start strumming.

Perhaps more than most camps, Meno A Kwena attracts a wide range of visitors, including independent travellers, safari-goers & a number of NGO workers. *US$350/500 pp sharing/sgl Dec–Mar, US$450/595 Apr–Jun & Nov, US$600/830 Jul–Oct, inc FB, drinks, all activities, park fees, road transfers, laundry. Self-drive US$250/355–310/420 pp FB only.* ⊕ *All year.*

OSTRICH BREEDING

Ostriches are particularly common in the eastern grasslands, and can often be seen from the main Nata–Maun road. These huge birds breed before the rains, with several females laying in a single scrape that may hold over 30 eggs. Incubation tends to rotate between the male at night (when his dark plumage is no longer vulnerable to overheating), and the female by day (when her drab plumage provides more effective camouflage). Youngsters from several broods gather together in large crèches, presided over by one adult pair, and can sometimes be seen gathering in the shadow of an adult for shade.

⌂ **Leroo La Tau** [map 425] (12 chalets) Contact Desert & Delta Safaris, page 176; ⊕ LEROOL 20°25.240'S, 24°31.277'E (turn off from road ⊕ LEROTO 20°26.231'S, 24°27.935'E). This long-established lodge, perched 15m above the Boteti River, lies in an area that can provide remarkable game spectacles. In 2008, under the Desert & Delta umbrella, the lodge was fully refurbished, its chalets completely rebuilt to a high specification. Most guests arrive by air from Maun, although self-driving is an option.

Until 2009, the star draw of the lodge was its extensive hide overlooking a large waterhole in the riverbed, with elephants & other wildlife in regular attendance. However, as water returned to the river, the waterhole rapidly disappeared, which in turn shifted the game dynamic of this area. The hide, & another above by the firepit, still looks out on to some fantastic scenery with game often coming down to drink on the opposite bank of the river, but the immediacy of the animals is gone.

Up a few steps, you'll find a small pool, surrounded by a large lawn set out with wooden loungers. Set back again is the main lodge, one long wall fronted by a shady veranda. Inside, it's light & modern, but not austere, the teak flooring & tables offset by leather directors' chairs & a neutral décor. Most visitors dine as a group, but there's plenty of flexibility, with individual tables always an option. Upstairs, above the bar, upholstered chairs & sofas are an enticing place to relax with a book, or to keep an eye on the river from the look-out window. Back at ground level, there's a good shop, selling reasonably priced curios & a range of books.

Accommodation is in smart thatched chalets, built into the treeline, overlooking the Boteti. Each has a large veranda with 2 day beds & a table, from which glazed sliding doors, backed by screens, lead into the bedroom. Furnished with a dbl & a single bed, bedside lamps, a dressing table & a comfortable chair, these are modern & unfussy. In the adjacent bathroom, with twin basins & a huge shower, the loo shares the channel view. Power is supplied by generator, & the hot water is efficient, though the water smells slightly of sulphur due to the natural chemicals in the area's groundwater.

Morning & afternoon game drives in 6-seater vehicles take visitors to explore beyond camp, either in a relatively narrow neck of land enclosed by a loop of the Boteti or into the park itself. Either way, this represents lots of riverfront – which is where the game is usually concentrated. Despite its location at the eastern end of a bend in the river inside the perimeter fence of the park, & surrounded by it on 3 sides, the lodge remains technically outside the park – which means that game drives can continue after dark. Guests staying 3 nights or more can opt for a full-day trip to Nxai Pan, but this must be pre-booked. *US$873/1,135 pp sharing/sgl Jul–Oct, US$495 pp Jan–Mar & Dec, US$573 pp Apr–Jun & Nov, fully inc.* ⊕ *All year.*

Å **Khumaga Campsite** [map 425] (9 pitches) Contact SKL, page 174; ⊕ KHUMAS 20°27.350'S, 24°30.978'E. Khumaga, sometimes written 'Xhumaga' or plain 'Kumaga', stands near the east bank of the (normally dry) Boteti River, close to one of the scout camps, & about 4km south of Leroo La Tau. It's a large, flat site, with extensive tree shade & a firepit for each pitch. There are 2 modern thatched ablution blocks, one for each sex, with flush toilets, washbasins, & showers heated by solar power, but the old facilities remain, too, perhaps in case the donkey boilers prove to be more reliable. *US$50 pp, exc park fees, bed levy.* ⊕ *All year.*

Å **Njuca Hills Campsite** [map 425] (2 sites) Contact DWNP, page 87; ⊕ NJUCA 20°25.807'S, 24°52.395'E. This basic site in the heart of the park, about 38km east of Khumaga, is slightly elevated (no more than about 20m), on one of a series of low, fossilised dunes, with an outcrop of trees for shade. Here you'll find no water or firewood, but there are pluses (aside from the seclusion): each site has a firepit, a newly built bucket shower & a long-drop toilet. Expect the main wildlife to be barking geckos & perhaps the odd curious yellow mongoose.

Just to emphasise the safety issues raised about travelling in any of the pans, visitors Richard & Vikki Threlfall wrote to me: 'We broke down at Njuca Hills Campsite, & were not found until the third morning after discovering the problem! And then it was only pure chance.' Note that this happened at one of only 2 official campsites in the park, & realise that it would have taken a full-scale air search to find them if they'd been off the main routes. Do take heed of the safety issues detailed in *Getting around*, pages 415–16, before you travel anywhere in the pans area. *P30 pp, exc park fees.* ⊕ *All year.*

14

⚠ Tree Island Campsite [map 425] (3 sites) Contact DWNP, page 87; ✪ TREISL 20°29.417'S, 24°55.053'E. Situated on the edge of a deep pan, about 8km southeast of Njuca Hills, this is one of the most remote & isolated campsites in northern Botswana. Opened in 2012, it's the newest camp in the area & again there is no water: just long-drop toilets & bucket showers. *P30 pp; exc park fees.* ⊕ *All year.*

WHAT TO SEE AND DO Like the bulk of Sua Pan or the rest of Ntwetwe Pan, the Makgadikgadi Pans National Park is really an area for experienced Africa hands to explore in their own vehicles – though bear in mind my comments on safety under *Getting around* on pages 415–16. That said, in the late dry season you won't be quite so isolated if you stick to the road in the park which runs beside the Boteti River and the Khumaga Campsite, which will then have quite a few visitors. Alternatively, and much safer, stay at one of the lodges outside the park, exploring each area with their expert local guides: the pans on the eastern side with Uncharted Africa, or the contrasting Boteti riverfront with Leroo La Tau or Meno A Kwena.

TOWNS AROUND THE PANS

The small towns around the pans, from Nata west to Motopi then south to Rakops, tend to be used by visitors driving themselves simply as places to refuel and replenish basic supplies; those flying into the area's camps will probably never see any of them. All the towns along this route have mobile-phone coverage, but don't expect any signal between them.

NATA Nata itself is a very small place at the junction of the tar road to Maun, Kasane and Francistown. For many years it was little more than a filling stop for most people, where the vital garage relied on hand-cranked petrol pumps, and the well-stocked Sua Pan Bottle Store was always busy. Fuel is still the main reason for people to stop, though now the town boasts three modern fuel stations at the junction (NATA ✪ 20°12.693'S, 26°10.859'E), each with either a shop or a fast-food outlet. With these, plus a branch of Barclays Bank with an ATM, a post office and a handful of local shops, including a baker and a butcher just over the river, Nata is a reasonable place to get organised. There's even a cash and carry at the junction, useful for larger groups wanting to stock up on basic supplies. And if you're in need of repairs to your vehicle, try contacting Nata Garage on the Kasane road (🖀 621 1450).

In 2013, a small arts and craft shop, Fresh Bright (m 7411 9788), had just opened, selling some good-quality local baskets and beads. You'll find it near the bridge heading out of town towards Francistown.

With some decent places to stay, Nata is also a good choice for an overnight stop. Those planning to linger might seek out the nearby Nata Sanctuary (see pages 418–19), on the northern edge of Sua Pan, or use it as a base for exploring the pan as a whole. As an aside, staff at both Northgate Lodge and Pelican Lodge talk with enthusiasm about the wildlife at Dzibanana Pan, about 5km north of town close to the Zimbabwean border, which is reported when filled with water (roughly between April and August) to attract buffalo and sable.

🏠 **Where to stay and eat** When a fire destroyed the established Nata Lodge in 2008, other accommodation options opened up to fill the gap. Now, with the lodge rebuilt and the opening of the new Pelican Lodge, there is plenty of choice. It is also possible to camp at Nata Sanctuary (see page 419). For campsites and lodges north of Nata, see *Chapter 8, Kasane to Nata* (pages 203–4).

Most visitors to Nata are either self-catering or eat at their lodge. For those just passing through, the restaurants at Nata, Pelican and Northgate lodges are all open to non-residents. Alternatively, there's fast food in the form of Barcelos Flame-Grilled Chicken at the Engen garage, or a Wimpy at Caltex.

🏠 **Nata Lodge** [map 397] (22 chalets, 10 Meru tents, camping) ✆ 620 0070; e reservations@ natalodge.com; www.natalodge.com; ⊕ 20°13.448'S, 26°16.052'E. Nata Lodge lies about 10km east of Nata towards Francistown, & is well signposted just off the main road. It stands in a patch of sparse woodland with real fan palms & marula trees. It was completely rebuilt in 2009, following a fire that destroyed the original building.

The new-look lodge builds on the success of the old. Thatched wooden chalets raised on stilts have AC & twin beds, & their en-suite facilities incorporate a bath & outdoor shower. Two of the rooms have extra bunk beds, for families, & a 3rd is designed for improved access for those with limited mobility. The en-suite safari tents, also with twin beds & an outdoor shower, are tucked into the bush.

One room (23) has decking leading straight into the main area, where there are disabled toilets, making it suitable for those with limited mobility. Nearby is a very large campsite with space for 150 campers & separate male & female ablution blocks. The restaurant has seating indoors & out. At lunchtime there's a 'terrace menu', with evening meals either à la carte or, when it's busy, a braai dinner (P150). The pool is right in front of the bar area, & there's also a shop selling curios as well as books, maps & clothes. On an ad hoc basis, there are trips into Nata Sanctuary & on to the pans (P165 pp/3hrs, min 3 people). **$$$** *exc b/fast; camping P80 pp.* ⊕ *All year.*

🏠 **Northgate Lodge** (22 rooms) ✆ 621 1156; e northgatelodge@yahoo.com. Right in the centre of Nata, adjacent to the Caltex garage, this deceptively large lodge opened in 2008. It's urban in concept, with good-sized twin, dbl & family rooms built in blocks. Painted a deep red & with tiled floors, they're pleasant & modern with walk-in mosquito nets, kettle & TV, plus AC & a fridge in the more expensive rooms. Best are those overlooking the free-form pool or small garden rather than the garage. The bar & restaurant are open to non-residents, as are the internet facilities (P30/½hr), & there's Wi-Fi throughout. There's also a limited amount of safe parking. Activities include trips to

Dzibanana Pan & Nata Sanctuary. **$$$** *exc b/fast.* ⊕ *All year.*

🏠 **Pelican Lodge** [map 397] (38 rooms, 4 suites, camping) ✆ 247 0117; e reservations@ pelicanlodge.co.bw; www.pelicanlodgebotswana. com. About 7km south of Nata, on the Francistown road, Pelican Lodge opened in 2012. More a stark hotel than a lodge, it dominates a vast site with a series of large concrete, thatched buildings linked by thatched walkways on concrete slabs. The whole property is surrounded by an indiscreet 3m fence, which at least helps to keep out the livestock.

There isn't really just one main area here. The reception area & à-la-carte restaurant are in different sections of one building, there's a bar in another room & a totally separate building houses the 'Boma Bar' – a more informal restaurant where b/fast is served. And there's another well-stocked bar & big-screen TV. At the front of all this is an inviting swimming pool which, in keeping with everything else, is large & spread out. Most of the rooms are twin or dbl, but 3 are for families. All come with AC, satellite TV, tea & coffee station, writing desk, safe, fridge & phone , plus a couple of wicker chairs & a table. En-suite bathrooms have both a bath with a shower & an outside shower – though if privacy is your thing, go for the indoor option. Furthest away from the road, a well-designed campsite has a central braai & washing up area, as well as a large ablution block for both sexes & a communal firepit. 3 sites sport their own private ablution blocks & braai stands. Activities include a tour of a local village, trips to Nata Sanctuary & game drives to Dzibanana Pan.

Pelican Lodge is adequate for a 1-night stopover; the staff are helpful & friendly, & the food is varied & very tasty. That said, it does feel as though it's trying to be all things to all men. With a campsite, a conference centre & guest rooms up to the 'presidential' suite, it's tempting to wish that they would concentrate on just one market. **$$$** *exc b/fast; camping P80 pp.* ⊕ *All year.*

🏠 **Nata Guest Inn** (8 rooms) ✆ 621 1156; m 7145 0066; e nata.guest.inn@gmail.com. For a clean, inexpensive 1-night stopover, Nata Guest Inn is a good option. Built in 2004, its twin or dbl rooms are en suite with a bath or shower, & for a larger group there's a family room. Most rooms have AC, with plans to roll this out across the remainder soon. A small bar & restaurant is strictly for guests only, but activities will need to be organised elsewhere. **$$** *exc b/fast.* ☺ *All year.*

🏠 **Maya Guest Inn** (8 chalets) m 7673 1521, 7701 7707. On the left of the main road towards Francistown, just before the river, this simple inn opened at the end of 2008. It's a small complex of square, thatched chalets, with AC, kettle with tea & coffee, & TV. For meals you'll have to go elsewhere,

but at least security should be thorough, as it's opposite the police station & there's a security guard on duty throughout the night. **$–$$** *exc b/fast.* ☺ *All year.*

🏠 **Riverside Campsite** (7 pitches) ✆ 621 1155; ⊕ 20°10.801'S, 26°10.751'E. Some 2km north of Nata towards Kasane, this very open campsite overlooking the Nata River is owned by the former owner of Northgate Lodge. There's a bar, several camping pitches each with its own braai area, & a unisex ablution block. *Camping P45.* ☺ *All year.*

GWETA

Gweta (⊕ GWETA 20°11.434'S, 25°15.888'E) is a small, old village about 2km south of the road between Nata and Maun, about 205km from Maun and 100km from Nata. The **fuel station** just east of the junction (⊕ GWFUEL 20°11.438'S, 25°15.896'E) is conveniently situated for those exploring Makgadikgadi and Nxai pans, and usefully has a shop selling the basics, sometimes fresh produce such as bread and tomatoes. They also serve Zambian dishes such as goat's liver or beef to order. In the village, the rather grandly named Maano **supermarket** (advertising 'Restaurant, arms & ammunition') sells the basics, plus some freshish fruit and vegetables, but offered little in the way of service when last visited.

Getting there and away Gweta is very clearly signposted from the main road, in an area of mostly stunted mopane woodlands with the odd small clay pan. Turning off you'll come to a fork, with a couple of shops on your right, and a post office on your left, before reaching the lodge.

For those using public transport there are very regular bus services between Maun and Francistown, with up to five a day to and from Nata. They usually turn into town and stop in the centre, near the Maano Supermarket. If not, ask the driver to stop on the road beside the turn-off to Planet Baobab. From here, the trip to Maun is about three hours and costs around P50; Francistown is some four hours away, at about P70.

🏠 **Where to stay** The choices here are starkly different: the recently upgraded but traditional Gweta Lodge in the village itself, or the funky, rustic-trendy Planet Baobab about 4km to the east. Both can be used as a base to explore Ntwetwe Pan or the Makgadikgadi Pans National Park, although most self-drive visitors will probably opt to camp nearer the pans instead. That said, both also offer day and overnight trips on to the pans, including quadbike excursions, so can be ideal for those without a vehicle. For accommodation right on the pans, see pages 422–3. There are also campsites in the national park (see pages 431–2).

🏠 **Gweta Lodge** [map 397] (15 rooms, camping) ✆ 621 2220; e gwetalodge@botsnet. bw; www.gwetalodge.com. This old restcamp has undergone something of a transformation in recent years. At the centre is a thatched bar & lounge area, with a small but sparkling pool in front. Twin, dbl & family en-suite rooms have fans, mosi nets & tiled floors. The smaller rondavels are

much nicer than they look, with fans & modern en-suite facilities. Across the entrance track is a level, grassy campsite, with toilets & showers, some pre-erected tents, & 3 further twin rooms. It used to be quite compact, so could get noisy as the site is popular with groups, but a recent redesign has spread things out somewhat. Campers can use the bar, pool & lounge at the lodge. Meals are served in the homely if old-fashioned restaurant, which is entirely separate.

Activities include village tours (P100 pp) & overnight fly-camping excursions into Nxai Pan, the Makgadikgadi, Ntwetwe Pan & the Central Kalahari for 2–30 guests (around P1,200 pp/day; discount for groups over 10). Quadbiking onto the pans, although no longer offered in late 2013, may be restarted in 2014. **$$** *exc b/fast; camping P60 pp.* ☺ *All year.*

⌂ **Planet Baobab** [map 397] (18 huts, camping) m 7233 8344; contact Uncharted Africa, page 422. From the giant aardvark at the entrance (⊕ PBAOBA 20°11.344'S, 25°18.330'E) to the subterranean feel of the reception 'tunnel', it's clear that Planet Baobab is indeed on another planet. Set in a grove of giant baobabs, it is just south of the main Nata–Maun road, & combines a Makgadikgadi Pans experience for a clientele who can't afford the prices of the trio of camps on the pans with somewhere interesting to stop for those driving past.

A sense of fun is evident in the well-furnished lodge, with bold local designs used to exuberant effect on the extensive surfaces of polished concrete. The focus is a funky bar area, dominated by a large, curved bar & lit by chandeliers made from local beer bottles. Seating is on hide-covered chairs at small concrete-plinth tables & there's a fine collection of interesting artefacts on the walls. Service is friendly, though food – served here or in the similarly styled restaurant – is nothing special (think chips with everything). That said, those booked on a fully inclusive itinerary can choose dishes from a pan-African menu. Outside is a superb 18m diameter circular pool, with a shallow area for children & thatched gazebos at the side: a great place to relax.

Traditional thatched 'mud' huts – actually brick clad in cement – offer intriguing accommodation, with everything inside rounded as if it were made of mud. Although similar in design, the Baobab chalets are slightly more spacious than the Bakalanga. A sgl bed is built into each side of the room, under a mosquito net, & there's an en-suite washbasin, toilet & shower. 3 family huts have a central dbl bed too, & a designated parking spot outside. All are well designed, with glazed windows & trendy wall mirrors, but lighting is really poor, so take a torch. All the huts have parking.

The campsite has 4 showers & toilets (separated for men & women) built into a large & stylish thatched rondavel – complete with lights set into the walls & clothes-hooks made from branches. Each site has a thatched shelter with power & washing-up facilities to hand.

A variety of trips can be organised out of Planet Baobab. These include a guided 2hr village & cattlepost tour (P480 pp) which takes in a visit to the local primary school, Gweta's *kgotla* (traditional court), & a stop at the traditional healer, as well as a meal with a local family (typically of sorghum, mealie meal, *seswaa* (beef stew), wild spinach, mopane worms in season, wild beans & perhaps creamy baobab fruit milkshake). There's always a chance to sample some of the local sorghum beer, too (it's an acquired taste!). With advance notice, a similar meal can be prepared in the restaurant, at P125 pp. A second option is a 2hr baobab bushwalk & sundowner (P190 pp), concentrating on the environment, the traditional uses of plants & animals, the history of the area & perhaps some local stories. Further afield are ½-day, full-day & overnight trips to Ntwetwe Pan (P930–1,610 pp, inc quadbikes), & a full-day Nxai Pan excursion (P1,985 pp) – or, between Nov & Mar, a full-day game drive to follow the zebra & wildebeest migration inside the national park. All excursions are for a min of 2 people, & on Nxai Xini Pan can involve sleeping out on a bedroll under the stars. With minimal dangerous game around, this is all you need & is a great way to sleep. **$$$/$$$$** *low/high season; camping P73/49 adult/child under 12. Visa & MasterCard accepted.* ☺ *All year.*

MOTOPI A few kilometres west of the Makgadikgadi Pans National Park, this large village is now linked to the main Maun–Nata road by a bridge (⊕ MOTOBR 20°12.723'S, 24°07.600'E) over the Boteti River. The timing couldn't be more apt, since in 2009 the river flowed at this point for the first time in 16 years, making the original crossing point impassable. Apart from a general dealer on the left by the bridge, there's nothing to delay visitors. (Though as an aside, the original gravel road, signposted to Moreomaoto, leads to the river, affording some lovely views and a nice picnic spot.)

From Motopi, a good tarred road runs parallel to the western bank of the river as far as Rakops (126km) and Mopipi, then around to Orapa and Letlhakane. From here the road splits, with one fork heading for Francistown, and the other for Palapye; both are now tarred and of good quality. Most of this area is flat, cattle-farming territory, much of it lush and green during the rains, though with the vegetation thinning out as you head south towards Rakops. If you don't fancy pulling off into the bush, several picnic spots along the side of the road offer the chance to stop.

KHUMAGA The village of Khumaga just east of the main road marks another gate (KHUMGT 20°28.321'S, 24°30.888'E) into the Makgadikgadi Pans National Park, leading directly to the scout post and Khumaga Campsite via a ferry across the Boteti River.

RAKOPS Useful as a refuelling stop and reachable now entirely on tarmac from Maun, Rakops (✪ RAKOPS 21°02.136'S, 24°24.432'E) is notable as the last outpost passed on many trips into the Central Kalahari Game Reserve.

The village itself sprawls to the east of the road. A ragged remnant of tar runs down the centre of the road, flanked by widely spaced huts and bungalows, and a few general stores. The small fuel station is about 500m from the main road; just bear right after the first crossroads and it's on the right. If you're in search of bread, continue along this road past Morningside General Dealers and you'll come to Tsienyane Leathercraft – where, somewhat surprisingly, there's an excellent bakery. Following this road to the end eventually brings you back to the main road towards Orapa.

 Where to stay While there is nowhere to stay in Rakops itself, there's a useful little lodge and campsite just 7km north of the turning off the main road and a similar-size motel just south of the town.

⌂ **Xere Motel** [map 396] (11 rooms) ☎297 5068; m 7267 5568; ✪ XERMOT 21°02.834'S, 24°24.008'E. Continuing south along the main road, pass the 1st turning to Rakops on your left, & after a further 3km you'll arrive at the Xere Motel. Established in 2004, its identical dbl rooms are small but clean & comfortable, with AC, satellite TV, fridge & en-suite shower, bath & toilet. There's an à-la-carte restaurant on site & laundry can be done at extra cost. **$$** *exc b/fast.* ☺ *All year.*

⌂ **Rakops River Lodge** [map 396] (10 chalets, camping) ☎393 2711; m 7143 4129; e enquires@ rakopsriverlodge.com; www.rakopsriverlodge.

com; ✪ RKRLO 20°59.189'S, 24°21.748'E. Close to the eastern side of the road, this simple but clean & very friendly motel – formerly the Sekgwa Sa Metsi Motel – opened under this name in 2012. Its small chalets each have a dbl or twin beds & tiled, en-suite facilities with bath & shower attachment, & 6 have AC. A couple of family rooms were being constructed in late 2013. Visitors can cook up their own braai, or eat in the large if rather empty dining area. The 9 pitches at the campsite have running water & a unisex ablution block, with power available on request. **$** *exc b/fast; camping P50 pp.* ☺ *All year.*

ORAPA AND LETLHAKANE **Orapa** is at the heart of Botswana's diamond-mining operations, producing around 12% of the world's gem-quality diamonds. This makes it by far the most important town in the country to Botswana's economy, and hence security there is very tight. You're not allowed in, or out, without permission from the diamond company Debswana, which isn't given easily. Hence it's effectively off-limits to visitors and there's a road that detours around the south side of the mine.

LIONS VS LIVESTOCK

When Graham Hemson worked as a guide at Jack's Camp, he was studying for a PhD on lion ecology and conservation in the Makgadikgadi area as part of Oxford University's Wildlife Conservation Research Unit. In 1999 he estimated that there were about 39 lions in the Makgadikgadi area, where he investigated their impact on people, and vice versa.

Every year lions kill hundreds of domestic animals in and around the Makgadikgadi Pans National Park, which brings them into conflict with the herders and owners. In retaliation people have, in the past, laid out traps and poison, and hunted lions outside the park with ruthless efficiency. As a result, between November 1999 and May 2000, at least 12 lions were killed.

However, contrary to common belief, Graham's research indicated that livestock predation does not happen mainly inside the kraal, but rather out in the grazing areas and sometimes inside the park. Although lions will tackle livestock in the villages, often they can simply pick off the many untended stragglers. An interesting ecological response to the predictability of livestock as prey is that lions that eat livestock have substantially smaller home ranges than those that are dependent on migratory prey, or scarce desert species.

Typically, this livestock predation is only a problem when wild prey is scarce. When zebra and wildebeest migrate out of their territories, lions are forced to change their preferences abruptly.

After surveying the local inhabitants, Graham found that many of the people in charge of the livestock were elderly women; often their husbands were living in town, running more lucrative family businesses. These women were physically unable to keep track of their cattle – resulting in a large number of stray animals which made a veritable manmade buffet for lions.

Following Graham's conclusions, Botswana's Department of Wildlife has lobbied its Veterinary Department to consider re-routing a proposed disease control fence around the Makgadikgadi, to help prevent the wildlife from straying into cattle country. Meanwhile strategies have been developed to help the local people minimise their losses, and to discourage them from killing more lions before the fence is built.

There's also a major diamond mine at **Letlhakane**, about 30km east of Orapa, on the Serowe road, and there's active prospecting continuing throughout the region for more diamond pipes. More usefully for visitors, Letlhakane is also one of the few places where you can buy entry permits for the national parks.

For the safari visitor, the road south from Orapa is notable in that it leads, after some 220km, to the **Khama Rhino Sanctuary** (*www.khamarhinosanctuary.org. bw*). Described by one mobile safari operator as 'a really well laid-out and cared for park with good wildlife and excellent facilities', it's a refuge for both white and black rhino. While its location falls outside the scope of this guide, it's a good stopover on the road between Maun and the south for self-drive tourists and thus is worthy of mention.

14

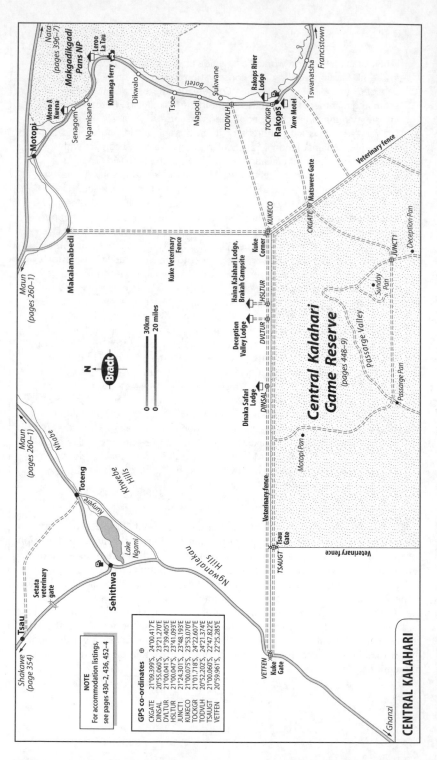

CENTRAL KALAHARI

Makgadikgadi
Pans NP
(pages 396–7)

Nata

Leroo
La Tau

Meno A
Kwena

Motopi

Senagom

Ngamisane

Khumaga ferry

Dikwalo

Tsoe

Boteti

Magodi

Sukwane

Rakops River
Lodge

Boteti

TODVLH

TOCKGR   Rakops

Xere Motel

Tswanatsha

Francistown

Veterinary fence

KUKECO

CKGATE ⊕ Matswere Gate

Makalamabedi

Maun
(pages 260–1)

Kuke Veterinary
Fence

Kuke
Corner

Haina Kalahari Lodge,
Brakah Campsite

HSLTUR

JUNCT1

Sunday
Pan

Deception Pan

30km

20 miles

0

0

N

Bradt

Deception
Valley Lodge

DVLTUR

Passarge Valley

**Central Kalahari
Game Reserve**
(pages 448–9)

Passarge Pan

Dinaka Safari
Lodge

DINSAL

Motopi Pan

Maun
(pages 260–1)

Nhabe

Kunyere

Toteng

Khwebe Hills

Lake
Ngami

Sehithwa

Ngwana|ekau Hills

Veterinary fence

Veterinary fence

Tsau
Gate

TSAUGT

Setata
veterinary
gate

Tsau

Shakawe
(page 354)

VETFEN
Kuke
Gate

Ghanzi

NOTE
For accommodation listings,
see pages 430–2, 436, 452–4

GPS co-ordinates ⊕

CKGATE,	21°09.399'S,	24°00.417'E
DINSAL,	20°55.060'S,	23°21.270'E
DVLTUR,	21°00.041'S,	23°39.405'E
HSLTUR,	21°00.047'S,	23°41.093'E
JUNCT1,	21°24.301'S,	23°48.193'E
KUKECO,	21°00.075'S,	23°53.070'E
TOCKGR,	21°01.718'S,	24°22.607'E
TODVLH,	20°52.202'S,	24°21.374'E
TSAUGT,	21°00.060'S,	22°47.822'E
VETFEN,	20°59.961'S,	22°25.285'E

15

The Central Kalahari

Covering about 52,800km², the Central Kalahari Game Reserve (or the CKGR, as it's usually known) is one of the world's largest game reserves. It dominates the centre of Botswana, the wider region that I refer to in this chapter as simply the 'Central Kalahari'. This is Africa at its most remote and esoteric: a vast sandsheet punctuated by a few huge open plains, occasional salt pans and the fossil remains of ancient riverbeds.

The CKGR isn't for everybody. The game is often sparse and can seem limited, with no elephants or buffalo; the distances are huge, along bush tracks of variable quality; and until 2009, the facilities were limited to a handful of campsites. So without a fully equipped vehicle (preferably two) and lots of bush experience, it was probably not the place for you. The converse is that if you've already experienced enough of Africa to love the feeling of space and the sheer freedom of real wilderness areas, then this reserve is completely magical; it's the ultimate wilderness destination.

In a recent change of policy, however, the authorities have permitted the establishment of two small lodges within the reserve, thus opening it up to those who don't have the experience, the time or the equipment to come here alone. As a middle ground, there are also a handful of mobile safaris operating in the area.

Due to limitations of space, this is only a short introduction to the area. It's intended to give you a feel for the Central Kalahari and the CKGR (the area of it which most visitors will see) and tell you how to get there and what it's like. I've assumed that most visitors will only be visiting the northern section of the park – Piper Pans and north – as that's generally regarded as the most interesting area. It's also the obvious part of the reserve to link into a trip with the more popular northern regions of Chobe and the Okavango.

BACKGROUND INFORMATION

HISTORY The Central Kalahari Game Reserve was declared a game park in 1961, on the very eve of independence. At that time, there was increasing international publicity about the San. With the prevalent view of their 'idyllic' hunter–gatherer lifestyle came a growing concern that this was threatened, and that they might become 'extinct'. The British Protectorate of Bechuanaland was the focus for this, so the authorities decided to protect the heart of the Kalahari for the San.

At the time, there was no way to set aside one particular area for an ethnic group. Neither the British authorities nor the Tswana, who were being groomed for government, wanted any discrimination amongst its citizens based on race. This would have set a dangerous precedent, with echoes of the tribal 'bantustans' created by the apartheid regime in South Africa.

Back in the 1960s, legislation to proclaim a separate area for a separate ethnic group didn't exist. Nor was any wanted by a new country anxious to avoid ethnic divisions. Hence the heart of the Central Kalahari was protected from further development or agricultural encroachment as a 'game park' – even though it was intended as a place of sanctuary for the San. Thus the Central Kalahari Game Reserve was proclaimed. (Still to this day the Botswana government has a strict policy of not discriminating – positively or negatively – between any of the ethnic groups in the country. 'We're all Tswana' is their wise approach, designed to minimise any ethnic tensions. However, there lies the nub of a problem. If a group like the San are allowed to live and hunt in a 'game reserve', why shouldn't any other Tswana citizen? Many who are concerned for the San argue that they need positive discrimination, whilst others maintain that such moves would be racist.)

In keeping with its origins, the CKGR remained largely closed for around 30 years; visitors needed special approval and permits, which were not lightly granted. During this time its most famous visitors were probably Mark and Delia Owens, a couple of young and idealistic animal researchers from America who lived on a tree-island in Deception Valley for about seven years (1974–80), and subsequently wrote a best-selling book, *Cry of the Kalahari* (see *Appendix 3, Further information*), based on their experiences.

Then in the late 1980s and early 1990s the park started to open up more, first allowing in organised groups with tour operators and, only in recent years, individual travellers in their own vehicles. However, despite the opening of two small lodges in 2009, numbers remain largely limited by the number of campsites available, so it still feels very much a wilderness destination.

PEOPLE When the CKGR was declared a reserve, a population of around 5,000 San people lived within its boundaries. In the 1990s a borehole had been installed at the small village of Xade, where some of the park's game scouts were based. Research in 1996 estimated that the population in the reserve had fallen below 1,500, a significant proportion of whom had moved to live in the vicinity of Xade, near this fairly reliable source of water.

In the 1980s, the government's stated policy was to encourage relocation of the people to New Xade, a village which was created outside the reserve. The resulting removals of the people, and the highly controversial court case that resulted, are discussed in detail in *Chapter 2, People and Culture*, pages 28–32. Note that this remains a very contentious and political topic.

GEOGRAPHY AND LANDSCAPE Despite its huge area, the Central Kalahari has relatively little scenic variation. Most of it is covered by an enormous, undulating sandsheet. Within the CKGR itself, the north of the park contains the most varied scenery; here you'll find a network of vegetated salt pans and a few fossilised riverbeds. There are two places within the reserve, at Letiahau Pan and Piper Pans, where water is pumped by the park's authorities.

FLORA AND FAUNA If you're expecting to find stark differences between contrasting environments within this Kalahari reserve, you'll be disappointed. There are subtle changes between its different landscapes, but there isn't the variation here that you'll find around Chobe or the Okavango. Because of this, the animal species found here vary little from area to area – and this is one reason why the Central Kalahari is an area for old Africa hands, and not first-time safari-goers.

Flora People on their first trip through the Kalahari are often struck by just how green and vegetated it is, in contrast to their mental image of a desert. In fact most of the Kalahari is covered in a thin, mixed bush with a fairly low canopy height, dotted with occasional larger trees. Beneath this is a rather sparse ground-covering of smaller bushes, grasses and herbs.

To be a little more precise, the Central Kalahari's vegetation is dominated by *Terminalia sericea* sandveld (see page 57), standing on deep sand. The most common species within this are the silver terminalia itself (*Terminalia sericea*), the Kalahari appleleaf (*Lonchocarpus nelsii*) and Kalahari sand acacias (*Acacia luederitzii*), which occasionally form thickets. These vary from bushes to substantial trees, growing to a maximum height of around 10m. (Their flattened canopies are easily confused with the umbrella thorn (*Acacia tortilis*), earning them the alternative name of bastard, or false, umbrella thorn.)

Other common trees include the distinctive purple-pod terminalia (*Terminalia prunioides*), which seem to grow best in areas where there is more clay in the soil; shepherd's trees (*Boscia albitrunca*), with their characteristic whitish bark; and feverberry trees (*Croton megalobotrys*). Bladethorns (*Acacia fleckii*) and their close cousins the bluethorns (*Acacia erubescens*), are common bushes with fine, feathery foliage but keen, curved barbs. Inevitably you'll spot plenty of old, gnarled camelthorn trees (*Acacia erioloba*).

Beneath these you'll commonly find a variety of low bushes and shrubs including wild seringa bushes (*Burkea africana*) and bushwillows (*Combretum collinum*). Meanwhile on the ground one of the more common grasses is the lovely silky Bushman grass (*Stipagrostis uniplumis*).

Look carefully, perhaps helped by a good guide, and you'll find plenty to interest you here including, during the wetter months of the year, many flowers and herbs. The beautifully curving flowers of the cat's tail (*Hermbstaedtia odorata*) form spectacular pink patches in damper areas. More entertaining are the bright red fruits of the balsam pear (*Momordica balsamina*) which, when ripe, fall to the ground and pop themselves open automatically if disturbed. In *Common Wild Flowers of the Okavango Delta* (see *Appendix 3, Further information*), Veronica Roodt reports that the young leaves of this plant are used as a vegetable, and while a few will use the fruits in cooking, many communities treat them as poisonous or use them in medicines.

Fauna Game viewing anywhere in the Central Kalahari area can be a stark contrast to the amazing densities of game that can often be seen in the Okavango–Linyanti–Chobe region. To get the best out of the CKGR, you'll require lots of time and patience, often just watching and waiting. The big game is here, but on average it occurs in very low densities – as you'd expect in such a harsh, arid environment. The only way to get around this is, as mentioned below, to visit when it congregates on the open pans in the north.

Springbok are probably the most numerous of the **large herbivores** in the park today. That said, the game populations in the Central Kalahari seem to have been fluctuating fairly wildly, at least for the last century, and perhaps longer. In his book, *A Comment on Kalahari Wildlife and the Khukhe Fence* (see *Appendix 3, Further information*), Alec Campbell suggests that over this period human activities and interference have altered the balance of the wildlife populations in the Kalahari substantially, and led indirectly to population explosions and crashes.

Currently springbok disperse in small herds across the park during the dry season, but congregate in very large numbers on the short grass plains found on pans and fossil riverbeds during and shortly after the rains. (Note that this is exactly the opposite of the usual situation for many mammals, including elephants and buffalo, which gather in larger herds as the dry season progresses, only to disperse during the rains.)

These successful antelope are both browsers and grazers, which can derive all the moisture that they need from their food, provided that the plants they eat contain at least 10% water. They'll often rest by day and eat at night, thus maximising the moisture content of their fodder by including dew on it.

Springbok populations are very elastic: they are able to reproduce very speedily when conditions are favourable, allowing them to rapidly repopulate after a bad drought. With good conditions females can produce two calves in 13 months, while even six-month-old ewes will conceive, giving birth to their first lamb when they are barely a year old. To maximise the survival of their offspring, the females gather together in maternal herds and synchronise their births, thus presenting predators with a short-term surplus of easily caught young lambs.

The Central Kalahari's population of blue wildebeest has, at times within the last century, swelled to enormous proportions. In his work *A Comment on Kalahari Wildlife and the Khukhe Fence* (see *Appendix 3*, page 505), Campbell describes them as peaking in the 1960s when 'herds of 50 and 100 had so accumulated in the Matsheng and Okwa area that they stretched unbroken for many kilometres and numbered hundreds of thousands'. Thane Riney, an ecologist there at the time, was familiar with the vast herds of the Serengeti yet still referred to these as 'the largest herds of plains game left in Africa today'. Wildebeest populations were then estimated at up to 250,000 animals, but within a few years lack of water, grazing and the existence of veterinary cordon fences had conspired to wipe them out from much of the Central Kalahari. Today you'll find small groups of wildebeest in the CKGR, but I've never seen them in large numbers.

Probably the area's most common large antelope are gemsbok (also known as oryx), which can be seen in congregations of hundreds on the short grass plains during the rains, but usually occur in smaller groupings during the rest of the year. These magnificent antelope are supremely adapted for desert living. They can survive fluctuations of their body temperature up to 45°C (when 42°C would kill most mammals) because of a series of blood vessels, known as the carotid rete, located immediately below their brain. These effectively cool the blood before it reaches the animal's brain – the organ most adversely affected by temperature variations.

Red hartebeest can also be found here in good numbers, as can eland and – an amazing sight – giraffe. Kudu occur, but generally in quite small numbers: either small bachelor groups or family groups consisting of an old male, several females and a number of youngsters. Common duiker are occasionally seen, too, but if you catch a glimpse of a small antelope bounding away from you, it's much more likely to be a steenbok.

The main **predators** here are lion, cheetah, leopard and spotted hyena, which generally occur in a low density, matching their prey species. The lion prides range over large territories and are bonded by loose associations; members spend most of their time apart from each other, living alone or in pairs, and meeting relatively infrequently. Individual lions will often hunt a variety of smaller prey, like bat-eared foxes and porcupines, as well as the larger antelope more commonly thought of as lion fodder.

Similarly the Central Kalahari's leopard have a very catholic diet, ranging from mice and spring hares to ground squirrels and wildcats, plus steenbok, springbok and calves of the larger antelope.

The park's cheetah seem to be more nomadic than the lion or leopard. In other parks, where game densities are higher, cheetah often lose their kills to these larger cats. Thus the CKGR's relatively low density of predators makes it a good place for cheetah. Hence this is one of sub-Saharan Africa's better parks for spotting them – at least at times when the springbok concentrate on the pans and riverbeds.

Amongst the **scavengers and insectivores** found here are the brown hyena (the original object of study for Mark and Delia Owens; see *Appendix 3, Further information*), black-backed jackal, caracal, Cape fox, bat-eared fox, aardwolf, genet and wildcat. However, as there is no facility for night drives in the reserve, only black-backed jackals are commonly seen as they aren't strictly nocturnal.

TUNNEL VISION

Just below the surface of the Kalahari lies a labyrinth of tunnels excavated by the Damara mole-rat (*Cryptomis damarensis*), the only member of this endemic African family to occur in the Kalahari. Mole-rats are rodents, and unlike true moles, which are insectivores, they feed entirely on plant matter – specifically underground storage organs such as bulbs, corms, tubers and desert cucumbers.

They have plump, cylindrical bodies, short, sturdy limbs and formidable projecting incisors for chiselling out the tunnels in which they live their entire lives. Earth excavated by the teeth is shuffled backwards by the forefeet, and when enough has accumulated the mole-rat reverses up a side tunnel, pushing it to the surface to form a 'molehill'. Digging is easiest when the soil is wet, so the rains prompt a flurry of activity: in one month, one colony of 16 Damara mole-rats was recorded digging 1km of tunnels and shifting 2.5 tonnes of soil to the surface. Not bad for an animal that weighs no more than 300g.

This Herculean effort uncovers enough food to last the colony through the dry season until the next rains. Meanwhile soil is shifted around and burrows modified to create a complex of chambers, passageways and latrines.

Damara mole-rats are the most sociable of their family. This is a necessary adaptation to the harsh Kalahari environment, where numbers bring more success to a team of blind foragers in search of an erratic, scattered food supply. Their complex societies are more like those of a social insect than a mammal. A colony averages around 15–25 members, occasionally up to 40, but only one pair – the dominant male and female – are reproductive. All others help forage, dig and rear the young, but suppress their fertility, being effectively like sterile worker-termites.

The dominant female breeds all year, producing a litter of between one and five pups after an 80-day gestation in a nest chamber 2m below ground. Hierarchies are reinforced aggressively, and each year about 10% of a colony's members leave to breed and found new colonies. Mole-rats communicate underground with snorts and squeals, and drum with their hind feet on tunnel walls to relay seismic messages to mates or rivals.

Though the casual visitor is unlikely ever to see a mole-rat, a range of canny predators, notably the mole snake (*Pseudaspis cana*), have learned to watch as a pile of fresh soil accumulates and will snatch the digger just as it approaches the surface.

Meanwhile the diurnal yellow mongoose is sometimes seen scampering around in search of insects, and families of meerkats (or suricats) are amongst the most entertaining and endearing of all the park's residents.

Birdlife The birdlife here is very varied, with Africa's largest bird, the ostrich, doing particularly well. I've never seen more free-roaming ostriches during May, when Deception Valley seemed to be dotted by large flocks of them.

Weighing 14–19kg, kori bustards are the world's heaviest flying birds and are also common, stepping around the plains in search of insects, small reptiles and mammals.

Closely related to the kori are the smaller korhaans; the northern black korhaan (or white-quilled korhaan, or white-winged) is one of the area's most obvious birds. The conspicuous black-and-white males have a harsh, raucous call and can be seen flying up and then falling back to the ground in endless display flights. Related red-crested korhaans are a little less obvious, and less common, though equally spectacular when displaying.

Doves are well represented with Cape turtle doves, laughing doves and, especially, Namaqua doves all being very common. All the species of sandgrouse found in southern Africa – double-banded, Burchell's, yellow-throated and Namaqua – live here. Watch in the mornings as flocks of Namaqua sandgrouse fly to waterholes. They drink and also wade into the water, where each male has specially adapted feathers on his breast, which act like a sponge to soak up water. He then flies up to 80km back to his nest, where the chicks drink from the feathers.

Large flocks of red-billed queleas resemble leaves blowing on a stiff autumn breeze as they swarm down from the trees in search of grass seeds or to drink from a muddy puddle. Even more colourful in the summer months are the male whydahs – pin-tailed, shaft-tailed and paradise – whose exuberant breeding plumage includes a disproportionately long tail. These are brood parasites – laying their eggs in the nest of other birds (see box, page 406).

The Central Kalahari's most common raptor is the pale-chanting goshawk: a light-grey bird, with pink legs and black ends to its wings and tail. It's usually seen hunting from a conspicuous perch, perhaps a fence post beside a track or the top of a small thorn bush, or occasionally hopping about the ground foraging. If disturbed it'll usually fly off low, swooping to land on a similar perch – even if that's another fence post from which it'll shortly be disturbed again. Equally visible during the summer months is the yellow-billed kite.

Black-shouldered kites and rock kestrels, both of which often hunt by hovering in flight, are common here. Bateleurs, black-breasted and brown snake eagles, martial and tawny eagles, and lanner falcons are also around, with the last making something of a speciality of hunting birds as they come to drink at waterholes.

PRACTICAL INFORMATION

WHEN TO VISIT The Kalahari is really unlike any other game area in sub-Saharan Africa in that its game is probably at its most spectacular during and shortly after the rains – from around January to April. Then the animals gather where the best rain has been and the sweetest grazing is, which usually means on the pans. These can be a magnificent sight, with very large herds of springbok and gemsbok, accompanied by good numbers of giraffe and ostrich plus groups of blue wildebeest, hartebeest and eland. Inevitably these attract increased predator activity from lion, cheetah and the odd leopard.

Having said that, this is also the time when the weather, and in particular the driving conditions, can be at their least hospitable. If there has been much rain then the road from Rakops to the Matswere Gate and beyond becomes a series of mudholes lined by black-cotton soil, which is rock-hard when dry, but feels like treacle when wet. Meanwhile areas of pans in the park become large, shallow lakes where both navigation and traction present a challenge to any vehicle. Any group coming at this time must be fully prepared for heavy rain, and should expect to have to dig out their vehicle from the mud a number of times.

As a compromise for those who are not fond of endless mud, a favourite time to visit is just after the rains, around March–May, depending on when the rains stop. Then most of the surface water has disappeared, and the black-cotton soil isn't nearly as treacherous as it would have been a few months earlier. The game concentrations will still be good, albeit perhaps not *quite* so spectacular, but your overall experience will probably be much more enjoyable. That is, unless you really enjoy digging your vehicle out of knee-deep mud …

GETTING THERE AND AWAY There are four entrances into the CKGR. Of these, the most widely used is the Matswere Gate, which is on the eastern side of the reserve. From here it's just 38km to the north end of Deception Valley and the nearest campsites.

The new Tsau Gate (✪ TSAUGT 21°00.060'S, 22°47.822'E), in the northwest corner of the reserve, lies 39km east of the main Maun–Ghanzi road, along the southern side of the veterinary fence that defines the reserve's northern border. The closest campsites to the gate are at Motopi Pan.

The other entrances, Khutse Gate in the far south and Xade Gate to the west, some 80km from Piper Pans, are best suited to those exploring the more southerly areas of the reserve.

Driving yourself Driving yourself into the Central Kalahari is only a viable option for experienced and bush-wise adventurers with their own fully equipped 4x4s. Even they need at least two 4x4 vehicles and some fail-safe plans for back-up assistance in the event of an emergency. There are now four usual routes to the reserve, three to the Matswere Gate on the eastern side, and one to the new Tsau Gate at the northwest corner.

From the Maun–Ghanzi road to the Matswere Gate About 119km from Ghanzi and 167km from Maun, on the tarred Maun–Ghanzi road, you'll have to stop and pass through the Kuke Veterinary Fence (✪ VETFEN 20°59.961'S, 22°25.285'E). Immediately north of this, you'll find a good, wide gravel road that heads off on a bearing fractionally south of east. After a few kilometres, this thoroughfare bends round to the left, and there's a small turning into the bush on the right. Take this, and you'll find a simple sand track with two clear ruts for your wheels (welcome to the Kalahari!). The veterinary fence will be literally inches from your right side.

Expect only the occasional 4x4 to pass you; this isn't a busy track. Beneath your wheels you'll sometimes find patches of hard ground with bands of calcrete rocks. Then there are mud-holes, where thick clay is a sticky hazard during the rains (when this route is perfectly possible, but time-consuming). However, most of the track is good, fairly hard sand on which a reasonably experienced bush driver should be able to average 50km/h.

At times now you'll find yourself travelling parallel to several fences, and sometimes with one on each side of you. Beware of startling antelope here; they'll run in front of the vehicle with no escape, and become exhausted easily if you drive too fast.

Around 128km after the tar you'll reach a left turning (⊕ DVLTUR 21°00.041'S, 23°39.405'E) which is clearly signposted to Deception Valley Lodge (see pages 452–3). The lodge is about 9km north from here along a winding track that crosses the lodge's own airstrip (⊕ DVLAIR 20°58.897'S, 23°39.515'E). Back on the main track, a further 3km brings you to the entrance to Haina Kalahari Lodge (⊕ HSLTUR 21°00.047'S, 23°41.093'E).

Almost 23km after passing this, you'll reach Phefodiaka veterinary checkpoint, widely known as Kuke Corner (⊕ KUKECO 21°00.075'S, 23°53.070'E; ⊕ 06.00–22.00). Here a gate marks the junction of four veterinary fences. As at other vet-fence checkpoints, you will probably be asked if you're carrying any red meat, which cannot be taken east across the fence. To the left a straight cutline heads due north to Makalamabedi. Continuing straight on brings you after 52km to the main Maun–Rakops road, coming out north of Rakops (⊕ TODVLH 20°52.202'S, 24°21.374'E). To the right, a well-used track follows the line of the fence, roughly south-southeast (bearing about 143°). This can be quite rutted and tedious driving, but after about 21.5km leads to the Matswere Gate into the CKGR (⊕ CKGATE 21°09.399'S, 24°00.417'E).

From the Maun–Ghanzi road to the Tsau Gate
The road east to the Tsau Gate is a turning off the Maun–Ghanzi road just south of the Kuke Veterinary Fence (⊕ VETFEN 20°59.961'S, 22°25.285'E). From here, it follows straight along the southern side of the fence for about 39km, to reach the Tsau Gate (⊕ TSAUGT 21°00.060'S, 22°47.822'E) into the reserve. After the gate, continue along the fence for a further 32km, before turning south (⊕ MOTCUT 21°00.194'S, 23°06.400'E) towards Motopi Pan. It's important to be aware that you cannot cross the vet fence into or out of the reserve at any point along its northern boundary.

From Rakops to the Matswere Gate
Between Rakops (⊕ RAKOPS 21°02.136'S, 24°24.432'E; see *Chapter 14*, page 436) and the CKGR's Matswere Gate there is one main track, fringed by a few detours and side-tracks. The turning from the tar road (⊕ TOCKGR 21°01.718'S, 24°22.607'E) is clearly signposted to the west, just 200m north of the turning to Rakops.

The track is pretty clear on the ground, following a bearing of about 250° until after around 41km you reach the veterinary fence that doubles as the park's boundary. This is the location of the smart new Matswere Gate (⊕ CKGATE 21°09.399'S, 24°00.417'E). When it's wet during the early months of the year, this is one of the muddiest, and hence trickiest, sections of track in the region, with patches of black-cotton soil that can trap even the most careful driver. I've heard tales of this section alone taking several days to pass, with frequent stops to dig out – so don't tackle it lightly. Later in the year, the track hardens to a roller-coaster ride where you bounce in and out of a succession of dry mud-holes; even then it's fairly slow going.

South along the cutline from Makalamabedi to the Matswere Gate
I haven't driven this route, but I believe it's probably the most scenic route between Maun and the CKGR, though with the advent of the tar road between Maun and Rakops it's probably no longer the quickest. You'll find the north end of this at the small village of Makalamabedi, southeast of Maun, and southwest of Motopi. If you're coming from Maun, turn south off the main Maun–Nata road just before

the Makalamabedi control post (✠ MAKACP 20°11.219'S, 23°51.739'E), and take the tar road to Makalamabedi. From here, simply follow the cutline due south (driving on the eastern side of the veterinary fence) to Kuke Corner (✠ KUKECO 21°00.075'S, 23°53.070'E), then continue south for a further 21.5km to the main Matswere Gate (✠ CKGATE 21°09.399'S, 24°00.417'E).

Without your own vehicle If, like most visitors to Botswana, you don't have the knowledge, experience or equipment for this kind of a trip, there are now several options to visit the CKGR.

Fly-in trips With the advent in 2009 of two exclusive lodges in the reserve (see pages 450–1), the option of incorporating a fly-in trip to the CKGR into a broader itinerary is now a reality.

Group trips A few of Botswana's larger safari companies have scheduled group trips, leaving on specific pre-planned dates, which include time camping within the CKGR; see the main listings in *Chapter 4, Planning and Preparation* (pages 77–8), *Chapter 7, Maun, Tour operators and safari companies* (pages 175–9) and *Chapter 8, Kasane and the Northeast, Tour operators, safari companies and travel agents* (pages 194–5). Check out what they have running and read between the lines to make sure you understand exactly how much of their time is within the CKGR: often, quite long trips will spend far too short a time in the park. Many of these trips will also feature Deception Valley Lodge, or even a private campsite on Deception Valley's reserve. Some of the better ones include a one-way flight, probably best done on your way out of the park at the end of your trip. Expect a return charter on a six-seater plane (up to five passengers) to Deception Valley to cost around US$380 per person.

Private mobile trips If you have a fairly generous budget, then the same operators (and many of the smaller ones) will be delighted to organise a private trip for two or more people, for which you'll be able to specify the departure date and the timings. Expect the costs to be high though – in the region of US$400–450 per person per night. (Larger groups and longer expeditions are generally less expensive than smaller groups and shorter trips.)

Book a short trip from a lodge If you just want a few days in the park, then it's worth checking with Meno A Kwena or Haina Kalahari Lodge (see pages 430 and 453). They will sometimes organise short, simple, guided camping expeditions into the park. Typically these come with a few nights either side at their lodge.

GETTING ORGANISED A visit to the CKGR requires a lot of organisation before you even start to drive there. You must book a place to stay and make arrangements to bring all your water, food, equipment and supplies. Brackish water is sometimes available at the Matswere Gate, but it isn't safe to drink and cannot be relied upon. Note that all the land outside the park falls into private farms and concessions, and so camping 'outside the gate' is not a practical option. Here, the nearest place to camp is the Brakah Campsite at Haina Kalahari Lodge.

GETTING AROUND The main entrance into the CKGR, and one of the few places where there's a break in the veterinary fence, is at the smart new Matswere Gate (✠ CKGATE 21°09.399'S, 24°00.417'E). Here you can sign in, check on the state of

15

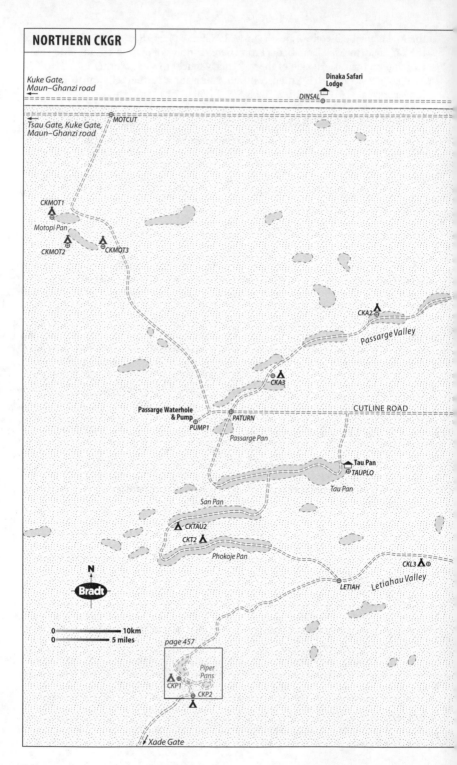

Kuke Gate,
Maun–Ghanzi road

Dinaka Safari
Lodge

DINSAL

Tsau Gate, Kuke Gate,
Maun–Ghanzi road

MOTCUT

CKMOT1

Motopi Pan

CKMOT2

CKMOT3

CKA2

Passarge Valley

CKA3

CUTLINE ROAD

Passarge Waterhole
& Pump

PATURN

PUMP1

Passarge Pan

Tau Pan

TAUPLO

Tau Pan

San Pan

CKTAU2

CKT2

Phokoje Pan

CKL3

LETIAH

Letiahau Valley

N

Bradt

0   10km
0   5 miles

page 457

Piper
Pans

CKP1

CKP2

Xade Gate

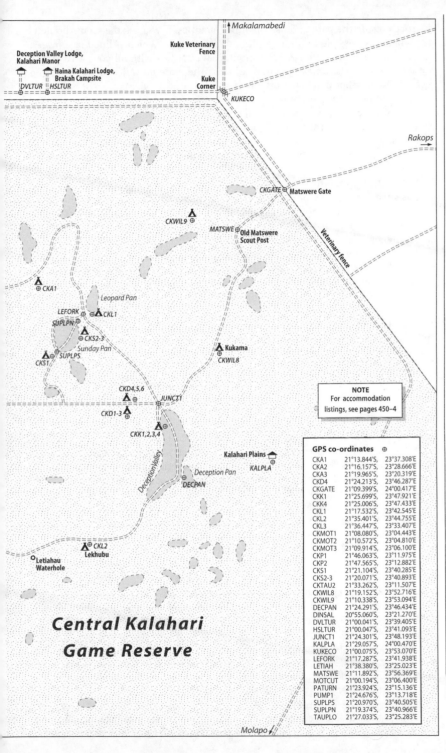

Makalamabedi

Kuke Veterinary Fence

Deception Valley Lodge, Kalahari Manor
Haina Kalahari Lodge, Brakah Campsite
DVLTUR HSLTUR

Kuke Corner
KUKECO

Rakops

CKGATE ⊕ Matswere Gate

Veterinary fence

CKWIL9 ⊕

MATSWE ⊕ Old Matswere Scout Post

⊕ CKA1

Leopard Pan

LEFORK ⊕ ▲ CKL1
SUPLPN ⊕
▲ CKS2-3
⊕
Sunday Pan

▲ Kukama
CKWIL8

▲ ⊕ SUPLPS
CKS1 ⊕

CKD4,5,6
▲ ⊕
JUNCT1

CKD1-3 ⊕

▲ ⊕
CKK1,2,3,4

Kalahari Plains
KALPLA

Deception Valley

Deception Pan
DECPAN

NOTE
For accommodation listings, see pages 450–4

⊕ CKL2
Lekhubu

Letiahau Waterhole

Central Kalahari Game Reserve

Molapo

GPS co-ordinates	⊕	
CKA1	21°13.844'S,	23°37.308'E
CKA2	21°16.157'S,	23°28.666'E
CKA3	21°19.965'S,	23°20.319'E
CKD4	21°24.213'S,	23°46.287'E
CKGATE	21°09.399'S,	24°00.417'E
CKK1	21°25.699'S,	23°47.921'E
CKK4	21°25.006'S,	23°47.433'E
CKL1	21°17.532'S,	23°42.545'E
CKL2	21°35.401'S,	23°44.755'E
CKL3	21°36.447'S,	23°33.407'E
CKMOT1	21°08.080'S,	23°04.443'E
CKMOT2	21°10.572'S,	23°04.810'E
CKMOT3	21°09.914'S,	23°06.100'E
CKP1	21°46.063'S,	23°11.975'E
CKP2	21°47.565'S,	23°12.882'E
CKS1	21°21.104'S,	23°40.285'E
CKS2-3	21°20.071'S,	23°40.893'E
CKTAU2	21°33.262'S,	23°11.507'E
CKWIL8	21°19.152'S,	23°52.716'E
CKWIL9	21°10.338'S,	23°53.094'E
DECPAN	21°24.291'S,	23°46.434'E
DINSAL	20°55.060'S,	23°21.270'E
DVLTUR	21°00.041'S,	23°39.405'E
HSLTUR	21°00.047'S,	23°41.093'E
JUNCT1	21°24.301'S,	23°48.193'E
KALPLA	21°29.057'S,	24°00.470'E
KUKECO	21°00.075'S,	23°53.070'E
LEFORK	21°17.287'S,	23°41.938'E
LETIAH	21°38.380'S,	23°25.023'E
MATSWE	21°11.892'S,	23°56.369'E
MOTCUT	21°00.194'S,	23°06.400'E
PATURN	21°23.924'S,	23°15.136'E
PUMP1	21°24.676'S,	23°13.718'E
SUPLPS	21°20.970'S,	23°40.505'E
SUPLPN	21°19.374'S,	23°40.966'E
TAUPLO	21°27.033'S,	23°25.283'E

the roads inside the park and use the toilet facilities. If you ask the scouts politely, it's sometimes possible to fill up with brackish water – which is fine for showers, but not suitable for drinking. (You should have arrived with all your own water, but if you didn't, then make the most of this. There are no waterpoints inside the reserve.) Remember that you must have pre-paid your park entry fees at one of the designated points; see pages 84–6.

The presence of a few signposts and distance markers within the reserve makes navigation a little easier than in the past, at least at first glance – but don't be fooled. Stray just a few metres from the main track and you could rapidly find yourself completely lost without a compass, a GPS, and a hefty degree of common sense.

Driving conditions In the dry season, the general quality of the tracks in the park is surprising. Many of them, particularly those which follow the valleys, are really very good. You might have expected to be constantly ploughing through deep sand, but it's not like that. Of course there are patches of deep and tricky sand, and also stretches of black-cotton soil (rock hard when dry; virtually impassable if very wet), but many of the road surfaces are easy and hard when it's dry. During the rainy months it's important to seek advice from the wardens at the entrance gate, and from other visitors to the park. Some sections can be particularly treacherous, and you could save yourself hours – or even days – of digging.

WHERE TO STAY Until 2009, visitors to the CKGR had two accommodation options: stay either within the park, using the park's demarcated campsites, or at one of the lodges outside the park boundary, which are not close enough for day trips (though they remain useful either as destinations in their own right, or as comfortable stops at the start and end of trips into the park). Now, however, two new lodges are situated inside the park boundary, which opens up the reserve to those who would not consider camping.

Inside the park While the lodges open up the CKGR to a wider range of visitors, there are plenty of challenges, including a relatively limited road network. These companies have a reputation for excellent guiding, though, so you should expect a real insight into the Kalahari's unique ecosystems, including the ways in which animals, birds & plants adapt to life in a region where lack of water is a serious problem.

Lodges

Kalahari Plains Camp [map 449] (10 tents) Contact Wilderness Safaris, page 177; ⊕ KALPLA 21°29.057'S, 24°00.470E. At the end of 2009, Wilderness moved their tented camp from its temporary home north of Deception Valley to an open, but entirely secluded pan further south, some 20km from the valley. Here, where permanent water has been found, accommodation is in good-sized, green, Meru-style tents, erected on wooden platforms & specially designed to mediate the Kalahari's extremes of temperature.

Each is simple rather than basic, with canvas doors, roll-up windows netted against mosquitoes, comfortable twin or dbl beds, electric lights & a fan (using solar power), & a small desk with chair. A couple of canvas chairs invite relaxation on the shaded veranda, while at the back are an en-suite shower, flush toilet & twin washbasins. Above each tent is a flat wooden deck which doubles as a sleep-out area, with mattresses made up on request for alfresco nights under the stars.

Similar in style is the main tent, reached along sand paths through the bush. This is long & narrow, open on all sides, but with roll-down panels to protect against the elements. To one side of the central bar is the dining area & a large fridge full of cold drinks; to the other, comfortable chairs with low tables & a small but relevant library. Outside, a swimming pool is surrounded by its own deck.

Access to the camp is either by air into an airstrip 5km from camp, or – for those with their own vehicles – by road. If you're driving yourself, follow the directions on page 446 for the Matswere Gate. From here, follow the signs towards Deception Valley for about 38km. Continue south through the valley, until the road forks at the end. Here you take the left fork towards Deception Pan for some 1km, then turn left onto a track known as the Northern Access Road. After a further 25km, you will reach Kalahari Plains Camp.

The location of the camp within the national park means that activities are limited to game drives during daylight hours, but they also organise walks from camp to learn about Bushman culture & history. *US$732 987pp sharing/sgl 11 Jan–31 May & Nov–Dec, US$586/841 Jun–Oct, inc FB, local drinks, park fees, activities.* ☺ *All year.*

⌂ **Tau Pan** [map 448] (8 chalets) Contact Kwando Safaris, page 176; ✪ TAUPLO 21°27.033'S, 23°25.283'E. Built on top of a low ridge, dominating the surrounding bush & with commanding views west across Tau Pan itself, this self-styled 'camp' has very much the feel of a lodge. If you're driving yourself, follow the main westerly track from the Matswere Gate for 78km, then turn south to Tau Pan (✪ TAUPTO 21°24.073'S, 23°25.656'E) for a further 6km to the lodge. The lodge is visible from miles around &, although its thatch is rapidly blending into the environment, the same can't be said for the metal-roofed kitchen, even with its coat of green paint. Most visitors, however, arrive by air at the new airstrip, just 3km away, so see none of this.

The light design hand behind the camp at Nxai Pan has clearly been at work here, too: witness the long, narrow central building built in a slight curve, the pool to one side of the deck, & the curio shop at the back. Similar, too, is the open view across the plains, with roll-down blinds to keep the elements at bay. Here, though, the wood is darker than at its

CAMPSITES

There are several designated campsites across the northern CKGR [map 448–9], with quite a good concentration around Deception Valley. Each of the sites is designed for just one group camping at any one time – with a maximum of two vehicles and six people – so once you have pre-booked a site, you should not be sharing it with anyone else. Until very recently, all these sites were totally undeveloped: just cleared patches of ground with no water, toilets or showers. Now, however, most of the sites have a long-drop toilet and a separate bucket shower, enclosed by simple rush screens, and a firepit. That said, you must still bring all the water you need, as well as all your food. And note that the vegetation around these facilities can get very overgrown, so digging your own toilet may be a more attractive option than fighting through the bush. (Don't forget a spade, and matches to burn any tissue paper before burying it.)

As with the rest of Botswana's parks, it's essential that you book and pay for these campsites in advance, as well as pre-paying your park fees, or you will not be allowed through the gate. See pages 84–7 for how to do this, and details of the costs. Within the CKGR, six sites – Lekhubu, Letiahau, Piper, Sunday, Passarge and Motopi – are operated by Bigfoot Tours (page 87), with rates for international visitors currently set at US$50 per person, excluding park fees. Other campsites within the reserve still fall within the remit of the DWNP, whose camping fees remain at P30 per person. It's worth noting, however, that there is a high expectation of park fees – and thus presumably attendant campsite and vehicle fees – being increased within the life of this book.

Each of the CKGR's campsites has a unique code. These are signposted on the ground as CKK1, CKK2, CKD1 etc, but for computer-booking purposes have been redesignated as CKKOR-01, CKKOR-02, CKDEC-01, etc. I've made notes on some of these under *What to see and do* on pages 454–8, identifying most of them with comments and GPS locations.

sister camp, & simple sand paths link the hub to each chalet. Here, sliding doors with mesh panels lead from a shaded deck into a spacious room, with roll-down blinds installed against the cold winter nights. Rooms are spacious but quite cosy, the centre taken up by twin or dbl beds. To one side are a desk & leather armchairs; to the other, a bathroom – with inside & outside showers, twin basins & separate toilet. Lighting for ceiling & bedside lamps is powered by solar panels. There's also a family chalet, sleeping up to 4 people.

Game drives explore the remote area around the camp, with day trips to Deception Valley a further option. There are also nature walks, conducted by the lodge's Bushman trackers. And with the huge Kalahari skies, stargazing is a must! *US$471/671 pp sharing/sgl Apr–Oct, US$554 Nov–March (sgl supp't 20 Dec–4 Jan US$80), inc FB, most drinks, activities, laundry.* ⊕ *All year.*

Campsites See box, page 451.

Outside the park There are 3 lodges close to the park's northern boundary: Dinaka Safari Lodge, Deception Valley Lodge, & the adjacent Haina Kalahari Lodge, which also has a campsite. Ideally these should be booked in advance, as if they're full it's a long way to the nearest alternative options. Note that they are at least 2hrs' drive from the Matswere Gate, & over 3hrs from the area within the CKGR known as Deception Valley. A possible alternative could be Meno A Kwena Lodge (page 430), which stands beside the western border of Makgadikgadi Pans National Park, at least 3hrs' drive from the park's entrance gate. While this is not an option for day trips, the lodge does offer overnight trips into the CKGR.

For those coming from the west, there are other accommodation options around Ghanzi, including Grasslands Bushman Lodge (m *7210 4270; www. grasslandlodge.com*), Motswiri Lodge (m *7211 8811; www.kanana.info*) & the tented Edo's Camp (m *7211 9400; www.edoscamp.com*), but these fall outside the scope of this book.

⌂ **Dinaka Safari Lodge** [map 448] (6 tents) ☎680 0251; e info@dinaka.com; www.dinaka.com; ⊕ DINSAL 20°55.060'S, 23°21.270'E. The newest lodge in the area, is the furthest west of the 3 lodges here, set in its own private concession.

It's quite accessible by road from the east, west & north, & also has its own airstrip.

Each of its Meru tents, including 2 for families of 4 or 5 people, is raised on a deck beneath an outer timber shell with a thatched roof. Simple furnishings make up the interior: twin or dbl beds, bedside tables & a couple of chairs, while at the rear are an open-air toilet, shower & washbasin. Power for the whole camp comes from solar panels.

Fronting the waterhole, Dinaka's main area encloses a few comfortable couches, a bar & the dining table – although private dining can be organised too. A small plunge pool is a boon during the hotter months. Morning & late-afternoon game drives form the mainstay of the activities, but walks with local Bushmen are also on offer. Dinaka also has a number of strategically positioned hides & we're reliably informed that these offer particularly productive game viewing in the dry season. Eland numbers are particularly good here, & leopard have also been seen regularly. *US$308 pp sharing Jan–May, US$374 Jun–Dec, inc FB, local drinks, laundry, activities.* ⊕ *All year.*

⌂ **Deception Valley Lodge** [map 449] (8 chalets) ☎+27 11 663 6948/9; e res@ deceptionvalley.co.za; www.deceptionvalley.co.za; ⊕ DVLOD 20°57.182'S, 23°38.988'E. Old-fashioned style & comfort are the watchwords at Deception Valley Lodge, which is also in one of the country's more remote locations, & its relative lack of big game suits old Africa hands more than 1st-time visitors. The lodge has its own airstrip, but if you're driving yourself, see the directions under *Getting there and away* on pages 445–7.

From a narrow veranda with simple chairs & a table, sliding doors lead into each thatched chalet. Heavy teak furniture dominates the bedroom (or 2 bedrooms in the family chalet), which has copious wardrobe space & twin beds (or a king-size dbl) under 4-poster mosquito nets. Comfortable mattresses are covered with high-quality cotton sheets & down quilts – which you'll need as the Kalahari's temperatures plummet at night. A blanket box doubles as a lockable safe. The separate lounge has a sofa & a large glass coffee table on a colourful rug, while the bathroom – set between the 2 rooms,– has a free-standing, claw-foot iron bath, & a door leading to an excellent outside shower. Hot water is derived from a gas geyser, & electricity powers a ceiling fan in each room, a well-stocked fridge/minibar in the lounge

& any number of lamps & lights – yet in the daytime, the whole remains rather dark.

The chalets are widely separated from each other, & linked by low wooden walkways to a good pool with sunloungers & the lodge's main reception. Here, the lounge & dining areas are furnished with careful attention to detail, including ostrich-eggshell lampshades, framed Bushman artefacts on the walls, & hand-crafted wrought-iron chairs. A small curio shop sells an unremarkable range of T-shirts as well as quilted jackets.

The veranda incorporates a large 'apron' deck, where leather couches & low tables create an appealing outdoor seating area, while beyond is an outdoor dining area, a prime spot for watching the porcupine that roams through camp in the evening. About 75m in front is a productive waterhole, which when visited in 2013 attracted a constant stream of animals: giraffe, oryx, zebra & wildebeest all turned up regularly.

Activities focus on day & night drives & walks on the lodge's 150km^2 concession, which shares its southern boundary with the CKGR. (Note that drives don't normally visit the game reserve, which – because of the location of the park gate – is too far for a comfortable day trip.) The landscape, flora & fauna are similar to that found on the fringes of the main reserve, although being much smaller & fenced, the concession doesn't get the large wet-season congregations that are a major attraction of the CKGR between Dec & May. In fact, the best season to visit Deception Valley Lodge is the more traditional game-viewing period of Jun–Sep. That said, it does encompass a number of waterholes & natural pans surrounded by larger trees, with a bird-hide beside one. Despite the relative lack of big game (lions are present but not always seen), there's plenty to look at, & with good guiding – helped by San trackers – visitors should spot many of the smaller attractions. 'Bushman' walks, accompanied by the lodge's San guides, incorporate demonstrations of their traditional skills. Children are welcome, but families must take a private game vehicle. *US$484–578 pp, inc FB, drinks, laundry & activities.* ⏀ *All year.*

🏠 **Kalahari Manor** [map 449] (max 4 people) www.kalaharimanor.com. Contact via Deception Valley Lodge. This exclusive house is under the same ownership as Deception Valley Lodge, but lies in a secluded setting just a short drive away. The label 'manor' is slightly misleading, for the building is practical rather than grand, at least on first appearance. Designed in the style of a British colonial house, it has high ceilings under a metal roof & a wide, north-facing veranda (to catch the winter sun), set with a dining table at one end, & casual chairs at the other. French doors lead into an extensive living room, where elegant chairs are set round a large fireplace, & a dining table seats 6 in comfort. All is spacious & traditionally stylish, the dark-wood furniture offset by full-length curtains, bold *nguni*-skin rugs, & well-placed Baines' prints on the walls. On each side is a rather grand bedroom with twin beds (or a dbl), & adjoining this is a huge contemporary bathroom, with free-standing bath, twin basins, a toilet & dbl shower. Thus, the manor is ideal for 2 couples travelling together as well as for families. Guests benefit from a private butler, chef, guide & game-drive vehicle, ensuring total privacy, although they are also welcome to use the facilities at the main lodge itself. *US$4,000 per night, fully inc.* ⏀ *All year.*

🏠 **Haina Kalahari Lodge** [map 449] (10 rooms, camping) ☏ 683 0238/9; e reservations@hainakalaharilodge.com; www.hainakalaharilodge.com; ⊕ HAISAL 20°56.964'S, 23°40.689'E. On a 120km^2 concession to the east of Deception Valley Lodge, Haina benefits from the same environment & wildlife. This, though, is an altogether simpler affair, appealing predominantly to self-drivers & self-flyers (it has its own airstrip), & suited to those who wish to be at least semi-independent. It is accessed from the same track (⊕ HSLTUR 21°00.047'S, 23°41.093'E).

Central to the lodge is a rustic canvas-&-pole structure under thatch, open on 2 sides, with a bar, dining area & comfortable chairs. To one side is a firepit & braai, so that guests can cater for themselves if they prefer, & to the front is a small pool. Accommodation is in dbl or twin Meru tents. All are en suite, but the 4 larger ones ('super luxury') are thatched & finished to a higher specification than the others, & one will sleep a family of 4. That said, all have good beds under mosquito nets, a stove to make hot drinks, a lockable box, & a deck at the front with chairs. Distances between the tents are considerable, with the furthest too far to walk to the central area even with a guide, so do check this if you don't want to have to drive – or be driven – everywhere. Hot water & power comes from solar panels, with a

15

generator as back-up, while water is desalinated to make it drinkable. Batteries can be charged at any time.

In addition to day & night game drives, guided walks & an opportunity to find out about Bushman culture, the lodge organises quadbike excursions (US$45/hr pp). It also operates both day trips (US$100 pp) & mobile safaris (2 nights US$340–515 pp) into the CKGR, each for a min of 4 people. Campers can drive around the concession, or pay to take part in walks or night drives. *US$340–410 pp sharing, 'super luxury' US$420–550, inc FB, local*

drinks, some activities; exc quad bikes, CKGR trips. ⏲ *All year.*

⅄ Brakah Campsite [map 449] Contact Haina Kalahari Lodge, above; ✪ 20°59.299'S, 23°41.910'E. A drive of some 6.5km from Haina Kalahari Lodge brings you to its secluded campsite, with space for up to 24 campers on tree-shaded pitches. There's a simple, reed-fenced ablution block with 2 flush toilets, a washing-up area with saline water, & firewood at P45 per bundle. Otherwise, you'll need to bring all your own fuel, food & fresh water. *Camping P195 pp, plus P50 per vehicle.* ⏲ *All year.*

WHAT TO SEE AND DO

For most visitors, being in a pristine area that is as remote as the CKGR is an end in itself. Just being able to camp, move around and watch the wildlife at leisure in such a beautiful wilderness, with the certainty that you'll see very few other vehicles, is the real attraction here. So don't rush around looking for 'sights', as there really aren't any. Just take time to enjoy where you are!

That said, detailed here are some of the areas that you may visit, including a few notes on some of the various campsites, with their names, on-the-ground codes and new booking codes. Your permit for camping in the CKGR will specify the precise campsites booked for you on each night – and these can't be changed when you're here.

If you're entering and leaving via the Matswere Gate then a lovely week's circuit can be made by starting around Sunday and Leopard pans, then heading north and west along Passarge Valley, south via the western link to Piper Pans, and then returning northeast through Letiahau and Deception valleys. This is the order in which I've described these areas.

Should you want to stop closer to the Matswere Gate, there are two campsites along that route, the first, CKWIL-09, close to the old Matswere Scout Post (✪ CKWIL9 21°10.338'S, 23°53.094'E), and the second, CKWIL-08, about 12km further into the reserve (✪ CKWIL8 21°19.152'S, 23°52.716'E).

SUNDAY AND LEOPARD PANS Just north of Deception Valley are two fairly large pans, Sunday and Leopard. A waymarked 9km 'loop' – really more of a 5km semi-circular detour off the main track to Leopard Pan – allows you to drive around the edge of Sunday Pan rather than stick to the central track. It starts in the south at ✪ SUPLPS 21°20.970'S, 23°40.505'E, continuing round to rejoin the original track at ✪ SUPLPN 21°19.374'S, 23°40.966'E.

Any of the **campsites** around these pans make a good first stop if you enter the reserve via the Matswere Gate and plan on heading to the area around Passarge Valley. The more southerly Sunday Pan has three campsites. The first, CKS1, or CKSUN-02, is slightly left of the track when you're driving north, at ✪ CKS1 21°21.104'S, 23°40.285'E. Further on, the turn-off to the second and third sites (CKS2 and CKS3, or CKSUN-04 and 03) is to the right, at ✪ CKS2-3 21°20.071'S, 23°40.893'E. All are pleasant, in the edge of the bush close to the main open area of the pan.

Towards Leopard Pan about 5km further north, is a fourth campsite, CKL1, or CKSUN-01 (✪ CKL1 21°17.532'S, 23°42.545'E).

PASSARGE VALLEY This is a long valley with many pans and several campsites. Approaching from the east, it's easily reached from Leopard Pan by finding the junction of tracks to the north of the pan (⊕ LEFORK 21°17.287'S, 23°41.938'E), and heading north from there.

Initially the landscape is quite a thick mixture of small trees and bushes: typical Kalahari sandveld. Then after about 13km you'll find an old green sign saying: 'Passarge Valley. Help keep this valley pristine by staying on the track'. Gradually – now heading southwest – you descend into a valley with a more open landscape and more grassland. About 9.5km further there's a turning south to Manong **Campsite**, coded CKA1/CKPAS-01 (⊕ CKA1 21°13.844'S, 23°37.308'E), a lovely campsite set very much on its own.

A CAUTIONARY TALE

On one morning's game viewing, driving slowly north into the end of Deception Valley, we spotted something unfamiliar moving in the distance. Training our binoculars, we could see a woman waving. We signalled that we'd seen her and continued, eventually taking a right track to head in her direction.

Approaching with some trepidation, we found a distressed Tswana woman on her own. She'd been standing on the roof of the 4x4 all morning, trying to attract attention. In fact she was one of the park's staff who, together with a few colleagues, had been driving from the Matswere Scout Post to Xade (I never learned why they were on a side-track off the main route!).

It seems that late the previous day the fuel filter in their old Land Rover had sprung a bad leak, marooning them there. They'd slept overnight but, with little water or food, her colleagues had set off to walk the 50km or so back to Matswere, and perhaps find visitors on the way who could help.

I spent a petrol-soaked hour under the vehicle, attempting a bush repair with no success, before offering her a lift back to the park's office. However, it transpired that this was the scout camp's only vehicle, so they wouldn't be able to do much. Hours later a better-equipped, modern Land Rover approached; it carried a bush-wise South African couple who travelled with what seemed like a garage full of spares and tools. The park workers had managed to flag this vehicle down and enlist the couple's help.

They were lucky. The park's remaining staff would have been virtually powerless to help, even if they'd known about the breakdown. Fortunately these visitors had the right tools and spare parts, so a repair was soon made. All set off again to Xade in their clapped-out Land Rover with few supplies. I hope they got there.

The morals of this story are simple:

* Don't expect any help from the park's staff: they probably won't have the vehicles or resources.
* Don't come to the CKGR without some basic spares, a simple tool kit and another vehicle to help you out.
* A satellite phone isn't totally necessary, but is a wise back-up, so bring one if possible.
* Ample food and water are absolutely essential: bring more than you expect to need.

Continuing in the valley for another 18km you'll then find a track to the north signposted to Kgokong Campsite, CKA2/CKPAS-02 (⊕ CKA2 21°16.157'S, 23°28.666'E). Here the valley is really stunning: open grassland dotted with a few small tree-islands. The campsite is in the thickets just off to the side, slightly above the floor of the valley.

Further southwest, the third of Passarge's campsites is Kukama Campsite, CKA3/ CKPAS-03 (⊕ CKA3 21°19.965'S, 23°20.319'E), in a small group of trees beside a fairly scrubby pan. This is about 12km northeast of the junction with the park's main east–west cutline track, at ⊕ PATURN 21°23.924'S, 23°15.136'E.

PASSARGE PAN AND MOTOPI PAN A little beyond the southwest end of the Passarge Valley track, Passarge Pan is on the south side of the track which leads to a water pump (⊕ PUMP1 21°24.676'S, 23°13.718'E). North of here a track leads through some lovely country dotted with small pans to Motopi Pan, where three new **campsites** have been established: CKMOT-01 (⊕ CKMOT1 21°08.080'S, 23°04.443'E), CKMOT-02 (⊕ CKMOT2 21°10.572'S, 23°04.810'E) and CKMOT-03 (⊕ CKMOT3 21°09.914'S, 23°06.100'E). This track leads ultimately to the double fence which is the northern boundary of the reserve (⊕ MOTCUT 21°00.194'S, 23°06.400'E). Note that there is no open gate here, and no direct way in or out of the reserve at this point. However, when you reach the fence you'll find a decent track that lies parallel to the fence. To the right, this runs east beside the fence, and then southeast from Kuke Corner (still confined within the park's boundary fence) to the main Matswere Gate. To the left a similar track runs west to the new Tsau Gate (⊕ TSAUGT 21°00.060'S, 22°47.822'E), and from there to the Kuke Gate on the main Maun–Ghanzi road.

THE WESTERN LINK On the northeast side of Passarge Pan, the track south towards Phukwi, Tau, San and Phokoje pans starts at ⊕ PATURN 21°23.924'S, 23°15.136'E. This track is the start of the 'western link', which eventually heads south towards Piper Pans.

You'll see from the map that this track seems to zigzag, always heading either north–south or east–west; this is because the inter-dune valleys (with their string of pans) run east–west. These valleys usually make the best game-viewing areas. They are linked by tracks running north–south, across the top of the dunes.

Note that on this track, the first few kilometres south of the main cutline track (⊕ PATURN) is very boggy; I'd expect this to be exceedingly challenging during the rains.

For an alternative route south, you can enter the western link via Tau Pan. To do this, first turn east along the cutline towards the north end of Deception Valley. About 18km from ⊕ PATURN, there's a track which heads almost due south to Phukwi Pan. For many years there has been a **campsite** on this route, at Tau Pan, but that was set to close at the end of 2009. In its place comes a new site, CKTAU-02, at San Pan (⊕ CKTAU2 21°33.262'S, 23°11.507'E). In addition, there is CKT2/CKTAU-03 (⊕ CKT2 21°35.278'S, 23°16.332'E), which is roughly halfway along the track that follows Phokoje Pan. Heading east along this, the track splits off southeast from Phokoje Pan about 18km before its junction (⊕ LETIAH 21°38.380'S, 23°25.023'E) with the main track from the Letiahau Valley to Piper Pans.

PIPER PANS Piper Pans are as far south as most people visit in the northern section of the park, and as far as I'll describe in this chapter. If you are wondering if it's worth the effort to get here, the answer is a resounding 'yes'. And that's despite a badly corrugated section of road just north of this area.

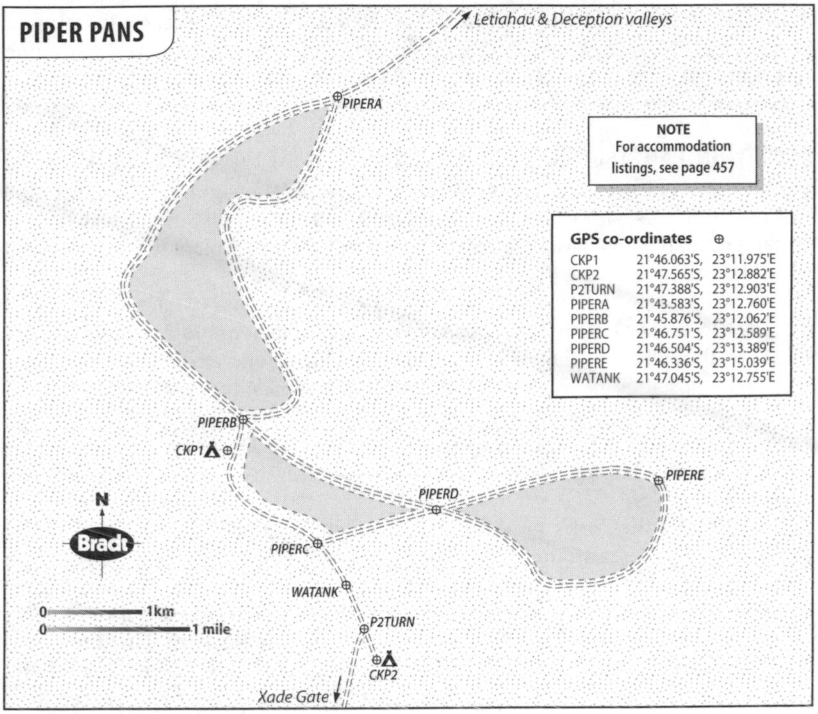
PIPER PANS
Letiahau & Deception valleys
PIPERA
NOTE
For accommodation listings, see page 457
GPS co-ordinates
CKP1 21°46.063'S, 23°11.975'E
CKP2 21°47.565'S, 23°12.882'E
P2TURN 21°47.388'S, 23°12.903'E
PIPERA 21°43.583'S, 23°12.760'E
PIPERB 21°45.876'S, 23°12.062'E
PIPERC 21°46.751'S, 23°12.589'E
PIPERD 21°46.504'S, 23°13.389'E
PIPERE 21°46.336'S, 23°15.039'E
WATANK 21°47.045'S, 23°12.755'E
PIPERB
CKP1
PIPERE
PIPERD
N
Bradt
PIPERC
WATANK
0 1km
0 1 mile
P2TURN
CKP2
Xade Gate

The complex of pans is only a few kilometres across, but it's a stunning stretch of perfectly flat grass. In the rains it's green, and often covered with springbok and gemsbok. By as early as May, it has usually turned a beautiful gold, like a field of ripe barley.

There are two **campsites** here. CKP1/CKPIP-01 (⊕ CKP1 21°46.063'S, 23°11.975'E), slightly further north, is in a grove of rather lovely trees on the west side of the track, but close to the edge of the pan.

The second site, CKP2/CKPIP-02 (⊕ CKP2 21°47.565'S, 23°12.882'E) is further south, up higher on a low fossilised dune. This is just beyond a prominent green water tank (⊕ WATANK 21°47.045'S, 23°12.755'E) which stands at the top of a fossilised dune, beside the track which leads, around 72km later, to Xade.

Around the outside edge of the pan itself there's a 7km circular track that is well worth exploring, although impassable during the rains. The eastern side of this (around ⊕ PIPERE 21°46.336'S, 23°15.039'E) is particularly treacherous black-cotton soil, while it often seems to disappear on the southern side. It's a lovely circuit, but very slow driving even when dry, as the hardened earth is very uneven.

LETIAHAU VALLEY Approaching from the south and Piper Pans, the road to Matswere leads first through Letiahau and then Deception Valley. About 12km northeast of the junction (⊕ LETIAH 21°38.380'S, 23°25.023'E), which is the turning north for the western link, the track enters the picturesque Letiahau Valley. A further 4km on there's a small turning south from the road which, after about 100m, leads to a group of trees in a bushy plain where the Letiahau **Campsite**, coded CKWIL-06 (⊕ CKL3 21°36.447'S, 23°33.407'E) is situated. Around 6km further east, a tiny loop takes a closer look at the permanent Letiahau waterhole.

About 20km east of the first campsite is a second one called Lekhubu, CKWIL-07 (⊕ CKL2 21°35.401'S, 23°44.755'E), off on the south side of the road. Continuing east from this, the track backs around to take a more northerly line as it approaches Deception Valley.

DECEPTION PAN This open pan (⊕ DECPAN 21°24.291'S, 23°46.434'E) at the southern end of the valley is found by taking a short detour, about 1.5km from the main track. It fills with water during the rains, but for the rest of the year it's flat, cracked mud, tinged a vivid red colour by a small red water plant which flourishes when it's full.

DECEPTION VALLEY This is a broad inter-dune valley running roughly north–south; it's thought to be the bed of a fossil river. During and after good rains this is carpeted in luscious green grass that attracts dense concentrations of game. It's the park's most famous location, and where Mark and Delia Owens (see *Appendix 3, Further information*) lived. If you are visiting the northern section of the park for five to six days, then my advice is for you to save this as a highlight for your last couple of days.

Because it is the park's most famous area, and relatively close (35km) to the Matswere Scout Post entrance, this is the place where you're most likely to see other visitors. It's also the area with the most campsites.

Towards the northern end of Deception Valley, on the west side, a track splits off to pass beside the four Kori campsites (CKK1–CKK4, or CKKOR-01 to CKKOR-04), which are spread across a distance of almost 1km. The most southerly one is located at ⊕ CKK1 21°25.699'S, 23°47.921'E, and the most northerly at ⊕ CKK4 21°25.006'S, 23°47.433'E. They're in fairly sparse bush on the edge of the main pan, and generally very close to any animal action there – though with the exception of CKK4, views of the pan are usually obscured by vegetation. There's also limited privacy, as a track runs almost through some of the sites.

Deception Valley's other campsites are all set north of the pan, higher up in fairly thick woodlands with some of the best shade in the park. There are six of these (CKD1–CKD6, or CKDEC-01 to CKDEC-06), three on either side of the cutline road. CKD4 (⊕ CKD4 21°24.213'S, 23°46.287'E) consists of a roughly circular area that has been cleared of trees and bushes. Each campsite is separated from its neighbours by a few hundred metres, making them very secluded and private.

When you leave the park, simply drive towards the north of Deception Valley. There you'll find several small junctions with signposts, as the tracks along the valley are intersected by the straight cutline road. Head east to ⊕ JUNCT1 21°24.301'S, 23°48.193'E, and continue on to sign out at the Matswere Gate (⊕ CKGATE 21°09.399'S, 24°00.417'E).

16

Livingstone and the Victoria Falls

I've included here a brief chapter on Livingstone and the Victoria Falls as many visitors to northern Botswana will either start or end their trips here. The Victoria Falls are a magnificent sight, and few can resist a couple of nights here in addition to time on safari.

Until the 1990s, Livingstone often remained unseen, and some even viewed it with suspicion, being bigger and less well known than the small Zimbabwean town that shares the name of the waterfall. Today, though, Livingstone has become popular in its own right; its riverside lodges are close to the Falls, and yet a perfect complement to Botswana's small camps, and it offers all the thrills and spills that have come to characterise the area. While Zimbabwe's small town of Victoria Falls is re-emerging from the country's recent troubled politics, most visitors now choose to stay on the northern (Livingstone) side. Yet the two sides of the Falls offer different views, and it is worth seeing both to appreciate the whole waterfall. Thus many visitors still venture across the border for an afternoon to see the waterfall from the Zimbabwean side.

This chapter aims to give you an overview of Livingstone: what to do, where to stay and how to get organised. For comprehensive details on Livingstone and the Falls, and on Zambia as a whole, see the latest edition of my *Zambia: The Bradt Travel Guide*.

LIVINGSTONE

GETTING THERE AND AWAY

By air Livingstone's international airport (✆ *0213 324235*) is just 5km northwest of the town centre. The airport has recently undergone an extensive programme of upgrading and redevelopment, including the construction of a brand-new international terminal, which opened in August 2013.

At the time of research, all facilities remained in the old terminal building, which will in time become the domestic terminal. Expect pleasant waiting rooms, airline offices, a bank (⊕ *08.00–16.00 Mon–Fri, 08.15–14.30 Sat*) with ATM, a post office, several car-hire kiosks and a desk for Bushtracks Africa. You can also buy curios and sundries such as sweets and postcards. A simple snack bar (⊕ *08.00–18.00 daily*) serves local dishes, but once you've passed through passport control, neither the bar nor the small 'private' lounge (*US$15 pp, inc unlimited drinks*) offers anything more substantial than snacks. As if in recompense, you'll find a duty-free shop and a couple more curio outlets, including Kubu Crafts.

Airlines Both Comair and South African Airways have daily flights between Johannesburg and Livingstone, taking around 1½ hours. Kenya Airways flies thre

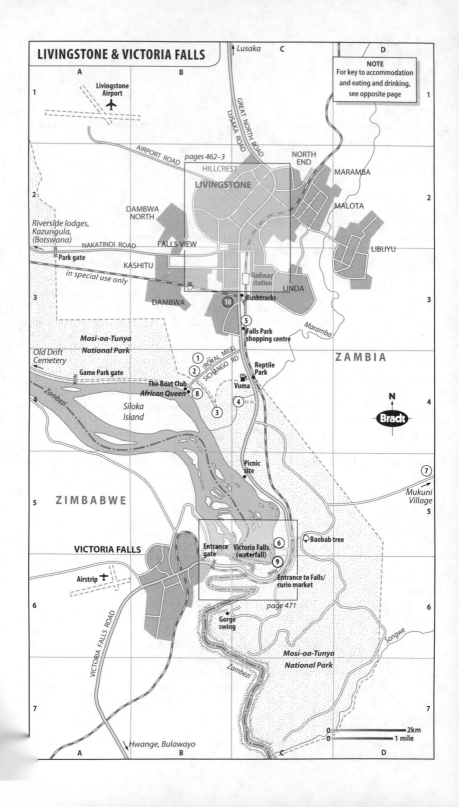

LIVINGSTONE & VICTORIA FALLS

↑ Lusaka

NOTE
For key to accommodation
and eating and drinking,
see opposite page

Livingstone
Airport ✈

GREAT NORTH ROAD
LUSAKA ROAD

AIRPORT ROAD

pages 462–3

HILLCREST

NORTH
END

LIVINGSTONE

MARAMBA

DAMBWA
NORTH

MALOTA

Riverside lodges,
Kazungula,
(Botswana)

NAKATINDI ROAD

FALLS VIEW

LIBUYU

✕ Park gate

KASHITU

Railway
station

in special use only

LINDA

DAMBWA

Maramba

⑩ ● Bushtracks

ZAMBIA

⑤ ● Falls Park
shopping centre

Mosi-oa-Tunya
National Park

Old Drift
Cemetery

① ● ROYAL MILE
② SICHANGO RD

● Reptile
Park

Game Park gate

The Boat Club ●
African Queen ⑧

🅟 Vuma

Zambezi

③

④

Siloka
Island

N

Bradt

● Picnic
site

⑦

Mukuni
Village

ZIMBABWE

⑥ ◖Baobab tree

VICTORIA FALLS

Entrance
gate ✕

Victoria Falls
(waterfall)

⑨

Airstrip ✚

Entrance to Falls/
curio market

page 471

VICTORIA FALLS ROAD

● Gorge
swing

Mosi-oa-Tunya
National Park

Zambezi

Songwe

↓ Hwange, Bulawayo

0   2km
0   1 mile

times a week between Nairobi and Livingstone, while SA Airlink flies four times a week to Nelspruit in South Africa.
Internal and charter airlines include:

✈ **Proflight** ☎0213 324745; e reservations@ proflight-zambia.com; www.flyzambia.com

✈ **Wilderness Air** ☎0211 271051; m 0978 770484 (24hr); e reservations@wilderness-air. co.zm; www.wilderness-air.com

By bus A brand-new state-of-the-art bus station [463 B6] was scheduled to open in December 2013 on Nakatindi Road, just west of the town centre. Once it opens, all bus companies will relocate their booking offices there, including one of the town's most reliable companies, Mazhandu Family Bus Services, making the service much easier for passengers.

Most buses are headed to Lusaka, but for visitors to or from Botswana, your best bet is to board the Mazhandu Family Bus to Mongu, which stops in Kazungula and Sesheke. It's wise to buy tickets the day before, and to be at the bus station at least half an hour before departure, since buses may leave early if they're full.

Driving west Those heading west, into Botswana, Namibia's Caprivi Strip or western Zambia, should take the Nakatindi Road – signposted as the M10 – that runs west, parallel to the river. After about 70km this comes to Kazungula – where you can take the ferry across the Zambezi into Botswana, near Kasane, or continue northwest within Zambia to Sesheke.

GETTING AROUND Livingstone town is small enough to walk around, as is the Falls area. To travel between the two, or to the airport, use one of the light-blue taxis that congregate at the main taxi stand [462 B2] or on Mosi-oa-Tunya Road opposite the craft market [462 E3]. A taxi between town and either the Falls or the airport will cost around Kw50–60/US$10–12 for up to four passengers. To the riverside lodges, you'll be charged from around Kw80/US$16, depending on the location. Be sure to agree on the price in advance.

By bus Minibuses run to the Falls [460 C6] from the Town Centre Market in the centre of Livingstone throughout the day, departing when they are full.

Driving yourself Driving yourself in Livingstone is pretty straightforward. Most lodges and hotels have secure parking, as do many restaurants. Cars can be hired with or without a driver (the former can even be a cheaper option). For a self-drive safari, you can rent a 4x4 with full kit.

In town, you're likely to come across any number of volunteers to look after your car. If you're prepared to trust someone then – in spite of considerable protestations to the contrary – a tip of

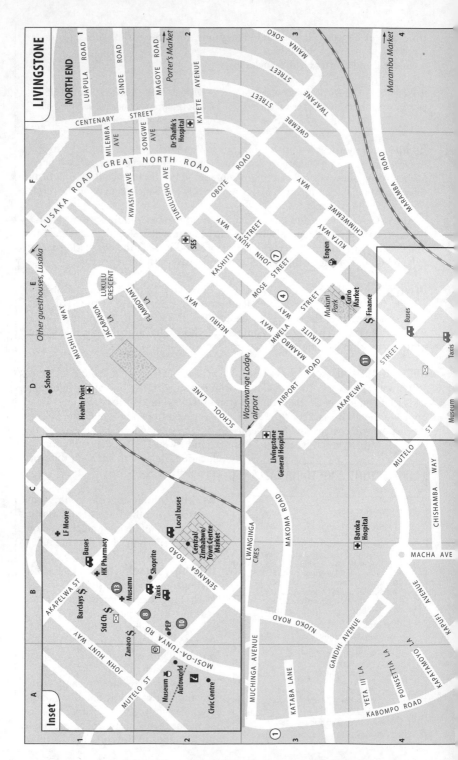

LIVINGSTONE

NORTH END

LUAPULA ROAD
SINDE ROAD
MAGOYE ROAD
Porter's Market
KATETE AVENUE
CENTENARY STREET
MILEMBA AVE
SONGWE AVE
Dr Shafik's Hospital
MAINA SOKO
TWAFANE STREET
GWEMBE STREET
MARAMBA ROAD
Maramba Market

LUSAKA ROAD / GREAT NORTH ROAD
KWASIYA AVE
TUKULUSHO AVE
OBOTE ROAD
WAY
CHIMWEMWE
KUTA WAY
Engen

Other guesthouses, Lusaka
MUSHILI WAY
JACARANDA LA
LUKULU CRESCENT
FLAMBOYANT LA
SES
KASHITU WAY
HUNT STREET
JOHN STREET
MOSE STREET
KUTA WAY
⑦
④
Mukuni Park
Curio Market
Finance
Buses
Taxis

School
Health Point
NEHRU WAY
MAAMBO WAY
MWELA WAY
LIKUTE WAY
AKAPELWA
⑪
STREET
Museum

SCHOOL LANE
Wasawange Lodge, airport
Livingstone General Hospital
AIRPORT ROAD

Inset

LF Moore
Buses
HK Pharmacy
Musamu
⑬
Shoprite
Local buses
Taxis
Central/ Zimbabwe/ Town Centre Market
AKAPELWA ST
Bardays
Std Ch
Zanaco
⑧
PEP
⑩
MOSI-OA-TUNYA RD
SENANGA ROAD

JOHN HUNT WAY
MUTELO ST
Museum
Autoworld
Civic Centre

LWANGINGA CRES
MAKOMA ROAD
Batoka Hospital
MUTELO
CHISHAMBA WAY
MACHA AVE

MUCHINGA AVENUE
NJOKO ROAD
GANDHI AVENUE
KATABA LANE
YETA III LA
KABOMPO ROAD
POINSETTIA LA
KAPATAMOYO LA
KAPUTI AVENUE

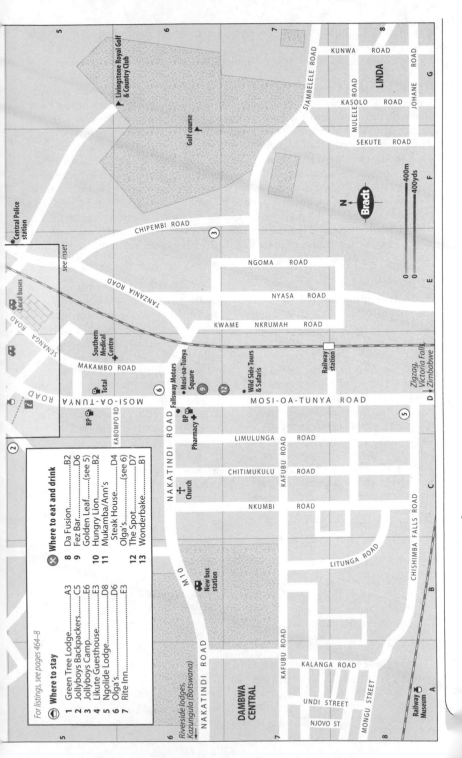

For listings, see pages 464–8

Where to stay

1 Green Tree Lodge.............A3
2 Jollyboys Backpackers.......C5
3 Jollyboys Camp..............E6
4 Likute Guesthouse...........E3
5 Ngolide Lodge...............D8
6 Olga's......................D6
7 Rite Inn....................E3

Where to eat and drink

8   Da Fusion.................B2
9   Fez Bar..................D6
10 Golden Leaf............(see 5)
    Hungry Lion.............B2
11 Mukamba/Ann's
    Steak House.............D4
    Olga's................(see 6)
12 The Spot.................D7
13 Wonderbake..............B1

CENTRAL POLICE STATION

Livingstone Royal Golf & Country Club

Golf course

CHIPEMBI ROAD

NGOMA ROAD

NYASA ROAD

KWAME NKRUMAH ROAD

STAMBELELE ROAD

KUNWA ROAD

LINDA

KASOLO ROAD

MULELE ROAD

JOHANE ROAD

SEKUTE ROAD

TANZANIA ROAD

SENANGA ROAD

Local buses

see inset

Southern Medical Centre

MAKAMBO ROAD

Total

BP

KABOMPO RD

MOSI-OA-TUNYA ROAD

Mosi-oa-Tunya Square

Fallsway Motors

BP

Pharmacy

Church

Wild Side Tours & Safaris

Railway station

Zigzag, Victoria Falls, Zimbabwe

NAKATINDI ROAD

LIMULUNGA ROAD

KAFUBU ROAD

CHITIMUKULU ROAD

NKUMBI ROAD

LITUNGA ROAD

CHISHIMBA FALLS ROAD

M10

New bus station

Riverside lodges, Kazungula (Botswana)

NAKATINDI ROAD

KAFUBU ROAD

KALANGA ROAD

DAMBWA CENTRAL

MONGU STREET

UNDI STREET

NJOVO ST

Railway Museum

400m
400yds

N

Bradt

about Kw1.50–2.50/US$0.30–0.50 should be about right, depending on the length of time you're away.

There are several 24-hour fuel stations on the main Mosi-oa-Tunya Road.

WHERE TO STAY Along the Zambezi River, numerous bush lodges occupy lovely situations, some close enough to enjoy the attractions and activities of the Falls, others further upstream and more remote. Closer to town, and to the Falls, an increasing number of upmarket hotels, some on the river, and others in a more urban setting, offer Western creature comforts. At the cheaper end of the market, staying in a guesthouse or in-town lodge, where you may meet African travellers or volunteers from overseas, can add a multi-cultural dimension to your visit, while backpacker accommodation tends to cater strictly to the international budget traveller.

Accommodation options listed here are among the best in an increasingly crowded market. For the purposes of this guide, we have concentrated on those that are relatively close to the Falls or within easy reach of the Botswana border at Kazungula. For full details of these and other options, see my companion guide, *Zambia: The Bradt Travel Guide*.

Game park and close to the Falls

🏠 **David Livingstone Safari Lodge & Spa** [460 B4] (77 rooms) ☎0213 324601; e lodge@ dlslandspa.com; www.thedavidlivingstone.com. This efficient, 4-star hotel under steep thatch makes the most of its wide river frontage with commanding views of the river from the rooms, restaurants & infinity pool. Huge basketwork lampshades & wooden sculptures dominate the communal areas, & concrete walkways with rustic railings lead to tastefully appointed rooms with small balconies. There's Wi-Fi throughout, with a laptop-loan scheme, plus a highly exclusive spa, a gym, wine cellar, gift shop & activity centre. Moored just in front is the lodge's own riverboat, the *Lady Livingstone*, which offers a discount to lodge guests. **$$$$$**

🏠 **Royal Livingstone** [460 C5] (173 rooms) Mosi-oa-Tunya Rd; ☎0213 321122; reservations ☎+27 11 780 7800; e zambia.reservations@ suninternational.com; www.suninternational. com. If the broad, low, white frontage is rather disappointing at 1st glance, inside all is spacious & elegant, with an old-world attention to detail & service that befits a 5-star hotel. Sweeping lawns lead down to an unparalleled frontage along the Zambezi, just a 15min walk (or a short buggy ride) along the river from the Falls. Zebra, impala & giraffe are often seen grazing in the grounds – an unusual sight from the swimming pool & riverfront massage tents. **$$$$$**

🏠 **Stanley Safari Lodge** [460 D4] (10 cottages) Robin Pope Safaris; reservations ☎+265 179 4491/5483; m 0967 848615; e info@ robinpopesafaris.net; www.robinpopesafaris.net. With sweeping views down towards the Zambezi & the spray of the Falls in the distance, this friendly lodge is best suited as a place to chill out, relax &

ACCOMMODATION PRICE CODES

Based on a double room with breakfast in high season. Single supplements usually apply, averaging 20%, but often significantly higher. VAT may be charged extra. Note that the Kwacha was rebased in 2013, effectively knocking off the final 000s.

$$$$$	£150+; US$250+; Kw1,125+
$$$$	£100–150; US$150–250; Kw750–1,125
$$$	£50–100; US$80–150; Kw400–750
$$	£25–50; US$40–80; Kw200–400
$	up to £25; up to US$40; up to Kw200

unwind. Inside the high electric fence, large, fairly formal gardens with a central pool are backed by a beautifully designed thatched building with an open-aspect lounge, bar & dining area, & a 'map room' with a laptop & free Wi-Fi, & a wine cellar for candlelit tastings. Stylish 'cottages' with king-size or twin beds are all laid out differently, some with a 'loo with a view' & some with an outside shower & bath. The honeymoon suite has its own plunge pool & fireplace, & children will love the family room, with a paddling pool, & bucket shower around a tree. *Cottage US$390–490; open suite US$430–575; closed suite US$490–640. All pp sharing inc FB, local drinks, activities laundry, airport transfers.*

🏠 **Zambezi Sun** [460 C6] (212 rooms) 393 Mosi-oa-Tunya Rd; 📞 0213 321122; reservations 📞 +27 11 780 7800; e zamres1@ suninternational.com; www.suninternational.com. The lively 3-star sibling of the Royal Livingstone is more reminiscent of a north African mosque than of southern Africa. Vervet monkeys cavort through the grounds & a large pool snakes through the centre. Although there are no views of the river, the location is unbeatable: just a few hundred metres' walk from the lip of the Falls & the curio market, & with unrestricted access. **$$$$$**

🏠 **The Bushfront Lodge** [460 B4] (14 chalets, camping) Sichango Rd; 📞 0213 322446; reservations 📞 0213 320428; e info@bushfront.com; www.bushfront.com. Set a few kilometres upriver from the Falls among indigenous vegetation, The Bushfront's thatched chalets have en-suite bathrooms with potted plants & 3 individual tent pitches with modern ablutions & a braai area. There's a large bar/lounge with satellite TV, a restaurant & a small pool. **$$$$** *Camping Kw55 pp.*

🏠 **Chrismar Hotel** [460 B4] (59 rooms) Sichango Rd; 📞 0213 323141; e guestrelations@livingstone. chrismar.co.zm; www.chrismarhotels.com. This mid-market hotel near the entrance to the national park is well thought out & offers good value for money. While it is not on the river, its bush setting is enhanced by numerous fountains & water features, including the largest swimming pool in town, complete with a bar in the middle. A 2nd, less flashy pool costs Kw20 pp for walk-in guests. Rooms, in a range of styles up to executive suites, are set around spacious grounds, & wouldn't disgrace a hotel of far better quality – despite the faux-fur fabrics. **$$$$**

🏠 **Maramba River Lodge** [460 B4] (9 chalets, 23 tents, camping) 📞 0213 324189;

e reservations@marambariverlodge.com; www. maramba-zambia.com. This established lodge & campsite is a real oasis in the bush, with green lawns & mature trees, hippos, elephants & birds aplenty. With an activity booking office, pool, children's play area, craft shop, fully licensed riverside bar & simple restaurant, the lodge is particularly good for families. En-suite accommodation ranges from bright-yellow chalets to simple twin-bedded safari tents, while campers share an ablution block. **$$$$** *Camping Kw53 pp.*

🏠 **The Zambezi Waterfront** [460 B4] (23 rooms, 24 tents, camping) off Sichango Rd; 📞 0213 320606–8; m 0968 320606; e waterfront@ safpar.com; www.safpar.net. Right opposite the entrance to Mosi-oa-Tunya National Park, the Waterfront is large, secure & affordable & incorporates a range of facilities on one of the best sites to view the sunset over the Zambezi. It's broadly split into 2 sites, 1 with a spacious restaurant with a pizza oven & a teak bar (with satellite TV), a sunken pool, & the best of the accommodation; the other housing the Adventure Village with a natural-style rock pool, another bar & an auditorium, plus permanent tents & a decidedly noisy camping area that's popular with overland trucks. **$$$** *Tent Kw132 pp; camping Kw55 pp.*

Beside the Zambezi: upriver [off 460 A2] Lodges & camps are listed here in order of their proximity to the Falls.

🏠 **Toka Leya** (12 tented chalets) Contact Wilderness Safaris, page 177. Some 5km from Livingstone, Toka Leya's canvas & natural wood chalets face the river from wide wooden verandas. Glass sliding doors lead to a bedroom & dressing area regaled with 4-poster beds enveloped by mosi nets, temperature controlled by AC/heating & a fan. It's airy & spacious but understated, enlivened by Persian-style rugs & bright lamps. Wooden walkways link chalets to the main lounge & restaurant area, bar, tree-shaded deck & firepit – as well as a small infinity pool, & simple riverside spa. Explore with boat trips, game drives & birding/nature walks, or book trips further afield. *US$620 pp sharing FB, inc local drinks, laundry, 2 activities/day, exc spa treatments.*

🏠 **Thorntree River Lodge** (9 chalets) 📞 0213 327480; reservations: +27 11 794 1446; e ceres@ threecities.co.za; www.thorntreeriverlodge.com.

From Thorntree's comfortable bar, lounge & dining area with riverside deck, you can watch elephants moving between the islands in the Zambezi – & its massage rooms overlook a waterhole frequented by buffalo, elephant, hippo, waterbuck & bushbuck. Simple but attractive brick-under-thatch chalets & suites line the riverbank, each with electricity, en-suite bathroom & small veranda. And to complete the picture, there's a figure-of-8 swimming pool. Thorntree is also the base for Livingstone's elephant-back safaris where guests can meet the resident herd. *US$350–400 pp sharing FB, inc 1 activity/day (sunset cruise, game drive or Falls tour), exc VAT, drinks, transfers & park fees.*

🏠 **The River Club** (11 chalets) ✆ 0213 327457; 📱 0977 892179; ✉ riverclub@iconnect.zm; www. theriverclubzambia.com, www.wilderness-safaris.com; for reservations, contact your tour operator. The distinctly colonial style here marks an exclusive & intimate lodge, set in extensive & secure grounds with magnificent views over the Zambezi. Large, thatched chalets boast plenty of creature comforts, alongside teak furniture, quality fabrics & beautifully polished floors. These are split level, but 3 suites with private pools are on a single storey. It's all elegant & very classy – yet with a stunning infinity pool, a gym, tennis court, sauna & jacuzzi, AC, & Wi-Fi throughout, there's more than a nod to the modern era. *US$682 pp sharing inc FB & activities.*

🏠 **Tongabezi** (5 cottages, 6 houses) ✆ 0213 327450/68; ✉ reservations@tongabezi.com; www.tongabezi.com. Set on a sweeping bend of the Zambezi, 15km west of town, Tongabezi's setting is matched by excellent service. Individual & tastefully decorated cottages & houses are all different – & carefully secluded – with the services of a private valet. The newly revamped & beautifully designed Dog House re-opened in August 2013 after being destroyed by fire. Sumptuous meals are served on the riverside deck, close to a natural-looking swimming pool & campfire, or in the open-sided dining room. You can even arrange to dine on a floating 'sampan' – perhaps after a relaxing massage. *Cottage US$535/640, house US$650/755, Nut House US$755/860, all pp sharing, low/high season (Nov–May/Jun–Oct), inc FB, local drinks, activities, laundry, levies; exc transfers, park fees. 40% sgl suppt high season; no children under 7.*

🏠 **Sindabezi Island** (5 chalets) Contact via Tongabezi, above. For barefoot luxury on an island retreat, Sindabezi is *the* place, with hippo & river birds in regular attendance. A short boat trip downstream from Tongabezi, its en-suite chalets are private, comfortable & deceptively spacious. During the day, mealtimes are taken high up with commanding views of the river; in the evening, enjoy a drink by the campfire, then dine by paraffin lighting in the central teak 'gazebo'. *Chalet US$450/515 pp sharing low/high season (Nov–May/Jun–Oct), honeymoon chalet US$490/585, inc FB, drinks, activities, laundry, transfers to/from island.*

🏠 **Waterberry Zambezi Lodge** (7 chalets) ✆ 0213 327455; enquiries +44 (0)1379 783392; ✉ reservations@waterberrylodge.com; www. waterberrylodge.com. More affordable than most along the river, but 35mins' drive from Livingstone, the understated Waterberry is set in a secluded position with a lagoon at the back that makes a good focus for bird & nature walks. Although the site is open, & frequented by hippos, children are welcome – but parents need to exercise a degree of caution. Rooms – most grouped around the 2-storey main building & pool – are all en suite with fans & mosi nets. The colonial-style River Farmhouse with stylish modern interiors was added in June 2013. Its 4 bedrooms, spacious lounge & dining room with its own chef make it well suited to families. *US$335 pp, farmhouse US$395 pp up to 4 guests (additional guest US$350), inc FB, local drinks, laundry, 2 activities/day, airport transfer.*

🏠 **Islands of Siankaba** (6 chalets, 1 honeymoon/VIP chalet) ✆ 0213 327490; 📱 0977 720530; ✉ info@siankaba.net; www. siankaba.com; reservations ✆ 0211 260279; 📱 0977 720530. Luxury & superb cuisine are the hallmarks of this exclusive lodge – though at 42km from Livingstone, it's more a place to enjoy for its own sake. Reached by a short boat ride, it has 2 islands. One houses large chalets that nestle like bird hides among the trees, regally furnished with 4-poster beds & a claw-footed bathtub. On the other you'll find the restaurant & bar/lounge area, with natural décor & tables on the terrace for alfresco dining. A secluded pool & spa are hidden among the trees, a nature trail runs round the island & bikes & mekoros allow you to explore. *Chalet US$445–505 pp;*

honeymoon chalet US$500–600, inc FB, drinks, their own activities, Livingstone airport transfers. No children under 10.

🏠 **Royal Chundu Zambezi River Lodge**
(10 chalets) Lodge ☎0213 327060; reservations: ☎+27 13 751 1038; e lodge@royalchundu.com; www.royalchundu.com. Just over an hour's drive from the Falls, the upmarket Royal Chundu is on a wooded stretch of the river, visited by just the occasional canoeist, & a haven for birds. At its heart, linked by walkways to solid & very smart chalets that boast all the accoutrements of a 5-star hotel, a sparkling infinity pool overlooks the river. A TV lounge, small library & computer room are tucked well away, but more typical are the floating riverside spa & formal dining room – complete with fireplace, polished silver, fine wines & cigars. *US$490 pp inc FB, sundowner cruise.*

In town

🏠 **Protea Hotel Livingstone** [460 C3]
(80 rooms, 13 apts) Mosi-oa-Tunya Rd; ☎0213 324630; e reservations@phlivingstone.co.zm; www.proteahotels.com. This surprisingly elegant hotel has an attractive courtyard with a fish-filled pond & a swimming pool, a restaurant & bar, & plenty of loungers. Dark-wood furniture & classic styling define the rooms. As well as a formal restaurant, the hotel has its own activity centre, free Wi-Fi, secure parking & a business centre. **$$$$**

🏠 **Ngolide Lodge** [463 D8] (16 rooms)
110 Mosi-oa-Tunya Rd; ☎0213 321091/2; e ngolide@gmail.com; www.ngolidelodge. com. More of a mini-hotel than a lodge, this thatched building fronted by gardens is well built & compact, if a bit dark. Small but comfortable & well-equipped rooms under high thatch lead off a central quadrangle that is surrounded by a shallow 'moat'. There's Wi-Fi access across the whole site & the Indian restaurant is among the best in Livingstone. **$$$**

🏠 **Olga's Guesthouse** [463 D6] (8 rooms)
Nakatindi Rd; ☎0213 324160; e info@ olgasproject.com; www.olgasproject.com. This popular pizza place (see page 468) added simple rooms in 2012, all surrounding its pretty little garden. Clean & comfortable with mosi nets & fans, rooms also offer the feel-good factor as all proceeds go to the Local Youth Community Training Centre, which provides training to local orphans & disadvantaged youths. **$$$**

🏠 **Green Tree Lodge** [462 A3] (5 chalets, camping) 2015 Kombe Dr; ☎0213 322631; m 0977 630159; e greentreelodge@livingstonezambia. com; www.greentreelodgezambia.com. Individual en-suite chalets with secure parking are set among fruit trees. Each boasts dbl or twin beds, AC, fridge, TV, Wi-Fi & kettle, & its own veranda looking over the pool & bar, where meals are available. **$$**

🏠 **Likute Guesthouse** [462 E3] (13 rooms)
62 Likute Way; ☎0213 323661; m 0978 06510, 0954 36074; e likuteguest@zamnet.zm. Within a small walled complex, the clean & welcoming Likute has en-suite rooms with AC, mosi nets, satellite TV, kettle & fridge. The staff are hard to find but friendly, meals are available on request & there's secure parking. **$$**

🏠 **Rite Inn** [462 E3] (10 rooms) 301 Mose St; ☎0213 323264; e riteinn@gmail.com. Clean, attractive rooms in a small, secure courtyard are among the nicest we've seen in this price range. Twin, dbl & family rooms have tiled bathrooms, AC, fridges, coffee/tea service, digital safes & satellite TVs. A sparkling swimming pool is surrounded by a large tiled patio, & there's a small bar & restaurant. **$$**

🏠 **Jollyboys Backpackers** [463 C5] (13 en suite chalets, 10 with shared ablutions, 50 dorm beds, camping) 34 Kanyanta Rd; ☎0213 324229/322086; e enquiries@backpackzambia.com; www. backpackzambia.com. The ever-popular but unpretentious Jollyboys occupies a central, tree-shaded site with attractive gardens. Facilities are set within a thatched courtyard, & at its heart is a wonderful sunken lounge with firepit & cushions. As well as a pool table, table tennis & enticing rock swimming pool, there's an open-plan bar with satellite TV, a restaurant, & a self-catering kitchen. Internet access, an activity centre, bike hire, laundry service, secure parking & a book exchange complete the picture. **$–$$**, *exc b/fast. 4/8/16-bed dorm Kw97/65/54 pp, camping Kw43 pp.*

🏠 **Jollyboys Camp** [463 E6] (28 dorm beds, 9 en-suite rooms, 4 twin chalets, camping) 80 Chipembi Rd; ☎0213 324756; e enquiries@ backpackzambia.com; www.backpackzambia.com. This offshoot of Jollyboys has a greater focus on family accommodation – there's even a jungle gym for the kids. **$–$$** *exc b/fast. Dorm bed Kw62; camping Kw31 pp.*

RESTAURANT PRICE CODES

Based on average cost of a main course

$$$$$	£12+; US$20+; Kw90+
$$$$	£9.50–12; US$14–20; Kw70–90
$$$	£6–9.50; US$9–14; Kw45–70
$$	£4–6; US$6–9; Kw30–45
$	under £4; under US$6; under Kw30

WHERE TO EAT

Restaurants Livingstone's independent & hotel restaurants offer a wide variety of cuisine at fairly decent prices. It's worth remembering that hotel establishments, while usually more expensive, often cater to foreign tastes.

✗ **Royal Livingstone** [460 C5] Mosi-oa-Tunya Rd; ✆0213 321122. Sun's flagship hotel has a fabulous restaurant with surprisingly reasonable prices. The setting is lovely, the service excellent, & the food the best in town. Booking essential. $$$$$

✗ **Zambezi Sun** [460 C6] Mosi-oa-Tunya Rd; ✆0213 321122. There's an alfresco grill by the pool, ideal for light lunches & snacks. In the evening, try the buffet dinner for Kw215: a selection of grilled kebabs, burgers, omelettes to order, salads & desserts. $$$$$

✗ **The Zambezi Waterfront** [460 B4] Sichango Rd; ✆0213 320606–8. Enjoy b/fast, lunch or dinner with magnificent views of the Zambezi at affordable prices. The food is good & plentiful with the usual variety of chicken dishes, burgers & chips, soups, sandwiches & daily specials served by friendly staff. The new pizza oven is an especially popular addition & there is also a full bar. $$$–$$$$

✗ **Zigzag** [460 B3] Industrial Rd; ✆0213 322814; ⏰ 07.00–21.00 Sun–Wed, 07.00–23.00 Thu–Sat. A welcome respite from the hustle & bustle of town, Zigzag is shaded by guava, lemon & mango trees. It's popular for b/fast, coffee & cakes, lunch, or an evening meal, & also has a children's menu & play area, & a fully licensed bar. $$$–$$$$

✗ **The Spot** [463 D7] 125 Mosi-oa-Tunya Rd; m 0978 170791; ⏰ 11.00–late Tue–Sat, 11.00–15.00 Sun. Funky, rustic & recommended, this light & breezy bar & restaurant is set in a colonial railworker's house, decorated with traditional masks & ornaments. Frequented by locals & tourists alike, it serves both traditional & Western dishes & has a licensed bar. There's indoor & outdoor seating & a children's play area in the pleasant gardens. $$$

✗ **The Golden Leaf** [463 D8] 110 Mosi-oa-Tunya Rd; ✆0213 321091/2; ⏰ 07.00–10.00, 12.30–14.00 & 18.15–22.00. One of the better places to eat in town, this small Indian restaurant has a varied menu, from fish masalla to kadai chicken & loads of veggie options. It's very popular, so do book in advance. $$–$$$

✗ **Olga's** [463 D6] Nakatindi Rd; ✆0213 324160; www.olgasproject.com; ⏰ 11.00–22.00 daily. This is *the* place for pizzas cooked in a traditional wood-fired oven, as well as pasta & salads. A thatched eating area incorporates crafts & furniture made by members of the Local Youth Community Training Centre & a school for disadvantaged youngsters, with profits fed back to the centre. $$–$$$

✗ **Mukamba/Ann's Steak House** [462 D4] 97 John Hunt Way. Down the road from Jollyboys, this is a great place to chill out with some cheap Zambian food & drinks, often accompanied by live, local music. $–$$

Take-aways and fast food There are several take-aways in town, including Wonderbake [462 B1], one of the best & most popular, & the Hungry Lion on the corner with Mutelo St [462 B2], serving the usual fare of chips, burgers, samosas, sandwiches & soft drinks. Falls Park shopping centre [460 C3] is also a useful source of fast food.

ENTERTAINMENT AND NIGHTLIFE Livingstone's nightlife centres largely around ncing and drinking, although if you simply want to relax and chat the bars at ous restaurants offer a pleasant atmosphere. For sundowners, join the crowd at the

Zambezi Waterfront [460 B4], overlooking the river. The Fez Bar [463 D6] is a lively venue most nights – a favourite hang-out for expats after a tough day looking after visitors. Other popular options are Da Fusion [460 B2] and Mukamba [462 D4]. For live music, there's a band at the Zambezi Sun [460 C6] most evenings and at weekends.

SHOPPING With both the Falls Park shopping centre [460 C3] and the newly built Mosi-oa-Tunya Square [463 D6] (commonly referred to as the 'Shoprite Centre'), options for shopping in Livingstone have improved considerably in recent years. There are also a couple of markets, and several shops along the main Mosi-oa-Tunya Road. Opening hours are usually around 09.00–17.00 Monday to Friday, and Saturday mornings, unless otherwise stated.

For books and magazines, Bookworld [463 D6] (*Mosi-oa-Tunya Sq;* \ *0213 321414*) has the best stock in Livingstone and also sells stationery, games and the like. Several of the curio shops stock wildlife reference books and regional travel guides. If you like bargaining and have lots of patience and time, then head for one of the craft markets (page 473) for **curios and gifts**. If not, then one of the tourist-orientated shops might suit you much better: many of these can be found along Mosi-oa-Tunya Road, or you could try the shop at the Livingstone Museum (page 472).

Pharmacies For cosmetics, toiletries or medicines there are several good pharmacies on and around Mosi-oa-Tunya Road, stocking a selection of items including insect repellents, beauty products, suncreams, medical supplies, baby supplies, batteries and more. Each has a trained pharmacist, who can offer advice on medications and fill prescriptions. Otherwise, both the Spar Super Store in Falls Park shopping centre [460 C3] and Shoprite in Mosi-oa-Tunya Square [463 D6] sell a variety of beauty products and the basics.

BANKS AND CHANGING MONEY Livingstone has several major banks near the main post office [462 B1], and various bureaux de change dotted throughout town. Most of the banks have ATMs, for which you'll generally need a Visa card rather than MasterCard. More convenient, but with the least favourable exchange rate, is to change money at a hotel or lodge. Avoid the freelance 'money-changers' who tend to congregate around the town centre and at the border.

COMMUNICATIONS
Internet As well as internet cafés around town, virtually all places of accommodation offer Wi-Fi (usually free for guests). While rates are low and comparable, the standard of computers, speed and service varies.

Post Livingstone's post office [462 B1] (\ *0213 21976;* ⏱ *08.00–18.00 Mon–Fri, 08.00–14.00 Sat*) lies in the centre of town in a sprawling complex of banks and shops, adjacent to the main road.

Telephone SIM cards for both Airtel and the state-owned Zamtel are obtainable from numerous outlets across town; look out for their signs at shopping malls and on Mosi-oa-Tunya Road.

OTHER PRACTICALITIES
Car repairs and spares The two biggest workshops in town are Foley's Africa (*Industrial Rd;* \ *0213 320888;* e *info@foleysafrica.com; www.foleysafrica.com*), which caters for Land Rovers; and Bennett Engineering, also known as Harry's

1

workshop [460 C3] (✆ *0213 321611/322380;* m *0978 308936;* e *hbennett@iconnect. zm*), opposite Falls Park.

For more basic repairs, contact Fallsway Motors [463 D6] (✆ *0213 321049*) at the corner of Nakatindi Road, or Channa's Motors (*Mosi-oa-Tunya Rd;* ✆ *0213 320468*), just across the railway line. Punctures and tyre repairs can be handled by the Total fuel station on Mosi-oa-Tunya Road [463 D5], while for parts or vehicle accessories, head for Autoworld [462 A2] (*Mosi-oa-Tunya Rd;* ✆ *0213 320264;* e *autoworld@zamtel.zm*).

Medical facilities The local hospitals are not up to the standard of those in the West, but there are several small clinics, and the two Sun International hotels, Zambezi Sun and the Royal Livingstone, have a mini-clinic with a nurse for their own guests. In the event of an emergency, contact:

✚ **SES** [462 E2] Speciality Emergency Services, cnr Likute Way & Obote Rd; ✆0213 322330; emergency control centre ✆0211 273302–7; m 0977 740307/8; e seslivingstone@zamnet.zm; www.ses-zambia.com. The local base is staffed with South African-trained paramedics.

Tourist information The Zambia Tourism Board [462 A2] (*Mosi-oa-Tunya Rd;* ✆ *0213 321404/87;* e *zntb@zambiatourism.org.zm; www.livingstonetourism.com, www.zambiatourism.com*) has an office at the tourist centre next to the Livingstone Museum, although resources are limited.

WHAT TO SEE AND DO

The area around Victoria Falls has been a major crossroads for travellers for over a hundred years, from the early missionaries and traders, to the backpackers, overland trucks and package tourists of the last few decades. Apart from simply marvelling at one of the world's greatest waterfalls, there are now lots of ways to occupy yourself for a few days. Details of the options listed here are available at most places to stay, but should you be at a loss, try one of the following:

Bushtracks Africa [460 C3] Mosi-oa-Tunya Rd; ✆0213 323232; e victoriafalls@bushtracksafrica. com; www.bushtracksafrica.com
SafPar [460 B4] The Zambezi Waterfront; ✆0213 320606/7; m 0973 403270 (Waterfront), 0977 434143 (head office); e zaminfo@safpar.com; www.safpar.net
Wild Side Tours & Safaris [463 D7] 131 Mosi-oa-Tunya Rd; ✆0213 323726; e wild@iconnect.zm

VICTORIA FALLS We can be sure that the Falls were well known to the native peoples of southern Africa well before any European 'discovered' them. After the San/Bushmen hunter-gatherers, the Toka Leya people inhabited the area, and it was probably they who christened the Falls Shongwe. Later, the Ndebele knew the Falls as the aManza Thunqayo, and after that the Makololo referred to them as Mosi-oa-Tunya. However, their first written description comes to us from Dr David Livingstone in November 1855:

> It had never been seen before by European eyes; but scenes so lovely must have been gazed upon by angels in their flight.

The Falls are 1,688m wide and average just over 100m in height. Around 550 million litres (750 million during peak months) cascade over the lip every minute,

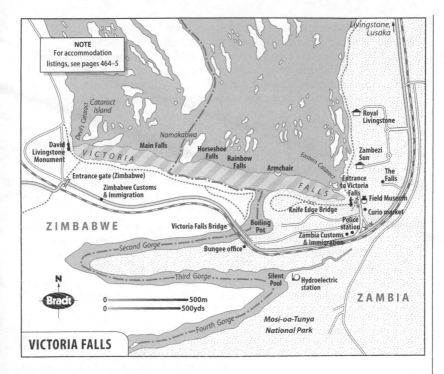

NOTE
For accommodation
listings, see pages 464–5

VICTORIA FALLS

making this one of the world's greatest waterfalls. Closer inspection shows that this immense curtain of water is interrupted by gaps, where small islands stand on the lip of the Falls. These effectively split the Falls into smaller waterfalls, which are known as (from west to east) the Devil's Cataract, the Main Falls, the Horseshoe Falls, the Rainbow Falls and the Eastern Cataract.

Around the Falls is a genuinely important and interesting rainforest, with plant species (especially ferns) rarely found elsewhere in Zimbabwe or Zambia. These are sustained by the clouds of spray, which blanket the immediate vicinity of the Falls. You'll also find various monkeys and baboons here, whilst the lush canopy shelters Livingstone's lourie amongst other birds.

The flow, and hence the spray, is greatest just after the end of the rainy season – around March or April, depending upon the rains – then decreases gradually until about December. During low water, a light raincoat (available for rent on site) is useful for wandering between the viewpoints on the Zimbabwean side, though it's not necessary in Zambia, but at high water a raincoat is largely ineffective as the spray soaks you in seconds. Anything that you want to keep dry must be wrapped in several layers of plastic.

The Falls never seem the same twice, so try to visit several times, under different light conditions. At sunrise, both Danger Point and Knife-edge Point are fascinating – position yourself carefully to see your shadow in the mists, with three concentric rainbows appearing as halos. (Photographers will find polarising filters invaluable in capturing the rainbows on film, as the light from the rainbows at any time of day is polarised.) Moonlight is another fascinating time, when the Falls take on an ethereal glow and the waters blend into one smooth mass which seems frozen over the rocks.

On the Zambian side viewing the Falls could not be easier. For photographers, the area is best in the early morning, when the sun is behind you and illuminates the Falls, or in the late afternoon when you may catch a stunning sunset. When the river is at its lowest, towards the end of the dry season, the channels on this side may have dried up, yet while the Falls will be less spectacular then, their fascinating geology, normally obscured by spray, is revealed.

You can easily explore on your own, or organise a professional guide for a detailed explanation of the formation of the Falls and gorges, the river, local history and flora and fauna.

From the Zimbabwean side, viewing the Falls is more regulated, and may be easiest organised through a tour operator, who will also handle visas and transport. If you're planning to visit independently, allow at least half a day, and expect a fair delay at the border. Tickets are valid for the whole day, so you can return for no extra cost during the same day – though be prepared for the generally pleasant but very persistent vendors and 'guides' along the way.

LIVINGSTONE ISLAND Accessed exclusively through Tongabezi (page 466), Livingstone (or Namakabwa) Island is where Dr Livingstone first viewed the Falls. Trips are run between July and March, subject to water levels. Gaze over the edge, perhaps chancing a thrilling dip in the Devil's Pool right on the Falls edge, or having a gourmet meal – breakfast, lunch or high tea – in an exclusive setting. When the water's at its lowest, around October and November, you can sometimes even walk across the top of the Falls.

RIVER CRUISES Floating on the Upper Zambezi with a glass in one hand, and a pair of binoculars in the other, is one of the region's highlights. Nowadays booze-cruise boats operate round the clock – and sometimes all congregate close together – but this is still a great way to take a gentle look around the Zambezi's islands, with national parks on both sides of the river.

Most elegant of the river boats are the *African Queen* [460 B4] and the *Lady Livingstone*, whose most popular excursions are the sunset cruises. Smaller, less formal craft ply the same route at rather lower cost.

FISHING EXCURSIONS If you dream of hooking a tigerfish then a day on the Zambezi with a knowledgeable guide can help make it come true. Half- and full-day fishing trips can be organised for both novice and experienced anglers as well as fly-fishermen, to include fishing tackle, boat hire, fuel, transfers, a qualified guide and refreshments.

THRILLS AND SPILLS The Falls area is indisputably *the* adventure capital of southern Africa. There is an amazing and seemingly endless variety of ways to get your shot of adrenalin, though none comes cheaply. If you wish to do multiple activities, check out the many combination packages on offer as these can be slightly cheaper than booking individually. Whatever you plan, expect to sign an indemnity form before your activity starts.

On the Zambian side there is a single cable car at Rapid 25 to bring clients out of the gorge after river trips, with the cost often included in the activity price.

Flight of Angels Named after Livingstone's famous comment, 'Flight of Angels' describes any sightseeing trip over the Falls by microlight or helicopter. This is a good way to get a feel for the geography of the area, and is surprisingly worthwhile. If you're arriving from Kasane, or leaving for there, consider combining a sightseeing flight and an air transfer.

Microlight Essentially sightseeing from a propeller-powered armchair 500m above the ground, this is the closest you'll get to soaring like a bird over the Falls.

Microlights are affected by the slightest turbulence, so if you book in advance, it's best to specify early morning or late afternoon, when conditions are ideal.

Helicopter The most expensive way to see the Falls is tremendous fun. A 15-minute trip takes in the Falls and the national park, or for 30 minutes you will fly over the gorges below the Falls as well; at extra cost, you can stop in the gorge for a picnic, or – if you plan to raft or riverboard – you save yourself the walk up and take an exhilarating helicopter lift instead, gaining an aerial view of the Falls and Zambezi gorges.

Bungee jumping Organised by an offshoot of the original New Zealand bungee pioneers, you jump – solo or tandem – from the middle of the main bridge between Zambia and Zimbabwe. With the Zambezi 111m below you, it is among the highest commercial bungee jumps in the world, and not for the nervous.

Bridge walks There's no-one better positioned to show you the ins and outs – no, make that ups and downs – of the Victoria Falls Bridge than the bungee folks, whose intimate bridge knowledge will not only fascinate you but have you clambering around and underneath the bridge like a monkey. With safety harness on and accompanied by guide, you have the opportunity to explore the bridge's superstructure while hearing all about its construction and riveting history. While not as adrenalin-charged as bungee jumping, it's still bound to get your heart beating faster as you navigate your way high above the Zambezi.

Abseiling, high-wiring, gorge swing and slide A popular option on the adventure menu is the Zambezi swing, a cable swing set across the gorge which, together with a 90m-high cable slide (flying fox), abseiling (rappelling) and 'rap' jumps (rappelling forwards) down the side of the gorge, offers daring fun for all ages.

Swing participants are harnessed to ropes attached to the cable's sliding pulley and, after stepping off the cliff face, experience a heart-stopping 53m, three-second free-fall, followed by an exhilarating pendulum-like swing across the gorge, accelerating up to 140km/h (with a pull of roughly 2.5 times gravity) for some two minutes before being lowered to the ground. It's definitely not for the faint-hearted, though participants as young as eight and as old as 76 have braved it. It's even possible to try it out in tandem.

Slightly tamer is the high wire or flying fox, set on another static cable stretched across the gorge. With harness and pulley, you leap off a platform and 'fly' (slide) across the gorge some 90m above the ground. It can be done in either a sitting or a flying position, and is suitable for children.

Canoeing on the Upper Zambezi Canoeing down the Upper Zambezi is a cool occupation on hot days, and the best way to explore the upper river, its islands and channels. Zimbabwe's Zambezi National Park stretches all along the western shore providing ample opportunity for game viewing, while lodges, farms, villages and bush dot the Zambian side as you head downstream. The silence of canoes makes them ideal for floating up to antelope, elephants or crocodiles. Birdlife is prolific – you may hear the cry of the African fish eagle or see pied kingfishers hover and dive. Hippos provide the excitement, and are treated with respect and given lots of space. All canoe trips are accompanied by a licensed river guide, and sometimes also a motorboat for additional safety. Canoes range from two-seater open-decked kayaks to inflatable 'crocodiles'.

No prior canoeing experience is necessary, and once you are used to the water, the better guides will encourage you to concentrate on the wildlife.

White-water rafting The Zambezi below the Falls is one of the world's most renowned stretches of white water. The rapids below the Falls are mostly graded IV and V – somewhere between 'very difficult' and 'for experts only' – but the majority of them don't need skill to manoeuvre the boat once it is within the rapids, so absolute beginners are usually allowed to take part. Nevertheless, although a trained river guide pilots every raft, you should think very carefully about committing yourself if you have no experience. Boats do flip over, and the consequences can be severe. It's also important to ensure that your chosen operator will give a thorough safety briefing before departure, explaining what to do in the event of a capsize.

Rafting is offered from both Zambia and Zimbabwe, but the entry points and length of trips vary according to the water levels. From July to January, when the water is low, and the river's waves and troughs (or 'drops') are more pronounced, there are full- or half-day trips, while in high-water months (February to July), only half-day trips are offered. If the water is too high, rafting is suspended until it recedes to a safer level.

Riverboarding Thrilling for the fit who swim strongly, riverboarding is not for the faint of heart. After donning fins, lifejacket and helmet, you and your foam board (the size of a small surfboard) will be taught the basic skills before getting an opportunity to 'surf' the big waves of the Zambezi – accompanied by a safety raft.

White-water kayaking Even those without experience can try tandem kayaking with a qualified guide, who manoeuvres the kayak through rapids while you assist with paddle power. All participants must be confident swimmers.

ROYAL LIVINGSTONE EXPRESS The whistle of a steam loco rarely fails to stir a frisson of excitement, and Livingstone's foray into steam is no exception. Restored with meticulous attention to detail, the locos and wooden carriages are polished until they gleam, attracting plenty of attention from trackside villages. Large windows, as well as an observation car, ensure good visibility for all, and – if elephant, buffalo or other game are spotted inside the national park – the train will sometimes stop for a better view. As the journey progresses, drinks are served before an unhurried dinner, enhanced by soft lighting and classical music.

CULTURAL ATTRACTIONS AND TOURS
Museums
Livingstone Museum [462 A2] Livingstone's main museum more than justifies a visit. To start with, there's an excellent three-dimensional map showing how the Zambezi River flows over Victoria Falls and downstream into the gorges, which puts everything into good perspective. Then there are exhibits on the Stone Age, and features on Zambian culture, politics, history, animals and traditional village life. Watch out, too, for the 'History' exhibition – it's easily missed but, with a unique collection of David Livingstone's personal possessions, including many of his letters, it's a must. Staff are friendly and knowledgeable and guided tours are included.

Railway Museum [463 A8] This collection of beautifully preserved old steam locomotives and memorabilia celebratIng the iron horse's history in Livingstone was badly damaged by fire and is now more for extreme railway buffs, Fortunately, though, the 1922 10th Class 156 out of Glasgow that used to take pride of place has now been put to work hauling the *Royal Livingstone Express*.

Field Museum [map 471] Directly across from the entrance gate to Victoria Falls, this is signed as an information centre, but is more of a small interpretation centre. It's well worth a visit for an understanding of the geology, archaeology and history of the Falls.

Markets Livingstone has many colourful local markets offering everything from fresh produce to secondhand clothes (*salaula*), from hand-fashioned metal pots to live chickens, from *chitenjes* (the traditional African cloth) to hand-crafted wood furniture and more. In addition to the large and fascinating Maramba Market [off 462 G4], there is also Porters' Market, further north [462 G2]. For something smaller and closer to town, try Zimbabwe, Central or Town Centre Market (take your pick of the names!), down the road from Shoprite and next to the minibus station [462 B2].

Craft markets Livingstone is one of the best places in Zambia to buy crafts – either from the outstanding curio market near the Falls [map 471], where the goods come from as far as the Democratic Republic of Congo and Malawi, or at the equally good Mukuni Park Curio Market [462 E3] in town, where local artisans, craftsmen and traders sell their wares. The best buys are *makenge* baskets from Zambia's Western Province, malachite and heavy woodcarvings: hippos, elephants, rhinos, giraffes and smaller statues, though do consider the ethics of encouraging any further exploitation of hardwoods. Note, too, that some wooden items, especially wooden salad bowls and tall giraffes, are prone to cracking once you get them home due to changes in climate, and that very rarely are 'antiques' sold at craft markets anything other than fakes.

The curio markets are places to bargain hard, but are more sophisticated than they appear; traders will accept most currencies and sometimes credit cards.

Village visits While some of the lodges organise independent visits to local villages for their guests, there are organised trips to different villages. Most popular among these, although somewhat commercial, is **Mukuni Village** [off 460 D5], where you can visit local huts, view villagers at work, watch curio-making and even sample traditional beer and food.

Historical tour of Livingstone A guided historical tour traces Livingstone's fascinating history, taking in many historical buildings and accented by colourful characters, intriguing tales and a once-vibrant social life.

SPORTS AND SPAS Many of Livingstone's hotels and lodges have small gyms or even tennis courts for their guests to use, or trained massage therapists on hand, but some facilities are open to all. Of note are the **spas** at the Royal Livingstone Hotel ([460 C5]; see page 464) and David Livingstone Safari Lodge and Spa ([460 B4]; see page 464).

Golfers can play at the Livingstone Royal Golf and Country Club [463 G6] (\ 0213 320440; e info@livingstonegolf.com; www.livingstonegolf.com), which has an 18-hole course and a renovated colonial-style club building.

WILDLIFE ENCOUNTERS
Mosi-oa-Tunya National Park Much of the Zambian area around the Falls is protected within the tiny Mosi-oa-Tunya National Park. You can drive yourself around easily, or go by 4x4 with a tour operator. There are even walking safaris, led by licensed safari guides.

A few hours' driving could yield sightings of most of the common antelope and some fine giraffe, as well as buffalo, elephant and zebra. There is also the chance of spotting white rhino. Even wild dog are present, but there are no lion, leopard or other big cats.

Birdwatching Even the casual visitor with little interest will often see fish eagles, Egyptian geese, lots of kingfishers, numerous different bee-eaters, Hadeda and sacred ibis, and various other storks, egrets and herons. Meanwhile, avid twitchers will be seeking the more elusive birds like the rare Taita falcon, rock pratincoles and African skimmers.

Elephant riding Zambezi Elephant Trails, based at Thorntree River Lodge, offer the only elephant-back safaris in Zambia. Here you and your *nduna* (elephant guide) will ride African elephants through the bush and along the river in the upper reaches of the Mosi-oa-Tunya National Park, where you may encounter a variety of game. In addition to the hour-long ride, there is the chance to interact with the elephants close up.

Livingstone Reptile Park ([460 C4]) This attraction offers the opportunity to see some huge crocs at close quarters. Picnic tables are set in the landscaped grounds and there's a café serving the park's signature 'Croc Bite'.

Walking with lions For visitors, the appeal of this encounter is the opportunity to walk with lion cubs, which are bred specially for the programme. Clearly this is very appealing to some people – but it's also very controversial; do consider the ethics before deciding whether or not to take part.

Appendix 1

WILDLIFE GUIDE

This wildlife guide is designed in a manner that should allow you to name most large mammals that you are likely to see in Botswana. Less common species are featured under the heading *Similar species* beneath the animal to which they are most closely allied, or bear the strongest resemblance.

For much more detailed information, see *Southern African Wildlife: A Visitor's Guide* by Mike Unwin, also published by Bradt Travel Guides.

CATS AND DOGS

Lion (*Panthera leo* Shoulder height 100–120cm. Weight 150–220kg) Africa's largest predator, the lion, is the animal that everybody hopes to see on safari. It is a sociable creature, living in prides of five to over 20 animals and defending a territory of 20–200km². Lions often hunt at night, and their favoured prey is large or medium antelope such as wildebeest and impala. Most hunting is done by females, but dominant males normally feed first after a kill. Rivalry between males is intense and takeover battles are frequently fought to the death, so two or more males often form a coalition. Young males are forced out of their home pride at three years of age, and cubs are usually killed after a successful takeover.

When not feeding or fighting, lions are remarkably indolent – they spend up to 23 hours of any given day at rest – so the anticipation of a lion sighting is often more exciting than the real thing. Lions naturally occur in any habitat, except desert or rainforest. They once ranged across much of the Old World, but these days they are all but restricted to the larger conservation areas in sub-Saharan Africa (one residual population exists in India).

Lions occur throughout Botswana, and are very common in the main northern areas of Chobe, Linyanti–Kwando and the Okavango. They also range across the Kalahari, in the Nxai/Makgadikgadi areas and the Central Kalahari Game Reserve, though the relative scarcity of prey leads to small, dissociated pride structures which have vast territories.

In the northern reserves, where food is plentiful, the converse is the case. Large prides are the norm and some, like those around North Gate and Savuti, have become so big that they make a speciality of killing young and juvenile elephants in order to have enough meat to go around. Even visiting these prolific reserves for just a few days, you're unlikely not to see at least some lions!

Leopard (*Panthera pardus* Shoulder height 70cm. Weight 60–80kg) The powerful leopard is the most solitary and secretive of Africa's big cats. It hunts at night, using stealth and power, often getting to within 5m of its intended prey before pouncing. If there are hyenas and lions around then leopards habitually move their kills up into trees to safeguard them. The leopard can be distinguished from the cheetah by its rosette-like spots, lack of black 'tearmarks' and more compact, low-slung, powerful build.

ANIMAL TRACKS (drawn to scale)

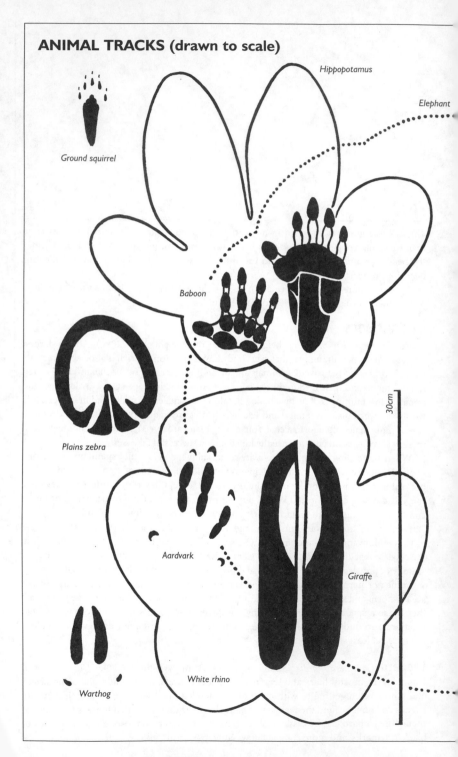

Ground squirrel

Hippopotamus

Elephant

Baboon

Plains zebra

Aardvark

Giraffe

White rhino

Warthog

30cm

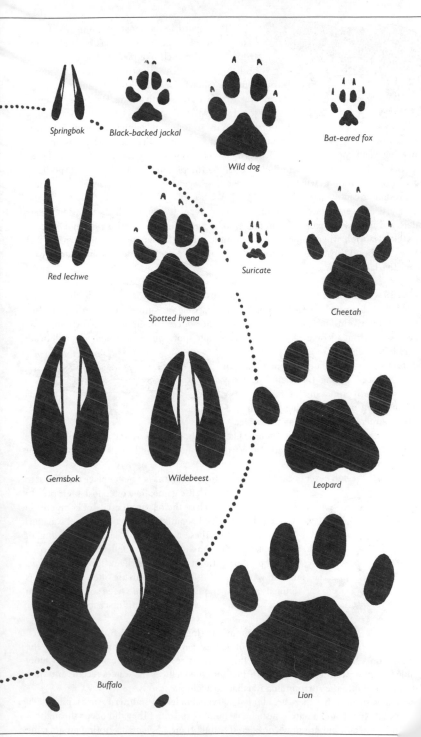

Springbok

Black-backed jackal

Wild dog

Bat-eared fox

Red lechwe

Spotted hyena

Suricate

Cheetah

Gemsbok

Wildebeest

Leopard

Buffalo

Lion

The leopard is the most common of Africa's large felines. Some of Botswana's bush is perfect for leopard, which like plenty of thickets, cover and big trees. The riverine woodlands found throughout the Chobe, Linyanti–Kwando and Okavango areas are firm favourites with them. Here they're quite often seen by sharp-eyed observers who scan low-hanging branches for these lounging felines. Meanwhile drives around dusk and early evening in the private concessions will sometimes yield good sightings of leopard going out on hunting forays as the light fades. Remarkably, leopard often seem unperturbed by the presence of a vehicle and spotlight, and will often continue whatever they are doing regardless of an audience. Watching a leopard stalk is captivating viewing.

Leopard are very adaptable. There are many records of individuals living for years undetected in close proximity to humans, for example in the suburbs of major African cities like Nairobi, where they prey on domestic dogs. Given this, it's no surprise that they're also found throughout the Kalahari, though in lower densities commensurate with the relative lack of prey.

Cheetah (*Acynonix jubatus* Shoulder height 70–80cm. Weight 50–60kg) This remarkable
spotted cat has a greyhound-like build, and is capable of running at 70km/h in bursts, making it the world's fastest land animal. Despite superficial similarities, you can easily tell a cheetah from a leopard by the former's simple spots, disproportionately small head, streamlined build, diagnostic black tearmarks, and preference for relatively open habitats. It is often seen pacing the plains restlessly, either on its own or in a small family group consisting of a mother and her offspring. Diurnal hunters, cheetah favour the cooler hours of the day to hunt smaller antelope like springbok, steenbok and duiker; plus young wildebeest, tsessebe and zebra, and also warthog, large birds, and small mammals such as scrub hares.

Given that cheetah never occur in high densities, Botswana is a better place than most to see them. In areas of dense game, they often lose their prey to lion or spotted hyena, so the relative scarcity of competition in areas like Nxai, Makgadikgadi and the Central Kalahari make these ideal. These also harbour large populations of springbok – a cheetah's ideal prey – and their ability to go for long periods without water gives them flexibility to move far from waterholes. Although cheetah are often thought of as animals of the open savannah, they do need some cover from which to sprint – so the Kalahari's thin scrub is perfect for them.

Having said that, all of my sightings of cheetah in Botswana have been in some of the central Okavango's areas of densest game – on Mboma Island and in the Mombo Concession! Looking through the sightings records at the camps, it's certainly notable that many of these cats move further into the Delta as the waters recede, and then move back out into the surrounding Kalahari to avoid the floods.

Estimates suggest that there are about 4,500 cheetah left in southern Africa, plus 2,500 or so in east Africa, and a barely sustainable number in Iran. (They did occur throughout ...a and Pakistan, but are now considered extinct there.) Scientists, noting an amazing lack of genetic diversity amongst all living cheetah, have suggested that the species must have gone through a 'genetic bottleneck' in the past – thus perhaps all living cheetah are descended from one female. This goes some way to explaining why they are very susceptible to disease.

Serval (*Felis serval* Shoulder height 60cm.

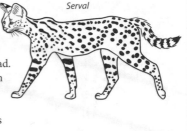
Serval

Weight 9–18kg) This long-legged cat is the tallest of Africa's 'small cats'. It has a similar build to a leopard, but with black-on-gold spots giving way to streaking near the head. Seldom seen, it is widespread and quite common in moist grassland, reedbeds and riverine habitats throughout Africa, including northern Botswana. It's largely absent from the drier areas of the Kalahari.

Serval do particularly well in wetter areas where there is lots of long grass – and are common throughout the Okavango and Linyanti–Kwando area – although they're relatively rarely seen. Until recently, there have been consistent reports of good sightings from night drives alongside the Savuti Channel, but now that it is flowing again, this is no longer the case. Serval prey on mice, rats, small mammals, birds, snakes, lizards and will sometimes even take fish or the young of small antelope. They use their big ears to locate their prey precisely by sound, and their long legs to see over tall grass, and to help them jump high as they pounce.

Caracal (*Felis caracal* Shoulder height 40cm. Weight 15–20kg) Smaller but heavier than

the serval, caracal resemble European lynx, with their uniform tan coat and tufted ears. They are solitary, mainly nocturnal hunters which feed on birds, small antelope and young livestock. Caracal are remarkable hunters for their size, and will often take prey as large as, or even larger than, they are. Their style is very much like small leopards; they normally stalk their prey as closely as possible, before springing with surprise. They also take many of the same species, even caching their prey in

Caracal

trees to return and feed later, and can be quite acrobatic hunters: they have been known to bat birds out of the air as they fly.

Caracal occur throughout sub-Saharan Africa, easily adapting to a variety of environments. They're found throughout Botswana and whilst night drives in the early evening provide your best chance of a glimpse of them, they're still very rarely seen.

Similar species The smaller **African wildcat** (*Felis sylvestris*) ranges from the Mediterranean to the Cape of Good Hope, and is similar in appearance to the domestic tabby cat. It has a ringed tail, a reddish-brown tinge to the back of its ears and an unspotted torso – which should preclude confusion with the even smaller **small spotted cat** (*Felis nigripes*), a relatively rare resident of the central and southern Kalahari which has a more distinctively marked coat. Both species are generally solitary and nocturnal, often utilising burrows or termite mounds as daytime shelters. They prey upon reptiles, amphibians and birds as well as small mammals.

Wild dog (*Lycaon pictus* Shoulder height 70cm. Weight 25kg) Also known as the painted

hunting dog, the wild dog is distinguished from other African dogs by its large size and mottled black, brown and cream coat. Highly sociable, living in packs of up to 20 animals, wild dogs are ferocious hunters that literally tear apart their prey on the run. The most endangered of Africa's great predators, they are now threatened with extinction. This is the result both of relentless persecution by farmers, who often view the dogs as dangerous vermin, and of their susceptibility to diseases spread by domestic dogs. Wild dogs are now extinct in many areas where they were formerly abundant, like the Serengeti, and they are common nowhere. The global population of fewer than 3,000 is concentrated in southern Tanzania, Zambia, Zimbabwe, Botswana, South Africa and Namibia.

African wild dog

Wild dogs prefer open savannah with only sparse tree cover, if any, and packs have enormous territories, typically covering 400km² or more. They travel huge distances in search of prey, so few parks are large enough to contain them. Northern Botswana has one of the healthiest and most prolific populations in Africa, and Botswana is the best place on the continent to see them. These range right across Chobe, the Kwando–Linyanti and Okavango areas, and spreading out beyond these into Namibia and the northwest areas of the Kalahari.

They generally den around July to early October, and this is the only time when you can be fairly sure of seeing them in any given area. Sometimes they'll den in the same area for several years running, whilst at other times they'll change from year to year. For the best chances of seeing them – and a possibility of following a pack as they hunt (an amazing, exhilarating experience) – choose a mainly dry reserve with plenty of open ground. Make sure that off-road driving is permitted, or you'll never be able to follow them, and ideally night drives should be allowed. Selinda, southern Kwando, Kwara and Vumbura would all currently be high on my list – and I've seen dogs in all of these. Better still, ask someone who knows the Delta and the reserves well where specific packs have denned the previous season, and go there.

Given that dogs will take most antelope and always run down their prey, the only strategy that their prey can adopt to avoid death is to run as far, and as fast, as they can. They will do this as soon as they realise that dogs are in the area. Thus if you ever see game seriously sprinting with a purpose, and just not stopping, then look hard: maybe there's a pack of dogs behind them!

Black-backed jackal (*Canis mesomelas* Shoulder
height 35–45cm. Weight 8–12kg) The black-backed jackal is an opportunistic feeder capable of adapting to most habitats. Most often seen singly or in pairs at dusk or dawn, it is ochre in colour with a prominent black saddle flecked by a varying amount of white or gold. It is probably the most frequently observed small predator in Africa south of the Zambezi, and its eerie call is a characteristic sound of the bush at night. It is found throughout Botswana, with the exception of the far north of the country around the Chobe and Linyanti–Kwando areas, and is fairly common in the drier areas of the Kalahari.

Black-backed jackal

Side-striped jackal *Canis adustus* Shoulder height 35–40cm. Weight 8–12kg) Despite its prevalence in other areas of Africa, the side-striped jackal is common nowhere in Botswana. It occurs in the far north of the country, including Chobe, the Linyanti–Kwando

area and the Okavango. It is about the same size as the previous species, but greyish in colour, with an indistinct pale horizontal stripe on each flank and often a white-tipped tail. These jackals are also usually seen singly or in pairs, at dusk or dawn. Both the side-striped and the black-backed jackal are opportunistic feeders, taking rats, mice, birds, insects, carrion, wild fruits and even termites.

Bat-eared fox (*Otocyon megalotis* Shoulder height 30–35cm. Weight 3–5kg) This

endearing small, silver-grey insectivore is unmistakable, with its huge ears and black eye-mask. It can be found throughout Botswana, anywhere that the harvester termite (*Hodotermes mossambicus*) occurs. The best areas are usually short grass plains that receive relatively low rainfall – Savuti Marsh was certainly a favourite habitat – when the marsh was dry.

Bat-eared fox

It is mostly nocturnal, but can sometimes be seen in pairs or small family groups during the cooler hours of the day, usually in dry open country. It digs well, and will often 'listen' to the ground (its ears operating like a radio-dish) whilst wandering around, before stopping to dig with its forepaws. As well as termites, bat-eared foxes will eat lizards, gerbils, small birds, scorpions, beetle larvae and other insects.

Insect populations vary with the seasons and bat-eared foxes will move with them, but when conditions allow, some areas will have very high densities of individuals.

Similar species The **Cape fox** (*Vulpes chama*) is an infrequently seen dry-country predator which occurs throughout central and western Botswana, but is absent from Chobe and the north side of the Okavango. The Cape fox lacks the prominent ears and mask of the bat-eared fox, and its coat is a uniform sandy-grey colour. I once had a Cape fox approach me cautiously, after dusk, whilst camping in Namibia's Namib-Naukluft Park, but have never seen another.

Spotted hyena (*Crocuta crocuta* Shoulder height 85cm.

Weight 70kg) Hyenas are characterised by their bulky build, sloping back (lower hindquarters), rough brownish coat, powerful jaws and dog-like expression. Contrary to popular myth, spotted hyenas are not exclusively scavengers; they are also adept hunters, which hunt in groups and kill animals as large as wildebeests. Nor are they hermaphroditic, an ancient belief that stems from the false scrotum and penis covering the female hyena's vagina. Sociable animals, hyenas live in loosely structured clans of about ten animals, led by females, who are stronger and larger than males, and based in a communal den.

Spotted hyena

Hyenas utilise their kills far better than most predators, digesting the bones, skin and even teeth of antelope. This results in the distinctive white colour attained by their faeces when dry – which is an easily identified sign of them living in an area.

The spotted hyena is the largest hyena, identified by its light-brown, blotchily spotted coat. It is found throughout most of Botswana, only absent from the eastern areas around Ghanzi, and perhaps the country's furthest southern edge. They are a common predator throughout the north, and will frequently scavenge around camps and campsites at night. Savuti's campsite was, for years, completely plagued by them, whilst few camps in the Delta are without a story of hyena breaking into kitchens or eating their way through larders.

Although mainly nocturnal, spotted hyenas can often be seen around dusk and dawn, and their distinctive, whooping calls are one of the most wonderful, yet spine-chilling, sounds of the African night.

Brown hyena (*Hyaena brunnea* Shoulder height 75–85cm. Weight 40–47kg) Although rare (with only about 8,000 animals left in the wild), this secretive, apparently solitary hyena occurs in the most arid parts of Namibia, and throughout Botswana; it is absent only from the far north. It is unmistakable, with a shaggy, dark-brown coat – not unlike a large, long-haired German shepherd dog – with faint black stripes and sloping back.

Brown hyena

In contrast to the spotted hyena, brown hyenas do tend to scavenge rather than hunt, and are generally solitary whilst doing so. They are the dominant carnivore in the drier areas of the Namib and Kalahari, where clans (typically two to ten animals) will defend enormous territories against neighbouring clans. Individuals normally forage on their own and eat whatever they can, from small birds and mammals to the remains of kill, as well as fruit and vegetables. They can go without water for long periods, gaining moisture from tsama melons as well as other food.

Brown hyena are very rarely seen on game drives, although in the last few years researchers based at Jack's Camp have habituated a small clan of hyena to their presence – making this probably the best place in Africa to see them. (See *The clans of Makgadikgadi* on page 428 for more information on brown hyena.)

Aardwolf (*Proteles cristatus* Shoulder height 45· Weight 7–11g) With a tawny brown coat and dark, ve stripes, this insectivorous hyena is not much bigger than a jackal and occurs in low numbers in most parts of Botswana. It is active mainly at night, gathering harvester termites (specifically those of the genus *Trinervitermes*), its principal food, with its wide, sticky tongue. These termites live underground (not in castle-like termite mounds) and come out at night to cut grass and drag it back down with them. Occasionally the aardwolf will also take other insects, mice, birds and carrion.

Aardwolf

Thus open grassland or lightly wooded areas form the typical habitat for aardwolves, which can sometimes be spotted around dusk, dawn or on very overcast days, especially during the colder months. The *Trinervitermes* termites often thrive on overgrazed land, which means that aardwolf are often more common on farmland than in national parks. I don't know of anywhere in central or northern Botswana where they're seen frequently.

PRIMATES
Chacma baboon (*Papio cynocephalus ursinus* Shoulder height 50–75cm. Weight 25–45kg) This powerful terrestrial primate, distinguished from any other monkey by its much larger size, inverted-U-shaped tail and distinctive dog-like head, is fascinating to watch from a behavioural perspective. It lives in large troops that boast a complex, rigid social structure characterised by a matriarchal lineage and plenty of inter-troop movement by males seeking social dominance. Omnivorous and at home in almost any habitat, the baboon is the most widespread primate in Africa, frequently seen in most of Botswana. The centre of the Kalahari (including the CKGR) is the only area from which they are absent.

There are three African races, regarded by some authorities as full species. The chacma baboon (*P. c. ursinus*) is grey, and confined largely to areas south of the Zambezi. The yellow baboon (*P. c. cynocephalus*) is the yellow-brown race occurring in Zambia, northern Mozambique, Malawi, southern and eastern Tanzania and eastern Kenya. The olive or anubis baboon (*P. c. anubis*) is a hairy green-to-brown baboon found in Ethiopia, Uganda, northern Tanzania and Kenya.

With a highly organised defence system, the only predator that seriously affects them is the leopard, which will try to pick them off at night whilst they are roosting in trees or cliffs. Campers in Chobe and Moremi should treat these animals with respect; long exposure to humans has taught them to steal, and not to be afraid.

Vervet monkey (*Cercopithecus aethiops* Length (excluding tail) 40–55cm. Weight 4–6kg)

Vervet monkey

Also known as the green or grivet monkey, the vervet is probably the world's most numerous monkey and certainly the most common and widespread representative of the *Cercopithecus* guenons, a taxonomically controversial genus associated with African forests. An atypical guenon in that it inhabits savannah and woodland rather than true forest, the vervet spends a high proportion of its time on the ground. It occurs throughout the northern and eastern parts of the country, but is absent from the drier areas of central, western and southern Botswana. Vervets like belts of tall trees with thick vegetation within easy reach of water, and much of northern Chobe, the Kwando–Linyanti area and the Okavango is ideal for them.

The vervet's light-grey coat, black face and white forehead band are distinctive – as are the male's garish blue genitals. Vervet monkeys live in troops averaging about 25 animals; they are active during the day and roost in trees at night. They eat mainly fruit and vegetables, though are opportunistic and will take insects and young birds, and even raid tents at campsites (usually where ill-informed visitors have previously tempted them into human contact by offering food).

Lesser bushbaby (*Galago senegalensis* Length (without tail) 17cm. Weight 150g)

Bushbaby

The lesser bushbaby is the most widespread and common member of a group of small and generally indistinguishable nocturnal primates, distantly related to the lemurs of Madagascar. In Botswana they occur throughout the northern half of the country, including Nxai and Makgadikgadi.

More often heard than seen, the lesser bushbaby can sometimes be picked out by tracing a cry to a tree and shining a torch into the branches; its eyes reflect as two red dots. These eyes are designed to function in what we would describe as total darkness. Lesser bushbabies feed on insects – some of which are caught in the air by jumping – and also eating sap from trees, especially acacia gum.

They inhabit wooded areas, and prefer acacia trees or riverine forests. I remember being startled by a small family of bushbabies once; they raced through the trees above us, bouncing from branch to branch whilst chattering and screaming out of all proportion to their size.

LARGE ANTELOPE

Sable antelope (*Hippotragus niger* Shoulder height 135cm. Weight 230kg)

The striking male sable is jet black with a distinct white face, underbelly and rump, and long decurved horns – a strong contender for the title of Africa's most beautiful antelope. The female is chestnut brown and has shorter horns, whilst the young are a lighter red-brown colour. Sable are found throughout the wetter areas of southern and eastern Africa, but are common nowhere.

In Botswana they occur in the north, as far west as the central Okavango. The Chobe riverfront is a good place to look for them in the dry season, usually between Kasane and Chobe Game Lodge, where several herds frequent the valleys and come down to drink.

Sable antelope

Similarly, they're occasionally seen near the Kwando and Linyanti rivers. They're not common in the Delta region, but are seen periodically. Good sightings have been recorded around the Gomoti River, and in NG20 and NG21. The Vumbura Concession (NG22) probably offers the highest density of sable in the Delta, whilst they're generally absent from NG26, NG27, NG30 and further west.

Sable are normally seen in small herds: either bachelor herds of males, or breeding herds of females and young, which are often accompanied by the dominant bull in that territory. The breeding females give birth around February or March; the calves remain hidden, away from the herd, for their first few weeks. Sable are mostly grazers, though will browse, especially when food is scarce. They need to drink at least every other day, and seem especially fond of low-lying dewy vleis in wetter areas.

Roan antelope (*Hippotragus equinus* Shoulder height 120–150cm. Weight 250–300kg)

This handsome horse-like antelope is uniform fawn-grey with a pale belly, short decurved horns and a light mane. It could be mistaken for the female sable antelope, but this has a well-defined white belly, and lacks the roan's distinctive black-and-white facial markings. The roan is a relatively rare antelope; common almost nowhere in Africa (Malawi's Nyika Plateau being the obvious exception to this rule). In Botswana, small groups of roan are found in the Chobe and Kwando–Linyanti areas, and occasionally some will wander as far as the drier parts of the Okavango Delta – but they're always something of a rarity. Ngwezumba Pans is probably the best location to search for them, but they're not seen regularly even there.

Roan antelope

Roan need lots of space if they are to thrive and breed; they don't generally do well where game densities are high. This alone precludes them from success in most of the Delta. Game farms prize them as one of the most valuable antelope. They need access to drinking water, but are well adapted to subsist on relatively high plateaux with poor soils.

Oryx or gemsbok (*Oryx gazella* Shoulder height 120cm. Weight 230kg)

This is the quintessential desert antelope, unmistakable with its ash-grey coat, bold black facial marks and flank strip, and unique long, straight horns. Of the three races of oryx in Africa, the gemsbok is the largest and most striking. It occurs throughout the Kalahari and Namib and is widespread all over central and western Botswana. They are the dominant large antelope in the CKGR, where they can be seen in large numbers during the early months of the year.

Oryx

As you might expect, gemsbok are very adaptable. They range widely and are found in areas of dunes, alkaline pans, open savannah and even woodlands. Along with the much smaller springbok, they can sometimes even be seen tracking across open plains with only dust-devils and mirages for company. Gemsbok can endure extremes of temperature, helped by specially adapted blood capillaries in their nasal passages that can cool their blood before it reaches their brains. Thus although their body temperature can rise by up to 6°C, their brains remain cool and they survive. They do not need drinking water and will eat wild melons and dig for roots, bulbs and tubers when grazing or browsing becomes difficult.

Waterbuck

Waterbuck (*Kobus ellipsiprymnus* Shoulder height 130cm. Weight 250–270kg) The waterbuck is easily recognised by its shaggy brown coat and the male's large, lyre-shaped horns. The common race of southern Africa (*K. e. ellipsiprymnus*) and areas east of the Rift Valley has a distinctive white ring around its rump, seen on the left of the sketch. The defassa race (known as *K. e. defassa* or *K. e. crawshayi*) of the Rift Valley and areas further west has a full white rump, as indicated on the right.

Only the common waterbuck are found in Botswana, and they're restricted to the Chobe, Kwando–Linyanti and eastern sides of the Delta. Favourite areas include the northern side of the Linyanti Concession (NG15), and also Vumbura (NG22), but they're relatively uncommon elsewhere. They certainly used to occur at Savuti when the channel flowed, but they deserted the area when the marsh dried up.

Waterbuck

Waterbuck need to drink very regularly, so usually stay within a few kilometres of water, where they like to graze on short, nutritious grasses. At night they may take cover in adjacent woodlands. It is often asserted that waterbuck flesh is oily and smelly, which may discourage predators.

Blue wildebeest

Blue wildebeest (*Connochaetes taurinus* Shoulder height 130–150cm. Weight 180–250kg) This ungainly antelope, also called the brindled gnu, is easily identified by its dark coat and bovine appearance. The superficially similar buffalo is far more heavily built.

Blue wildebeest

When they have enough space and conditions are right, blue wildebeest can multiply rapidly and form immense herds – as perhaps a million do for their annual migration from Tanzania's Serengeti Plains into Kenya's Maasai Mara.

In Botswana during the middle of the 20th century they were probably the most numerous large herbivore, forming herds estimated at a quarter of a million individuals. Although they are still found throughout Botswana, these numbers have reduced drastically. (See *Fauna* in *Chapter 15, The Central Kalahari*, page 442, for further discussion of this.)

Wildebeest are best adapted to take large mouthfuls of short, nutritious grasses, and they need access to drinking water every two or three days. This limits them to remain relatively close to a source of water, and if that dries up they will journey as far as necessary to find another.

Hartebeest

Hartebeest (*Alcelaphus buselaphus* Shoulder height 125cm. Weight 120–150kg) Hartebeests are ungainly antelopes, readily identified by the combination of large shoulders, a sloping back, a glossy, red-brown coat and smallish horns in both sexes. Numerous subspecies are recognised, all of which are generally seen in small family groups in reasonably open country. Though once hartebeest were found from the Mediterranean to the Cape, only isolated populations still survive.

Hartebeest

The only one native to Botswana is the red hartebeest, which is found throughout the arid central, southern and western areas of the country. They can be seen in Nxai and Makgadikgadi, and they're one of the more numerous large mammals in the CKGR. Hartebeest may occur in the drier, southwestern corners of the Delta, or in the drier parts of southern Chobe, but I've no records of them being seen in either location.

Hartebeests are more or less exclusively grazers, and although they like access to water they will eat melons, tubers and rhizomes when necessary. In the Central Kalahari they'll range widely, often with wildebeest, following thunderstorms in search of fresh, green shoots.

Tsessebe (*Damaliscus lunatus* Shoulder height 120cm. Weight 125–140kg) Tsessebe are basically a slightly smaller, darker version of hartebeest, coloured red-brown with an almost purple sheen, though their lower legs are distinctly paler. (A closely related subspecies is known as topi in east Africa.) They look similar in profile or at a distance, although often in the field you can make a good guess from the environment which antelope you're looking at long before you're close enough to examine its colouring.

Tsessebe are found in northern Botswana, and are one of the most common antelope in some parts of the Okavango Delta. Its favourite habitat is open grassland, where it is a selective grazer, eating the younger, more nutritious grasses. This makes it efficient in pastures where some grasses are old and some fresh, or in more broken country, but less efficient than, say, wildebeest where the pasture is uniformly short, good grass. The tsessebe is one of the fastest antelope species, and jumps very well.

Kudu (*Tragelaphus strepsiceros* Shoulder height 140–155cm. Weight 180–250kg) The kudu (or, more properly, the greater kudu) is the most frequently observed member of the genus *Tragelaphus*. These medium-sized to large antelopes are characterised by their grey- brown coats and up to ten stripes on each side. The male has magnificent double-spiralled corkscrew horns. Occurring throughout Mozambique, Zimbabwe, Zambia and Namibia, kudu are found all over Botswana with the exception of the Kgalagadi Transfrontier Park, in the extreme southwest.

Kudu are particularly common in the well-wooded areas of Chobe, the Kwando–Linyanti area and the Okavango, though they also occur throughout the drier areas of the Kalahari. They are browsers that thrive in areas with mixed tree savannah and thickets, and the males will sometimes use their horns to pull down the lower branches of trees to eat.

Kudu

Wherever they occur, kudu are normally seen in small herds, consisting of a couple of females and their offspring, usually accompanied by a male. Otherwise the males occur either singly, or in small bachelor groups.

Eland (*Taurotragus oryx* Shoulder height 150–175cm. Weight 450–900kg) Africa's largest antelope, the eland is light brown in colour, sometimes with a few faint white vertical stripes. Relatively short horns and a large dewlap accentuate its somewhat bovine appearance. It was once widely distributed in eastern and southern Africa, though the population has now been severely depleted. Small herds of eland frequent grasslands and light woodlands, often fleeing at the slightest provocation. (They have long been hunted for their excellent meat, so perhaps this is not surprising.)

Eland

Eland are very rare in the Okavango area and although they probably occur throughout Chobe, they are seldom seen. Better areas to see them are in the Kalahari's salt pans or, better still, the Central Kalahari. They are opportunist browsers and grazers, eating fruit, berries, seed pods and leaves as well as green grass after the rains, and roots and tubers when times are lean.

They run slowly, though can trot for great distances and jump exceedingly well. Eland have a very special significance for the San people – illustrated by the highlight of the famous 'van der Post panel' at the Tsodilo Hills (see page 383), which is a painting of a particularly magnificent eland bull.

MEDIUM AND SMALL ANTELOPE

Bushbuck (*Tragelaphus scriptus* Shoulder height 70–80cm. Weight 30–45kg) This attractive antelope, a member of the same genus as the kudu, is widespread throughout Africa and shows great regional variation in its colouring. (The animals found in sub-Saharan Africa are often claimed to be a subspecies, the 'Chobe bushbuck' – though it seems likely that they're simply a colour variation of the main species.)

They occur in forest and riverine woodland, where they are normally seen singly or in pairs. The male is dark brown or chestnut, while the much smaller female is generally a pale reddish brown. The male has relatively small, straight horns and both sexes are marked with white spots and sometimes stripes, though the stripes are often indistinct.

Bushbuck

Bushbuck tend to be secretive and very skittish, except when used to people, when they relax and become almost tame. They depend on cover and camouflage to avoid predators, and are often found in the thick, herby vegetation around rivers – and are the only solitary antelope in Africa which do not defend a territory. They will freeze if disturbed, before dashing off into the undergrowth. Bushbuck are both browsers and grazers, choosing the more succulent grass shoots, fruit and flowers. In Botswana they have a limited distribution around the Okavango, beside the Kwando–Linyanti and the Chobe. Look for them slowly picking their way through the thick bush near the water. (Serondela used to be a favourite spot, and the island on which Kwetsani stands had several fairly relaxed resident pairs when I last visited.)

Impala (*Aepeceros melampus* Shoulder height 90cm. Weight 45kg) This slender, handsome antelope is superficially similar to the springbok, but in fact belongs to its own separate family. Chestnut in colour, and lighter underneath than above, the impala has diagnostic black and white stripes running down its rump and tail, and the male has large lyre-shaped horns. The impala is one of the most widespread and successful antelope species in eastern and southern Africa. It is often the most common antelope in wooded savannah habitats, including most of Chobe and the drier, more forested parts of the Okavango Delta – though is rarely seen west of the Okavango, or south of Nxai Pan. Although they can survive without drinking, impala prefer to live near water and are largely absent from the Kalahari.

Impala

As expected of such a successful species, it both grazes and browses, depending on what fodder is available. Despite some people's tendency to overlook them as common, take a close look and you'll realise that they're exceptionally beautiful animals. Socially you'll normally see large herds of females and young, lorded over by a dominant male, and small bachelor groups of males.

Springbok (*Antidorcas marsupilis* Shoulder height 60cm. Weight 20–25kg) Springbok are graceful herbivores, similar in size to impala. Visitors from east Africa, noticing their passing resemblance to Thomson's gazelle (*Gazella thomsonii*), will not be surprised that they're southern Africa's only member of the gazelle family.

Even from a distance, springbok are unlikely to be confused with anything else; their finely marked short coats have fawn-brown upper parts and a white belly, separated by a dark brown band. Springbok generally occur in herds and favour dry, open country, preferring plains or savannah, and avoiding thick woodlands and mountains. They can subsist without water for long periods, provided that there is moisture (minimum of 10%) in the vegetation that they graze or browse.

Since springbok are more dependent on food than water, they congregate in huge numbers during the rains on areas where they can find fresh, green shoots – like the pans of the CKGR. In contrast, during the dry season they spread out across the vast arid parks of the Kalahari. This is exactly the opposite pattern to that followed by most water-dependent antelope, which typically congregate during the dry season (around rivers to remaining pans), whilst spreading out during the

Springbok

rains. This explains why the Kalahari's game is at its densest during the rains, whereas the game in Chobe and the Okavango is at its most prolific during the dry season.

Springbok occur throughout central and southern Botswana, where they are usually the most common small antelope by far; in Nxai, Makgadikgadi and the CKGR they number in the thousands.

Reedbuck (*Redunca arundinum* Shoulder height 80–90cm. Weight 45–65kg) Sometimes referred to as the southern reedbuck (as distinct from mountain and Bohor reedbucks, found further east), these delicate antelope are uniformly fawn or grey in colour, and lighter below than above. They are generally found in reedbeds and tall grasslands, often beside rivers, and are easily identified by their loud, whistling alarm call and distinctive bounding running style.

In Botswana they are found only where there is close access to water in the north: in northern Chobe, the Kwando–Linyanti region and throughout the Delta. They live in monogamous pairs that defend a territory. You'll often see just a pair together, and they have a distinctive rocking gait as they take flight by bounding away through tall reedbeds.

Reedbuck

Klipspringer (*Oreotragus oreotragus* Shoulder height 60cm. Weight 13kg) The klipspringer is a strongly built little antelope, normally seen in pairs, and easily identified by its dark, bristly grey-yellow coat, slightly speckled appearance and unique habitat preference. Klipspringer means 'rockjumper' in Afrikaans and it is an apt name for an antelope which occurs exclusively in mountainous areas and rocky outcrops, from Cape Town to the Red Sea. Klipspringers are mainly browsers, though they do eat a little new grass. When spotted they will freeze, or bound at great speed across the steepest of slopes.

Though often thought to be absent from all but the extreme southeast corner of Botswana, there were several reliable reports of sightings on Qumxhwaa Hill, near Savuti Marsh, at the end of the 1970s. Given that they only live in rocky hills and kopjes, and that most of Botswana is amazingly flat (or gently rolling at best), it's

Klipspringer

no surprise that only the odd isolated population exists. It's the same in other parts of their range. I've no reports of them at the Tsodilo Hills, but it would be a perfect habitat for them!

Red lechwe (*Kobus leche* Shoulder height 90–100cm. Weight 80–100kg) Red lechwe are sturdy, shaggy antelope with a chestnut-red coat, paler underneath than on top, and beautiful lyre-shaped horns. They need dry land on which to rest, but otherwise are adapted for life in the seasonal floodplains that border lakes and rivers. They will spend much of their time grazing on grasses and sedges, standing in water if necessary. Their hooves are splayed, adapted to bounding through their muddy environment when fleeing from the lion, hyena and wild dog that hunt them, making them the most aquatic of antelope after sitatunga.

Lechwe

Lechwe reach the southern limit of their distribution in the Okavango and Linyanti areas. They are also found in the DRC, Angola, Namibia's Caprivi Strip, and in Zambia, their stronghold. Wherever they occur, the males are generally larger and darker than the females. When conditions are right, they can be found in huge numbers, and they are the most numerous antelope in the shallow-water environments of the Delta.

Sitatunga (*Tragelaphus spekei* Shoulder height 85–90cm. Weight 105–115kg) This semi-aquatic antelope is a widespread but infrequently observed inhabitant of west and central African papyrus swamps, from the Okavango in Botswana to the Sudd in Sudan. In Botswana they're concentrated in the Okavango – which has a strong population – though they're also seen periodically in the Kwando–Linyanti

Sitatunga

NILE CROCODILE   *Mike Unwin*

Nile crocodile (*Crocodylus niloticus* Length over 5m. Weight over 1,000kg) Many visitors to northern Botswana will get to see this antediluvian creature. With its powerful serrated tail, horny plated skin and up to 100 peg-like teeth crammed into a long, sinister smile, the Nile crocodile is the stuff of nightmares and action movies. Contrary to the more lurid myths, crocodiles generally avoid people (understandably, given the slaughter they have suffered). Yet while they will not launch themselves into boats or come galloping after you on land, humans are still potential prey for a big one, and tragedies do occasionally occur. When in crocodile country, it is sensible to keep your distance from the water's edge.

Crocodiles can live up to 100 years, but reach sexual maturity at 12–15 years. They inhabit lakes, rivers and swamps. Whereas youngsters are boldly marked in black and green, adults are generally a muddy grey-brown colour – usually lighter in rivers than in lagoons. Theirs is an amphibious life: basking on land, jaws agape to lose heat, or cruising the waters, raised eyes and nostrils allowing them to see and breathe undetected. As well as eating fish such as bream and barbel, adult crocs will ambush mammals up to the size of buffalo, grabbing them with an explosive sideways lunge from the water, before dragging them under to drown. Large numbers of crocodiles gather to scavenge big carcasses, churning up the water as they thrash and spin to dislodge chunks of flesh. They will even leave the water to steal a nearby lion kill.

and Chobe systems. The best places to spot them are deep-water areas with plenty of papyrus, including Moremi and in NG21, 22, 23, 24 and 25 concessions.

Because of their preferred habitat, sitatunga are elusive and seldom seen, even in areas where they are relatively common. They are also less easy to hunt/poach than many other species, although they are exceedingly vulnerable to habitat destruction. Sitatunga are noted for an ability to submerse themselves completely, with just their nostrils showing, when pursued by a predator.

Puku (*Kobus vardonii* Shoulder height 80cm. Weight 60–75kg) Easily confused with the lechwe at a glance, the puku has an orange-red colour overall, which is lighter underneath than above. Its legs are uniformly red, and its tail is a lighter yellow. Puku are smaller and slightly shaggier than lechwe, and the males have smaller, stouter, lyre-shaped horns when compared with the lechwe.

Puku are found all over eastern and central Africa, and are one of the most common antelopes in Zambia. Typically they inhabit open areas near rivers and marshes, though in Zambia are found in a wide variety of habitats. In Botswana their distribution is restricted to the floodplain areas of the Chobe riverfront, and often virtually the only place that you'll see them is around the aptly named Puku Flats, just west of Chobe Game Lodge.

Steenbok

Steenbok (*Raphicerus cempestris* Shoulder height 50cm. Weight 11kg) This rather nondescript small antelope has red-brown upper parts and clear white underparts, and the male has short straight horns. It is one of the most commonly observed small antelope, especially on farmland; if you see antelope fleeing from you across grassland, then it is likely to be a steenbok. Like most other small antelopes, the steenbok is normally encountered singly or in pairs and tends to 'freeze' when disturbed, before taking flight.

Similar species The **Oribi** (*Ourebia ourebi*) is a relatively widespread but generally uncommon antelope, which occurs in very localised areas throughout sub-Saharan Africa. It is usually found only in large, open stretches of dry grassland, where there are also patches of taller grass for cover. It looks much like a steenbok but stands about 10cm higher at the shoulder and has an altogether more upright bearing. In Botswana it is thought to occur in Chobe, and specifically in the Ngwezumba Pans area – although sightings of it even there are not common. **Sharpe's grysbok** (*Raphicerus sharpei*) is similar in size and appearance, though it has a distinctive white-flecked coat. It occurs alongside the steenbok in the far northeastern corner of Botswana, around northern Chobe and the Kasane area, but is almost entirely nocturnal in its habits and so very seldom seen.

Common duiker (*Sylvicapra grimmia* Shoulder height 50cm. Weight 20kg) This anomalous duiker holds itself more like a steenbok or grysbok and is the only member of its (large) family to occur outside of forests. Generally grey in colour, the common duiker can most easily be separated from other small antelopes by the black tuft of hair that sticks up between its horns. It occurs throughout Botswana, and across virtually the whole of southern Africa, with the exception of the Namib Desert. Common duikers tolerate most habitats except for true forest and very open country, and are tolerant of nearby human settlements. They are opportunist feeders, taking fruit, seeds and leaves, as well as crops, small reptiles and amphibians. Despite their widespread occurrence, duiker are relatively rarely seen.

Common duiker

OTHER LARGE HERBIVORES

African elephant (*Loxodonta africana* Shoulder height 2.3–3.4m. Weight up to 6,000kg) The world's largest land animal, the African elephant is intelligent, social and often very entertaining to watch. Female elephants live in closely knit clans in which the eldest female plays matriarch over her sisters, daughters and granddaughters. Their life spans are comparable with those of humans, and mother–daughter bonds are strong and may last for up to 50 years. Males generally leave the family group at around 12 years to roam singly or form bachelor herds. Under normal circumstances, elephants range widely in search of food and water, but when concentrated populations are forced to live in conservation areas their habit of uprooting trees can cause serious environmental damage.

African elephant

Elephants are widespread and common in habitats ranging from deserts to rainforest; but they require trees and access to drinking water. They are very common in the north of Botswana.

The Chobe, Kwando–Linyanti and Okavango areas have one of Africa's strongest populations of elephants. During the rains, from December onwards, these disperse in the interior of the country, into the vast expanses of mopane forest and into the drier areas of the northern Kalahari. They split up into smaller family groups and spread out as they can then find water all over the place (the clay pans of the mopane woodlands are especially valuable as sources).

Despite their range having become more restricted by human expansion over the years, individuals will often wander widely, turning up in locations from which they have been absent for years.

However, as the dry season progresses and the waterholes dry up, they gradually coalesce into larger herds, and head for the permanent sources: the rivers and the Delta. Thus by September and October you can normally see huge herds of elephants along the Chobe, Kwando and Linyanti rivers. The number and size of herds in the Okavango increases also.

In many areas elephants have no natural predators (the huge prides of lion in the Savuti and North Gate areas are an exception to this rule); they are generally constrained by lack of suitable habitat (ie: trees and water), by man and by diseases such as anthrax. Thus in many confined national parks in southern Africa, there are programmes to cull elephants to restrict their numbers. This is controversial, even amongst ardent conservationists. Botswana has no such policy. The result, some argue, is an over-population of elephants here, and the severe environmental degradation to be seen around the riverfront in Chobe, where the riverine forests have been decimated. Whilst not denying the observation, it's well worth remembering that there was a sawmill in this area, and extensive logging during the 1930s and early 1940s – so humans should take part of the blame for this.

Black rhinoceros (*Diceros bicornis* Shoulder height 160cm. Weight 1,000kg) This is the more widespread of Africa's two rhino species, an imposing and rather temperamental creature. Black rhino were once found all over northern Botswana, but were thought to have been poached to extinction here, whilst becoming highly endangered in many other countries within their range.

Black rhino exploit a wide range of habitats from dense woodlands and bush, and are generally solitary animals. They can survive without drinking for four to five days. However, their territorial behaviour and regular patterns of movement make them an easy target

Black rhinoceros

for poachers. Black rhino can be very aggressive when disturbed and will charge with minimal provocation. Their hearing and sense of smell are acute, whilst their eyesight is poor (so they often miss their target): keep a low profile and don't move.

Now, following the successful reintroduction of white rhino to Chief's Island, black rhino have been reintroduced here also (see page 289). The environment is very suitable, and the island is effectively isolated within a large area devoted to wildlife; so it is hoped that poaching them from here would be difficult. If you want to help with this work, then see *Travelling positively* on page 114.

White rhinoceros (*Ceratotherium simum* Shoulder height 180cm. Weight 1,500–2,000kg) The white rhino is in fact no paler in colour than the black rhino: 'white' and 'black' are *not* literal descriptions. The description 'white' derives from the Afrikaans *weit* (wide) and refers to its flattened mouth, an ideal shape for cropping grass. This is the best way to tell the two rhino species apart, since the mouth of the black rhino, a browser in most parts of its range, is more rounded with a hooked upper lip.

White rhinoceros

Unlike their smaller cousins, white rhino are generally placid grazing animals which are very rarely aggressive. They prefer open grassy plains and are often seen in small groups. In the accounts of the first trips across Africa by the early white explorers, rhino were found (and shot) in huge numbers.

As with the black rhino, hunting and poaching reduced the population of African white rhinos drastically, reaching a crisis in the 1980s, when only a few South African reserves remained with really strong populations (notably Umfolozi and Hluhluwe). Amongst other countries, Zimbabwe retained remnants whilst Botswana, Zambia and others were effectively poached out.

Since then those parks which effectively saved the species have been used as reservoirs, to slowly re-populate a few protected areas. In 2001, a small group was reintroduced into the Chief's Island area of Moremi, with encouraging success (see page 289). It's hoped that this will continue, and that once again Botswana will be able to boast at least one area where rhino are prolific.

Hippopotamus (*Hippopotamus amphibius* Shoulder height 150cm. Weight 2,000kg) Characteristic of Africa's large rivers and lakes, this large, lumbering animal spends most of the day submerged but emerges at night to graze. Strongly territorial, herds of ten or more animals are presided over by a dominant male who will readily defend his patriarchy to the death. Hippos are abundant in most protected rivers and water bodies and are still quite common outside of reserves.

They are widely credited with killing more people than any other African mammal. They are clearly very, very dangerous – but I know of no statistics to support this, and many reliable sources suggest that crocodile, elephant and lion could all vie for this dubious title. So, whilst undoubtedly dangerous, perhaps they don't quite deserve their reputation.

In Botswana you'll find hippo in good numbers in all of the major river systems: Chobe, Kwando–Linyanti and the Okavango. It'd be difficult to go on safari in any of the wetter areas of northern Botswana without seeing large numbers of hippo.

Buffalo (*Syncerus caffer* Shoulder height 140cm. Weight 700kg) Frequently and erroneously referred to as a water buffalo (which is actually an Asian species), the Cape, or African, buffalo is a distinctive, highly social, ox-like animal that lives as part of a herd. It prefers well-watered savannah, though also occurs in forested areas. Buffalo are primarily grazers and need regular access to water, where they swim readily. Lion often follow herds of buffalo, their favourite prey.

Huge herds are generally fairly peaceful, and experienced guides will often walk straight through them on walking safaris. However, small bachelor herds, and especially single old bulls, can be very nervous and aggressive. They have a reputation for charging at the slightest provocation, often in the midst of thick bush, and are exceedingly dangerous when wounded.

African buffalo

Buffalo smell and hear well, but it's often claimed that they have poor eyesight. This isn't true, though when encountered during a walking safari, if you keep still and the wind is right they won't be able to discern your presence.

Common and widespread in sub-Saharan Africa, in Botswana the buffalo is limited to the north of the country, largely by the absence of sufficient water in the rest of the country. Their annual movements mirror those of elephants in general terms. During the rains, from December onwards, they disperse into the mopane forests and into the drier areas of the northern Kalahari, splitting up into smaller groups and spreading out.

However, as the dry season progresses, they gather together into larger herds, and congregate near permanent sources of water: along the Chobe, Kwando and Linyanti rivers, and throughout the Okavango Delta. Then you'll see them in most reserves with water, though the open plains of NG23 (Duba Plains) seem to have particularly high concentrations of buffalo.

Giraffe (*Giraffa camelopardis* Shoulder height 250–350cm. Weight 1,000–1,400kg) The world's tallest and longest-necked land animal, a fully grown giraffe can measure up to 5.5m high. Quite unmistakable, giraffe live in loosely structured herds of up to 15 head, though herd members often disperse, when they are seen singly or in smaller groups. Formerly distributed throughout eastern and southern Africa, in Botswana these great browsers are now found only in the centre and north of the country. The CKGR has a very healthy population, as do Makgadikgadi and Nxai, and they are also found through the Chobe, Kwando–Linyanti and Okavango areas.

Giraffe are adapted to browse vegetation that is beyond the reach of all the other large herbivores, with the exception of elephant. They prefer *Acacia* and *Combretum* species, and a 45cm tongue ensures that they can extract the leaves from the most thorny of branches.

Plains zebra (*Equus quagga* Shoulder height 130cm. Weight 300–340kg) Also known as common zebra, this attractive striped horse is common and widespread throughout most of eastern and southern Africa, where it is often seen in large herds alongside wildebeest. There are many subspecies of zebra in Africa, and most southern races, including those in Botswana, have paler brownish 'shadow stripes' between the bold black stripes (which are present in all races).

Plains zebra

Zebra are common in most conservation areas, from northern South Africa, Namibia and all the way up to the southeast of Ethiopia. In Botswana they occur in Makgadikgadi, Nxai and to the north – but I don't believe that they still occur within the CKGR. If the rains have been good in the Makgadikgadi Pans area, then during the first few months of the year you can witness huge herds of zebra roaming across the open plains in search of the freshest new grass.

Warthog (*Phacochoreus africanus* Shoulder height 60–70cm. Weight up to 100kg) This widespread and often conspicuously abundant resident of the African savannah is grey in

Warthog

colour with a thin covering of hairs, wart-like bumps on its face, and rather large, upward-curving tusks. Africa's only diurnal swine, the warthog is often seen in family groups, trotting around with its tail raised stiffly (a diagnostic trait) and a determinedly nonchalant air. They occur throughout Botswana with the exception of the far south, although they don't usually fare well near settlements, as they are very susceptible to subsistence hunting/poaching. Wherever they occur, you'll often see them grazing beside the road, on bended knee.

Similar species Bulkier, hairier and browner, the **bushpig** (*Potomochoerus larvatus*) only occurs in the wetter areas of northern Botswana – northern Chobe, the Kwando–Linyanti and the Okavango. Like the warthog, they don't survive well near settlements: they damage crops and so are persistently hunted. That said, even where they do occur, they are rarely seen due to their nocturnal habits and preference for living in dense vegetation.

SMALL MAMMALS

African civet (*Civettictis civetta* Shoulder height 40cm. Weight 10–15kg) This bulky, long-haired, rather feline creature of the African night is primarily carnivorous, feeding on small animals and carrion, but will also eat fruit. It has a similarly coloured coat to a leopard, which is densely blotched with large black spots becoming stripes towards the head. Civets are widespread and common throughout a band across northern Botswana, including Chobe, the Kwando–Linyanti and Okavango areas. They occur in many habitats, and make frequent cameo appearances on night drives.

African civet

Note that although they are occasionally referred to as 'civet cats', this is misleading. They are more closely related to the mongooses than the felines.

Similar species Both the **small-spotted genet** (*Genetta genetta*) and the **large-spotted genet** (*Genetta tigrina*) are members of a large group of similar small predators found in Botswana. All the genets are slender and rather feline in appearance (though they are *not* cats), with a grey to gold-brown coat marked with black spots (perhaps combining into short bars) and a long ringed tail. However, as even experts often can't tell the various species apart without examining their skins by hand, precise identification of genets is difficult.

You're most likely to see genets on nocturnal game drives or occasionally scavenging around game-reserve lodges. The small-spotted genet is found all over Botswana, whereas its larger cousin is thought to be restricted to the northern areas of Chobe, Kwando–Linyanti and Okavango. Genets are excellent climbers and opportunists, eating fruit, small birds, termites and even scorpions.

Banded mongoose (*Mungos mungo* Shoulder height 20cm. Weight around 1kg) The banded mongoose is probably the most commonly observed member of a group of small, slender, terrestrial carnivores. Uniform dark grey-brown except for a dozen black stripes across its back, it is a diurnal mongoose occurring in playful family groups, or troops, in most habitats throughout northern and northwestern Botswana. It feeds on insects, scorpions, amphibians, reptiles and even carrion and bird's eggs, and can move through the bush at quite a pace.

Banded mongoose

Similar species Another six or so mongoose species occur in Botswana. Some are social and gather in troops; others are solitary. Several are too scarce and nocturnal to be seen by most visitors.

The water or **marsh mongoose** (*Atilax paludinosus*) is large, normally solitary and has a very scruffy brown coat; it's widespread in the Chobe, Kwando–Linyanti and Okavango regions.

The **white-tailed mongoose** (*Ichneumia albicauda*), or white-tailed ichneumon, is a solitary, large brown mongoose with long, coarse, woolly hair. It is nocturnal and easily identified by its bushy white tail if seen crossing roads at night. It has a similar distribution, where it can also be found in a few cattle-ranching areas, where it eats the beetle-grubs found in manure.

The **slender mongoose** (*Galerella sanguinea*) is also widespread throughout Botswana where there is lots of cover for it. It, too, is solitary, but it is very much smaller (shoulder height 10cm) and has a uniform brown or reddish coat and blackish tail tip. Its tail is held up when it runs.

The **large grey mongoose** (*Herpestes ichneumon*), also called the Egyptian mongoose, is a large mongoose with coarse, grey-speckled body hair, black lower legs and feet, and a black tip to its tail. It's found in the same northern areas of Botswana, but is common nowhere. It is generally diurnal and is either solitary, or lives in pairs. Large grey mongooses eat small rodents, reptiles, birds and also snakes, generally killing rather than scavenging.

Selous' mongoose (*Paracynictis selousi*) is smaller, with fine, speckled grey fur, and a white tip at the end of its tail. It likes open country and woodlands, occurring in many areas of northern and the further eastern areas of Botswana. It is nocturnal and solitary, eating mainly insects, grubs, small reptiles and amphibians. It seems especially fond of the larvae of dung beetles, and so is sometimes found in cattle country.

The **yellow mongoose** (*Cynitis penicillata*) is a small, sociable mongoose with a tawny or yellow coat, and is commonly found across most of Botswana – even in the drier areas of the Central Kalahari. It normally forages alone and is easily identified by the white tip on the end of its tail.

Finally, the **dwarf mongoose** (*Helogate parvula*) is a diminutive (shoulder height 7cm), highly sociable light-brown mongoose often seen in the vicinity of the termite mounds where it nests. This is Africa's smallest carnivore, occurring in a higher density than any other. It is widespread throughout the Chobe, Kwando–Linyanti and Okavango areas, and often seen. Groups of 20–30 are not unknown, consisting of a breeding pair and subordinate others. These inquisitive little animals can be very entertaining to watch.

Meerkat or suricate (*Suricata suricatta* Shoulder height 25–35cm. Weight 650–950g)

Found throughout central and southwest Botswana, and much of neighbouring Namibia, meerkats are absent from Makgadikgadi and further north. The best places to see them are the CKGR and further towards the southwest corner of Botswana (eg: the KD1 concession, south of Ghanzi, and the Kgalagadi Transfrontier Park).

These small animals are sandy to silvery-grey in colour, with dark bands running across their backs. They are exclusively diurnal and have a distinctive habit of sitting upright on their hind legs. They do this when they first emerge in the morning, to sun themselves, and throughout the day.

Living in complex social groups, meerkats are usually seen scratching around for insects, beetles and small reptiles in dry, open, grassy areas. Whilst the rest forage, one or two of the group will use the highest mound around as a sentry-post – looking out for predators using their remarkable eyesight. Meerkats' social behaviour is very complex: they squeak constantly to communicate and even use different alarm calls for different types of predators. Because of their photogenic poses and fascinating social behaviour, they have been the subject of several successful television documentaries filmed in the southern Kalahari.

Honey badger (*Mellivora capensis* Shoulder height 30cm. Weight 12kg) Also known
as the ratel, the honey badger is black with a puppyish face and grey-white back. It is an opportunistic feeder best known for its allegedly symbiotic relationship with a bird called the honeyguide which leads it to beehives, waits for it to tear them open, then feeds on the scraps. The honey badger is among the most widespread of African carnivores, and also amongst the most powerful and aggressive for its size. It occurs all over Botswana,

Honey badger

but is thinly distributed and infrequently seen, except when it has lost its fear of people and started to scavenge from safari camps.

Similar species Other mustelids occurring in the region include the **striped polecat** (*Ictonyx striatus*), a common but rarely seen nocturnal creature with black underparts and a bushy white back.

Cape clawless otter (*Aonyx capensis* Shoulder height 20–30cm. Weight 3–5kg) This
is the larger of the two species of otter that occur in southern Africa. It has a chocolate-brown coat with a pale cream-to-white chin and throat. In Botswana, it is restricted to the northern river systems of Chobe, Kwando–Linyanti and the Okavango (it's not found in broad, tropical rivers like the Zambezi), though will occasionally move away from there, across dry land, in search of other pools and waterways.

Cape clawless otters are active mostly around dusk and dawn, although they will sometimes be seen in broad daylight or at night. Rough skin on their paws gives excellent grip, and with this they prey mostly on frogs and fish. They'll also take freshwater mussels, and will use rocks to help them crack these open.

Although very shy (they'll usually flee when approached by a boat or people), they're delightful to watch, seeming very playful, with a variety of aquatic acrobatics, and cleaning their face and paws scrupulously after every meal. Visiting Botswana, you're most likely to see otters in the shallow floodplain areas of the Okavango when on a quiet mokoro trip.

Similar species The smaller **spotted-necked otter** (*Lutra maculicollis*) is darker with light white spots on its throat – though difficult to distinguish from its larger cousin unless you're familiar with them both. Their distribution and habits are similar to the Cape clawless, though they are more diurnal, and more tied to bodies of water.

Aardvark (*Orycteropus afer* Shoulder height 60cm. Weight up to 70kg) This singularly
bizarre nocturnal insectivore is unmistakable with its long snout, huge ears and powerful legs, adapted to dig up the nests of termites, on which it feeds. Aardvarks occur throughout southern Africa, except the driest western areas of the Namib. Though their distinctive three-toed tracks are often seen, and they are not uncommon animals, sightings of them are rare.

Aardvark

Aardvarks prefer areas of grassland and sparse scrub, rather than dense woodlands, so much of Botswana's bush suits them well. You're most likely to see them on a late-night game drive, and many guides say that they are seen more often during the rainy season, from December to March.

Pangolin (*Manis temmincki* Total length 70–100cm. Weight 8–15kg) Sharing the aardvaak's diet of termites and ants, the pangolin is another very unusual nocturnal insectivore, with distinctive armour plating and a tendency to roll up in a ball when disturbed. (Then it can swipe its tail from side to side, inflicting serious damage on its aggressor.) Sometimes known as Temminck's pangolins, or scaly anteaters, these strange animals walk on their hindlegs, using their tail and front legs for balance. They are both nocturnal and rare, and their distribution is uncertain, although they are thought to occur throughout

Pangolin

Botswana. Sightings are exceedingly rare; thus an average of three sightings of pangolin per year in NG31 Reserve counts as a remarkably prolific record by the standards of most areas in Africa!

In some areas further south, particularly Zimbabwe, local custom is to make a present of any pangolin found to the paramount chief (often taken to mean the president). This has caused great damage to their population.

Porcupine (*Hystrix africaeaustralis* Total length 80–100cm. Weight 15–25kg) This is the largest rodent found in the region, and occurs all over southern Africa, except for the western reaches of the Namib Desert. It is easily identified by its black-and-white-striped quills, generally black hair and shambolic gait. If heard in the dark, then the rustle of its foraging is augmented by the slight rattle of its quills. These drop off fairly regularly, and are often found in the bush.

The porcupine's diet is varied, and they are fairly opportunistic when it comes to food. Roots and tubers are favourites, as is the bark of certain trees; they will also eat meat and small reptiles or birds if they have the chance. You're most likely to see porcupines on night drives, as individuals, pairs or small family groups.

Similar species Also spiky, the **Southern African hedgehog** (*Erinaceus frontalis*) has been recorded in eastern and southeastern areas of Botswana, though it is small and nocturnal, so rarely seen even where it does occur. Hedgehogs are about 20cm long (much smaller than porcupines), omnivorous and uncommon.

Rock hyrax (*Procavia capensis* Shoulder height 20–30cm. Weight 4kg) Rodent-like in appearance, hyraxes (also known as dassies) are claimed to be the closest living relative of elephants. The rock hyrax and similar **yellow-spotted rock hyrax** (*Heterohyrax brucei*) are often seen sunning themselves in rocky habitats, and become tame when used to people.

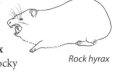

Rock hyrax

They are social animals, living in large groups, and are largely herbivores, eating leaves, grasses and fruits. Where you see lots of dassies, watch out for black eagles and other raptors which prey extensively on them. In Botswana they're restricted to the southeast of the country, although places like the Tsodilo Hills would seem an ideal habitat for them.

Scrub hare (*Lepus saxatilis* Shoulder height 45–60cm. Weight 1–4.5kg) This is the largest and most common African hare or rabbit, occurring everywhere in Botswana. In some areas a short walk at dusk or after nightfall might reveal three or four scrub hares. They tend to freeze when disturbed.

Similar species Very similar, the **Cape hare** (*Lepus capensis*) has been recorded in Botswana, both in the southwest and in an area to the north of the great salt pans. However, distinguishing between these two similar species at night, when they are most likely to be seen, would be very difficult.

Ground squirrel (*Xerus inauris* Shoulder height 20–30cm. Weight 400–700g) This terrestrial rodent is common in the more arid parts of Botswana, including the Central Kalahari, and southeastern areas. The ground squirrel is grey to grey-brown with a prominent white eye ring and silver-black tail. Within its range, it might be confused with the meerkat, which also spends much time on its hind legs. Unlike the meerkat, the ground squirrel has a characteristic squirrel mannerism of holding food in its forepaws.

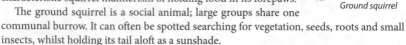

Ground squirrel

The ground squirrel is a social animal; large groups share one communal burrow. It can often be spotted searching for vegetation, seeds, roots and small insects, whilst holding its tail aloft as a sunshade.

Bush squirrel (*Paraxerus cepapi* Total length 35cm. Weight 100–250g) This common rodent is a uniform grey or buff colour, with a long tail that is furry but not bushy. It's widely distributed all over southern and east Africa, and occurs throughout northern Botswana in most woodland habitats, although not wet evergreen or montane forests. Bush squirrels are so numerous in mopane woodlands that it can be difficult to avoid seeing it, hence its other common name, the mopane squirrel.

Bush squirrels live alone, in pairs or in small groups, usually nesting in a drey of dry leaves, in a hole in a tree. They are diurnal and venture to the ground to feed on seeds, fruit, nuts, vegetable matter and small insects. When alarmed they often bolt up the nearest tree, keeping on the side of the trunk away from the threat, out of sight as much as possible. If they can find a safe vantage point with a view of the threat, then they'll sometimes make a loud clicking alarm call.

Appendix 2

LANGUAGE   *based on an original compiled by Phil Deutschle*

Setswana is the national language of Botswana, while English is the official language. In practice, though many people speak other languages at home, most will be able to converse in Setswana. English will be spoken by those who have been to school, or who have been outside the country. In a country with a high level of education, this means most people, with the exception of the older generation in rural areas.

Learning to speak a little Setswana is easy and, even in educated circles, trying to speak a few words of the language will mark you out as showing respect for the country's culture. It will open many doors, and will really make a difference to how you are received. Carry the most important phrases on a slip of paper, and practise whenever you can.

PRONUNCIATION The only difficult sound in Setswana is the g, usually pronounced like ch in the Scottish 'loch' or German 'ich'. If you have trouble with that, just say the g like an ordinary h. The r is often rolled, especially if it's written 'rr'. Vowels and other consonants are pronounced as follows:

a	like a in China
e	like ay in day
i	like ee in see
o	like o in go
ph	like p in put
th	like t in table
u	like oo in too
x	like k in kite (also used to represent a click, as in Nxai)

Note, however, that Setswana is not entirely phonetic, and some letters may not be pronounced at all.

GREETINGS Greetings are relatively easy to master, as you can practise them with everyone you meet. They'll also get you instant results; using them is almost guaranteed to bring a smile to the face of those you greet – whilst sending out the message that you're not an arrogant foreigner who can't be bothered to learn a word of Setswana. So even if you never master anything else in Setswana, do learn the basic greetings and it'll make your trip so much easier and more pleasant.

English	Setswana
Words in underlined italics are optional	

Hello (literally 'Greetings Sir/Madam')	Dumela Rra/Mma
How did you rise?	O tsogile *jang*?
I have risen *well*	Ke tsogile <u>sentle</u>
How did you spend the day?	O tlhotse *jang*?
I spent the day *well*	Ke tlhotse <u>sentle</u>
How are you? (informal)	O kae?
I'm fine (lit, 'I'm here')	Ke teng
It's OK	Go siame
I am going	Ke a tsamaya
Stay well (said to someone staying)	Sala sentle
Go well (said to someone going)	Tsamaya sentle
Sleep well	Robala sentle

ESSENTIAL WORDS

Yes	Ee
No	Nnyaa
Thank you	Ke aleboga, Ke itumetse (lit 'I am happy')
Excuse me!	Sorry!

BASIC QUESTIONS AND ANSWERS

What's your name? (formal)	Leina la gago ke mang?
My name is …	Leina la me ke …
Who are you? (informal)	O mang?
I'm …	Ke …
How goes it?	Wa reng?
It goes OK	Ga ke bue
Where are you from? or	
Where are you coming from?	O tswa kae?
I'm (coming) from …	Ke tswa kwa …
Where are you going?	O ya kae?
I'm going to …	Ke ya …
What's the time?	Nako ke mang?
Where's the shop?	Shopo e kae?
What do you want?	O batla eng?
I want …	Ke batla/kopa …
There is none	Ga go na
How much?	Ke bokae?
It's expensive/cheap	Go a tura/tshipi
What is this *in Setswana*?	Se ke eng ka <u>Setswana</u>?
What do you do? (your job)	O dira eng?

NUMBERS Unusually, numbers are said in English.

FOOD AND DRINK

water	*metse*	sugar	*sukiri*
tea	*tee*	mealie meal	*dupr*
coffee	*kofee*	meat	*fnama*
milk	*mashi*		

OTHER USEFUL WORDS AND PHRASES

I don't know *Setswana*

I't tastes good

I'm satisfied (regarding food)

Men/Women (written on toilets)

Far/near

I'm asking for money/tobacco

I have no money/tobacco

Ga ke itse <u>Setswana</u>

Go monate

Ke kgotshe

Banna/Basadi

Kgakala/gaufi

Ke kopa madi/motsoko

Ga ke na madi/motsoko

Appendix 3

FURTHER INFORMATION
BOOKS AND JOURNALS
Historical interest

Andersson, Charles John *Lake Ngami and the River Okavango* Originally published late 1850s; republished as a facsimile reprint by Struik, Cape Town, 1967. Records Namibia and Botswana in the 1850s through the eyes of one of the first traders and hunters in the area.

Baines, Thomas *Explorations in South-west Africa* London, 1864. Although linked more with the countries further east, the travels of Baines, as he accompanied Livingstone and others, makes good reading and is well illustrated by the author.

Henk, Dan 'The Botswana Defence Force: Evolution of a Professional African Military', *African Security Review*, Volume 13, No 4, 2004.

Lane, Paul, Reid, Andrew and Segobya, Alinah (eds) *The Archaeology of Botswana* Co-publisher Botswana Society, Gaborone, 1998. This is a detailed and academic overview of the archaeology of Botswana, as well as how archaeology has progressed in the country to date. It's an excellent reference, but not a light read.

Fawcus, Peter and Tilbury, Alan *Botswana: The Road to Independence* Co-publisher Botswana Society, Gaborone, 2000. The authors of this were two of Britain's most senior administrators during the final decade that led to Botswana's independence. Their book paints a rare picture (quite densely packed with detail) of a country's smooth transition from a colonial protectorate to an independent state – and has a particularly interesting foreword by Sir Ketumile Masire, one of Botswana's former presidents.

Gordon, Robert J *The Bushman Myth: The Making of a Namibian Underclass* Westview Press, Colorado and Oxford, 1992. If you, like me, had accepted the received wisdom that Bushmen are the last descendants of Stone Age man, pushed to living in splendid isolation in the Kalahari, then you must read this. It places the Bushmen in an accurate historical context and deconstructs many of the myths we have created about them. Despite being mainly based on facts about the San in Namibia, it's still well worth reading for an understanding of their position in contemporary Botswana.

Grant, Sandy *Botswana and its National Heritage* Melrose Books, Ely, 2012. This is as much a history of Botswana pre-independence than a dry record of its culture. Accessible text adds colour to many historical events and anecdotes, but it's the monochrome photographs from the archives that bring it to life. By the same author is *Botswana: An Historical Anthology*.

Head, Bessie *Serowe: Village of the Rain Wind*, Heinemann, UK, 2008. This fascinating collection of oral-history transcripts records villagers' memories of their past, and especially the deeds of their enlightened leaders, Khama the Great, who ruled from 1875 to 1923, Tshekedi Khama (1926–59), his son from a second marriage, and Sir

Seretse Khama, Khama's grandson by his first-born son Segkoma II (1923–25), who became first president of the independent Botswana.

Livingstone, David *Missionary Travels and Researches in South Africa* John Murray, London, 1857. This classic is fascinating reading, over a century after it was written.

Reader, John *Africa: A Biography of the Continent* Penguin Books, London, 1997. Over 700 pages of highly readable history, interwoven with facts and statistics, to make a remarkable overview of Africa's past. Given that Botswana's boundaries were imposed from Europe, its history must be looked at from a pan-African context to be understood. This book can show you that wider view; it is compelling and essential reading. (Chapters 41 and 42 deal with the early settlers in the Cape, and are largely devoted to the Lozi people.)

Shortridge, G C *The Mammals of South West Africa* Heinemann, London, 1934. This is more of historical interest than a practical field guide.

Tlou, Thomas and Campbell, Alec *History of Botswana* Macmillan Botswana, Gaborone, 1997.

Williams, Susan *Colour Bar: The Triumph of Seretse Khama and His Nation* Penguin, UK, 2007. This recent book documents the impact of the marriage of Sir Seretse Khama and Lady Ruth Williams Khama.

Botswana Notes and Records The Botswana Society (see page 114) has published an annual journal, *Botswana Notes and Records*, since 1969. It contains 'scientific, and semi-scientific articles and notes, written by amateur as well as professional experts on subjects of permanent interest relating to Botswana'. This is an amazing archive of reliable information, which I've only scratched the surface of here – it's a real treasure trove for anyone interested in Botswana. During my researches I've read many articles and made reference to some of them, including the main ones, which are mentioned here:

Andringa, J 'The Climate of Botswana in Histograms', Volume 16 (1984), pages 117–26.

Campbell, Alec 'A Comment on Kalahari Wildlife and the Khukhe Fence', Volume 13 (1981), pages 111–18.

Campbell, Alec 'The Riddle of the Stone Walls', Volume 23 (1991), pages 243–50.

Cooke, H J and Baillieul, T 'The Caves of Ngamiland: An Interim Report on Explorations and Fieldwork 1972–74', Volume 6 (1974), pages 147–56.

Cooper, Dr S M 'Clan Size of Spotted Hyenas in the Savuti Region of Chobe National Park, Botswana', Volume 21 (1989), pages 121–33.

Garner, R A and Ritter, R C 'Resurvey of Gcwihaba Cave and Exploration of the Aha Sinkhole Caves', Volume 26 (1994), pages 183–8.

Gieske, A 'Modelling of Surface Outflow from the Okavango Delta', Volume 28 (1996), pages 165–92.

Hitchcock, Robert 'A Chronology of Major Events Relating to the Central Kalahari Game Reserve', Volume 31 (1999), pages 105–17.

Mann, P M and Ritter, R C 'Further Exploration and Resurvey of !WaDoum Cave', Volume 27 (1995), pages 13–20.

Parsons, Q N 'Franz or Klikko, the Wild Dancing Bushman: A Case Study in Khoisan Stereotyping', Volume 20 (1989), pages 71–6.

Ramsay, Jeff 'Some Notes on the Colonial Era History of the Central Kalahari Game Reserve Region', Volume 20 (1989), pages 91–4.

Renew, Audrey 'Some Edible Wild Cucumbers of Botswana', Volume 1 (1968), pages 5–8.

Ritter, R C and Garner, R A 'Discovery and Preliminary Exploration of a New Cave in the Gcwihaba Valley', Volume 26 (1994), pages 55–65.

Ritter, Ron and Mann, Paul 'Discovery and Exploration of Two New Caves in the Northwest District', Volume 27 (1995), pages 1–12.

Robbins, L H and Campbell, A C 'The Depression Rock Shelter Site, Tsodilo Hills', Volume 20 (1989), pages 1–3.

Robbins, L H, Murphy, M L, Campbell, A C and Brook, G A 'Excavations at the Tsodilo Hills Rhino Cave', Volume 28 (1996), pages 23–45.

Robbins, Lawrence H 'The Middle Stone Age of Kudiakam Pan', Volume 20 (1989), pages 41–50.

Sommerlatte, M W L 'A Preliminary Report on the Number, Distribution and Movement of Elephants in the Chobe National Park with Notes on Browse Utilisation', Volume 7 (1975), pages 121–9.

VanderPost, Cornelius 'Putting the Bushmen on the Map of Botswana', Volume 32 (2000), pages 107–15.

Viljoen, P C 'New Locality Record for the Klipspinger', Volume 12 (1980), page 169.

Williamson, D T & J E 'An Assessment of the Impact of Fences on Large Herbivore Biomass in the Kalahari', Volume 13 (1981), pages 107–10.

Yellen, J E, Brooks, A S, Stuckenrath, R, and Welbourne, R 'A Terminal Pleistocene Assemblage from Drotsky's Cave, Western Ngamiland', Volume 19 (1987), pages 1–6.

Language and culture

Davis, Ronald & researchers at Stanford University 'Y chromosome sequence variation and the history of human populations' *Nature Genetics* November 2000.

Dunbar, R 'Why gossip is good for you' *New Scientist*, 21 November 1992, pages 28–31.

Rantao, Paul Mmolotsi *Setswana Culture and Tradition* Pentagon Publishers, Gaborone, 2006. A straightforward introduction to the traditional Setswana lifestyle, covering everything from social structure and daily rituals to religious beliefs and practices.

Biography

Allison, Peter *Don't Run Whatever You Do: My Adventures as a Safari Guide* Nicholas Brealey Publishing, London, 2007. Light-hearted and easy reading, this behind-the-scenes series of anecdotes might just make you look at your safari guide in a new light.

Carruthers, Jane and Arnold, Marion *Life and Work of Thomas Baines* Fernwood Press, South Africa, 1995, reprinted 1996.

Davies, Caitlin *Place of Reeds: A True African Love Story* Simon & Schuster, London, 2006. Set in Maun in the early 1990s, this intensely personal and sometimes disturbing memoir is enriched by a very strong sense of place and a fascinating insight into the culture of northern Botswana.

Horton, Bernard *My Forever Heartache: Four Years of Discovery with the Kalahari Bushmen* Black Crake Books, Maun, 2013.

Owens, Mark and Delia *Cry of the Kalahari* HarperCollins, UK, 1986. A highly personal account of the authors' seven years in the Central Kalahari Game Reserve in the 1970s, during which time they conducted studies focusing largely on lions and brown hyena, and set up a conservation project.

Paton, Alan *Lost City of the Kalahari* University of KwaZulu Natal Press, South Africa, 2005. In 1886, the ruins of a 'lost city' in the Kalahari were described by G A Farin in *Through the Kalahari Desert*. Seventy years later, in 1956, seven adventurers set out in search of this mythical city, among them Alan Paton, author of *Cry, the Beloved Country*. This is the story of their expedition.

Randall, Will *Botswana Time* Abacus, UK, 2005. The author's stint as a teacher in Kasane makes light-hearted if hardly memorable reading.

Slaughter, Carolyn *Before the Knife: Memories of an African Childhood* Doubleday, UK, 2002. For a young white girl, growing up in the British Protectorate of Bechuanaland was in itself unusual, but even in this context the author's childhood was outside the norm. Beyond her personal horror is pre-independence Botswana, described with both affection and, at times, a stark realism.

van der Post, Laurens *The Lost World of the Kalahari* Hogarth Press, London, 1958; many subsequent reprints by Penguin. Laurens van der Post's classic account of how he journeyed into the heart of the Kalahari Desert in search of a 'pure' Bushman group – eventually found at the Tsodilo Hills. His almost mystical description of the Bushmen is fascinating, so long as you can cope with the rather dated, turgid prose. You then need to read Robert J Gordon's very different book, *The Bushman Myth* (see above), to put it in perspective.

Field guides The choice of field guides has increased significantly in recent years, but those listed here remain among the best.

Butchart, Duncan *Wildlife of the Okavango: Common Animals and Plants* Struik Nature, Cape Town, 2000. Slim enough to take on a game drive, this handy guide with generally good photographs is an ideal first reference – albeit no substitute for a dedicated bird book.

Coates Palgrave, Keith and Coates Palgrave, Meg (eds) *Trees of Southern Africa* Struik, Cape Town, 3rd edn 2003. The definitive guide to the region's trees is a must-have for natural-history buffs.

Estes, Richard *The Safari Companion* Russell Friedman Books, South Africa, 1993 (co-published Tutorial Press, Zimbabwe and Chelsea Green Publishing, Vermont). Whilst slightly too thick to be an ideal travelling companion, this is a real treasure chest of information on animal behaviour. It covers all the main animal species found in mainland Africa, from duikers and dwarf antelope to cats, dogs and the great apes. For each it includes a brief description of its social systems and forms of communication, along with helpful outlines of body postures and diagrams to explain typical forms of behaviour. If you've longed to decipher the language of animals, and have the time to stop and watch rather than simply tick game off a list, then you must bring this book.

Newman, Kenneth *Birds of Botswana* Southern Books, South Africa, 1999. Although the text is dedicated to Botswana, the cost of this book is likely to steer most ordinary birders towards the more general southern African text below.

Newman, Kenneth *Newman's Birds of Southern Africa* Struik Publishers, South Africa. This has been re-published numerous times since its first edition in 1988 and has become one of the standard field guides to birds in southern Africa, south of the Kunene and Zambezi rivers. It also covers most species found in Zambia.

Roodt, Veronica *Common Wild Flowers of the Okavango Delta* Shell Oil Botswana, Gaborone, 1998. The second book in Shell's 'Field Guide' series is a little more specialist than the first book on trees, but still manages to comment on diverse topics from the formula for gunpowder to the treatment of scorpion stings. It's well worth getting, even for flower identification beyond the Delta.

Roodt, Veronica *Trees and Shrubs of the Okavango Delta* Shell Oil Botswana, Gaborone, 1998. This first book in Shell's 'Field Guide' series isn't just about trees or shrubs, and doesn't restrict its comments rigidly to the Okavango – but it is a masterpiece. Veronica Roodt has lived and worked in Moremi for many years, researching the plants of the area. This book is ostensibly just a field guide to slightly over 60 of the more common trees and shrubs in the area, but in reality it's a fascinating treatise on the insects and animals associated with all of them, plus the medicinal uses and local superstitions attached to each. It's well worth buying a copy as soon as you get to Botswana, even if you're not that interested in trees; it reads very well!

Roodt, Veronica *Wild Flowers, Waterplants and Grasses of the Okavango Delta and Kalahari* Veronica Roodt Publications, South Africa, 2011. Bringing together coverage of Chobe and the Makgadikgadi Pans as well as the Delta and the Kalahari, this new field guide with excellent photographs is a must. There's also a companion volume, *Mammals of Botswana and Surrounding Areas.*

Sinclair, Ian, Hockey, Phil and Tarboton, Warwick *Sasol Birds of Southern Africa* Struik, South Africa, 3rd edn 2002. First published in 1993, so a more recent addition to the market than Newman's, this is particularly useful for the illustrations of birds at different stages of their development, and in flight.

Unwin, Mike *Southern African Wildlife: A Visitor's Guide* Bradt Travel Guides, UK, 2003. A compact, single-volume guide to the habitats, identification and behavioural characteristics of the region's wildlife. A well-written text, which includes sections on tracks and signs, is matched by exceptionally good photographs.

Other useful guides

Bulpin, T V *Discovering Southern Africa* Discovering Southern Africa Productions, South Africa (distributed by Book Sales). Part guidebook and part history book, this covers mainly South Africa but also extends into Namibia and Zimbabwe. A weighty tome with useful background views and information, written from a South African perspective.

Campbell, Alec *The Guide to Botswana* Winchester Press, Johannesburg, first published 1968. Alec Campbell is perhaps the leading authority on Botswana's natural areas and history, having not only lived in Botswana for most of his life, but also held posts as the Director of National Parks and later as the Director of the National Museum of Botswana. There were several very substantial editions to this early guide which give insights into what Botswana was like decades ago. It's also fascinating to contrast and compare his guides with more contemporary guidebooks.

Campbell, Alec and Coulson, David *African Rock Art: Painting and Engraving on Stone* Abrams, New York, 2001. Campbell's informative text underpins some stunning photography, making this so much more than a coffee-table book.

Chittenden, Hugh (compiler) *Top Birding Spots of Southern Africa* Southern Book Publishers, South Africa, 1992. This useful, practical book details about 400 sites for keen birdwatchers, listing local specialities and endemic species with a checklist of key species for each site. Some of its simple maps are now out of date, though I'm not aware of it being reprinted in the last decade.

Dodwell, Christina *An Explorer's Handbook: Travel, Survival and Bush Cookery* Hodder and Stoughton, London, 1984. Over 170 pages of practical and amusing anecdotes, including chapters on 'unusual eatables', 'building an open fire' and 'tested exits from tight corners'. Practical advice for both possible and most unlikely eventualities – and it's a great read.

Gifford, James and Stockhall, Steven *Wildlife Photography in Botswana: A practical guide* Enlivened, Botswana, 2010. From technical know-how and equipment to where and how to photograph wildlife in Botswana, this is a helpful manual both for first-time photographers and those seeking more advanced skills – with some superb images.

Main, Mike *Kalahari: Life's Variety in Dune and Delta* Macmillan, UK, 1988.

Main, Mike *African Adventurer's Guide to Botswana* New Holland, UK, 2001. Mike Main is a leading authority on all things to do with Botswana, and especially its wilder areas. This book builds on the earlier *Visitor's Guide to Botswana.* It features route descriptions for some very offbeat 4x4 trips, including a few GPS points and schematic maps of the routes.

Rattray, Gordon *Access Africa* Bradt Travel Guides, UK, 2009. An invaluable guide to Africa's major safari areas for travellers with limited mobility.

Coffee-table picture books

Bailey, Adrian *Okavango: Africa's Wetland Wilderness* Struik Publishers, Cape Town, 1998. Bright colour plates and an informative text make this a good coffee-table overview of the Delta.

Balfour, Daryl and Sharna *Chobe: Africa's Untamed Wilderness* Southern Books, Johannesburg, 1997. An almost day-by-day account of a year that this renowned couple spent in Chobe and Selinda. Good pictures and a readable diary-format style give a fair picture of the changing seasons and the wildlife.

Forester, Bob, Murray-Hudson, Mike and Cherry, Lance *The Swamp Book: A View of the Okavango* Southern Books, Johannesburg, 1989. This interesting and quirky coffee-table book includes highly readable sections on the Okavango Delta and some of its more common flora and fauna, as well as comments on a few interesting historical accounts of travel there. Photographs include several taken underwater.

Lanting, Frans *Okavango: Africa's Last Eden* Chronicle Books, San Francisco, 1993. Probably the ultimate in coffee-table books includes minimal text but many impressive and beautiful images that were originally commissioned for *National Geographic* magazine.

McNutt, John and Boggs Ross, Lesley (text), Heldring, Hélène and Hamman, Dave (photography) *Running Wild: Dispelling the Myths of the African Wild Dog* Southern Books, Johannesburg, 1996. Some beautiful pictures of dogs in the Delta (the 'Mombo Pack' in the early 1990s) plus informative text about their behaviour and group dynamics – put into the context of observations made throughout northern Botswana.

Pickford, Peter and Beverly *The Miracle Rivers: The Okavango and Chobe of Botswana* Southern Books, Johannesburg, 1999. A coffee-table book with some colour plates and grainy black-and-white shots. The text is a mixture of quotes and travelogue with attention (and almost homage) paid to various hunting operations.

Ross, Karen *Okavango: Jewel of the Kalahari* BBC Enterprises Ltd, London, 1987. Written by Karen Ross in parallel with her research for a short series of films, produced by Partridge Films for the BBC. The film series is stunning, and certainly raised the UK's awareness of the Okavango Delta considerably when it was first shown. The book's also first class. Its photography is good, though not exceptional, but the depth of its text raises it well above the normal standard of coffee-table books. Though perhaps slightly dated now, it is still well worth getting hold of.

Walker, Clive *Savuti: The Vanishing River* Southern Books, Johannesburg, 1991. Using many simple line drawings, and just a sprinkling of generally impressive photographs, this is less pictorial than most coffee-table books. It concentrates mainly on Walker's personal experiences in Savuti, where he spent time with Lloyd Wilmot, amongst others, and witnessed the final drying out of the Savuti Channel. It's a good read, though too large to travel with easily.

Health

Wilson-Howarth, Dr Jane *The Essential Guide to Travel Health: Don't Let Bugs Bites and Bowels Spoil Your Trip* Cadogan Books, London, 2009. Formerly simply *Bugs, Bites and Bowels,* this amusing and erudite overview of the hazards of tropical travel is small enough to take with you.

Wilson-Howarth, Dr Jane, and Ellis, Dr Matthew *Your Child Abroad: A Travel Health Guide* Bradt Travel Guides, UK, 2005. Full of practical first-hand advice from two leading medical experts, with updates on www.bradtguides.com. An indispensable guide if you plan to travel abroad with young children.

Novels

Dow, Unity *No 1 and Beyon'* Spinifex Press, Australia, 2000. Tackling the complex issues of the role of women in society, and the conflict of the traditional and modern world, this is the first of Unity Dow's novels. Botswana's first female high-court judge, she brings her experience of the legal profession to her deceptively simple stories. Later books, also published by Spinifex, are *The Screaming of the Innocent* (2002), *Juggling Truths* (2003), and *The Heavens May Fall* (2007).

Head, Bessie *Maru* Heinemann, UK, 1972. The uplifting story of a Masarwa orphan's experiences of racial prejudice at a time when the Bushmen were treated as slaves by the dominant peoples of Botswana. South African by birth, Bessie Head came to Botswana as a refugee and was granted citizenship after 15 years. Her other novels include *When Rain Clouds Gather* (1968) and *A Question of Power* (1974), both published by Heinemann.

McCall-Smith, Alexander *The No 1 Ladies' Detective Agency* Abacus, UK, 2003. Mma Precious Ramotswe and her detective agency have been taken to the hearts of readers worldwide, but her roots are firmly in Gaborone. McCall-Smith's gently humorous tales, of which this is the first, are set in the context of modern-day Botswana, and will enrich even the shortest visit to the country.

Children's books

Botumile, Bontekanye *The Elephant Story* (2006), *Patterns in the Sky* (2007), *The Seed Children* (2008), Thari-e-Ntsho Storytellers, Maun (*www.botswanastories.com*). This series of illustrated books for primary-school children combines Botswana legends with notes on topics such as traditional remedies.

McNeice, Angus, Maisie and Travers *The Lion Children* Orion Books Ltd, London, 2001. This entertaining scrapbook about life in the bush was written by three British children whose lives were transformed when their parents moved to the Okavango (around NG34) to research lions. Whilst basically a children's book, it's a lot of fun to read and occasionally quite insightful.

USEFUL WEBSITES A selection of the web's most interesting resources on Botswana might include, in alphabetical order:

http://anthro.fullerton.edu/Okavango A site by the Okavango researcher John Bock, which focuses on the peoples of the Okavango area – though it also includes numerous links to other sites of interest concerning Botswana.

www.bidpa.bw Home for the Botswana Institute for Development Policy Analysis (BIDPA). It's a fairly dry NGO site but includes some quite detailed papers on Botswana's economic development.

www.botswana-safari-guide.com I plan to post my guidebook live onto this website, with a facility to leave updates and comments.

www.botswanatourism.co.bw The official website of the Botswana Tourism Board, complete with useful contacts, is both colourful and accessible.

www.cbnrm.bw The home page of the Community Based Natural Resources Management support programme in Botswana. This is an extensive site used as a noticeboard for communities involved in managing areas. It has lots of information about concessions and community developments, if you're prepared to spend time digging through it, and some real gems.

www.columbia.edu/cu/lweb/indiv/africa/cuvl/Botswana.html Columbia University's Department of African Studies is a good starting place for information on Botswana, with basic summaries and lots of good links.

http://dmoz.org/Regional/Africa/Botswana The Open Directory Project's page on Botswana leads to a number of useful links.

www.expertafrica.com The home page for Expert Africa, run by this guide's author. UK residents can order maps from here, and it incorporates Google maps featuring many locations within Botswana.

www.gov.bw The home page of Botswana's government. It has links to a huge variety of sites, from the official tourist-information site (which is good) to the various government departments. If you want to email a minister, download the latest customs regulations or read the latest budget speech – this is the place.

www.info.bw A fast-loading site from one of the country's main ISPs. It includes a listing of virtually every Botswana website (no comments, just an alphabetical list), a useful page of links to the media on the web, and even weather forecasts for Botswana's various towns.

www-sul.stanford.edu/depts/ssrg/africa/bots.html With a long page of links to sites relating to Botswana – some useful, others not – this is a helpful starting point if you're surfing around seeking information.

http://ubh.tripod.com/bw/bhp1.htm Run by a part of the University of Botswana this includes an impressive section on Botswana's history written by Neil Parsons. Links to a number of other relevant web pages cover many topics, from tourism and the media, to history, geography and Botswana's literature.

Newspapers on the web

www.botswanaguardian.co.bw Clear and with broad coverage, the online version of the *Botswana Guardian* offers only a limited archive of articles published since January 2012.

www.dailynews.gov.bw The online version of the *Daily News*, the free, government-sponsored paper, also has a good archive going back to 1999.

www.gazette.bw Home to *The Botswana Gazette*, an independent paper which is issued every Wednesday. The site's archive search is limited to recent articles only.

www.themidweeksun.co.bw The *Midweek Sun* online – with a search facility that promises more than it delivers.

www.mmegi.bw An online version of the substantial *Mmegi* daily newspaper, with archive material dating from 2008.

http://ngamitimes.com The online version of *The Ngami Times*, which rather frustratingly has no search facility – though they do archive articles back to mid-2012.

Index

Page numbers in **bold** indicate major entries; those in *italic* indicate maps.

INDEX OF ADVERTISERS